Walker Evans

Walker Evans

James R. Mellow

BASIC BOOKS

A Member of the Perseus Books Group

A CIP catalog record for this book is available from the
Library of Congress.

ISBN: 0-465-09077-X

Printed and bound by RR Donnelley
United States

Published by Basic Books,
A Member of the Perseus Books Group

Contents

For Leslie Katz and John T. Hill

Acknowledgments

Jim Mellow's untimely death deprived him of the opportunity to acknowledge publicly and with his usual eloquence the gratitude he felt toward the people who — in one way or another and in varying degrees — helped him to bring this biography of Walker Evans to near completion. He would want me, I know, to give thanks in his place, however inadequately, to the individuals and the staffs of institutions, listed here. For any misspellings or omissions, I offer my apologies; the fault is not Jim's but mine.

Hiram Ash; Leslie Baier; Charlee Brodsky; Anne Borchardt; Georges Borchardt, Jim's long-time literary agent; Beverly Brannan, Prints and Photographs, Library of Congress; Leila R. Buckjune, Christie's; Albert Capaccio; Cass Canfield; William Christenberry; Joel Conarroe, President, John Simon Guggenheim Memorial Foundation; Leverett M. Cooper; Lynn Cox; Marcia Due; Doug Ecklund, Department of Photographs, The Metropolitan Museum of Art; Alvin Eisenman; Charles Henri Ford; Teresa Fox Cooper; Roy Flukinger, Curator, The Harry Ransom Humanities Research Center, University of Texas at Austin; Peter Galassi, Curator of Photo Department, The Museum of Modern Art; Edward Grazda; Sarah Greenough, Curator, Department of Photographs, National Gallery of Art; Maria Hambourg, Curator, Department of Photographs, The Metropolitan Museum of Art; DeAnna Heindall; Cathy Henderson, Research Librarian, University of Texas at Austin; David Herwaldt; Dorothy Hill; John Hill; Nick Jenkins, Executor, Lincoln Kirstein Estate; Constance Ives; Stephen Jones; Staff, Beinecke Library; Deborah Martin Kao, Fogg Museum, Harvard University; Leslie Katz; Gus Kayafas; Peter Kayafas; Judith Keller, J. Paul Getty Museum; Allison Kemmerer, Addison Gallery of American Art; John Kemmerer, Basic Books; Rodger Kingston; Lincoln Kirstein; Susan Kismaric, Permissions Editor, The Museum of Modern Art; Peter Koster; Esta Kramer; Hilton Kramer; Helen Levitt; Janice Loeb; special thanks to Sue Davidson Lowe who assisted in proofreading the manuscript; Jane Mayhall; Alma McArdle; John McDonald; James McNair; Gilles Mora; Alice Morris; Mary Newman, Trustee, James Agee Estate; Alston Purvis; Belinda Rathbone; Jeff

L. Rosenheim, Assistant Curator, Department of Photographs, The Metropolitan Museum of Art; Elizabeth Sekaer Rothschild; Alexandra Rowley, Robert Miller Gallery; Jane Ninas Evans Sargeant; Nora Sayer; Dennise Shannon; Sewall Silliman; Elena Simon, Executrix, Estate of Jay Leyda; James Sinquefield, John Simon Guggenheim Memorial Foundation; Norman Snyder; Caroline Sparrow, Basic Books; Isabelle Storey; James Storey; William Stott, Ph.D., University of Texas at Austin; Jerry Thompson; G. Thomas Tonselle, John Simon Guggenheim Memorial Foundation; David Travis; The Art Institute of Chicago; Patricia Willis, Curator, Beinecke Rare Book and Manuscript Library, Yale University.

Addison Gallery of American Art, Phillips Academy,
    Andover, Massachusetts
The Art Institute of Chicago, Chicago, Illinois
The Beinecke Rare Book and Manuscript Library, Yale University,
    Collection of American Literature. New Haven, Connecticut
Harvard University Art Museums, Boston, Massachusetts
The J. Paul Getty Museum, Malibu, California
The John Simon Guggenheim Memorial Foundation, New York City
The Library of Congress, Washington, D.C.
The Metropolitan Museum of Art, New York City
The Museum of Modern Art, New York City
New York University, New York City
The Robert Miller Gallery, New York City
The Harry Ransom Humanities Research Center, University of Texas at
    Austin, Austin, Texas

I am also grateful to Richard Fumosa, special projects director at Basic Books, Boulder, Colorado.

Special thanks and gratitude to Don Fehr, Jim's tireless and talented editor, who was instrumental in bringing this book to publication. His faith in Jim's monumental talent is truly appreciated.

Augie Capaccio,
Clinton, Connecticut
1998

Walker Evans

Introduction by Hilton Kramer

It has long been recognized that Walker Evans was the preeminent photographer of his generation in America. What is less often acknowledged is that he was also one of the emblematic figures in the art and culture of his period. For it was Walker Evans's eye — and the particular sensibility that governed it — that signaled a decisive shift from the high-art aestheticism of Alfred Stieglitz in the initial phase of American modernism at the turn of the century to something quite different a generation later: an acutely lucid, disabused photographic style that placed its trust in an unembellished, highly concentrated look at the given realities of American life. Evans was by no means alone in effecting this radical revision in the way we observe the objects and environments of modern experience, but his was the most incisive contribution to the art that resulted from it, an art that changed the very conception of what a photograph might be. In this respect, he was one of the principal artists who redrew the map of American visual culture in this century, and thus permanently altered the way we see ourselves and the world we inhabit.

Born in 1903, Evans belonged to the same generation as literary talents as diverse as W.H. Auden, George Orwell, and James Agee, with all of whom his outlook on art and life had something in common. It was a generation that had been spared the horrors of the First World War — this was what separated it from the so-called Lost Generation of Hemingway, Dos Passos, and e e cummings — and it came of age instead in the heady excitements of the 1920s. However, it was by the shocks and conflicts of the depression era and the Second World War that this generation was most decisively formed. It was especially the period that Auden looked back on in his poem, "September 1, 1939" as a "low, dishonest decade," that prompted the artists and writers of his and Evans's generation to place a radically accessible candor at the center of their creative endeavors.

This inevitably put them in a critical relation to the first great wave of twentieth-century modernism in the arts — the achievement represented by Eliot and Joyce, Picasso and Matisse, and their many acolytes — which

13

was firmly in place when Evans and his contemporaries arrived on the scene. That achievement could neither be ignored nor slavishly emulated if something truly of their own time, yet on a comparably exalted level of quality, was to be created. One of the crucial things that this break with early modernism entailed for Evans's generation was a rejection of its hermeticism in favor of more direct, even documentary forms of expression. It was in that interest that Auden collaborated on film documentaries and brought the landscape of industrial England into modernist English verse, and that Orwell wrote a classic prose documentary, *The Road to Wigan Pier*. A similar imperative led Evans to abandon his early ambition to be a writer in order to pursue a vocation in photography and collaborate with Agee on a documentary project like *Let Us Now Praise Famous Men*.

No one has described the implications of that vocation more succinctly than John Szarkowski, for many years the curator of photography at the Museum of Modern Art in New York and himself a distinguished photographer. Writing in *Looking at Photographs* (1973), Szarkowski observed: "Evans' work seemed at first almost the antithesis of art. It was puritanically economical, precisely measured, frontal, unemotional, dryly textured, insistently factual, qualities that seemed more appropriate to a bookkeeper's ledger than to art. But in time it became clear that Evans' pictures, however laconic in manner, were immensely rich in expressive content. His work constitutes a personal survey of the interior resources of the American tradition, a survey based on a sensibility that found poetry and complexity where most earlier travelers had found only drab statistics or fairy tales."

That the man who, by embarking upon this "personal survey," produced a seemingly impersonal art largely devoted to anonymous subjects, has himself remained something of an enigma, would come as no surprise to anyone who knew Walker Evans. An enigma was precisely what Evans the man wished to remain, preferring — indeed, insisting — that the "poetry and complexity" which Szarkowski spoke of in his work speak for him. He was an enigma to many who were closest to him in his lifetime, and he clearly wished to preserve that enigmatic mask for posterity. The once-famous admonition of André Gide, who early on exerted a considerable influence on Evans — "Don't understand me too quickly!" — might very well have been his own.

Alas, he was anything but unique in this respect. It is often the case, after all, that artists and writers, in the course of their careers, do tend to become inordinately resistant to and suspicious of personal revelation. With some, this resistance takes the form of an impenetrable and protracted silence. With others, however — and this was very much the case with Evans — resistance takes a very different form. They talk, and talk a lot. This was certainly true of Walker when I knew him in the last years of his life. When the spirit was upon him, he was an inspired raconteur. But that, too, often proved to be a strategy of resistance to revelation. For the man himself remained concealed behind the constant flow of engaging anecdote, pointed observation, and cavalier obiter dicta, which, without being exactly untrue, was nonetheless designed to preserve a privacy as essential to his inner being as it was to the spirit of his art.

Walker once admitted as much to me — though obliquely, of course — in one of our many conversations. He was then teaching at the Yale School of Art, and while it was my impression that he greatly enjoyed his new role as a mentor to younger talents, his life was otherwise fairly problematic. His recent marriage — his second — was in trouble. His health was failing, and so was his resolve to stay on the wagon. And although a succession of exhibitions brought a chorus of praise from the critics, some of it written by myself in the *New York Times*, he no longer seemed capable of adding much to the classical oeuvre he had already created. He was clearly searching for new interests or a new project, something that might revive his faltering spirits.

Over lunch in New Haven one day, we got to talking about the memoirs that some of Walker's contemporaries had lately published. He professed not to have read any of these memoirs of the 1920s and '30s, but he plied me with questions about those I had read, eager to elicit whatever unfavorable criticisms I might make of them. I then suggested to Walker that *he* write a book of memoirs, and, to my astonishment, he seemed eager to give it some serious thought.

Some months passed before I received a call summoning me to lunch again in New Haven. Walker promptly announced that since our last lunch he had spent much of his time reading through as many of those memoirs as he could lay hands on. Then, with an air of triumph, he declared: "They're all lies! They're nothing but lies!" "Well," I replied, "that's all the more reason for you to write *your* memoirs." This irritated him greatly. "No, no," he said. "You don't understand. I would write lies, too. You can't write anything but lies about the past." I thought of all the entertaining stories Walker had recounted to me — and to others — over the years that I had known him, and realized in retrospect that they had always served him as a kind of *blague* to keep the ghosts of the past at bay.

It is not the least of James Mellow's achievements in this biography that he has brought so many of these ghosts to life again, and has often managed to do so in Evans's own words or in those who were closest to him in the most pivotal and dramatic years of his life. The Walker Evans that we encounter in this book is a figure that has never before been so accurately described, so sympathetically portrayed, or so delicately judged. Both the man and his work are fully rendered for the first time by a writer who was himself a master of biographical portraiture. There is nothing like this Life, either, in the literature of modern photography to match its account of Walker's working methods, and nothing that comes close to its absorbing description of the man himself.

Jim Mellow came to the subject of Walker Evans at an important juncture in his own life as a writer. The history of American modernism had been one of the principal concerns of his work since the publication of his first book, a biography called *Charmed Circle: Gertrude Stein & Company* (1974), a finalist for the National Book Award and now regarded as a classic. That book initiated a trilogy — later completed with *Invented Lives: F. Scott and Zelda Fitzgerald* (1984) and *Hemingway: A Life Without Consequences* (1992) — devoted to the expatriate writers who set the standard for modern American prose in the period between the two world wars.

His second book — *Nathaniel Hawthorne in His Times* (1980), which won the National Book Award — was intended to be the first volume in a parallel series on nineteenth-century American prose writers. A life of Margaret Fuller, which was meant to be a counterpart to the Stein biography, had already been announced. But as often happens to writers who live by their pen, Jim was persuaded by his publisher to defer that project until the lives of Fitzgerald and Hemingway had been completed. By that time, however, he was offered the opportunity to write a life of Walker Evans, and he jumped at the chance. For this was a subject that would allow him to extend his account of American modernism into a later generation and expand its focus to the realm of pictorial art, which had long been another of Jim's professional interests.

As the editor of *Arts Magazine* in the early 1960s, and subsequently as a contributor to the Sunday art page of the *New York Times*, Jim had already published a good deal of art criticism when he turned his attention to the life and work of Walker Evans. Preferring to concentrate on his books, he had turned down an offer from the *Times* to join its staff as a full-time art critic, but he continued to write the occasional article for the paper. That was how he came to have his one and only meeting with Walker — an encounter that is vividly described in the prologue to this book.

It was precisely Jim's exceptional command of both literature and the pictorial arts in this century that made him an ideal chronicler of Walker's special genius, which was itself governed by an unusual combination of literary and visual interests. (In this connection, it is worth recalling that Walker also wrote a good deal of art criticism when he worked for *Time* magazine.) It was another advantage, of course, that Jim brought to this subject a comprehensive knowledge of the expatriate literary and artistic worlds in Europe in the 1920s and '30s, for it was in that milieu that Walker came to his vocation in photography from his apprenticeship as an aspiring author and translator. Exactly what Walker derived from his expatriate period and how it came to be applied to the work of his artistic maturity were therefore matters that Jim was uniquely qualified to deal with.

In much of Jim's writing — but particularly in the Stein and Hemingway biographies — one of the central themes is the role played by European culture and Europe itself in the development of an American artistic consciousness. It was in Paris, after all, and under the influence of Cubist painting where Stein effected her radical renovation of American prose, and Hemingway applied the lessons of that renovation in forging the style of his early stories of northern Michigan — a style that set the pace of American prose for several generations thereafter. About the nuances and consequences of this cultural paradox, in which French precedents functioned as a catalyst in the production of what came to be regarded as the most influential American prose style of its time, Jim had established himself as a connoisseur before ever turning to the art of Walker Evans.

Owing to the distinctly American subject-matter of so many of Walker's best-known photographs — and perhaps, too, to what many critics regard as his equally distinctive American response to his subjects — the expatriate experience is not a theme commonly associated with Walker's work. Yet Jim's own experience in chronicling the lives of American expatriate writers gave him an uncommon appreciation of what Walker *as an artist* derived from his early immersion in French literature. This was a subject that Walker himself often spoke about in his later years, citing Flaubert and Baudelaire as the crucial influences. As a veteran biographer, however, Jim knew better than to rely on such retrospective testimony. When he conducted his own research into Walker's papers, the debt to Baudelaire was confirmed, but Jim found there was little evidence that he had read much of Flaubert. The writers he was drawn to early on in his expatriate period were Joris-Karl Huysmans, Rémy de Gourmont, and Jean Cocteau, and those whose works he set himself the task of translating into English were André Gide, Blaise Cendrars, and Raymond Radiguet. It was Gide's prose style that Walker especially esteemed, but the entire list suggests a closer acquaintance with the aesthetic and moral interests of contemporary French literature than is usually supposed.

As for the particular qualities that Walker admired in Gide's prose, it needs to be remembered that it was its note of radical moral candor that made the author such a controversial figure in his day — precisely the quality that is now so admired in Walker's best work. And in his research into Walker's translations, Jim was struck by something else that might have stirred Walker's interest. About a little-known memoir of Gide's called "Conversation with a German Some Years Before the War," which Walker translated in 1927, Jim writes: "One of the things that may have impressed Evans about the [memoir] is Gide's nearly photographic attention to finical and revealing detail — 'He offered me a cigarette in the finest case I have ever seen. I admired too his match container, silver like the cigarette case. The smallest objects he had about him were of a somber and restrained elegance . . . '"

It is in observations of this kind that Jim was able to limn the relation that obtained between Walker's French literary interests and the aesthetic that subsequently governed his pictorial practice. No other writer has traced the course of that delicately negotiated shift from literature to photography with such a deep and detailed understanding of what it entailed for Walker, both aesthetically and intellectually. For it was never a question, in his case, of repudiating the literary origins of his art. Literature, as we are frequently reminded in this book, remained one of Walker's abiding passions.

Yet it was one of the defining features of his photographic art that it was never conceived to be any sort of illustration of a literary idea or a literary subject. It was indeed the essence of Walker's modernism to separate photography from its literary subject-matter and allow it to achieve an aesthetic autonomy of its own. Even in his most famous collaborative work — *Let Us Now Praise Famous Men* — Walker's pictures remained remarkably independent of James Agee's text in their utter detachment from the pathos of the social drama that is so eloquently evoked in the writing. What Walker contributed to the book wasn't illustration but a parallel succession of pictorial images that illuminated a moral landscape with a clarity and immediacy that are uniquely the province of photography.

In this respect, the influence of Baudelaire is certainly discernible in Walker's photographic style — the influence, that is, of Baudelaire the dandy, with his attitude of radical detachment from all he surveys, and of Baudelaire the *flâneur*, who selects objects of interest from his wanderings in the miscellany of the modern world without much regard for the status which received opinion has assigned to them. From this disabused Baudelairean perspective, a sharecropper's hovel or an unmade bed might prove to be quite as compelling, as a pictorial subject, as a Victorian mansion or a remarkable face. Everything would depend on the quality of the observer's aesthetic response, while all hierarchies of privileged subject-matter were consigned to oblivion.

It was undoubtedly Walker's French connection, as it may be called, that enabled him to secure his artistic independence from the powerful influence of Alfred Stieglitz. About this milestone in the history of Walker's artistic development Jim Mellow also gives us the most complete account we have. Walker was deeply conflicted about Stieglitz, and often contradictory in his avowals and denials on the subject. Understandably so, perhaps, for it was no small task to get free of the master's formidable mystique even in the crisis atmosphere of the 1930s. Stieglitz was the lion in the path of all the photographic artists of Walker's generation. He had undeniably been the single greatest force in achieving a new artistic status for photography in America, yet the atmosphere of aestheticism and mystagogy with which he surrounded his artistic mission was proving to be a handicap in dealing with the social realities of the Depression era. So was Stieglitz's condescending attitude toward America itself. He couldn't be ignored, yet he couldn't be emulated either. He had somehow to be overcome.

In the effort he made to secure his independence from the Stieglitz mystique, Walker had the good fortune of winning the support of an equally formidable but much younger visionary of the arts — Lincoln Kirstein. About this crucial relationship, too, Jim writes with an authority no other writer has brought to the subject. Had he lived, Jim's chronicle of American modernism would have been expanded even further with the biography of Kirstein he was planning to write after the completion of his life of Evans. It was in the course of his research for the present volume that Jim first met Kirstein, whose own role in Walker's life and work is so brilliantly recounted in this book. Kirstein — poet, critic, historian, aesthete, and impressario of the arts — was a famously difficult personality, yet when Jim approached him in his quest for first-hand information about Walker's life and work, Kirstein responded with extraordinary enthusiasm. It turned out that Kirstein had read and admired Jim's life of Gertrude Stein, and, as a consequence, he not only placed his voluminous papers at Jim's disposal but invited him to write a life of Kirstein upon the completion of Walker's — a proposal to which Jim readily agreed.

This was a project that interested Jim greatly, for Kirstein was, like Walker, one of the emblematic figures in the cultural life of our time. Known the world over today as the founder of the New York City Ballet — who, by bringing George Balanchine to America in the 1930s, made New York the dance capital of the world — Kirstein was also a connoisseur of photography, painting, sculpture, and architecture. In *The Hound and Horn*, the literary journal he founded while still an undergraduate at Harvard in the late 1920s, Kirstein had published Walker's first writings on photography, and he was subsequently tireless in promoting Walker's own photographs during the period he served as curator at the Museum of Modern Art in the 1930s.

Had he lived to write it, Jim's biography of Kirstein would have carried his history of American modernism down to the present day. It was not to be, alas, and the time which Jim devoted to Kirstein in the last years of his life proved to be unexpectedly costly, for it delayed the completion of this book. When Jim died suddenly on November 23, 1997, he had not yet completed the closing chapter of Walker's life, but fortunately for us all, what he has written, what you have before you, is both a landmark work on the life of Walker Evans as well as an extraordinary chronicle of the art of our time.

Prologue

The voice at the other end of the line sounded distant, faint. It was Walker Evans: "No, I'm in New Haven. Meet me here tomorrow morning at ten-thirty."

I was hesitant. I had made the arrangements earlier in the week and was sure that I had called the number he had given me for his home in Lyme, Connecticut, in case he wasn't at the apartment in New Haven. In my nervousness, perhaps I had mixed the numbers up when I took them down.

"Fine, at ten-thirty in New Haven," I said. Evans had, despite the wispy, faraway voice, seemed confident. I had been assigned by the *New York Times* to do an interview with him for the Sunday art section. It was intended to run during an exhibition of forty of his photographs at the Robert Schoelkopf Gallery in New York.

I was all the more confused the next morning, Saturday, when I arrived at the apartment building, the Madison Towers, one of the newer high-rises near the Yale School of Art, when the doorman told me that he doubted that Evans was home, that he hadn't picked up his mail the day before. He assumed Evans was in Lyme, where he usually went on the weekends. He suggested I call him there, which I did (it was the same number I had called the night before), but there was no answer. "Maybe he's on his way," the doorman suggested.

I had been told that Evans didn't like to give interviews and didn't often grant them. (I later learned that this wasn't altogether true: There are a considerable number of tapes and transcripts of interviews with him, particularly dating from later in his life, after he had begun teaching classes at Yale in 1965.) Faced with a no-show, I began to wonder whether Evans conveniently forgot or, worse, deliberately wanted to avoid the meeting. That would mean I would have to scrap the interview, since the Schoelkopf exhibition would be closing soon.

Three quarters of an hour later, I was relieved when, returning to the apartment, I learned that Evans was indeed in. At the door of his eighth-

Lyme, Connecticut,
February, 1973

floor apartment, he made no mention of the confusion about where he had been the evening before. And, certainly, I had no intention of asking. Evans seemed rather bleary-eyed, his eyes rheumy, his beard unkempt, as if he might have made a late rush to New Haven. I was ushered into the kitchen without a chance to look around or at least notice much about the sparse furnishings that might provide some background description for an article. Evans started off by pouring himself a hefty tumbler full of Rémy Martin. He asked if I would like a drink. I passed on the first offer; it was still too early in the morning, and I hadn't had much of a breakfast.

At first, Evans wasn't forthcoming: He sat in a kitchen chair, staring off into space. I suspected he had early on thought of the interview as an inconvenience and wanted to get through it. Under questioning, he made it clear, or intended to give the appearance, that he had a real distaste for what he called "artiness" and preferred to avoid the "fashionable photographic world." He hated galleries, he said. ("Almost any artist would hate art galleries by nature.") He hadn't even put in an appearance yet at his own exhibition. He seldom read the critics of photography: "Mostly dribble and rubbish — and boring," he said, with an abruptness that seemed targeted at some point directly above my head.

Most of what I knew about Evans was the photographic record, the work — those graphic rather than pretty or nostalgic photographs of country roads and sharecroppers, the photographic collaboration with James Agee for *Let Us Now Praise Famous Men*, which had made both of them famous in their own right when it was published in 1941. And what had impressed me about that work was its hard-edged, no-nonsense approach, which I classified with the other photographers I especially admired: Eugène Atget, whom I had first come across in Berenice Abbott's *Guide to Better Photography*, in high school, and later, Cartier-Bresson, whom I had first seen after the war, in his book *The Decisive Moment*.

It was far easier, therefore, to talk about the work. I had noticed that Evans seldom took photographs of flowers. He suggested that in the past his attitude was "probably snobbery or purity on my part. I felt you shouldn't photograph what was already beautiful. But Redon has made me change my mind about that." He had lately been taking some photographs of roses, he told me. In his Schoelkopf exhibition, however, the only flower on view — with nice irony — was an artificial rose stuck in the stone hand of a tombstone statue of a little Victorian girl, taken in the midst of winter in 1969 in Clarkesville, Kentucky.

He had little interest in photographing celebrities, he said when I asked him. "Celebrities are suspect," he said "It's an impure thing to do — too easy." For starters, people were more interested in the famous person than in the photograph. He had refused to photograph Hemingway, he said, and ee cummings and all those people. "Much to Hemingway's delight, I might add. I think he felt I wanted to be coaxed." Nor was he ever much interested in taking photographs of skyscrapers, a usual motif for other photographers of his generation. He had, he said, taken photographs of the structure of the Chrysler Building when it was going up in 1929; there were, too, the photographs he had taken of the Brooklyn Bridge that were later used in the Black Sun edition of Hart Crane's *The Bridge* (1930). And there were the early photographs of people who were to become famous later: Crane himself, the photographer Berenice Abbott, his painter friend Ben Shahn, and Lincoln Kirstein, who, as a patron and critic, had given the earliest boost to Evans's reputation.

Somewhere in the midst of the discussion, Evans offered me a drink again, and not wanting to cut off the interview too early, I had accepted. He poured one for me and replenished his own. When I pressed him on personal issues or about people he had known, he was not readily forthcoming. I had been intrigued by the photograph of Cary Ross's New York apartment; Ross was a little-known figure, a sometime poet and art entrepreneur, whom I had come across while researching a biography of Scott and Zelda Fitzgerald. (Ross had managed to put together an exhibition of Zelda's paintings in 1934, while she was in an asylum in upstate New York — a generous effort to get some recognition for a woman who was badly in need of it.) But Evans was clearly reluctant to talk about other people he knew, famous or not, and made it clear that he didn't welcome that line of questioning. Ross was a young man about town, was all he would venture.

As the interview wound down I had gotten more expansive, but less focused, under the influence of the brandy. Evans, too, was winding down, and it was clear that he was waiting for me to leave.

When the interview with Evans appeared in the Sunday, December 1, 1974 edition of the *Times*, it created an unexpected stir, not from any critical assessment on my part, but because of the tumbler of Rémy Martin. It was the signal to many of Evans's close friends that he had fallen off the wagon, and was the cause of real concern, if not a falling out, between Evans and the young photographer-assistant, Jerry Thompson, who had only recently been sharing the rental of the New Haven apartment and for a year or more had been watching over Evans's health, getting him off the regimen of painkilling drugs, including Demerol, which Evans had been taking indiscriminately ever since a serious operation for stomach ulcer. Evans had explained the missing bottle of brandy was due to the fact that the reporter from the *Times* had drunk it all. Thompson had had some inkling that Walker had been drinking of late, though he had been on the wagon since 1966. At a luncheon with Robert Schoelkopf and his family, Schoelkopf had been astonished when Walker had accepted a glass of white wine, saying that his psychiatrist had told him that it was all right to have a glass of wine now and then. (Prior to that there had been a full bar for guests at the house in Old Lyme and Evans had never seemed to have been bothered by it.) But, around the time of my interview, Thompson had been receiving reports from friends about Evans's making late-night calls to them with "alarmingly slurred" speech and bar-type music in the background. By late November, Evans had had to ask for help, and his friends, including Thompson, had unsuccessfully tried to find a place where he could dry out. Evans's psychiatrist eventually arranged to have him admitted to the psychiatric ward in New Haven hospital. While there for observation and evaluation, he fell, breaking his collarbone, and was removed to a medical ward. In December, it was recommended that he be transferred to Gaylord, for convalescence.

Evans wasn't one of the celebrities whose private lives had been lived out in the public domain. I didn't know that he had had a serious drinking problem years before and that he was purportedly on the wagon. Nor did I know that he had had a critical operation for ulcers and had a large part of his stomach removed. I was not aware that he had been married twice and twice divorced. None of which, perhaps, was relevant to the interview — except as life is always related, in devious ways, to the work of any creative artist.

A little more than four months later, Evans was dead. About his work I knew something; about Evans himself, I had everything to learn.

School Years

I

Walker Evans III, as he sometimes jauntily referred to himself, was born in St. Louis, Missouri, on November 3, 1903. His father Walker Evans, Jr., an advertising man, had married the lively Jessie Beach Crane in St. Louis on January 15, 1900. The Evans family, according to an unidentified three-page typed genealogical tree in the Walker Evans archive, traced the family roots back to a John Laurence, born in Wisset, England, early in the seventeenth century, who later settled in Watertown, Massachusetts. The Laurence family line married into a succession of venerable New England families: Tarbells and Shedds and Haddens and Fullers. A Levi Laurence, born in Thetford, Vermont, on August 14, 1759, served for three years in the Revolutionary War and later became a deacon and lay preacher of the Baptist Church in Thetford. It was Levi's daughter, Mary Anne, born August 17, 1809, in Thetford, who married (in 1833 in St. Louis, Missouri) an Augustus Heaslip Evans, of an uncertain birth date, born in Woodstock, Virginia.

There the family line becomes a bit confused in the unknown genealogist's research. The first Walker Evans, the photographer's grandfather, born May 29, 1844, in St. Louis, marries an Amanda Brooks, originally of Mexico, Missouri, on December 4, 1844, *and* December 4, 1877, in St. Louis. That their son Walker Evans, Jr., is listed as having been born on January 29, 1876, in Mexico, Missouri, a year or so before their marriage compounds the problem. Another complication is the notation that the photographer's sister, Jane Beach Evans (born January 5, 1902), attended the couple's fiftieth wedding anniversary in 1937 rather than 1927. And the notation for Walker Evans III incorrectly gives his birthdate as March 3, 1903, rather than November 3. There is also a pointed notation: "has no children."

Perhaps it matters little in the life of the photographer, except that his mother, Jessie Beach Crane Evans, set some store on family connections. Judging from early family photographs of the Evanses and Cranes, it was a convivial family of aunts and uncles, nephews and nieces, of family visits

Walker Evans II,
Walker Evans III,
Walker Evans I,
c. 1907

and outings. A wedding photo of Walker's mother shows her, dainty slipper peeking forth from her lacy wedding gown and her head tilted to one side, with a coy beguiling smile. A photograph of Walker Evans's father taken the same year, 1900, shows him as dapper in a neatly tailored suit and vest, with pince-nez and smoothly parted hair. Another shows the father playing a guitar with a broad grin, while Jessie, leaning back on a slipcovered divan at what might be the Evans's family homestead, Fern Valley, near St. Louis, is looking thoroughly appreciative. There is, too, a picture of the young marrieds on a sailing expedition with family or friends, a perfect expression of turn-of-the-century life and pleasure, with Jessie staring knowingly at the photographer while her husband, seated on the deck, leans against her knees.

It was in the nature of Walker Evans Jr.'s profession that the family moved a good deal and that the children's education was a chequered affair. Walker and his sister, Jane, attended a kindergarten in Kenilworth, Illinois, a well-to-do suburb of Chicago. From grade school, when he was about eight, he would recall, somewhat vaguely, a pair of teachers—sisters who

"were very sympathetic and good women. They were wonderful."

He claimed that he had been an apt pupil "until I discovered the choice of being bad and not doing well. But I was naïve. Maybe at the age of eight I was a star pupil, because I loved it. And I loved the teacher. But when I lost interest I became a very poor student," he admitted.

His defection must have occurred later at about the age of twelve or thirteen, when he was in the seventh grade of the Fuller School in Toledo, Ohio. Walker's father had been given the account for Willys Overland, the automobile manufacturer: "That was a big thing. That was why he had to move there. He couldn't turn it down." There is a postcard view of his class-mates: the boys of the "class of room 15," posed in shirts and ties and cardigan sweaters or more fashionable Norfolk jackets, a collection of prominent ears and professional smiles, betokening the seriousness of the occasion. It was in Toledo, apparently around the age of fourteen, "like every other child," that Evans first became interested in photography: "I did have a box camera, and I developed film in the bathroom." He was at that age, he said, "visual . . . But I was both graphic and visual in school as

well as literary, and I was always drawing. For example, in school we were supposed to draw some maps. I couldn't stop drawing maps, and I made fine maps. I just went on and on and on." He had painted, too, in childhood: "I'm a natural painter." But it was not all a matter of ease and facility: "I also went through a period of insecurity, shyness, and depression about it." When you were a child and then again when you were a young man, you looked at other people's paintings and realized that you couldn't do what they had done. "I had to get over that." In Toledo, Evans recalled, he attended high school for only a year or two. He was pulled out to attend a boys school, Loomis, in Windsor, Connecticut.

But in Evans's scattered recollections he would recall that around 1919 or 1920, when he was sixteen or seventeen, he had attended the Mercersburg Academy in Pennsylvania. Fifteen years later, in 1935, on a photographic assignment traveling through Pennsylvania and West Virginia, he made a special trip, first to a hotel in Bedford Springs, Pennsylvania, where he and his "Happy Evans family" had stayed. He had

Left:
School picture,
approximately age 8.

Right:
Circa 1915.

become aware of the distance he had traveled in time from the young boy in white flannel long pants who, at fourteen or fifteen, had strolled along the causeway to the source of the springs. In 1935, for the first time, he had been struck by the architecture of the hotel and sardonically noted his failure to have noticed it when a boy: "Observant boy remembers classic portico and swimming pool but not rooms slept in, not a trace of memory of this, or of food eaten or dining room or arrival." Given his adult interest in vernacular architecture, he noted that he had "completely overlooked the gingerbread wings of the hotel" when he and his family had visited there.

The following morning, leaving the hotel late in the morning, he continued his sentimental journey. "Visited Mercersburg Academy—deserted, touched by a mild rush of reminiscences that was I think me in 1919 or 1920. Discovered that some things did happen to me there and that I am at least partly the same person I was fifteen years ago. I liked something there more than I knew at the time. Discovered by comparison that space shrinks with advancing time, or seems to." There were reasons, it appears, for fixing the present in its irrevocable time: It would become a principle of his photography.

Evans's education continued in the same spotty fashion. When his mother and father separated, Evans moved with his mother to New York City and from there, he was sent to Phillips Andover in Andover, Massachusetts, a prep school for well-to-do young boys. His performance those two years at Phillips Andover was hardly spectacular. Nevertheless, he was admitted to Williams College in Williamstown in September 1922. Despite the poor showing of his Andover records, Evans would claim, "I started reading at Andover with a real love of reading and then I carried it on so much at Williams that I didn't do much else but read in the library." Judging from his grades at Williams College, it may well have been true. Evans's recollection, supported by his records, was that he had dropped out of Williams after only one year. It was the end of his education, he claimed, "although I left in good standing. I don't remember studying anything. Paid a little attention in class." Evans's education did mark the beginning of a lifelong interest in literature, for, as he claimed, his first ambition in life, in fact, was to be a writer.

Class picture,
Phillips
Academy,
Andover,
Massachusetts,
May, 1923

The Incandescent Center

2

"I went there," Walker Evans said of his 1926 trip to Paris, "because I had an intelligent and forbearing father who said if you want to leave college, which I did want to do, and go to Paris instead, and study there, go ahead and I'll pay for it. Of course, it was damned cheap, cheaper than going to college here; the exchange was so much in our favor . . . I went there because it was economically possible, because I wanted to."

In remembering his past, Evans did not always adhere to the strictly documentary line. There were minor discrepancies in his later claims about his Paris sojourn. It was not altogether true that he had gone to Paris to complete a college education. There had been almost a three-year lapse between the time he left Williams College, during which he worked in the New York Public Library (part of it in the Map Room) before he sailed for Europe. Presumably, it was during this time, possibly while working in the Map Room, that Evans met Hanns Skolle. The two would become important to each other as friends and critics of each other's early work. It was not until April 6, 1926, at age twenty-two, that he embarked for Europe on the R.S.M.P. *Orduna*, arriving in Cherbourg on April 16. Nor did he mention that in the first months of his year abroad, his freedom was hampered by the unwelcome presence of his mother, who appears to have made the voyage with him. References to Jessie Crane Evans do not turn up in Evans's known letters at the time and it was not often that she is mentioned in his later recollections. Understandably, the brave image of the young artist on his first trip abroad ("One lived in a sort of fiery cloud of excitement," he recalled. "You're excited when you're young anyway, but this was super excitement. Every day it took the top of your head off.") would have needed to be cropped once Evans admitted he had been chaperoned by his mother. There is some reason for speculation that Jessie, unhappy over the separation from her husband, had become tiresomely dependent on her son at the time. The price of his grand adventure may have included the presence of Jessie Evans. Clearly his mother was with Evans when Hanns Skolle wrote him on April 27, responding to Evans's account of the Atlantic crossing.

Shadow
Self-portraits,
Juan-les-Pins,
January 1927

Skolle pointedly offered "My best regards to your mother." In one of Evans's rare moments of admission, he acknowledged that his mother's presence on that trip became so burdensome that in the course of a disagreeable argument conducted on a park bench, he had flatly told his mother he wanted to be on his own and that she should go home. Evans remained close-mouthed about the episode until years later.

The declaration of independence nonetheless seems to have been emancipating. It seems to have doubled his sense of exhilaration at being in Paris. Forty-five years later, in a talk with young college students, he claimed: "Any man of my age who was sensitive to the arts was drawn as by a magnet to Paris because that was the incandescent center, the place to be." Even at that late date, the trip to Paris remained one of the sunniest recollections of his life: "Figure what was going on, who was alive: Proust was just dead; Gide was alive; Picasso was in mid-career; there was all the School of Paris art, which seemed revolutionary at the time. It was terribly exciting. The place as I say was incandescent. You had to go there."

After a preliminary stay at the Hotel Chambon, Evans settled at the Hotel Fleurus on April 21, according to a three-page itinerary he kept. Judging from Skolle's April 27 letter, the bantering style the two friends had adopted early in their correspondence was kept up, at least as far as Skolle's letters were concerned. Skolle was congratulatory about Evans's literary ambitions: "Your intention to write me masterpieces I applaud most sincerely." It was, indeed, Evans's ambition to become a writer and that was one of the chief purposes of his trip abroad. By June, when Skolle was addressing his letters c/o American University Union, Evans had enrolled in French classes. His homework assignments were corrected in a minuscule hand by a Mme. Berthier, whose annotations corrected his grammar and spelling, offered some encouragement and some criticism.

In one of his earliest exercises, written in the form of a letter addressed to "Chère Avis, Avis chère," Mme. Berthier found Evans's "Style moderne" somewhat "depouille et synthetique" but "assez surprenant." It was clear that the newly arrived student intended to impress his teacher with his familiarity with French literature. In "Chère Avis," supposedly written in the heat of his enthusiasm for Paris, Evans confesses to surrendering to the illusions created by the writers of the past. The names tumble out readily: Baudelaire, Verlaine, Huysmans, Rémy de Gourmont. But the Paris of these writers, he complains, no longer exists: "Le parfum reste, mais c'est tout." Instead he has encountered a different Paris, the Paris of the Dôme (American) and the Rotonde ("ecœurant" [disgusting, loathsome]), and the Paris of surrealism. "Even our André Gide is out of date. Cocteau and Picasso exist certainly and that is all to the good." What caught his attention were "the poseurs. Always the poseurs — everywhere." Barbey d'Aurevilly et Villiers de l'Isle Adam, both nineteenth-century poets, were his "friends." They lived with him, he said, in his "chambre intime."

In another of his class compositions, "A Bas Platon" ("Down with Plato"), having been asked to give his conception of happiness, he answered: "Mais hélas, c'est impossible, Madame; je suis trop jeune pour etre sage en parlant sur un tel sujet; et je suis trop sage pour etre franc."[1] The text is spirited, chatty, considering the poor grades in French he had received earlier in his education. Evans argues the case of youth against old age. Any serious definition of happiness would be a platitude. Considering himself the declared enemy of platitude, he would refrain from giving one.

Alors que dire! Seulement ceci; Pendant que nous sommes jeunes nous chercherons (et nous trouverons) le plus grand rapprochement vers le bonheur dans le plaisirs terrestres et meme mondains. Tandis que nous le pouvons nous danserons et nous dinerons; et, cela va sans dires, nous ferons l'amour.[2]

Our elders, he asked, weren't they a bit envious — and in some cases, jealous? Wasn't it true that they chewed their nails over each lost occasion of their youth? It seemed to him that the first stage toward the sagacity of age was "un pleine perception du monde et de tout ce qui en est ... le beau, le gai, l'amusant, et le ... je rougis ... l'erotique.

"Qu'il fasse beau!"[3]

[All French phrases, stories and notations are quoted directly from Walker Evans's diaries, notes and papers without editorial corrections.]

1 "But alas, it is impossible, Madame; I am too young to be wise in discussing such a subject; and I am too wise to be frank."
2 "What to say. Only this: While we are young we will search (and we will find) the greatest approach to happiness in earthly, even worldly pleasures. While we can, we will dance, we will dine, and, it goes without saying, we will make love."
3 "a full perception of the world and all that is in it ... the beautiful, the gay, the amusing, and ... I blush ... the erotic. May it be good weather!"

Evans, who, fortunately for his biographers, developed a lifetime habit of making lists — brief notes on his travels and activities, lists of possible projects, reminders to himself, antic lists of people to whom he proposed sending his published photographic books or invitations to his exhibitions — made a two-column list of his 1926-27 European adventures in addition to the more chronologically detailed three-page itinerary of his travels. It included such items as his commentaries on arrival: "Disgust in the boat train. The taxi horns of Paris. In the Tuileries gardens." He jotted down places: "Shakespeare and Company," the famed bookstore, and "The Dôme," the equally famed café of the expatriates which he seems to have frequented. In Parisian memoirs of the period, names and addresses appear and disappear without explanation. Threading through his list were repetitive and romantic indications of states of being at various stages of his travels: "Solitude" (at Cannes); "Solitude, soleil, santé" (at Juan-les-Pins).

Two titles that crop up on Evans's list — *Le bateau ivre* and *Si le grain ne meurt* — suggest that he was acquainting himself with or furthering his readings of the works of Rimbaud and Gide. Rimbaud's symbolist poem, full of hallucinatory images and one of the landmarks of modernist poetry, had served as the seventeen-year-old poet's introduction to poet Paul Verlaine, initiating their stormy friendship and the start of Rimbaud's brief transit to literary fame. (It would prove an inspiration for some of Evans's own attempts at poetry.) *Si le grain ne meurt*, Gide's scandalous memoir, was first published in 1920 in a limited edition of twelve copies. Four years later it appeared in a public edition with some names altered and a short passage omitted because one of Gide's cousins objected that his account was inaccurate. In the book, Gide daringly revealed his amorous episode with an exotic Ouled Nail dancer as well as sexual encounters with lithe young Arab boys on his trips to North Africa. Three months after Evans's return to America, he would translate a twelve-page episode from Gide's book — a safe passage dealing with Gide's early childhood. He may have intended to send it around to the magazines for possible publication. In that respect, Evans may have been more up to date than other would-be translators. Surprisingly, his translation, at points, is more down to earth — and perhaps more accurate — than Dorothy Bussy's later, more ladylike and literary translation for the 1935 Modern Library edition.

For a biographer, valuable lists such as Evans's can be frustrating.

Luxembourg Garden, Paris, December 25, 1926

Another of his entries, "Problem of JCE," obviously relates to his difficulties with his mother but offers no clues to what the problem was or to when or how it was resolved, whether by attrition or a quarrel. Equally frustrating is an unreadable notation after the name "Campagne 1er," following his trips to Cannes and Juan-les-Pins in July. A similar notation of the street "Hotel — rue Campagne 1er" after his return to Paris on August 1, 1926, was crossed out on his three-page itinerary. This is intriguing because 31 bis rue Campagne-Première was the address for the studio of the photographer and artist Man Ray, where Berenice Abbott, whom Evans would meet a year or two later in New York, was working as an assistant.

Further down the same street, at number 17 bis, was the studio of the documentary French photographer Eugène Atget. Both Abbott and Atget would figure importantly in Evans's career. The coincidence that the three were in Paris at the same time is intriguing, but there is no evidence Evans was aware of either of the two. Atget, still active as a street photographer (he had set himself the grandiose task of documenting Paris and its environs in a career that lasted thirty or more years), had photographed streets and shopfronts, ragpickers and prostititutes, the churches and parks of the banlieues (Saint-Ouen, Versailles). In his shabby clothes, his cumbersome view-camera and tripod bundled in a huge black cloth, he was still at work. In April, when Evans had arrived in Paris, Atget was rephotographing the gnarled trees and birches in the vast park of St. Cloud, a subject he returned to again and again over the years.

Berenice Abbott, thoroughly impressed with the documentary approach of Atget's photographs ("Their impact was immediate and tremendous. There was a sudden flash of recognition — the shock of realism unadorned."), had already begun to buy photographs from the pioneering but neglected seventy-year-old photographer whom she visited in his cluttered fifth-floor studio. She would later photograph him in her rue du Bac studio, surprised that he had arrived in a new overcoat rather than in the much-patched work clothes he usually wore. When she later took her prints to show him, she was shocked to learn that Atget had died (on August 4, 1927). Though it would take another year, she rescued a major portion of Atget's life work, including the glass negatives and prints remaining in his studio. Along with New York gallery dealer Julien Levy, she became Atget's most dedicated promoter in America. It was through Abbott, some two years later, that Evans would become acquainted with

the work of Atget.

There does not appear to be any strictly documentary evidence for the claim which crops up in the various chronologies of Evans's life (Evans was probably the source) that he had studied in the studio of the famed early French photographer Nadar. (Nadar was the pseudonym for Gaspard Félix Tournachon.) If true, this would have been the studio not of the original Nadar, who died in 1910, but his son Paul, who took over his father's studio in the 1880s, adopting the father's professional name as well. It was true that Evans, at this point, had taken up photography in a small way, using a pocket camera to take souvenir shots in France and later in Italy.

He also made a series of self-portraits, in Paris, one on a balcony against a window-shuttered wall, as well as a sequence of ghostly shadow shots of himself in profile, made in the South of France. One or two of these he sent to Hanns Skolle, who was full of admiration: "Upon my word," Skolle wrote, "the photos you took of yourself are superb. The one 'en face' is truly a treat of a picture. I wish I could paint as well as that." Few of these have survived. Evans, at the time, did not regard his early efforts at photography as serious, though he later acknowledged that they showed "something." And even though, back in New York, he kept at it with some unconscious drive, he still considered photography a kind of "left-hand

European souvenir snapshots, 1926–27

hobby." It was his friend Skolle and other acquaintances who made him take his photographic work seriously.

Important as Evans's trip to Paris was, he strangely, out of shyness or lack of confidence, seems to have made no special effort to meet any of the major expatriate writers who were settled in Paris at the time — a missed opportunity that would characterize his life in some ways, indicating a certain off-handed diffidence. Certainly, he was a customer of Sylvia Beach's bookstore, Shakespeare and Company, but he would later claim, with a certain pride, that when he had a chance to meet Joyce there, he did not seize it. His considered opinion of Joyce was that "he had very poor judgment of everybody around. He was ignorant of Proust; he was ignorant of all the great writers of the time. Yet look who he was."

Nor did he meet Ernest Hemingway, another of the favored customers at Shakespeare and Company. Hemingway was in Paris that spring finishing up the typescript for his novel of expatriate life in Paris, *The Sun Also Rises*. This was prior to leaving for his annual visit to the bullfights in Spain. True, Hemingway was only on the verge of real fame or notoriety. That would come later, in October, with the publication of his novel, though his ill-conceived and hastily written satire of such mentors and friends as Sherwood Anderson, Gertrude Stein, and F. Scott Fitzgerald, *The Torrents of Spring*, caused a minor stir in May. Hemingway, however, was already well known to the close-knit and gossipy expatriate society of Paris, and it is possible Evans might have heard about Hemingway, whom he would meet in person a few years later in Cuba. But in Paris, if the subject of Hemingway had come up, it would more likely have been in October, when the publication of *The Sun Also Rises* created a furor among former friends and acquaintances who turned up, thinly disguised, as characters in the book. As Janet Flanner alias Genet, the Paris correspondent for *The New Yorker*, phrased it: "All these personages are, it is maintained, to be seen just where Hemingway so often placed them at the Sélect." The two books published that year marked Hemingway's definitive break from the Paris crowd, with whom he was never quite comfortable.

Like Hemingway, Evans, too, did not consider himself part of the idle café society. He later would also make a distinction between his own generation of American artists and an earlier one: "I think mine was the first

Self-portrait,
5, rue de le Santé,
Paris, September
1926

generation that went to Europe and instead of studying European art and coming back and imitating it, went to Europe and got a European technique and applied it to America. Got a perspective and a technique."

Yet the curious thing is that, by chance, Evans seemed to be following in the migratory paths of the gregarious Parisian set. In July he began a month's vacation on the French Riviera. At Marseille he stopped at the Hotel Terminus overnight, proceeding to Cannes for a two-week stay at the Hotel Modern on the rue de Serbes. It was a modest hotel, only a few blocks from the harbor, with its yachts and fishing shacks and the fashionable casino on the Promenade de la Croisette, with its sentinel palms stretching along the glittering beach. The hills above the town were luxuriant with shrubs and groves of olive and orange trees, and, nestling among them, gleaming white villas and gardens blossoming with mimosa and paper bougainvillea. It says something for the spot that only months before Evans arrived, the painter Pierre Bonnard, transfixed by the rightness of the locale, had bought a villa in the hills above town. For a lifetime, he would devote himself to painting, with rigorous awkwardness and radiant color, his gardens at Le Cannet, which looked toward the blue sprawl of the mountains of L'Esterel beyond and the busy harbor and Gulf of Napoule, with its sudden summer squalls.

Evans, on the other hand, in all his lifetime as a photographer, would deliberately avoid the picturesque, even ignore it. Yet, at twenty-two (it is one of the many, bracing contradictions of his life) he seems to have been duly impressed by the Côte d'Azur. On the evening of July 12, he dined at a seaside restaurant at Juan-les-Pins, some eleven miles up the coast. In glowing French, but with a touch of asperity, he typed out an homage to "the animalities infantiles du monde de plaisir." The evening was "exotique," and the sky was "supernaturel," thanks to the lights, the ready violins, the décor of the restaurant. "We [A troublesome we. Was his mother still with him like a nagging ghost or had he taken some new companion out for the evening?] were visiting another world in reality . . . had happened on a temporary escape from the usual idea of reality . . ." Back in Cannes, standing on the balcony of his hotel room ("seul," he emphasizes) unable to sleep because of the champagne, the too richly sauced dinner, the too many cups of coffee, he catches sight of an incredible, theatrical star, a minuscule sun, on the horizon above Juan-les-Pins. ("Incroyable, tout a fait theatricale," he writes with some theatricality.) It turns out to be a balloon, rising, reflecting the lights from the casino below. A few days later, on July 15 or thereabouts, Evans moved to Juan-les-Pins to finish his vacation, apparently seduced by the charms of the place. He settles there in the Villa Myosotis. ("Chez Alliaume," he notes in his itinerary, a name that will have an interesting connection later.)

By the mid-twenties Juan-les-Pins and the nearby Cap d'Antibes had become popular for French writers and artists as well as for English and American expatriates. Evans's two-week stay occurred during a particularly festive and crowded summer: Picasso was in residence, painting for much of the summer at Juan-les-Pins. Among the other visitors were the painter Marie Laurencin and the lavish party giver and patron of the arts Count Etienne de Beaumont and his wife. On the beach that summer one could have seen Maurice Sachs, one of Cocteau's bedeviled disciples, fresh from a seminary and parading along the sands in his soutane, hand in hand with a young American boy, Tom Pinkerton, a minor whose mother found it necessary to protest to the bishop of Nice. The English writer Rebecca West and her son Anthony were there, as was the English novelist G. B. Stern. F. Scott Fitzgerald and his wife, Zelda, and their daughter, Scottie, were living in the Villa St. Louis near the beach and casino, having earlier vacated the Villa Paquita because Zelda had found it too uncomfortable and Fitzgerald seemed unable to work there. The Hemingways (Ernest; his wife, Hadley; and son, "Bumby") had come and gone (to the bullfights in Pamplona), having, for several weeks, occupied the Villa Paquita courtesy of the Fitzgeralds, because Bumby had to be quarantined for whooping cough. They were expected back in August. Only a few miles distant, at Cap d'Antibes, Gerald and Sara Murphy, having completed the renovations of their Villa America above the beach at La Garoupe, were entertaining in style. Among their guests and visitors were the poet Archibald MacLeish and his wife, Ada; Anita Loos, the author of *Gentlemen Prefer Blondes*; the critics Gilbert Seldes and Alexander Woollcott; playwright Charles MacArthur; and opera star Grace Moore, who had rented a villa at Antibes.

But it was not a happy time for either the Fitzgerald or the Hemingway families, especially the wives. Zelda, recuperating from an appendectomy, was left alone much of the time while Scott preferred the liveliness at Cap d'Antibes. "I wanted you to swim with me at Juan-les-Pins," she would later write to Scott from the depths of one of her breakdowns, "but you liked it better where it was gayer at the Garoupe with Marisse Hamilton and the Murphys and MacLeishes."

Fitzgerald was in a glum and irritable mood. It rankled him that the Murphys were so attentive to their new protégé Hemingway, praising his work. It nettled him even more that he was stalled on his long-delayed novel *Tender Is the Night*. He acted outrageously at a champagne and caviar party the Murphys gave in Hemingway's honor, sulking, making caustic remarks, tossing ashtrays around. Throughout the summer — much of the time leaving Zelda and Scottie to their own devices — Fitzgerald drank heavily and behaved so badly at the Murphys' soirées that he was banned for a week or two. Fitzgerald's disgruntled feelings toward Hemingway may partly explain the patronizing letter he sent to Hemingway after reading a manuscript copy of *The Sun Also Rises*, offering lengthy criticisms and suggestions for improvements, with assurances of good intentions that only served to underscore his dissatisfaction. (Zelda's appraisal of *The Sun Also Rises* was blunt. When a friend asked her what the book was about, she answered "bull fighting, bull slinging, bull — !")

Hemingway hardly needed the aggravation; he was in the midst of unusual marital problems, suffering pangs of guilt and anxiety over an adulterous affair he had begun with Pauline Pfeiffer, a fashion editor for Paris *Vogue* who had befriended Hadley. To make matters worse, well before departing for Pamplona, Pauline Pfeiffer had arrived at Juan-les-Pins, ostensibly to help with the ailing Bumby. Her arrival — she would accompany them to Spain, as well — created a strange ménage-à-trois, with uneasy days at the beach and solemn attempts at the usual civilities. As Hadley described life at the Villa Paquita: "Here it was that the three breakfast trays, three wet bathing suits on the lines, three bicycles were to be found. Pauline tried to teach me to dive, but I was not a success. Ernest wanted us to play bridge, but I found it hard to concentrate." Mounting trouble in paradise. It was understandable, then, though not to their stunned friends, that when the Hemingways returned to the Riviera in August (sans Pauline) it was only to announce their plans to separate.

Considering that Evans, in the presence of any body of water, was an incorrigible swimmer and beach lounger, one wonders what rumors and reports of the Hemingways and Fitzgeralds he might have heard on the beach at Juan-les-Pins. He met neither of the writers during his year abroad, but he would evolve certain opinions, some of them misguided, about Paris and the expatriate crowd, particularly Fitzgerald and Hemingway. "All people went to Europe differently," Evans would later maintain. "For example, I don't think Fitzgerald got anything much out of Europe and wasn't really interested in anything there." This was a miscalculation, considering the symbolic importance that Paris and the Riviera would play in several of Fitzgerald's stories and significantly in the novel *Tender Is the Night*. On the other hand, Evans contended that Hemingway did get something out of Europe. In another of his overestimations, he maintained, "Hemingway became a sort of master of all the languages. I mean he could speak French and Italian and Spanish. Fitzgerald didn't pay any attention to the French language."

II

Walker Evans's isolation from the frenetic expatriate life on the Riviera the summer of 1926 may have had a psychological cause. A note he had written on the back of a brief July 29, 1926, letter from Skolle reveals that he was suffering through a period of deep depression and some soul-searching:

I don't write to you because my erstwhile dashing spirit is dormant. I am dead and disgusted . . . My self-analysis is becoming self-laceration; my failures call for such ardent criticism (and get it) that I am in a fair way . . . to what? And the funny part of it is, I know exactly what I need to cure me but am too lazy to go out and get it. No, I don't think of suicide and I am ashamed of that too. Do you know what nothing means? There is something to discover. I think you do. Death is something you see.

The notations of "solitude," "bitterness," "hatred and shame," running

Hanns Skolle,
New York, 1929

like a leitmotif through Evans's one-page European list suggest that the down spells were recurrent and even perhaps drastic. His initial hopes for writing masterpieces appear to have been stalled. Years later he confessed that he had suffered from a serious case of writer's block: "You see I'd done a lot of reading and I knew what writing was. And if I tried to do it, what I did was ludicrous and I threw it away and blushed." But it must have been something more than writer's block that had affected him. Clearly the tone of his penciled note indicates he had touched that sense of "nothingness" in which the bottom of the world drops out from beneath one. He had been forced to confront an abyss against which even death was "something" one could hold on to. Skolle's letter, which was dated July 29, 1926, could not have reached Evans in Juan-les-Pins, so his black thoughts must have been written down sometime after August 1, when he was back in Paris.

It probably did not help that Skolle's letters were so full of energy, so full of projects in which he was engaged. He was selling drawings to the left-wing political magazine *New Masses*, making sketches for woodcuts of the prisoners at Sing Sing in Ossining, preparing for a possible exhibition at the Weyhe Gallery in New York. He had read De Quincey's essays on murder and the English mail system with great delight. Skolle asked Evans, if possible, to send him French books (with illustrations) on Modigliani and Gauguin. It would have been understandable if Evans, in his bleak mood, felt even worse hearing about his friend's relentless activities.

Evans may not have sent Skolle the letter he had drafted during the depths of his unhappiness, but he did at some later date tell Skolle, who had pointedly asked, "How are the literary masterpieces coming?" that in his depressed state he had destroyed all his manuscripts. Skolle answered with some seriousness: "I fear you made a deplorable mistake in destroying all your writing. Why incapacitate yourself? Especially when there is no immediate substance to take the place of the destroyed matter?"

Still, not all of Evans's manuscripts were destroyed. Two versions of a short story, begun in September 1926, which went through subsequent revisions until June 1928 and perhaps beyond, have survived. Titled "A Love Story," it involves a young man in a foreign country who has been taking his meals in a boarding house on the theory that it is one of the better ways to learn the language. In one version, the narrator is enrolled in unspecified classes at a nearby school. The other boarding house diners include a young

Scotswoman; a Pole and his unpleasant Danish wife; two English boys, one of whom thinks that no French writer came up to Galsworthy; and three English girls, one of whom wears glasses and is attracted to the narrator. There is, too, a rather vulgar landlady and her pregnant daughter-in-law. With the exception of the Scots girl, most of these characters have no bearing on the story, so the narrator readily admits.

At the noon and evening meals, the narrator prefers to sit with the young Scots girl. They strike up a friendship of sorts. Her afternoons, he adds, were spent in the library, where she read Tolstoi on art. "I knew," he comments rather dryly, "she would get thick ankles doing that and I just waited." The modern note of the story is struck when the narrator confesses that he cannot explain his attraction to the girl. She was "courageous and big and 'genuine' and socialistic. I was annoyed because I really don't like girls like that."

In an eerie episode, the narrator invites the Scots girl to his rooming house or apartment and shows her his "mysterious wall." It is at the end of the garden. High up in the expanse of stone there is a solitary, small iron-barred window. From time to time he can hear bells ringing inside and other noises as well. On Sunday mornings there is violin-playing and someone singing. Some nights a light shines from the window. The mystery of what is happening in the room behind the barred window defines the two characters: "The Scotch girl said something about smashing through to find out the human suffering." The narrator's suspicion is that the place is a madhouse.

At the end of the summer the girl plans to go to the coast for a week or more. The narrator agrees to meet her there. She writes to the mayor of a fishing village. He is a Communist and a local hero. A few years earlier, he had been shot by government forces during a fishermen's strike. In her letter, the Scotswoman explains that she is a comrade and that she would be bringing another comrade and wants rooms in the town.

The narrator arrives at the fishing village at night. Much to his satisfaction, it is out of season; there are no tourists or resorters around. The next morning he finds the Scots girl in the marketplace: "She puckered a little and said she hadn't thought I would come." They decide to have a picnic on a beach a couple of miles from the village. But abruptly, on the way, they separate and make no effort to get together again. "I didn't look back," the narrator explains. "She knew I was miserable and let me go on about a mile. I asked God some sharp questions and was told I was a spoiled child. I knew that."

At this point in Evans's shaky story, the narrative breaks down. The petulant narrator is disappointed that he hasn't been granted some vision or even some foresight into an unexplained event that he mentions as having happened to him after he returned to town. Had there been some apparition, he ruminates, he might have sat eating his sardine sandwiches while the abyss opened before him as he pretended not to notice. Instead, he claims, "I just lay there and imagined things of different shapes and colors and imagined what they would do and what I would do." Evans concludes these wanderings of the narrative mind with an ending sufficiently sharp to redeem the story somewhat:

After that the sea and the silence were not enough for me. The white figure of the Scotch girl running into the water a mile away reminded me that I was an unhappy fool.

Evans's enigmatic little tale of frustrated love was rooted in his recent experiences. On his page list there is a simple notation of "L'Ecossaise" (the feminine of Scot). And in September, as he vaguely remembered it, he had taken an excursion that included the Channel towns of Deauville, Dinard, and Douarenez, towns that had a tradition of fishing. Sometime, during the summer, he had certainly had his sobering glimpse of the nature of nothingness. The antic details of the story, to say nothing of the motivational lapses, leave the reader with the suspicion that they were part of a picture based on strong autobiographical elements rather than any necessary thematic consequences of the tale. Evans, perhaps, hadn't quite thought them through enough to establish a textual necessity.

It is also clear, based on two surviving homework assignments, one of them an essay on Baudelaire, that during the month of August, before making his trip to the coast, Evans was again enrolled in French classes. The essay, dated August 7, 1926, was presented as a few pages from a journal in which Evans confesses to feeling isolated and introspective and too young: "Voici mon journal par example — un temoin d'introspection et d'egoisme." (Take my journal for instance — a proof of introspection and egotism.)

Evans's journal-essay offers other tidbits from his personal life that were surely meant to impress the professor with his precocity. He chose to write about Baudelaire, he admits, because he had a beautiful edition of *Les Fleurs du Mal*. He claims to have been familiar with the poem, "Les bijoux," because, at the age of eighteen, of having heard it was one of Baudelaire's "condemned" poems. He had read it in the New York Public Library. (The poem, about the nature of desire and a woman in the firelight, nude except for her jewels, would have struck a reader of any age; its opulence, its Near Eastern rhythms seemingly stamping out some exotic dance, has a mesmerizing cadence.) But at the age of eighteen, Evans was enrolled at Loomis, the Connecticut prep school, and not working at the New York Public Library.

In his tribute to the talents of Baudelaire, Evans, imitating the poet's extravagant language, extols Baudelaire's gift for gorgeous and perverse imagery. Furthermore, he claims that his own affinities to Baudelaire were prompted by the deprivations of American culture. At home he was "tourmente, serre par la sante perverse d'Amerique" [tormented, constrained by the perverse well-being of America].

The second essay takes the form of a clever dialogue between two friends on the question of "l'art pour l'art," one of whom is required to write an essay on that subject, ostensibly dealing with Théophile Gautier versus Victor Hugo. The most vocal of the characters has read Gautier's forty-four-page preface to his novel *Mademoiselle de Maupin* and was shocked (when not bored) by the falsehoods of the "estimable Théophile"'s ideas. Not once, he maintains, does Gautier say a word about the part the sexual urge plays in art. Evans's outspoken character believes not only that artists knowingly or subconsciously have used their works to promote their own sexual ideas and sexual dreams, but that the audience, too, uses art for the same sublimational purposes. At points, his argument turns boisterously antifeminist. The audience that buys books and fills museums, he claims, consists for the most part of "femmes affamees," the clear implication being that they are sex-starved. He regards this as especially true of English and American audiences. He is particularly obsessed with the subject of the dry and ugly women ("living horrors"), always from the best families, who rush off to conferences on the Arts ("With a capital A").

What is significant about the two classroom exercises is that they underscore Evans's early (and, occasionally, late) views on two themes: the

*Shadow
Self-portraits,
Juan-les-Pins,
January, 1927*

aridity of American culture and the role of women in the arts. Evans regarded his first trip abroad as an escape from the dry, commercial culture of the United States: "I was really anti-American at that time," he admitted. "I was so scared and America was big business and the hell with it . . . It just nauseated me." Nor should his youthful antifeminist views — also relating to his ideas about culture — be overlooked. Remarkably, he still voiced some of those ideas forty-five years later, tempered but not by much from his youthful opinions: "Culture and art are in the hands of women and schoolteachers and nice dominant women in every community," he maintained. "They're always on museum boards and all that, or have been. That's been one of the things that's been the matter with American culture, left to the hands of women. And that's an anti-feminine remark, but I can't help it."

By November, Evans was enrolled in a new course, this one a study of "Civilisation Française." His compositions were even more ambitious and more opinionated. Writing on the subject of his literary preferences — the choice of period and genre was up to him — he admitted that he liked Gautier better than George Sand, even though he had not read a word written by that "ridiculous woman." The professor, perhaps a woman, judging from the delicate handwriting of the marginal corrections, remarked "Oh!!!"

Evans listed the authors and books that now gave him great pleasure and enormous satisfaction: Huysmans's *A rebours*, the criticism of Rémy de Gourmont, *Mademoiselle de Maupin*, Baudelaire, and Jean Cocteau. Evans went on to recount a personal episode. One day, reading Cocteau's early novel *Thomas l'imposteur*, a beautiful young woman approached him and sat down beside him on a beach. She was French, had red hair and green eyes, "the pure soul of a young bourgeois." She asked what book he was reading. When he told her it was Cocteau, she gave a hearty laugh. Evans argued strongly for Cocteau's boldness of approach, his ability to stir up intellectual surprises. It was true that Cocteau had a habit of playing droll, but he believed Cocteau was far from being that. Certainly he could be incredibly amusing. A writer's faults of worldly taste were less important when the writer possessed real talent, Evans claimed. As proof, he cited Cocteau's play *Orphée*.

Evans began the New Year, 1927, with a burst of energy. His itinerary details a trip south to the Riviera. (In the late twenties, the Riviera was still, primarily, a winter resort.) Was it only one of those mysterious coincidences that, having become so enthusiastic about the writings of Jean Cocteau, Evans, around January 4, should have booked himself into the Hotel Welcome at Villefranche-sur-Mer? It was there, in September 1925, that Cocteau, still in the haze of his opium addiction, had completed *Orphée*. And it was there, in late June 1926, just after the Paris production of the play, that Cocteau returned to the hotel for the summer.

Villefranche had other more artistic attractions: It was a haunt of Isadora Duncan, dowdy and well past her prime, and her entourage of febrile young males and nubile dance maidens, and of Man Ray, who in 1926 had photographed Picasso, bare-chested, and his mistress, Kiki, the famed and rowdy artists' model, on the beach at Juan-les-Pins. The blossoming young American writer Glenway Wescott, who completed his novel *The Grandmothers* in the stimulating atmosphere of Villefranche, would describe the scene at the Welcome aptly: "Life was not a series of parties, but one constant long party."

It is impossible to know just what Evans, in 1926, may have heard about Villefranche and its notorious hotel while staying only miles away at Juan-les-Pins. But it may not have been mere coincidence that he would begin the

New Year with a stop at the Welcome. One gets the feeling that no matter how diffident Evans might appear about meeting artistic celebrities, he seems to have been interested enough, when young, to have stalked them, albeit at a comfortable distance. But one thing is certain: throughout his life, Evans had too much pride and self-possession to ever become a fan.

By January 15, he was once again in Juan-les-Pins, this time staying, first, at the Villa Choupette until March 24, when he moved to the Hotel des Fleurs. Judging from the notations on his page list, it was a happy enough time: "Solitude, soleil, sante" at least suggests that he was enjoying himself. He appears to have met a Mme. A. and her daughter, or possibly became friendly again with the Alliaumes, with whom he had stayed the year before. "Bicyclette," "Musique," "La Follie" at St-Jean-Cap-Ferrat, suggest other possibly pleasurable activities.

But what was of more importance was that for the next two and a half months Evans would busy himself reading and occasionally translating from the works of French authors, mostly contemporary. And he was once again writing stories, some of which, both translations and stories, he sent to Skolle, who pronounced them "damn good." The translation, possibly, was from Blaise Cendrars's novel *Moravagine*, since Skolle, having received it in February, remarked that he was eager to read more Cendrars. The story unfortunately is unnamed.

Skolle's letters also carried interesting news. He had recently met a French woman, Elizabeth Chavanon, possibly older than he, who was visiting New York. She was from Paris, a "magnificent" pianist, and she knew a lot about books and editions. (Her father was a publisher.) What astonished Evans, evidently, was that within a month or two the pair was married. Responding to Evans's surprise Skolle answered:

Become sedate, old bean, and try to conceive me — a married man. No way out. How did it all happen? Might as well dwell upon the question how two deaf and dumb men of different nationalities would make each other understood.

Elizabeth, Skolle informed Evans, was returning to Paris for two weeks in March to settle some financial matters of importance. He hoped Evans would be able to meet her there. But the meeting did not take place since Evans did not return to Paris until May. It was not until he returned to America that he met the bride.

At Juan-les-Pins that January and for the next two or three years Evans would busy himself with the task of reading a number of modern and contemporary French authors and translating segments from their works. Evans was definitely reading Cendrars's *Moravagine* and perhaps others of Cendrars's works. (In 1929, his translation of Cendrars's hallucinatory story "Mad" would be published in the magazine *Alhambra*.) He also translated a section of *Le diable au corps*, the still scandalous novel by Cocteau's protégé and former lover Raymond Radiguet, who had died of typhoid in 1923 only months after the publication of his book. Evans's translation is dated Juan-les-Pins, 1927.

Evans was particularly impressed with Gide's style. "Gide's prose style," he would remark later, "was very mesmerizing almost, to me and everybody else. I learned a lot of French from Gide." But perhaps there was a stronger kinship beyond the matter of style. In the translated segment of *Si le grain ne meurt*, Gide, a boy, spies on the evening ball his parents are giving, and senses that he is on the point of a discovery:

It seems to me that I am about to be initiated suddenly into another life, a mysterious unusually real, a more brilliant and a more pathetic life, which commences only when little children are in bed.

Just beyond the point where Evans's manuscript translation ends, Gide develops the idea further with implications that might have impressed Evans as much as the precision and lucidity, the finical attention to detail, that marked Gide's authoritative literary style.

And before sinking into sleep, I thought in a confused way — there is reality and there are dreams and there is another reality as well.

The vague, ill-defined belief that something else exists alongside the acknowledged, above-board reality of everyday life, inhabited me for many years; and I am not sure that even to-day I have not still some remnants of it left . . . I think it was more a kind of unskillful desire to give life more thickness . . . and also a sort of propensity to imagine a clandestine side of things.

Evans was right in claiming Gide as one of his early mentors. He would also translate a brief segment from Gide's *Morceaux choisis* (1921), on "Individualism." In his diverting fashion, Gide chose to downplay the individual and at the same time use him as a stick to beat down the bourgeoisie and its mediocre values. Characteristically taking the offensive stance, Gide declared that greatness was a burden to society, its enemy: "Individualism — never, for pity's sake, out of pity [pity] individuals. Never encourage the great; and as for the others: discourage! discourage!" Evans's translation was not so apt as his episode from *Si le grain ne meurt*, but it caught the élan of Gide's perverse argument:

[G]reat individuals need no theories to protect them: they are conquerors. So let us leave the joy of being able to condemn them to the mediocre and the weak, and [to the] conquered and crushed themselves. Let them take an innocent revenge in conquering them in effigy.

The heady argument, perhaps, struck a chord with a young writer needing to assert his individuality, dissatisfied with his family's values. One of the more curious translations of Gide made by Evans was an episode obviously from a personal memoir, "Conversation with a German Some Years Before the War." (The translation is dated February 1927, Juan-les-

Evans with friends, French countryside, 1927

Pins.) It reveals another aspect of Gide's gifts that may have appealed to Evans. In this episode Gide has agreed to meet B.R., a German reader and admirer of Gide's works including the *Nourritures terrestres* and *L'immoraliste*. B.R. is engaged in translating both. He has just been released from a German prison, having served fourteen months for the crime of embezzlement. B.R. admits to being a constant liar and a man "passionately fond of luxury." He has come all the way from Cologne just to see Gide, probably in an attempt — despite his abrasive and erratic behavior — perhaps to engage the writer in some business dealing. (Or, as Gide suspects, to make a touch.) One of the things that may have impressed Evans abut the episode is Gide's nearly photographic attention to finical and revealing detail: "He offered me a cigarette in the finest case I have ever seen: I admired too his match container, silver like the cigarette case. The smallest objects he had about him were of a somber and restrained elegance . . ." What might also be nice to imagine is that what may have struck Evans was the irony that he, himself, was an erstwhile translator of Gide who was making the effort to escape from the prison of his family.

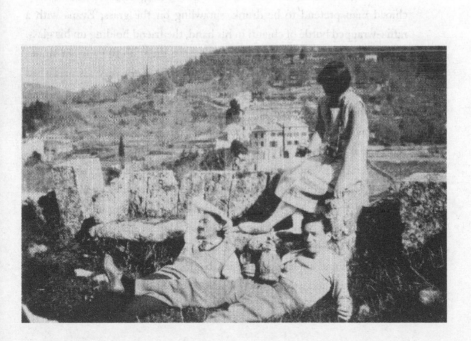

III

It was not, apparently, an eventful trip home. Other than the bare itinerary of dates, including a month-long tour of Italy, there are scant clues about the purpose or the pleasures of the journey. It began at midnight on the fourth of April at Villefranche, where Evans took the S.S. *Biancamano*, arriving at Genoa early on the morning of the fifth. The next day he was at Naples, which he later claimed he hated, though he stayed there at the Pensione Marcini Partinope for six days. Leaving Naples at midnight, there was not even a day's stay in Rome to break the trip to Florence, where he put himself up at the Pensione Constantin on the Via Solferino for a nine-day stop. Presumably, in that amount of time, he was able to go to the Uffizi; see the Botticellis, the Raphaels, the Tintorettos; and perhaps even visit the map room, given his childhood interest in maps.

Somewhere along the route he may have met companions, unless they had accompanied him all the way. There are snapshots of Evans and friends — a young man and woman of about his age or a little older — in what look to be the hills in the south of France; photographs of smiling faces, figures posing arm in arm against the luxuriant shrubbery, such as many a tourist might have taken. There is a bit of clowning: Evans and the mustachioed man pretend to be drunk, sprawling on the grass, Evans with a raffia-wrapped bottle of chianti in his hand, the friend holding up his glass. The woman, stylishly bobbed, is seated above them on the ancient stones of some ruin. In the distance what appears to be a not very distinguished country inn stands below a terraced garden or vineyard on a sparsely wooded hillside.

Evans seems to have had a penchant for midnight departures. He leaves Florence at midnight on Friday, April 22, traveling by way of Pisa, Genoa, Bordighera, and Ventimiglia to arrive at Juan-les-Pins at eight the following evening. What happened after that has fallen between the cracks of Evans's brisk itinerary. On May 10 he leaves Paris for Cherbourg and the voyage home, arriving in New York before noon on May 16, 1927, to begin his long career. He is twenty-three. But Evans, confronted by the unexpected compromises and antic opportunities that life presents, had made the break with his family and its past that his unique career seemed to require.

Standing Aside

3

A photograph of Evans, dated June, 1927, taken at 13 East Fourteenth Street, probably by Hanns Skolle, shows him as beatifically young but alarmingly thin. The likelihood is that Evans stayed with the Skolles for a while after his return from Europe. Earlier, in February, Skolle had already alerted Evans that the studio he had rented on East Fourteenth Street was "of huge dimensions," large enough for him to hang an exhibition of his work soon after moving into it and large enough to hold sketch classes and give lessons in making woodcuts. It had formerly belonged to the American artist Walter Pach—"sort of a famous man," Skolle mentioned. Pach was, indeed, well known in New York City artistic circles, one of the organizers of the famed 1913 Armory Show of modernist art, which offered such artists as Matisse, Picasso, and Marcel Duchamp to a broad but stunned American public. According to Skolle, the studio was "generally spoken of by hushed voices for its trick bathtub, partly collapsible, serving likewise as tub and kitchen table." One could only get into it by means of a step ladder or chair, thus producing "the eternal symbol of purity . . . on a fantastically high level."

It may not have been the happiest of occasions when Evans met the new bride, judging from the acerbic little short story, dated 1927, which Evans wrote sometime after his return from France. The presumed earliest manuscript, written in longhand, was titled "A Story in Which Something Happens." In it Evans used actual names throughout, even noting that he had been ill for a few days before calling on the couple, a detail that might account for his emaciated appearance in the photograph. But in an odd maneuver, he provided his tale with an "Introduction by Hanns Skolle," though it was clearly written in Evans's own hand:

Walker Evans, a figment of my mind, seems to have undertaken a sketch of my married life. Let him. He deserves, perhaps, a better outlet for his literary impulsions. I am his limitation. Ah, well; I have endowed him with all the common sense necessary. The rest is literature.

*Columbia
Heights,
Brooklyn,
New York,
October, 1928,
possibly a
self-portrait*

Evans, no doubt, intended the story to be a fairly factual depiction of the Skolle marriage, of which he was patently disapproving:

Hanns Skolle listened in the evening to the piano playing of Elizabeth Chavanon. They were legally married; the piano he rented.

Hanns' wife was thirty, and so was the piano. She was bien-pensante, the piano was upright, though dilapidated.

Evans proceeded to give the details of Hanns's life, how he had been brought up in Leipzig with intellectual and creative ambitions, noting, too, that he was an artist. With an apparent juggling of the actual chronology of their relationship, Evans indicated that Hanns was twenty-four at the time of the story, though only twenty when Hanns and he first met. Hanns, he explained, "found me in the New York Society Library, covered with dust." A brisk psychological analysis of the young Hanns is provided, relating how in Leipzig "he had learned the art of making himself sick with his own thoughts. He investigated strange places and strange moods." Evans then sets out the details of the marriage as he had learned of them: "Ellie married Hanns while I was in Paris. They were in New York. I had to figure it out for myself. First Ellie sat to, or posed, for Hanns, who found he could not paint her type. She conceived a child. Marriage was discussed and perpetrated. Hanns met me at the pier when I landed."

The narrator's first meeting with the bride at the studio was awkward: "Some sort of presentation was made, which we all passed off apologetically. Our breeding came into play. Together we all dined and made that evening as difficult as possible. All spoke English." He admits to feelings of guilt at his friend's changed status: "Where he had dreamed, now he worried. He had never mistaken his dreams for possibilities; now he found the suspicion that both belonged to the free state he had known before the funny thing happened to him." In his ambiguous account of his friend's dilemma, which bore some relationship to his own situation as well, Evans made a pointed comparison. In kicking out from under himself the prop of bourgeois life, Evans claimed, "Hanns had lost the conviction of his own social entity. Had I too not kicked — but I had; I had kicked as far as Paris and had left him with his guard down."

For a time, the expected baby brings the couple together. Evans becomes more cynical than ever when he views the parents' behavior after the birth of the child. Its sex, strangely enough, does not figure in the story: "The appalling red thing refused to recognize us. We all went in for child psychology. But none of us could think of a good name." The narrator is not impressed by the picture of the mother leaning on her man's shoulder before the cradle, even less by the sight of the father cavorting before the baby in a frantic effort to impress his personality on it. "I was surprised," the narrator claims, "and began to collect these experiences." He also becomes aware that the new mother, with increasing frequency, has begun to speak about her great-grandmother in France. The denouement is expectable:

Hanns grew fonder of the piano. We kept it; but Ellie and the child are in the bosom of an honorable French family — bien-pensante.

The "We kept it," is one of the subtleties of the story; with the departure of the wife and child, the two friends are now sharing the studio apartment.

Given what appeared to be the strained circumstances of the Fourteenth Street ménage, it was understandable that Evans, who tended to avoid unpleasant confrontations, did not stay long at the studio. By July he was living out of state. Elizabeth Skolle (variously known as Ellie, Lily, and eventually the Lil that Hanns called her) wrote Evans, in French, on Bastille Day, complaining that his absence was felt in the kitchen. Without his aid, the noodles had a tendency to "escape from the saucepan." From the same letter it is clear that Evans was off on an unspecified horticultural venture. Lil, in her bantering style, was sure he was about to make a fortune and would certainly develop some magnificent new floral species to be called "walkeria evantina." Whatever the nature of the summer project, it would engage Evans over the next three or four summers. According to one story it was connected with one of his father's extracurricular activities — the growing of hybrid varieties of gladiolas. The horticultural project begun at Stamford, Connecticut, in the summer months of 1927 seems to have been continued on in Ossining, New York, the following summer of 1928 and then definitely transferred to Darien in 1929.

The summer of 1927, at least in New York, was brutally hot, so hot in fact that Lil, in her letter, was hoping for violent and refreshing storms — but only in the city, thus sparing what she termed Walker's "seedbeds and cuttings." Hanns, over the next few years, playfully denigrating his friend's efforts as farmer, would inquire about his crop of "forget-me-nuts" or suggest that he transfer his "damned peanut bulbs" to a ranch in Denver where he could "enjoy the invigorating air and mountains of Alcoholorado."

In another letter he counseled Evans: "Yes, take my advice: you had better give up that supine flower growing and settle down to some fiery

writing. What the hell! A breeding station is nothing but a nursery of futilities . . . Better begin training for your inevitable future position as representative of immortality." Among Evans's early undated negatives there is a sequence of some forty photographs of gladiolas in bloom, a few of them named varieties ("Wm McGavin" and "W. Lind," e.g.), which may have been intended as possible illustrations for a nursery catalogue. It may say something further about Evans's horticultural enterprise that through most of his lengthy photographic career, he showed no great inclination to take pictures of flowers.

In the early years of their friendship, whenever Evans and Skolle were separated, they kept up an active correspondence on literary matters and sent each other anecdotal newspaper clippings. Skolle had an enormous interest in all things American. In many ways, he served as a goad for Evans, alerting him to new interests, new trends. A young man with a voracious literary appetite, his letters are full of commentaries on his readings. During the summer of 1927, the Skolles made a brief visit to friends in Cos Cob, not far from Stamford. On arrival, Hanns wrote Evans, informing him that he had brought along the typewriter and a volume of Stendhal that Evans had apparently requested. Skolle was full of praise for one of his new discoveries, Stephen Crane: "By Jove, there is an American for you! . . . Stephen Crane is colossal," he claimed.

Evans in East Fourteenth Street studio, New York, 1927

Financially, the Skolles were feeling the pinch. Hanns complained of being "under the stinking influence of some ignominious rot — daily bread, you know." He joked: "E. intends to sell your books. She, too, thinks that we are as much entitled to a hamburger steak now and then as the rest of mankind." He sent Evans a highly interesting Dadaist collage of figures cut from rotogravure sections, pasted into a boat, which he titled *Ulysses*. This was followed by a one-page Dadaist film scenario *Cinema, Deviation Number I*, which included in its action an "irascible giraffe successfully dodging boomerang and monkeywrench, insidiously fired by celibate arborculturist who is promptly attacked in turn by serpenticular viper." In one of his letters he advised Evans to consider staying at East Fourteenth Street when his agricultural labors were over: "I think you would do well in coming to our place. Consider our engaging fire-place as idyllic touch to the forthcoming study of Plato."

In all probability, Evans must have been eager to escape the East Fourteenth Street studio during the course of Lil Skolle's pregnancy. Yet he made himself available during the birth of the child, returning to New York to stay with the waiting father. A surprising, undated letter from Lil written from the maternity ward of the Womans' Hospital in New York confirms that, as in the story, there was some consternation and some comedy about the naming of the child — a girl, eventually named Anita. She also acknowledged that it was very "gentil" of Walker to offer to send champagne to the hospital but warned that it was not permitted on the ward. She pardoned his offense of treating "le père de ma fille" as a "grand stupide" and branding the circumstances as "criminelles." Nevertheless, she was expecting to find Walker at the studio when she returned from the hospital a few days later. She assured him the bébé would not be too much trouble. It was a perfectly healthy child and therefore would only cry at night under exceptional circumstances.

Lil Skolle's letters to Evans have a tone of warmth and sly familiarity: They are the letters of an older woman dealing with the affairs of two not so mature, younger men. They are not the letters one would expect from the "Marie" of Evans's brisk and bitter little short story. Nor did the events of the Skolle's married life end as neatly and finally as Evans's narrator had related it. There are unfortunate gaps in the chronology of this period in Evans's life, but evidence suggests that Evans may have stayed with the Skolles again after his return from Stamford, probably in late September. There are early photographs of Hanns and Lil, taken with Walker's vest-pocket camera, presumably on the roof of their Fourteenth Street studio building, Hanns looking pinched and intense, Lil a bit dowdy, but clearly past her pregnancy. From Lil's random correspondence with Evans it is clear that the marriage was not necessarily a happy one. Skolle did not slip easily into the role of husband and father. He was subject to dark moods which Lil, in a letter to Evans, explained with grim forthrightness: "For Hanns, I am 'sa femme'; is there any word more chilling than that to a man?" Evans's friendship with Hanns continued on for several years to come, but in the course of it he became a witness if not a collaborator in the eventual unraveling of the Skolle marriage. Like the narrator in "A Story in Which Something Happens," Evans had begun to "collect" such experiences.

Evans at New York Hospital,
1928

II

In the early summer of 1928, Walker Evans was hospitalized for unexplained reasons and an undetermined length of time. Hanns Skolle visited him at the hospital at least once and took a series of snapshots of Evans in the hospital, his face gaunt, with a thin growth of beard and a slightly bewildered expression. The face is perched above a slope of white sheeting. Skolle wrote his friend, apologizing for not having made another visit to the hospital before Evans was released, explaining that his "long islandish labours" had not yet ended. "You certainly look like D. H. Lawrence, junior, on the photos," he commented. He hoped that Evans was rapidly getting well. During the month of June, Evans was recuperating in Ossining, New York, at the newly acquired farmhouse on Somerstown Road owned by his sister Jane and her husband, Talbot Brewer. (Later, he would move to Liberty Street in town.) Tal Brewer, at the time, was working as a personnel manager for the Wall Street firm of Henry L. Doherty, with hopes of quitting the company and becoming a gentleman farmer on his thirteen-acre Berry Patch Farm. It is a possibility that that summer Evans had moved his flower-growing operation to his brother-in-law's sprawling acreage.

Out of the minutiae of the day-to-day life found in the letters (mostly Skolle's) a biographer may eke out a few significant facts. They indicate that Skolle made one or more visits to Ossining: in July 1928, in two of his letters he thanked Evans for driving him as far back as Yonkers and stressing his hopes that Evans had gotten back to Ossining all right. He also sent special thanks to Evans's mother, an indication that the feud between mother and son was sufficiently forgotten for Jessie Evans to be staying with her son on Liberty Street or, perhaps as likely, with her daughter at Berry Patch Farm. (Lil Skolle, too, in an August letter to Evans, would send "Respectueux souvenirs a votre mère," indicating that Mrs. Evans was in Ossining for a respectable stay.) And there are a few clues about Evans's slowly developing career in photography. On one of the Skolle visits, the two were on a photographic expedition in the vicinity of Sing-Sing and caused a fuss of some kind when Evans spotted a Model T Ford in shambles, the roofing torn to shreds and hanging loose, which he evidently wanted to photograph.

That summer the Skolles were on the verge of a decisive move, vacating their Fourteenth Street studio and planning to move to Denver. They were in the process of shipping their belongings west. That necessitated the removal of Evans's trunk. In the second of his thank-you notes, Skolle informed him: "Bad news: You will have to send a couple of strong men down in a car to fetch your trunk. It won't lock. Can't give it to the Express Company." Evans's answer on July 11, somewhat clouds the issue:

I shall come in town with automobile, make bonfire of most of contents of trunk; carry off everything left; have no more to think of same, nor you (will) nor your wife (will). The parentheses are for you not to think I think of saying I will have no more to think of you and wife; use them for this. We issue no coupons on account of the extreme quality of the product.

Having given up their studio, Skolle and Lil planned to stay with friends until their departure for the West. They had taken a place five miles from the town of Sharon where the painter Bertram Elliott and his wife were summering, and at Sharon, it turned out that "The joys of country-life," as Hanns titled his letter to Evans soon after arrival, were not so joyful: "The baby has been crying at all hours. Lil is 'reproaching' me for lack of affection, as usual, and there is a little boy staying out here who, soaked through with urine, asks questions, bangs doors and screeches all day long." To make matters worse there was nothing to paint within walking distance and Bert Elliott's car was not operative. The little family found themselves stuck in the wilds of Wassaic. "My nerves being set on edge," Hanns complained, "I can't afford to step on toads and copperheads walking through fields and woods." The weather was "rotten" for three or four days at a time. He begged Evans to send him something to read, preferably something by Dostoevsky. "In general, things are not quite what they might be out here," Skolle complained in another letter, "Not a bit inspiring. Matters between Lil and me seem to be coming to a point. I am getting very skeptical about Colorado."

Life at Sharon, it would seem, was a catalogue of woes. Hanns even found fault with the volume of D. H. Lawrence's short stories Evans had sent him: He thought "The Fox" was much too long, and "Ladybird" a little ridiculous. Walker had sent him some of the portrait photographs they had taken. Skolle responded with many thanks and a bit of dissatisfaction: "I deserve the 'baron' judging from the portrait of me. I wish it were photo-graphically as good as that of you." Since they were not living in town, but in the woods, when Evans drove up to visit them on a Sunday, he was not

Evans's sister Jane with her husband Talbot Brewer, circa 1929

able to find them or anyone who might give him directions. The Skolles regretted his failed attempt but were looking forward to Evans's promised new visit. Lil wrote him "Bonne chance et à bientôt:" Bert, she said, was expecting him; Anita was expecting him; she was expecting him. Hanns, however, was not expecting him "because he wants you to come and because he does not believe in anything good in this world."

But even Evans's successful visit to Sharon had an awkward mishap: On the day of Walker's departure, Skolle, out painting, failed to return home in time to say good-bye. He sent Evans a humorous letter of apology: "It was hinted in some quarters that my absence at the time of your departure may have cost you a spasm of chagrin. Forsooth, it pleased me not that thou shouldst leave my humble dwelling thus inclined." Skolle made a pointed request, asking whether his woodblocks were accessible at Ossining. "I shall have to pull a few prints for a friend of Weyhe if I can find the woodblock in question."

Evans reported that the woodblocks were available: "They are not even in the attic here, but clutter up my closet floor so that if I had as many shooz as a gentleman should have they would be in the way." He next asked Skolle if he wanted to pay a visit to Ossining; he had discovered some new diversions. One was a pool that was deserted at midday; another was a game of throw-the-ice-pick, which he had invented just that evening. "The point is that the [pick] travels through the air point first, sticks in doors, trembling dramatically the while. Just walk across the room, casually; suddenly, whirl about and sling the instrument at a portrait of Cal Coolidge hung on the door . . . Come and we will play this game." As an extra attraction Evans added: "There are also two girls to swim with and take riding. I don't know them very well but find that they will do very nicely for that sort of thing."

By the time that Evans transported the Skolle family to Cos Cob at the end of August or early September, it had been decided that Hanns would remain in New York for three months after Lil departed for Colorado. Evans and Skolle were planning to share quarters: "I am looking forward to the next three months as the proper chance for a reincarnation," Skolle wrote with evident relief. The Wertheims (Alma Wertheim was the sister of Henry Morgenthau, Jr., a public official later to become Secretary of the Treasury under Franklin Roosevelt) had generously offered their

Manhattan apartment to Skolle and his wife until Lil and Anita took the train to Colorado. Since Evans was still in Ossining in early October it might have been Skolle who found the apartment at 48 Columbia Heights in Brooklyn Heights, within sight of the Brooklyn Bridge, for himself and Evans. In some ways, the move to Brooklyn, when he was twenty-five, would prove to be an official beginning of Walker Evans's career as a photographer.

III

In later years, though acknowledging the early photographs he had taken with a vest-pocket camera in Europe, Evans would maintain that his real career began around 1928 in New York. That, reasonably enough, is the date established in the official chronologies probably supplied, unofficially, by Evans himself. It may be too simplistic: a man remembering how it had begun, making a point for history's sake. But the scattered correspondence

Portrait of
Elizabeth Skolle
by Hanns Skolle

of those years indicates that it was essentially true.

More important, it reinforces the idea that Evans's year abroad had served as a fulcrum, providing the leverage that allowed him to make a break with his family's expectations. In the same way, over the years, he would come to regard his year abroad as his decisive break with American cultural values, at least what he regarded as the rampant commercialism of the late twenties. "I was standing aside at the beginning of my life," he would tell a student audience at the University of Michigan in Ann Arbor, in 1971, "standing aside from the world I found myself in — which was a New York life. I couldn't bear to immerse myself in the problem of earning a living and getting a job. I felt that I would soon be stuck with that. I instinctively kept away from it. . . ."

His interest in French literature and culture provided him with an often-cited example of his generalized artistic aims, first as an aspiring writer and then as a photographer whose reputation, ironically, was tied to the American scene and to the New York life from which he claimed he

wanted to escape. Evans believed that the breadth of one's learning offered unconscious possibilities. He advised aspiring young photographers not to settle for less, that is, to remain simply photographers: "I always remember telling my classes that students should seek to have a cultivated life and an education; they'd make better photographs." It was especially important for what he termed "the psychology of camera work." In a bold moment, he added: "This is why a man who has faith, intelligence, and cultivation will show that in his work. Fine photography is literature, and it should be."

But it was precisely the counterculture of the New York life that made his career possible. Tracing back to the earlier influences on his career, Evans would remember that leafing through a back issue of Alfred Stieglitz's vanguard magazine *Camera Work* in the New York Public Library, he had been struck by a gravure printing of Paul Strand's 1916 photograph *Blind Woman*. Strand had had his debut in 1915 at Stieglitz's "291" gallery, one of the most influential New York galleries for the introduction of modernist art and photography. What strikes one as peculiarly apt about Evans's choice of the *Blind Woman* photograph is that it so accurately prefigured the elemental concerns of Evans's later photographs: the importance of signage (the blunt "Blind" sign on the woman's breast, the engraved peddler's license), the stark reality of the memorable face and damaged eye, taken front-on against the granite wall.

The photograph had appeared in the last (June/July 1917) issue of Stieglitz's magazine, an issue devoted solely to Strand's work. Stieglitz, whose praise meant something in the New York scene as well as in the history of early American photography, pronounced Strand's work "the direct expression of today."

The photogravures in this number represent the real Strand. The man who has actually done something from within. The photographer has added something to what has gone before. The work is brutally direct. Devoid of all flim-flam; devoid of trickery and of any attempt to mystify an ignorant public, including the photographers themselves.

Whether Stieglitz's words contributed to the notable effect of Strand's picture is not known, but Evans would describe the visual encounter at the library as significant: ". . . I remember going out of there overstimulated: 'That's the stuff, that's the thing to do.' Now it seems automatic [romantic]

*Lindbergh
Day Parade,
June 13, 1927*

even, but it was quite a powerful picture. It charged me up."

As a photographer, Evans moved easily into the documentary mode. Among the earliest photos he took after his return to the states were one or two vest-pocket-sized snapshots of the mammoth New York City parade in honor of Charles Lindbergh's historic transatlantic flight to Europe. On May 21, 1927, Lindbergh had been given a tumultuous welcome as he landed at Le Bourget airport near Paris. As much as anything, that event celebrated and symbolized the spirit of youth and daring in the Roaring Twenties. The young Ernest Hemingway, summing it up with dry envy, wrote critic Edmund Wilson: "Isn't it fine what the American embassy's doing for Lindbergh. It's as if they'd caught an angel that talks like Coolidge." (President Coolidge had sent an American cruiser to bring Lindbergh home, where he was given a hero's welcome and ticker tape parade.) Evans, oddly, did not focus on the main event, but snapped the celebration, the flags, the bunting, the blizzard of paper from a different angle, capturing the marchers at rest on a side street, possibly waiting to begin the long march up Fifth Avenue to cheering crowds. There are other, possibly early 1⅝ x 2½ snapshots of New York City streets and buildings that seem a continuation of the same-sized rare photos of the garden of his Paris apartment and the Riviera harbors taken in Europe. Caught up in the fervor of photographing, Evans admitted:

Oh yes, I was a passionate photographer, and for a while somewhat guiltily, because I thought that this is a substitute for something else — well for writing, for one thing. . . . But I got very engaged and I was compulsive about it too. . . . It was a real drive. Particularly when the lighting was right. You couldn't keep me in.

During this same period, Evans's father, as an encouragement, sent him another camera, his own Kodak Tourist 2½ x 4¼ inch format. Not that Evans ever assumed that his father would necessarily be pleased by the character of his work. Evans once described his photographic efforts as "a semi-conscious reaction against right thinking and optimism. It was an attack on the establishment. Wanted to disturb them. I could just hear my father saying, 'Why do you want to look at these scenes, they're depressing? Why don't you look at the nice things in life?' "

Hanns Skolle remembered the haphazard manner of Evans's photographic apprenticeship, so to speak:

Walker and I used to take long walks over the Brooklyn Bridge. In the very beginning, when I knew Walker, he didn't really know what he was going to do with himself. He had tried painting, he had tried writing, but nothing really clicked.

Skolle's evaluation was that Walker's paintings "were of two kinds. The first were superb little doodles, as his remarks often were — magnificent little arabesques. He also did small abstract things — none of those 'big as a house' paintings. . . . As to his writings, Walker was a great inventor and storyteller." What Skolle appreciated about the earlier years of their friendship was that Walker was "always extremely keen on everything — about going somewhere, in his method of seeing, his method of selecting and composing." It was a gratifying quality in a friend, Skolle felt. "On one of [our] walks over the Bridge, I said to him, 'you have a good eye. Look at the Bridge — why don't you photograph it?' He had the selective gift as the basis for his creativity. He had a funny little folding camera then that he used to use." It was with the little vest-pocket camera, and (apparently) with his father's Kodak Tourist, that Evans launched into his forty-six-year career.

But there was still a living to be earned. For a time, briefly it seems, Evans may have worked at a Fifty-seventh Street French bookstore. But by mid-October, Evans was working for the Henry L. Doherty Company, the Wall Street brokerage house where Talbot Brewer was personnel manager. Not only was Evans working there as a stock clerk, but he and Tal Brewer were instrumental in getting a job as a file clerk for the poet Hart Crane. Crane's biographer, John Unterecker, who had interviewed Evans for his 1969 *Voyager: A Life of Hart Crane*, noted that Crane and Evans had known about each other because Hart's father, C. A. Crane, a Cleveland candy manufacturer, knew Walker's father through business connections. But the poet and the photographer had first met each other only in the fall of 1928, when they were both living in Brooklyn Heights. Crane, off and on, had lived in the area since 1924, at first at 110 Columbia Heights, where, luckily, he occupied a room whose window overlooked the East River. The view, Crane wrote his mother, was the finest in all America:

Just imagine looking out of your window directly on the East River with nothing intervening between your view of the Statue of Liberty, way down the harbor, and the marvelous beauty of Brooklyn Bridge close above you on your right! All of the great new skyscrapers of Lower Manhattan are marshalled directly across from you, and there is a constant stream of tugs, liners, sail boats, etc., in procession before you on the river!

The view was, in fact, literally inspiring, since the Brooklyn Bridge would become the spanning metaphor for Crane's great poem *The Bridge*, which he was still trying to complete, without success, in the fall of 1928.

It was a difficult time for Crane. His parents, like Evans's, were separated. His mother, neurotic and extremely possessive, was a source of anger and anxiety, using his dependency as a weapon to get him back to California, where she was living. She sent him telegrams announcing that she was desperately ill or else would hold off answering his letters, tactics that angered Crane even more, since she was refusing to sign the necessary papers for him to claim his inheritance — five thousand dollars — from the death of his grandmother. Crane was going through another of his bouts of alcoholism. Like most of his relationships at the time, the friendship with Evans was troubled by the poet's drinking habits, characterized by sudden and extreme binges and brief days of sobering up. There were also the occasional brawls, some of them with taxi drivers over arguments about the fare; others occasioned by Crane's attempts to pick up sailors in the Sands Street bars near the Brooklyn Naval Yard.

During this period when the poet was living first at 77 Willow Street, then at the Columbia Heights apartment of Crane's dedicated Cleveland friend, Sam Loveman, who had recently opened a bookstore in Manhattan (and, it appears, for a time, at his favorite haunt, the 110 Columbia Heights boarding-house home of his merchant mariner friend Emil Opffer), several of his friends were called upon to rescue him from his binges and deliver him home. The brisk changes of address in Crane's life were often enough precipitated by visits from the police; in moments of drunken anger, he broke china or furniture and threw things out of windows.

Only the most stalwart of Crane's friends and the hardiest of believers in his talent could survive a friendship with the poet. It was not particularly easy for someone like Evans who hated displays of temperament or violence of any kind. "God no. Perish the thought!" he once remarked when asked if he and Crane had shared an apartment together in Brooklyn Heights. Evans did look after the poet in other ways, occasionally running essential errands. Among Evans's salvaged scraps of documentary paper is a signed note from Crane: "Kindly give bearer 1 pint of gin." Skolle, with whom Evans did share an apartment at the time, also remembered a bit of literary heroism on Evans's part. It was Walker, Skolle maintained with perhaps a bit of hyperbole, "who saved 'The Bridge.' He kept the manuscript hidden at our apartment because Crane was so completely irresponsible. He went on those drunken binges and he'd destroy everything — throw things out of the windows, even. He lived up the street from us at Number 110. Often we took him home after he'd passed out. So Walker kept 'The Bridge' for safekeeping. I think that is a very important, unknown thing about him." Yet Evans seemed to enjoy Crane's company when the poet, sober, accompanied him on some of his photographic expeditions along the docks in Brooklyn and New York, even perhaps when he first began taking photographs of the Brooklyn Bridge. (There is, however, a common misconception that the photographs were taken as illustrations for Crane's poem.)

Evans and Crane shared some literary preferences: Both were admirers of Baudelaire, for instance. And there are reasons to believe that Evans was struck by the vital imagery of Crane's poem. Whatever its sometimes florid language and its occasional Elizabethan address to the reader, *The Bridge* had the genuine imprint of modernism and remains one of America's great twentieth-century poems. The opening stanza of Crane's segment titled "The River," with its slogans and signboard references, would have been an appropriate accompaniment to the photographs Evans took only a few years later:

> Stick your patent name on a signboard
> Brother — all over — going west — young man
> Tintex—Japalac—Certain-teed Overalls ads
> and lands sakes! Under the new playbill ripped
> in the guaranteed corner — See Bert Williams what?
> Minstrels when you steal a chicken just

save me the wing . . .

Given Evans's belief in the value of unconscious literary associations, it seems more than likely that, a few years later, confronted by an actual instance of a torn poster for J. C. Lincoln's "Sunny South" Minstrels, one with a black man in hot pursuit of a chicken, he would have instinctively photographed it.

Like Evans, Crane, who was twenty-nine when he took his file clerk's job, had no ambitions to climb the corporate ladder. He could easily write about his strenuous efforts to meet the daily nine-to-five grind on the twentieth floor — after a binge. (Elevators, though not necessarily the ones at 60 Wall Street, assumed a certain poetic conveyance, in the "Poem" to *The Bridge*: "Till elevators drop us from our day," could certainly serve as a personal recollection of nadir at the end of the day at Henry L. Doherty Company.) In an ebullient letter to his friend the critic and poet Malcolm Cowley after a strenuous night out, he said: "It's me for the navy or Mallorca damned quick. Meanwhile sorting securities of cancelled legion ten years back — for filing — pax vobiscum — With Wall Street at 30 percent — and chewing gum for lunch." For Cowley's benefit he gave a detailed account of his night before: "But here I am — full of Renault Wine Tonics — after an evening with the Danish millionaire on Riverside — and better, thank God, a night with a bluejacket from the Arkansas — raving like a'mad. And it's time to go to work. So long . . ."

Evans recalled the November day that Crane dramatically quit his brief job at Henry L. Doherty Company, striding into the office in the now-rumpled suit he had worn the night before on leaving the premises, still drunk at noon. The clerks and secretaries watched attentively as he strode to a window and looking out proclaimed, "There's Scott's Emulsion." Sweeping aside the pile of stocks and bonds on his desk, he scattered them on the floor, announcing, "I never took a drop of that and I never will as long as I live!" After his proclamation he proceeded to the door, turned for a final and emphatic "Never!" and left.

Fortunately, Crane had managed to get hold of a portion of his inheritance — not all of it, but enough to allow him to make a trip to England on the Cunard Line's R.M.S. *Tuscania*. There was a round of celebrations of one kind or another: Crane attended a performance of the musical *Showboat* at the new Ziegfeld Theater ("Like greased lightning — the suave mechanical perfection of the thing.") and a party at Sam Loveman's apartment, "the best bat ever last night . . . finally two cops came in and joined the party at three o'clock." A bon-voyage party was in order, and Crane, with his newly acquired wealth, gave it himself at a Second Avenue speakeasy. He invited his stalwart friends: Cowley and his wife, Peggy; the poet e. e. cummings and his next wife-to-be, Anne Barton; Sam Loveman; the writer and editor Gorham Munson; Crane's painter friend Charmion von Weigand; and Walker. It was a bibulous and buoyant affair; Crane danced with all the women, recited limericks, played the piano — one of his favorite tunes, "Too Much Mustard," and something that sounded like Debussy. ("I fake it," he whispered confidentially to Evans.) Despite all the gaiety, Crane afterwards complained that his party was a failure; cummings and Anne Barton had failed to show up. He considered that a betrayal.

Hanns Skolle is not mentioned among the invited guests in the accounts of that evening. If Skolle didn't attend, it might not have been an oversight. Even in youth, Evans managed to be snobbish, tending to compartmentalize his friends. As Skolle himself admitted, "Walker had a lot of friends then that I didn't know and he went to social gatherings in which I had no part — deliberately, I may add."

Crane's departure was not the only one in the Brooklyn Heights circle. Hanns Skolle's three months of "reincarnation" ended on January 23, 1929, when he took the train to Chicago en route to Denver. The little rush of correspondence between him and Evans that followed suggests that the effect on the two might have been rather like the separation of Siamese twins. Before leaving, Skolle had worked up a hand-lettered Germanic testimonial "To Walker Evans, In greatful [sic] Acknowledgment of efficient Services rendered in the Year of Our Lord 1928" along with translations from two poems by Gottfried Benn, one of them an unidentified stanza that included the lines: "A child! Oh yes, a child! / But where to take it from — without blushing. / Once I dreamt a young birch-tree / had born[e] me a son.—" With it, Skolle included a brief newspaper clipping about an infant who had drowned in a big bowl of soup that his mother, Mrs. Louis Ollivier, of 31 Mercer Street, Lodi, New Jersey, had left on the kitchen floor to cool while she was out of the house. Young Roger Ollivier, fourteen months old and crawling, had lifted himself up to look into the steaming bowl "and his head fell in." It was one of Skolle's most successful, if ominous, finds.

Skolle kept Evans informed of the stops and delays of his three-day journey, the "dead-cold" at Albany, the stale sandwiches, his unsatisfactory reading material (Lawrence's *Old Calabria*: "Tough going after Lady Chatterley"). Evans and Skolle had begun reading Lawrence's just-published but banned erotic novel *Lady Chatterley's Lover* before his departure and Evans had promised to send him further typed passages. (Hanns reminded him of his promise, specified that he had broken off "where the game keeper makes love to her on his way to fetch the milk.") He couldn't say much for or against Chicago except that it was "intolerably cold" and much cleaner than he had expected: "But then the dirt was frozen to the pavement! What a sensation when I ordered tea for breakfast! The waitress thought I was French." Kansas was nothing but "brown and yellow." He was sure he had caught a glimpse of "buffaloes over yonder, by God, or domestic cows with artificial humps?" He decided that Anita Loos's bestselling *Gentlemen Prefer Blondes* was "disgusting rot . . . I swear I shan't read a woman's book again, not even 'satire.' The people who read such stuff didn't deserve to be amused."

On January 25 ("nom de dieu") Walker began a two-day letter to Skolle:

Thursday spent figuring best way to pass off departure of my melancholic companion. Dropped in at Haaga's [the local grocer's] and found you weren't missed yet there. Simple souls! They think everything is as it was. Dashed up to talkative picture framer. As soon as I put in appearance, and before I opened my mouth, he emerged from backshop holding Brooklyn Bridge. What flattery; I left him with his illusions intact.

The notable bit of news there being that Evans seems to have had one of his earliest prints of the Brooklyn Bridge framed well before the subject of his illustrating Crane's book had even been broached. (At the time, Crane, on the recommendation of Charmion von Weigand, was hoping to illustrate the poem with one of Joseph Stella's paintings of the Brooklyn Bridge in the collection of the Brooklyn Museum.) Evans, in his breezy and comic letter, mentioned that the wealthy Dr. Galdston, their neighbor in the Heights, had been very "touched" by Skolle's parting gift of a mask he had made. "I could see it through his violent efforts to make me believe it," Evans noted. "He looked at his gold wrist watch and at his platinum pocket watch, uttered choice literary words in four languages, stepped on the dog and gave me a drink. Also $1.25 herewith." As for himself, Evans admitted that he had returned "very casually" to 48 Columbia Heights alone, "put on Clair de Lune and fell to cleaning up the place, noting different items of my inheritance as I went along. Six trips to the garbage can." On Friday evening, he had splattered spinach on the kitchen ceiling: "Geyser," he explained. Then he had read some more *Chatterley* and typed up passages for Skolle's benefit.

Skolle was "highly pleased" with the letter. "Do that thing in a more impersonal way for literary purposes," he suggested. The five lines on Dr. Galdston, he remarked, "are a piece of perfection." Skolle added: "May I reward you with that dirty pair of pyjamas which you must have found on my table? They will look like new after a good cleaning."

In his second letter, Evans mentioned he was working at a new job — nights "from five to midnight or thereabouts." Whether at Doherty or a new firm is not clear: "The job is excellent, just what I was looking for: cut-and-dried, not much work, no women, gives me all day free." Evans also made an inventory (with commentary) of items Skolle had left behind:

Thanks for:	No thanks for:
ruler	LePage's Big Boy Paste
Rosmersholm [by Ibsen]	*The Miraculous Revenge*
Superior clips	by Bernard Shaw
Vick's Vaporub	Rock Island time table
twine	garbage
India ink	Burton's pure trade purity strength
Asia [a magazine]	delicacy of flavor mark
Monocle	extract of vanilla
The Missing Link	souvenirs of amorous adventures
hatchet	whiskey
Dos En Uno Pasta Superior	oil can

In a later letter, in response to Skolle's query about the new job, Evans expanded: "Situation very satisfactory here. Alone all day until teatime: much possibilities. . . . Last night sat late after work reading that wonderful chapter headed 'Waterparty' in Women in Love. Do you remember it? The drowning incident, the frantic supernatural atmosphere all along." One of the advantages of the new job was that he was free during the day to work with his camera. "Photography encouraging lately," he commented. "I want to hear about Denver now," Evans added. "The facts. The details. Photographs of anything you do." Skolle had taken with him on his journey one of Evans's cameras, apparently the small vest-pocket one. As an after-thought, Evans added, then scratched over in the carbon copy of his February 6 letter: "Perhaps you'd better send me that little camera when you can get yourself one. Didn't you take any snapshots on the trip out? In sending it, best get a wooden box and fill in space tight with cotton."

But it would be some time — and several complaints from Skolle about the contrariness of the piece of equipment — before the camera was returned.

Words, Etc.

4

Like many aspects of Walker Evans's career, his response to the work of pioneering photographer Alfred Stieglitz was tactically ambivalent. In the 1969 volume *Quality: Its Image in the Arts*, edited by Louis Kronenberger, Evans, discussing photography and Stieglitz's role, represented his then-current attitude as a legendary confrontation of the generations, referring to Stieglitz as "undoubtedly the most insistently 'artistic' practitioner of all time; with the adverse effect that it was he who forced 'art' into quotation marks and into unwonted earnestness." He was quick to add that there had been an obverse gain from Stieglitz's faults: "On the other hand, Stieglitz's overstated, self-conscious aestheticism engendered a healthy reaction." In the published text, without stating so, he presented himself as being in the camp of the antiart photographers. Characteristically the failure to name himself was not modesty as much as a result of his equally characteristic effort to distance himself from any ideological liabilities.

In the sixty or more pages of typed and handwritten drafts, revisions, and notes Evans wrote for the brief final text, one can see him maneuvering in his response to the older man: "There is reason to believe that Alfred Stieglitz may very well have been the father of serious contemporary photography. I hedge first because Stieglitz never really stopped being a 'salon' photographer; second because his most successful offspring have, in truth, worked in inspired *opposition* to his heavy tenets and manner." In an inserted notation, he pictured Stieglitz as a "19th century master in black hat and cape." The source of his irritation may well have been revealed in another deleted mention: "I think the fact that Stieglitz was such a screaming aesthete came from the [circumstance] that he had a private income of unearned money. The effect of this kind of concern upon artists seldom seems to be given the importance I think it has."

Evans's early response to Stieglitz, however, was more complicated than he later wanted to acknowledge. It is probable that he first met Stieglitz late in 1928, soon after his move to Brooklyn Heights. According to his best recollection, he had been sent to see the sixty-four-year-old Stieglitz by a

Port of
New York

Wall Street
Windows

Family on
street corner,
seen from
above

Vest-pocket
camera
photographs,
1929

Brooklyn acquaintance, the painter Stefan Hirsch. Stieglitz, having closed his pioneering art and photography gallery at 291 Fifth Avenue several years earlier, was running a small operation, the Intimate Gallery — so called for its twelve-by-twenty-foot space, an area ceded to him within the larger Anderson Galleries at 489 Park Avenue. With a third-person grandeur emphasized by Germanic capitalizations, Stieglitz announced that his new gallery was "not a business . . . but a Direct Point of Contact between Public and Artist . . . [to which] Alfred Stieglitz has volunteered his services and is its guiding Spirit."

For that remembered meeting, Evans had brought with him a box of his early snapshots: "I only had a few — they were small — they were contact prints of 2½ by 4¼ and vest-pocket." Stieglitz was not in when Evans arrived. Fortunately, however, Stieglitz's wife, the painter Georgia O'Keeffe, was minding the gallery. O'Keeffe told him to wait, that her husband would be back. The two had what Evans remembered as "a very nice conversation." He was, he admitted, immediately smitten with her:

And I loved her . . . I remember her charm, her niceness, and I was so — I was fond, attracted very strongly to her niceness. Oh she spoke intelligently about my work. Told me I could get a better print out of that — and said, 'that was interesting'—um — also she was charming — she was majestic and human at the same time. . . . Her smile I can see to this day, sort of a wry smile.

When Stieglitz did arrive, O'Keeffe and Evans were huddled in talk, still looking over his photographs — a fact that Evans felt had worked against him. Stieglitz's response to the photographs was disappointing: "He didn't say much. I know exactly what he said. I think he said nothing, 'I'm looking . . .'" Later Stieglitz added: "Well, they're very good. All I can say is go on working." Evans remembered the incident with a certain sourness: "At which I took my leave — with only ten cents in my pocket. . . . Didn't say to come back, show us something more — nothing."

In a letter dated March 17, 1929, Evans reported to Skolle on a later visit to the gallery, perhaps his second or third. (It may well have been during the month-and-a-half exhibition of some thirty-five O'Keeffe paintings, which ended on the seventeenth.) Evans told Skolle: "Saw Stieglitz again. He talked at length. He should never open his mouth. Nobody should, but especially Stieglitz. He showed me some excellent photographs he had

made: clouds, wet grass, the rump of a white horse, the bark of an old tree. As an example of his overstatement: he said of the tree bark photo: It was YEARS before I DARED to do it." Put off by his first visit, Evans was hardly complimentary and certainly less than awed by the impresario. But many another gallery goer, Edmund Wilson for instance, recalled Stieglitz's habit of buttonholing visitors with a flow of talk that was impossible to interrupt or to break away from. As Wilson observed, Stieglitz's "ribbon of talk was as strong as a cable."

Nevertheless Hanns Skolle claimed that Stieglitz was one of the early, precipitating factors in Evans's photographic career: "When I knew Walker, he thought Stieglitz was his absolute master — in the 20s and 30s." Hyperbole perhaps? Skolle's statement runs counter to many of Evans's

Paul Grotz,
1929

later remarks. On learning about Evans's late negative opinions, Skolle was surprised, but conceded, "I think I have always had the same feeling about Georgia O'Keeffe that Evans seems to have developed about Stieglitz — greatly overrated." Even so, he still maintained, "But it wasn't like that when I knew him."

Other evidence corroborates Skolle's view that Evans was at first impressed by Stieglitz *and* his work. In a letter to Skolle dated June 23, 1929 (but marked "Not sent"), Evans asked: "Did you ever see Stieglitz's photographs in the Metropolitan? I went the other day and found three or four of them very exciting." In the letter that he did send, Evans narrowed down his choice to one: "Did you ever see Stieglitz's photographs in the print room at the Metropolitan? He has a portrait of O'Keeffe that must be one of the best things I'll ever see. Great Guns."

It must have been at the Strand exhibition that followed the O'Keeffe show in the spring of 1929 (the photographer showed Colorado and New Mexico landscapes as well as close-ups of rain-dappled cobwebs, rocks, roots, and a sequence of studies of broad-leaved garden iris taken in Maine the year before) that occasioned Evans's comic account of seeing Stieglitz the dealer at work: "He was concentrating on a rich Westchester matron. . . . Strand's stuff was particularly technical, absolutely beautiful. Platinum prints. . . . And she said 'I believe I'm going to have that. How much does it cost?' and he said $250. . . . You won't believe this, but I thought he meant $2.50 and I thought. Jesus I could get one — if I saved up. . . . Just shows how naïve I was."

Over the years, Evans would recall other, occasional gripes about the character of the pioneering photographer: "You know, really, when you come right down to it," he once claimed, "Stieglitz was not very sure about himself. All that declamation and breast beating, it sort of came from insecurity I think. He once made a very revealing remark to me. He said, 'I would have been one of the greatest painters ever born, had I painted.' That gave me plenty of thought."

There is no doubt that Evans could be quite contradictory in his opinions of Stieglitz. Stieglitz's cloud photographs, from a sequence of near-abstractions titled the *Equivalents* as well as the "horse's rump" photograph, which in 1929 had impressed him as "excellent," would be cited in Evans's last years, when he was clearly editing his views for posterity, as examples of what he disliked most about Stieglitz's work. The cloud pictures Evans claimed "mean very little to me." Asked what he thought of Stieglitz's work at the time, he stated: "I didn't like it. It bugged me. It helped me as something to react against. Oh my God, Clouds? Or O'Keeffe's hands, breasts — I was doing junk cars." He was even more adamant about the significance of Stieglitz's title for the picture of the white horse's hindquarters (if not the photograph itself)—"Spiritual America." "I know it well," he said of the famous photograph, "only too well. . . . It's an interesting picture, but I just hate what he said by that — I hate his caption."

The image itself, however, stuck in his mind. Among his early photographs, there are several of white horses in a field, close-up shots that one could only assume had been taken with Stieglitz's image in mind — but with no tendentious titles. Few things in biography, however, are as clear-cut and decisive as one would like. Fewer still — thankfully — provide certified examples of the nature of artistic influences. There are other photographs of the same white horses in a field that may have been taken with a 35-mm camera by a new friend of Evans's, Paul Grotz, whom

Evans met in late 1928. The similarity of the photographs by the two men suggest the two were photographing the same subject together or, perhaps, the contrary proposition that Evans may have been using Grotz's Leica, as he sometimes did. Grotz, trained as an architect in Munich, had only recently arrived in New York from Germany. His English was not perfect, he remembered, and he had needed help in looking for a reference book in a Dutton book shop. Grotz recalled that he and Evans were introduced to each other by a helpful French salesgirl.

In February, Evans reported to Skolle: "My job: at four-thirty, I have bang-up tea, at five I enter big office, no cheers. I am handed instead pkg. of bonds on which are written knames [sic]; and a list of knames. Then I match them until seven, when I begin to get hungry. Dinner is at eight, so I read SONS AND LOVERS. From nine to midnight or so there is more of same. Then dramatic passage under East River, me standing in front vestibule of train in exaltation. Hot Ovaltine (nothing like it for exaltation); puttering around among books papers photos memories and chagrins: bed." He was enjoying his solitude. "Living alone is so pleasant," he told Skolle, "I am considering putting off Paul Grotz."

He had sent Skolle a copy of his latest literary endeavor, a short story entitled "Brooms." It was a bachelor's reverie in the modernist style. The narrator, attempting a change of mode, is dissatisfied with his journal: "Have decided to continue but to omit dramas, crises, eruptions, explosions, simmerings boiling and all manifestations of the chaos of my inner life." He is a man in distress: "full of hate; have wanderlust not only in Spring; am firmly entrenched in physical life and love it; am alone, have soul, to which I hereby bid farewell."

He is also a man of reduced means, without even a broom to his name. "Couldn't buy anything. Sold in fact, books, cameras, pawned watch. There was no broom until I found one in the alley back of the abandoned factory. . . . I carried it home and swept bitterly." In a commercial district, he spies a cluster of "super-brooms" swaying in the breeze, their handles "dipped in robin's egg blue for youth and happiness." But he does not buy one. (Interestingly, Evans cribbed the color and its symbolism from the ice pick used in his summer game at Ossining the year before.) "I was sick of an old passion," he explains cryptically. He lists his imperative needs:

"suspenders/drawers/collar pin/bath slippers/*Crime and Punishment/*
rubber cement" — the necessities of a bachelor of modest fashion and,
judging from the rubber cement needed probably for mounting prints — a
photographer.

In a disjunctive, first-person narrative style that owes more than a little
to Blaise Cendrars's *Moravagine*, Evans ends his charged little tale in
respectable literary fashion:

*Words: the bottom of my life is a shadowy pattern of unreality, imposing enough
in its own private way. I look into it coming out of deleria or even out of sleep
on summer mornings before dawn, having set my will to go off at 4:30. Moi
intime. My happy hunting-ground. My little core of humanity. Later it is shot
through with cold sparks of intellect or words of that effect.*

*Soon after I left the house, before I had even turned the corner, I saw a worn-out
broom lying in the gutter. It is nothing, I said; it will pass. But I saw another,
and yet another. All had that horrible, suggestive triangular shape. It was too
much. Today, this dateless day, I walked myself into Macy's and bought a vacuum
cleaner.*

Now I shall suck the dust out of chaos.

Skolle wrote him: "*Brooms* is remarkably good. Certainly the best thing
extant. The apparition on the last page is a trump, the final sentence the
finest you have let loose, the puns are matchless." He offered one or two
"unimportant criticisms" and returned the manuscript asking Evans to sign
it for him. "Twang away, Muse," he concluded. Evans, more than pleased
by Skolle's response, nonetheless lacked inspiration for the moment. "Most
encouraging, that letter of yours about BROOMS. I have lost the mood, but
when it comes again I'll go over it with your suggestions." Still he was
encouraged enough to send the story to Bruce Blivens, the editor of *The
New Republic*: "got a decent letter about it, explaining why they couldn't use
it, and asking to see something else." It might well have been Skolle's
encouragement that also made him undertake the French translation of the
story, titled "Balais," found among his papers.

The two friends kept up a lively correspondence all through the spring,
Evans typing up a sheaf of extracts from *Lady Chatterley's Lover*, with intermittent commentaries:

Lawrence the prophet all right. One sentence I remember, something said by Mellers-Lawrence near the end:

"I stand for the touch of bodily awareness between human beings and the touch of tenderness."

The sentence of the book, as far as prophetic writing is concerned. But besides, what a strapping piece of literature, genuine literature, pas?

I am enclosing two rather long excerpts which I couldn't resist copying out word for word. Also a newspaper interview in which Lawrence speaks of the book.

Skolle shot back: "Thanks for that superbest of all treats. Just the first sheets. Saving the rest for special pow-wow. . . . Your cadenzas in the Lawrence synopsis are first-rate." Evans mentioned his uneasiness about sending the banned erotic passages through the mail: "I suppose you and I would both be arrested if the post office knew; along with Lawrence, what an honor." The two were on a Lawrence binge in fact, reading through and commenting on much of the Lawrence canon at the time, Evans promoting *Sons and Lovers* which has "made a very deep impression on me. I shall always treasure it. *Women in Love* too. The latter is more intimately touching but not as big a book." Skolle registered his own complaint ("'Plumed Serpent' ugly; some rather dopy questionable writing") but praised *Kangaroo*: "It's a hum-dinger! . . . With D. H. Lawrence, more than Blake even, I feel that his art is an uncontrollable curse of a gift which he didn't have to fight for, a question of spurt-away or bust . . . Say what you like, this is more awesome than the slick art of Greece, though it be no solace." Evans responded: "Excellent observations on D. H. Lawrence. But slick I would not call the art of Greece. Too beautiful is perhaps what you mean; too comfortably lofty? Just started *Kangaroo*; like it so far (7 pages)."

As usual, Skolle was afire with projects. His painting was going well: "Did a very successful watercolor today, probably the best in the whole lot. Too bad Lil can't say anything decent when I show her my new work. Makes me think sadly of our exhibitions at Col[umbia] Heights. *Nulle rose sans epines* [There is no rose without thorns]." He sent Evans a photograph of a large group portrait (in oil) he had completed. It pictured a remembered and raucous New York party in the apartment of their mutual friend, the Singapore-born hostess Ena Douglas. (She crops up in one or two of

Evans's early stories and in his letters to Skolle.) Evans tried to imagine what the colors might be:

It is a large picture, I hope. That sort of thing makes one feel the stupidity of photography. I missed none of the details: Ena aloft with the cup that cheers: myself so subtly draped over the keyboard; Rusty somebody being spanked (the perfect touch there: Somebody HAD to be upside down in that picture.) The Swede departing in search of more drink; his dark face . . .

A recent exhibition of Skolle's work in Denver was the occasion for an article by no less a light than Arnold Ronnebeck. Like Skolle, a transplanted German, Ronnebeck was an accomplished artist and sculptor recently appointed Director of the Denver Art Museum. He was a man of considerable experience. A close friend of the vanguard American painter Marsden Hartley, Ronnebeck, before World War I, had been one of the regulars of Gertrude Stein's Parisian salon. (Both Stein and her companion Alice B. Toklas, however, were convinced that he might have been a German spy because of his habit of photographing panoramic views of Paris and its environs.) Typically, Skolle was double-edged about Ronnebeck's review: "I was very pleased with his article in spite of certain inanities. Still, he is something of a toad-eater, you know." He was pleased enough that Ronnebeck had bought one of his woodcuts. Skolle appears to have included in his exhibition a recent watercolor portrait of Evans, since he reported: "The Denver Museum took quite a shine to my watercolor of you. It has been requested as a 'permanent loan,' whatever that means." When Evans informed him that "Permanent loan means that the artist is permanently unable to collect anything for the picture," Hanns decided to forgo the honor.

Throughout the spring, Evans kept up his end of their dedicated correspondence. (They appear to have been feeling pangs of separation.) Early in March he informed Skolle: "Paul Grotz is coming here to live after all. Must say I'm pleased enough." His letters were full of suggestions, opinions, new enthusiasms. He proposed that he and Skolle should enter an amateur photography contest sponsored by Eastman Kodak Company. It had been advertised on the back cover of the current *Saturday Evening Post*: "The whole thing sounds *on ne peut plus bête* [a ridiculous thing], but I think both of us can make the judges at least fart briefly." He asked if

Skolle had been doing any writing lately: "After all literature is the noblest of the arts. Yes. Give me the ramifications of the intellect preferably abnormal. For instance I like your painting most when it is evidence of your sardonic diseased perverted suspirated excruciated convulsed mind your surrational fantastical ecstatical extravaganzical hamletical mind sic."

Having read and reread Thomas Mann's *The Magic Mountain*, at first finding it "a subversive . . . insidious book; essence of first-rate corruption," Evans had second opinions: "More impressed than at first with its artistic qualities. I was too dumfounded the first time to notice some of its fine points. But now I have it as a unified piece. And after all, it is so first-rate as a work of art that one can hardly care whether one's mind is shot up by it or not. But one's mind certainly is. Whew. Up and to pieces." Having recently seen Dreyer's *La passion de Jeanne d'Arc*, and finding it excellent he wrote Skolle, "Don't miss it. Jeanne in the picture is reminiscent of Lil." He also sent a bit of evidence that he was taking his photography more seriously. "You will have received," he wrote Skolle on March 17, "the enlargement of you as Hamlet which I sent last week. I ought to explain why I waited so long to send it, and why I am sending the others we took only now: I saw what a good enlargement the Hamlet would make but hadn't the money to get it done: and I wanted that one picture to crash into your consciousness alone, instead of weakened by the others." He also advised Skolle that he would soon be through working on Wall Street. "Am in for another summer of gardening, but it won't be as bad this time. In fact I shall enjoy it, perhaps. Don't yet know where I'll settle."

II

Evans's new friendship with Paul Grotz had an awkward beginning. Around Easter, not long after Grotz had moved into the Columbia Heights apartment, they were visited by a young woman, Dorothy Rogers, whom Evans had known earlier when she worked in a French bookstore. The two had apparently had a brief romantic involvement that had been broken off by mutual consent. Still, having heard that Evans was ill, Rogers paid him a visit, bringing him an Easter egg. The awkwardness of the situation was that Grotz and Dorothy were immediately attracted to each other and soon began dating, a matter of some chagrin for Evans. For several months it posed a threat to the friendship between the two men.

Nevertheless, as Evans wrote Skolle on May 24 from Darien, Connecticut, he and Grotz had made plans together:

Rented a house here, moved in a week ago, and have been digging and cooking like mad since. Preparing to plant my famous flowers. Have been alone, but Grotz arrives tomorrow and will stay here until he leaves for his Grand Tour d'Amerique. The moving and digging and cooking had kept me from answering your May 7 letter (though now that I see that date I realize I should have sent you a card.)

His garden patch in Darien was, apparently, no extensive affair; Paul Grotz remembered it as about the size of two large rooms. In the few photographs of Evans standing with a proprietary air in front of the house itself, it was not prepossessing either, a quaint cottage, really, almost dwarfed by the large Ford touring car parked beside it. Evans had also acquired a dog, a ragtag mutt which he promptly named Aspasia after the fifth century B.C. intellectual consort of the Athenian statesman Pericles. In mid-June he was visited by Lil Skolle and Anita, who were staying with friends in Darien before voyaging to Paris. Evans drove over to pick them up. He was flattered when the child Anita had toddled down the stairs pronouncing his name. "We came back to my place," he wrote Skolle, "and I pumped information from thy wife. I gather that things are not half bad. Certainly your daughter is a gem. Lil is in much better shape than she was. In every way . . . I was altogether pleased and amused. So was my dog, Aspasia."

That spring Evans, with Skolle's encouragement, had been busy concocting plans for future travel to New Mexico or Mexico City, though conceding, "I'll never manage to get away four months in the summer unless I make some money. Or even one. But another idea is the West Indies next winter. I've sighed long enough for the tropics and here are islands at our door, run by our greedy fatherland." But for the meantime he was contemplating a motor trip to Canada: "Summer has been a success so far in Darien. I have written nothing, but have read some Dostoevsky and have been so definitely touched by him that the experience is enough in itself for a while. Paul Grotz has been with me, as I believe I told you. Next week he is quitting his job in town and we are setting out for Maine and

Quebec in the car, after about ten days of which P. will leave for the West Coast."

He had good news to report, what could be considered officially as the start of his recognition as both a photographer and a writer/translator: "I met one Angel Flores, editor of a pretty good new magazine here in New York, and sold him a photograph (for twenty-five bucks)." In addition, in the same issue of *Alhambra*, Flores also published a segment, "Mad," of Evans's translation of Cendrars's *Moravagine*. As Evans explained:

Flores is a man of taste, widely read and widely travelled, and would be the man to edit a good literary review if there were a public for it here. He is going to try to place MORAVAGINE *with an American publisher so that I can have the job of translating it. (The Cendrars fantastic adventure novel.) Flores would certainly like to see some of your woodcuts. You can almost surely count on selling him a couple of the New York series if you care to.*

Evans's photograph *New York in the Making* appeared on page twenty-seven (cropped and enlarged, evidently, from one of his vest-pocket negatives). It gave evidence of his early progress as a photographer: a striking vertically elongated shot of skyscrapers and an industrial crane with a construction worker perched perilously atop it. The Cendrars translation, "Mad," a brief two and a half pages long, consisted of a black surrealistic passage in which the narrator, Moravagine, the last descendant of a family of royal exiles, gouges out the eyes of his faithful dog and beats it to death "like a slut from the streets," then brutally eviscerates his young wife, the princess Rita, who has told him she intends to leave him for good. At the age of eighteen, he is thrown into the Pressbourg prison for ten years, then transferred to the Waldensee asylum. In one of the racier passages, one that Evans translated with considerable verve, the narrator, stricken with insomnia, describes his nocturnal fantasies:

Carnal visions pursued me. Women surrounded me, women of all sizes and colors, of all ages and epochs. They lined up in front of me, rigid, like the pipes of an organ. They arranged themselves in a circle, lying down, upside down, lascivious stringed instruments. I mastered them all, arousing some by a look and others by a gesture. Standing, straightened like an orchestra conductor, I beat time for their debauches, speeding up or slowing down their transports, ad libitum; or abruptly stopping them in order to make them start all over again thousands and thousands of times, a capo, to make them again go through their motions, their poses and their sporting; or dismissing them all at the same time, tutti in order to throw them into a dizzy delirium. This frenzy was killing me. I was totally consumed, shrunken. Circles around my eyes, hollow cheeks.

The passage might easily have stirred up memories — for Cendrars, perhaps, if not for Evans — of such period icons as Picasso's fierce *Demoiselles d'Avignon* (1907), or Man Ray's sensual photographic portrait of his mistress Kiki as *Le Violin d'Ingres* which made its first public appearance in the June 1924 issue of *Litterature*. Evans's dual appearances in *Alhambra*, decidedly placed him on modernist ground. Even the contributor's note, undoubtedly supplied by Evans, struck the impertinent modernist chord: "Walker Evans is uneducated, unattached and unemployed. He has lived in Montana, Antibes, the Quartier Latin and

Building and Crane, 1929

Connecticut. Has been working with a camera on Manhattan for the last year or so."

True to his word, in late August, Flores brought *Moravagine* and presumably Walker's translation to the attention of Maxim Lieber at Brentano's bookstore, which at the time published books as well as sold them. Flores pulled out all the stops, hailing the novel as "a prolonged *Walpurgisnacht*, cinematic in conception and bristling with the fireworks of a daemonic quixoticism." He compared it favorably to Gide's *Lafcadio's Adventures* and Joyce's *Ulysses*, though claiming for it a "higher sense of humor." He further announced that Cendrars was "a Flaubert who, touched [by] the cynicism of Aldous Huxley and the savage cruelty of Barbey d'Aurevilly, decided to write a 'Bouvard and Pecuchet' but full of our contemporary sensibility and poison." Evans, encouraged by the editor's interest, gave Flores his story "Brooms." Several months later, however, he took it back dissatisfied with the editor's failure to publish. As he wrote Skolle: "Dear old BROOMS is on display in the editorial offices of *The New World Monthly*, a new literary monthly not altogether unsympathetic. I got sick of Flores's crowd and withdrew it from him."

Still, his publication in *Alhambra* represented Evans's first useful appearance with the international avant garde. Flores was well connected in his role as editor. Earlier in the summer, he had befriended the Spanish poet Federico García Lorca, then visiting in New York prior to a trip to Cuba. A selection of Lorca's *Ballads*, as well as an article about them, were published in the same August issue of *Alhambra* in which Evans's contributions appeared. Sometime later, not long after Hart Crane had returned to the States, Flores took the Spanish poet to meet the American poet at one of Crane's noisy parties in Brooklyn Heights. Crane was then in another of his periods of intensive work, interrupted by extensive drinking, trying — and failing — to complete the promised remaining sections of *The Bridge*. Crane knew no Spanish so he and Lorca conversed in halting French. But by the time Flores quit the party he noticed that the two poets had drifted apart, each the center of a little orbit of sailors.

Evans may not have been back in Brooklyn at the time of the party. It was not until the late fall, seemingly, that he moved into 78 Columbia Heights for a brief period. In a letter dated "end of November, 1929," he wrote Skolle, "Complicated and bewildering things happen. . . . Since you left I have been in a dark brown coma, punctuated by the arrival and departure of Paul." Thereby hung a tale, he said, much of it relating to Grotz's relationship with Dorothy Rogers. The two were definitely in love and had taken a recent trip together as a test. It was successful and they had just left for Germany. Evans now claimed that he and Skolle had been wrong about Rogers:

Anyway my mind has been completely put to rest about the whole affair. Rogers turned out to be much better than I thought. At first I didn't see her. Then, since that was spoiling the end of our friendship, P and I had a talk which led to a famous interview with Rogers which I wish I could describe. It didn't come off until the eleventh hour; up to the last day I doubted I could manage it at all. As to my conversion, you will have to take my word for it.

"Hart Crane is in very bad shape, but it is impossible," Evans wrote Skolle at the end of November, "so much so that I don't believe I can have anything to do with him. He is really a case now, muttering about 'the end' and his mother's beautiful white skull and syphilis and the ingratitude of his friends. This is all theater and he knows it; which enrages him more."

For Crane it was a chaotic period. Having come back from Paris with the Crosbys' agreement to publish a limited edition of *The Bridge*, he was suffering from the nervousness of "letting go" a work that he recognized from the beginning was meant to be a major achievement in his career. He was trying to complete the final promised segments, "Quaker Hill" and "Indiana," as well as revise significant passages in the "Cape Hatteras" and "The River" sections, driven by the need to complete an overriding thematic structure. As usual he had fallen back on drink as a source of inspiration. He was also in full flight from what he dreaded would be an impending visit by his mother (the source, no doubt, of the grim metaphor of the "mother's beautiful white skull" echoed in Evans's letter). That was the cause of hurried visits to his father (and his father's new wife) in Chagrin Falls, Ohio; his hideaway in Patterson, New York; and abrupt returns to his apartment at 130 Columbia Heights, all the while fitting in periods of serious work on his poem.

Evans, once more swept up in Crane's frantic life, could hardly avoid a growing sense of the destructiveness that sometimes accompanies genius. Edgy about personal claims on his own time and friendship, he was relieved that Sam Loveman, Crane's devoted older Cleveland friend, was living in the Heights and keeping an eye on the poet. "Thank heaven," Evans wrote Skolle, "I won't have to be the friend to put him to bed and witness his staged insanity. But it depresses me to see it."

A series of photographs Evans made of Crane (probably in 1929 or 1930) concentrated on the features from a close angle, the face squeezed into the format, suggesting aggressiveness or an intensity to bore in on the personality as if it were a specimen. Another of Crane shows him in suit and tie, standing against a darkened window, with a cigar in a stubby hand. The hair is cropped and bristling; the brown eyes have seen much — or too much. There is an air of self-consciousness about the occasion. Evans photographed Loveman as well: Like Crane, he is thick-featured, but balding. The photograph does not tell us that this is one of those dedicated lives on whom Crane's erratic genius depended for survival, stability, generous loans, rescues from difficult situations. There is, too, at least one portrait of the two friends together, both white-shirted against a white wall: Loveman with just the cusp of a smile; Crane, head tilted, interested and assured. Long study might yield hints about the nature of the friendship; but photographs do not reveal everything. Other revelations would still depend on the facts — not nearly indisputable — obtained from letters, diaries, the memoirs of friends and enemies.

There is no definite date for when Crane decided to ask Evans to provide photographs of the Brooklyn Bridge as illustrations for the Crosbys' edition of *The Bridge*. In January 1929, Crane was courting the painter Joseph Stella, hoping to use one of his dramatic paintings of the bridge as a frontispiece. In a letter to Stella, he was cordial, making a point of the "remarkable coincidence that I should, years later, have discovered another person, by whom I mean you, should have had the same sentiments regarding the Brooklyn Bridge, which inspired the main themes and pattern of my poem." A bit of flattery perhaps, but not insincere; Crane had the genuine artist's talent for recognizing real talent. Even as late as September 6 he was offering to get the Crosbys a "fresh photo of Stella's picture within a few days." Between then and late December the plans had been changed and Crane asked Evans to supply the illustrations. Evans offered three vest-pocket-sized 1⅝ x 2½ photos which were produced the same size on the page. (Evans remembered Crane's friend the critic

Hart Crane,
1929

102

Malcolm Cowley telling him it was "precious to do it that way.") For a later addition a larger, dramatic horizontal photo was used as a frontispiece. Small though they were, they were effectively dramatic and angular, verging toward an abstractionism that Evans, himself, would later claim was too romantic for his taste. It is clear that he had had some say in the layout of the illustrations. When Crane wrote Caresse Crosby about the matter, he stressed:

By the way, will you see that the middle photograph (the one of the barges and tug) goes between the "Cutty Sark" Section and the "Hatteras" Section. That is the center of the book both physically and symbolically. Evans is very anxious, as am I, that no ruling or printing appear on the pages devoted to the reproduction — which is probably your intention anyway.

The Paris edition of *The Bridge* did not appear until the following February. But early in December — on the seventh — Crane arranged a party in Brooklyn Heights to celebrate the forthcoming publication. Harry and Caresse Crosby, in New York on a visit, were the guests of honor and Evans, as illustrator, was asked to attend. Crane had also invited the poets William Carlos Williams and e e cummings and their wives. Crane's friend Margaret ("Peggy") Robson, who had helped type up the final copies of the poem, organized the party and served as hostess. It was a convivial affair, with toasts and compliments, so successful in fact that Robson and Harry Crosby had to search the neighborhood for more bootleg gin. Crosby's diary for that day says little about the party itself, only that cummings was there. That morning he had visited the premier exhibition of the new Museum of Modern Art on the twelfth floor of the Hecksher Building at the corner of Fifth Avenue and Fifty-seventh Street. It was an exhibition of Cézanne, Gauguin, Seurat, and Van Gogh. He had been particularly impressed by a Gauguin decorative panel and Van Gogh's painting of his room at Arles. He did note in a curious addition that his young mistress, Josephine Rotch, his "Fire Princess" as he sometimes referred to her, had appeared "all young and sparkling, her eyes goodbye in that grey city." It is not clear whether an out-of-sequence diary entry assigned to that date referred to something that happened at the Crane party or not: "Pack of Cards. I said I like Hearts the best. I drew and I drew the Ace of Hearts, the card I wanted."

But both entries give an ironic twist to the tragic ending that followed Crane's celebration party. Three days later Crosby, in a love/death pact with his mistress, committed suicide in a borrowed studio-apartment at the Hotel des Artistes. Crosby had failed to show up for the pretheater dinner party at the Caviar Restaurant, where Crane, Robson, Caresse, and Crosby's mother were waiting. Nor did he appear at the Lyceum Theater, where Leslie Howard was starring in *Berkeley Square*. It was only later, midway through the play, that the news came that the police, who had been called by a friend, broke down the door to the apartment and found the couple dead, lying fully clothed in bed and in each others' arms, both shot through the temples with Crosby's .25 Belgian automatic.

The Center of Things

5

Toward the end of 1929, while living at 78 Columbia Heights, Brooklyn, Evans took on a job in the Wall Street district. Without explaining his function there, in a late November letter he gave Skolle a brief report on the 111 John Street office, itemizing "the liquid soap squirters that work, the beautiful tomato bisque files, armpit odors, maddening motion of pimpled jaws on wads of chicklets, awe-inspiring nostrils of homely anonymous girls, one completely bald head." His list also included "the three flirts that have saved me from hysterics and murder: (1) a sort of improvement on Peggy Wood, (2) a Greta Garbo with the most exquisite little ears I have ever seen, (3) AND a really glorified Ena Douglas, a sight that would make you weep and blow saliva out of your ears." The third proved useful as a model for a now missing story: "I will say no more than that she is the inspiration of the enclosed composition entitled FILE CLERK FILING IN BLUE."

Early in 1930, however, the twenty-six-year-old Evans embarked on a new career and rented a new apartment, concrete evidence that he had begun to take a professional, if slightly sardonic, view of his photographic work. "I am not working downtown any more," he wrote Skolle. "Not 179 Columbia Heights. I sailed right past the 101 intervening houses without lowering my flags and signed a lease here, papered the walls dead white and am a sort of professional photographer who will do sort of advertising work on a paying basis."

He was keeping up an active life in the midst of the New York creative world just beginning to feel the effects of the Great Depression. He had read Robert Coates's Dadaist novel, *Eater of Darkness*, and found it "no good." He approved, however, of the thirty-two-year-old art critic for the *New Yorker*, who years earlier, fresh out of Yale, had made a canoe trip on the rivers and canals of Normandy. (Along the waterways, curious natives speculated that Coates and his companion were latter-day "peaux-rouges.") Evans found the tall, red-headed Coates a most "interesting and amusing person." Another recent acquaintance, the poet e e cummings, so Evans informed Skolle, "has married the lady and she is fat with a child and that

*Brooklyn
Bridge,
1928–29*

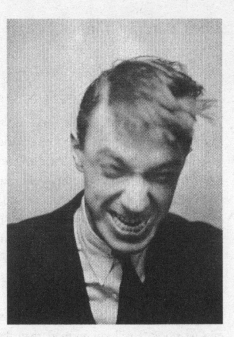

Photomat
portrait of Evans,
1929–30

seems awful." He had attended a recital by the dancer Martha Graham and
her group at the Maxine Elliot Theater, where she premiered her solo
dance, "Lamentation," with music by Zoltán Kodály. Wearing a tubing of
[orange] tricot that clung to her body, Graham's every grieving movement
became a sculptural gesture. Evans announced that the dancer "was better
than ever." Presumably he had shouted himself hoarse: "That's how I got
tonsillitis," he claimed. He also had attended the inaugural exhibition at
the new Museum of Modern Art, a show of Gauguin, Van Gogh, Cézanne,
and Seurat. It was, he reported, "a great stampede of the art world and its
fringes. Mobs of awful awful awful people and talk talk talk — and many
wonderful paintings." He could barely afford the two dollars and fifty cents
for the illustrated catalogue and was not able to send a copy to Skolle.

Of his early years in the profession, Evans would admit: "I used to try
to figure out precisely what I was seeing all the time, until I discovered I
didn't need to. If the thing is there, why, there it is." Early in 1930, he was
assuring Skolle "I am learning something about photography." To be sure,
he had his quirks. Like any serious young professional, he had acquired

certain dogmas. He was then extolling panchromatic film because it captured gradations of tone. He preferred absolute flat matte printing papers — "no reflection of light" — preferably double weight. He was still roaming the streets in search of subjects and bemoaning the fact that he had no close friend who could give him worthwhile criticism of his efforts. (It was a frequent complaint in his letters to Skolle: "I need some good criticism on photographs I am doing for myself. I have some things done which I am very anxious to show you. . . . I have specialized lately in crumbling gravestones: they are wonderful camera subjects.") These presumably were the early photos of an ancient Boston graveyard. By 1930, when he had set up shop so to speak, he had become proficient with two large format cameras (negative sizes of 5 x 7 and 6½ x 8½, with ground-glass viewing), which meant working with a tripod and required set-up times, as well as the earlier hand-held cameras he had begun with.

He was also exploring the possibilities of the medium with an eager curiosity. Early in 1930 he had experimented with the local photographic machines or photomatons that had become popular. He took a sequence of some fifteen or more self-portraits in a local photomat, mostly in the comic vein, to judge from the report of Skolle, to whom Evans sent his only copies. "Tableau No. 2 is disgusting," Skolle wrote, "5 very lifelike, 8 calls for birdies in the upper left corner. No. 10 looks as though had sold a Buick a minute ago. In No. 11 the customer seems to have cancelled his order. . . . Of course, 15 takes the cake." The latter Evans had decided to call *Opium*, but Skolle, in a show of expertise, corrected him on his choice of title: "Opium is a worthy experiment and good fun, though I suggest Cocaine — which really causes facial contortions quite in contrast to opium which is a soporific." Evans said he would be happy to make a 5 x 7 enlargement of the picture to send Skolle, but he would need ninety cents to have it made. Photomat portraits, he informed his friend, were made as direct prints on sensitive paper in the machine. There were no negatives; that was why he had requested the return of the prints.

His first official year as a photographer with a studio began on a promising note. In January, Hart Crane was promoting him in advance of the publication of both the Paris and New York Liveright editions of *The Bridge*, which carried Evans's photographs as illustrations. Evans, who was seeing a great deal of the poet at the time, was appreciative: "Besides

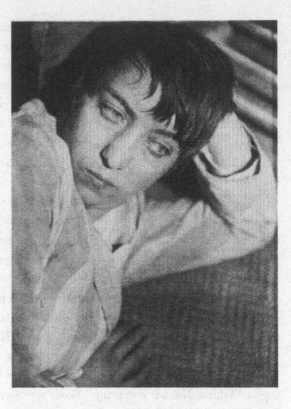

amusing me beyond words he has been ballyhooing me among the great and neogreat of the city — really generous and *sans arriere-pensée* [without thinking twice]." But his gratitude was phased out a few months later when Crane began acting up: "I got fed up with Crane," he informed Skolle, "and am not seeing him. Had a quarrel in fact, and am disgusted at myself for allowing things to get to the point where a quarrel was necessary. Thank God there were no actual 'words,' though, an outcome of the sort of thing I once described. He is beyond recall, I suppose. Anyhow, impossible as far as I'm concerned. God, how I hate that sort of thing."

It is possible that the connection with Crane's book may have resulted in the use of one of his Brooklyn Bridge photographs as a cover photo for the summer issue of *USA*, a new and trendy literary quarterly published in Philadelphia. But in March Evans was already in touch with the New York-based art editor of the magazine, hoping to interest him in his photographs.

At around the same time, so he informed Skolle, he had received a check for six hundred dollars from an unnamed advertising firm in Philadelphia for a set of six photos he had made in one afternoon. It might not be as good as it sounded, he admitted, "since I have borrowed twice that much and more to get myself into a position to bring off such a deal." He preferred to keep the fee secret since his regular asking price was one hundred and twenty-five dollars per photo. A month later, however, he complained about the vagaries of the marketplace: "Couldn't say what happened to Philadelphia. Mysterious of them to throw me hundreds of dollars worth of prostitution, make a fuss over me, then shut off. Now I'll have to storm the New York agencies, God help me." Even so, Evans was convinced that New York was where he ought to be with respect to his career. He reprimanded Skolle for having deserted the city, telling him about a young painter-friend of Crane's, Peter Blume, who had sold a large oil to Mrs. Rockefeller for twenty-five hundred dollars. Blume was "pretty good, of course, but he has nowhere near your depth." Also Skolle should have been in the American show just held at the Museum of Modern Art. "Damn it," he scolded, "you get out of the center of things when you stay long in the provinces."

The truth is that, despite the depression, the year 1930 was to be a year of good fortune, not only in the commissions that came Evans's way but in the people he met. It is not exactly clear how or when he first met the photographer Berenice Abbott, who in late 1929 had returned from Paris and was for a time living in a studio at the Hotel des Artistes. Abbott had brought with her the collection of Atget glass plates and prints that she would tend and preserve for years to come. (In 1930, the New York art dealer Julien Levy acquired an interest in the collection.) In February 1930, Evans was writing about her to Skolle in terms that suggest he only recently had met her: "You would like Berenice Abbott with her hair brushed forward and her woozy eyes." That was precisely the look in a series of photographs he took of her during this period. Presumably, it was around the same time that he became acquainted with the work of Atget. It was to be one of the seminal documentary influences of his own career, though a bit defensively in later years he would insist he had already achieved his own style before seeing Atget's photographs. It is significant, however, that both Abbott and Evans, as much as any contemporary photographers, would make careers of documenting New York's architecture, street scenes, and shop fronts, introducing Atget's vital urban documentary style into American photography.

Evans's friendship with Abbott would survive the years, though she would sometimes feel hurt or disappointed that Evans never gave the impression that he thought highly of her work — or told her that he did. Evans could maintain a strange silence about the work of women photographers with whom he was otherwise very friendly. But at the beginning, the relationship between the two was solid enough that Evans was given the use of Abbott's darkroom facilities. And she was eager to promote his work — too eager, it appears, for Evans. In June, he wrote Skolle: "Berenice Abbott let a French publisher have some of my best photographs for a book and I am furious because that is a total loss all around and I am going to try to cable nothing doing; all this is very tough on Knerves."

There was another item in his letter which he perversely included as "Further news not worth recording except that I have some photos in international (Lichtbild) exhibition in Munich." It is not clear whether Evans was aware of a notice of his work in the exhibition that appeared in the November 15, 1930, issue of the Parisian *La Revue Moderne*. The reviewer, C. De Cordis, however, was thoroughly familiar with Evans's career to date, noting his illustrations for the Parisian edition of Hart Crane's *The Bridge*, and his appearances in such American magazines as *USA*, *The Architectual Record*, *Hound & Horn*, and *Creative Art*, some of which were still forthcoming. It is possible that Evans himself or a friend with a French connection, like Berenice Abbott, may have supplied the information. But certainly Evans was either being cavalier or unduly modest about this earliest and important international recognition of his work. The *Revue Moderne* had even included a severely cropped reproduction of his photograph of a billowing wash line and a fence with torn political posters against a backdrop of smoke stacks of the Brooklyn power house, a thoroughly appropriate image for what the reviewer praised as *"un remarquable champ d'experience dans les visions architecturales si fortement caracterisées de New York, Walker Evans vient d'achève cette serie imporant de clichés."* (A remarkable range of expertise in the architectural visions that characterize New York, Walker Evans has just finished this important series of photographs.) Though the other photographs in the exhibition are not indicated, de Cordis went on to state: *"Il continuera par l'étude de la vie et du movement dans la rue."* (He will continue the study of life and movement in the street.) De Cordis was convinced that in large measure Evans had been influenced by the work of Atget (not altogether a familiar name even in Paris except in vanguard circles like the surrealists) as well as by the American Paul Strand and, less convincingly, the Russian filmmaker Sergei Eisenstein. Nonetheless, he noted, accurately enough, that "Walker Evans veut une photographie pure sans aucun romantisme, et il ne craint pas que son oeuvre soit dure, et meme impitoyablement revelatrice des defauts que peut presenter le sujet." (Walker Evans wants a pure photography without any romanticism, and does not fear that his work might be hard, or even pitiless in revealing the potential flaws of his subject.)

In the summer of 1930, Evans spent some time on Cape Cod with a new friend, the painter and illustrator Ben Shahn, whom he had met earlier at the home of his Brooklyn Heights patron and collector, Dr. Iago Galdston. Evans's recollection was that there were others present but that the conversation was mostly superficial: "I was, with Ben, by far the brightest man in the room. Ben noticed it too. Ben took a fancy to me and I think when I left he decided to leave too, walked with me a bit." Evans couldn't remember what they talked about, only that Shahn was something of a braggart: "He was too forward, I was more reserved and usually respected it in others." Still, the friendship took. Shahn, five years older than Evans, had been born in Kovno, Lithuania. At the age of eight his family made the voyage to America, settling in Brooklyn. He was eleven when the tenement the family lived in on Lorimer Street caught fire. His father managed to drop the four children into the arms of a friend waiting below. As a youngster Shahn grew up in the predominantly Jewish Williamsburg district, attending high school at night and working as an apprentice to a lithographer during the days. When Evans met him he was a burly man in his early thirties, mustachioed, intense, looking more like a laborer than an artist. Hard-working, he had managed to save enough to take his family to Europe in 1925 and again in 1927, twice traveling to North Africa, drawn there by his interest in the art and writings of Eugène Delacroix. In April 1930, he had his first exhibition at Edith Halpert's Downtown Gallery, largely a show of his drawings and paintings of Africa.

Evans conceded that Shahn was "a tough Jew," that he needed to be, growing up in Williamsburg. He was apparently impressed by Shahn's rise from near poverty. When he first met the artist, Shahn was living in very close quarters with his wife Tillie and their daughter Judith in a basement flat in Brooklyn. Evans was not impressed with Tillie, thought her "a quite uninteresting, very hard-working woman." On the one or two occasions that Shahn took him to meet his parents in their Brooklyn home, Evans made a fastidious social distinction: "There was a factory next to it and it shook all the time."

The two men's paths had not crossed in Paris, but Evans heard about the family's struggles at surviving in the French Capital. Evans recalled: "For a boy who had been living in the slums of Brooklyn, [Paris] was even cheaper because he had a wife." But not that cheap: "She'd go around and buy seconds or tripe or even horse-meat, I don't know what, and lived on nothing. . . . Tillie," he said, "was working herself to the bone and he [Shahn] lost interest in her so she must have been pretty miserable."

In his June 1930 letter to Skolle, Evans claimed that he had gotten a

touch of sunstroke from not wearing a hat while out taking photographs in a "peculiar landscape." The Truro photographs that turn up in his Cape Cod negatives reveal no specifically "peculiar" scenes. But it may well have been on the summer visit (he would make another trip to Truro in late November) that Evans took one of the early sign photographs of the words "Gas A" scrawled in dripping paint on torn and paint-besmeared posters. A notation on a negative sleeve indicates it had been taken on a road near Truro. As an image it has an almost abstract expressionist quality, twenty years before the fact, and it has remained one of the much-reproduced Evans photographs. Another less familiar Truro shot is of a row of beach houses silhouetted against the sky, models of routine sameness on a grassy slope. Quite probably, too, the portraits of Tillie Shahn and Shahn's daughter, Judy, date from this earlier visit to Truro.

It is more likely that some of Evans's most significant photographs taken in Cape Cod that year were taken during his Thanksgiving visit. These were interior views of the house belonging to the De Luzes, a family of Portuguese fishermen, from whom the Shahns rented their cottage. There are photographs of a cluttered kitchen, full of the detritus of daily life: a water pail and tin dipper, a sink pump. Above it on a shelf is a *Roadside Gas* kerosene lamp and a small hand loom with a bit of weaving. Another *Sign, 1929,* kitchen shot is a scene equally unkempt: a kitchen sink with a cloth skirt *Truro,* that hides the plumbing (à la thirties improvised). Beside it there is a *Cape Cod* makeshift drying board with recently washed down-turned cups and a rusty bread box in the background. The only element of order and organization in this disorder is a pair of identical kitchen chairs jammed tightly together. (Evans had a kind of fixation for objects in series.) The atmosphere speaks of a hard-times rental unit and poor housekeeping. And it is true that in a November letter to Skolle, Evans makes it clear that he is roughing it on Cape Cod. The telephone, the gas, and the electricity had been disconnected. "But we manage. Oil lamps, you know. Oil stove you know and fire place." Since he was inviting Skolle to a Thanksgiving feast on the premises, he emphasized "BOUGHT TWO OIL HEATERS," and included a sketch of stoves radiating heat lines. Skolle, having come east sometime in the summer, had been staying at Ossining and New York. The condition Evans attached to the invitation was that Skolle should bring a bottle of schnapps. There was some cause for celebration: Just when

Evans's "financial barometer" had hit lower than the actual barometer, he had received an unanticipated two hundred dollars in the mail. "So mon ami, we shall eat. In fact if you come very soon we shall have a turkey and lots of schnapps." His early professional career was a matter of such unexpected windfalls and second-rate accommodations.

At Truro, Evans noted, there had been a severe three-day northeaster. "The only thing one goes out for is to pee." Nevertheless, he made a daily trek to the village and the post office as well as to get milk and bread. "Walking to the village in the face of above N.E er with slicker slapping around your legs and getting entangled in your pants and pulling them up to your knees almost makes me feel like Captains Courageous." Evans launched into an account of hitching a ride with Antony de Luze and his father in their Chevy: "All in heavy oilskins, boots, Southwester hats. I tell you if an artist painted it or O'Neill wrote it nobody would believe it."

It is possible that some of the kitchen photos may be of the De Luze kitchen: a plaster saint in a niche (probably Saint Therese of Lisieux, a popular icon in the thirties) and a hanging bird cage with cuttlebone suggest something more personal than a short-term rental affair. The most famous of the Truro photographs are definitely identified on negative sleeves as the De Luze home interior. They are, in their way, monuments to horticultural ugliness, Evans's droll way of puncturing the romanticism of nature's beauties. A monstrous, misshapen cactus plant sits in a wooden bucket on a Victrola cabinet in what appears to be the corner of the parlor. Beside it is a wedding photograph. In a larger take of the same scene, the jumble of life in the corner is more apparent still: Family photographs and snapshots are arranged on the mantle of the closed-off fireplace and are hung on the floral-papered wall. On a nearby table is a meager bouquet in a vase and a sickly fern. In the disarray around the cactus plant, there is the wedding bouquet on the woman's lap in the wedding photograph and above it a bouquet of wilted flowers and the dried palm fronds from a Palm Sunday mass long past. One may dig deeper and find more: The woman in the photograph on the mantle wears a flower on her bosom; the frame on the photograph on the wall is carved with rosettes. In the background of this floral and familial confusion, the tip of a furled American flag asserts itself. Was the floral confusion a mere coincidence that Evans was unaware of when he clicked the shutter?

Interior Detail of Portuguese House, 1930

What haunts many of Evans's photographs of interiors is the absence of the occupants. By pictorial means — in the same manner as a writer might do with words — Evans confirms the presence of these living ghosts in the oh-so-homely details of their existence. The photographs-within-the-photographs supply, in fact, a family genealogy of occupants and relatives. The profusion of floral motifs may be an instance of someone's character and taste, probably that of the wife of the household — her instinctive love of flowers, etc., revealed in a particular convergence. There is the feminine touch of the box of Houbigant powder or perfume on the shelf. The presence of the American flag may offer no reference to gender or nationality, but it might possibly be attributed to the new-found patriotism of an immigrant. One is invited to pore over the evidence like a Sherlock Holmes. What is there is truly there, as Evans maintained; the photographer has only to capture its fullest expression in the jumbled corner.

Years later, in an interview, Evans maintained, "I think I incorporated Flaubert's method almost unconsciously, but anyway I used it in two ways: Both his realism or naturalism, and his objectivity of treatment. The nonappearance of the author. The nonsubjectivity. That is literally applicable to the way I want to use a camera and do." He was perhaps right that he had adopted Flaubert's method unconsciously, for although he cites that source, there is no great evidence — so far — that he had read Flaubert with the same diligence that encouraged him to translate Gide or Radiguet or Blaise Cendrars. But it is true that his photographs of the De Luze interiors appear to have been taken with a novelist's eye. If not Flaubert, perhaps Balzac, on similar grounds. (Although there is no evidence that Evans had read Balzac widely either.) Yet every detail of the mise-en-scène of the De Luze pictures is as evidentiary as those in Flaubert or Balzac. The pictures on the walls, the poverty of taste, the carelessness of the housekeeping, the hands of the clock on the shelf, the calendar on the wall — all define character and circumstances, time and place. The eye collects; the camera frames.

It is said that Evans had a small exhibition of his photographs and Ben Shahn's paintings in a Truro barn in 1930. If it took place during the summer, it might well have been — officially — his first unheralded American exhibition. But by Thanksgiving time, Evans had appeared in a far more prestigious exhibition in Cambridge, Massachusetts, and had some of his photographs reproduced in an influential magazine, *Hound & Horn*.

II

Few of the friends and acquaintances Evans made in the 1930 and 1931 professional years were to prove more useful to his career than Lincoln Kirstein, the son of a wealthy Boston paterfamilias, Louis Edward Kirstein, a partner of William Filene's Sons department store as well as President of the Boston Public Library. Kirstein, four years younger than Evans, had managed to attend Phillips Exeter as briefly as Evans had attended Phillips Andover. Kirstein had had rather precocious and varied artistic experiences as a youth. At the academy, he had published a play, *The Silver Fan*, in the *Phillips Exeter Monthly*. In the summers, on trips abroad with his mother and other family members, he had been introduced to the Bloomsbury circle in London, meeting art critic Clive Bell and Virginia Woolf as well as the Sitwells. He had entrée into the studio of painter Duncan Grant. John Maynard Keynes, economist and art patron, had escorted him to an exhibition of Cézanne watercolors at the Leicester Galleries. His mother, who had a passion for Wagner, took him on pilgrimage to Bayreuth, where he became acquainted with the antisemitism of the grand hotels. His mother was told that there were no accommodations at Der Schwarze Adler and that they might be "happier" in the private home of Frau Steinkraus, a co-religionist. At Bayreuth, Kirstein particularly remembered a performance of *Die Meistersinger* at which, after the finale, the audience rose in a burst of postwar patriotic vengeance chanting "Deutschland, Deutschland Über Alles."

Kirstein's father, thinking it would be better that his son have a glimpse of the working world before entering college, allowed him, at the age of eighteen, to be apprenticed (without pay) in the stained-glass studio of Charles Connick in Boston. (While there, he made roundels of male and female figures in sports clothes representing the Four Seasons. They were later installed in his sister's farm in Ashfield, Massachusetts.) Kirstein entered Harvard in the fall of 1926, graduating with the class of 1930. During his college years, he was the initiating force behind the vanguard quarterly *Hound & Horn*, funded by his father and patterned after T. S. Eliot's *The Criterion*. During its seven years of existence from 1927 to 1934, and under varying editors, it published stories and poems by Kay Boyle, Stephen Spender, Erskine Caldwell, Katherine Anne Porter (her early masterpiece "Flowering Judas"), e e cummings, William Carlos Williams, Marianne

Moore, and Wallace Stevens. Its premiere September 1927 issue included a two-part essay on T. S. Eliot by Richard Blackmur with a bibliography of Eliot's work by Varian Fry. Its critical articles covered the field of modernism from art and architecture to film, theater, and dance.

Ezra Pound, whose two lines from an early poem "The White Stag" (" 'Tis the white stag, Fame, we're a-hunting / Bid the world's hounds come to horn!") provided the magazine with its title, served as a European mentor, contributing ranting diatribes against "Murkin" values in the form of letters. The magazine also published his "Cantos XXVIII–XXX." But the relationship ended when the editors declined two of Pound's contributions. Pound withdrew his support, disgusted, he claimed, with writing for "a pair of rich fahrts and not getting paid." When the magazine began publishing illustrations, it featured drawings by Picasso and the sculptor Gaston Lachaise (one of Kirstein's favored artists) as well as photographs by Harry Crosby and Evans. Evans's first appearance in the October/December 1930 issue (he was identified as a "Brooklyn photographer") consisted of a series of four New York scenes: "Traffic," "Wash Day," "Sixth Avenue (42nd Street)" and "Port of New York." The first quite probably is a view looking down at the entrance to the Borough Hall Brooklyn subway entrance with traffic speeding past. The second seems to be a variant or cropped and enlarged view from a sequence of shots he made of a wash line strung against the backdrop of the chimney stacks of the Brooklyn Power House, an anthropomorphic ballet of shirts and drawers and socks billowing in the wind. (Pound, still involved with the magazine, commented, "Evans photos. good; especially Wash Day.")

Kirstein's undergraduate ambitions did not stop with *Hound & Horn*. In 1928, along with his well-to-do undergraduate colleagues at Harvard, John Walker III and Eddie Warburg, and the art scholar Agnes Mongan, he became the driving force behind the Harvard Society for Contemporary Art, a precursor of New York's Museum of Modern Art, which opened officially the following year. Although the Harvard Society's initial exhibition in February 1929 was something less than vanguard, it did include works by Edward Hopper, Kenneth Hayes Miller, Maurice Sterne, Georgia O'Keeffe, John Marin, and the sculptors Alexander Archipenko, Robert Laurent, and Lachaise. Its second show, The School of Paris: 1910-1928, which included paintings and sculptures by Braque, de Chirico, Modigliani, Gris, Brancusi, and Maillol, among others, was more satisfyingly controversial and had an attendance record of 3,500 during its three-week run.

Although it is not quite clear when the strapping six-foot-plus Kirstein first met the five-foot-seven-and-a-half Walker Evans, it would seem to have been sometime prior to Evans's appearance in *Hound & Horn*. Kirstein, however, does have a recollection that Evans had visited the Harvard Society exhibition in which ten of his works were shown. Opening on November 7, 1930, it was, for conservative Boston, a groundbreaking exhibition of modern photography, including ten works by Berenice Abbott, ten Atget photographs from her collection, as well as ten photographs apiece by such contemporary photographers as Ralph Steiner, Edward Weston, Tina Modotti, Alfred Stieglitz, and Paul Strand, among others. In a bold gesture Kirstein and his colleagues had included examples of press and aerial photographs, X rays, and astronomical photographs from the Harvard College Observatory. The introductory note, probably written by Kirstein, declared:

Photography exists in the contemporary consciousness of time, surprising the passing moment out of its context in flux and holding it up to be regarded in the magic of its arrest. It has the curious vividness and unreality of street accidents, things seen from a passing train and personal situations overheard or seen by chance — as one looks from the window of one skyscraper into the lighted room of another forty stories high and only across the street.

Evans's photographs stressed the down-to-earth urban origins of his early work, notably New York scenes: a sewer grating, electric signs, a detail from the Brooklyn waterfront, the S.S. *Leviathan* at its North River dock, a group of Coney Island bathers, all dating from 1928-30. By contrast, Abbott emphasized her recent French connections, portraits of the celebrities she had met during her eight-year stay in Paris: photographs of André Gide, André Maurois, and Jean Cocteau (including a vivid portrait of Cocteau's hands) as well as James Joyce.

Evans obviously appreciated the éclat that his appearance in the exhibition brought him. He boasted to Skolle: "Is it art or is it caricature seems to be the theme song of all the papers. Hit me on the shoulder. Slap me on the back. I MADE the tabloids. On the same page with pictures of Kiki Roberts, (Legs Diamond) Garner. Police Routing Striking Miners. I feel a little bit sorry for me. So young and already so famous."

The Indigenous Past

6

But it was not until early 1931 that Evans's friendship with Kirstein developed in full, largely, it seems, in the heady artistic, sexual, and political context of Muriel Draper's New York salon. Draper was a nineteenth-century daughter of New England. Born in Haverhill, Massachusetts, in 1886 (d. 1952), she was a woman of twentieth-century inclinations. An erstwhile interior decorator and author, she wrote occasional articles on interior decoration for the *New Yorker* under the backward byline "Repard Leirum." Her lively memoir, *Music at Midnight*, published two years earlier, had covered the pre–World War I years when she and her husband, the tenor Paul Draper, ran a noted musical salon in Edith Grove in London. In the golden years at the end of an era, she and her husband had hosted musical and literary evenings that featured the likes of the young pianist Artur Rubenstein, the cellist Pablo Casals, or the Belgian composer and later more famous conductor Eugene Goossens. Draper even managed to bag a childhood hero, Henry James. (At an early age she had been told that James was a genius.) She was also well acquainted with the painter John Singer Sargent. According to Kirstein, Muriel's first-hand accounts about these and other celebrities were even more entertaining than her written ones. But the radiant years of her London salon ended abruptly with the beginning of the war and the desertion of her husband. One day at the London docks, Paul Draper, while seeing off the actress Jeanne Eagels on a voyage to America, decided to make the journey with the star, leaving behind his wife and two small sons, Paul, Jr., and Sanders.

In the New York of the thirties, Muriel Draper was the quintessential hostess of what Kirstein referred to as Manhattan's "high bohemia." Her salon at 312 East Fifty-third Street was awash with the theories of Russian mystic and guru George Ivanovich Gurdjieff, whom Kirstein had first met in 1927 at Gurdjieff's *Fontainebleau Institute for the Harmonious Development of Man* in France. (In 1931, the master was giving inspirational sessions in New York, which Draper and Kirtsein attended with some regularity.) Draper had also taken an ardent interest in the politics of Soviet Russia

Muriel Draper Apartment, 1931

that would lead to an extended stay in Russia in the mid-thirties. At her "evenings" one met the New York critics Edmund Wilson and Gilbert Seldes, the black poet Langston Hughes, singer and actor Paul Robeson, even, occasionally, rival New York saloniste Mabel Dodge Luhan. Wilson, who for a time lived next door to Draper in a little wooden house at 314 East Fifty-third next to her little wooden house at 312, once in a testimonial letter apologizes for having missed one of Draper's soirées: "I enjoy your parties more than anybody else's in New York, and never stay away without a reluctance which lends bitterness to my obstinacy" [March 17, 1930].

Kirstein, some twenty years younger than Draper, had met her as early as 1927, when he was a precocious Harvard freshman. It was at one of her Thursday evenings at her loft above an old coach house on East Fortieth Street that he had first met Carl Van Vechten, friend and promoter of Gertrude Stein, novelist and photographer of the Harlem Renaissance figures Zora Neale Hurston, Langston Hughes, Jean Toomer, and Claude McKay. Van Vechten, Kirstein remembered, looked like a "large, blond, faintly Churchillian baby" wearing a bright red fireman's shirt. Through Van Vechten he was introduced, at that tender age, to the Harlem of the Savoy Dance Hall and the Apollo Theater, "a Harlem far more parochial, private, remote, less dangerous" than it would later become. "To us," Kirstein recalled, "Harlem was far more an arrondissement of Paris than a battleground of New York."

Kirstein was indebted to Van Vechten for another important experience. At the age of nine he had developed a fateful lifetime interest in the dazzling figure of the dancer Vaslav Nijinsky. It had started with the odd circumstance of not having seen Nijinsky dance when in 1916 Diaghilev's Ballets Russes performed in Boston. (Kirstein's mother, Rose, was convinced that her son was too sensitive to witness what was reported to be the violence of Nijinsky's performances in *Scheherazade*.) Van Vechten, who had been present at the riotous 1913 first-night performance in Paris of Stravinsky's *Rite of Spring*, which Nijinsky had choreographed, gave Kirstein so vivid a first-hand account of Nijinsky in performance, that Kirstein admitted, "I often used his description later as a personal lie, pretending to have experienced this dancer, who in real life, I had never seen."

It was early in 1931 that Walker Evans first cropped up in the lively, decade-long diaries in which Kirstein recorded his coming-of-age, his New York life, and his adventures in the arts. Evans cuts an odd figure among the leisurely entries. Kirstein, ever observant, noted that Evans "had the curious New York Manner, a mixture of complete agreement with you — almost before you speak, an insistence on making you believe he actually really was in sympathy with you, instead of waiting to let you discover it for yourself. I suppose everything here works so fast that sensitive people have to keep up with the rush, and when they meet each other they can't let time slip." It was a quality that Kirstein, professing himself something of a newcomer to the scene, detected in other men-about-town like Cary Ross, whom he had recently met, and Jere Abbott, a former Harvard graduate and contributor to *Hound & Horn* and assistant to Alfred H. Barr, the recently appointed director of the new Museum of Modern Art. "It slightly embarrasses me," Kirstein noted, "because I feel they are exposing more than I am willing to concede myself and in losing the personal equilibrium it is somehow subtly degrading." Kirstein's innocence is somewhat suspect, however, considering the extent of his experiences in the world.

Walker Evans's entrée into the sophisticated world of the Draper salon brought with it certain hazards. He seems to have made a hit with a number of the homosexual and bisexual men who regularly frequented Muriel's evenings. Kirstein, in his diaries, routinely recorded the episodes he had witnessed and those in which Muriel reported on the general campaign of assault against Evans's masculine virtue. There was the case of the aspiring young member of the American diplomatic corps, an intimate of Jean Cocteau's, who, high on drugs, took Walker out for dinner "and horrified him by acting camp and taking dope which he got in Harlem and which he decided was half talcum powder after all. He would scream at the rails of the elevated and tell them to stop. He made a pass at Walker and was generally difficult." On a different occasion another of Muriel's young blades had been so attracted by Evans that when he finally took the plunge of asking him for lunch, he did it in such a "transparently flirtatious and ass-humping" manner that he was no longer attracted. Muriel, bemused, commented on "the very subtle and powerful influence that Walker Evans exerted on all of us, mainly in the mysterious quality that he projected — did he know his own power or not?" At a dinner at 312 East Fifty-third that Evans and the publisher Joseph Brewer had attended, Muriel reported she had behaved like a "perfect school girl" flirting outrageously with Brewer, purely to hide her interest in Evans. "I preened for him and Joseph preened for him." All the while Evans went on "looking like a Coptic head, or an Etruscan vase."

In a droll moment Kirstein reported on his and Muriel's sexual intentions toward Evans. He had been at one of Muriel's all-night parties and confessed to having talked too loudly and drunkenly. In the gray New York morning Kirstein walked Evans home — or at least from Fifty-third to Twenty-third Street:

The buildings in the gray precast of dawn looked larger than I ever saw them, more massive and realized. We spoke of ourselves, of our standards of affection. He spoke of Hanns Skolle, the boy he lives with in a difficult strain of emotional pins and needles. Back to Muriel's to say good night to her. She baited me for my walk with Walker. "Which of us shall take him to bed?" I told her she could for all of me.

Among the habitués of the Draper salon, studies in the psychology of sex could take remarkable twists and turns. Kirstein remembered one of the more unusual discussions:

*Tin Relic,
1930*

Walker and I took the bus down to his place. He said the trouble with us was that we were just lesbians. I told this to Mools. She said she felt the same way about men. That is, homosexuals. Only the male part of her liked men. I said I was sick of the limits of my single attitude towards sex. She said she agreed but the trouble was that there are damn few women, women as such, left in the world.

Kirstein also remarked — several times in the spring of 1931 — on the near poverty in which Evans and Skolle were living in their apartment at 92 Fifth Avenue, before Skolle returned to Europe in May:

Went over to 14th Street and Fifth Avenue to call on Walker Evans. . . . Walker lives with his German friend Hanns Skolle in a particularly depressing hole in the wall. Their poverty is really so sad, always implied but never mentioned. I hated to feel my very presence compelled a comparison, and it probably did in my eager mind.

Yet out of the shabbiness, Evans managed to salvage a pair of striking photographs. It so happened that the building at 92 Fifth Avenue was being reroofed and in the debris he recovered some damaged tin soffits which he subsequently photographed. Two of them would appear as *Stamped Tin Relic* and *Tin Relic*, forming the entablature photographs for the opening and closing of Part II, the architectural segment of Evans's first important book *American Photographs*.

They were not the only photographs to commemorate Evans's ascendancy in New York's bohemia. However grimy or humble his Fifth Avenue apartment seemed to Kirstein, it was the setting for a series of droll portrait photographs that Evans took of his new friend. Kirstein noted an early, clowning session at the apartment:

Walker first took me as a convict — front and side views — as in a Rogue's Gallery. Then as the afternoon progressed we got crazier and crazier and ended up in an orgy of gaga poses, I cutting the tube or nipple off a funnel, or like a monkey. The fun of doing it was probably more fun, that is, better than the

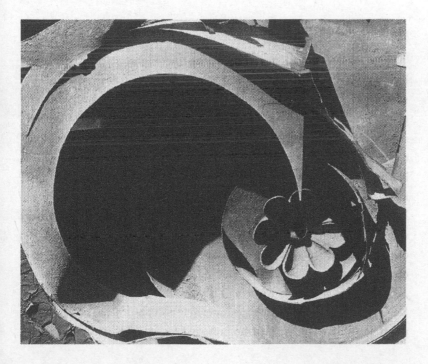

photographs will be.

The session gave Kirstein the idea that he might use photographs to illustrate his nearly completed novel-in-progress *Flesh Is Heir*. Much of the novel was autobiographical — indeed Kirstein claims that it is all autobiographical — and based on his recent experiences in the world of art and society. Kirstein claimed: "It's not a novel. I hope it's not literature in a traditional sense. The pictures would be like photographs handed out to illustrate a conversation, a correct image or metaphor." Days later, Kirstein's misgivings were justified. When Evans showed him the photographs at lunch, Kirstein decided they "were not as good as he [Evans] thought they were." The photographs were, as he judged, more fun in the making. One of the portraits, a double exposure, shows Kirstein nude to the waist, the exposures creating superimposed left and right profiles. Evans labeled it *Janus Portrait of Lincoln Kirstein*. The fact that he did not show it to Kirstein suggests that he either considered it unsuccessful or perhaps more psychologically revealing than he preferred to let on. Kirstein was much

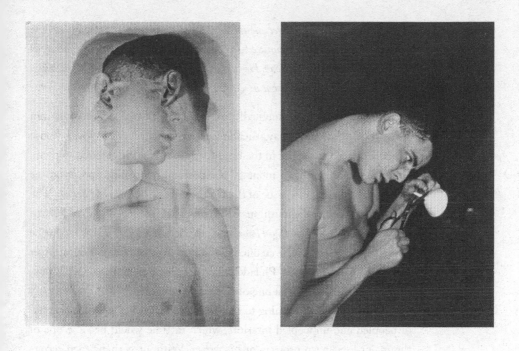

more satisfied with a later shot, his "gangster photo," showing him wearing a black derby tipped rakishly forward and a cigarette dangling from his lips, which fit into one of his current enthusiasms. Kirstein had developed a brisk obsession for the force and tempo of the gangster movies of the early thirties (*Public Enemy*, *Little Caesar*) and would refer to the photograph as his Cagney pose.

Early in the year, Evans and Kirstein were seeing each other with some frequency, trudging the New York streets, lunching or dining out. Kirstein's diaries of these sessions carried useful glimpses into Evans's personal woes and his random professional activities:

Dinner with Walker Evans. We were both feeling very poor. It's extraordinary the way I feel about money, always having had all I wanted. More than most other people so that I feel a certain obligation to pay for meals, etc. Walker told me he felt the same only much worse, since he had no money anyway. He hates to sell his photographs or leave them places where they might be seen, copied, or have ideas stolen from him. It's all part of his disappointing fear of getting tired easily.

Perhaps he actually doesn't get enough to eat and his vitality is actually low, but I told him I thought he submitted too easily to his terrors. He has a job to do bright light signs on Broadway. He carries a tiny Leica camera around with him always and stopped to snapshot as we walked across.

The photographs undoubtedly were related to a sequence of 35-mm photographs of Broadway theater advertisements and movie house marquees, "lurid metaphor in the bright lights" as Kirstein referred to them. Evans turned them into a montage composition that would appear on the cover of the June 24, 1931, issue of the trade journal *Advertising & Selling*. The photo credit for the composition, which included marquee lights of Metro-Goldwyn Mayer's *The Big House* and an electric sign for Lucky Strike cigarettes ("It's Toasted"), credited the Third Annual Exhibition at Ayer Galleries (most likely in Philadelphia), a heretofore unlisted exhibition, which had included at least one of Evans's photographs.

Evans was also continuing to build his personal collection of "portraits" of peopled and unpeopled interiors, which in time would become one of the major long-term projects of his career. Without perhaps then recognizing it as such, it became an anthology of the lives and personalities, homes and living quarters of the people who crossed his path and the acquaintances whose lives and careers ran parallel with his own. It might have been termed, à la Trollope, "The Way We Live Now," extending through the length of Evans's career as a kind of underground autobiographical sequence, an artist's day-book indicating his personal commitments, his travels and concerns, completing a dedicated investigation of contemporary American life.

In early 1931 Evans found an occasion, the impending marriage of eighteen-year-old Smudge Draper to his girlfriend Marcia Tucker, to produce another notable addition to the sequence. Some days before the wedding, Muriel Draper hosted a bachelor party at 312 East Fifty-third Street. The guests included Smudge's dancer-brother Paul Draper, Jr., Lincoln Kirstein, and Evans as well as other male friends. Walker photographed the occasion but not the people; he focused instead on the aftermath of the party. There is no attempt at commercial swank or of a commission for some glossy house and garden magazine. What Evans captured was a *memento mori*, the remains of a jovial night: the dinner tables with half-empty wine glasses, the soiled napkins, the scattered crumbs and cigarette ashes, the coffee service, the metallic-sheened drapes, the prodigious bouquets beginning to wilt, a snuffed-out, broken candle, bibelots, vases, empty wine bottles — an air of seediness and raffishness. Over the marble mantelpiece hangs a bleached cow's skull, an item of décor that may have been prompted by Georgia O'Keeffe's recently exhibited paintings of animal skulls gathered in the New Mexican desert.

In one of his diary notes in *The Thirties*, Edmund Wilson created a still-life version of Muriel's white downstairs sitting room that certifies the authenticity of Evans's photographic record, down to the wilting bouquets: "stale white calla lilies in a big white vase, cameo china ashtrays with cupids on them, white skull of a cow hung on the wall." Is that, perhaps, Evans's hat, a fedora, sitting on the mantel, considering that he liked to leave some telltale mark of his presence on the scene — his long shadow in the foreground, his reflection in a plate glass shop window? As in a passage in a Balzac novel, Smudge Draper's bachelor party, memorialized by Evans, is an evening of New York society now past, recorded without sentiment or any attempt at Hollywood glamour, only with ruthless down-to-earth veracity. The inevitable temptation is to see Evans's photographic work in terms of the novel and short story and its range as a *comédie humaine* — character as revealed by detail.

II

It was before late February that year that Kirstein first broached the subject to Walker Evans: "Suggested he come up to Boston to photograph the Victorian Houses." It was an ambitious project Kirstein had been considering a year or two earlier in collaboration with John Brooks Wheelwright, his former Boston mentor — a writer and architectural critic with quixotic tastes who regularly attended mass at the priory of the Anglican Cowley Fathers near Charles River Drive. Kirstein once described him as "a Brahmin of Boston's best, an Anglican Trotskyite and a most interesting theological poet." Wheelwright, tall as a secretary bird but wearing a raccoon coat, was the son of a Boston architect and a spare-time architect himself. He was planning to write a book on Victorian architecture for which the photographs would serve as illustrations. He and Kirstein were also considering the possibility of mounting an exhibition on Victorian and industrial architecture at the Harvard Society for Contemporary Art.

It was not the only generous effort Kirstein made on Evans's behalf. Within weeks he began an active campaign to get Joseph Brewer to publish a book of Evans's photographs. A few days later Evans and the painter Mark Tobey were visiting the Metropolitan Museum when they encountered Kirstein. In a burst of enthusiasm, Kirstein suggested that Evans make photographs of the museum's sculpture collections. He commandeered the two and briskly paraded them through the galleries. Evans, who had left his glasses behind, got eyestrain. Kirstein noted in his diaries: "I so much wanted them to share my enthusiasm that I talked too fast and rushed around tiring Walker. . . . I think he felt I had an arrogant, arbitrary and proprietary interest in the object." It would prove to be an early warning sign that the two men would not always see eye to eye and that Evans was cautionary, at best, in his dealings with Kirstein. Nevertheless, some days after, Kirstein, having tea with Brewer, proposed his scheme: "Spoke to Joe of trying to publish small books of photographs of objects in the Metropolitan Museum, etc." He was not successful; Brewer, he noted, "didn't think it would be a good business proposition."

Evans and Kirstein continued to maintain their active social life in the last weeks before beginning their photography project. Evans was invited to dinner at Kirstein's sister Mina Curtiss's apartment. (The other guest was Hyatt Mayor, one of the editors of *Hound & Horn*.) Kirstein noted his pleasure with the fact that Walker had gotten along so well with Mina. Afterward, they all went to a movie and then to Roseland, the Broadway dance hall where the Cuban rumba was being introduced to New York. Twenty Cuban couples took part in a competition, dancing to the monotonous rhythm of one tune, "The Peanut Vendor." The best of the couples was a Spanish half-breed and a stout Cuban woman, all in white except for the man's green sash. According to Kirstein their performance was a case of "incipient rape." Dining out on another night Evans and Kirstein told each other stories of "boyhood bawdry at boarding school," Walker relating how at Andover there was an epidemic of boys lighting each other's farts, which burnt with a dull blue flame. From there the talk graduated to Maurice Sachs' "extraordinary tale" of the attaché in the Ministère de la Marine, never once absent in thirty years. In spite of the changing of ministries, the man had become indispensable since he knew where every dossier was. When he failed to show up for two days, they broke down his door and found him "hung up from a rafter, his little gray beard and all, in a ballet dancer's costume."

Kirstein had given Evans a manuscript copy of his novel *Flesh Is Heir* to read, and the two had some talk about it. In his diary, however, Kirstein made no mention of what Evans said about the book. (When it was published, Evans wrote Skolle, referring to it as a "doubtful novel," saying he would not send it because it was "meaningless.") But in the novel, Kirstein described an autobiographical episode dealing with the hero Roger's relationship with a sadistic and menacing classmate with whom he was nevertheless fascinated. Evans claimed he had had a very similar relationship with a college friend (unnamed in Kirstein's diary) and admitted that "he can't even see the guy anymore. No interest there."

On another of their movie nights, Evans and Kirstein went to see Joseph von Sternberg's *Dishonoured*, starring Marlene Dietrich in the role of Mata Hari. Kirstein thought it the most accomplished talking movie he'd ever seen despite the failures of taste, the trick double exposures, the borrowing from Eisenstein. He also recorded Evans's opinions: "One of Walker Evans's convictions is that nothing any good can happen except by mistake. He thinks it's only a break that anything the least good gets done in the movies, and the technical difficulties are so enormous that a man of intelligence hasn't a prayer."

Late in March, they were at a party given by the editors of the *New Republic* in a Fifth Avenue penthouse (Wilson, critic Paul Rosenfeld, and Dwight Macdonald, a brash young Yale graduate on the staff of *Fortune* magazine, were among the other guests) when Hart Crane made not one but two noisy drunken appearances. The first ended when Crane was thrown out for having started a fight. A half hour later he returned, banging on the door to be let in, followed by an angry cabdriver he had hired to take him to the Sands Street bars. Crane had no money to pay the fare and so had to return to the party to collect the funding from friends. Kirstein was struck by the "patient penitence, muffled apologies and small boy's pathetic, instinctive good manners" displayed on Crane's second appearance. But like Evans he was wary of becoming too personally involved with the poet. What was ironic about Kirstein's account of the incident is that he revealed that it was Evans (smaller and not a man of bravado on such occasions) who nevertheless introduced Kirstein to the rough and tumble Brooklyn bars that Crane usually attended. Kirstein slyly acknowledged that although he was suitably "costumed" in cut-rate clothes from Army-Navy stores, he "was not wildly successful as a male impersonator." Evans, a most unlikely Virgil to the underworld of sailors' bars, usefully advised Kirstein to keep his mouth shut in such places.

In these early stages of their friendship, the two men were positioning themselves, taking stock on matters of sexuality as well as esthetic conviction. Late in life, Kirstein remained convinced that Evans had no homosexual inclinations, even though his own bisexual tendencies were evident and despite the eager attention to Evans paid by the young men of Muriel Draper's social circle. Kirstein maintained this view even when there was some later evidence to suggest that Evans may have had a homosexual relationship or two. Perhaps his conviction was reinforced by one of the bits of sexual gossip regularly traded in the Draper circle. Muriel told Kirstein of a visit that Walker, full of champagne from a family wedding party, made on Saturday night: "He achieved, she said, a not inexpert attack on her virtue, but she finally put him off with one of her head-thrown-back speeches about 'Walker, go now. We musn't spoil this,' etc. Like she did me the first time I ever tried to make love to her and me drunk."

III

Oddly enough, the prelude to the great search for Victorian architecture in New England was an assignment to photograph a modern house built by Kirstein's young architect friend Lyman Paine at Naushon on one of the Elizabeth Islands in Buzzards Bay. Early in April Evans, Kirstein, Paine, and his wife, Ruth, took a boat from New York to Fall River, then taxied to New Bedford, where they caught another boat to Woods Hole. Paine had made the prior arrangement because Walker was expected to photograph his new house. Through Kirstein, Evans had met Paine earlier, and much to Kirstein's satisfaction the two had "liked each other at once." Walker, at the time, showed them "some very good advertising work" he had done for Columbia Records. But, as Kirstein, in his stock-taking phase, observed: "His persecution mania is fed by such information that all the photographers are [banding] together into a society which will only further itself and we will be excluded, etc. Why, one can't tell." At a later lunch, the men, joined by Paine's assistant, talked about Russia and the recently exhibited model for the Radio City complex, which they all agreed was "very bad." Kirstein, with his connections as one of the junior advisors for the Museum of Modern Art, was soon to be involved in mounting an exhibition of suggested painters and sculptors, European and American, who might provide murals and sculptures for the complex.

The trip to Fall River and Woods Hole had its comic aspects: the boat carved with 1901 pseudo-Renaissance detail, for one. "Lechery presupposed with a thick coat of gentility," Kirstein observed. As they cruised up the East River the sun was going down and the Empire State Building with its just-finished moving mast was dominating the scene. Lyman Paine, suffering with back problems, took to his cabin, and Evans and Kirstein joined him for drinks before going to their own cabin. Kirstein, finding that he didn't have enough money and that Evans had none, borrowed some from Paine, who, it was presumed, had plenty. In their cabin, there were awkward moments: "Walker and I talked in our bunks with some degree of self-consciousness at the proximity of intimacy," Kirstein noted. Walker, perversely perhaps, made the situation more difficult by confiding that Paine had joked a bit consciously about having gotten the two of them a stateroom together. He rather pointedly hoped Evans wouldn't mind. Kirstein, nettled, admitted, "Until I found out the exact nature of his character, I made this worry me." It was to become a troublesome problem during the early stages of the journey. When they reached Naushon, the party put up first at the Stone House, where Paine and his wife had the bridal chamber with its big four-poster bed. Kirstein had the room opposite, and Evans, possibly relieved, had a room down the hall.

At Naushon Evans took several shots of the exterior of the three-storied Paine house with its stained wide-board clapboarding and its antic semicircular porticos looking like a moderne afterthought. The wide Wright-style windows and the second-story deck looked out over a woodsy site of trees not yet into leaf. Still it was warm enough for the modernist deck chairs that appear on the extended ground-floor porch. Evans's photos of the house, at least those that have survived, were not exactly inspired. Kirstein's friend, the architectural critic Russell Hitchcock, had already declared the Paine house, despite its many faults, as the best "modern" house to date on the East Coast. Kirstein felt that on a human scale it was a fine achievement, but disapproved of the interior décor, which he considered too cute, too Wiener Werkstadt for his taste. It was a criticism confirmed by one of Evans's interior shots of the living room, with its patterned hangings against the stark plastered walls and its geometric-style rug.

In the evenings, Paine lay on the floor in front of the fire resting his back while Kirstein outlined Thomas Craven's "lousy" book *Men of Art*, which he was nonetheless planning to send out to be reviewed for *Hound & Horn*. He also brooded over Evans's remarks on the Fall River boat but tried not to show "any childish animus or vengeance," and partially succeeded. But his diary notes revealed the full extent of his aggravation. His description of Evans was pointed:

Colorless, pleasant before and exerting a kind of small but concentrated animal magnetism, he somehow seemed to allow his small size to lead him into the exaggerations of a strutting compensation. His actions are governed by springs pretty far below the surface. His jealousy or irritation manifests itself after the initial impulse by a long interval. His self-consciousness and localized egotism I found so difficult to put up with that I knew I must be affected pretty subjectively.

Still the preliminary trip had its moments for both men. Kirstein enjoyed an early morning ride on the island with Ruth Paine, seeing the deer scatter, flicking their tails over the gray-brown land. This was on the day that Evans and Paine spent photographing the house from room to room. On the final day, Evans discovered an island character named Bill, a fisherman who for twenty years had lived docked on the island in his boat, reputedly never changing his clothes to bathe or sleep. Evans, Kirstein noted, "kept snapping Leica photos of him constantly under his nose and he either didn't see or didn't mind." The photographer, comfortable at least, was adding to his photographic stock-in-trade.

Jack Wheelwright and Walker Evans and I started our photographic campaign to get all the good Victorian houses in the vicinity from New Greek, through the influence of Viollet-le-Duc through English Gothic and Italian and French Renaissance ending up in the McKinley period. We worked hard for five days, morning and afternoon, threading in and out the streets of Boston, Brookline,

South Boston, the South End, Somerville, Salem, Medford, Charlestown, East Boston, Cambridge, Belmont, Lynn, Swampscott, Beverly, Watertown, Waltham, Dedham, Revere, Dorchester, Chestnut Hill and Arlington, looking for whatever landmark or beckoning spire that presented itself above the common roofline of the other houses. We often felt like thieves snapping the houses, for fear the owners might object, for in some cases they were disagreeable. We had some difficulty in keeping our impulses straight on this stuff, i.e. did we want the best of the romantic stuff, or the best and the most eccentric, or a historical survey of the whole period . . . ? We also took a certain number of industrial subjects because I was more interested in getting the older things because they are all in mortal danger of imminent destruction or disrepair.

It was an ambitious program for a mere five days and not without difficulties, technical as well as personal. The process was complicated, Kirstein admitted:

. . . even aside from the actual sighting, clicking, etc. of the camera itself. The sun had to be just right and more often than not we would have to come back to the same place two or even three times for the light to be hard and bright. I felt like a surgeon's assistant to Walker. Cleaning up neatly after him, and he a surgeon operating on the fluid body of time. Some satisfaction in exhausting a given locale of its definite formal atmosphere — so rich, exuberant, gracious and redolent of a distinguished past. . . .

There were the recognizable satisfactions in the work, which Kirstein duly noted:

The Victorian houses that Jack Wheelwright and Walker Evans and I have been photographing are really remarkable. At least a part of my life consists in filling up the ledger of the indigenous past, in recording these places, and in time which by accident and preference I know best . . . South Boston was extremely gracious and clean-looking, not poverty stricken at all and Salem is a miracle of provincial grace and wealth.

But the personal problems were also apparent. One of the difficulties was that for Kirstein's taste, Evans was being too much the purist, wanting to photograph the architecture about which he fussed. Kirstein thought they should also be photographing the inhabitants. He felt that the houses were not just "artifacts," that people lived in them, and Walker's reluctance went a long way toward convincing him that Evans was "not too interested in people." If Evans was still the victim of the early timidity he felt about taking photographs of people, that may have been one of the reasons. He had, of course, been taking photographs of people on the streets, crowds at Coney Island, and had even done a certain amount of portrait photography. But he may, simply, have been resisting Kirstein. In any event, Kirstein lost, as is apparent in the photographs that make up the Victorian architecture series; people are rigorously excluded. The growing friction between the two is apparent in Kirstein's daily notes: "Walker Evans I find a considerable disappointment insomuch that he has to be constantly amused: he seems perennially bored, thin-blooded, too easily tired. I find it impossible not to bully him by rushing him or telling him just what to do. His feelings that he is only a paid photographer, etc."

Otherwise the Victorian architecture junket had its sociabilities. After a dinner out one night, Wheelwright and Kirstein had amused themselves — for Evans's benefit — by "eviscerating" Mr. and Mrs. Edward Weeks, "Ellery Sedgwick's most efficient bootlickers." (Weeks was the editor and Sedgwick the publisher of the Boston-based, staid old *Atlantic Monthly*.) On another evening Evans was invited to dinner with Kirstein's parents, his mother regaling them with stories of her recent committeewoman's visit to Washington and her meeting with the very starchy Herbert Hoover. Evans, Kirstein, and Wheelwright had lunch at the Adams House in Marblehead ("a great conglomerate eating factory for all the Americans that are most penetratingly loathesome"). Wheelwright's malice, apparently, was in great form and they all sent postcards to Muriel Draper. Wheelwright made a point of not returning them to the woman who sold them "for fear she would read the insults of the Adams House and then not send them." That evening, Kirstein noted: "Tonight Walker was feeling the little gangster or Don Juan of the people and I was feeling the big equivalent so we went down to see life on the Common. But it was a cold night and the sailors and their girl friends weren't sporting." It was not until April 21 that Evans and Kirstein took the train to New York, ending the first phase of the architecture expedition.

IV

Evans was to be always chary of attending the opening nights of exhibitions of his work. That may be the principal reason he remained photographing in Boston, missing the opening of the first important exhibition that would introduce him to the New York audience, "Photographs by Three Americans," which opened at the John Becker Gallery on April 18. The other two photographers were Margaret Bourke-White and the New York photographer Ralph Steiner, who would play a helpful role in Evans's development. The exhibition received some worthwhile attention. Critic Walter Knowlton reviewed the show for the "Around the Galleries" column in the May issue of *Creative Art*. M. F. Agha, also reviewing the exhibition, linked the three photographers to various trends in the earlier development of the medium which led up to the fundamentals of what he identified as the "new photography." The term would be affixed to Evans's name in the early years. Agha placed Evans among those who had heeded Ruskin's admonition: "Go to nature, in all singleness of heart, rejecting nothing, selecting nothing."

Walker Evans is one of the objectively recording photographers, these glorified reporters supremely indifferent to the technical side of their trade, who go to Nature, in all singleness of heart and armed with a Kodak.

Agha compared Evans to Atget in a dismissive manner, but made a necessary distinction: "Atget's vision of life was full of horse buggies, headless dressmakers' dummies and corset shop windows; whereas Evans understands life in terms of steel girders, luminous signs, and Coney Island bathers." His account at least provides some helpful hints to the lost list of Evans's photographs that were included in the show. One definite choice was *Traffic*, the photograph that appeared in the October-December 1930 issue of *Hound & Horn* and that the *New York Times* used as an illustration in its notice of the Becker Gallery exhibition. The steel girders may well fit the series of New York construction sites that Evans was photographing around that time. And the Coney Island bathers represented a significant group of photographs of bathers and strollers along the boardwalk.

Agha was no less dismissive of Bourke-White, whose subjects were "mostly mechanical and therefore modern, but her personal attitude is that of an industrial romantic. There is a great deal of pathos about her factory chimneys and her machinery is rather sentimental." Her attitude had its sociological justifications, Agha noted, "and would appeal both to American executives and Bolshevik officials"—a sly commentary on her apparent left-wing sympathies. Steiner's photographs Agha described as quaint Americana with a literary flavor and "a certain decorative and intellectual bitterness." But it was Steiner's purely photographic technique, the critic acknowledged, which best expressed the spirit that was the "very basis of the modern movement in the plastic arts."

It is quite possible that Agha's affirmative view of Steiner's technical skills as opposed to Evans's indifference "to the technical side of the trade" prompted Evans to seek professional help. Weeks later he wrote Skolle that he was about to take lessons: "Ralph Steiner the photographer has turned out to be most generous and has offered to teach me photography. He is a bitter little Jew, intelligent, whose limitations are skillfully blurred. Probably not clear in his mind about what he is doing (he can make money with tragic ease)." The perception that intelligence and style were necessary corollaries was an important one and an indication of Evans's quickness of mind — as well as proof of his own intelligence. With the self-assurance and opportunism of the young, he added: "I will let him work on me as much as he likes. He has made a few of the best street snapshots of people I have seen, but he doesn't show them. People greeting one another, showing off, et cet. Not enough done, though. Like all superior Jews, he has married an inferior Nordic who has pushed him in the wrong direction."

It was not until mid-May, three weeks after his return from Boston, that Evans completed a first batch of the photographs from his trip. Kirstein, eager to see the results, was more than pleased: "To see Walker Evans and obtain from him the finished plates of the Victorian architecture he took for me in Boston, which are, except for a very few, better than I had dared hope." Evans too was pleased, at least pleased enough to write Skolle, then in Europe, that he was sorry he hadn't been able to show him some prints before he left. He promised to send some of the more amusing ones. Evans had used a minor deception in telling Kirstein that it was the death, on May 8, of the "mad painter" Merton Clivette on the floor below him at 92 Fifth Avenue that had prevented him from working for several days. Clivette's death was in its way a chastening experience, confirming the hazards and neglect that trail after the creative life even into old age:

Dreadful goings on [he wrote Skolle] . . . He [Clivette] had been ill, and expired I supposed as all elderly sick people do; but those terrifying women must dramatise themselves into a nausea, further to cheapen one's conception of human dignity. Of course I had to be on the spot, very much so, with my door wide open, while Madame banged at my neighbor, who was, of course, sound asleep. He put on his pants (4 minutes) to preserve his human dignity. The rest of the morning will work itself out in my nightmares of the future. You may be spared the details.

Actually, three days later, when he wrote Hanns, Evans and Paul Grotz were in Ossining on a visit to his sister, Jane Brewer. He and Grotz were enjoying their drives around the back-country lanes and he had had a swim in a woodland stream. Evans was also seeing to the Ford, which had been given "two coats of brilliant black enamel and seems to run." He was planning to take it to Boston on his next architectural junket.

Although Evans and Kirstein continued to see each other frequently and Kirstein was continuing his efforts to promote Evans's opportunities, the friendship was not wearing well, it seems. One day at lunch Evans presented Kirstein with a print of the "gangster" portrait of him which he had taken in Boston. "This pleased me greatly for some time," Kirstein duly noted. But he was filled with second thoughts about their relationship. After dinner together one night, Kirstein confided to his diary: "I don't much want to see him anymore, yet I feel I ought to go on photographing with him the Victorian houses and factories that we started together. Got tired of him."

The situation did not noticeably improve when, on June 13, the two were once again in Boston "cleaning up" on the houses they had not managed to photograph earlier. In their tour they visited Revere Beach and Salem. (Kirstein on Salem: ". . . architecturally speaking, a town of the most astonishing grace, breadth, and dignity.") There were some disappointments: In Newburyport, strangely, since it is a city crowded with architectural gems, examples of the Federal and early-nineteenth-century homes, they found nothing to photograph. (Kirstein had once rather narrowly established the dates 1830–65 as the parameters for his collection.) In Essex, where he wanted to get photographs of boat-building activities, he found there were no boats being built. Possibly these disappointments had something to do with it, but in any event, Kirstein's dissatisfaction rose to a level of high complaint:

Increasingly bored with Evans. No resilience of energy. He resists one only on tiny details. Now a door should be shut, etc. If ever opposed in conversation he says, "I don't know." Tired, inert, reminds me of a constipated and castrated bulldog, old and squatting before his time. However I try to treat him as an exercise, try to hide my animus not out of grace to him . . . because I can't see that he needs or deserves it but merely as a discipline to myself.

On Cape Ann, visiting Hyatt Mayor, who was summering in Annisquam, things were not much better. Passing a nearby quarry:

Walker Evans made a great to-do about jumping from a big high point into the fresh water. He later confessed he cracked his balls. . . . Lots of little Annisquam boys swimming in the quarry naked. Poor Kirstein trying to get a glimpse of them almost drove his car into the quarry. A too neat fate.

Kirstein's appreciation of the visit with Hyatt Mayor, his appreciation of Mayor's "great precision and dispassionate warmth," seemed only to provide a sour contrast to Evans, whose "only interest in documenting is from the point of view of social [missing words], disintegration, inertia. Hence the skimmed decadence of so much of his work." Back in Boston, before their departure for New York, the two had dinner with the visiting Lyman Paine at the Somerset Hotel overlooking the Fenway. Kirstein and Paine indulged in an argument over Frank Lloyd Wright's lectures at Princeton, Paine extolling Wright's fine, "juicy," earthy style and Kirstein maintaining that the architect was "hopelessly vague and self-seduced." All through the discussion, much to Kirstein's aggravation, Evans was "silent, exercising to the full the negative personal magnetism which is his only and suicidal claim on people. Lyman and I put him to bed and then we took a very long ride out late to Concord and back."

Nonetheless, back in New York, Kirstein once again began promoting Evans and his work, this time writing to Lewis Mumford, the architectural critic whose *The Brown Decades* was soon to be published, offering to show him his collection of recent photographs: "The work itself has been done by a very able photographer, Mr. Walker Evans. The examples, generally speaking, are from Boston, Salem, West Massachusetts, and Connecticut." Months later, he would also try to interest Mrs. Juliana Force, the director of the newly opened Whitney Museum of American Art, in publishing Evans's Victorian architecture photographs as one of a projected series of monographs on American art. In neither case was he successful.

In the meantime Evans and Kirstein, on the surface at least, were being sociable enough. Kirstein took the trouble to have dinner with Evans and Berenice Abbott: "She is nice in a way, a face with no edges, boy's cut hair and enormous kewpie eyes." The three discussed Jean Cocteau's recently translated book, *Opium*, dealing with his addiction and one of his periodic stays in a drug clinic. In the book, Cocteau declared, "The past, the future torment me, and passionate acts are few. Well, opium mixes the past and future, making of them a *present of One*. It amounts to the photographic negative of passion." Abbott, fascinated by the book, said it made her want to smoke. Walker maintained that he was bored so much of the time, he had often wanted to take it. Kirstein took the adversarial view: "I said I had not yet explored the possibilities of my rational dreams."

V

For Evans the summer and fall of 1931 were to be a busy time. The results of his second trip to Boston had been successful: "Augmented the series of Victorian architecture photos with a rather better series. . . ." he wrote to Skolle. He was working with Ralph Steiner and for the time being was staying with Paul and Dorothy Grotz. But Paul was out of work and Evans, feeling he may have worn out his welcome, was planning to move: "[W]ill have to have a place where I can work and sleep (not live, note). And try to make some money. Summon my most hard-boiled manner." He had been reading Waugh's *Decline and Fall*, "indeed a good book, indeed excellent, splendid," and H. G. Wells's *Outline of History*, which he found "not a book" but a "fascinating conglomeration." Wells, he claimed, was "such a funny man about improving the race. I am unable to understand his approach. Not a poet, not an artist, not an historian. Just a goddam little socialist I suppose." "Me," he added, "I am a Fascisti and I think the human race should be kicked around a great deal more than it is, and that I should do the kicking. It is sad that men like Wells and B. Russell and Shaw too, who can get into things brainfully, should come out of them that way. I am told that Spengler is the guy to investigate from our point of view." His other news was random. He had spent some time in the country. Possibly in Ossining visiting the Brewers again, but Evans doesn't say where: "The country is magnificent for the senses, offering smells of greenery and faroff [sic] noises of train whistles going still farther off, objectively of course. I always sit quite still under the circumstances." He mentions having run into Avis Ferme, "the artist's model" (possibly an earlier flame), crossing Fourteenth Street; and there was a rumor that Kathleen Young, "the trage-dienne" and poet, was in town. Young had reputedly been caught up in a ménage à trois with Evans and Skolle when the two, earlier, had shared an apartment together. "But that would be another matter to encounter in traffic," Evans added. Skolle's response was minimal: "Best regards to Kathleen, hum."

In early October, Evans was back in New York, living at 63 Park Avenue, having earned "seventy-five dollars" for some unspecified job, but not enough or soon enough to pay his bills. His telephone had been shut off. He had just returned from a month in Provincetown, including a side trip to Martha's Vineyard, where Jane and Tal Brewer were vacationing. Jane, so Evans informed Skolle, was three months pregnant though not yet "protuberant." He was glad to be back in the city "to get mail and to go to the newsreel theater and to eat breakfast. The world as you may know it is about to collapse and what I say is it jolly well deserves it."

It was a productive trip with a good many photographs. (He was working on them.) In Provincetown, he photographed one of the more notable and often depicted intersections in the glare of sunlight: clapboard houses at the conjunction of wayward streets, a civic building looming above, gathering in the cluster of frame buildings. What was elemental about the photograph was that he made no attempt to disguise the welter of telephone posts and telephone wires that were as indigenous as the quaint architecture. In another photograph, a weathered window provides a frame for a water-stained portrait of President Hoover and a prophetic reliquary bunch of artificial flowers. There is, too, a photo of a decrepit Ford with a door off and a rubber tire missing, stationed like a pilgrimage shrine on a journey not completed, that was taken along a country road.

Another of Evans's "finds" taken in Martha's Vineyard is now too hard to identify among the many Gothic wonders he photographed before and subsequently in his travels. In the center of a little village of wooden cottages, built around the eighteen seventies, Evans noted a tabernacle built in "jig-saw gothic and completely god damn nuts and very funny to see."

On October 7, Kirstein, still touting Evans's works, wrote Wheelwright: "Walker Evans has got some amazing new photographs of New Bedford, Martha's Vineyard, and New York State. We are going to get some more soon." (The mention of New York State is important: a first notice that at least some of the New York sequences, presumably under Kirstein's auspices, had been taken already.) Two weeks later he wrote Hyatt Mayor proposing that some of the photos might be used in an upcoming issue of *Hound & Horn*: "Walker Evans has done some magnificent photographs of circus posters on barns and drug stores, ripped by the wind and rain, so that they look like some horrible accident. There are two circus ones and two movie ones and I think they would be admirable in conjunction with Dudley Fitts' poem about the Southwest. God knows they are American." The photographs were not used, but Kirstein was right about the stark, metaphorical value of the pictures, the most dramatic of which shows a man and woman clutching each other against some impending menace. The ravaged poster is plastered over with torn banners announcing Friday and Saturday. That this was taken in the early phases of the Great Depression has some bearing on the timely and timeless effectiveness of its imagery. It is an announcement of ephemerality: the ephemerality of the American Dream, of American advertising, of circuses and movies — the whole host of disillusionments swept up by economic reality. It was not that Evans was superbly indifferent to the history of the time (or Kirstein either for that matter). One incident in Kirstein's diary makes clear that by 1931 the fact of the depression had been borne home: "Thousands of men sell apples — really fine apples — on the street for a nickel apiece. The apparent desperation that one meets everywhere is really terrifying. If this goes on all winter Walker Evans was saying the Communist Party might have something to work with — all the young artists or writers who [are] unemployed, or because to get a living, have a horrible cloud of fear constantly over them, more so now than otherwise." Strangely the hard facts of life in the depression did not show up prominently in Evans's photographs, or only metaphorically at best. He had not yet taken note of ragged men selling apples on his beat. In 1931, perhaps, the wear and tear of such lives had not shown up yet on their clothing, at least in New York City streets. But the shabbiness would show up in time. For Evans the recognition of poverty would come a few years later.

For the moment Evans had found a miraculous escape. The once dreamed-of journey to the South Seas presented itself in a commissioned voyage as official shipboard photographer for Oliver Jennings, who was planning a South Seas cruise for himself and his wealthy friends. Lincoln Kirstein, just returned by train from Boston, noted the departure in his diary:

Dec 30, [1931]: To New York out of my berth at the crack of dawn. . . . Saw Walker Evans off to the South Seas giving him Virgil, Marcus Aurelius and Dante in small editions. His friends Paul Grotz and Ben Shahn stuffed an extra suitcase half full of films for movie camera with a light bulb, a New York telephone directory and toilet paper. We told the taxi driver to go to Papeete. He said, "Oh the South Seas."

Walker was, as usual, nervous, jerky, devitalized and displaying ½ filament of magnetism.

Broadway Lights (cover photograph of Advertising & Selling, June 24, 1931)

Voyages

7

At 1:45 A.M. on New Year's Day, the *Cressida*, the German-built 170-foot top sail schooner, left Jekyll Island off the coast of Georgia. The New Year's party prepared for the passengers before departure brought out the ambivalent and cynical character of Evans's feelings about the wealthy. The ship's lights had been turned on as they approached the dock; an all-in-white steward had helped the ladies aboard. There was a handshake from the captain, who was, Evans noticed, cross-eyed. They had boarded in "alphabetical disorder" under what Evans conceded were the utmost romantic conditions: "southern moon, odorous water, savannahs, flowers, musing remarks of gay people with buttonholes and alcohol; people who have to be that way." He listed his fellow passengers: Polly Campbell, "a nice girl" with whom he would form a platonic and talky romance of sorts; Oliver Jennings, the organizer of the cruise, and his Ecuadorian wife, Isabel; Adolph Dick; and Lawrence Noyes. (During the cruise he may or may not have learned that Noyes was Scott Fitzgerald's less-than-boyhood-friend in St. Paul and later the Greenwich Village roommate of Edmund Wilson.) Of male passengers Evans had little good to say: They were "gentlemen, flanneled fools without wickets, fleurs du capitalist mal." Of the celebration Evans was equally sarcastic. At the dock that evening a black choir sang "It Is the Needy Time" and a rather dubious spiritual; "If religion was a thing that money could buy, the rich would live and the poor would die." The New Year came in over the radio, "after which pink portly robber-barons stumped around the room shaking hands, and sons were nice to their mothers."

There were rough seas on the voyage out. On the first few days the passengers, including Evans, were stricken with seasickness. Boredom, or what he termed "indolence on tap," also set in. There was, he confessed, too much to be done on the way from indolence to action:

morning toilet, the morning wireless news-report of the death of a Jewish phil-anthropist, the decay of civilization; there are too many books and too many unlearned ropes. Points of danger, bowsprit, flirtation and masthead . . .; the

Crew of the Cressida, Tahiti voyage, 1932.

tidying of a cabin; always another member of the crew to cultivate. Then one can never tell when a conversation may break out among the passengers. This has to be fanned, and one must drop whatever is at hand and rush to the scene with bellows and poker.

For want of something to do, Evans availed himself of the ship's library — volumes of Beerbohm, Conrad, *Alice in Wonderland*, Hardy, and Gide — as well as the books Lincoln Kirstein had given him. Otherwise, as he informed Skolle in a New Year's day letter: "Four tiled bathrooms, no official sex life." Kingston, Jamaica, where the ship anchored early on the morning of January 6, was a relief. He went ashore, but kept to himself. As the official photographer of the cruise, he took his camera along. In a run-on page of his travel itinerary he announced that Jamaica was just what he expected, adding: "Color, heart, rum, palms, colonialites, carriages, rum, markets, rum." The subjects proved less than inspiring it appears: "My eye ceases to select, I abandon all idea of recording anything with the cameras

until a little moor in red and white rags stumps after the carriage. He has no feet, and a language I never heard."

What had begun as "Days at Sea" turned into just "Days." The passengers were becoming even more bored:

Adolph Dick is sleeping in a low wicker deck-chair. Nap after lunch. Light breeze and following sea. One bird. Three people reading, one musing. Adolph Dick wakes. Leaves the deck, has movement of bowels. Wanders back, with hair freshly combed and nails cleaned. Sees tin box of fruit cake, attacks it. Three people want some too. Light horseplay, Polly Campbell gets fruitcake down her back. Adolph Dick stands munching at the lee rail and sings What is this thing called piggly-wiggly? A game of something is suggested but no one knows where the implements are. Adolph Dick sits down again and closes his eyes.

On January 9, they reached the Colón breakwater and proceeded through the Panama Canal. Evans thought the canal itself uninteresting:

It takes a long time to go through but efficiently and the town at the other end is full of international desperation. There are many people stranded there, women and sailors and many people who are professionally busy and contemptuously unaware of the other kind. Many of the people are hard and unpleasant looking at all hours and there are clubs for the upper classes as in Kansas City. There is dancing and commercial activity and perhaps some gaiety.

Untitled Tahiti portrait, 1932.

The whores, he decided, were out of central casting. Apparently he was more impressed with the natives, for Skolle responded, "I must say, your convincing descriptions have an almost sinister aspect despite the waving palm frond behind the type, a stunt whose technical method eludes my bleary eyes." Evans had described, too, a Cocle Indian ceremony and bought some native souvenirs. That, too, had impressed his friend, for Skolle wrote, "Judging by the dexterity with which you caught the detail, you must have acquired the objects in question." The following day, setting sail from Balboa was less than Homeric. "The Pacific Ocean is like the Atlantic Ocean," Evans claimed. Nor, after five more days at sea, were the Galapagos Islands as enchanted as the name "The Encantadas" seemed to suggest. He found them "a dreadful conglomeration of lava and the stink of pelicandroppings, reptiles, prehistoric desertion, silence." Herman Melville, cruising the same waters ninety years before, was of the same

opinion: "It is to be doubted whether any spot on earth can, in desolateness, furnish a parallel to this group." Evans seems not to have photographed any of it.

The voyage to Nuku Hiva in the Marquesas Islands, which they reached on the morning of January 30, was uneventful except for one dramatic incident four nights earlier: Sudden squalls had carried away the port square sail yard. The little village and port of Taiohae in Anna Maria Bay was not the best introduction to the islands. It was a penal colony, mostly for Tahitians, in which the prisoners, in their canvas shirts, were allowed to roam free. Evans met a French Catholic priest who, having known Gauguin, referred to him as "pitoyable." "Certainly he was," Evans commented. "Strange no one ever talked to this guy about Gauguin; he knew nothing of his renown as a painter, and asked me to send him book by and about him, which I certainly will not do." But there was, that evening, a lively Saturday night barn dance in which all the villagers took part. The women lined up on one side and the men, with flowers behind their ears, lined up on the other. At first the natives were shy, dancing in European fashion to the music of a guitar and an accordion, playing a heavily rhythmic and distorted version of "Ukelele Lady" and "Mr. Gallagher and Mr. Sheen."

But we were gay that evening, we had drunk at dinner, and danced ourselves with some abandon. Which thawed the Marquesans into their natural form of dancing. . . . It went on to perfection in that barn: two girls who were the best of all, and a half-dozen men revolving round them, hip swinging and arm movement in their best tradition. Delighted with themselves and with us, with the music and the hot sexy rain outside.

On the following day they took the *Cressida*'s launch to Typee Valley (the setting for Melville's *Typee*) and the village strung along a small river with bamboo huts and palm-thatched roofs.

It is a Sunday, and the priest who has even here set up his disgusting establishment is away. God be praised, the natives are bored and sing. Thirty in a little room, a drawn out repetitious air carried by women's voices, tones filled in by chorus of men. Marked rhythm, variations of volume. The best music we will hear. They were still at it when we passed by later on our way back from up the valley above.

It appears to have been at Fati Hiva in the Marquesas that Evans began his first effort as a motion picture photographer. It is possible that earlier he had taken some of the shipboard movies of sailors athwart the boom, climbing the shrouds, and views of the rigging and sails, the ship's bow cutting the waters. According to Evans's reel notations and the ship's log, the Fati Hiva sequences were taken between noon on February 1, when the *Cressida* anchored at Hana Vara Bay, and 5:00 the next morning, when the ship sailed south. Mostly — again according to the reel notations — these were panoramic views of the island and the bay, landscape views of coconut palms and native huts along the beach. Beginning as early as January 5 he seemingly had used his still cameras with a Dupont panchromatic film for shipboard photographs, catching the mast, sails, ropes, and shadows, using a #3 filter to bring up the sky. That there were some rough seas early in the cruise is clear from several dramatic shots from high in the rigging looking down at the deck. There were, as well, close-ups of the captain and the passengers: Noyes in his sailor's shirt, Adolph Dick in stripes, Polly Campbell and Isabela Jennings talking on deck. Shots of the crew unfurling sails on the boom, sewing. In a rare photo, Evans, gone native and naked, stands on a beach, at the ready with a long fishing harpoon much taller than he.

Evans was never the political soldier and in his lifetime seldom became publicly engaged concerning the subject. But sailing toward Tahiti, he became uncharacteristically philosophical and a bit polemical. On February 4, he wrote Skolle: "The sadness of the Marquesans is indescribable. Strange beauty of landscape and vegetation, yes; there up to the hilt of imagination. But evidence of the death of the native race too painful and infuriating to look at for long. I say this not only because I have read of it again and again, and have been prepared in advance to find it; but because the reality is ten times more powerfully drawn than this acquired knowledge." Cruising past atolls, green archipelagos, and islands the *Cressida* could not visit because of the size of the ship and the dangerous shoals, he grew reflective:

I suppose it is worth coming in a boat to see islands in the southern ocean. However, what one comes to see is gone years ago and is furthermore very well saved preserved between the covers of a book or books in libraries both public and private as well as in book shops. So that those who for one reason or another cannot or will not travel may sit in solid chairs and glean the essence of exoticism right in the midst of loved ones and all the comforts and conveniences of modern life with its joys and sorrows. Alas for adventure and illusion, fleeting beauties, and visions of the mind's eye.

Whatever his misgivings about the failures of the tourist trade, it was at Papeete, where they arrived on the afternoon of February 6, that Evans got down to serious work as ship's photographer. For the next month he toured Tahiti and such neighboring Society Islands as Bora Bora and Huahine. He took the several reels of film ("a few thousand feet") that made up the bulk of the movies he filmed. He was shooting in the dark, so to speak, and was understandably nervous. "The thing is," he wrote Skolle later, "I went in fear and trembling because I knew next to nothing about how to operate my machinery; and couldn't tell what I was getting until we got back to New York." And it was in the islands that he took most of the still photographs that resulted from the trip. Judging from the chronological listings, the introductory material for the projected film consisted of shipboard activities that Evans took either in the Caribbean or in the Pacific en route to the Marquesas. The crew members and the passengers are in summer wear.

Untitled. Tahiti landscape, 1932.

Evans was remarkably close-mouthed about his personal life, but he did mention, once, that on arrival in Tahiti he had been warned by a doctor to avoid any sexual contact with the natives because venereal disease was rampant. The two things he told his first wife, Jane Ninas, about his Polynesian adventures was first that he was proud of having climbed the rigging (evidenced by the stunning shots, taken from aloft, of the deck, the masts, and sails of the *Cressida*). The second was that he had shunned the native women, no matter how attractive.

They appeared, however, frequently enough in film sequences and in the still photographs: Dorothy Lamour types in flowered sarongs, graceful with frank and engaging smiles. Notations about discarded segments from the film carry identifications like "Cutie and friend, seated," a sequence of two young beauties with floral headdresses, a theme primed perhaps by Evans's glimpses of Gauguin's Polynesian paintings at the opening exhibition of the Museum of Modern Art in 1929. Evans exhibited a decided fascination with palm trees framing views of distant mountains or, in another sequence, braceleting the shoreline of Moorea, its rocky crags, and cloud covering as the ferry approached the island. For some of his effects, he depended on color filters and telephoto lenses.

The dance sequences seem to have provided the major action in the film: male dancers proceeding forward in marching file; cut to women seated, clapping; cut to close-up of man drumming. One of his notations: "Telephoto closeup of the circle dance uh uh uh uh quite long. Use only a little, say 10 sec., 20 ft. of any part where screen is covered with bodies." He later confessed: "Movies are more difficult than I realized. I seem to be able to get striking individual pictures but have difficulty in composing any significant sequence. Hard to dramatise my subjects."

II

Evans's feelings about the interlopers in Polynesian edens — such travelers as himself and his fellow passengers — was the theme of an inconclusive short story at first titled "A trip around the Island" and then "The Italics Are Mine." (He was still pursuing his literary career and the italicized portions represented the stream-of-consciousness thought of his unnamed narrator, à la Joyce.) Written in Tahiti in February, it is an eerie tale, the scenario somewhat vaporous but with undercurrents of wandering sexuality. The narrator is searching for a friend named Steve. There is a party in progress at the new house of a bootlegger named Smith, who opens the story with a brusque command: "For Christ's sake come in and have a drink, what's your name? Never mind, nobody asks questions around here. This is my party but I'm having a rotten time." The narrator muses: "*This is going to be awful.*" In the description of the affair, "the flower-bedecked banquet table, the drunken guests, the dancing couples, the customary natives with guitar and accordion smirkingly doing what was expected of them, except not playing Mr. Gallagher and Mr. Sheen at the moment," the various people moving from place to place "according to the laws of alcoholic paralysis" are all presented as routine at such island affairs.

Smith continues: "Come and meet my friends. I'm opening my new house." He then apologizes for the drink: "Fearful stuff, I'll get you something better." In the most casual manner, he adds, "You can have Bixby's girl." Sitting next to the narrator is Bixby himself. Bixby asks:

"Do you know who I am?" Then "Never mind, it doesn't matter. I'm a famous author huh?" As a matter of fact I had read a book which was no good and he had written it. I told him I knew him and he said I could have Smith's girl.

Neither Smith's nor Bixby's girl ever appears in this story. There are deft touches: the way Bixby, for example, after getting the narrator a tall glass of red wine, propositions him, or seems to proposition him:

"I'm drunk now but you come with me to my house. I want to get away from here anyway. I'll be sober in a half an hour. You're an intelligent man, we can talk, and you stay with me tonight. I always sleep on the floor, huh. We'll go duck shooting tomorrow and you can take the boat back Tuesday. I'll come over with you, the mail'll be in. But you won't though."

My hedging was quickly felt. We were both frantic with indecision. He groped for something he didn't want, some obscure form of self-justification. And I wanted to find out what he was ashamed of.

If one takes Evans's title literally, then the curious italicized passage that follows is part of the narrator's stream-of-consciousness reflections:

An underdog past. This is better than what you had but you'll always resent what has happened to you, and what hasn't. You part-time criminal, you want to get back in somewhere. But there isn't enough to go around bigboy, never will be. . . .

In the earlier version of the manuscript, however, Evans had first made the phrase "an underdog past," part of the narration, then crossed it out and made it part of the italicized ruminations. The crux of the story here is ambivalent. Is the passage a bit of self-analysis on the part of the narrator/author or a rumination on the character of Bixby? Does the "you part-time criminal" then refer to Bixby or to the narrator himself?

The story at this point trails off into a series of brief, surreal encounters with island types, lives lived in a tropical limbo. Driving off with Bixby further along the shore they stop at a "sad elaborate place" where the narrator is introduced to "a tall Jew whom I had seen before in Seattle, Toledo, New York, and parts of Boston, usually playing the oboe in a good symphony orchestra." His name is Mike Hahn. There is a slight suspicion that Hahn's politics, if not his profession, have been borrowed from Ben Shahn since Hahn, after shaking hands, brings out rum "together with political generalizations, slightly red liberalizations and musical reminiscences." Hahn next insists that the narrator, when he gets back to New York, introduce himself to a violinist friend of his who would be delighted to take him out to dinner.

Driving back to the Smith party, the narrator, thinking about his friend Steve as the night begins to darken, gives way to some pointedly odd reflections: *"My plans are less protuberant but still in the forefront of my consciousness. Drop Bixby and go by the housewarming for a hasty glance at Steve."* (He had left Steve drinking heavily on Smith's porch.) Another character now enters the tonneau in which he is riding. This time it is a woman, "a local character of average proportions. She had evidently been attracted by the velocity of our vehicle and was prepared to ride by my side, making gratuitous gestures at regular intervals." The woman, too, disappears from further consideration. Everywhere, this is a story of missed connections. It ends at Smith's party with a final flourish:

> By now it was night-dark, Steve nowhere to be seen. Instead an astrologer in a bad green shirt invited himself to go with me wherever I was bound and did in fact enter the tonneau with this in mind. But he thought of two lonesome friends behind in the full blare of the housewarming, and went off to find them. Whereupon, keen to be off again, I spurred on my driver and left him, the astrologer, gently calling to his friends there in the tropical night.

It may be no coincidence that a segment of Gauguin's account of his first trip to Tahiti, *Noa Noa*, was titled "Trip Around the Islands"—Evans's original choice for his story. In it Gauguin reports on his search through the remoter villages of Tahiti for a *vahine*, a young more-or-less-temporary wife. As in the book itself, Gauguin glories in his joyous escape from the prudery of European morals. In the Evans story, the narrator does comment on the off-handed way in which both Smith and Bixby offer him each other's girls. He also describes his own maneuvering to escape the

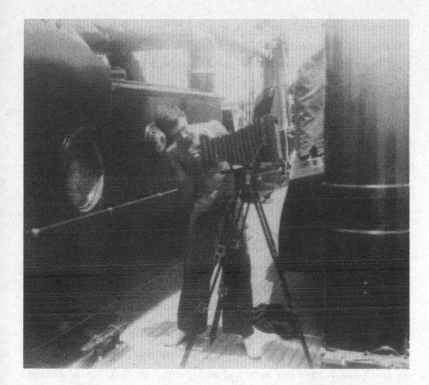

*Evans aboard
the* Cressida,
*Tahiti voyage,
1932.*

attentions of the various males he encounters. The story certainly suggests
the sensual laxity of the island population if not the native population. But
where Gauguin found the easy sexuality of both the men and the women a
praiseworthy feature of life in Tahiti, Evans, for his part, was hardly so
uninhibited. (In one of the italicized passages, the narrator confesses: *"All
I've got to do is keep my head. What an effort. You'd think for once I'd let go, but
after all, my boy, this is no place to be careless."* He seems rather to have given
the situation a comic twist, passing it off as a bit of vaudeville like the
repartee in "Mr. Gallagher and Mr. Sheen.") "The Italics Are Mine" has its
effective moments, its mood, but the italicized passages in particular tend
to be disruptive and too self-consciously modern.

April 4, 5, 6, or 7, 1932: the winds moderate or light or variable or gentle
northerly and the seas invariably smooth on any of those days. Evans
wrote:

Letter to Hanns Skolle, written as much to pass the time as to convey greetings, exchange sentiments and the like. For here I am afloat in a vast salt ocean and have been for one month now, without having seen nothing but a exasperatingly circular horizon which in itself is too big to see all at once. Not that I would want to. The annoying thing is that this spacial emptiness grows within. Thus I perish. . . . New York is probably in total crash by now; must be absolutely nothing going on there, judging from the state of affairs when I left three months ago. Great guns I have been on this rocking peanut since the first day of January. . . .

I have tried drinking, staying up all night, painting in watercolor, climbing to dangerous heights in the rigging — in short everything but masturbation. Hasten to add that of the two ladies present only one is attractive to me and she is in love, rather spiritually, with our host. Oh, yes, I have also tried playing jazz records on the victor. Don't ever try that if you're cooped up in a small escapeless place. The tune begins the next morning in your head and continues with the rhythm of the engines for from thirteen to sixteen days running, at the end of which time you jump overboard (tomorrow).

As for this girl I said was on board with me she is good comic relief to hear her laugh and get tight and dance and see her roll on the floor, but she is a nice girl. Sometimes we all dance and roll on the floor because there are soft carpets and we are way out in the ocean with a certain sense of isolation, as it were. And there is much jealousy and sometimes she likes me because I am all wrong but have an interesting mind while she is unhappy in the love affair mentioned and she is proud in suffering and I discovered it with my intuition. Now we can talk about love late at night in her cabin or bunk and eat crackers and use our intuitions on the others, who are all unhappy too. Thus we uncover and analyze cruelties and heartaches and dark unmotivated surprises in our companions, some of whom are married but not living, I mean, not going to bed occasionally. And small wonder, for the husband is really incapable of going to bed with his wife, she stinks and has too much ego and is Spanish anyway. And he doesn't want to in the beginning owing to shall we say psychological deformities of a unmentionable nature. The 1st steward too is a fairy but is not prospering.

Also there has been a fistfight in the crew over a game of checkers or perhaps for some deeper reason. Mutiny is not thought probably but I don't see why unless they realize that someone has got to make the ship go on, and we in the poopdeck certainly couldn't.

On April 20, the *Cressida* docked in Havana harbor for a one-day layover. There is evidence that Evans spent some time ashore. (Skolle, responding to one of Evans's missing letters: "Yes, Havana has something about it. I must have told you about my friend the charming nigger pimp, the pineapples, and the odour of fresh tobacco.") It was another week before the yacht reached New York at the end of its 14,000-mile voyage. The long weeks at sea had given Evans much to think about and time for second thoughts to harden into convictions:

There was nothing much to the South Sea Islands [he wrote Skolle]. Exotic yes for a day or so, and I suppose living there would be a little pleasanter and a little easier than in an American or a European city, but there can't be much choice, and if there were even, I'd choose the American city. For because there is nobody to talk to in the South Sea Islands and nobody to do evil and diverting and stimulating and diverting things with. And it is too hot and bad food and venereal disease and rain. Apparently life is just awful anywhere, as someone has said . . . .

It was not long after his arrival in New York when Evans learned that on April 27, 1932, Hart Crane, 254 miles out from Havana Harbor, had jumped to his death from the deck of the *Orizaba*. The night before, according to one story, Crane had been so drunk that he had to be locked in his cabin by the purser. He was on his return voyage from a long stay in Mexico, made possible by a grant from the Guggenheim Foundation. He was accompanied by Peggy Cowley, who was in the process of divorcing her husband. Much to the surprise of friends, Crane announced that he was planning to marry her. The two had been living together in Taxco for a time, Peggy bringing some moments of needed stability to Crane's disordered life. His death occasioned a number of stories and rumors, most of them salacious: that he had picked up the wrong sailor in Havana; that aboard ship he indulged in sex with a cabin boy or one or more members of the crew and had been beaten and robbed. On the following morning, he had already begun drinking again when he appeared at Peggy's cabin in his pajamas, saying, "I'm not going to make it, dear. I'm utterly disgraced."

Evans had not seen Crane off on the first phase of his Mexican sojourn on April 4, 1931, when, after several days of celebration and flush with his Guggenheim money, he gave a party for friends in his cabin. But a few days later Evans wrote Crane's friend Margaret Robson: "I wish I had gone to the boat to see Hart off — I hear you were all there and gai comme les oiseaux. I saw H, spent a very speedy afternoon with him, our stimulating fulminating friend. We fulminated up and down Manhattan buying dungarees. . . ."

Evans's final disturbing glimpse of Crane had come on August 29, four months before his own voyage to Tahiti. Crane, home for his father's funeral, was returning to Mexico once again for what was intended to be a serious and sober period of work. But the poet was so drunk that Evans, afraid he would not get off in time, made a determined effort to get him to the boat and safely in his cabin.

Damaged,
New York,
1931

Crane's suicide may have shocked Evans but it did not surprise him. In May 1932, writing to Skolle, he sketched out some of the details:

> *Hart Crane did away with himself jumping off a steamer in the Caribbean Sea last month. He was drunk, made a spectacular dive from crowded deck at high noon, was completely lost immediately, sharks probably, although boats were lowered and search lasted an hour. Had been unable to write anything in Mexico. . . . Don't let this upset you. Crane a goner long ago, as you will remember.*

It was a cold remembrance.

III

Once again Evans was traveling when important exhibitions of his work opened. On February 1, 1932, the Julien Levy Gallery on Madison Avenue featured a joint exhibition of photographs by Evans and George Platt Lynes. Levy was another of the young and ambitious group of Harvard students, graduates, and tutors — including Kirstein, Alfred Barr, Henry Russell Hitchcock, A. Edward "Chick" Austin, Jr., and Philip Johnson — who promoted the modernist movement in America. Levy had introduced Atget's work to America, and had advanced the one thousand dollars to Berenice Abbott to buy the Atget collection and another thousand dollars to preserve it. It was Levy who had induced Erhard Wehye to produce, with Abbott's help, the French volume *Atget: Photographe de Paris*

and the follow-up November-December 1930 exhibition of the book and Atget prints at Weyhe's Lexington Avenue bookstore. (He was working there at the time.)

Levy had opened his own gallery in November 1931 with a retrospective view of American photography that included Stieglitz and Steichen, Clarence White, Paul Strand, and Gertrude Kasebier, the first of many exhibitions of modern photography. Later he arranged a second exhibition of Atget coupled with works by the nineteenth-century French photographer Nadar. Levy's gallery, which survived until 1949, became one of the most persistent agencies of the surrealist curia, promoting the works of Dali, Marcel Duchamp, Max Ernst, Man Ray, Giacometti, and de Chirico. (His first surrealist exhibition had included Dali's *The Persistence of Memory*, famous for its limp watches.) In another of his innovative services, the Film Society, Levy gave screenings of such vanguard films as the Buñuel-Dali films *Un chien andalou* and *L'Age d'or*, and Léger's *Ballet Mechanique*.

There is an element of mystery about Evans's association with the Levy Gallery. Since he appeared in the February show with Lynes and three years later in an exhibition with Cartier-Bresson and the Mexican photographer Manuel Alvarez Bravo and in at least one group show, the assumption is that Evans considered it an important connection. Yet in Evans's letters and diaries, there is little mention of Levy or the exhibitions there. And Levy in his brisk *Memoir of an Art Gallery* mentions Evans only once in passing in a listing of photographers he showed. The memoir reads like an old film fast forwarded, spinning off eminent names. But the most eminent names and important associations are each given the full weight of racy anecdotes or developed chapters. Levy cites his own preeminence and pioneering efforts (many of them justified), and boasts of his having set major artists on the right paths to glory. (He claimed, for instance, that it was he who had advised Alexander Calder to give up motorized mobiles and rely instead upon perfect balance, gentle breezes, or the delicate touch of a finger to motivate sculptures, and that it was he who persuaded Joseph Cornell that in his assemblages, he should give up the kind of imagery Max Ernst culled for his collages.) Published in 1977, when Evans's fame was a fact of history, one can only wonder what grievance was the source of Levy's threadbare mention of Evans in his memoir.

The Evans-Lynes exhibition in February drew highly respectful notices, with most of the critics emphasizing the youth and earnestness of the two photographers. From the reviews, one can identify some of the photographs included, all of them from 1931 or earlier, before Evans's voyage to Tahiti. In a brief review in the *New York Times*, K.G.S. referred to Evans as "a sort of New York Atget." (It would become a frequent and not altogether unwarranted comparison for both Evans and Berenice Abbott, who also showed at the Levy Gallery.) The *Times* reviewer, like many of the others, fastened on the photographs of torn movie and circus posters "grotesquely pockmarked by wind and rain." He also singled out one of three burly workmen either in the process of installing or carting off a huge marquee sign spelling "Damaged." For Evans it served as an outright visual pun, a riddle of ambiguity, and further evidence of his growing interest in theater and advertising. Evans, the critic maintained, photographed his subjects "without sentiment and with only the faintest undercurrent of satire."

From the reviews it is also clear that Evans had begun to exhibit his photographs of Victorian architecture. Helen Appleton Read, in the *Brooklyn Daily Eagle*, noted the "jigsaw details of suburban houses of the Garfield and

McKinley periods. . . . Without exaggeration or falsification," she commented, "Mr. Evans gives his subject a quality of independent life. He goes to the life about him for his subject matter, but he sees and is interested in aspects of the visual universe which have hitherto been disregarded as ugly or negligible." She saw Evans's efforts as reclamation work: "He does what many artists who strike out new paths for themselves have done before him — he liberates his subjects from the taboos of his time." For not the only time in Evans's career, she made a comparison between the unsentimental quality of Evans's work and the chilly urban cityscapes of the painter Edward Hopper. But she also attempted to separate Evans's reputation from a too-easy identification with Atget, "whom the moderns have canonized as a pioneer of the new objectivity." She insisted on Evans's American difference. Where Atget had made thousands of photographs of Paris streets, Evans's vision "is a series of stills from the motion picture of contemporary America." It was not the clearest of distinctions, more a matter of geography. Lynes's scope, she thought, was broader, since he was also interested in portraiture and figure studies. But Read praised them both for what she considered the objectivity of their work. She compared and complimented them by way of an aperçu from novelist Thomas Mann: "What else, I should like to know, have art and artists ever done," ran the Mann quotation, "except to perceive the individual thing, isolate the object out of the welter of phenomena, elevate it, intensify it, inspire it and give it meaning."

Both the *Times* critic and critic for the Sunday *Art News* cited the photographs of the crumpled metalwork from the roofing at 92 Fifth Avenue. Both Lynes and Evans, the *Art News* critic added, demonstrated "proof that the camera is an instrument of great flexibility according to the operator's deft or temperamental manipulation." Lynes, he decided, "goes after his subject matter with stylistic intent, particularly in his group of antique figures, while Mr. Evans, with deeper penetration, gets at the very heart of its subject, be it a battered metal cornice or the close-set backyards of some suburban hillside." The latter photograph was clearly the photograph of frame houses on a summer hillside that Evans had taken on one of his prescribed family visits in Ossining. The *Brooklyn Times* critic, noting the pictures of suburban streets, graveyard statues, and once again the torn posters, suggested that Evans's talent "is to reveal in the most ordinary subject an element of independent life, sometimes surprising and almost fabulous."

For Evans, it turned out to be a full exhibition schedule. While the Levy Gallery show was in progress, he was also included in the group exhibition "Modern Photography: At Home and Abroad" at the Albright Art Gallery in Buffalo, New York (February 7-25, 1932). Though smaller, the exhibition was linked to the 1930 show at the Harvard Society and included several of the more notable American and European photographers with whom he would be associated: Bourke-White, Charles Sheeler, Ralph Steiner, Doris Ullman, Paul Outerbridge, Edward Weston. Many of the pictures chosen — the Berenice Abbotts, the Atgets, the Sheelers, for instance — were repeats. The biographical information, in most instances, was reprinted from the Harvard Society catalogue with some updating: Evans's biography mistakenly noted, "He lives in New York City and in Europe." But the seven photographs included in the Albright show were more up-to-date. They were all lent by *Hound & Horn*, suggesting that Kirstein, once more, had had some hand in the exhibition. (Perhaps by way of A. Conger Goodyear, the former trendsetting president of the Albright Gallery and at the moment the Museum of Modern Art's first president.) At least four of Evans's pictures came from the recent New England architectural series. Another *Damaged* photo may have been a variant of the one included in the Levy show. The photograph titled in the catalogue as *Negress on Sixth Avenue* may have been the photograph of a black woman in a fur-trimmed coat standing at the entrance to an el station. Evans would single out this photograph, more usually catalogued as "42nd Street" and dated 1929, as the precursor for his later important series of subway photographs.

On March 8, while Evans was setting sail from Nuku Hiva for the journey homeward, the Brooklyn Museum opened its International Photographers exhibition. Significantly, the catalogue note expressed its gratitude to Condé Nast Publications and extended thanks for the services of *Brooklyn Eagle* critic Helen Appleton Read; Evans's two dealers, John Becker and Julien Levy; and the art director of *Vanity Fair*, M. F. Agha, who had reviewed Evans's 1931 show at the Becker Gallery. Seven of the photos, taken with a view camera with 6½ x 8½ glass plates, were loaned by Charles F. Fuller. (The remaining five were borrowed from the Levy Gallery.) Some of the Fuller pictures must have been taken as late as November 1931, when Evans was photographing Greek Revival architecture in such upstate New York sites as Pleasant Valley in Dutchess County;

Fly Creek and Cherry Valley in Otsego County; Mycenae, Marcellus, Skaneateles, and Syracuse in Onondaga County; indicating a fairly wide-ranging tour. There must have been some haste in processing the plates and providing the prints for the exhibitions before Evans's December 30 departure for the South Seas. And one wonders about the irony in the fact that the photographs from his summer expeditions with Lincoln Kirstein were shown out of town in Buffalo and those from his November trips in upstate New York were exhibited in Brooklyn. Considering this burst of exhibitions, it was clear that Evans had made all the right connections. By the winter of 1931–32, even with his absence from the scene, the twenty-eight-year-old Walker Evans's career was well launched.

Evans had missed the hubbub of the February opening at the Julien Levy Gallery and the minor satisfaction of reading his reviews while they were hot off the press, but he may have been gratified by a low-key show after his return to New York. In May, Levy mounted a group exhibition, New York by New Yorkers (May 2–June 2, 1932). Among the photographs by Stieglitz, Abbott, Steiner, Lynes, Bourke-White, and others, the unidentified critic for the *New York Times* singled out Evans's photo titled *Mirror*. It appears to have been the circa 1931 photograph of a mirrored dresser standing on a Brooklyn sidewalk in the process of being moved, that piece of information provided by the confusing image of the mover's truck reflected in the glass. It was only one of many photographs of mirrors, some taken from an angle reflecting only a silvered void, that would provide Evans with a teasing and recurrent existential theme. This one, the *Times* critic praised as an "incredible study of chaos."

Three weeks back in the United States, Evans, in a letter to Skolle, took stock of his personal situation, which seemed to reflect the country's situation as well. First, he advised his friend to stay on in Europe and not return to New York unless he were prepared to "spunge [sic] off a few crumbs dropped by our still oversupplied upper crust; do what you are told to do." The only advantage to that would be looking forward to a time when the upper crust cracked, allowing him, at least, to "enjoy the sight of anguish suffered where it should be." As for his own circumstances:

I am beginning to understand what sort of a period we are living in. Now

I am thrown on my own resources (which thank heaven are something at present, through photography). There is nothing to be done but go after money by the nearest means to hand. For instance, I have "contacts" and "leads." People in such bastard trades as advertising, publicity, etc., have sometimes heard of me because I have two exhibitions of photos. So I may get a job.

The immediate prospects (none of which were realized, however) were that he might do photomurals for Bloomingdale's department store. Another was to make theatrical posters for Roxy's Theater in the new Rockefeller Center complex, which was a-building. ("As they want them, of course, not my way.") Then, too, something might come of the South Seas trip.

The film by the way is good in spots. That is, there are a few irrelevant shots that are beautiful and exciting in themselves. What can be made out of the whole thing remains to be seen. If I can sell the whole works to movie people, I will, of course.

If not, he was prepared to make something short and original and show it to the Guggenheim Foundation or the banker/philanthropist Otto Kahn in hopes of getting a grant or funds to make more films. Perhaps he and Skolle should collaborate on a movie venture. It was not, apparently, a new thought: "You remember the 'Men Working' idea?" he asked.

By now Evans was ready to carp about his Pacific adventures. "You don't understand the awful, bloodcurdling conditions I was travelling under, the sort of millionaire's joyride I was on, conditions of the people, manner of the inhabitants, native craftsmanship, indeed. I was fighting (I hope) for my life and the wonder is I observed anything at all. Some day, I'll detail the extraordinary personal situation I got into with those people." But Skolle too had been traveling in North Africa under the auspices of a wealthy Englishwoman. (His wife and daughter were at home in Yonkers.) He took a more sanguine view. "We are both doing rather extraordinary things:" he wrote Evans, "you the visitor to a wrecked paradise, I in the devilishly pleasant position of a young man travelling, if you like, with a much older but none the less dashing woman. It will be a very special pleasure to meet again after all this."

In his letter to Hanns, Evans apologized for having done nothing about

a prior invitation to edit the photo section of Samuel Putnam's Paris magazine the *New Review*. First published in 1931, in opposition to Eugene
Jolas's *Transition*, its aim was to provide a kind of international cultural
reportage. It published work by Pound, Cocteau, Henry Miller, the
American Marxist critic V. F. Calverton, the Russian novelist Andrei Biely,
the Spanish writer Miguel de Unamuno, and Skolle's current financial
patron the composer George Antheil. Evans claimed he was not impressed
with the publication but nevertheless asked Skolle to put in a good word
for him: "You can do me a favor there by telling him [Putnam] I have been
out to Tahiti doing wonderful things . . ." His reasoning was clear: "I do
think you and I ought to show up as strongly and as often as possible in it."
He was planning to send Putnam something, "but I want him to believe
the reason I had for not contributing sooner and not think me merely [an]
irresponsible faker." Unfortunately he was too late. In the volatile,
contentious literary atmosphere of Paris in the early depression years, the
New Review had folded with its fifth and final issue in April.

Evans mentioned in passing that since his return, he had been seeing
few of his painter friends, with the exception of Ben Shahn. He was still of
the opinion that Skolle's work was better than Shahn's. He confessed, "I
must say I miss being in on a painter's work, your work, I mean. As I
remember it the birth of your pictures was giving me a lot more than I
knew." Shahn's work, he conceded, was much improved, but "he'll never
excite me as you did through painting." Shahn, he reported, had hit upon
a good thing, the past winter, by exhibiting a series of gouaches illustrating
the Sacco-Vanzetti affair, the trial of the two Italian anarchists and immigrants who in 1920 were arrested for allegedly killing a paymaster and a
guard in a robbery in a Massachusetts shoe factory. The gouaches, Evans
said, were extremely well done "in an entirely new manner which I didn't
think he had in his hand." They had sold well and brought the artist a good
deal of public attention. The controversial subject matter — the two men,
executed in 1927, became international martyrs of the capitalist system and
saints of the Marxist cause — had propelled Shahn into something of a
celebrity. Through the good offices of Lincoln Kirstein, Shahn had hung a
huge mural depicting Sacco and Vanzetti in an exhibition at the Museum
of Modern Art. The mural depicted:

Sacco and Vanzetti in coffins, presided over by the Lowell Committee holding lilies, almost photographic likenesses of President Lowell of Harvard and two other powerful gents who are naturally friends of the museum directors. Our friend Lincoln Kirstein had charge of the show and invited Ben to hang one mural along with about forty other Americans. It seems a big new two-block skyscraper development is in doubt about how to decorate its walls, so this show was supposed to be a hint and suggestion. The whole thing is a delicate capitalist confusion. Kirstein was badly damaged for insisting upon hanging Shahn's picture, so is now a hero.

It mattered little how far Evans traveled in the early thirties; politics would remain an inescapable theme.

Evans on
Tahiti beach

Cuba Libre

8

Quite probably, it was Ernestine Evans, a close friend of Katherine Anne Porter, who had proposed Walker Evans as the photographer for Carleton Beals's controversial book *The Crime of Cuba*, a scathing left-wing exposé of the murderous and corrupt eight-year regime of President Gerardo Machado, sustained in power by powerful American business and banking interests. Ernestine Evans, since 1930, had been the high-powered associate editor of J. B. Lippincott, the Philadelphia firm that was publishing the Beals book. A matronly woman thirteen years older than Evans, she took up the promotion of the young photographer with a persistence and faith that, strangely, left Walker Evans less than grateful. For unspecified reasons (her letters suggest she could be as direct and directorial as Evans's mother) he regularly found her efforts on his behalf grating.

As an editor and journalist, Ernestine Evans was a woman with important political and professional connections. She had served as a foreign correspondent for many years, covering Russia and the Balkans. (Her husband of ten years, Kenneth Durant, was the American representative for Tass.) In the early twenties, writing from Russia, she had correctly predicted that Stalin would be Lenin's successor despite the acknowledged importance and the brilliance of Trotsky in the Soviet politburo. As a journalist Ernestine Evans had served on the staffs of such New York newspapers as the *Tribune* and the *Evening Post*. Later she became a feature writer for the *Christian Science Monitor* and a literary editor for the publishing house of Coward-McCann.

Havana Citizen, 1933

Before Beals had turned in his manuscript (he had spent some six weeks in Cuba in September-October 1932 to research the political scene), the editors at Lippincott, particularly Evans, had pushed the author to accept Walker Evans as the photographer for what they expected would become a very topical book. That judgment was based on the fact that the political situation in Cuba had become headline news in the American newspapers since early in the year. The brutality of the Machado regime was reaching a climax in a sequence of bloody political murders and equally bloody reprisals. Machado's opponents — politicians and newspaper editors opposed to the wholesale corruption and mounting violence, student activists (Machado had shut down the University of Havana in 1930 as a hotbed of insurrection), and members of a small but growing Communist Party — were being routinely imprisoned or murdered in clandestine raids. In some instances, the victims were taken out on boats and fed to the sharks. Students arrested and jailed were disposed of through a familiar, dictatorial Cuban practice, the *ley de fuga*, that is, they were released on deserted roads and told to run, then shot, on the supposedly legal grounds that they had been killed while attempting to escape. This was the case with a seventeen-year-old high school student, Juan Mariano González Rubiera, who, according to a *New York Times* report by Russell Porter on February 4, 1933, had been found dead in the street, his hands and feet still bound, even though it was claimed he had tried to escape. On Good Friday, April 14, 1933, another *Times* reporter, James Phillips, together with his wife Ruby, had witnessed the murder of one of two brothers, both students named Valdés Daussa, who had been gunned down in broad daylight in the street beneath their balcony window near the Principe Fortress prison. They saw the boy running and shouting "No tire más" ("Don't shoot anymore") while fusillades from waiting prison guards brought him down in front of a monument to former Cuban president José Miguel Gómez. The guards had been stationed on the banks of the Avenida de los Presidentes for expressly that purpose. The other Valdés Daussa brother had been shot at the same time but further down the Avenida, out of the Phillipses' line of sight.

Not all of the atrocities, however, were committed by Machado's army forces or his "porristas," the club-carrying strong-arm squads, many of them hardened criminals released from jail for the purpose of breaking up street demonstrations by bludgeoning protestors. The ABC, a terrorist society funded largely by young well-to-do professionals and business men, more or less centrist or right-wing in their politics, but with strong ties to radical right- and left-wing student groups, were equally notorious in their tactics. The case of the two Valdés Daussa brothers, which occurred little more than a month before Evans's arrival, was indicative of the mounting violence. Bombings by the ABC student cells had been stepped up, probably as a political tactic to force the hand of the new Franklin D. Roosevelt administration, which had just taken office in March. (Under the Platt Amendment, the U.S. government was obligated to come to the aid of Cuba in case of civil unrest or foreign invasion; but historically both the Cuban governments-in-power and opposition forces had used the threat of American intervention as a strategic political weapon.) It was at this time that the Valdés Daussa brothers were arrested on suspicions of having connections with the ABC and were murdered.

Evans, to some extent, must have become aware of the worsening Cuban situation when first approached about the Beals assignment. As early as March, through Ernestine Evans, he may have met Beals, who was in New York, writing his book. The editor had written Beals: "Will you write Walker Evans, 23 Bethune St., and see him? He is the photographer — artist rather — who might do illustrations for your book. I want him to know all the possibilities for pictures you have seen." At the time Walker, in financial straits again, was living in the front room of the Bethune Street house where Ben Shahn and his family had taken a studio apartment. In April, another of the Lippincott editors, Walter Goodwin, having received the first chapter of the Beals manuscript, wrote the author, convinced "more truly than ever what an important thing it would mean to this book to have Walker Evans do the photographs for it." Beals had first suggested using recent news photographs from the *New York Mirror*. But Goodwin argued that something better than routine news coverage would get them "all kinds of publicity." He added, "I feel perfectly sure that Evans has the possibilities for another Margaret Bourke-White and it would be nice to get the publicity of the illustrations through the rotogravure sections if he did as good a job in Cuba as the other did in Russia." Only at the last moment, on May 4, was the Evans assignment firmed up. Goodwin suggested that Beals see the photographer: "I am sure the boy will do a fine piece of work on the book and will make this a really great black and white book. If you can help Evans in any way, I know you will do so, but I had better explain that I had only an opportunity to telephone him about it this afternoon and I hope he will be started soon."

In later years, Evans would claim that he had not read the Beals book before his trip to Cuba. That was essentially true — Beals had not completed the manuscript by the time Evans left for Cuba in the middle of May. Evans took with him two cameras, a medium format 2½ x 4¼ camera and a 6½ x 8½ view camera with tripod, giving him some measure of flexibility with the quicker hand-held shots and the inevitably more static shots necessitated by the setting-up of the tripod exposures. For a photographer who was barely making a living and, moreover, who was not exactly famous at the time, the Cuban assignment was a significant opportunity. Yet Evans, according to Beals's recollection of their only interview, had appeared sullen and scowling, even a bit truculent, making it a condition of his accepting the commission that he would not specifically illustrate Beals's text and that his photographs would be presented as a portfolio — an independent photo essay in fact — at the end of the book. There may be some truth to that as well, but the fact is that given the fast developing political situation in Cuba, and the last-minute nature of Evans's photographic assignment, it made far more sense to have the text, which included two appendices, a bibliography, and an index, set up in type and galley proof, leaving a free page in the front-matter for the photographic captions. Evans's photographs could then be printed up at the last moment as an independent portfolio at the end of the book.

Evans arrived in Havana in mid-May. In an undated diary entry written shortly after his arrival, he noted: "The political situation was critical at the moment." He then crossed it out: testimony, it would seem, to a certain ambivalence as to whether his mission was political or professional. He also noted that new cities always "excited" him. Whether he was feeling a sense of danger or the sense of a new city is debatable: "When you are still bewildered," he wrote, "you notice more things, as in a drunk. I was drunk with a new city for days." The photographs do indicate that, excited by the new city, he must have been on the streets daily. He had arrived early enough to photograph the festivities of Cuban Independence Day, May 20, a Saturday, celebrating Cuba's liberation from Spain. Judging from the brief sequence of photographs, it was a sunny day, with crowds gathering at the Capitol, congregating on the steps, surging through the streets. People are gathered on the balconies of the better-class apartments. The police were in attendance, dressed in white linens. The photographer — from what height or vantage point? — stares down into a crowd congregated near a touring car, its hood draped with the Cuban flag, motorcycle policemen ready for escort. The back seat, open, awaits some public official — El Presidente? At the bottom of the photograph, some members of the milling crowd stare up, making contact with the photographer.

Havana, Evans claimed, was still "a frontier town"—an odd judgment for a city which, under the ambitious building program of Machado and his Minister of Public Works, Carlos Miguel Cespedes, boasted a new Capitol building patterned after the U.S. Capitol, a new Central Highway, and an ambitious program for widening the streets. It was also a city of grand neo-baroque theaters and concert halls. As early as the mid-nineteenth century, Havana supported a famed opera house, introducing the works of Verdi to the Western Hemisphere. The city, at the time, was the first stop of the stars of the French and Italian opera houses who extended their tours to include Boston, New York, and New Orleans. In the thirties it could boast of a lively cultural life and numerous publications, including weekly reviews and vanguard literary magazines. In 1930, following his New York triumph, the Spanish poet Federico García Lorca made a celebrated three-month visit to Cuba. Unknowingly, perhaps, Evans, in photographing the Parque Centrale, focused on the dramatic façade of the Alhambra Theater, a men's-only establishment off-limits to respectable persons that Garcia Lorca boldly frequented. It specialized in political satires, pornographic playlets, and naked rumbas with audience participation. (After Castro's rise to power, it was renamed after the poet.) With its brothels and rampant gambling houses, Havana also had a reputation for bohemianism and dissipation. Machado, reputedly one of the secret owners of the Molina Rejo, the second of the two disreputable theaters noted in Evans's diary, nonetheless had embarked on a plan to make Havana the "Athens" of the Caribbean. Officially a Liberal, he had also become an admirer of Mussolini. Following in the Duce's footsteps, he was efficiently ridding himself of labor leaders, anarchists, and communists, and even the more troublesome members of the Cuban bourgeoisie.

Beals had given Evans letters of introduction to newsmen he knew in Havana: Phillips of the *Times*, Haas of the United Press, José Antonio Fernández de Castro of the influential Cuban paper *Diario de la Marina*, and his brother Jorge, all of whom were thoroughly familiar with the Cuban scene and proved useful. Havana, Evans soon noted, was a city crowded with men in uniform, a number of them armed blacks (who may have been part of Machado's militia, assigned to do the dirty work of polit-

ical assassination) as well as soldiers in tan uniforms with "heavy, shouldered guns." All this, he noted, "to keep their master gangster in power —
the only way." Evans was alert to the violence behind the cosmopolitan
façade of Havana. In his diary notes he even tried writing about it as a
cloak-and-dagger affair. But the military presence does not figure prominently in the more than four hundred photographs he took in Cuba. On
his first attempt to meet José Antonio Fernández de Castro, he made the
mistake of taking a bus. The bus (he exaggerated) was "full of spys [sic],
counterspies, plainclothesmen, secret agents and ordinary thieves." As a
precaution, he had left half his money in the hotel safe and hid the rest in
a money belt, along with the "compromising ('I hope,') letters of introduction to well-known oppositionists." But on the bus, he claimed, he more or
less had to "undress" in order to pay the fare. Despite his precautions, when
he got off, he discovered that his money had been stolen. There were other
dangers: "No American takes a bus in Havana," Evans wrote. "'They'
would suspect something and follow me. And of course everyone who is
seen near Fernández de Castro's person is immediately filed in some official card index somewhere; then shadowed."

To make matters worse, Fernández de Castro was not at home. Free for
the evening, Evans spent it investigating "some of the charming and many
nice places of the city. There was still the other half of my money in the
hotel safe and the other half of the world in the back of my mind." But this
view of Havana was to be colored by the outskirts and the drearier streets in
which he wandered. He thought of it as half savage and unsafe: "There is
history, of course, but history with pirates, the extreme heightened actions
of a decayed race, recurrent instability." Badly paved streets gave way to no
pavement at all, although they were lined with marble "palaces." Rainwater
torrents had eroded the red earth and weeds had grown up with tropical
speed and strength. Taxis refused to go down such streets and on hills the
drivers shut off the motors because of the tax on gasoline.

Evans soon enough learned that Havana was also a city of secret
errands, clandestine operations. That was the lesson of his first meeting
with Fernández de Castro. Evans met him the following day at his office
and gave a brisk account in his diary:

He said good! We will go to lunch and we will talk. (I could see that.) He wore his mind on his sleeve of white linen, white one day longer than possible. There was no reserve because the letter was from Beals . . . But a good man in one of the various shades of meaning I give to the word. . . .

Coming down in the elevator and out onto the street, Fernández de Castro gesticulated a lot, talked rapidly. The Cuban's volatility added to Evans's impression of the man: ". . . and I was thinking about his good latin face and how it was all right for him to flash the way he did, there in his city, and to seem to have no manners." But there was, Evans decided, something sinister in the way a taxi arrived suddenly at Fernández de Castro's bidding. They drove off in search of some unnamed address. Evans was puzzled by an additional passenger:

Some underfed person with us who seemed to know the driver. He sat in front and was not introduced, leaving me to think, bodyguard. It got easier to think anything during that ride. We stopped somewhere and Fernández de Castro got out but not for long and I don't know what he did. The bodyguard stayed in the car. I knew I would learn reasons for all these things . . . Motivation, I thought in the car, is tiresome and inevitable. . . .

It was at that point that Evans's on-the-spot diary account of his Cuban adventure breaks off. But not without his asking himself: "Is this man knocking around between money, sex, boredom, or has he something else up his sleeve?"

II

It was mere coincidence that brought Evans and Ernest Hemingway together in Havana in that late spring of 1933. Hemingway had arrived in early April on a fishing expedition on the *Anita*, a thirty-foot cruiser rented from one of his Key West cronies. It was the only meeting between Evans and Hemingway, though the two men would remember the encounter well in later years. Evans, who may have been introduced to Hemingway by one of Beals's newspaper connections in Havana, considered himself lucky: "I had a wonderful time with Hemingway. Drinking every night. He was at loose ends . . . and he needed a drinking companion, and I filled that role for two weeks." The drinking quite probably took place at the famed

Floridita, Hemingway's usual hangout, or the bar at The Pearl of San Francisco Café in the seaport area of Old Havana. One or the other — or perhaps both — served as the model for the bar in the opening action of Hemingway's novel *To Have and Have Not*.

When Evans ran out of money — fortunately he had already paid for his return passage — Hemingway loaned him enough to stay on for another week. Evans would later claim that he disliked taking photographs of famous people: "Photographically speaking the face of a celebrity is a cliché." In Havana he was true to his word and made a point of not photographing the highly famous Hemingway. "Much to Hemingway's delight I might add," Evans commented. "I think he felt I wanted to be coaxed." But in a devious way, he managed to commemorate their meeting by taking photographs of two Havana movie theaters which happened to be showing *Adiós a las Armas*, the film version of Hemingway's *A Farewell to Arms*. When, precisely, he met Hemingway is not clear, but the probability is that it was within the first week of his arrival, since the theaters, one of them the gaudy Apollo with its gilded columns, were still advertising *Adiós a las Armas* for Saturday, May 27, and the other for Sunday. Yet on the subject of Hemingway, Evans could be uncharacteristically loquacious. In a later interview, he said:

> *I had a very instinctive bond between him and me, and he knew it. But I was very wary of him. He was very secretive — that's not the word — he was a very hard man to come close to. But in one way I did. I really thought he was a great artist at that time and he loved that recognition. He could see that I knew what he was about. I could see him in his work. And he knew it right away. Very intelligent, very sensitive man. But I decided instinctively to keep my distance, not to carry on a friendship with him.*

A Document of the Terror (Collected by Evans from Havana newspaper files, 1933)

For his part, Hemingway remembered the photographer as a "nice kid" who took "beautiful" pictures. (Actually, Evans, a very youthful twenty-nine, was only three years younger than Hemingway.) The relationship was chummy enough that Hemingway told Evans about his planned trip to Spain in August and, perhaps, about his intended trip to Africa — his first — later in 1933. Hemingway, at least, recalled a bit of camaraderie in a cause: "We were both working against Machado at the time," he remembered. That was something of an exaggeration; both may have been sympathetic to the rebels who were opposing the entrenched Machadistas, but there is no evidence that Hemingway, and certainly none that Evans, were actively engaged in toppling the regime, other than artistically.

Still it was a meeting at a dangerous time. Aside from the four hundred or more photographs Evans took during his month-long stay in Cuba, he also collected a small file of atrocity photographs probably gotten from local newspaper sources. They provided the strongest evidence of the brutalities of the Machado regime: mutilated corpses, policemen routing protesters, students behind bars, police officials consulting one another. Among his illustrations for *The Crime of Cuba*, he included one of the bloodied corpse of the teen-age González Rubiero and another, captioned "Document of the Terror," of a young black in a deadly still life, the man laid out with a coiled rope and a sinister knife.

But the most gruesome file-photograph he acquired was that of a stool pigeon named Manuel Cepero, the victim of an ABC reprisal. Months before the arrival of either Hemingway or Evans, Cepero had made the mistake of warning one of Machado's most notorious henchmen, Major Arsenio Ortíz — guilty of wholesale atrocities, murders, and mutilations — that an assassination attempt would be made against him. Ortíz, forewarned, managed to kill his assailant. But Cepero was found a few nights

later with his throat cut, his tongue and ears cut off, and a sign reading: "El ABC dará esta muerte a todos los lenguilargos." One historian, Hugh Thomas, gives a polite version of the message: "The punishment of ABC on those who see and talk too much." A shorter, more colloquial version suggests that the ABC was declaring "Death to all big mouths."

Hemingway in 1934 used the anti-Machado revolution as the political backdrop for two short stories, "One Trip Across" and "The Tradesman's Return." Both would eventually be melded into *To Have and Have Not*, his 1937 novel of political corruption and terrorism in Cuba. He almost certainly must have used the Cepero incident and the ABC role in it — without naming either — in a particularly grim exchange at the outset of the novel. His hero, Harry Morgan, has been approached by three young Cubans offering a thousand dollars apiece to take them from Cuba to the U.S. mainland on his boat: "They were nice-looking fellows all right and I would have liked to have done them the favor," Harry admits. But Harry, who otherwise would be occupied in several shady affairs — bootlegging, for instance, and an attempt to transport illegal Chinese emigrants to the United States — tells the Cubans he can't; he makes his living with his boat and isn't willing to take the risk of losing it. One of the men, Pancho, turns sour and threatening. Harry argues that he won't carry anything that can talk: "Sacked liquor can't talk. Demijohns can't talk." Pancho, nastily, confronts him in turn: "You're not a lengua larga, are you?"

"I don't think so," Harry says.

"What's that? A threat?"

"Listen," Harry tells him, "Don't be so tough so early in the morning. I'm sure you've cut plenty of people's throats. I haven't even had my coffee yet."

"So you're sure I've cut people's throats?" Pancho answers.

Repetitions in Hemingway's terse writing style are not often slack editing; insistence in mere description usually has a point, and the unspoken association with the ABC seems clear. As the three men leave, Harry observes once more: "They were good-looking fellows, wore good clothes; none of them wore hats, and they looked like they had plenty of money. They talked plenty of money, anyway, and they spoke the kind of English Cubans with money speak." It is altogether probable that Hemingway was aware of the murder of Cepero and was using it, as he would later write about the murderous activities of both the Loyalists and the Fascists in the Spanish Civil War in his novel *For Whom the Bell Tolls*. His insistence on the wealth and youth of the three young Cubans (who are, incidentally, gunned down probably by machadistas as they step out of the café) suggests that they were members of the ABC involved in the revolt against Machado and were currently in danger of their lives or trying to involve Harry in some gun-running scheme to bring back illegal weapons from the United States.

Evans, strangely enough, had his own albeit slight connection to the rampant mayhem Hemingway would depict in his Cuban stories. Among the letters of introduction Carleton Beals had given him was one to Orestes Ferrara, the ubiquitous Secretary of State and Finance as well as editor of the *Heraldo de Cuba*, the official organ of the Machado regime. "Missed Machiavelli the Ferrara, I regret," Evans later informed Beals in a letter. It was probably just as well that Ferrara was out of the country at the time. It was Ferrara, in fact, who wrote to the *New York Times* on February 9, 1933, indignantly protesting Russell Porter's account of the murdered González Rubiera, asking the name of the Cuban newspaper that had shown the photograph of the dead student lying in the street with his hands and feet bound. "All is fiction," Ferrara claimed, "Porter could not prove anything of the kind." Porter's reply, published in the *Times* as well, indicated not only that the picture had been published in the December 31, 1932, issue of *El Pais*, but that the editor, Enrique Pizzi, had gone into hiding and had only returned to work after receiving assurance from Dr. Ferrara (unfortunately through an intermediary) that he would not be harmed. "According to reliable information in the writer's possession," Porter added, "[Pizzi] was arrested on Jan. 31 and is now held incommunicado in Principe Fortress in Havana." Clearly Ferrara was not a source to be trusted.

It is clear that Evans processed and printed some of his Cuban film in Havana. (There is an address for "Am. Photo Studios" on Calle Zenea 43 in his diary.) But more important there is a clue that he was concerned that his pictures might be a source of danger or might be confiscated by Machado operatives if they fell into the wrong hands. Hemingway clearly remembered that as a precaution Evans had given him a set of his prints to take back to the States on his boat the *Anita*.

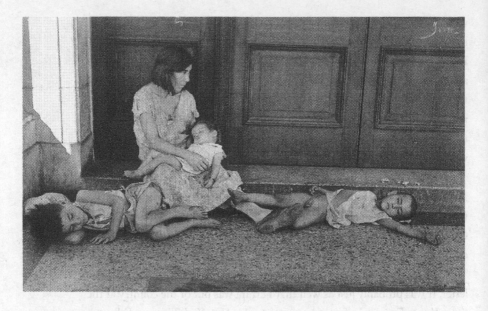

There is little in the photographs Evans took in Cuba, however, that hints at any political fears. More can be found in the less-than-thousand words recorded in his Cuban diary notes or the otherwise unsubstantiated claims that would appear on the dust jacket of *The Crime of Cuba* when it was published on August 17, where it was stated that Evans "was stopped and searched by soldiers everywhere and once stoned by 'toughs,'" which might or might not have been true. Otherwise his fears appear to have been sublimated by the excitement of what he was seeing. His Cuban photographs constitute, rather, a working dictionary of Havana in the year 1933: its people, its ethnic diversity, its shops, its professions — all itemized for a posterity Evans may not even have considered yet. He enlarged on the inventory of fruit stands he had begun earlier in New York: There is an interesting sequence of photographs of stalls and peddler's carts with pineapples, melons, bananas arranged in tight drill formations. There are shots of siesta time: civic sleepers in the torpor of the day, sprawled on park benches, in shaded doorways. For the most part they are of poor people. (The rich, presumably, slept comfortably behind shuttered windows.) Two women, one with an injured foot, doze on a hard bench in the glare of noon. A woman with three children sits guard while they sleep in front of a doorway. She cradles the youngest; another, a boy nude except for a dirty shirt, sprawls out against a step. A man in torn trousers sleeps on a marble slab; another, dead to the world, lies on a park bench. Is it a matter of the photographer's intent that both sleepers lie with their hands in or on their crotches, as if guarding their wallets while in a vulnerable state? They are echoes of Evans's earlier photo of a drunk with his fly open sleeping it off in a doorway on South Street, New York: Drunkenness has no geography.

Evans was clearly caught up in the ethnic diversity of the country — the Spanish, the blacks, the mixed bloods — with the exception of the Chinese population. Although he made a note of the Chinese district in his diary, he seems not to have taken photographs there. (Cuba had a significant Chinese population, but of men only. Chinese women were not allowed to emigrate there, a deliberate effort to keep down the Chinese population.)

Woman and Children, Havana, 1933.

There is a certain larkiness about the photographs Evans took of a group of soot-blackened coal shovelers and dockworkers, using both the smaller hand-held camera and the 6½ x 8½ view camera with tripod. Which means he must have cajoled the workers into posing for him against a blank wall. "Those people [the dockworkers] have no self-pity," he once commented. "They're just as happy as you are, really." The well-intentioned remark is more patronizing than the actual photographs. Like the early abandoned drafts of a writer, subsidiary photographs (those not published for lack of opportunity or not deemed worthy) leave clues, suggestions of the photographer's mysterious intentions, his state of mind. Judging from this ancillary evidence, Evans may have spotted the men with their shovels at the pay window first, then arranged to take the group portraits. In a group, with their blackened faces, their grins, their cocky poses, they offer a parody version of the society photograph. In the individual portraits, with their sweat-rags tied around their necks, their straw boaters, jockey caps and makeshift hats, they are the fashion plates of grime. It was clear that Evans had found himself a "subject" and diligently turned it into an exercise of wit.

Given Evans's penchant for signs and signage, he could hardly have resisted photographing a government lottery stand, with its barrage of

hanging number plates. Did Evans know that the whole government lottery system was one of the great sources of public corruption in Cuba? The privilege of vending tickets was routinely bought by healthy bribes to public officials, the vendors taking lucrative profits from off the top. Are they perhaps a symbol of the rampant political corruption?

While photographing a corner dairy shop, Evans became fascinated by a young and stylish dark-skinned woman in a thin dress standing in front of a dairy shop on the opposite side of the street. A light breeze tugs at the hem of her dress. (But even with photographic evidence, there are no definitive truths to be had. Given his interest in attractive women, he might have photographed her first, then, circling around, took a second shot from behind, catching sight of another opportunity, a kitchenware store across the street.) In any event, he zeroes in, too, on the primitive cartoon-image of a kitchen stove painted on the shop wall and a three-dimensional sign for a Yale key. What attracts him here is the irrepressible chaos of street corner graphics, the Yale key a minor leitmotif, perhaps, of American influence abroad. One of the more striking and possibly most famous of Evans's Cuban photographs (though it was not included in *The Crime of Cuba*) underscores that possibility. A tall black man in a white linen suit and straw hat stands in front of a newsstand. The magazine racks are loaded with movie magazines and other periodicals. The eyes of Kay Francis, a reigning white queen of the silver screen in the thirties, peer out from the picture on a level with the black man's sullen stare. With the devious simplicity of photography, the picture says Man and Woman, black and white, and raises other unspoken visual issues. It says Hollywoodism and American enterprise. (A Coca-Cola sign appears prominently above.) Perhaps it is only coincidence that the newspaper a newsboy is reading blazons "GRAN TRIUNFO DE CHOCOLATE," a reference to "Kid Chocolate" (Eligio Sardinas), the 1932 black Cuban featherweight boxing champion. Beneath the headline is the image of Kid Chocolate upside down. The eyes of an astute photographer, one wants to believe, are trained to pick up the desiderata of a scene or situation. "Your eye is a collector," Evans once told a group of students. "It runs down this and that byway, some of them false and some of them very fruitful. You don't often know whether you're on the right track or not, but you do get on it and follow it." This perhaps refers to Evans's belief that through "luck" or the trained eye, the photographer becomes a "medium," a prophet of social changes he is unaware of at the moment of taking the picture.

Havana Dockworkers, 1933

He noticed the women of Havana, some of them probably prostitutes — rather attractive ones — standing or sitting in a cramped foyer with straggly potted plants or palms near doorways that revealed the bedrooms beyond. A dark-haired woman wearing a pearl necklace, leans, looking out, from a narrow opening in a barred gateway, but despite the doorbell, there is no access there; two stout stalks of a vine are tied to the immobile iron bars. A stylish young woman sits at a café table and obligingly turns her head this way and that and looks frankly at the photographer. ("None of the pictures with people is posed," Evans wrote for his dust-jacket blurb.) He completed a series of portraits of a rather sickly and wistful nymphet who posed against two different backdrops — one of gauze, another a plaid blanket. Presumably he had to have arranged for a room to photograph her. Another, older, more vivacious woman appears in two different outfits.

Evans had a reputation of being a charmer where women were concerned.

And there was the woman who decidedly attracted him — Dorothy Butcher, an English woman who worked in one of the offices he frequented. There is no identification, no detail to place her definitively, and no indication that she is one of the women he photographed. But Evans gave her a good deal of thought later when he was back in the States. He mused about her in the draft of a letter in his diary. He may or may not have written her. Portions of the letter were crossed out:

> *I had better write you after all, six weeks late, some thanks for making me remember [little things, kindnesses, the grotesque futility of my conversations with you in that business place . . . and to admit I wanted to know you more than I seemed to be able.] I have been often amused at my not being able to talk to you of anything other than whatever we did talk about over the mahogany barrier in your office.*

It was a timid letter suggesting the relationship had not proceeded very far. Or that Evans was cautious about giving away too much. On one of the diary pages, there was a sketch, in a scratchy hand, of an old graybeard, presumably by Evans, and an admission (crossed out): "And behind your back, I took all sorts of liberties in trying to find someone in Havana who knew you."

In Havana and its outskirts, Evans did concentrate on the abject poverty that could hardly be ignored: a battered beggar on the sidewalk, his hand out to a passerby; poor people in the breadline, waiting for the gates to open to the free kitchen run by the newspaper *El País*; a shabbily dressed country family munching on pineapple slices in front of an imposing mansion. Outside the city he took the more dramatic photographs of the purgatory of crowded, thatched, stick-and-palm-leaf huts — the votive *bohíos* of the poor — collected like unanswered prayers below a church on a hill. He moved along the dirt road to the settlement and down the irregular streets strung with washday clothes and small children at play. The message perhaps is that poverty is poverty everywhere.

In Havana, Evans took in the ancient sites, the tourist attractions, though far less extensively: the city viewed from the Malecón Wall; the Teatro Nacional; the Parque Central; the Christopher Columbus Cathedral

Woman,
Havana, 1933

(officially the Cathedral of the Immaculate Conception), where supposedly the bones of Columbus and his son Diego were at one time buried; the empty university with a solitary guard patroling the street. And in the midst of these photo-taking sessions, he found time to insert his shadowy personal appearance: the photograph of a barbershop with his autobiographical image of the photographer taking the photograph reflected in the mirror. In another, if one looks sharply, one catches sight of him in a straw hat, bent over his camera, wreathed round with artificial roses on the reflecting glass front of a peddler's stand selling "Lechon Asado" (roast pork).

By June 25, a week after his return to New York, Evans was writing to Carleton Beals (in California) that he had turned over his selection of Cuban photographs to Lippincott. He had evidently taken some care about the sequencing of the pictures to be used, warning that "the number of prints and order and titles seems not to bear any changing at all, and have prayed Mr. J. Jefferson Jones to leave it thus." He was convinced that the arrangement would make "something noticeable, and that ought to help the book." Cuba was a "grand place," he said, and he would be sorry not to go there again: "You I suppose are permanently banned, though mightn't Machado's enemies honor you. The old butcher seems firmly in, still, for some time to come."

He had sent sixty-four prints in all to Lippincott, though only thirty-one were to be used in the final publication. Still pushing, he noted that Ernestine Evans had approved of his selection and hoped that that would carry weight with the publisher. It was a perplexing job, he said, "so many different courses to follow. I wonder if the illustrations will seem Cuba to you as you know it." He was acknowledging, then, two different versions of reality: that of the polemical author and his own as photographer.

Throughout the thirties, Evans gave every evidence that he was consid-ering photographs and images in sequential terms, not just as individual pictures. The photographic sequence Evans devised for *The Crime of Cuba* within a week or so after his return (whether editorial changes were made is not clear) is not the searing indictment it might have been, considering the bitter text he was illustrating. It is more subtle than one might find effective. He started with the ethnic diversity of a crowded street (the photograph was also used on the dust jacket), then moved immediately to the Cuban woman, the possible prostitute, in the inset of a doorway, followed by a statue of St. Rocco in a Havana church — a too-obvious contrast between the profane and the sacred. There were the various aspects of the busy city: the siesta sleepers, peddlers' carts, butcher shops, the "public spectacle" of a crowd on the Capitol steps, the sweeping shot of a village of *bohíos*, a sugar plantation in the off-season.

It was not until the end of the sequence that Evans provided a dramatic

Tintype of Evans with young woman, possibly Dorothy Butcher, Havana, 1933.

climax, noting the military presence in Cuba by showing a single guard-soldier on patrol outside an ancient wall, then the political terror of the anonymous news photographs of the murdered young black and the brutalized face of the student González Rubiera. Just before the end, there is an ironic sequence of newsboys climbing up the barred windows of a newspaper plant, waiting for deliveries. This was followed by the haunting file photograph of young student terrorists looking out glumly from behind prison bars. The photographs are not, in the most emphatic sense, indictments, statements of innocence or guilt, but images of the observant eye. The sequence ends with a picture of words, political slogans scrawled on a wall: "We support the strike of the cigar workers," probably from some labor party, and "Down with the Imperialist War," signed P.C. for the Communist Party. Evans's effort received a minor commendation in the front-page review of the book in the August 20 issue of the *New York Times Book Review*: "Especial mention should be made of Mr. Evans's photographs. They form an appendix of thirty [sic] views of Cuban life, including two or three mementoes of the horror." But the review did carry a full-width horizontal of his photograph *Village of Havana Poor*.

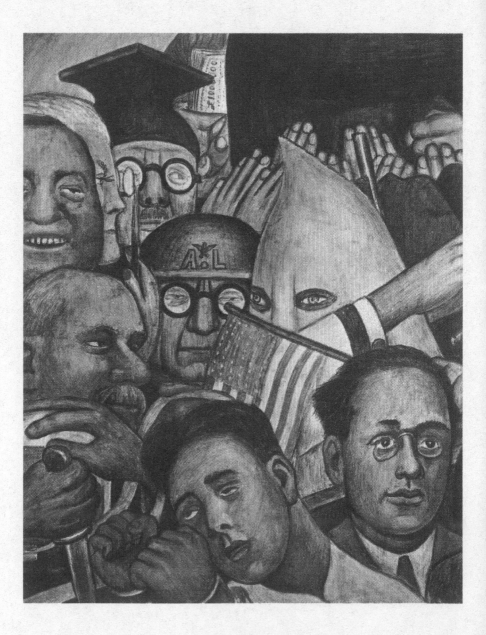

Seeing Red

9

July 13, 1933: A day in the life of an itinerant photographer. Evans was still in straitened circumstances, forced to cadge a midday meal with friends who were as badly off as he. "Hungry, so walked to see Noda; they were in and I ate." He was referring to the twenty-five-year-old Japanese painter Hideo Noda and his wife or mistress, Ruth, who had an apartment on Sixteenth Street. Considering Evans's situation, he was taking it with a certain equanimity: "Not panicky, nor yet careless-bohemian about it." He had at least one prospect, a possible assignment from publisher Tim Coward, of Coward-McCann, Ernestine Evans's former employer, who was preparing a book about the South. Evans had read the manuscript the day before and found it "very bad." Interviewed by Coward on the afternoon of the thirteenth, he learned the assignment meant a $250 fee and a trip South the following week. He was to provide sixteen "background, documentary-atmosphere" photographs. It seemed to be a more or less settled affair. Yet the meeting with Coward left him dissatisfied: "As usual I couldn't think well when under fire about money. It seemed almost ridiculous anyway, me sitting there with a dime in my pocket before puffy Tim Coward and his cigar, and me not resenting anything and wondering why I didn't grow hysterical and scream out some scene. Always wondering if past experiences with poverty have or have not depleted me."

In the late afternoon he visited Leonie Sterner ostensibly for tea, but really to ask her if she wanted to back a book by him as she once had suggested. She was one of several people Evans met that year who were interested in filmmaking as was her husband, Harold. Nothing came of the hoped-for discussion: The tea was superseded by cocktails, then company arrived — a homosexual movie critic and a sailor in civies (flannel, pocket handkerchief, etc.). The conversation turned to "night violence" in New York. "Leonie attracts me," Evans noted. "The repellent Leonie. She says people are making money on the stock exchange again." As Evans was leaving her house — "cocktailed," as he put it — he ran into the photogra-

Diego Rivera mural for New Workers School, 1933, detail framed by Evans

195

pher Ralph Steiner on the street, but they had little to say to one another.

Once more he was confronted with a familiar problem: "No money for dinner. Noda and Ruth in at Sixteenth Street, also without money. I got three dollars from Ethel Goldwater and we ate a horrible steak dinner in a restaurant." To add to his problem, his habitual interest in and attractiveness to women was creating difficulties. Ruth Noda was in pursuit of him, openly in the company of her husband. "I don't know what to think about Hideo and Ruth. She hides nothing much when we are all together, and suggests openly going south with me. I can see no signs of what his feelings are," Evans confided to his diary on July 13. "None of us, unless it is I, are embarrassed. Tonight she was more appealing than ever, and of course knew it."

That evening, another near-starving friend, the artists' model Avis Ferme, with whom he had once pursued a courtship if not an affair, telephoned him. He acknowledged a certain coldness in his attitude:

I feel careless about it and don't know what that's a sign of. A sign that I am tired of the hypocrisy of sending stranded people around to unstranded people. Weary of this perpetual inability we all share to be strictly honest about our indifference. I don't care if Avis Ferme starves to death as long as I don't have to watch her do it; so I feel like writing that down.

II

It was a summer of difficulties with women. Ruth Noda continued to torment Hideo, with whom Evans began to sympathize. At dinner with them the following night — the Nodas had invited the photographer Leo Hurwitz, a former lover of Ruth's — the awkwardness was critical. Hurwitz's presence spoiled the occasion for Evans, partly because of the taint of his antisemitism ("So much Jew, me so much Nordic") and partly because he felt depressed in the presence of another photographer. Also he felt that Hurwitz's presence altered the balance of his relationship with Ruth and Hideo: "Hurwitz and I painfully conscious of each other all the time. Ruth discreet for his benefit, really for my relief." When Hurwitz left, the trio moved the last act of the drama to Evans's Bethune Street lodgings, where it worsened substantially. He described the scene with the analytical fervor of a French novelist:

[Ruth] promptly went into a madcap mood and tried everything to upset us all. Hideo wavered pitifully, and I wasn't very solid myself — though the stake is smaller for me. Finally Hideo left with the understanding that she was to stay the night with me. It is impossible to recapture just what happened, and I see the relation of the actual movements indicates nothing but the situation. It is so difficult to read an Oriental face. Anyway H. left with his smile, after I had tried to prevent that several times. In the midst of it all I perceived how little I cared, and found I was working for nothing but the status quo.

No sooner had Hideo left than an unspecified opportunity for escape presented itself. Evans used it to get Ruth out of the apartment. They found Noda standing on a corner. Ruth went into action once more:

Her cruelty galvanized, he got it and tried to go away again. Then to my relief called definitely for her to speak to him alone. They went off out of sight. She came back to me skipping and being mysterious. I guessed she would walk around with me for an hour or so, long enough to torture him fairly thoroughly, then let me take her back where she hates to feel she belongs. Torture me too of course . . .

It was not the end of the matter: ". . . I think she lost interest in what she was doing, for she suddenly asked me if I were tired and wanted to go home — and I knew she meant alone. Home I went from her doorstep, but not much affected by all this."

Two days later there was a birthday party for Hideo that brought this stage of the affair to a crucial point: "Tonight at least crystallized an attitude in me. He suffers too much," Evans noted. Early in the evening he and Ruth went out for a walk around the block. Hideo, "gayish with liquor," waved his blessing. But later, as the party was breaking up, Ruth and Evans went out for another walk. Noda was apparently distraught: "He was going to bed, even suggested I sleep with them. Then half an hour later when we were sitting on the doorsteps he came down in an obviously desperate state, paid no attention to me but implored her to come up with him. He begged but with a really powerful insistence, so that even that careless girl saw it and simply went."

Evans claimed he felt disgusted with Ruth, but still playing the role of matchless observer, he was not inclined to take any decisive action. His reasoning was that a sudden break would only cause the worst trouble between them. "All sloppy," he commented in the on-going saga of the affair. The following morning Ruth phoned him and he had breakfast with her at a nearby restaurant. "Since nothing is important to her, least of all my relation to her, she dropped the information, casually, averted, that 'we wouldn't see each other anymore.' And something of her talk with Hideo last night after they retired came out; and I learned more than I have known what he is going through. He doesn't know what to think of me." Three days later, with understandable relief, he had breakfast with the couple and saw Ruth off on a trip to Vermont.

But having escaped from one awkward situation Evans propelled himself into another. He arranged to have dinner with Leonie Sterner, who talked that evening mostly about her proposed movie about Indians. "Mysterious Leonie still attracts," he wrote in his diary. "It sometimes seems she wants someone to go with her to New Mexico and Hollywood — someone like me for instance. A fascinating piece of cheese is she and every once in a while I like her." That was more than he could say for her "awful friends." The friends tended "to drop in at midnight while her awful husband is away." "Maurice Sachs, oh, my!" he commented.

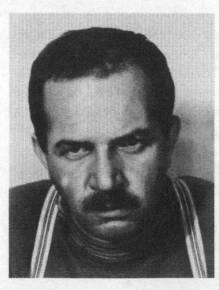

There were other thoughts on his mind as well. He had been taking portraits of a young model named Jo-Jo who seemed to interest him. But when, a few days later, she and a troop of five lesbians showed up at the studio, he confessed, "I didn't like it." The news of a general strike in Cuba set him wondering about the English girl in Havana: "How is Dorothy Butcher, will she lose her job before I get in touch with her?" He asked himself, "Why do I like her so much?" He worried, too, about not having paid Hemingway the "small amount of money" he had borrowed. In the meantime he also reported: "Leonie Sterner has ditched me because I forgot to telephone her." He still wondered, however, whether she would want to finance the book by him. A trip to Coney Island with Leonie a week later fared no better: "We got nowhere." By late August, she became a name among the other women's names in an end-of-season entry: "Leonie Sterner, Peggy Osborn reappears. Summer over . . . Ruth Noda comes back."

His were not the only sensual and sexual tremors that summer. Ben Shahn was dividing his time between the Bethune Street studio in New York and Truro on Cape Cod, where his wife Tillie was lumbering through pregnancy. Shahn periodically returned to Bethune Street, providing Evans with small sums of relief money as well as lunches and dinners. Evans's diary reveals that Shahn, too, was otherwise involved:

In the restaurant we talked about Mary Badger and his ten day fling with her. He asked me if I liked her better because of it, or not, and I couldn't tell him what I really felt about that — I couldn't find out quickly enough for words on the spot. More, I think.

Ben Shahn,
1933

Later that summer, the two men would have another "personal" discussion of sexual matters:

Ben's private dilemma seems to be the discovery that he is polygamous and at the same time honest to a point which makes it necessary to inform one woman of another. Just how much he enjoys hurting other people he neglected to say. His latest theory, several times lately underlined to me, is, you hurt someone every time you take a breath; so you should breathe in and then out too.

To illustrate his point Shahn held a glass plate in front of his lips so that he could see the moisture of his breath.

III

In late July and early August, a jumble of days in a terrific heat wave. Evans refreshed himself by sitting under the hose in the back garden. The bank failure loomed in the news; "Roosevelt may do something like closing exchange," he wrote in his diary. There had been some persistent, sad letters from Ernestine Evans, who was in Berlin: "Berlin bad, Ernestine bad, me good somehow." Shahn and he were seeing each other with some regularity. For Shahn's benefit, he attempted to describe Hemingway's character without much success. (Hemingway was decidedly out of favor with liberals and fellow travelers for his apparent lack of concern for the proletariat.) And there were days in their relationship that Evans was reluctant to record: "Let myself be led around all day and evening by Ben. A day I wouldn't like to describe." Once Tillie Shahn came to New York for a few days, very much pregnant. Too pregnant, it appears, for the fastidious Evans: "I dislike other men's wives in that condition."

Evans noted: "The government launches the National Recovery idea." Harold Ickes, officially Roosevelt's Secretary of the Interior, was appointed one of the administrators of the new agency. In 1933, uncharacteristically, Evans was paying attention to politics and the policies of the New Deal, probably because of his friendship with Harry Hopkins, whom Roosevelt had appointed head of the Federal Emergency Relief Administration. Perhaps he hoped to benefit from the connection. Writing to Skolle, he reasoned: "America is changing though I don't think you'd like it any the better. At least though, none of the cocksure prosperous ones are cocksure now. That's a great help psychically even though it means the almost complete disappearance of art patronage. May I add, fuck art patronage; it never was right when it *could* be lavish." He obviously had heard talk of state patronage under the guise of unemployment relief for artists. He thought it might be more honest than in the period of former prosperity since it would mean less "decorating of Park Avenue retiring rooms." "Fortunately," he wrote, "Harry Hopkins will have charge of this money and he has sense enough to ask people who know, how to manage it. When I first got wind of it I was apathetic but now I feel it might be really a good

*Ernestine
Evans*

thing." Hopkins would be in a position to do enormous things for artists. "It's important," he added, "because at the moment there is *nothing* doing; no artists, even the best, are working with any spirit at all." Evans was obviously connected to the right sources; it was not until two years later, however, that Roosevelt actually appointed Hopkins head of the Works Progress Administration, the agency that handled all federal arts projects.

Professionally, Evans had been in the doldrums for most of the year. In April, before his Cuban trip, he had made some money photographing American folk art paintings and objects from the collection of Edith Halpert's Downtown Gallery. ("I could support myself copying paintings I think, but don't relish the work," he informed Skolle.) He had reedited his South Sea Islands film into something better "but not yet really a film," and there was a chance of selling a print to the London Film Society but for not much money. Eugene O'Neill's *The Emperor Jones* with Paul Robeson was being filmed in New York by director Dudley Murphy. "Murphy," Evans claimed, "is dumb as they come, a racketeer but rather honest and likeable. I may do something for him by way of stills." The deal with Tim Coward had fallen through; Coward's publicity person was against photographic illustrations for the book.

By mid-July he was reduced to selling some of his books: "No money for eating so I took some books to Walter Goldwater and lunched with him." Afterwards, at loose ends and standing on Fourteenth Street, he decided, "I couldn't do anything with people until I had a haircut and that

I didn't want to do anything with people anyway. That settled by being unable to get a haircut even for myself." With a bad taste in his mouth, he puttered back to Bethune Street and went to sleep. "Spending pennies," Evans noted again in his diary. "How I eat three times a day is a mystery," he wrote a few days later, "I saw a homeless boy asleep near the docks early one morning." He made no other comment, just the bare recognition of the visual reality. A recently married friend, Freddie Paine, brother of Lyman Paine, wrote him: "Your telephone is disconnected. Are you?" It was true; he hadn't paid his bill. His mother, too, found out about it: "Mrs. Evans," he wrote with suspicious formality, "writes that she wants to send me some money and suspects I need it. . . . More and more sympathy because of the telephone!" "I can't remember for two days running," he wrote in his diary. "The usual key to a day's events is simply the chronological disposition of time (whatever that means), but two of these days is [sic] only a mass of hellish vagueness. I perceive that I am unhappy."

Modest financial relief came in the form of work for the radical Mexican muralist Diego Rivera and his painter-wife Frida Kahlo: meager sums of ten dollars or so for taking detailed photographs of the series of murals Rivera was then painting at the New Workers' School on West Fourteenth Street. Of the two, Evans took an immediate liking to Frida, a fiery and down-to-earth individualist. She seemed to be the more generous and responsive, paying him for taking pictures of her paintings at their West Thirteenth Street apartment. Other than "a few petty borrowings and scrapings," it was the only cash Evans got over a period of ten days. Besides, Frida liked his work, as Evans reported in his diary: "Incredibly set up by Frida's appreciation of my Cuba pictures." When Rivera paid him a little something a couple of days later, Evans suspected it was for other motives: "He insists we have a telephone here, and knows any money coming in will go to reinstallation of the thing."

Probably through Ben Shahn, Evans had first met the couple in the spring, when Rivera had begun painting his controversial and ill-fated mural for the RCA building in Rockefeller Plaza. "Shahn is working with Rivera on a mural (fresco) in Radio City, and that *is* exciting." Evans wrote Skolle in April: "I go up often and watch the procedure. The thing is confused at present or I'd regale you with a description." The theme of the mural was Man at the Crossroads, a grandiose moral fable about the struggle of good against evil, socialism against capitalism. On the left-hand side of the huge mural, working-class demonstrators were being beaten by policemen with raised billy clubs in contrast with the degenerate pleasures of the rich, who were comfortably seated in a nightclub. (One of the more vivid segments depicting the crimes of capitalism included chemical warfare, illustrated by hordes of marching soldiers, bayonets raised and wearing gas masks, in Hitlerized Germany. It serves as an interesting premonition of the clippings of figures in gas masks that Evans used to create a featured sequence in his scrapbook.) On the right-hand side of Rivera's unequal political equation, in the painter's own words, were "the organized Soviet masses, with the youth in the vanguard . . . marching towards the development of a new social order trusting in the light of History." Although a Communist, Rivera was, at the time, out of political favor because of his pronounced anti-Stalinist views. His American friend and biographer Bertram Wolfe suggested that Rivera wanted to prove that despite his Trotskyite leanings, he was more a Communist than the rank-and-file members of the party.

If so, he had made his statement in one of the bastions of capitalism. A fact not lost on the news media. A catchy headline in the *New York World Telegram* blared: RIVERA PAINTS SCENES OF COMMUNIST ACTIVITY AND JOHN D. JR. FOOTS THE BILL. The reporter noted: "The dominant color is red — red headdress, red flags, waves of red . . . in a victorious onsweep." In the left-wing *New Masses*, however, editor Joseph Freedman condemned Rivera's Rockefeller Center mural as "reactionary" and "counterrevolutionary." But the real crisis came (appropriately on May 1) when Rivera transformed what had originally been a sketch of a worker-leader wearing a cap into an unmistakable portrait of the balding Lenin. Despite his earlier claims, nowhere in Rivera's preliminary sketches nor in his written explanation was Lenin mentioned as a figure in the painting or as the intended labor-leader. It fell to the young Nelson Rockefeller, as executive vice president of Rockefeller Center and spokesman for the family, to write Rivera politely requesting that he "substitute the face of some unknown man where Lenin's face now appears." Rivera refused (partly on the urging of some of his assistants, who said that they would go out on strike). During the several silent days that followed, reporters were forbidden to photograph the mural. Then, on the morning of May 9, Rivera was called down from the scaffolding, handed a check for the remaining $14,000 of the $21,000 commission, and told to quit the premises. The building's security guards took over; a crew proceeded to screen the unfinished mural from view.

Rivera's dismissal became a cause célèbre, eliciting protests from both partisan and conservative artists and public figures. The Communist party, as Bertram Wolfe noted in the revised 1963 version of his Rivera biography, "was caught in no man's land. It did not want to defend nor praise Rivera, nor take the side of his millionaire patron, nor did it have any 'Marxist explanation' to offer. A revolutionary painter for millionaires, a millionaire patron of revolutionary painting, and a Communist party silent on the fight between them constituted a triple absurdity." Despite the pledge that the fresco would not be mutilated, only withheld from view "for an indefinite time," it was destroyed nine months later in February 1934, causing another furor.

Panel from New Workers School Mural, Diego Rivera, 1933

The Rivera mural sequence that Evans photographed in midsummer 1933 was titled *Portrait of America*. Rivera began painting it on July 15 at the New Workers' School, free of charge, purposely using up the Rockefeller money. Bertram Wolfe, the director of the school, was also Rivera's acknowledged collaborator on the involved schema of the mural. This time Rivera painted his ambitious project on moveable panels, particularly since the school was housed in rented and rundown quarters. Judging from Evans's diary, he began taking pictures on July 21 with a photographer friend, Jay Leyda, and developed them immediately. The negatives were underexposed but he found the pictures interesting. Presumably, he reshot them soon afterwards.

Though the mural was supposed to be based on American history, Rivera nonetheless resurrected Lenin and Marx and the Russian pantheon of Communist heroes, which included even Stalin, in a panel, *Proletarian Unity*. The title was particularly inappropriate since the painting included Stalin's arch enemy Leon Trotsky as well as several quarreling American Communists: William Z. Forster, representing the Stalinist faction; Jay Lovestone, the oppositionist leader; and James Cannon, the secretary of the American Trotskyites. It was a large concession on Rivera's part, since as recently as 1932, complaining publicly about the sorry state of Soviet art, he had placed the blame on "the international functionaries, petty leaders and intellectual lackeys of Sir Joseph Stalin." The most savage panels dealt with Mussolini and the ranting Adolf Hitler, beneath whom Rivera painted the battered figure of a Jew and beside him a woman with a shorn head, a placard hanging from her neck stating: "I have given myself to a Jew." Among the American themes, there were lethal caricatures of J. P. Morgan and the withered John D. Rockefeller, a background glimpse of a slave market, and, whether coincidental or not, a map of Cuba as a symbol of American exploitation. These were compensated for by admiring portraits of Jefferson and the patriot forces of the American Revolution. The Cuban reference may have had nothing to do with Evans's recent visit and his photographs. Certainly the Cuban situation was much in the news while Rivera was painting the mural. Evans took a second set of photos, which he considered successful, in early August and a third on August 7. A number of his detailed, graphic shots would be published in *Portrait of*

America with Wolfe's extended explication of the text of the New Worker's School mural and a personal account of the debacle of the RCA mural.

Rivera made it plain that he appreciated Evans's work, even suggested that the photographer come back to Mexico with them. On the seventh, when Evans visited the New Workers' School, the painter was with M. F. Agha and editor Frank Crowningshield of *Vanity Fair*. Rivera, rising to the occasion, Evans noted, "gave me a nice puff to them and they asked me to come up. I will but I don't expect much from that crowd." He was wrong; a sequence of his mural photographs appeared in *Vanity Fair*. It featured a panel depicting Benjamin Franklin, Thomas Paine, and a colonial tax collector being tarred and feathered, which Evans thought one of the weakest segments. He was paid fifty dollars. ("Thank the lord.")

Despite Rivera's favors, Evans was cautious in his feelings:

Curiously unemotional about him when I could be expected to get into a hero attitude toward him. Frida I suppose is much more the hero of the two. Talked about American women and [reached?] vehement agreement. I suppose much of my character is based on irrevocable revolt against them.

He seems to have had a particular target in mind: "Which reminds me," he added, "I wrote a note to my mother telling her I was all right."

IV

That summer Evans had been seeing a good deal of Jay Leyda, the energetic twenty-three-year-old photographer and filmmaker who had assisted him in photographing some of the Rivera murals. Evans in turn offered his darkroom facilities at Bethune Street and his help in making stills from Leyda's films. Leyda had at one time been a darkroom assistant for Ralph Steiner. He was as well a portrait photographer. (Julien Levy had included him in a 1932 group exhibition of portrait photography.) His portraits of creative people like the young Alfred Barr, Lincoln Kirstein, and Evans's difficult lady friend, the poet Kathleen Tankersley Young, tended to be studied, intense, artfully posed, and artfully lighted. He admitted to having "victimized" his sitters; his portraits, he said, were never candid. His dramatic portrait shot of Evans made him look like a moody actor auditioning for the role of Cyrano de Bergerac. Walker, he claimed, sat through the session very patiently. Later in his career Leyda would become curator for the Museum of Modern Art's film department, and later still a noted Herman Melville scholar who compiled *The Melville Log* (1951), one of the essential reference works in the Melville canon.

For Leyda the summer of 1933 was to be an eventful period in an eventful year: he had been accepted by the Moscow Film School to study with Sergei Eisenstein and was planning to leave for Russia in the early fall. His views were decidedly left wing and during one of their darkroom sessions Evans had been unexpectedly "pleased" to have the younger man talk to him "about background, revolution, communism, his subjection to the influence of Joe Freeman, disappointment in but respect for Steiner." There were occasions when Evans tried to "poison" Leyda's communism, "or at least he accuses me of trying." Evans enjoyed his company; he was convinced that Leyda was the only Communist he knew with a sense of humor. Out of generosity, Leyda arranged for Evans to meet Freeman, with the expectation that the editor might buy some of his photographs.

The dinner with Freeman at Leyda's apartment did not go well. Whether it was a matter of disaffected politics or ingrained prejudice or both, Evans disliked Freeman on sight:

I didn't like him. Never saw such atypical Jewishness of just the kind that bothers me. They poke at you. This one is fearful that way. He'll get nothing from me, in case he wants anything. Dinner there was altogether awful for other reasons: Freeman's wife; Jay's older woman protector, a Jewish liberal lawyer, militantly unattractive female, not minding being so. Hell with liberals, intellectuals, artists, communists. Human society is a failure.

Evans felt differently about a recent Jewish acquaintance, Irving Jacoby, a budding filmmaker who would later become a founder of Affiliated Films. On more than one occasion on hot summer evenings, Jacoby would drive Evans out into the country and they talked: "Talk of things for me to do with movie camera." Over the next few years, they thought up film projects which unfortunately did not materialize. One night, accompanied by Joseph Losey, another filmmaker, they drove to Ossining and back:

Full moon, Westchester, misty valleys. Losey was with us. All talked late after coming back here. Talk of Ernestine Evans and I was disloyal to her. Talk of ourselves and the times and this country. Liked Jacoby for some things said. He is very race-conscious.

There were besetting problems that summer. In mid-July Evans made a hurried visit to Bellevue Hospital to give blood for a friend, Harry Alan Potamkin, the film critic for *Hound & Horn.* Potamkin, thirty-three, was dying of leukemia. On July 19 Evans reported in his diary: "I was just able to go through with it, and must have strained myself considerably because I vomited in the middle of the proceeding and then lost control of my emotions and wept like a baby." It was one of his rarely confessed bursts of emotion. The hospital's good whiskey and his interest in the proceedings helped him through the ordeal. "Scared of course because P. was dying there next to me and looked it. He died a few minutes after I left the hospital." Afterwards Evans made his way to Leyda's apartment and had a good meal. "Felt all right physically, don't know how much blood lost."

Kirstein, abroad in London at the time of Potamkin's death, was distressed. He considered Potamkin, although a card-carrying Communist, "one of the good guys." He had taken a perverse pleasure in having hired him in the first place and claimed that Potamkin's "charm, his untamed outrage, raised hackles of my slumbering guilt," as far as proletarian issues were concerned. In his brief career at the magazine, Potamkin had written pioneering essays on such vanguard film directors as Réné Clair, Pabst, Pudovkin, and Eisenstein. Kirstein, on his return to the States, commiserated with Potamkin's widow, asking if there was anything he could do. She told him: "Yes, buy me a red silk dress and yourself a bright red tie; wear it for Harry."

A little more than two weeks later, through Leyda, Evans learned that Kathleen Tankersley Young had died in Mexico:

It sounds very much like a sort of suicide — her sort. And very depressing to imagine in some Mexican town. She was sick in all ways. I will always be sorry for my experiences with her.

The sudden reminders of mortality, along with his money troubles ("Got two dollars out of the bank."), may have had something to do with the physical complaints that began to trouble him: "My stomach is bad. I think often about ulcers, or why the strange sharp pain. Ulcers, inflamed prostate gland, whatnot. Makes me very tired of myself. I suppose I will see a doctor." He began drinking milk. A few days later he announced, "I have had a new pain in testicle dammit." He considered talking to the physician who was treating Frida Kahlo, Dr. David Glusker: "I will ask him what the devil is the matter with my insides." Finally, in late August, after consulting another doctor, he was relieved: "I am told there is nothing the matter with my lungs, no ulcerous stomach."

In early August the Cuban crisis was reaching its climax. Evans had received a letter from Jorge Fernández de Castro indicating that things were happening there to their mutual liking: "Asks me to send photos for an exchange arrangement Cuba-Russia, things as they are." Evans was frequenting the newsreel theaters and, occasionally accompanied by Shahn, reading up on events in the library: "I've rarely spent so much time reading the papers." A general strike on the island had thrown Havana into turmoil, and there was a gasoline shortage. Strikers threatened to burn every vehicle on the streets; people were strewing nails in the roads, throwing rocks at passing automobiles. Machado it was rumored was waiting for violence to break out between the police and the strikers so that he could place the island under martial law. Ambassador Sumner Welles's efforts at mediation between the government and the oppositionists, including the ABC terrorists, were effectively stalled.

Cuban news more and more exciting [Evans wrote in his diary]. Tonight it looks like intervention. Had the idea of getting someone to send me down to cover it with movies. But I am not ready to do that . . . Ten people were killed in one of these marches on the President's palace, so it may well have been one of the brothers Fernández de Castro. Jorge would certainly be standing by in that crowd. Hemingway no doubt has left for Spain.

Evans tried peddling his Cuba pictures around town with no success. At the *New York Times*, he met a woman who knew his work, but the results were the same: "No sales." Luckily, Oliver Jennings invited him out to Cold Spring Harbor for the weekend. Evans was glad to escape the struggles of Bethune Street. He claimed he wanted to see "if American society is still functioning. (Long Island Division.)" He concluded that it was. It was a dramatically different scene. Jennings had taken his guests to a dull country dinner party: "Delicious food and luxury," however. Hawaiian singers played off the porch during cocktails. There was one attractive woman—"our girl hostess." After dinner there was much talk about international politics, none of which he claimed to understand. Coincidentally, the former Mrs. Sumner Welles was one of the guests, but she could tell him nothing about Cuba. It was from the afternoon papers on August 12, that he got an "exciting account" of Machado's flight and the sacking of the presidential palace. Machado's plane to Miami, with his family and a few close officials aboard, had barely gotten off the runway ahead of the pursuing ABC revolutionaries. That night, Ruby Hart Phillips, watching from the top of a building on the Prado, saw the angry crowds gathering, heard scattered gunfire, and realized that the killing of Machado's *porristas* had already begun. "The terrible things which happened," she wrote later, "Civilization was stripped away in one stroke. Relatives of boys who had been tortured and killed started on vengeance hunts and they knew the men they were seeking." Some victims, trapped in buildings, were hurled out the nearest windows; the body of another, caught in front of the Capitolio, was completely unrecognizable when the mob had finished with him. Crowds stormed the presidential palace, carrying off weird assortments of booty; boys toted ferns and uprooted calla lilies from the presidential garden, offering them to strangers; a man pushed a water cooler along the street; a woman walked off with a pair of pillows, another with a stalk of bananas. Orestes Ferrara, whose offices at the *Heraldo de Cuba* had been thoroughly sacked, managed to escape with his wife on a Miami-bound seaplane, the pilot having left behind a group of American tourists whose luggage was stolen by the mob.

There was more than a hint of irony in Evans's final note on his Long Island weekend: "Report on American rich would be that they seem richer than ever." Back in New York, he had a welcome change of luck. Oliver Jennings wanted photographs from his South Seas expedition. Evans rushed the job, collecting $68, "undreamed of riches." The woman from the *Times* phoned for Cuban pictures: "If they use some, I'll be rich for a few days." He had a pointed argument with Shahn about the Cuban revolution: "Shahn of course thinks it is a social revolution for good of proletariat." Evans, with the wisdom of foresight, thought differently: "[It] was nothing of the kind. The proletariat gets nowhere from it. Good for more respectable bourgeoisie and intellectuals."

*Evans portrait
by Jay Leyda,
c. 1933*

The Politics of the Vernacular

"I'm interested in what's called vernacular," Evans claimed. ". . . finished, I mean educated, architecture doesn't interest me, but I love to find American vernacular." It was the largesse of Lincoln Kirstein who, early in the year, had donated some one hundred of Evans's nineteenth-century architecture photographs to the Museum of Modern Art that occasioned an exhibition of thirty-nine of them after Kirstein's return from Europe in the late summer. The exhibition, directed by Kirstein, was Evans's first at the Modern and it was held in the architecture room of the museum's new quarters at 11 West Fifty-third Street from November 16 to January 1, 1934. What is remarkable about the event is the persistence with which Kirstein promoted Evans's career in the early years of their relationship. (In later years, he would claim, "If I hadn't known him, he wouldn't have interested me.") What also is amazing is the alacrity with which exhibitions at the new Modern could be mounted. Kirstein's diary indicated that he first proposed the show to Alfred Barr at lunch on November 9, only a week before the exhibition opened. ("Talked about a show of Walker Evans's Victorian houses to be held . . . in conjunction with Hopper show.") It was possibly one of the longest-running exhibitions of Evans's career: It circulated to other museums until 1940 and was probably the exhibition that firmly established Evans in the public mind as a documentary photographer, not always to Evans's liking — and with some reason. He took a narrow, more subtle view of documentary photography than many of his critics recognized. He claimed, for instance, that the newsreel films that he went to once a week in the 1930s were documentary with a vengeance — and quite wonderful. But documents were not art: "Documentary? That's a very sophisticated and misleading word. And not very clear. You have to have a sophisticated ear to receive that word. The term should be *documentary style*." Something as vernacular as a police photograph of a murder scene, he maintained, could be considered a literal document: "You see, a document has use, whereas art is really useless. . . . I'm sometimes called a 'documentary photographer,' but that supposes quite a subtle knowledge of

Maine Pump,
1933

the distinction I've just made." He boasted, "A man operating under that definition could take a certain sly pleasure in the disguise. Very often I'm doing one thing when I'm thought to be doing another." But that subversive admission had further ambiguities. One of the transcripts of the tapes read: "And very often I'm doing one thing and I thought I was doing another"—a more mundane alternative. The term *documentary* had other implications Evans preferred to avoid: he suffered, he claimed, when "philistines" referred to his work as "nostalgic":

I hate that word. That's not the intent at all. To be nostalgic is to be sentimental. To be interested in what you see that is passing out of history, even if it's a trolley car you've found, that's not an act of nostalgia. You could read Proust as "nostalgia," but that's not what Proust had in mind at all.

Yet Lincoln Kirstein, in his introductory text for the exhibition, published in the *Museum of Modern Art Bulletin* of December 1933, made a strong case for the documentary importance of Evans's work:

Photography [Kirstein stated] is in essence a scientifically accurate process for the reproduction of objective appearances, a stationary magic that fixes a second from time's passage on a single plane. Its greatest service is documentary.

Wooden Gothic House Near Nyack, New York, 1931

He found that Evans's photographs were such "perfect documents" that their excellence was not "assertive" enough. He went on to note that the photographs were taken as illustrations for a "monumental" history of nineteenth-century American Federal and Victorian architecture "in its most imaginative and impermanent period. These wooden houses disintegrate, almost, between snaps of the lens. Many shown in these photographs no longer stand." Kirstein's text is important in other respects, partly because it gives us one of the early accounts of Evans in action. Shorn of the personal, sometimes biting, remarks of his diary notes, Kirstein's text rose to the public occasion:

Evans's style is based on moral virtues of patience, surgical accuracy and self-effacement. In order to force details into their firmest relief, he could only work in brilliant sunlight, and the sun had to be on the correct side of the streets. Often many trips to the same house were necessary to avoid shadows cast by trees or other houses; only the spring and fall were favorable seasons.

He gave a few of the humble details: that the search for examples had been conducted by automobile, that the equipment had been carried in the rumble seat, that the general itinerary of the sites included the New England states, metropolitan Boston, and upstate New York. He promised, sardonically, that "Detroit, Cleveland, Chicago, St. Louis and Philadelphia await the tender cruelty of Evans's camera. It is a painfully haphazard method limited by time, money, and insufficient information." Evans's progress, it would seem, was like that of an itinerant portrait painter in colonial days, scouring the landscape for possibilities and work.

The thirty-nine photos in the exhibition actually ranged architecturally from Gothic and Greek Revival specimens to ornate gingerbread cottages, and geographically from Columbia Heights in Brooklyn and Ocean Grove, New Jersey, to Kennebunk, Maine, as well as to the urban sites Kirstein had mentioned. A spic-and-span Kennebunk house with its sheltered pump stand is a marvel of Gothic traceries, finialed spires, elaborate fencework — a personal monument to extravagance and quixotic taste, thrust up against a main road like a sprawling architectural valentine. So, too, is the gabled façade of a wooden house near Nyack, with its lathework columns and

peaks, or the caretaker's gate house near Poughkeepsie. They are the American equivalents of English follies. Doorways and entrances intrigued Evans, but they also must have interested Kirstein, since they are among the choices he made. (He had no recollection of Evans's having helped him in making the selection.) Essentially the exhibition illustrated a dictionary of American taste carved in stone or crafted in wood.

Kirstein, in passing, paid tribute to the works of Edward Hopper, whose retrospective of some twenty-five oils, thirty-seven watercolors, and eleven prints ran concurrently with Evans's show for a period of two weeks. Kirstein's praise had a slight edge: "The focus [of Evans's photographs] was sharpened until so precise an image was achieved, that many of the houses seem to exist in an airless atmosphere, much as they exist in the airless nostalgia for the past to which Edward Hopper in his noble canvases pays a more personal tribute."

It may have been the first time, but certainly would not be the last, that a critic compared Evans's urban photographs to the chill reality of Hopper's work, with its stark architectural emphasis. Evans's pictures in the Modern's show gave little evidence of the human figure that Hopper, already a master, made a dramatic presence in the plate glass reality of his urban scenes. Critical distinctions can be high-wire performances based on narrow premises. But Kirstein had seen enough of Evans's New York photographic work and his comparison was apt. Where the city was concerned, Evans tended to insist on straightforwardness whereas Hopper could be brooding. But the urban scene provided them both with a stead-fast theme over the years. The two shared certain other career similarities: Paris had been important in the early years of their development, and they both appreciated literature.

Gothic Gate Cottage, Near Poughkeepsie, New York, 1931

It is worth recalling some of the views Hopper expressed in his "Notes on Painting," published in the catalogue for his show; Evans might well have shared them. Hopper was frank about the need to divorce American art from its French precedents. The period of American apprenticeship, he felt, had already been served: "Any further relation of such a character can only mean humiliation to us. After all we are not French and never can be and any attempt to be so is to deny our inheritance and to try to impose upon ourselves a character that can be nothing but a veneer upon the surface." It was not mere chauvinism; Hopper was prepared to view modernist art as a universal call for independence:

In its most limited sense, modern art would seem to concern itself only with the technical innovations of the period. In its larger and to me irrevocable sense it is the art of all time; of definite personalities, that remain forever modern by the fundamental truth that is in them. It makes Moliere at his greatest as new as Ibsen, or Giotto as modern as Cezanne.

In later years Evans discouraged any inference that Hopper had had a direct influence upon his photographic work: "This is a case of parallel," he claimed. "I didn't know Hopper or what he was doing. I was doing very similar things. It just happens. It's one of the wonders of the art world." But those were later disclaimers.

One gets a clearer view of Evans's work esthetic at the time from some sharp remarks about the work of another young photographer, Ansel Adams. Writing to Jay Leyda in Russia, Evans complained that the Adams show was "disappointing. His work is careful, studied, weak Strand, self-conscious, mostly utterly pointless. An abandoned steam roller, quite

beautiful, in the middle of a desert, titled 'Capitalism 1933.' Wood seasoned, rocks landscapes, filtered skies. All wrong." His own efforts were evidently more promising: "I have done some more interiors you would like, I think, I hope. What would happen if I sent photos to you I wonder. Tell me, please."

A tantalizing undated list of thirty-six early photographs "Sent to Russia with W. Goldwater" suggests that Evans, through the agency of Goldwater, the Greenwich Village bookseller who specialized in books about radical politics, may have taken part in a photographic exhibition in Russia in the early thirties. Goldwater, who had been to the USSR in the late twenties, was still a believer in Stalinist communism, though he would become a Trotskyite in short order. The listed items, since they ranged from the earliest 1927 photographs of the Lindbergh and Byrd parades in New York City to circa 1930 pictures of construction work on Bloomingdale's

department store, could well have constituted a kind of retrospective of Evans's earliest work. Some of them were important works, like the picture of the black woman in the cloche hat and fur-collared coat at the Forty-second Street entrance of the Sixth Avenue el (the same site where he photographed the stairs lettered Royal Baking Powder).

The list also included photographs of a Coney Island ferris wheel and a swarming group of bathers; sportsmen in knickers at the Danbury Fair in Connecticut; a black longshoreman standing in a [South Street] doorway; the Chrysler Building under construction; and two formal abstractions of Montreal grain elevators. The thirty-six photographs tend to suggest that Evans might have been slated for a more extensive exhibition within the group show.

Other evidence indicates that the impetus for the show — if it, in fact, took place — might have come from Jay Leyda and that it was promoted by the always energized Ernestine Evans, with the collaboration of the dealer Julien Levy. Ernestine Evans, who had met Leyda one evening while Walker was finishing work on his Cuban pictures, wrote Leyda on April 24, 1934: "Julien Levy has shown me your note saying an exhibit of photographs from America to Moscow would be desirable." She also had heard from her husband, Kenneth Durant, just returned from Russia, "that an exhibit that sets some standards for them is indeed desirable." With her brisk efficiency, she had already talked to the people at the American Russian Institute, recently reorganized after the Roosevelt administration's diplomatic recognition of Russia. She needed further details: "Levy says you spoke of the *Museum of Western Art*," and she asked that Leyda cable her to that effect. In her peremptory way she had already more or less organized the scheme for a four-part exhibition: "photographs by artists; photographs of astonishing technique; a few portraits; and a section of action and news photographs drawn from the files of anonymous agency stuff — this section to have a double aim . . . to show what news photographers can do; and to present the American social scene." It was her version of the vernacular. She was well aware that a request to do the show should probably come from some diplomatically correct source in the States to some official there: "Though my experience is that on either end there must be a Black man to put the heart in it. You would be just that there; and I, here."

Evans photographing Chrysler Building construction, 1929.

There was some urgency involved; Leyda would be closing his gallery in the following week, but would open it for a two-day show before the works were sent to Russia: "On receipt of your cable we shall go ahead if I can get the money for good mounting, and then when your letter comes we can add or subtract perhaps to conform to your advice."

II

Good news was balanced by the bad: Evans's illustrations for the Cuba book had been honored by the American Institute of Graphic Arts and the book had been selected as one of seventeen included in a traveling exhibition of illustrated books. The judges had included Agha, art critic Thomas Craven, and print expert Carl Zigrosser. "I'm sure it all means work for me," he wrote Jay Leyda, "if I only have a good idea and gumption, faith hope and charity." The bad news was that a prospect for a world cruise in which he, acting as the cameraman, and Irving Jacoby, serving as director, would film a travelogue under the aegis of Hendrik Van Loon, the popular historian and biographer (*Story of Mankind*, 1921, and *Van Loon's Geography*, 1932) had fallen through for lack of money. Evans still had hopes, however:

We (largely J. who has a good head for such things) pulled something out of the fire and I'm sure we're going to make pictures either in connection with Van Loon or somehow on our own. Really we were in a good spot with Van Loon — in a position to make pretty nearly anything and market it with his name. He himself of course is quite a fat-head, and a man out for his pocketbook, an opportunist. But not as bad as I thought he would be. . . .

The new plan would only pay expenses plus royalties for making a series of travelogues in America and Europe, "entirely as we see fit, call it Van Loon's Occident or whatever he likes." They needed a sufficient period of practice together, and Evans was hoping that Leyda would meet them in Europe and join the project.

At the moment, however, Evans had another assignment, taking publicity photographs at Hobe Sound, Florida, a resort developed by his wealthy Phillips Andover classmate Joseph Verner Reed. He was staying, in some luxury, at the Island Inn, he wrote Ernestine Evans in an unfinished letter written soon after his arrival. He had acquired a car and a 4 x 5

Graflex with a good lens, perhaps on the strength of the assignment. "I motored down [that was his elite version of driving] . . . Carolina & Georgia, a revelation. I have to do something about that too," he said. "Florida is ghastly and very pleasant where I am, away from the cheap part. One feels good, naturally, coming out of New York winter. This island a millionaire's paradise and I'd like to be a millionaire as you know. A few week's I'll get hopping too, to earn some money." Apparently he and Ernestine had argued before he left New York; his near poverty had made him testy. "I was in a bad temper," he wrote, "I'll answer your letter now that the climate is agreeable and the food served regularly."

Ernestine Evans, it appears, was pushing him to publish a book of his photographs, possibly with Lippincott, on the strength of his AIGA honors. What is important about his unfinished letter was that it provided him with an occasion to set forth a lively agenda for the future: "What do I want to do? Where did the conversations with the publishers end? I know now is the time for picture books." He had given some attention to the matter:

An American city is the best, Pittsburgh better than Washington. I know more about such a place. I would want to visit several besides Pittsburgh before deciding. Something perhaps smaller, Toledo, Ohio, maybe. Then I'm not sure a book of photos should be identified locally. American city is what I'm after. So I might use several, keeping things typical. The right things can be found in Pittsburgh, Toledo, Detroit (a lot in Detroit, I want to get in some dirty cracks, Detroit's full of chances), Chicago business stuff, probably nothing of New York, but Philadelphia suburbs are smug and endless.

The "dirty cracks" suggest she [Ernestine] was leaning these days toward some form of political statement. So too did his next item: "People, all classes, surrounded by bunches of the new down-and-out." It would later become a common criticism of Evans's career that when he later went to work for *Fortune* magazine, he had lost the natural touch of his earlier photographs. But in the agenda put together in his unfinished 1934 letter, one finds that he had already spelled out many of the subjects he would simply transfer to the portfolios that visually enlivened *Fortune* when, in 1945, he was formally given the post of staff photographer. The 1934 list spelled out further possibilities:

Billboard Painters,
Florida, 1934

Automobiles and the automobile landscape

Architecture, American urban taste, commerce, small scale, large scale, the city street atmosphere, the street smell, the hateful stuff, women's clubs, fake culture, bad education, religion in decay.

The movies.

Evidence of what the people of the city read, eat, see for amusement, do for relaxation and not get it.

Sex.

Advertising.

Sex, admittedly, would never have fit into the *Fortune* format. (Nor, in fact, does it crop up, and only with rare exceptions, in Evans's entire photographic oeuvre; he was plainly prudish about exploiting it.) Otherwise, much of the agenda would (and often did) provide themes for his later *Fortune* portfolios. His brush with the politics of the thirties added a certain acerbity to his work. There is a hint of it in the conclusion of his letter to Ernestine Evans: "You ought to see West Palm Beach and die," he wrote. "There is among other things a walkathon, if you know what that is, going on at present. Oh, the Florida whites! Even Negroes bad in Fla. Me, I play tennis and drink iced tea in grateful seclusion."

He was working with three cameras, the Leica, his 8 x 10 view camera and the 4 x 5 Speed Graphic, a press camera with a viewfinder and range finder, which could be used on a tripod or hand held. The photographs he took in Florida and en route down and back to New York were varied: Foy's Used Tire garage, the painted window sign for "Horice's Fish Market," rows of bleak workers' shacks in a rain-sodden compound. One of the most comic ventures, in Florida, was the photographic sequence of two men painting a huge billboard advertising a resort hotel, the painted version obliterating the real landscape. Evans's view of the joys of nature was often sardonic. In this fugue of the real in contrapuntal arrangement with the painted, the actual human figures cast their shadows into the fictional landscape; the lush stylized palm tree pops up behind the billboard; and the painted rooftops and the turret with its unflappable wooden flag rise up into a real sky. Judging from the progress of the painted sequence Evans

223

must have spent some time photographing the episode or else returned at various intervals to record the development. (On the seventh day did the painters rest?) It is pure Evans; a jeu d'esprit about the random contract between art and nature.

The sequence of photos of the *Interior of Negro Preacher's House* and the portraits of the preacher himself in a vest, natty tie, and gold watch chain, as well as those of other members of the family, also belong to the Florida session. The flowered lamp stand, the starched cloth on the mirrored dresser in the corner, and the ornate cloth hangings speak of refinements put up against the poverty of the living quarters, with its cracks in the wooden walls letting in the light and weather. It is another of those Evans interiors in which mirrors provide a picture within the picture.

Still, the Florida assignment was not exactly the happiest of occasions — so, at least, he informed Leyda: "I am in a lousy resort hotel living room surrounded by bridge players and golf conversation — fearful, and no place to write clearly." He was, he claimed, "fantastically mixed up as usual, politically, and have often wished you were around for a conversation on certain events and theories." By the time he returned to New York, late in March, the hoped for film project was a good deal dimmer for "the same old story, lack of money." He was almost broke, he noted, but there were a couple of jobs in sight.

One of the political events he may well have wanted to talk over with Leyda was the destruction of Rivera's Radio City mural, accomplished in secret over the Lincoln's Birthday holiday. John D. Rockefeller, Jr., had the work destroyed without informing his wife, Abby Aldrich Rockefeller, or his son, Nelson. Both had been active sponsors of the Rivera cause and young Nelson had had hopes of having the mural removed and installed — if it were feasible — at the Museum of Modern Art. The clandestine action created a stir in the New York cultural world, not that Evans was ever inclined to stand up and be counted with those who protested visibly or vocally. Leyda was of the opinion that Evans "was never active politically, as far as I know. He wouldn't do anything to commit himself to one party or the other, or to one cause. He had his own cause — maybe it was that of anonymous people — at heart." He had good reason to think as he did. Evans had complained bitterly in his November 1933 letter to Leyda that the Film and Photo League, decidedly left-wing in its membership, had used his name as a sponsor "after I had declined the honor with reasons. Very foolish of them to antagonize that way."

Oddly, Evans's published work that summer and fall had a political tinge. *Hound & Horn*, in its July/September issue, carried a two-page spread of his Cuba pictures (*Cuba Libre*); Evans's photographs had served the cause equally well both prerevolution and postrevolution. Strangest of all, in mid-July he was given an assignment to photograph a bustling Communist summer camp in Westchester County in New York. He accompanied Dwight Macdonald, a brash young Phillips Exeter/Yale graduate and staff writer for *Fortune* magazine, who was researching an article on the Communist party, and Geoffrey Hellman, a writer for *The New Yorker*. It was the first of Evans's assignments for *Fortune*, presumably the capitalist flagship of Henry Luce's publishing empire. But, oddly enough, Luce was nurturing a brood of such liberal and left-wing writers and editors as Ralph Ingersoll, who a few years later started up the left-liberal daily *PM*, and young turks like James Agee, Dwight Macdonald, and John McDonald, who joined Evans's expanding circle of politicized friends. Dwight Macdonald, already immersed in Marxism, would soon move into the Trotskyite, anti-Stalinist camp. (He and his wife-to-be, Nancy Rodman, took the party names James Joyce and Elsie Dinsmore!) As Macdonald remarked about the heady political scene: "Such whirligig changes, such conjunctions were typical of the period."

The junket to Camp Nitgedaiget ("not to worry" in Yiddish) took place on a Saturday in blistering heat. Macdonald, experiencing a bout of polit-ical claustrophobia, was revulsed by the thought of "bathing in a slightly dirty pool with other comrades and eating off slightly soiled plates with other comrades and applauding mass violin solos with the other comrades" (not the prescribed Marxist response toward the masses). He admitted to a "fundamental dislike of living as one of a herd" and the "love of living in each other's laps that you can observe any day at Coney Island." Writing to Nancy he complained that he was "disgusted by humanity whether Yiddish or Racquet Clubbish, when it presented itself as a squirming mass." By Sunday afternoon, he, Evans, and Hellman hastened to the Westchester Embassy Club, where they "bathed in a clean capitalist pool and drank a couple of Tom Collinses in capitalistic solitude." Whether intentionally or not, Evans was as fastidious as the *Fortune* staff writer. His photographs for Macdonald's "The Communist Party" article in the September issue seemed to reflect Macdonald's private views if not his published opinions. Having photographed the bourgeois hordes at play at Coney Island, Evans now cast a cold eye on the anticapitalist lemmings sunbathing on the lawns of Camp Nitgedaiget.

Jane

When, early in 1935, the thirty-one-year-old Walker Evans headed south, escaping the winter once again, he had no idea that it would involve an important change in his life. He had a promising commission from Gifford Cochran, a wealthy carpet manufacturer. Young, dapper, balding, Cochran was also a part-time theatrical entrepreneur and co-producer of the 1933 film version of O'Neill's *The Emperor Jones*, starring Paul Robeson. Evans may well have first met Cochran when he was being considered for taking still photographs of the production. (His more fashionable rival, Edward Steichen, however, shot the moody and dramatic photo of Robeson that appeared in *Vanity Fair*.) Cochran wanted Evans to take photographs of antebellum architecture in New Orleans and the South for a proposed book. (Evans's friend, architect Charles Fuller, mockingly referred to it as "Cochran's American Vitruvius.")

This time, Evans traveled south in style in Cochran's chauffeured sedan. On February 4, he made an initial entry in his diary: "First day, Savannah." It was his trial run, in a sense, for the more productive weeks he would spend in and around New Orleans. On that Monday he made several test exposures using a green filter that he considered successful, photographing three or four houses, ending with the Hermitage Plantation and its tidy brick slave quarters, a kind of doll village that masked the life of economic bondage within. The next day he took some two dozen exposures with his 8 x 10 view camera, which, given the required preparation and setup time, must have made him a noticeable feature on the scene himself. In the afternoon while Cochran "researched," fruitlessly hunting for fine specimens, the chauffeur, James, drove Evans to the marketplace and the Negro quarter, where he took some "good" photographs, using the 8 x 10 view camera and the 4 x 5 Speed Graphic. Most of the shots, including a few 35-mm frames, show a juncture of two bleak avenues with ramshackle row houses and a few occupants sitting on the stoops.

In Evans's photographs, roads end elsewhere and distant horizons only restate the obvious: that there is always something beyond the chosen point

Jane Smith Ninas, Bourbon Street, New Orleans, 1935

of view. *Savannah Negro Quarter, 1935* may at first have been one of the test exposures; it lacks the clarity and emphasis that mark most of Evans's work and the distance in the foreground is unusually deep for him. But the fact that he shot the subject both with his cumbersome 8 x 10 setup and with his Leica suggests he saw something there of enduring interest. Throughout his southern junkets in 1935 and 1936, he would make it a point of photographing the life of the black quarters in the cities he visited. He thought well enough of the subject to use a shot, more dramatically cropped, in his major exhibition, "American Photographs," three years later. His brisk diary note for the day also indicates that, using his Speed Graphic, he found much that was worthwhile in the market area — clothing shops and waterfront buildings — exposing one and a half packs of film. That night he and Cochran and the chauffeur visited a waterfront joint and talked to the girls there. Evans found it "depressing, unappetising." Then, on his own on the sixth, he had an "extremely active morning," after which the little caravan drove on to Atlanta. His Savannah pictures included houses with grillwork balconies or Tudor detail, one of them with a masonic emblem, churches, the Telford Academy.

Savannah Negro Quarter, 1935

In New Orleans, Cochran had rented a furnished apartment in the Upper Pontalba Building in the French Quarter on the uptown side of Jackson Square. He hired a black cook who also did the housecleaning. There is no indication of where Evans stayed for the first several days, but his luck was good. Within the week Cochran had to return to New York, leaving the apartment to Evans and putting the car at his disposal.

The more important bit of good luck was that at a lunch with Charles Bein, the director of the New Orleans Arts and Crafts Club, Evans met an attractive young woman, Jane Smith Ninas, and her husband, Paul Ninas, one of the instructors at the Arts and Crafts Club. Dark-haired, sultry-eyed, Jane was an up-and-coming artist of the quarter. She and her husband lived on Bourbon Street. She had a penchant for sketching the batture architecture of the levees and Negro shacks at Gretna in a carefully deliberated style. She exhibited regularly in the Arts and Crafts Club exhibitions and in 1934 had won a prize in one of their shows.

Jane Ninas was acquainted with the work of the modernists, admired Matisse and Picasso both, as well as Bonnard and Van Gogh. She was born (1913) in Fond du Lac, Wisconsin, where her father ran the Bijou and the

Orpheum, two of the local movie theaters. He was a man with artistic interests who subscribed to art magazines but whose ambitions along those lines were never fulfilled. He did, however, become a skilled draftsman. It was her father who had encouraged Jane's interest in art. She had come to New Orleans in 1929, studying for four years at Sophie Newcomb College, the women's college of Tulane. At Newcomb, she remembers, she learned much about design and color, but it was later and from Paul, whom she had met through a sculptor-friend, that she learned a good deal more about the art of painting. Paul Ninas was a prominent New Orleans artist with a solid reputation, having studied abroad, in Vienna and elsewhere. His mother was American; his father, Russian in origin, had taught engineering at the Roberts Academy, an American school in Constantinople.

Ninas and Jane were married in 1933: she twenty, Ninas ten years older. But by the time Evans appeared on the scene, the marriage had already suffered some erosion. Ninas, a man of the quarter, by then had a mistress, Christine Fairchild, an acquaintance and supposed friend of Jane's. An architect with the WPA, Christine had studied at Columbia University (where she had struck up a still on-going relationship with a young

German, Freedie von Helms). Her family were natives of New Orleans and she was then working on the restoration of the Lower Pontalba Building in Jackson Square. Despite the obvious complications, the ménage à trois between Paul and Christine and Jane had reached a stage of silent accommodation that was to become more complicated with Walker Evans's arrival.

Evans was clearly struck by Jane. She was very attractive, bright, open-minded. Whether it was her looks, the penetrating gaze of her blue eyes, her interest in art, or a certain impulsiveness that screened a deeper timidity, or some momentary clue about her situation with her husband, Evans appeared decidedly interested. Despite childhood bouts of anxiety that bordered on agoraphobia, she had overcome such problems sufficiently to move out of Fond du Lac and begin her career. None of that, however, was evident on her first meeting with Evans. Her recollections of that lunch meeting are not expansive. What she remembers was Walker's "extraordinary charm." "He was very witty," she said, "That was one of the things that drew me to him, that he was such fun when I first met him."

Evans, born to the manner, was quick to entertain the Ninases, inviting them to a dinner in Cochran's rented apartment. He even suggested that Ninas and Jane accompany him on one of his photographic expeditions along the river road. But on that first offer, Paul was too busy with his regular classes. Jane went alone; there was never an occasion when Paul went with them. On their first trip, Cochran's cook prepared a picnic lunch for them. In a "typical Walker gesture," Jane remembered, Evans brought along copies of *Harper's Bazaar* and *Vogue*, worried that she might be bored while he worked. For the next several weeks, during February and March, it became routine, in good weather, for the pair to drive out together along the river road toward Baton Rouge. Walker, arriving in Cochran's car, would pick her up at the Bourbon Street apartment. In the evenings, there were a number of occasions when Evans joined Jane, Paul, and Christine for nights of dancing on the *Capitol*, one of the Mississippi riverboats. The arrangement, apparently, suited all four.

Occasionally Evans drove out along the levees, sometimes alone, sometimes with Jane. Evans photographed the blacks walking, relaxing on the banks to the sounds of a guitarist. Young blacks, in their white shirts and Sunday neckties, congregating at worn meeting spots in the rise, groups of

*Levee scene,
Vicinity
New Orleans,
1935*

232

children on the banks clustered together, curious about being captured by the camera eye. He photographed the sights along the road, sometimes from the car: the black quarters and the Godchaux sugar plantation in Reserve, the largest of the sugar producers and refiners in the United States at the time; groups of blacks in their Sunday clothes, passing, with a stare, along the roads; distant men on horseback, silhouetted against the sky, herding a few lean cows. The Leica shots, most of them, gave him an opportunity to photograph people in motion, as opposed to the fixed photos of his more cumbersome view camera. With the 4 x 5 Speed Graphic he stopped to photograph Ormond, an eighteenth-century "raised cottage" plantation house near Destrehan and, spanning the centuries, a prize example of steamboat Gothic, San Francisco, in the lumber town of Garyville.

Further upriver he and Jane toured the decaying yet still elegant remains of plantation architecture. Evans found the subject of the Belle Grove mansion at White Castle worthy enough to make two or more expeditions. On one of those trips, Christine accompanied the couple. Walker photographed the two women, laughing, looking down at him from the balcony. Built in 1857 by the New Orleans architect James Gallier, Jr., it was one of the most elaborate and luxuriant examples of Greek Revival: the

two-story main structure of brick covered with pink stucco, the soaring Corinthian columns of the entrance topped by elaborately carved cypress capitals. He photographed the exterior in a series of several long shots, emphasizing the building as a monument in a broad plain, a relic of past glory surrendering to inexorable ruin. Even after the Civil War, it had had a second burst of reclame when it was acquired by the Ware family, who entertained lavishly, even maintaining a private racetrack. In a rare interior shot, Evans photographed the abandoned drawing room with its shuttered light and moldering Corinthian columns and pilasters. (It has come down to posterity with his mislabeling as the *Breakfast Room*.) Touting up the plantation for a later photographic proposal, he described Belle Grove as "the most sophisticated example of [a] classic revival private dwelling in the country."

Most of his plantation photographs, perhaps because the buildings were still occupied or because the interiors were in shambles, were exterior shots. Near Convent, there was the Uncle Sam plantation taken as the light etched out the colonnades, a rescue of time, since it was demolished in 1940 to make way for a levee. When Evans photographed it and its surrounding porch of twenty-eight Doric columns and its flanking *garconnières* and *pigeonniers*, it was still one of the few remaining complete old plantation groups in the state. The Belle Hélène plantation house (formerly called Ashland) in Geismar was in incipient decay but still occupied by the remnants of the once-prominent du Plessix family. The chicken coop and hen yard unceremoniously abutting the house proper indicated how low the family fortunes had fallen. A more commanding and unasked for metaphor was the huge dead tree that had fallen, uprooted, in front of the once-grand but rotting colonnade — the ruin of a gone society. Jane sometimes sketched while Evans photographed. It was her impression that Walker knew in advance the subject he wanted to photograph; she was not familiar with some of the plantations they visited.

When not photographing antebellum plantations, she and Evans walked the streets of the quarter, Evans sighting subjects he would later photograph. The much published photograph of the woman in the doorway of the French Opera Barber Shop — *Sidewalk and Shopfront, New Orleans, 1935* — with the bold antic zebra stripes of the storefront and the sinuous stripes on the blouse of the woman standing in the doorway, was just such a picture. It is a glimpse of the realities of commercial life: "Ladies Neck Trim 15 cents;" "Home of Perfecto Hair Restorer." It represents a pocket of resistance to more conventional good taste, a kind of manic display of barber pole striping down to the light globe above the doorway — an antic moment; a celebration of an unexpected convergence.

What, after all, were the chances of a photographer at just the right moment finding a woman in a striped blouse standing in the stripe-framed doorway? The four or five exposures Evans took indicate that he had had to set up the tripod to take the shot and then, perhaps, was surprised to see the woman emerge. The sequence seems to indicate that he had taken the first shot just as there was a blur of activity within the shadowy doorway, as the woman was about to emerge from the dark interior. Then, seemingly,

The Breakfast Room, Belle Grove Plantation, 1935

he asked her to pose. The variations of the woman's expressions, from quizzicality to amusement, as well as the expressions of the shadowy barber seated in the barber chair, which barely show in the published (and variously cropped) final prints, support that probability. Had there been only the one shot, it might have been a moment of pure art (which is perhaps the way Evans preferred to exhibit it). But the irrepressibility of the life that yields the art is revealed in the sequence.

There is more to the photograph, however, than the dramatic convergence of stripes; the vital reality of the plump woman with the feather in her cap (even with her plucked eyebrows) offers an invidious comparison with the bland unreality of the woman of allure in the placard advertising lemon cleansing cream in the drugstore window next door. In any full-fledged Evans photograph, stories run in several directions. Narrative, caught in the fixed moment (like Zeno's arrow), was one of Evans's principal talents. His eye gathered in the composition of things as they are. His was an art of juxtaposition, visual wit, droll happenstance. Jane remembered him, during the first New Orleans visit, as being tremendously excited by what he was doing.

Among the street photographs, there is one of her in a flouncy-collared blouse posed arm-akimbo near a pair of automobiles. If Evans had wanted to emphasize her beauty, he might have photographed her in a garden or against a sunlit wall or, perhaps, à la Edward Weston, nude on a sand dune, her sleek skin contrasted with every wind-ripple of the dune. But Evans preferred to photograph her in context, in actuality, not as an artifact. He took her in the street, against uncompromising aspects of modern life; in the actual location in which he found her, or, for the moment, preferred to take her. At times, in his photographic excursions, he even used Jane as a decoy, employing a right-angle view finder to capture the real subject while giving the appearance of taking a shot of Jane straight ahead. It was not the only time he would resort to deviousness to get the picture he wanted.

Evans's street scenes during his first New Orleans trip — pictures of a young black girl of the quarter, for instance, taken in sequence with a Leica — have the vitality that characterized his best work. But for all the fame of New Orleans architecture — the lacework cast-iron balconies, the changing variations of pattern — the strictly architectural photographs have a monotonous static character not found in his dramatic plantation

Sidewalk and Shopfront, New Orleans, 1935

shots. Generally it is the street life that comes alive: women and men, mostly black, on balconies, following the photographer's progress as he proceeded down the mean streets, past tattered advertisements — a sight different from the equally poverty-stricken Cubans he had photographed against the elegant façades of Havana buildings two years before.

During this phase of the excursions that Evans and Jane were taking, Paul Ninas seemed not to be noticeably suspicious or even jealous about the growing relationship between his wife and the photographer. Jane felt that was due to the fact that Paul was too caught up in his affair with Christine to be concerned. But it was clear the relationship was becoming serious. Both she and Evans were aware of it. One night after an evening of dancing, Paul took Christine home and Evans walked Jane to her Bourbon Street apartment. "Suddenly," so she remembered, "Walker pushed me up against a fence and kissed me." The whole tenor of the relationship had led her to expect it, and they both took it as natural. Walker, she recognized, was flirtatious with women, but after that, when they were together, he flirted with her "more wildly and openly." They began to find reasons for saying they were going here or there but wanting to be alone together. Even so, neither of them was prepared to take the final step; they did not sleep together. "I didn't go to bed with him," she says. But moldering and romantic plantations were no longer the most pressing engagements on their minds. One or two days before his departure, Evans tried to make an appointment to photograph Oak Alley, one of the most historic and still elegantly maintained plantations in Louisiana. Jane, unable to recall the reason that the expedition to Vacherie failed, remembered that they just as happily spent the afternoon together in Walker's apartment.

When Evans left at noon on March 23, she knew she was going to miss him. They wrote one another, she recalled, and Walker began sending her little gifts: a copy of Thomas Wolfe's *Look Homeward, Angel*, drawing pads, a pair of beautiful silver buttons he found in a New York shop — none of which, she recognized with some dismay, bothered Paul to any degree.

According to his diary, Evans arrived at the Auld Lang Syne plantation in South Carolina late on the evening of March 25, a long trip for such a brief time (little more than a day and a half). It did not allow much time for extensive photographing. There he was the guest of Julia Peterkin, a writer of some national renown at the time, author of *Scarlet Sister Mary* and *Roll, Jordan, Roll* and whose most recent book, *A Plantation Christmas* (1934), extolled the virtues of the old traditions: black house servants "bestirring themselves industriously in order to have every piece of glass and silver bright and shining" for the holidays; pantry shelves stocked with rows of jars filled with jellies and jams and preserves of figs, peaches, apples, and watermelon rinds. Peterkin noted the happy laughter and singing of the cotton pickers in the fields "as they pick the last scattering white locks out of belated bolls for every extra pound of cotton means extra coins for Christmas." In one of her poetic passages Peterkin described the old houses in the Negro quarter "weathered by long years of rain and wind and sunshine into a soft gray, but underneath this gentle color their yellow wood stands as solid and steadfast as it was a hundred years ago." Evans appears not to have taken pictures of the black quarters at Auld Lang Syne. He had already seen too many of the mean streets of Savannah and the forlorn shacks along the Mississippi levees. On the morning after his arrival, Evans drove Peterkin to Columbia and back. The stay at Auld Lang Syne was a stopover he would make on other later trips to the South. Leaving the plantation early on the morning of the twenty-sixth, he stopped overnight in Virginia. The following evening at 5:30 he arrived at his Bethune Street apartment. Full of news about his activities, he had dinner that night with Gifford Cochran.

Evans's return was none too soon; an exhibition scheduled at the Julien Levy Gallery was due to open within a month — on April 23 — and there were the films from his southern trip to process. On April 7, after a long day of developing negatives and prints, he was fairly well pleased: "[F]ive dozen or so finished, very successful, very exciting, some very good, some shocking errors. Tend to overexpose, tend to raise lensboard too much, leaving top corner-rings." No checklist for the exhibition survives among Evans's papers and he left no notes on the forty prints that the gallery dealer had requested. It is not clear how many of his southern prints may have been included in the show. It was an exhibition with distinguished company: the French photographer Henri Cartier-Bresson, and the Mexican Manuel Alvarez-Bravo, both of the photographers in the new mode.

By the early thirties, Cartier-Bresson had already established his inimitable documentary style — direct and graphic, mixed with a certain French intellectual élan. The images he created (though not necessarily those shown in the 1935 Levy exhibition) would become icons both of his work and of the years between the two wars. Younger than Evans (he was born in 1908) his first ambition had been to become a painter. Like Evans he had come to photography as a second choice around 1930. He was already a shrewd observer of the Parisian scene, and had traveled much in Europe. His 1933 work in Spain — children playing games in a partly demolished building, a blind boy feeling his way along a wall — were eerie precursors of the civil war that ravaged the country three years later. Cartier-Bresson had had some notable exhibitions: in 1933 at the Atheneo Club in Madrid and in 1934 with Alvarez-Bravo at the Palacio de Bellas Artes in Mexico City. Evans, quite possibly, had seen his earlier exhibition at the Levy Gallery in the fall of 1933 and made some estimation of the Frenchman's work. The tagwords for the new exhibition, "Documentary & Antigraphic," seem to have caused some concern for the unnamed critic (probably Henry McBride?) for the *New York Sun* who defined Cartier-Bresson and Alvarez-Bravo as "anti-graphic." The term had been coined by another critic, Peter Lloyd (actually a pseudonym for gallery-owner Julien Levy himself), who praised the new photography as "a moral photography, equivocal, ambivalent, antiplastic, accidental photography. Call it anti-graphic photography." The *Sun*'s critic deferred to Lloyd's definition: "If you must have a word for Cartier-Bresson's work, that will do as well as another, I suppose." He found the Cartier-Bresson photographs "distinguished," work of "the greatest legibility and precision. It is all done in a flash and abounds in happy accidents, although this time 'accident' really isn't the word. Acceptable accidents only happen to artists and M. Cartier-Bresson is a very gifted artist."

By contrast the works of Alvarez-Bravo were not discussed at all. Evans fared better. Among New York critics, he had come into his style; his previous exhibitions of urban views, nineteenth-century architecture, and the excursion into sociology of his Cuban photographs had gained him a reputation. The *Sun*'s critic described his photographs as "documents" that were beginning to become well-known, adding that "the better they are known the better they are liked." It is clear that Evans had exhibited some photographs from his Savannah to New Orleans trip. "The present series of Southern façades with iron-grilled balconies," the critic concluded, "are among his most enchanting."

Evans had been delayed in printing up some of the southern photographs by a sudden offer from Alfred Barr, who wanted archival photographic prints made of a stunning exhibition of African art that was running currently at the Modern. Arguably the most important exhibition of primitive art to be mounted in New York in the thirties, it included some four hundred and fifty works of sculpture, textiles, ritual objects, and utensils drawn from museums, galleries, and private collections, with significant examples loaned by Dadaist Tristan Tzara, art critic Roger Fry, and painter André Derain. The project entailed a good deal of work; photographing the items alone involved tricky lighting problems and the use of filters to impart proper color values to the painted African masks. "Enormous undertaking for me at this time," Evans noted, "but would clear $1,000." He told Thomas Mabry, Barr's new assistant, that he would do it for two dollars a negative, and fifteen cents a print but would need to delay delivery. Evans had met Mabry, a close friend of Lincoln Kirstein, when he was assistant director of the John Becker Gallery. He was less comfortable with Alfred Barr. "Barr so nice and so confused," Evans confided to his diary. "Quite a *useless* man, I'd say; though a sweet one." The director and assistant director had different ideas about what exactly was to be done. "Tom knows what he's doing," Evans conceded, but he had a feeling that their relationship had entered a new phase. Mabry was "[a] little mysterious to me; he seems to have changed a lot — or I have. Both have." Nonetheless, the two men, in time, became life-long friends.

The project involved more than the taking of the negatives. The museum planned to issue some seventeen portfolios of five hundred mounted prints each as study archives. The Modern's highly energized publicity department promptly announced the project, noting that seven sets were to be distributed to Negro colleges and one to the Harlem branch of the New York Public Library. The remaining sets were to be sold to museums and colleges at a nominal fee. The March-April *Museum Bulletin* carried a similar announcement: "The museum has been fortunate in securing the services of the distinguished photographer, Walker Evans, whose series of photographs of nineteenth-century American houses is in the museum's permanent collection." The news coverage in the *Times* and elsewhere pretty much repeated the wording of the press release and the *Bulletin*; it was another step forward in Evans's reputation.

The assignment could not have come at a better time; Gifford Cochran gave every evidence of abandoning his book project, although he at one point appeared delighted with the negatives. Charles Fuller was urging him to state his position and put up lots of cash. At lunch on the eighteenth with Cochran and Evans, Fuller pushed for two thousand dollars over a five-year period — unsuccessfully. Evans noted in his diary: "C[ochran] wriggled lamely. Detestable . . . G annoyed all around, especially that I didn't bring any prints." There were other worries. Sylvia Bernice Baumgarten of the Brandt and Brandt Agency had had no luck with his work: "Apparently all the first-rate publishers she has approached with my photos have turned her down." He seems to have had a momentary falling out with Ernestine Evans that was related to the matter; he told Miss Baumgarten that he "didn't want Ernestine Evans ever to have anything to do with my affairs." Nor were these the only problems he had at that moment. He was suffering with a toothache and paid a visit to the dentist to have the tooth extracted. There was a night of heavy drinking which left him with a hangover that cut into the work he was able to do the following morning. It was understandable, then, that his diary carried the following notation: "Feeling of life disappearing at high speed up a blank alley."

Despite all that, the new commission proved useful. It drew him into the Modern's high-powered if disorganized operation. He lunched with Barr and James Johnson Sweeney, the organizer of the African Negro Art exhibition, and met the architects Philip Johnson and Alan Blackburn, both former staff members of the museum, who had only recently resigned to take up a political crusade. Johnson had been instrumental in organizing two ground-breaking exhibitions at the museum: Modern Architecture: International Exhibition (1932) and Machine Art (1934). Impressed by Hitler's political success, however, he and Blackburn had decided to throw their support behind the Louisiana politician and demagogue Huey Long — without much encouragement from Long himself. One afternoon at the museum, Johnson and Blackburn demonstrated what Evans perceived to be "a photo taking arrangement they've gotten up to sell Huey Long."

Evans was less than impressed: "They're both mad, madder than Long by a long shot, and with less ability. Johnson expects to have dictatorial power one day."

Needless to say, Evans was more taken with Dorothy Miller, a recently hired hard-working and attractive assistant, whose job it was to work with him on photographing the African sculpture in the evenings after the museum was closed. Evans kept a separate, very detailed notebook on the filters used, the timing of the shots, the background cloths, the numbered items, and whether the objects were the same size as the photos. After a few days of testing and experimenting, he seems to have begun shooting in earnest on April 24, the day after his exhibition at the Julien Levy gallery opened. His diary note for April 19, though written later, was accurate: "From here to Memorial Day entirely occupied with museum job, working with Dorothy Miller."

Jane Ninas,
Belle Grove
Plantation,
1935

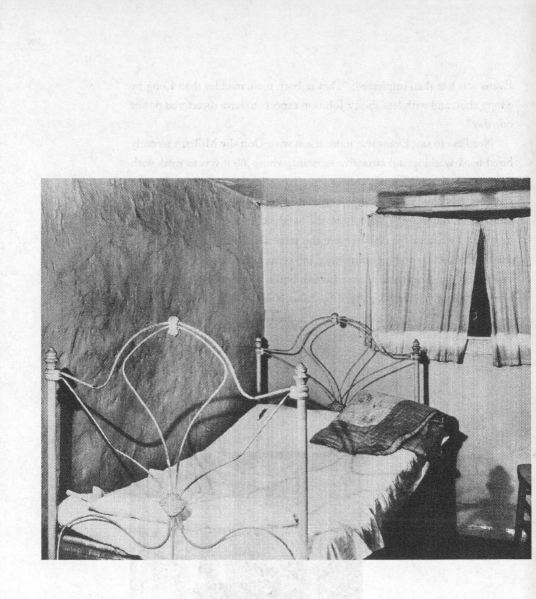

Love in the Thirties

12

In New York, Evans was once more caught up in the widening circle of friends and interrelated projects that helped shape his career. In his brief stop at Savannah, for instance, he had made a point of sending notes to several of the friends: "Postcards to Morrie, Cheever, Ben, J.C.E., B., Irving." The J. C. E. was not a friend but his mother Jessie Crane Evans, whom he habitually referred to in initial terms. The others included Ben Shahn and M. R. ("Morrie") Werner, a biographer and historian whose dark-haired wife, Hazel, a fiction writer, Evans photographed around this time. The Werners, originally from Boston, were dedicated liberals and occasional contributors to Lincoln Kirstein's *Hound & Horn*. Cheever was John Cheever, a protégé of the Werners', a struggling twenty-two-year-old writer, eking out a bare subsistence in New York reviewing books for the liberal/left-wing *New Republic*. Cheever's story "Bock Beer and Bermuda Onions" had appeared in the April-June 1932 issue of *Hound & Horn*, along with a story by Hazel Hawthorne Werner. Kirstein at that time had taken the two writers to a notable lunch in Boston at which Cheever, nervous about his first meeting with the editor, fortified himself with some heavy drinking in the morning. At lunch, he made a point of arguing with Kirstein when the conversation turned on the subject of Henry James.

It was during the early period of Cheever's friendship with Evans, presumably when Evans was living and working at one of the Bethune Street addresses, that Cheever's homosexual seduction by Walker Evans took place — if, in fact, it ever did take place. Cheever's story of a one-night stand is revealed in a letter written years later when Cheever was fifty-one and out of the closet far enough for certain friends and younger men to be aware of his propensity. The episode, as vividly described as one of Cheever's gloomy urban tales, is sardonic, briskly paced, and full of seemingly authoritative detail:

When I was twenty-one Walker Evans invited me to spend the night at his apartment. I said yes. I dropped my   clothes (Brooks). He hung his (also

Hudson Street Boarding House Detail, New York, 1931

(John Cheever's room)

Brooks) neatly in a closet. When I asked how to do it he seemed rather put off. He had an enormous cock that showed only the most fleeting signs of life. I was ravening. I came all over the sheets, the Le Corbusier chair, the Matisse lithograph and hit him under the chin. I gave up around three, dressed and spent the rest of the night on a park bench near the river. In the morning I drove to Massachusetts, embraced my dear brother and swam in the sea.

The Brooks Brothers clothes tidily hung in the closet and the Corbusier chair seem right. There are Evans photos of a neatly arranged closet in one of his apartments that attest to his fastidiousness when it came to clothes. Others show a modern Corbusier-type chair. The Matisse lithograph is doubtful; at least there are no mentions of it in letters or diaries and it does not show in photos of Evans's various apartments.

Beatrice Jacoby,
c. 1935

There are those, mostly women friends, who doubt the authenticity of Cheever's late report. Purportedly it would have taken place after Cheever had made his decisive move to New York in the late summer of 1934 after a two-month stay at Yaddo, the writer's and artist's colony in Saratoga Springs. He was then living on little more than a ten-dollar weekly allowance from his "dear brother" in Boston and paying three dollars a week for the miserable room in a Hudson Street boarding house that Evans photographed — dingy iron bedstead, sagging mattress, the dirty folded quilt, and a drawn dark shade on the one small window that suffused the light. On the scruffy dresser, a book, matchbook, and folded spectacles give witness of an occupant. It was in that dingy room, at five dollars a book, that Cheever read and made synopses of novels for M-G-M for possible movies. The other tenants were mostly out-of-work longshoremen or cooks. Whores used the downstairs toilet as a professional convenience. Although traditionally dated 1931, Evans's photograph — one of the bleakest of the bedroom characterizations that continued to intrigue him — was more than likely taken in 1934 or early 1935. Cheever was convinced that Evans took the picture "because he couldn't believe that anyone could live in such a miserable place."

The Irving of Evans's diary was Irving Jacoby while the B. undoubtedly was Jacoby's sister Beatrice whom Evans was courting, or at least trying to romance. Beatrice was young (she graduated from Hunter College in 1933), dark-haired, and attractive. Evans courted her in late night drives, sitting and holding hands, or took her to hear Count Basie at the Savoy in

Harlem. It was so crowded, Beatrice recalled, she had to be lifted off the floor to sit on a railing, her feet dangling. In the early stages of the romance, Walker invited her to his Bethune Street apartment where he cooked dinner. Although he was poor at the time, when he did take her out to dinner it was usually to someplace elegant. Evans had introduced her to Ernestine Evans, Jay Leyda, and Dorothy Miller, and apparently thought about her seriously enough to take her to Ossining to meet his sister Jane Brewer, possibly in 1933, while the Brewers' son, Tad, was still an infant. The romance, however, never became sexual.

Beatrice Jacoby's most detailed memory is of a trip she and Evans made to Copake, New York, around the Christmas season on a visit to the Nadelberg family. (Her brother, Irving, was dating the Nadelberg's daughter, Rose.) Although she knew nothing about cooking, Beatrice got up early one morning and made oatmeal, putting a huge amount of salt in the pot. The others laughed at her, but Walker had been calm and kind about it. The photographs that Evans made of the interiors of the Copake house are among his finest. The distilled light of the several bedrooms, the dark-stained furniture, the ornate wallpaper borders, the Jacquard bedspreads and the patchwork quilts, the oil lamps gathered on a table speak, even in the early 1930s when the photographs were taken, of a time past, placed somewhere in mid-nineteenth-century America. Above all the silence, the absence of living beings fixes a mood. A passage from Walt Whitman, which Evans would use as an epigraph for his career in the catalogue for his 1971 retrospective at the Museum of Modern Art, states the case equally well for the eloquence of Evans's Copake interiors:

I do not doubt but the majesty & beauty of the work are
    latent in any iota of the world...
I do not doubt there is far more in trivialities,
    insects, vulgar persons, slaves, dwarfs, weeds,
    rejected refuse, than I have supposed....
I do not doubt interiors have their interiors, and
    exteriors have their exteriors...

*   *   *

Evans's Savannah postcards to his friends were not a mere tourist obligation. By the mid-thirties at least (and quite probably earlier) he had developed a collector's passion for vintage, five-for-a-nickel postcards from what he specified as the McKinley to the Taft period. With Evans, as with any major artist, seemingly minor interests may stretch out into a larger context. His passion for postcards (not too dramatic a way of characterizing it) continued throughout his lifetime. Over the years his collection would amount to some nine thousand, most of them filed and kept in shoe boxes. The collection favored pictures of main streets, east and west, from Norwich, Connecticut, to Hicksville, Ohio. But he also collected such exotica as pictures of a woman from the Ouled Nail tribe; Flemish lacemakers; a Normandy wedding party; an Indian from Tierra del Fuego; actresses from the English stage; French authors Theodore de Bainville, Edmond About, Dumas Fils, and others (par Nadar); "The only authentic photograph of His Majesty King George V in coronation robes"; the Prince of Wales in his Knight of the Garter investiture ("Below the left knee is the Garter with the inscription *Honi-soit-qui-mal-y-pense*, in choice diamonds"). In an envelope marked "Madness," the pictures included a *Tumbler of Marvelous Nerve* doing a handstand at the very edge of Overhanging Rock at Yosemite Valley and a mountainous backside view of a sumo wrestler.

As a major artist, Evans gave status to the postcard as another of his pursuits of the vernacular. During his career he produced two portfolios on postcards for *Fortune* magazine, another for *Architectural Forum*, and a ground-breaking lecture on the subject for the intelligentsia and students at Yale. In articles and lectures, he used postcards (chiefly from his own collection) to deliver his obiter dicta on art and history, announcing in one of the *Fortune* portfolios:

In the 1900's sending and saving picture postcards was a prevalent and often a deadly boring fad in a million middle class family homes. Yet the plethora of cards printed in the period now forms a solid bank on which to draw some of the most charming and, on occasion, the most horrid mementos ever bequested one gener-ation by another. At their best, the purity of the humble vintage postcards shines exceedingly bright in 1948.

In Evans's chronology, that was where it ended: "For postcards are now in an aesthetic slump from which they probably will never recover." In the late 1940s he deemed postcards had become the "quintessence of gimcrack." But vintage postcards from the turn of the century, he claimed, constituted "some of the truest visual records ever made of any period." Hyperbole perhaps, but he made a point of their historical importance. Appropriately enough, the self-styled disappointed writer had found a medium that combined an image and, on its reverse side, space for the thousands of words that friends and members of families sent to one another. It was a duality that marked Evans's art and career more notice-ably than it did most of his colleagues and rivals.

Evans was interested not only in the images, the historical evidence of bygone days, however tinted or prettified. It is clear, too, that he was a collector of the messages the cards carried. The unsigned correspondent of the postcard of Main Street, Norwich, Connecticut, writes on November 6, 1910, to Varian B. York of North Stonington: "The bill for the use of a handkerchief with an 'H' inscribed in one corner thereof will be sent at a later date." Another reads: "Well, if she doesn't care any more than that I don't either. See you Tues." And a third: "Your ma and I stopped at this hotel before you were ever heard of." He had quoted the card in his *Fortune* portfolio "Main Street Looking North from Courthouse Square." (No matter that Evans didn't get the last message quite right. The note sent to Master Foster French actually read: "Your Ma & I stoped at this Depot before you was ever heard of." (Perhaps he considered his transcript an editorial improvement.) But these were authentic voices out of the past. The comments, anarchic or absurd, pertinent or impertinent, are archeological finds. The circumstances, often, one can only guess at.

In the darkroom, oddly enough, Evans would use postcard paper to make test exposures, and even to compose enlarged segments of other negatives. As far as is known, he never used these to write to friends. But commercial postcards, old and new, would serve as Evans's preferred, usually droll, method of communication. Friends, in turn, sent him choice specimens for his collection. To one younger colleague, Jerry Thompson, Evans once sent a card of seven nubile Amish girls, pretty maids all in a row, striding down a country road. His only comment was "Hm."

II

Presumably, the earliest mention of James Agee in Walker Evans's extant diaries comes on Friday, April 5, 1935: "Evening at Agee's unpardonably dull; went dancing Cheever, Emma Agee and someone. Drank." It was not a characteristic episode in one of Evans's most important friendships. Agee was many things other than unpardonably dull. His all-night talkathons might be exhausting; the jazzy riff of some train of his thoughts could be exhilarating; the sudden twists of his variations on themes of sensuality and sexuality might be astonishing or embarrassing; but dullness was not one of his plebeian virtues. By April 1935, when Evans set the name down in his diary, Agee was twenty-five, only two years married to Olivia ("Via") Saunders, a Bryn Mawr graduate. He was already restive under his marital ties as well as his three years as a staff writer for Henry Luce's *Fortune* magazine. A graduate of Phillips Exeter and Harvard, he was a young man with the right friends in the right places, acquired not through scheming or manipulation but through sheer energy, talent, and charisma. It was Dwight Macdonald, a former Exeter graduate, who had made Agee's entrée to the *Fortune* job easy. It was another *Fortune* writer, poet Archibald MacLeish, who had provided the glowing foreword to Agee's first volume of poetry, *Permit Me Voyage*, published by Yale University Press in its prestigious Yale Series of Younger Poets. (MacLeish praised Agee's "poetic gift which no amount of application can purchase and which no amount of ingenuity can fake.") It was Lincoln Kirstein who had first met Agee in Harvard and published his poem "Ann Garner" in the Spring 1929 issue of *Hound & Horn* and who, in the February 27, 1935, issue of the *New Republic*, praised *Permit Me Voyage*, noting Agee's unique talents and his absorption of seventeenth-century prose and eighteenth-century verse. He described Agee's highly charged autobiographical prose poem "Dedication" as a "hymn of praise, compassion, and a curse of genuine proportions."

Tall, gangling, awkward in movement, with dark curly hair and pene-trating blue eyes, Agee had an easy intimacy about him. Women, including women with talents and ambitions, found him immediately attentive and attractive. It is possible that Evans had met him as early as the summer of 1934, when Evans was on assignment with Dwight Macdonald photographing the Communist summer camp for the September 1934 issue of *Fortune*. In that same issue, another of Evans's photographs, a not very distinguished shot of a tourist cabin dubbed "miss Florida," appeared in Agee's zesty article "The Great American Roadside."

Evans's recollections of Agee in that early time were vivid. A fastidious dresser himself, he cast a cool eye on Agee's preference for cheap clothes and workmen's garb. He understood it was not just because Agee was poor, but because he was making a statement: "Cleaning and pressing would have undone this beautiful process. I exaggerate but it did seem sometimes that wind, rain, work, and mockery were his tailors." He was also impressed by Agee's verbal panache:

He seemed to model, fight, and stroke his phrases as he talked. The talk in the end was his great distinguishing feature. He talked his prose, Agee prose. It was hardly a twentieth century style; it had Elizabethan colors. Yet it had extraordi-narily knowledgeable contemporary content. . . . It wasn't a matter of show, and it wasn't necessarily bottle-inspired. Sheer energy of imagination was what lay behind it.

If, as seems likely, Evans read Agee's piece "The Great American Roadside," he would have found him another colleague in pursuit of the American vernacular. Like a number of Agee's exuberantly styled articles for *Fortune*, it began (and ended) with a literary thrust. (The obligatory statistics and factual matter, mostly supplied by the busy research staff of the magazine, were sandwiched into the middle.) In his incantatory openings, Agee hustled the reader into a comfortable familiarity with the principals of the story, which in this case included the American continent, "an open palm spread frank before the sky against the bulk of the world." He went on: "The automobile you know as well as you know the slouch of the accustomed body at the wheel and the small stench of gas and hot metal." There followed the various ramifications of the highway: "How like a blacksnake in the sun it takes the ridges, the green and dim ravines which are the Cumberlands, and lolls loose into the hot Alabama valleys." Following that, the piece lifts to a paean to the open road:

Oh yes, you know this road; and you know this roadside. You know this roadside as well as you know the formulas of talk at the gas station, the welcome taste of a Bar B-Q sandwich in mid-afternoon, the oddly excellent feel of a weak-springed bed in a clapboard transient shack, and the early start in the cold bright lonesome air, the dustless and dewy road and the stammering birds, and the day's first hitch-hiker brushing the damp hay out of his shirt.

The oddity, of course, is that such prose should ever have graced the pages of a magazine bent on extolling the virtues of the capitalist system and the successes of American businessmen. The affinity of Agee's prose with the vision of Evans's photographs was clear to many of their contemporaries. Lincoln Kirstein, for instance, was not surprised that Evans and Agee should have found common ground: "It is no chance that, after Crane, Walker Evans should have worked with James Agee . . . whose verse, springing at once from Catholic liturgy, moving pictures, music and spoken language, is our purest diction since Eliot. Walker Evans's eye is a poet's eye. It finds corroboration in the poet's voice."

Whether by chance or from report, Agee, during the summer of 1935, would be dealing with a subject that Evans had already assayed — Saratoga in upstate New York. "For *Fortune* I am now working on a story about Bookies (at horseraces), and Saratoga," Agee informed a friend. "Difficult and one of the very few interesting assignments I've had here. Different pieces of the day-night poem are scattered around in different hideouts downtown." Evans had concentrated on the off-season architectural grandiosities of the spa, its ornate high-Victorian hotels, the black Fords lined up on its blackened streets glistening in a cold rain. Agee in his "day-night" poem democratically covered the racing-season clientele, the

Whitneys and the Vanderbilts, as well as the seamier customers: "Add gentlemen of the persuasion of The Little Augie and of Charlie (Lucky) Luciano (Capone's numbers man) and of Dutch Schultz, whose hideout is visible from Saratoga's highest point." He noted the night spots on Congress Street and the smarter edge-of-town clubs where the music was cooler. ("Saratoga runs less to the hot than to the potted palm styles of music and entertainment.") He even managed to give a certain urgency to the statistics: the racing receipts from 1929 to 1934; the average wage of a staff man (around fifteen dollars a day); and the botanical clues for spotting a bookie: "Keeps his real name or number out of the phone book, has wide underworld sports and stage and political connections, winters in Florida and dresses a lot more conservatively than you probably expect him to — only shirts and ties, as a rule, give him away." But these were racy spots in the informational body of the article compared to the energetic beginning and ending.

Agee closed the article with a picture as graphic as one of Evans's photographic sequences. He described the abrupt end of the racing season with the departing horse lorries lumbering out of town, leaving a September silence: "And every next morning the streets are as strangely empty as a new-made corpse of breath. The cottages are being boarded up; the windows of the big hotels whitened with Bon Ami; the furnishings in the smart clubs shrouded in white sheets. Over the bare porches and the elaborate colonnades and the pitiable slums behind the big hotels "there settles, delayed a little but by no means dispelled . . . the chill and the very temper and the very cold of death."

* * *

But in the early spring of 1935 Evans was not so concerned with the occasional dull evening at the Agees' basement apartment on Perry Street. He was, for the time being, caught up in an affair with Agee's sister, Emma. Two years younger than her brother, Emma was a secretive poet who would not show her verses to others, a young woman overshadowed by her more talented brother. She liked drinking, was fond of jazz, and frequented Nick's on Seventh Avenue, where the band, which began playing on a Sunday afternoon, continued on well into the night. She was also fond of dancing. Aside from the fact that the affair with Emma had begun sometime earlier, Evans's diary spells out the details of their meetings:

April 6 . . . Evening Emma Agee came and spent the night with me, first time she'd done that here me not surprised, quite pleased but a little annoyed at myself later.

April 7 . . . Emma Agee came, dinner, back here and slept again with me. She's being nice about it. I like her but not that well.

That for Evans this was to be a period of involvements with women became clear on April 8:

. . . Letter from Jane this morning says she might come to NY wants to know what I would do if she left Paul.

Dinner at Jacoby's house. Beatrice annoys me by paying attention to her brother at my expense.

April 10 . . . Emma came again tonight and stayed with me.

April 11 . . . Home, toothache, bed, Emma came.

On April 12, Evans learned that the African sculpture assignment for the Museum of Modern Art had been settled. Sensing that he would be swamped with work he noted in his diary: "Called off everything, consisting of engagement with Beatrice. Emma appeared with charm before dinner."

On April 13, he wrote to Jane Ninas. After that point — in his diary at least — the mentions of Emma Agee became a diminishing echo.

III

Jane Ninas has no recollection of having been as direct or aggressive as Evans's April 8 note suggests: "I can't remember having the nerve to write him that," she says. "Absolutely insane. He must have asked me because I certainly didn't suggest that I was coming to New York." Evans, she maintains, was aware that Paul spent his summers in Texas, teaching in summer school, and that it was her custom to go to Wisconsin to visit her family: "I think he wrote and said that someone had lent him this house [on Jane Street in the Village] and would Christine and I like to come up and visit.

I'm sure that's how this thing must have started." Probably, she suggests, Walker had initiated the idea of having Christine come with her as a chaperone. The deceptions of New Orleans were again in force: Christine had her own reasons for making the trip; she was still involved with a young German friend at Columbia, Freedie von Helms. She could manufacture her own cover story as well: an intended visit to her half sister in Manhattan. Eventually it was arranged that Evans would meet the two women in Washington, D.C., and drive them to New York.

In the meantime, Ernestine Evans had been busy on Walker's behalf, trying to arrange an assignment for him with one of the new work-relief programs begun by the Roosevelt administration. There was the continuing possibility that Evans might find some post in the Works Projects Administration, headed up by family friend Harry Hopkins. But another opportunity was the Resettlement Administration, a newly established division of the Department of Agriculture, under the direction of Rexford Tugwell. Tugwell was a prominent member of Roosevelt's Brain Trust, the president's hand-picked team of economic advisors. With her usual effectiveness and wide-ranging connections, Ernestine Evans was prodding John Franklin Carter, director of the agency's Division of Information, to take Evans on on a trial basis.

Franklin Roosevelt had no great interest in art per se. His taste ran to paintings of ships and boating scenes; his critical standards seemed based on the correctness of the rigging. But he was persuaded that in the current economic situation, artists, like construction workers and ditchdiggers, could work equally well for the public good, providing murals and paintings for public buildings. The painter George Biddle remarked, "Roosevelt has almost no taste or judgement about painting, and I don't think he gets much enjoyment out of it; yet he has done more for painters in this country than anybody ever did." Eventually the WPA program was extended to provide work for musicians and actors who toured small-town America and writers who were put to work on a statewide series of guidebooks or the "Living Newspaper" productions of the Federal Theater.

That Evans had given thought to such prospects is clear from a series of draft memoranda indicating what equipment might be required and how he envisioned the jobs themselves. He made a list of assistants needed for a WPA photo unit which included a secretary and a file clerk as well as "routine" photographers and project photographers. The latter he originally described as "Creative" photographers; then, sensibly recognizing that that might seem too creative for the bureaucracy, crossed it out. But it was clear from the beginning that he considered such projects as relating to his own special interests and possibly to his recognition of Atget's work-agenda. He also expanded on the ideas he had sketched out for Ernestine Evans a year earlier. Evans listed such diversified photographic projects as "the trades," "set of shop windows," "the backyards of N.Y.," "national groups," "children in the streets," "subway," and "interiors of all sorts." Still feeling his way in the spring of 1935, when a job with the Resettlement Administration appeared to be possible, he made it clear (in a handwritten draft of a memorandum) that he intended to be his own man and not a government factotum: "Mean never [to] make photographic statements for the government or do photographic chores for gov or anyone in gov, no matter how powerful — this is pure record not propaganda. The value, and, if you like even the propaganda value for the government lies in the record itself which in the long run will prove an intelligent and farsighted thing to have done. NO POLITICS whatever." The one concession he seemed willing to make was to supply the agency with "the outright gift on my part of complete collection of year's work (prints only) in America together with a stipulation: 'All rights retained by me.'"

Evans's arrangement to meet Jane and Christine in Washington, D.C., on June 7 was undoubtedly determined by a scheduled meeting with Ernestine Evans, who had been making appointments for him, most notably with John Carter. Once there, he learned that the assignment was pretty much settled; he was to return in another two weeks "and do some work (as expert!) on government projects, Cumberland plateau." On the evening of the seventh, Jane and Christine arrived on a 7:30 P.M. train. Evans took them to the Powhatan Hotel. The next day, they set out on the drive to New York, making an overnight stay at a charming old inn at New Castle, Delaware. (Dorothy Miller, another of Evans's feminine interests that spring, had recommended it.) On the afternoon of the ninth, the trio arrived at the Jane Street apartment.

* * *

It was Jane Ninas's first adult visit to New York; as a child she had been there with her parents. There was a sense of excitement not altogether attributable to her adventures in the city. The days were crowded with activities: Walker took her to the Museum of Modern Art and to the new Radio City Music Hall, where she saw the screen version of Thackeray's *Vanity Fair* with Miriam Hopkins as Becky Sharp. At the New Workers' School, he showed her the controversial Rivera murals he had photographed two years earlier. Most nights, they went out to dinner together; Christine, using the Jane Street house largely as a base of operations, had other engagements. They were glad to have the time alone. It was at Jane Street that the relationship between Jane and Evans became sexual. Christine, presumably aware, had no grounds for comment on the secret visits between bedrooms. Jane took a rational approach: "Not only was she [Christine] trying to take my husband away from me; she had a boyfriend in New York."

New York life had its behavioral oddities, but nothing that fazed Jane, who had lived in New Orleans. She and Christine paid a call on Christine's wealthy and eccentric half sister, who preferred to live in an illuminated darkness: The windows of her apartment had been painted black to shut out the offending light. At Jane Street, late one night, a loud knock at the door woke Evans: It was Jim Agee, tousle-headed and intense, come to pay a visit. Nothing would do but that Walker put on his robe and settle down for a talk. Jane and Christine, roused from their beds, were encouraged to come down as well. It was the first of Jane's encounters with Agee's indefatigable conversations; this one lasting well into the early hours of the morning. Walker also took Jane to see the Bethune Street studio he was sharing with Lou Block and Ben Shahn, both of whom were now into photography, partly through Evans's encouragement. (Block remembered that he and Shahn would "work both sides of the street like a couple of peddlers, snapping everything." Shahn discovered that the street photos were useful as sketches for the murals he and Block were commissioned to paint for the new Riker's Island penitentiary.) By a strange coincidence, when Jane visited the studio, Block and the ever-helpful Agee were covering the windows with black cloth to make a darkroom for Evans.

It was, however, a brief if eventful holiday in New York. Evans managed to persuade Jane to return with him to Washington rather than proceed on to Wisconsin as she had told Paul. Christine remained at the Jane Street apartment. For the trip, Jane had packed her large leghorn hat in an innocuous-looking cardboard hatbox. Evans eyed it critically and on the road glanced at it from time to time. Finally, at Havre de Grace, in Maryland, he made up his mind. Stopping at a stylish shop, he came back with an expensive patent leather hatbox. In Baltimore, he also bought her a copy of Fanny Burney's *Evelina*. It was a slow trip, Jane remembered: "It always took a *long* time to get anywhere with Walker." It was a lesson confirmed on many later trips. They arrived in Washington at 8:30 on the evening of the twentieth, registering once more at the Powhatan.

The FSA assignment did not begin auspiciously. The morning after, a Friday, Evans learned, much to his dismay, that his photographic equipment and supplies had not arrived. (He had requested a Leica and an 8 x 10 Deardorff, considered the Cadillac of view cameras, and a Protar Triple Convertible lens which allowed for three different focal lengths, giving the 8 x 10 formats greater depth and detail versatility.) He and Jane salvaged the weekend, however, by taking a trip to Harper's Ferry. A marvelous trip, she recalled, during which they stayed at a bed-and-breakfast. By Monday only some of the supplies had turned up, the requested Leica among them. Evans busied himself with viewing some Department of Agriculture films and the next day ran into Alan Blackburn who was demonstrating his Visograph for officials in Washington. The evenings with Jane were pleasant, spent walking in the nighttime capital.

The continuing delay of the supplies was aggravating. On the morning of the twenty-sixth nothing came. Evans was fussed; it was not until after lunch that the films for the Leica showed up, along with the Deardorff camera, for which, unfortunately, he had been sent the wrong film plates. Exasperated, he and Jane, early that evening, took off for Leesburg, Virginia. He was hoping the film for the Deardorff would reach him on the road. Crossing the Alleghenies on the twenty-seventh, he fulfilled the first stop of his assignment, photographing the Hoffman Tannery and the workers' houses at Gormania in West Virginia. A photograph of a bleak row of workers' houses close upon the highway, with figures on the stoops and a curious young girl standing on a slope, is vignetted by a dark semi-circle at the top, suggesting that Evans was pushing the lens beyond its limits. That evening they put up at the Youghiogheny Lodge in Aurora. Jane's recollections of the trip, thus far, were fond: They were both deeply in love, she felt. In some sense it was a preliminary honeymoon.

It was a slow trip to Reedsville: Evans became lost in the byways; there were brake troubles with the car. En route, he took some shots of Rowlesburg, its frame houses perched on a hillside, the town a kind of background extension of the simple tilted gravestones of the roadside cemetery in the foreground. On the outskirts of Reedsville they put up at the Indian Rock tourist camp, which became their base of operations for the next eight days. Each day they drove out to nearby towns like Arthursdale, Masontown, Morgantown, Scott's Run, and Osage in Preston and Monongalia counties. Jane remembered Evans's excitement about the work in the early days of the assignment. The countryside, Evans admitted, was good though he was alert to the poverty marked by the deserted mining towns along the way. In Morgantown, it was the "wonderful rows of frame houses" on the hills that caught his eye. In Scott's Run, the "series of half starved brutal soft coal mining camps, company owned," impressed him. He met a "wonderful dumb local politician," a Mr. Boyle, connected by marriage to the mine operators, who purportedly worked "for good of miners." A strike, he learned, was brewing. "Marvelous material," Evans claimed, noting his own sense of "well being." In the Scott's Run area he shot three rolls of film with his Leica. But he made a point of scouting the back roads as well as the assigned projects. On one of these byway excursions he passed a wide but shallow stream and stopped the car, stripped, and waded in, splashing himself in the cool waters. Afterwards he sat down on the bank by the fully-clothed Jane and, "very typically," as Jane noted, became amorous. It was not an opportune moment; suddenly on the opposite bank there loomed up the figure of a country bumpkin who, taking in the situation, was astonished, turned on his heels, and fled. Both Evans and Jane began to laugh; he dressed hastily and turned on the ignition. The two started down the road, raising the dust on their bucolic interlude.

On July 2, the film for the Deardorff finally arrived. Evans drove to Morgantown, where he loaded the film holders in a photographer's darkroom, and began a new round of shooting at Scott's Run and Arthursdale. In the latter town he photographed the new constructions of a vacuum cleaner factory, a near-Bauhaus modern expanse of glass and brick. He also photographed the trim new frame workers' houses under construction, part of the Subsistence Homestead Project, promoted through the efforts of Eleanor Roosevelt. Back at the tourist camp, Evans's notebook entry of July 3 testified to his spirit of work and well-being: "Much affection for Jane, for this cabin, for my car, for Dorothy Miller, Lincoln Kirstein, Jim Agee, Bea Jacoby, for myself."

But his moods were becoming ambivalent. The Fourth of July began with a heavy rainstorm and he admitted to a sense of "leisure, solace, (what?)." When the rain stopped he and Jane drove to Terra Alta ("pronounced Teralta," he noted), where a homecoming of natives was in progress. It was not to his liking: "very degenerate natives, mush faced, the pall of ignorance on all sides. Photographed the most gruesome specimens." Several of these were probably taken with his right-angle viewfinder, Jane serving as the decoy. The day was somewhat redeemed when they went to a W. C. Fields movie, which he thought funny. But that evening he and Jane had a first serious quarrel — over what is now unremembered. Jane Ninas thinks it might have been over the question of commitment, though she is also sure no thought of her divorcing Paul was ever discussed between them. Evans took the blame: "very bad, my fault, stupid of me," he wrote in his diary. On the following day Evans made a return trip to Arthursdale, photographing the workmen on the project with his Leica. That evening at five, he and Jane drove to Pittsburgh. It was the night before her departure for Wisconsin.

Interior, West Virginia Miner's House, 1936

July 6 was a glum day; Evans felt "hot, depleted, unsexed." They kept busy in the morning, visiting the Carnegie Institute, looking at casts of Greek architectural orders, looking at the very bad paintings, looking at specimens of black lace and Staffordshire china. By the time they returned to the hotel, they both had headaches. It was a time of "love and tears, all unreal to me," Evans confessed. "What we were really doing all day was parting." At the Pittsburgh station it was hot and dirty, not a porter to be found anywhere. The image that remained stuck in his mind was of Jane's head, looking but not seeing, from the train window as the cars pulled away. He also remembered: "The way I induce myopia when things look too sharp." Sharpness of focus was a necessity in his photographs, but at painful times in life, he reserved the right to avoid it.

* * *

In the days that followed he tried to make an assessment of his state of mind: "slight depression, not thinking of J, if possible, unable completely to eliminate the face in the train, confusion, some fear, some shame." (Were these signs or symptoms of love in the thirties?) He kept busy, this time taking a cabin in Morgantown, photographing there again "some interiors" he noted. It is not clear whether on this occasion he photographed one of the more deceptive, straight-on but still haunting, photographs among his West Virginia series: the interior of a coal miner's house. (First identified as *Vicinity Morgantown West Virginia, July, 1935*, it was later, and probably incorrectly, identified as *Coal Miner's House, Scott's Run, 1936*.) A lonesome-looking boy sits awkwardly, dutifully, in an oak chair in the beam-and-board interior. The walls are insulated with folded cardboard,

pathetically decorated with near life-sized advertising placards of smiling mothers, a Santa Claus, a hunting dog. It is definitely worth remembering that the photographer himself grew up, a small boy, amid the promissory notes of American advertising. Evans's father, however, had advertised brand names other than Armour's Cloverbloom butter or "Rinso: Soaks Clothes White" and benefits other than those of the Kentucky General Life & Accident Insurance Company. Evans trapped other visual clues that provide commentaries on the scene: the blurry mirror with its distorted reflections; the little still life of a shaving mug and empty Mason jars and the touch of gentility introduced by the draped table scarf on the side table in which the drawer pulls are missing. But the principal focus of the picture is the boy in his playsuit, barefooted, scuff-kneed, immured in his environment temporarily, and staring back, trancelike, at the photographer. It is one of Evans's vital pictures of the decade, an ironic metaphor of the American Dream in disrepair.

What makes the precise date of the photograph questionable is Evans's dissatisfaction with his last series of photos in West Virginia. "Rather discouraging, not getting much," he wrote of the shoot three days after Jane's departure. (The mood, perhaps, may only reflect an artist's sense of failure of the moment; it had been written before he had even seen the results.) But it is quite probable that the photograph (and possibly one or two companion photographs) was taken during Evans's 1935 excursion in West Virginia, if not during the shoots when Jane Ninas accompanied him. She has no recollection of the boy or the miner's house.

A letter and telegram from the Resettlement Administration informed him that he was expected to do another project across the border in Westmoreland County, Pennsylvania. On his way he traveled through Carnegie Mellon and Frick coal country, reaching the Frick Hecla Mine #1, near Mt. Pleasant, in the late afternoon of July 10. That evening a Czech miner who was a union official as well as a politician took him down into the mine: "cold and terrifying," he noted. The next day, at the Westmoreland Subsistence Homestead Project, he photographed construction workers and carpenters, and, curiously, shot a sequence of inquisitive young boys who frankly took an interest in the proceedings. But he confessed that evening that he "worked badly and listlessly. By night dead bored." He had nothing much else to do but listen to the union official's stories of local scandals, corruption, and violence. Still, photographing around Mt. Pleasant that day, he had taken a series of views of the streets and environs of the town: the white picket fences, the clipped hedges, the plainspoken frame houses, roads leading down and away with the blur of distant pedestrians, as if, in the drowse of high summer, life was untouchable and guaranteed against hardship.

On Evans's return trip to Washington, he stopped at the hotel in Bedford Springs for dinner. "As a joke on myself," he noted, adding, "Sad joke." He was in a nostalgic mood: "I find I completely overlooked the gingerbread wings of the hotel when the happy Evans family [was] here in 1917 or 1918." The "happy Evans family" clearly carried an edge of irony or even bitterness. "Observant boy," he added, "remembers classic portico and swimming pool but not rooms slept in, not a trace of memory or of food eaten, or dining room, or arrival." But Evans did recall how at the age of fourteen or fifteen, wearing white flannel long pants, he had strolled along the causeway to the source of the springs.

The next morning soured the occasion. After a "mad, unnecessary" telephone conversation with Ernestine Evans, he had a "ludicrous row with the operator, me trembling and ashamed." What prompted the excursion into his past is not clear, but it became a search for a lost identity. Later that day he stopped at the Mercersburg Academy, "touched," he noted, "by a mild rush of reminiscences — that was I think me in 1919 or 1920." In the flush of that recovery, he noted:

Discovered that some things did happen to me there and that I am at least partly the same person I was fifteen years ago. I liked some things there more than I knew at the time. Discovered that space shrinks with advancing time. Or seems to.

A Subsidized Freedom

13

"Typical Washington day," Evans wrote in his diary on July 15, 1935. "Lunched with one Stryker, a Tugwell man, with all sorts of ideas about photography." The "typical Washington day" and "all sorts of ideas about photography" are the telling phrases. At the beginning of what was to be an important if aggravating opportunity, they certify Evans's initial response to officialdom and fallibility of official art. "I went down there at the suggestion of Ernestine Evans, when Roy Stryker didn't know what he was doing, didn't know why he was there," Walker would later recall, with some bit of distortion. "He was just a friend of Tugwell's. I think he had been a history teacher." In later years he also quarreled with any suggestion that he had been under the sway of Stryker's authority or a disciple of Stryker's views about the purposes of the Resettlement Administration's photographic unit: "I've been particularly infuriated by reading here and there that he [Stryker] was 'directing' his photographers. He wasn't directing *me*; I wouldn't let him."

Contrary to Evans's querulous view, Roy E. Stryker did know something about photography. As a graduate student at Columbia under the aegis of his professor, Rexford Tugwell, he had selected the photographic illustrations for Tugwell's heavily illustrated 1925 volume (with Thomas Munro) *American Economic Life and the Means of Its Improvement*. He was also well aware of the documentary photography of Jacob Riis and particularly of the pioneering work of Lewis Hine. (Roughly one-third of the two hundred photographs Stryker chose for Tugwell's book were by Hine.) As a result, in 1935, Tugwell picked his former student and later colleague to head up the RA's photographic unit. Tugwell readily admitted that the idea for the unit "was mine and Stryker's, and we wanted to make as complete a record as we could of an agonizing interlude in American life."

As a representative of the New Deal's bureaucracy of good intentions, Stryker's dogma was assertive: "Truth is the objective of the documentary attitude," he claimed. "A good documentary," he maintained, "should tell not only what a place or a thing or a person *looks* like, but it must also tell

Gas Station,
Reedsville,
West Virginia,
1936

the audience what it would *feel* like to be an actual witness to the scene." Stryker had his own pragmatic agenda, pressing RA photographers to document "not the America of the unique, odd, or unusual happening, but the America of how to mine a piece of coal, grow a wheat field or make an apple pie." An interesting, if not a revolutionary proposition; but one that grated on Evans's firm commitment to the here and now. As an artist, Evans's feelings were too closely guarded to allow him to become the spokesman for easy sentiments or political generalities, creeds, or slogans. His concern was the hard evidence of time and place.

By Evans's standards, Stryker's aims in photography were both sentimental and propagandistic. Where Stieglitz, in a negative way, had helped define Evans's esthetics, Stryker's New Deal sympathies confirmed Evans's distrust of political authority no matter how necessary or beneficial in a crisis, or how well-meaning: "It was crazy, you know. Nobody could take it seriously. It was just mad, inefficient bureaucracy." He didn't "give a damn about the office in Washington — or about the New Deal really," Evans maintained. Still, he was not oblivious to the opportunities it afforded him at a critical phase of his own career: "Well, a subsidized freedom to do my stuff! Good heavens, what more could anyone ask for! . . . I had a whole hot year tremendously productive."

But he would never become the grateful public servant. After his return to New York, he promptly began work on the harvest of West Virginia and Pennsylvania photographs, sending the 35-mm films to Willoughby's for developing. He processed the 8 x 10 film himself. It was not soon enough; on the twenty-second — by which time he had begun printing up the Leica photos — he received word from Ernestine Evans urging him to make delivery of the work. Evans's answer was expectable; the next day, he noted, "E.E. wired admonishingly." Still, on the twenty-fourth, he admitted in his diary to having finished the Leicas and even to having titled them. On the twenty-fifth, he mailed the Leica prints to Washington. On the same day, having bought himself a contact printer, he began printing up the 8 x 10 photographs and two days later, on the twenty-seventh, finished printing and mounting the government 8 x 10s. He was satisfied with the work, at least to the extent of noting that the prints "Look good." But he was, in the meantime, "dispirited and worried" about the delays in working on the African prints for The Museum of

Modern Art. When Ernestine Evans stopped by his studio on the after-noon of the twenty-ninth, probably as a means of speeding up the process, he finished captioning the material. The next day he mailed thirty-two of the mounted prints to Washington. In effect, his assertion of independence was something of a pose. Not only had he worked steadily on the project, but it was clear that he had wanted to make a very good impression by mounting and captioning the Deardorff prints.

John Franklin Carter wrote on August 1, commending the work done so far as valuable. Later, there was also an encouraging call from Stryker. Still involved in printing up more film for the government, he had a rush call from film director Pare Lorentz, another member of the RA staff, asking for additional prints. Next came a telegram asking for negatives. In a letter to Carter written on the seventeeth, Evans was conciliatory but firm. He hoped Carter would agree with him "that the only really satisfac-tory prints of a careful photographer's negative must be made by the original photographer and that you will appreciate a certain craftsman's concern on my part over the quality of the prints of my negatives." Not quite truthfully, he attributed the delays to his work for The Museum of Modern Art but assured Carter that he was "exceedingly interested" in his work for the Information Division, "which seems to me to have enormous possibilities, of precisely the sort that interest me." He added, "Please be good enough to excuse the length and possibly the egotism of this letter. They have seemed unavoidable."

* * *

Evans and Jane Ninas kept up a correspondence while she was still in Wisconsin. One of her letters, however, was disturbing. She was concerned that she might be pregnant, a worry that bothered Evans for a week, until, on July 22, he noted: "Thank God letter from J. all right; her innocence established. My breathing regular." But while Jane was experiencing a certain amount of astonishment — and guilt — about the audacity of their deepening relationship, Evans, that summer, was keeping up an active social life with various women friends and acquaintances.

He saw Beatrice Jacoby with some regularity, taking her out to dinner and for walks in the park. Taking her to the movies one night he noted,

"Considerable excitement." There were dinner dates with earlier flames Ruth Hedoni and Leonie Sterner, the latter caught up in political activities and nurturing hopes of producing films for the government. Another disturbing letter from Jane was cause for further concern: "Bad letter from J. Paul is at her again with divorce and all the [various] tortures. Tiresome as can be." Occasionally he had drinks or dinners with Freedie von Helms; bachelors both, they discussed the problems of their affairs with Christine and Jane. Evans found it a relief.

Dorothy Miller seems to have established a continuing presence in Evans's diary notes even though she was involved with Holger Cahill, then director of the Federal Art Project in Washington. On one occasion when Cahill was in New York, Evans met the couple for "beer, poor conversation." He was not impressed; Cahill was "disappointing and depressing," a "defeated, frustrated man." Possibly it was a reflection of his general feelings about Washington bureaucrats.

Through August he worked steadily on developing the African sculpture negatives for the Modern, printing up a selection for Tom Mabry. Mabry was pleased with the results and Evans's immediate financial situation was helped considerably by a promised four-hundred-dollar payment

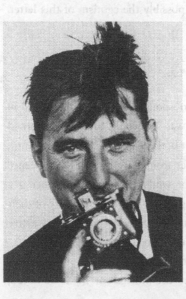

Peter Sekaer,
1935

from the museum. Within days, Evans hired an assistant, Peter Sekaer, a thirty-four-year-old Dane, an ambitious sign painter and photographer who for the past year or more had been studying under Berenice Abbott at the New School for Social Research and had been active photographing New York City street scenes, the El, shopfronts, and the homeless — subjects that were highly compatible with Evans's point of view. Sekaer started work with Evans at the Bethune Street studio on August 19. The two had been introduced to each other by Ben Shahn, whose liberal/left-wing views Sekaer shared. What loomed ahead for Evans at this point was a prodigious amount of work printing and mounting the subscription sets of the African sculpture series. It would become more of a problem with the firming up of another of Evans's government windfalls.

* * *

The official memo from Roy Stryker of the Division of Information, dated October 9, 1935, read: "Mr. Walker Evans has agreed to join our staff on a permanent basis. It will be necessary in order to hold him to increase his salary to $3,000." Some weeks earlier, Evans had actually been offered an appointment as Assistant Specialist in Information at a salary of $7.22 per diem, effective as of September 24, but he seems to have held out, successfully, for better terms. The Stryker memo spelled out his new duties, noting the fact that he was given "wide latitude for the exercise of independent judgement as Senior Information Specialist to carry out special assignments in the field." Evans's job would be "to collect and create photographic material to illustrate factual and interpretive news releases and other informational material upon all problems, progress and activities of the Resettlement Administration." As Senior Information Specialist, he would, from time to time, also be in charge of a small group of assistants, depending upon the size and importance of the assignments.

At the time of the appointment, Evans was in Washington and duly recorded his satisfaction: "Job looks excellent as it is written." A diary note for August 30, however, indicates that he had originally asked for $3,600 starting October 1, so he appears to have agreed to the lesser sum. But the language of the official appointment was more than encouraging and in an administration as anxious to put people to work as F.D.R.'s New Deal, the cut in salary would have been part of the waltz of the accommodation in which other new political appointees were similarly engaged. Evans was less successful in getting an RA job for Sekaer who, after two months of working with Evans on the African sculpture project, was in Washington with him. It was not until the eleventh that Evans noted: "Think Peter can get job but not as good as mine by any means." On that same day, Evans had a talk with Holger Cahill about "art and culture" in America and what should be done about it: "He is pessimistic and I don't think he can do much anyway." But the prospects were hardly as gloomy as Cahill envisioned. The Roosevelt-sponsored art programs, aside from putting people to work, constituted one of the most revolutionary and ambitious efforts to promote the legitimacy of painting and sculpture, literature, theater, music, and architecture as public professions in America's cultural history. Cahill himself would be responsible for an important WPA project, the Index of American Design, an extensive illustrated catalogue of American folk art — quilts and coverlets, kitchen utensils, plain-style furnishings — recording the "great reservoir" of the country's heritage in the practical and decorative arts.

In terms of opportunity — if not always in terms of individual taste or achievement — the government's art and history programs proved to be a godsend for Evans and many of his colleagues. Historian Morris Werner had already made his pilgrimage to Washington. Berenice Abbott, whose West Fifty-third Street darkroom and enlarger Evans used in printing up some of the government prints, had submitted a proposal for an index of urban architecture which the WPA accepted. Partly through the good offices of Ernestine Evans, Ben Shahn was engaged by the Special Skills Department of the Resettlement Administration as a painter, poster maker, and photographer. In mid-September, he left for Washington on a photographic tour of the South. (Two weeks earlier, Evans, in his sister Jane's borrowed car, had driven Ben to the capital for preliminary talks.) Evans, jealous of Shahn's abilities as a hustler, commented, "He could wrap Mr. Stryker around his finger; and did. . . . Ben really worked Washington for all it was worth." (Tillie Shahn, as well as Lou Block, would serve in supervisory positions for the Federal Art Project's Index of American Design.) Whether on Evans's recommendation or on his own initiative, Shahn took sequences of graphic shots in West Virginia, around the Scott's Run area and further west around Red House. (In his three years of working for the agency, Shahn made some five to six thousand photographs; whereas Evans, in the same time span, produced less than half as many.) Where Evans was willing, even preferred, to work with a cumbersome Deardorff to get a shot he wanted, Shahn used a fixed-lens Leica, at the ready for spur-of-the moment shots. It was another example of Shahn's bravado about which Evans confessed to a certain envy: "That always irritated me because he would do things that would embarrass me, that I wouldn't do." One can understand the differences between the two by comparing Evans's West Virginia photographs with Shahn's. Where Evans was cautious and reflective, hardly disturbing the dust of the road, or using his Leica with a right-angle viewfinder to catch unsuspecting natives at a Fourth of July celebration in Terra Alta, Shahn was aggressive, pushing in to capture the startled and suspicious expressions of a group of blacks in their Sunday suits, hats and ties, standing on a street corner, or to trap a group of whites on the porch of a Scott's Run country store. Shahn attacked in close and up front.

The work of both men, nevertheless, impressed Roy Stryker: "Walker Evans's pictures, Ben Shahn's trip, all those things began to come back and we began to see the need for doing this; doing that." Stryker's photographic unit was one of the most active agencies in what was renamed the Farm Security Administration in 1937. It would produce some 270,000 photographs, the work of photographers like Evans, Shahn, Dorothea Lange, Russell Lee, Carl Mydans, Arthur Rothstein, John Vachon, Marion Post Wolcott, and Jack Delano among them, several of whom would move on to positions with the major news and photo magazines of the period. It was the policy of Stryker and his agency, as a form of propaganda, to supply free photographs to *Fortune*, *Life*, *Look*, *Time*, and the *New York Times*, as well as to book publishers. The FSA was, as well, a political tool of some value by way of its exhibitions. Shahn, for instance, designed an exhibition of FSA photographs for the 1936 Democratic Convention, and major shows of such photographs, sponsored by camera manufacturers and distributed by museums like the Modern, established the iconography of the "Great Depression" nationwide.

II

"Still photography, of general sociological nature," was the all-encompassing term Evans used in the proposal he worked up for Roy Stryker. What he had in mind was an ambitious (probably too ambitious) automobile tour of the southeastern states to begin on November 1. With the skill of a veteran applicant for government support he pinpointed his first objectives: "Pittsburgh and vicinity, one week, photography, documentary in style, of industrial subjects, emphasis on housing and home life of working class people." His next target was the Ohio Valley: "rural architecture, including the historical, contemporary 'Middletown' subjects; Cincinnati housing; notes on style of Victorian prosperous period." The "Middletown" mention was a canny move since Robert Lynd, the author, with his wife, Helen, of *Middletown* (1929), the bible of the liberal social scientists of the period, were two of Stryker's close friends and advisors.

View of Easton, Pennsylvania, 1935

Evans's itinerary included places with which he was already familiar and those which it seemed unlikely he could cover in the allotted time: Indiana, Kentucky, and Illinois river towns; "Ditto Mississippi river towns. Select one of these, such as Hannibal, Missouri, for more thorough treatment, if time allows." He produced some questionable and some solid bits of expertise based on his earlier travels — for Natchez, for instance, he suggested "Antebellum plantation architecture, flower of which is concentrated in Natchez." For Louisiana plantation architecture, he offered Belle Grove, which he had already photographed in its poignant decay: "The most sophisticated example of classic revival private dwelling in the country." He also suggested further work on other Louisiana plantations: "historical records and notes of present use, present owners," little of which he would actually gather. It was, nonetheless, a worthy project for a well-meaning administration with preservation on its mind. The "industrial documentary pictures" of Birmingham, Alabama, and the "rural subjects" of Alabama and Georgia provided the more achievable projects on his list.

Yet the remarkable thing about Evans's proposal, though he was not the most prolific photographer in the FSA stable, is that he managed to produce some of the most important and striking photographs in the department's archives. He even managed to complete a good portion of the task while furthering his own interests. Of that first year of work for the RA, he remembered, "We were working at a pretty white heat."

* * *

In the last days of October and into early November, as his sometimes contradictory diary entries and photographer's record sheets indicate, Evans took a night train to Washington, from where he began a circuitous automobile trip through York and on to Bethlehem, Pennsylvania. On the road once again, he photographed what had become routine for him: another service station (this one in York), a farmhouse between York and Hillam on Route 30, a Victorian house in Lancaster. In Bethlehem he resorted to his Leica, photographing men and women on the streets, a pair

of glum-faced women out shopping in their dowdy fall coats and hats, a pair of boys in the lobby of a movie theater. On November 2 he spent a day with the Deardorff, catching first the view from the window in his room at the Hotel Bethlehem in the full morning sun at 8:30. Then, as the day wore on, he shot from the roof of the hotel, scanning the sky west and south, fixing on the jumble of frame houses, factories, the massive arched Hill-to-Hill and Broad Street bridges. And in the afternoon, he took to the streets on the east end of town. There was a haze and the sky had darkened. Using the "smallest stop" he focused on the steep hills and the clustered houses nestled around the city towers, or the view from behind the smoking mill stacks. The oddity, though it was a Saturday, is that in most of the views the streets were unpeopled, bereft of activity, except once, according to the record sheets, for the blurred ghost of a moving car. It was a city becalmed as if by the photographer's will.

On November 3, Evans took a few days break, returning north to New York to have dinner with Alfred Barr and his wife and to pick up his mail, which included, so he reported in his diary, an "inexplicable" letter from Jane. (The letter is now missing and she has no recollection of what might have been inexplicable about it.) She and Paul were now back in New Orleans and had moved to an attic apartment in the downtown Pontalba Building. Since they had no phone, the Ninases took their calls in the ground-floor liquor store. Evans's itinerary included a return trip to New Orleans; it may have been around this time that he had begun contacting Jane by phone, alerting her to his trip south. Things were not going well with her and Paul. Christine, who had an apartment in another section of the building, was an ever-intrusive presence in their lives. The three of them were still going out together and sometimes spent a weekend at her family's house in Waveland, Mississippi. Jane admitted to doing anything to stall or thwart Christine's management of their lives, which included leaving notes for errands to be done or a movie she wanted to see. Jane routinely destroyed them. It was an unhappy period. Though Walker was writing her with some regularity, Paul showed little concern, and Jane was becoming more and more aware of Christine's "take no prisoners attitude."

Part of Phillipsburg, New Jersey, 1935

By Wednesday, November 6, according to his field notes, Evans was back in Pennsylvania. With his Deardorff 8 x 10 he began a sequence of notable photographs in the Phillipsburg, New Jersey/Easton, Pennsylvania area using a Zeiss double-Protar lens. He chose the longest focal length, 69 cm, which compressed the distance, flattening the perspective, a practice he used effectively throughout his two-week assignment in the Lehigh Valley. Collapsing the depth of the view allowed subjects in the foreground to be equated with things in the distance, producing what Evans's young assistant of the late years Jerry Thompson accurately describes as the "epic vistas" of the 1935-36 photographs. Evans's own commentary on the photographs of the Easton-Phillipsburg Free Bridge spanning the Delaware River and the cluster of frame houses on the hillside beyond is revealing. They were taken at three in the afternoon in full sun, using a G filter to bring up the cloud formations in the sky. (Time as well as place and the changing light are as important in a photograph as they are in a painting by Monet.) The scene — the lacy structure of the bridge, the railroad car on the opposite bank — is as Evans termed it, "a very American view." He acknowledged the ugliness and the crazy jumble of different architectural styles: "Look at the quite handsome, charming building down front. While to the left is a ridiculous house with a crenellated castle on it. The first is honest, the second is not honest; both are American." That he was excited by the afternoon's shoot is probable; that night he developed the films and on the following day — a rainy one — he printed the results.

On the eighth, he made another fresh assault; this time beginning in Bethlehem. (By now the Biblical associations of his setting must have borne in on him as a kind of ironic counterpoint.) He photographed the stolid railroad station, a solemn sprawling structure perched on a landscape of slag and rubble with a bare sapling tree in the foreground and a row of monotonous steelworkers' houses edging down an embankment. At noon Evans began photographing in St. Michael's cemetery, unkempt and weedy, high on a hill looking down at the company blast furnaces, where he took some of the most vividly remembered photographs of his career. "Graveyard, Houses, and Steel Mills," in particular, has become one of the several icons of his oeuvre. Burial grounds and burial monuments would remain a persistent theme through much of his career. But this one afforded him a confrontation between the dead-at-peace lying in the wake of the industrial age. In Evans's view, the large solid granite cross surveys the workers' houses, the steep descent to the mill, and the array of smoke stacks barricading the sky. (Did Evans intend for us to recognize one of Eliot's objective correlatives between the buried dead and the lives of the *Joe's Auto* working-class families boxed away in their row houses across the street?) *Graveyard,* From a different angle he took at least two side views of a gravesite *1936* surrounded by a broken balustrade and in the middle distance a curiously wrought stone monument that he seems to have kept in mind for a later day.

It was his further luck that afternoon that, en route to Easton again, he ventured upon a graveyard of another sort, "Joe's Auto Graveyard," a procession of wrecked automobiles stretched out along Route 22. It was another of his "finds," even considering how often Evans had been and would be detained, photographically, by the sight of automobiles lined up on city streets or abandoned in fields. In this case it was a major metaphor, though for what, precisely, has remained something of a mystery for Evans 276 criticism. The most familiar of the auto graveyard pictures itemizes what looks like a herd of disabled animals moving through a wide savanna. Atop the distant hill a line of trees stands defoliated. A less familiar, though equally effective, shot overtakes the cars from behind as they converge, helter skelter, toward some forlorn destination. (Only a few years later, the latter could serve as the visual equivalent of newsreel shots of crowds of human refugees fleeing along the escape routes of war.) Some critics have seen the picture as an indictment of American wastefulness or the image of the devastation the automobile has wrought on the American landscape. With a more personal insight, Evans's last assistant, Thompson, sees it as something more than "a simple complaint at the encroachment of the automobile; rather it describes, with considerable wit and penetration, a fine manifestation of the entangled and contradictory energies that drive American culture." That seems nearest the mark, though one might add that the automobile was the modus operandi, the necessary vehicle, of Evans's search for subjects for much of his life. It had quite personal associations. (Then, too, Evans fancied stylish automobiles and late in life acquired the prize of a Jaguar.) Rather than a criticism of the car, his photographs delighted (flagrantly) in everything that followed in its wake: the antic billboards, the doll-house motels, the roadside stands plastered with signs. The man who photographed "Joe's Auto Graveyard" was not

the mere ecological critic.

On November 9, Peter Sekaer and his wife, Elizabeth, arrived in Bethlehem and were caught up in photographic excursions. At some point during the Armistice Day holiday weekend, Evans used his Leica to catch two of the most graphic images of his tour. If one can judge from the irritated expression of the American Legionnaire in full uniform — staring, hostile — standing with a group of legionnaires, Evans did not use the right-angle viewfinder for this shot. Bespectacled, with a pert, pointed mustache, the man glares toward the camera, suspicious of why he is being singled out. Evans got a different reception from the lineup of "sons of American Legion" in the second shot. It presents an array of boyhood reactions — from puzzled curiosity, grimace, and disinterest to bland acceptance — as the lads stand in a row in caps, white shirts, and ties. (It was, it would seem, a warm day for November.) In the uncropped version in the FSA files, a disembodied hand reaches in from the left-hand side to turn around a boy with his back to the camera so that he, too, can have his picture taken. As he did with his earliest photos of the Lindbergh and Byrd parades in New York City, Evans chose not to shoot the parade in its full march down the street. Instead he took his shots from the sidelines while waiting for the parade to begin or to break up after it had ended, the moment of inaction.

Midday on the tenth, a Sunday, Sekaer accompanied Evans to St. Michael's Cemetery, stopping first while Evans made a couple of shots of

Right:
Graveyard,
Houses, and
Steel Mills,
Bethlehem,
Pennsylvania
1935

Below:
Evans
photographing,
Bethlehem,
Pennsylvania,
1935

the Christ Rescue Mission on East Third Street and some more interesting shots of the window of a housewares store near the cemetery on Fourth Street. Evans tended to use shop windows as anthologies of the human condition: stacks of unshaped felt hats behind plate glass, a zombie-eyed mannequin straightening his tie. The window of the Bethlehem furnishings store spoke of domestic life in saws and cabbage slicers, an alarm clock, a flatiron, bathroom plungers at attention, a menacing syringe — the complete household inventory at the ready.

The real purpose of the excursion, it seems, was a retake of the views he shot two days earlier in the cemetery, showing the large cross on the left and looking beyond the workers' houses toward the Bethlehem Steel works. Evans used the focal length of 69 cm as before and an aperture of f45, timing the shots at one, three, and six seconds. It was a gray afternoon and he noted the lack of sun at 3:00 p.m. The implication is that he wanted to make sure he had gotten satisfactory shots of what he considered an important subject: "It's transcendent. You feel it . . ." he would say of the excitement of such discoveries. "An instance of chance, action, and fortuity. It's there and you can't unfeel it."

For good measure, Evans then took a closer look at the monument that had appeared in one of the Friday shots, a grandiose stone monument for Antonio Castellucci and his wife, Maria, a cross festooned with intricately carved roses and below it, vignetted in bas relief, portraits of the pair. It may be that he was amused by the image of leafy and transient nature fixed in stone or by the bland carved portraits of Castellucci and *sua moglie*, their faces turned toward eternity and the cold blasts of winter. Peter Sekaer, as witness to the event, took a photograph of the photographer taking a photograph atop the embankment wall, camera settled on its tripod, bellows extended, at that precise moment either inserting or withdrawing

the film holder — the paradox that is one of the riddles of photographic action.

* * *

Evans's trip had its rewards but also its aggravations. While in the Lehigh Valley, he received a note from Stryker reminding him of his official duties. It was written on November 9, the day before Sekaer caught him in the act of photographing the Castellucci monument. (He did, nonetheless, submit it to the RA.) The agency was coming under fire to produce meaningful propaganda; an election year was coming up, and Stryker thought it expedient to mention that Ben Shahn had returned to Washington "with some 32 rolls of Leica and nine rolls of 16 mm movie film. He is busily at work today printing up his stuff. He was in hopes that you might come back down through Washington to chat about the territory he covered and to show you what material he obtained. This (to) avoid duplication in other areas."

III

American Legionnaire, 1936

For Evans, the summer-to-summer year of 1935-36 would become his American journey. As much as any man can, he became identified with — and instructed by — the vagaries of the country he was photographing. "I developed my own eye, my own feeling about this country," he would later claim of the experience. "Oh, gosh, yes, that was great for me!" But the experience would also, in his mind at least, set him apart from the other photographers in the FSA, with the possible exception of Shahn, whom he respected or did respect at that time. "I look at those other photographs," he claimed, "and I see that they haven't got what I've got. I'm rather egotistical and conceited about that. I knew at the time who I was, in terms of the eye and that I had a real eye, and other people were occasionally phony about it, or they really didn't see. I know that's immodest, but I have to say it."

Whatever the pressures of Washington, he did not perform all the services his earlier itinerary suggested. In late November, after an overnight stop at Harper's Ferry, he drove on toward Johnstown, Pennsylvania, passing Windber, which he described summarily as "a mining town on a hill with uniform dirty frame houses and a huge dump heap." Nor was he impressed with Ferndale or Moxham, which he considered equally grim, arriving in Johnstown in late afternoon. The photographs he took (he seems to have spent some time there printing the results) indicate that it was cloudy, with a dusting of snow on the rooftops of unheated outbuildings and the open porches of the frame houses. Evans evidently thought it worth making a sociological footnote about working conditions in the bleak and wintry city in the nadir of the Depression: "The hotel chambermaids in the best hotel in Johnstown get $9 a week without lunch or carfare and contribute to community chest by threat of loss of jobs." Considering the 425 miles he had traveled in and around the Lehigh Valley, the 15 or so miles devoted to the Johnstown area, reported in his diary, suggest he did not consider it an important assignment. Nor, in the first few days of December, did he spend much time in Pittsburgh. Having earlier described it as a "complex, pictorially rich modern industrial center" worth a week of study, he gave it only three days. *Waterfront and Hillside Houses*, nevertheless, is the promised view of a modern industrial center but in the grip of winter: chill and gray, smoke rising, the rubble along the riverside absolved by a blanket of snow.

After that, his trip continued southward through Zanesville, Ohio, to Wilmington (an overnight stop), then to Carrollton, Kentucky. He appears to have only stopped en route at Cincinnati. ("Hills in this city offer revealing views for records of architecture, chiefly nineteenth century," he had noted in his proposed itinerary.) In Carrollton, his diary made note of Courthouse Square, the 1870 architecture, a Main Street moviehouse and some Wild West posters. Evans arrived in Nashville at noon on December 9 and spent a week there. On December 10, Stryker wrote him, concerned about not having received any work and not having heard from him. He jokingly wondered whether Evans "had been waylaid and were sleeping in a ditch somewhere in the South." He also advised him, "[Y]ou must push as hard as possible and get your pictures done because no one knows how long we will be holding forth here."

Whether or not Evans took Stryker's words to heart is uncertain, but he appears to have remained in Nashville for a week and may have settled down to work on developing and printing some of his negatives and writing up his field notes. (Leica numberings for the American Legion photographs are written on the back of a piece of stationery for the Andrew Jackson Hotel in Nashville.) On December 16, he headed further south, stopping overnight at Decatur, Alabama, en route to Clanton. Acknowledging his responsibilities to the FSA, he photographed a neat, relatively new row of miners' houses at Lewisburg near Birmingham and a disreputable cluster of ramshackle huts on a hillside in the same vicinity. His real interest seems to have been a trove of circus and minstrel show posters first sighted at Hartselle, then Clanton, and at Demopolis two days after that. Where the photographs of the miners' houses were dutiful, Evans relished every shred and tatter of the posters: bold illustrations of giraffes, a rampant lion, tigers in cages, parading mandarins and Arabs on steeds, the posters hanging like worn tapestries in the winter sun. In Demopolis what caught his eye was the lively poster for the Silas Green Show—"From New Orleans"—sporting lithe dancing girls shimmying in beaded skirts. The brick wall was already showing through the tatters although the event was little more than two months past. It was an effect that Evans appreciated: the hard wall of reality revealing itself behind the gaudy illusion. It took on added significance when a mule team with wagon stopped to graze in front of the poster.

Remarkably at Selma, though Evans's field notes indicate he spent only one day there, he put in a full day of photographing with full sun: streets and signage (Fixings for Men, a clothing store), main street architecture ("Selma vs. Tuscaloosa," the whitewashed announcement in the shop window), black men seated on benches, and a shoeshine stand along a row of brick storefronts. In his diary, Evans began collecting random snippets of local talk: "Come Back Boss Man," "Mortified to death, as I'm right." There was much to gather up in southern streets.

Nearing Christmas, he made a brisk trip into Mississippi through Forest to Brookhaven, evidently skipping Jackson for the moment. A missing page presents a gap in his diary, and there is no notation for December 23. On Christmas Eve he left New Orleans in the afternoon for the roughly two-hundred-mile trip back north to Jackson. On Christmas Day he is on the road back to New Orleans — a flurry of activity that remains unexplained. Though he had obviously alerted Jane Ninas about his arrival, they did not see each other on the holiday. Two days later, Evans and Jane in one car and Paul and Christine in Paul's car drove out to

Waveland for a weekend at Christine's family cottage on the Mississippi Sound. The "cottage" was definitely a find, a two-story Victorian display of gingerbread traceries, though Evans did not photograph it until two weeks later when he returned on his own. But the weekend was a loss, two couples uneasy about their situation, Jane suspecting that Christine had invited them "out of obvious evil," wanting to prove to Paul that something was going on between Walker and her. It was "a nightmarish time," she remembered. It was cold and they had to huddle around the fireplaces. "It was just tension," she remembered, "very high tension all the time. Nothing overt at all; everybody was being civilized and nice." After they returned to New Orleans, Evans reverted to calling her up by way of the downstairs liquor store.

Photographing in the city once again, he stayed on for another week or more; a run of Greek Revival houses in the city; the waterfront markets; the Liberty movie theater; a house in the Negro quarter teeming with life and laundry on the second floor balcony; the Margaret Statue, a tribute to one of the city's benefactors (a seated woman and child, the woman's crocheted shawl a marvel of fragility worked in stone, like the carved roses of the Castellucci monument); the grillwork of a house on Felicity and Orange streets. One of the curiosities was the sequence of four photographs of a garage mechanic which he took with the Deardorff rather than his Leica. (The mechanic would play an odd role in Evans's life some months later.) Before leaving for Washington on the train (he planned to leave the car in New Orleans) he journeyed out to Waveland on January 11 to take what, under the circumstances, might have passed for a souvenir of his uncomfortable weekend at Fairchild Cottage as well as an assignment for the FSA.

In the meantime, Peter Sekaer in New York was writing him repeatedly (and receiving no replies) about the mounting expenses at the studio. He was also negotiating with Tom Mabry for additional money for the printing and mounting of the African sculpture portfolios he and John Cheever were assembling. Sekaer was expecting Evans to return to New York on January 15 so that he could accompany him to Washington; there was a possibility of his accompanying Evans on the next phase of his assignment. He was apparently aware of the mounting pressure from Stryker that Evans turn in more work. On December 26, he wrote Evans with the suggestion that he turn in some of his prior work in the South: "You can always count your 4 x 5 as well as your Leica negatives if you wish to impress Washington with your industry!" He admonished Evans, "For Christ's sake write!"

Belle Hélène Plantation Manor House, Louisiana, 1935

On January 2, he wrote again: "Still not so much as a postal from you . . ." The burden of this letter was that the Edison Company had shut off the electricity at 20 Bethune Street, where Cheever was working. He planned to hit up Mabry in order to settle the bill: "I don't like this errand particularly, but poor John can't sit over there in the dark. . . ." He supposed that Evans was not getting his letters. "Or are you lying dead by the road-side?" he asked. "Or have you been fatally shot by a jealous maniac?" His query was almost prophetic.

IV

The directives from Washington were becoming insistent. In February, Roy Stryker wrote Evans at length outlining the projects he was expected to complete during the final phase of his FSA assignment. He also indicated that Ernestine Evans would be meeting him in Birmingham, where the two could work out further details. Stryker was deferential: "Of course, we concede your right to modify, since you are on the ground and may see good reasons why you should go one place instead of another." The first assignment was in Tupelo, Mississippi, where the RA project was being returned to local management. "There is an insistent demand here for additional photography to be used for publicity purposes," Stryker told him, "so it is absolutely essential that you get in and take a set of pictures showing the present state of the building and some additional local color, also people and activities. . . . This is one of the emergency jobs that I hate to bother you with, but it must be done." There was no need, he felt, to go into detail about Birmingham: "I am sure that you will have a grand time here with your eye for industrial landscapes." In Georgia there were the Piedmont plantations and the Coastal Flatwood projects near Monticello and Waycross, both Resettlement assignments. In the latter there were cut pine lands and turpentine workers. "Get us some good 8 x 10 shots and also some good Leica shots of the turpentine workers."

Mindful that some of these assignments would be irksome to the photographer, he recommended the Piedmont project: "I am informed that you will find some very excellent examples of plantation homes. Incidentally, most of them are in a sad state of decay." He was shipping Evans a case of film; one of the reasons it was necessary that Evans keep him "posted of your whereabouts every few days." Stryker had also ordered a wide-angle lens, which Ernestine Evans would bring to Birmingham if it arrived in time. "This will give you a chance to do some interior stuff while you are out on this particular trip. If possible, get us some interiors of the country stores." It was election year and the Republicans were making an issue of what they considered the wasteful programs of the Roosevelt administration, the Farm Security Administration's Photographic Unit being an easy target. It was important that the photographers in the field produce. He was explicit about what the agency needed: "good land

Barbershop,
Southern Town,
1936

pictures, showing the erosion, sub-marginal areas, cut-over land. These should be taken wherever possible, showing the relationship of the land to the cultural decay. Cotton planting is probably now going on. Try to get us a few nice 'syrupy' pictures of agricultural scenes and general pictures for cover pages." Stryker stressed the point: "I realize this is a nice big order, but remember you've got to deliver or else I am going to catch the devil. Take time off to develop your film occasionally and keep sending it through."

Evans complied with some of Stryker's suggestions, though not all. On this trip, Peter Sekaer was with him and by mid-February, in advance of Stryker's directive, the two were based in New Orleans where Evans picked up his car and made side trips to Pontchatoula, Louisiana, and up to Edwards, Mississippi. At Pontchatoula, on February 13, setting up his Deardorff in the bright slanted light of mid-afternoon, he photographed George's Place, a roadside stand with baskets of fruit at the curbside that offered oysters at the counter. The following morning, with only faint sun,

looking down from a high vantage spot, he took a sequence of lovely shots of the railroad station at Edwards: the tracks veering round a bend, the station bereft of activity except for a few stragglers in conversation, and a lone figure walking beside the distant rails. The scene has a peculiar kind of American poetry: the stillness, the emptiness that lingers after departure.

By the fifteenth, Evans and Sekaer were once more in New Orleans, Evans now in familiar territory photographing a group of houses along South Clairborne Avenue and a grimy rundown house in the factory district, behind it a huge gas tank and beside it a spruce new billboard picturing a schoolboy studying his geography lesson. The image, it seems, was meant to alert viewers to the hardship of "defective vision." For Sekaer, the city was a broadening experience; he roamed the streets — some of them the same streets Evans had photographed on earlier visits — busily photographing. His politics drew him to the Negro quarter, and he made many photographs

there. But he also savored the street life, photographing toughs (white) on a street corner, prostitutes at their profession. (The captions he wrote for his family in Denmark were sly: "Behind the window screen sits a naughty girl and offers herself to the passing gentlemen! New Orleans.") During this and later visits he also photographed the architecture and elaborate grillwork balconies. He was captivated by the old Napoleon House, which, according to legend, had been built by Napoleon's American friends, who had planned to send the pirate Lafitte to rescue him at St. Helena "when word came that the Emperor was dead." Like Evans, Sekaer was intrigued by the shop signs, among them a gypsy phrenologist's chart: "She reads your head like an open book. She speks servel langues. Step in." Jane Ninas recalls having met Sekaer for the first time with Evans at a fancy New Orleans tea shop. She was wearing a thin coat and Evans had pointedly asked Sekaer, "Do you think that coat's warm enough to get back to New York in?" For Jane the remark came from out of the blue. It was her first realization that Walker was thinking seriously about their going off together.

On February 16, Evans and Sekaer were traveling north on Route 61 to Baton Rouge en route to Vicksburg. At Baton Rouge Evans took the trouble of setting up his Deardorff to photograph what he termed a "surrealist clothing sign," photographing it against the sun, the subject entirely in the shade. Another of the clues to the ride north was the photograph of a pair of hitchhikers, a man and a woman, standing by the roadside, the man's arm raised thumbing, with the road and the leafless trees stretching endlessly ahead in the gray day. What gives one pause is that the photograph is not a snapshot taken from the car window but an 8 x 10, which required that Evans set up his Deardorff while the couple assumed their poses. Quite probably it is "Negative D103" of his photographic record for February 18 taken on Route 61 North traveling toward Vicksburg. That the caption reads "Jack Forest & wife" suggests that Evans and Sekaer had given the couple a ride.

Street Scene, New Orleans, 1936

For the latter part of the month, from February 18 to March 2, 1936, with gaps of a few days here and there, Evans's records indicate he was in Vicksburg and its vicinity. He and Sekaer were staying at the Carroll Hotel, which is where Stryker's lengthy letter had reached them. They were already photographing industriously and with a certain amount of rivalry. It was little wonder that Sekaer would later complain to his wife that Evans

289

got to the subjects before he did. A case in point may have been the striking sequence of photographs of ferry boats along the Mississippi at Vicksburg that Evans took on February 21 and again on the twenty-seventh. On the first occasion, according to his records, he photographed the Mississippi sternwheelers the *Charles J. Miller* and the *George W. Miller*, docked at Desoto Island. The shots were taken from the east bank of the river, with river men and cargo flats in the foreground. Sekaer, on that same day apparently, photographed the ferry *Chicot*, puffing upstream past Evans's two ships and, a little further downstream, he caught the New Orleans sternwheeler *Destrehan*, docked at the ferry landing. What attracted his attention, too, was a handsome black youth whom he seems to have encountered on the riverbank and of whom he made several portraits. It would be true of most of their shoots together during that trip that Sekaer was particularly interested in depicting the life of the blacks in the South, the sociology of the place. Sekaer made a point of photographing water fountains labeled "Colored" or the similarly desig-

nated outside stairs leading to the balconies of the local movie houses.

The twenty-first was a busy day; late in the afternoon, both men began taking photographs in the Vicksburg black quarter. From the vantage point of a high private backyard, as Evans noted, he took a long shot of what he designated as "nigger houses." (The term was an exception in his records; he generally used the term "Negroes," as did Sekaer.) Evans took only three or four shots of the clustered houses in the south end of town, but he and Sekaer returned the following day for more, with Evans catching a group of black women in conversation on a porch. It was a domestic scene, caught from a distance, that added a different dimension to what might otherwise have been a sociological exercise for the agency's benefit.

The most striking of their finds in the quarter was a trio of black barbershops in a row. Both took shots, Evans still using his Deardorff, which must have aroused a certain amount of curiosity in the men and the one woman sitting or standing outside in the bright sunlight. Evans, by this time, had become a fancier of the minor social dramas of barbershops; as in Havana he had caught the barbers at their trade. In New Orleans, the year before, there had been the wonderful surprise of the fat lady in the striped blouse emerging sequentially out the door with a flurry of move-ment behind her in the darkened interior. The Vicksburg sequence now offered a kind of street ballet as Evans, proceeding downhill, closed in on the prize: the two connecting shots encompassing the three barbershops (the Brother in Law, the New Deal, and the Savoy), the figures trapped against the raked lighting of the clapboards. One can, with some justice, imagine the rival choreographies of the photographers: Evans moving first and Sekaer beginning further up the slope, following Evans down, taking two wide-angled horizontal shots at some distance from the curb. The man seated next to the woman in Evans's shot has gotten up and moved further down the street. (Is that he standing in the doorway of the barbershop next door?) In the Sekaer pictures, another woman has started downhill, and a third in a dark coat and carrying a package is on her way up. She has stopped to talk to the loungers in front of the New Deal Barber Shop. This is, at least, a probable scenario for the dance in time captured by the two photographers on a bright late morning or early afternoon in Vicksburg.

According to Sekaer's recollections, another of the subjects in their ongoing competition, a black man standing against a movie billboard

Garage in Southern City Outskirts, 1936

for the 1936 film *The Loves of Bugle Ann*, starring Lionel Barrymore and Maureen O'Sullivan, was taken in Vicksburg as well. One can see the difference between the confirmed professional and the younger photographer in comparison. It is a 35-mm shot and Evans has closed in and cropped the subject with only a bit of the lettering so that the figure of the black man is juxtaposed against the larger-than-life faces of a beaming white couple. In an enlarged print, he cropped the white man's face drastically, creating an immediate confrontation between the black working man and the glamorous sparkling-eyed Maureen O'Sullivan. In essence the photograph is a repeat of Evans's Havana shot of the black man in the white suit against the rack of movie-star magazines. Sekaer, on the other hand, seized on the subject at an awkward moment, too far back, with the man blotting out O'Sullivan's face and losing the dramatic point.

The last of the Vicksburg photographs were taken on February 27 and into the first days of March. Evans photographed the Islamic-style arches on the side entrance of the Carroll Hotel, where he was staying, automobiles angled and parked at the curbside — a familiar refrain in his work. As if to satisfy one of Stryker's demands, he photographed the interior of a seed store, the wares neatly arranged; shots requiring long five-minute exposures and an .45f-stop. There were, then, obvious technical reasons for avoiding people and the blur of motion when taking some of his photographs. The seed store photographs, if they were meant to satisfy an official request, were still among the more memorable commonplace subjects of the trip, ineffable reminders of a time and a place. The tidy rows of seed corn and beans in burlap bags, the brightly illustrated packets of vegetable seeds. High on the shelves shiny bird cages were arranged in drill formation, and beneath, ranks of packaged canary food products and poultry prescriptions, giving testimony to a storekeeper's obsession with order in the midst of threatened chaos. There would be other store photographs on this and many another Evans trip. Stores were a persistent genre in his photographs; they served him as inventories of domestic life and household activities. But beyond that they were catalogues of American aspirations. Very late in life Evans would spell out the appeal such subjects had for him: "I am fascinated by man's work and the civilization that he's built. In fact, I think that's *the* interesting thing in the world, what man makes."

Negro quarter, Tupelo, Mississippi, March, 1936

Few of the Evans Vicksburg photographs — Negro shacks, a moldering antebellum townhouse, an array of histrionic sculptures in a battlefield park — could be classified as pretty or scenic. Yet it was one of the peculiarities of his case that Evans developed a vestigial affection for the southern landscape and he viewed his Vicksburg sojourn as a special one. Late in life, asked by a young southern writer and photographer, Bill Ferris, if he remembered Vicksburg, he remarked, "Of course I remember Vicksburg. You know, to someone who hasn't been there before, it has a tremendous appeal to the eye. I can understand why Southerners are haunted by their own landscape and in love with it."

293

V

Nothing could have prepared Evans for the misfortune of his return trip to New Orleans to see Jane Ninas. Ninas believes it was in the spring, mindful that spring comes earlier in New Orleans than elsewhere. She thinks it was probably while Evans and Sekaer were still operating around Vicksburg, which could have been late February. One evening Evans visited her and Paul in their Pontalba apartment. The strain of the uncomfortable holiday visit to Waveland was still in the air. Paul Ninas, in a rare acknowledgment that his wife and Evans were possibly having an affair, abruptly decided to make an issue of it. The three of them, Jane remembers, were standing in the living room when Paul suddenly pulled out a pistol and began waving it around. He pointed it directly at Evans, declaring that Walker should either take Jane with him or get out of their lives. (She hadn't known that Paul had a gun; she thought it must have been something he recently acquired following his father's death, along with a collection of oriental rugs and brass objects from Constantinople.) The results were disastrous. Evans turned pale and immediately took his leave. Paul's threats and Walker's abrupt departure left Jane shaken. For her it was a traumatic event; for the next two or three days she was sick in bed. During those few days, unknown to her, Evans was parked outside the Pontalba Building, worried that something might have happened to her, watching to see if she came out. In a melodramatic step, he wore a disguise, having borrowed an Auto Supply Company cap and outfit from the garage mechanic he had photographed weeks earlier. The surveillance did not last long, however; Evans soon left the city. Within a few days, from Vicksburg or possibly elsewhere in his travels, he sent Jane a long letter explaining that their relationship had become too complicated, too hazardous, and that they had better end it. Jane was shocked; her recollection was that she promptly blocked out every memory of her affair with Walker. She suffered, she thinks, from a form of amnesia. After the episode, however, she noticed that Paul and she quarreled often.

Evans at work, in the southeastern United States. Center: Evans kneeling to load film in darkens of bedcovers. 1936.

* * *

It is not clear, either, when Evans finally made the trip to Tupelo that

Stryker had designated as a priority assignment. Presumably it was after he quit Vicksburg and began his journey northward. Whatever his distress over the humiliating incident with Jane and Paul, Evans kept on working. On March 3, he stopped at Edwards again, this time photographing shop fronts, including the "Dew Drop In Cafe Kelly," as well as a folksy sign of a bull's head painted on the brick wall of a butcher shop. On Route 80, outside Edwards traveling toward Jackson, he photographed a Mississippi farm scene. In the photograph the buildings are cited at a distance, the trees behind them still barren of leaves, and in the foreground the fields still in their winter furrows. Noticeably, he heeded Stryker's request and began a number of photographs, meant to illustrate the devastating effects of soil erosion, most of them taken around the vicinity of Edwards and Jackson and possibly on up to Oxford. On occasion, however, the erosion shots took on an eerie beauty, the wind and rain having sculptured the land forms until they looked like cratered moonscapes except for the sentinel pines standing on top of the plateaus. He and Sekaer, then, had kept busy along the way north. By March 11, Evans's records indicate that they were photographing in Alabama. The probability, then, is that the trip to Tupelo was made during the intervening gap in his records. In the FSA catalogue of his photographs, the erosion and Tupelo shots are all dated as March 1936.

The Tupelo sites provided shots of the local Negro quarters, too. These were similar to those taken in the Negro quarter at Vicksburg, except that the shacks, on the outskirts of the county capital, were even more ramshackle, some with the eroded landscape showing in the background. Once more he and Sekaer were competing for the same subjects, Sekaer shooting a family group of blacks sitting on a cabin stoop, Evans using his Deardorff, trying for the more classical pose, focusing on three youngsters in shabby clothes sitting on the ground. The many shots Sekaer took suggest that the session may have taken some time or perhaps that they had returned on a second day. The young black boy who appeared in very badly torn dark pants in Evans's photograph appears in Sekaer's boisterous family group wearing a pair of ragged dark shorts.

Houses and Billboards in Atlanta, 1936

On several occasions during the trip, Sekaer amused himself by photographing Evans in flagrante delicto in the very act of photographing, for example, under the blackcloth (this was at Vicksburg). On another occasion, he is lounging at some unknown site in front of "The Grand Man," a folk art mural of the Vitruvian man, with signs of the zodiac pointing to related body parts. He also photographed Evans in his hotel room kneeling by his bedside, not in prayer but loading film under the blanket. In Tupelo, Sekaer photographed Evans's Deardorff at ease in the landscape and what appears to be Evans giving a group of black children a glimpse through the ground glass screen of the camera.

The most mysterious photo Evans took at the Tupelo sites was a marvel of subtlety. At first one takes in the scene as a whole and only later notices the figure of a black man in the middle ground. Seen from the back, he is neatly dressed in a dark suit and cap, leaning against the tilted wall of a shack, peering cautiously around the corner at some unseen person or event. In the distance the tower of a stolid civic building rises above the general dilapidation of the setting. The clock in the tower stands at 10 past 10 A.M.

What is he looking at, hiding there? One is left to guess at the circumstances, but it is a photograph about the mysteries of human behavior and the unknowable events in human life. It is also an admission that there are times when vision can tell us only so much and nothing more.

* * *

One might say of Evans what was once claimed for Henry James: that as an artist, he had a mind so fine, no idea could violate it. Wherever the venue, Evans, put down in any place, would find something remarkable to photograph, something not to be tied to esthetic theory or to any political agenda. He had a purist's eye. His 1935-1936 excursions through the South would produce a body of work that stands on its own as a remarkable American pilgrimage. And the final stages of his journey with Sekaer in the spring of 1936 added more to his achievement. He had, indeed, as Stryker had requested, spent some time in Birmingham, photographing a sequence of carefully organized formal views of the workers' houses and the dark and intricate silhouettes of the steel mills on the plain. But this attention to duty was also relieved by more personal interests. On March 11, according to his records, he made several shots of the gingerbread porch of a run-down boarding house at 2416 Fourth Avenue in Birmingham. It is not only the insistent architectural decoration with its frieze of roundels and the ornately cut arches that strike one's imagination, but the bits of life encapsulated in the façade, like episodes in an illuminated medieval psalter; a man dozes on the porch, another gazes off into space. At a second story window, behind a makeshift bit of screening, a woman is bent over her sewing. In nearby Bessemer, he caught sight of a billboard for the McDonald Furniture Company which appears to be the "furniture sign" noted in his records. With its picture of a living room as vast as the American Dream, with overscaled furniture and diminutive family members, it was a piece of primitive art Evans could hardly have passed up.

Penny Picture Display, Savannah, 1936

* * *

Evidence suggests that, as originally planned, Evans met up with Ernestine Evans in Birmingham. Belinda Rathbone, in her book *Walker*

STUDIO

Evans: A Biography, indicates that it was only after some difficulties in communication that they managed to get together. But the Birmingham stay could not have been long. By March 13, Evans and Sekaer were in Georgia. Judging from the fact that Sekaer took photographs of the outside "Colored" balcony entrance of a movie house in Anniston, Alabama, it is probable that the pair had taken Route 78 into Georgia. For the remainder of the trip, whether chastened by Washington or not, Evans followed Stryker's directives more or less to the letter. From March 13 through 16, the two were — productively — operating in Atlanta, staying at the Kimball House. (Rooms 651 and 653, according to Sekaer's copies of the bills, which may mean that Sekaer had footed the six-dollar-bill for the two of them.) Evans took a lengthy and detailed sequence of photographs of the black quarter there, the housing units cramped together but often more solidly built than what he had seen elsewhere. Either then or perhaps at a later stop in Atlanta, he made several photographs in a Negro barbershop, and one of his signature studies of two movie billboards: one of Carole Lombard with a black eye advertising *Love Before Breakfast* and one of Anne Shirley in *Chatterbox,* both plastered against a board fence and backed by twin begrimed frame houses.

It is clear from Sekaer's captions that they visited Dalton, north of Atlanta, where Sekaer photographed the local farmers coming into town on a Saturday afternoon. Also in Atlanta, Evans photographed the Cherokee Parts Store which was located at 973 Marietta Street. Against the backdrop of a garage, Evans was to witness a little roadside drama that involved a woman in a fur jacket watching while an unusually well-dressed garage attendant studied the problem of her car. Next to him, a young man has caught sight of Evans at his bulky camera and is clearly interested in the procedure. To the left in the sequence, a young woman, backed by a composition of hanging tires, inner tubes, hub caps, and wheelspokes, is bored, then bemused by the little drama in the interior of the garage. The theater of the wayside played a more important part in Evans's photographs than he has been given credit for; the specificity of detail could have been influenced by Balzac — if Evans had ever read Balzac — but the concentrated narrative is straight out of Flaubert.

Following Stryker's itinerary, the two moved on to Monticello and Eatonton in Jasper and Putnam counties, Evans more taken by another plantation house and a field of dead trees in the Monticello vicinity but dutifully recording a sequence on the operations of the FSA project near Eatonton, where he found spruce modern houses under construction; carpenters at work fixing doors, hanging windows; a farmer plowing a field. At Macon, Evans took a long shot from aloft of the busy Main Street, another addition to his records of downtown America. The pair moved further south toward the coastal plains. Somewhere in their southern pilgrimage, possibly on their way to St. Mary's Georgia, Evans and Sekaer came upon a chain gang of blacks working along a broad barren highway. Fascinated by the sight, they stopped and, without intervention from the armed guards, began to take photographs. They took rather similar shots; the blacks in zebra-striped uniforms, bent over their hoes and shovels, one of them circulating with a pail of water and a dipper. Evans recorded the blunt facts of the case. Sekaer, in his captions, added a bit of sociological observation: "Negroes are used to build roads. They are unjustly treated. When a theft occurs and it is thought that a Negro did it, a Negro gets arrested. That it isn't the same Negro doesn't matter — he goes to prison anyway. This system is quicker and cheaper."

At St. Mary's on the coast, Evans was struck by the ruins of what was

Walker Evans,
c. 1936

purported to be an ancient Spanish mission but was actually a colonial sugar mill. The intriguing feature of the remaining structures were the coarse tabby walls made of oyster shells, lime, sand, and saltwater — a structural material dating back to colonial times. In the photographs, Evans avoided any aspect of artfulness or the use of dramatic angles; clearly the subject was dramatic enough. The structures, relics of a lost time, had a rough-hewn solemnity, standing, as they did, in a field of new growth dotted with spring wildflowers. A small pile of rubbish served as a reminder of the careless human presence. At St. Mary's, too, he took a few photographs of the small rural wooden churches that were a familiar type in the region. Receding north toward Savannah, he photographed a grander, more historic example, the Midway Church at Midway in Liberty County, which had been burned in the American Revolution and rebuilt in 1792.

Evans had already visited Savannah a number of times and had photographed there often. The mystery of this later visit is the mystery of his photograph *Penny Picture Display, Savannah*, taken of a window of a photographer's studio, which he afterwards attributed to his 1936 Savannah visit. The FSA records, however, describe the photograph as having been taken in Birmingham, Alabama. A quite different shot of a photographer's window display in Birmingham, taken from a slight angle and the photographs held together with paper clips, also exists. The Savannah photograph, however, is one of the most famous and at the same time most poetic and personal of Evans's career. It serves as a metaphor for the photographic profession itself and its historic connection with portraiture by taking it to the *n*th degree. It also serves as the summary photograph of an important phase of Evans's career — his uncanny recognition of his subject, wherever it happened to be. The photograph is a celebration of the fact that he had become, however focused, the commentator on American ways and mores. Under the bold studio logo, he had found the human comedy: a gallery of quizzical infants, boys in sailor suits, sweethearts, youthful buddies, businessmen, housewives, doting grandpas. All of the subjects were white and dressed for the occasion. They represent, presumably, all members of the middle-class clientele that patronized such establishments. The original photographer had worked at pairing and comparing prints, combinations, contrasts. When Evans came on the scene, the faces were still fresh and current. For viewers half a century later it is another story. The inspiration — not for the operator of the studio, but perhaps for Evans with his literary bent and his admiration for T. S. Eliot — might almost have been the lines from *The Waste Land* about the crowds flowing over London Bridge: "so many / I had not thought death had undone so many." But the definitive text is Evans's own later commentary: "The only reason this photograph has any value is an instinct is touched in it. 'This is for me.' It's like the meaning of a person. The singular importance of this spoke to me that way. It's uproariously funny, and very touching and very sad and very human. All these people had composed themselves in front of the local studio camera, and I bring my camera, and they all pose again together for me. That's a fabulous fact. I look at it and think, and think, and think about all those people. It was made in the thirties, in Savannah."

It says something about the occasional offhandedness of Evans's technical approach that of the three negatives he made of what he seemingly recognized as a major picture, he eventually cut down two in order to make suitable 5 x 7 negatives for his 5 x 7 enlarger. (He had no enlarger for 8 x 10 prints at the time and resorted to contact prints for his Deardorff photographs.) Luckily the third negative was in the safe hands of the FSA and has remained intact.

Of the final phase of his trip, traveling through South Carolina, he added to his anthology of rural churches with a sequence of Negro churches with shallow porches and slender unornamented beam-pillars, only the varied spires differentiating the style from place to place. In Beaufort, presumably on his way to Charleston and the expected meeting with Julia Peterkin in Columbia, he made a lucky find: a single building, part store, part office, freighted with a conglomeration of signs. Combining the illustrious past with the mundane present, it struck the American note. The most impressive feature was the sign announcing that General Lafayette had spoken from its porch in 1824. (A cat's head, a mere speck in the composition, peers over the bottom railing.) The remaining signs indicated that the house was a veritable ark of American civilization: Under the one roof could be found the Beaufort Art School, a public stenographer, and, on the ground floor, a fish company and a market for fruits and vegetables. The latter sign carried a delicate still life of fruits and vegetables that Evans obviously cherished, all the more so since the painted banana was

303

juxtaposed against a huge bunch of the real thing hanging in the doorway of the gloomy interior. "This struck me as very funny, absurd, naïve, and unconscious," he later admitted. ". . . much more humor in it than in pop art. The still life of fruit is a lovely piece of primitive painting." The building had weathered the ages from the postrevolutionary period to the depression year of 1936, carrying its burden of culture and commodities. In Evans's photograph, it now served as a souvenir of his remarkable southern tour under the auspices of the federal government.

Signs,
South Carolina,
1936

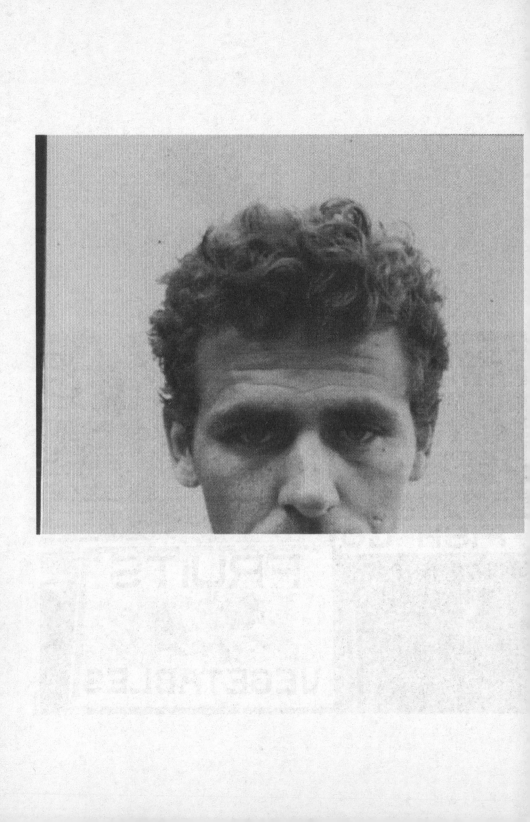

A Curious Piece of Work

14

Is it of some consequence that the most successful activities in Walker Evans's working career should involve a relationship with a male friend who was likely to be more ambitious, more hard-headed, more informed about opportunities, and better placed to make use of them? By the summer of 1936, Evans — if he had chosen to do so — could have looked back over a series of such involvements. There had been Hanns Skolle, who, for all his opportunistic ways, was a serious influence and source of encouragement in Evans's pursuit of an artistic career. There had been the efforts, in more minor ways, of Hart Crane and Paul Grotz. More important, he owed an acknowledged debt to Lincoln Kirstein, who had given him financial support, published his work in *The Hound and Horn*, promoted him in important circles, including the Muriel Draper salon with its wide connections, and the new Museum of Modern Art. At the Modern, Tom Mabry eased Evans into the African sculpture project. Ben Shahn, full of the self-assurance that Evans lacked (in Evans's eyes at least)—a man indefatigably in pursuit of the main chance — had made a mark on Evans's character, though never persuasively when it came to his radical political views. More recently there had been the companionship of his go-getter friend, Peter Sekaer, who, like Skolle and Grotz, was a transplanted European.

In the summer of 1936, it was James Agee who provided one of the most important collaborative efforts in Evans's career. Agee and his wife, Via, had only recently returned to New York from his leave of absence in Anna Maria, Florida. In the spring of that year Agee had it in mind to quit *Fortune*, but by a stroke of luck Managing Editor Eric Hodgins offered him an opportunity he could hardly resist. It was the chance to write an article on tenant farming in the Deep South. It was slated for the magazine's "Life and Circumstances" series, intended to inform its readership of well-to-do businessmen about the less fortunate members of American society. Given Agee's Tennessee origins and his earlier articles on New Deal topics, he was the logical choice for the project. Thrilled, Agee stopped by the office of his friend Robert Fitzgerald with the news.

Tenant Farmer with Daughter, Hale County, Alabama, 1936

Fitzgerald, only recently hired as a staff member of *Time*, remembered the scene vividly: "One day Jim appeared in my office unusually tall and quiet and swallowing with excitement (did I have a moment?) to tell me something in confidence." Agee was, as Fitzgerald quaintly put it, "stunned, exalted, scared clean through, and felt like impregnating every woman on the fifty-second floor." Although the deal hadn't been definitely settled, the two were in a mood to celebrate. They repaired to a Third Avenue bar where Agee spelled out "not for the first time nor the last, the genesis of *Let Us Now Praise Famous Men*." He also told Fitzgerald his hope that the magazine would hire Walker Evans as the photographer for the project. Agee was equally exuberant writing to his friend Father Flye: "The best break I ever had on *Fortune*; feel terrific personal responsibility toward story, considerable doubts of my ability to bring it off, considerable more doubts of Fortune's ultimate willingness to use it."

Evans, oddly, would remember that the assignment was "eagerly grabbed by Agee but not by me." Certainly he was not aroused by the New Deal aspects of the offer. His political stance, as described in later years, was plain: "The problem is one of staying out of Left politics and still avoiding Establishment patterns. I would not politicize my mind or work. . . . The apostles can't have me. I don't think an artist is directly able to alleviate the human condition. He's very interested in *revealing* it." As far as his work for the FSA was concerned, Evans took no credit for the kind of humanist motives Agee might have considered: "I was interested, selfishly, in the opportunity it gave me to go around and use the camera. I did anything I pleased and *ignored* what I was expected to do. . . . Such a bore; I wouldn't touch it." It was Evans's conviction that *Fortune* "didn't really know what role it should play during the depression. They didn't know what they were doing, since they were founded to describe in a stimulating and interesting way, American business and industry and that was falling apart." He had also grown tired of the "subterfuge," as he called it, by which he was operating in the Photography Unit, that is, ignoring administrative orders as best he could. "I remember once somebody wanted one of those stupid building projects photographed. I photographed it but I said this is the last time I'm going to do that; I'm not interested in this; to hell with it, I won't do it." He may well have been referring to the Eatonton project, which accounts for some of the dullest photographs in his FSA catalogue, though it was not the last of the assignments he covered for the government.

All the same, he requested a leave from the FSA and took on the *Fortune* offer. Officially his leave ran from July 16 to September 17, longer, in fact, than the month *Fortune* had originally proposed. A serious drawback, however, and one that Evans later regretted, was that the FSA laid claim to whatever photographs he produced on the *Fortune* assignment. In later life Evans confessed he was not sure why he had agreed to it, only specifying that it was one of the conditions of his leave.

* * *

"During July and August 1936," Agee remembered, "Walker Evans and I were traveling in the middle south of this nation and were engaged in what, even from the first, has seemed to me rather a curious piece of work." Evans had already scouted the Hale County territory (the year before) but he and Agee had difficulties finding a proper subject: a single sharecropper family that would serve as model for the whole condition of the tenant farmer in the Depression South. Their random forays turned up some interesting false starts which would serve Agee as a kind of prelude in the later *Let Us Now Praise Famous Men*. On a hot Sunday morning in the company of a New Deal agent named Harmon and a local landlord they paid a visit to a compound of black sharecropper families. They stopped first at the foreman's house, set in a cluster of oaks with a dozen or more two-room sharecropper shacks nearby. Their unexpected arrival created a stir. The foreman was entertaining relatives: The women, interrupted in the midst of preparing dinner, were quietly hostile; the men, in their Sunday best, stood respectfully in attendance and then withdrew while the landlord talked with the foreman. Beforehand, Evans had pointedly asked if it would be all right to take pictures. The landlord had answered, "Sure, of course, take all the snaps you're a mind to; that is if you can keep the niggers from running off when they see a camera." Not a propitious answer, and, oddly, in the files, there don't seem to be photos of this earliest visit. Some of the neighboring blacks began to congregate, among them an older man with a pair of stripling boys. What followed, in Agee's excruciating study of race relations in the South in the thirties, may have had more to do with the undercurrent of sexuality that Agee brought to the scene than to the actual sociology of the case. The landlord teased the old man: "An you, you ben doin much coltn lately, you horny old bastard?" One of the neighbors jokes, "He too *ole*, Mist-So-and-So, he don't got no sap lef in him." The landlord singles out the two young sons and Agee reports the conversation with the father in a run-on passage that would certainly give any magazine editor pause before publication:

These yer two yere, colts yourn ain't they?—and the old man said they were, and the landowner said, Musta found <u>them</u> in the woods, strappin young niggers as that; and the old man said, No sir, he got the both of them lawful married, Mist So-and-So; and the landowner said that eldest on em looks to be ready for a piece himself, and the negroes laughed, and the two boys twisted their beautiful bald gourdlike skulls in a unison of shyness and their faces were illumined with maid-enly smiles of shame, delight, and fear; and meanwhile the landowner had loosened the top two buttons of his trousers, and he now reached his hand in to the middle of the forearm, and, squatting with bent knees apart, clawed, scratched and rearranged his genitals.

A child is sent running to fetch the male members of the church choir and Evans and Agee are treated to a chorus. The men dressed for church in their starched white shirts, pinned with the purple and gold ribbons of a burial society, assemble in the oak shade on that bright Sunday morning. Agee gives a full and odd account of the singing, its pitch and tone and rhythm: "it tore itself like a dance of sped plants out of three young men who stood sunk to their throats in land, and whose eyes were neither shut nor looking at anything . . ." When the performance ends abruptly, the landlord smiles coldly. Agee pointedly makes a request for a second number: "I had a feeling, through their silence before entering it, that it was their favorite and their particular 'pride;' the tenor lifted out his voice alone in a long, plorative line that hung like fire on heaven, or whistle's echo sinking, sunken, along descents of a modality I had not heard before. . . ." Finally the landlord, complaining of too much howling and religion on end, asks for "something with some life to it" and the trio strikes into "a fast, sassy, pelvic tune whose words were loaded almost beyond translation with comic sexual metaphor." At the end, embarrassed and "in a perversion of self-torture," Agee hands the leader fifty cents and thanks the singers, apologizing for having held them up. In his stylized and colloquial manner, the whole episode is as graphic as a photograph, or more like a film clip that captures the forced deference of the blacks, the raunchiness of the landowner, the self-consciousness of the northern visitors woven into the picture of the black choral group fixed in the dappled shade, straining at their song. The effect could only reinforce Agee's challenging notion — ironically expressed in the book — that the camera was "next to unassisted and weaponless consciousness, the central instrument of our time."

A second random episode depicts a porch visit with a down-and-out white family they had stopped to question in their search for suitable share-cropper farms. The young man is invalided from asthma, his wife forced to do most of the work with only a weak steer to do the plowing. The third figure is a retarded young man, slobbering, his conversation reduced to a loud "Awnk, awnk," one more burden, another mouth to be fed, in an already overburdened family. They are clients of a rehabilitation agency who, having planted too late, already owe the government for seed and fertilizer, while their sparse crops lie withering in a drought. The depth of their poverty is such that they are receiving the charity of a family of blacks living two or three miles down a back road who have supplied them with dried corn and peas from their own dwindling rations. At the least sign of attention or interest the retarded man begins to pester and tug at Agee. (Evans does not make an appearance in this episode except as Agee's unnamed companion on the drive.) The woman speaks to the boy/man sharply but not unkindly:

as if he were a dog masturbating on a caller, and he withdrew against a post of the porch and sank along it to the floor with his knees up sharp and wide apart and the fingers of his left hand jammed as deep as they would go down his gnashing mouth, while he stayed his bright eyes on me. She got up abruptly without speaking and went indoors and came back out with a piece of stony corn-bread and gave it to him, and took her place again in her chair.

The vignette forms one of the most painful and graphic snapshots of Agee's early account of the trip.

The third episode of this prelude describes a seemingly innocent encounter, but it carries the same painfulness, the same psychological edge as the earlier segments. Agee and Evans have stopped to inspect a rural church whose door is locked. They peer through a window, wondering whether to force it. In the meantime a young negro couple walks on by: "Without appearing to look either longer or less long, or with more or less interest, than a white man might care for, and without altering their pace, they made a thorough observation of us, of the car, and of the tripod and camera." Agee decides to go after them to ask if there is a minister nearby or someone who could let them into the church. But as the couple hears him coming up the road behind them, they panic. The young woman slips in the loose gravel like a wild animal startled into flight. Agee apologizes profusely and the couple, not very convincingly, assures him that they were not scared. "Their faces were secret, soft, utterly without trust of me, and utterly without understanding; and they had to stand here now and hear what I was saying, because in that country no negro safely walks away from a white man, or even appears not to listen while he is talking."

Such episodes, graphic as they were and lacking any sense of uplift, were not likely to fit the *Fortune* assignment. At this stage of their effort, both Agee and Evans seemed to be on the loose. In their wandering approach it was probably typical, perhaps even intended, that when the *Fortune* office tried to get in touch with the two men through their New Deal contact, they were missing in action if not AWOL. The magazine's contact, Harmon, was forced to admit that he didn't know where they were. As Agee confessed, it was a frustrating time. According to the magazine's schedule: "I should have been back at my typewriter and Walker at his tanks" and they had not even begun. Moreover, *Fortune* had set up a number of contacts and obligations that they found irritating. The result was a kind of "constant dissimulation" on their part.

* * *

It was Evans who made the essential contact. One day, in search of some likely prospect, he and Agee stopped in Greensboro, the county seat of Hale County. While Agee was checking in at the local relief office, Evans struck up a conversation with a fifty-four-year-old tenant farmer, Frank Tengle. He was idling in the courthouse square, seated at the base of a Civil War monument. Tengle, full faced, still jet haired, wearing a straw hat and dark denim overalls, was a compulsive talker more out of nervousness than sociability. Sizing up the camera equipment, Tengle's interest perked up when he learned that Evans had connections with the Resettlement Administration in Washington. Agee, coming out of the courthouse, joined them. He particularly noticed how Tengle showed his pink gums whenever he gave vent to his strained laughter. He and Tengle (Evans having moved off, surreptitiously taking photographs with his 35-mm camera with right-angle lens attached) were shortly joined by Bud Fields and Floyd Burroughs, both tenant farmers and both related to Tengle. Fields, fifty-nine, a thin, grizzled man, was Tengle's brother-in-law. He was also Burroughs's father-in-law. Burroughs, thirty-four, tall and muscular, was married to Field's daughter Allie Mae. All three were tenant farming near each other on Hobe's Hill, fifteen miles north of Greensboro. It was not a prospering summer — there had been a drought — and they had come to town trying to sign up for relief or, failing that, to apply for relief work. They had just learned that as tenant farmers they were technically considered employed and therefore not eligible.

In Greensboro, Evans took some photographs of the men, but few of these earliest 35-mm shots seem to have survived. Agee remembered that Evans, cagily, took a dozen or more photographs of Tengle while they chatted. One of them seems to be of Tengle sitting in front of the blurred Civil War monument. Surprised that Tengle was unaware of the ruse, he noted "how much slower white people are to catch on than negroes, who understand the meaning of a camera, a weapon, a stealer of images and souls, a gun, an evil eye." But Evans did get some shots of the three men lounging in the full sun in what is presumably the town square. He would later credit Agee's gifts of persuasion in getting the three men to allow him to photograph their families and farms: "[W]e told them exactly what we were doing," Evans remembered, "and they said all right. I think it was really largely because they liked Agee who had a great gift of making people not only like him but love him. They only had to listen to him a little bit and they took him in. I just sort of followed his lead that way. Although I did pick up the family first, he took on from there." It was arranged on the spot that he and Agee would drive Tengle home, with Fields and Burroughs joining them there. The luck of having found not one tenant farmer but three must have come as a relief. It is possible, too, that either before the chance meeting or after, Evans made several shots of the town of

Greensboro: near-noon photographs of the stores down the street from the courthouse, the Fords lined up in front of McCollum's Grocery and C. A. Johnson and Son store, and across the street, the sidewalk with the hanging sign of the Alabama Power Company. He used both the 35-mm and 8 x 10 cameras.

At the Tengle farmhouse they sat and talked, were given some small sweet peaches that had been heated on a piece of tin in the sun. Walker set up his 8 x 10 camera with a studied carefulness that Agee described as somehow a bit sinister: "the terrible structure of the tripod crested by the black square heavy head, dangerous as that of a hunchback," with Walker "stooping beneath cloak and cloud of wicked cloth and twisting buttons; a witchcraft preparing, colder than keenest ice and incalculably cruel." His account of the session is expansive, romantic, partly hinting at later psychological inferences that would provide a sexual subtext to what was supposed to be an innocent documentary assignment. The setting up of the 8 x 10 was another ruse, a delaying tactic. Evans's secret 35-mm shots reveal what Agee also described: that the children's faces have been freshly scrubbed (with rainwater) and the older girls, Dora Mae and Elizabeth Tengle, were drying their hair. Evans took the shots impromptu with seemingly no intent of formal composition. The children are grouped helter-skelter on the rickety porch, with its clutter of old cans and paraphernalia. A dog is stretched out in the heat. Floyd Burroughs appears to be rolling and moistening a cigarette: "Walker made a picture of this," Agee reported in an imaginary conversation with Tengle: "You didn't know, you thought he was still testing around." What is remarkable about this little episode is that the heroic description given by Agee is far different from what Evans caught in the camera eye: "the children standing like columns of an exquisite temple, their eyes straying, and behind, both girls, bent deep in the dark shadow somehow as if listening and as in a dance, attending like harps the black flags of their hair." His prose suggested something far more eloquent and poetic than the scruffy reality Evans captured, picturing the older girls in their sack dresses, fixing their hair, while sitting on the steps are two of the younger Tengle children and three-year-old William Fields, naked under his loose shirt, hugging his homemade doll.

For the Fields family had now arrived: Fields's buxom wife, Lily ("whose eyes go to bed with every man she sees," Agee claimed), much

Floyd Burroughs on Tengle family porch, 1936

315

younger than he, and her daughter, Pearl, by an earlier marriage; baby Ellen, only twenty months old carried athwart her waist; and her mother, "Miss Molly," in her fifties. The Burroughs children also had appeared — Lucille, George, Jr., and young Charles, though not Burroughs's wife, Allie Mae, or their twenty-month-old son, Othel Lee, nicknamed "Squeakie." Agee had a story to tell about this congregation of related families. Alert to minor social distinction, he noticed that Floyd Burroughs was not eager to have his children photographed with the rag-tag, gregarious crew of the Tengles, even though Lucille, with her keen gray eyes, the most handsome of his children, had been dressed for the picture-taking session in a clean, cheap thin dress and wore a ribbon in her hair. Agee apostrophized: "Your father will not let you get into the pictures on the porch: your picture will be later to yourselves. (He is not unfriendly or 'pointed' about this, just open, and quiet.") Later family sessions make it clear that both Evans and Agee preferred the fastidiousness of the Burroughs clan; it shows in both the photographs and the prose. Not surprisingly most of the photographs of the families were taken with the 35-mm camera on the porch or outdoors; Evans used the 8 x 10 for his pictures in the darkened interiors. Eventually Floyd Burroughs relented and he and the children posed for more formal shots away from the shambles of the Tengle's porch:

The background is a tall bush in disheveling bloom, out in front of the house in the hard sun; George [Floyd Burroughs] stands behind them all, one hand on Junior's shoulder; Louise [Lucille Burroughs] (she has first straightened her dress, her hair, her ribbon), stands directly in front of her father, her head about to his breastbone, her hands crossed quietly at the joining of her thighs, looking very straight ahead, her eyes wide open in spite of the sun; Burt [Charles Burroughs] sits at her feet with his legs uncrossing and his mind wandering.

Considering the badge of guilt Agee wore for having intruded into the lives of the families, it was not strange that he was apologetic for having kept the Tengles from their dinner for at least an hour. If so, this would mean that the initial photographic session was not a lengthy one. Yet Evans managed to take several interior shots with the big camera, perhaps some of the most important ones he would make: the entrance to Frank Tengle's bedroom, with its clutter of old calendars, magazine illustrations, hats hung on nails, and on the mantel the small oil can and the package of Health-O shaving cream. (Balzac, as indices of character, would have noted that the calendars predominantly advertised laxatives and various medical cures. Agee, more graphic, reported a bit of crude landowner gossip about Frank Tengle: "Why, that dirty son-of-a-bitch, he *brags* that he hasn't bought his family a bar of soap in five year.") There is a shot of the fireplace in what was called the Cotton Room. There is a gaping hole in its back open to the elements and presumably to stray animals. Above it a hand-lettered notice reads "Pleas! be Quite. Everybody is Welcome," a cryptic, mixed message encoded in the family's daily life.

It was more than probable that on the first visit Evans made the 8 x 10 portraits of Frank Tengle and his wife. (The latter, for effect, is cropped to a narrow vertical.) Tengle stands searching-eyed, confronting the camera lens and the cameraman behind it. Mrs. Tengle is apprehensive and a bit shamed, standing barefoot, wearing a torn and grungy work dress, waiting for the ordeal to be over. ("But all this while," Agee maintained, "it was you I was particularly watching, Mrs. Ricketts [Tengle]; you can have no idea with what care for you, what need to let you know, oh, not to fear us, not to fear, not to hate us, that we are your friends.")

Possibly on that first day Evans hit upon one of his private epiphanies, poignant and lovely in itself. He took a photograph of two old photographs positioned against an interior wall. One is a bleached photograph of an old woman standing with arms straight down, frowning in the sun in a nondescript country setting. It is torn at the lower left corner. Next to it is a photograph of small children in old-fashioned clothes seated in front of dark greenery. The pictures are nailed side by side against the rude grain of the wood, the protruding nails hinting, almost, at crucifixion. They are souvenirs of time past: the woman perhaps a dead mother; the children possibly Tengle brothers and sisters from an earlier generation. If one examines the photograph of the old woman, one realizes that it had appeared earlier in the cluttered photograph of the calendars and magazine illustrations above the mantlepiece. Evans must have asked to put the two photographs together. (Whether on the first visit or on a later one is not certain.) Pinning a photograph against a wall was not a new device for him; he had taken a picture of a picture using the portrait photograph of Joseph Verner Reed tacked against a wooden fence some years earlier. This newest version was another variation on the theme of the multiple portraits of anonymous clients seen in the windows of photographers' studios in Birmingham and Savannah.

After that first family session, Agee and Evans drove to Birmingham for a few days, putting up at the Hotel Tutwiler, a businessman's hotel. Evans planned to use the hotel bathroom for developing some of the test shots he had made. There was also a possibility of getting help or information from a New Deal architect "whose goodness and understanding Walker felt some certainty of in advance." Agee thought he might connect up with some Communists he had met in Tarrant City. But mostly it was the chance to "walk through lobbies whose provincial slickness we could simultaneously rest upon and ridicule and in both ways delight in. . . ." Until the sweltering Sunday that he left to drive back to Greensboro (Evans was to follow him back by train), Agee took a perverse delight in the shop windows and building façades, the meals taken in chilled rooms, and the emptiness of the streets at night. In some ways, he claimed, it reminded him of his visit to New York City at the age of fifteen, when he had "first walked in the late brilliant June dusk into the blinding marvel of Times Square."

But it was soon enough the day, a sweltering Sunday, when he planned to drive back to Greensboro. That morning he and Evans sat in their hotel room, drinking sloe gin, reading the funny papers and the latest news of the Spanish Civil War. Agee shaved and put on a clean shirt. They had a cold and expensive lunch in an air-conditioned coffee shop. Then Agee said good-bye and settled into the drive back. En route he thought about the whore he and Evans had met at the filling station/luncheonette on the drive up, confessing, "I knew I very badly wanted, not to say needed, a piece of tail."

What followed, however, was not fulfillment. On the road back, he did catch sight of the woman, lounging against a Plymouth with one foot on the running board chatting to a man in a white hat. But he preferred to drive on by, indulging a blunt and prolonged sexual fantasy about her while traveling the road to Greensboro in the breezeless heat. Not a leaf was stirring on the trees; parked cars were broiling in the sun. "All the porches were empty, beyond any idea of emptiness. Their empty rockers stood in them; their empty hammocks hung in them." The smoldering heat, the whole experience only served to recall his childhood days in Knoxville, Tennessee, when, eleven years old, bored and drowsy, he would be stretched on the porch suffering and nursing an erection and feeling heartily guilty. The account of the return to Greensboro was one of the long passages of the nonfiction marvel Agee later wrote. His bravado style sent the reader pushing through thickets of adjectives to arrive at the vital noun, describing "the slow blue dangerous and secret small-town eyes" that followed a stranger in the smaller towns of the South or the local crazy-eyed young toughs in Gaffney's Lunch, "talking low in sexual voices and sniggering without enthusiasm," who might be looking for a fight with a stranger. "Of all the christbitten places to spend a few free hours alone," he would confess, "and of all the days to do it on." Alabama in the summer of 1936.

* * *

But, as Agee reported, the return trip did provide both him and Evans with the substance of their book. Before the trip to Birmingham, he had sounded out Bud Fields about staying with him and his family; but Fields cagily suggested it would not look good to have two young men hanging around with his young wife: "You understand, taint I don't *trust* yuns, but I know young feller git too nigh a womurn, may not know hisself what he's lible to do next. Don't want to take no chanstes." Back near Greensboro, Agee decided it would be better to seek out Burroughs and his family as a more appropriate subject for the article: "His yellow eyes and very slow way of talking had stayed with me most," he remembered. He thought Burroughs the most direct, the most bitter, and the most intelligent of the three men. Unfortunately he did not know where Burroughs lived. On the Sunday of his return, however, he decided to scout out the terrain. He wanted to avoid running into the nearby Tengles on the way but fortunately or unfortunately, with a brewing thunderstorm, he did run into Frank Tengle, who offered to accompany him to the Burroughs place down one of the narrow overgrown back roads. They arrived there just as the storm broke, the corn stalks bent with rain, the melons lying like hogs in the field, their dusty backs pelted with rain. They made their way to the farmhouse porch, soaked. Floyd Burroughs took them into the bedroom, where the family was huddled in the dark. His wife, Allie Mae, frightened by the thunder and the rips of lightning, was lying on the bed with the smaller children. There is the roar of drenching rain on the roof and varied sounds of drip and splatter from the leaks. The detail with which Agee describes the scene is intimate, querying, psychological, and insistently photographic, from the lighting of an oil lamp picked up in the kitchen to the repeated attempts to strike the damp matches. He deals out itineraries of the furniture, including the iron bedsteads and the crude little table next to the fireplace with its piece of flour sacking pathetically embroidered with pink and blue thread. The prose images are graphic enough to have been the inspiration for the photographs that Evans took some days later, except that the photographs were taken well before Agee wrote his text. It is part of the mystery of their collaboration that word and image should be so closely allied even though legend claims (wrongly, one thinks) that the two were distinctly separate operations. Taken together the book and the photographs are an exercise in word and image that remains one of the fascinations of the book and of its mysterious staying power.

The thunderstorm at the Burroughs house, with its icy cold, its constant dripping from the leaky roof, passes through Agee's narrative. Since Evans was not there, it is from Agee's account that we know of the personal awkwardness, of the lack of any social introductions because Allie Mae is so terrified, and of Frank Tengle's chattering away that Allie Mae, squinched up on the bed as she is, looks like "devil hisself was after her, yes sir, devil hisself." Nobody bothers to answer. Agee has a gift for dialogue, particularly for southern talk, that matches Hemingway's conversational style in the short story form.

There is a sense of relief when the storm is over and the shutters are opened. Allie Mae takes her hands from her ears; Agee notes the tear streaks on her face. There are still no introductions made, Agee observes, "as if a definite avoidance of any of these issues [w]as too complicated to try to cope with." It is here that one recognizes that the book is indeed a collaboration; he and Evans are separate but equal. For all his deference to photography and his admiration for Evans's skills, Agee is intent on demonstrating the moments of intuition that can't so easily be rendered through the eye of the still camera. The nervousness in the air, for instance, or his sense of his own intrusiveness, until after the storm breaks: "Our voices and our bodies, take shape and loosen and we get up off our chairs and the bed and the floor, and come out of the room to see what the rain has done." It is then that Agee notices "how they are very careful toward me, puzzled by me, yet glad rather than not to see me, and not troubled by me." Outside, the hens have come out from under the house, murmuring. (In some of Evans's later photographs, one can pick them out, patroling under the porch.) A hog grunts in its wallow. Out by the cotton field, a peach tree has been split by the storm; the family and Agee collect the fallen peaches, selecting the ripe and usable fruit, sorting out the remainder for the hogs. The sun breaks through with light and country shine, one of those moments that Agee, not without some taint of romanticism, acknowledges "can fill you with love which has no traceable basis."

He was asked to stay overnight, but passed up the opportunity — reluctantly.

He thanked Burroughs but said he had better not. He drove Tengle home, then started back to the highway on a muddy road hoping for some excuse to return. Whether accidentally or on purpose — he was never sure which — he slid into a ditch and gunned the motor so hard that there was no hope of getting out of it. There was nothing to be done but trudge back to the Burroughs's place, knowing, he conceded, "I had at least half-contrived this." The house was now dark; they were already in bed. Nevertheless Floyd and his wife got up and welcomed him once again. Allie Mae, despite his protests, made supper for him, causing him further guilt, enough so that he consumed four fried eggs, a serving of fried pork, two plates of field peas, some warmed-over biscuits, and a jelly glass full of buttermilk — all, he conceded, in the attempt to stave off any suspicion on their part that he felt "superior" or that he didn't like their food. He was clearly a man surrendering to an excess of conscience, a theological disease common mostly to only the obsessively religious. Still Agee enjoyed sitting and chatting with both of them into the night, bonded, he felt, by a sense of intimacy which was "not of our creating." Nor had it anything to do with their talk, though it "increased in our tones of voice, in small quiet turns of humor, in glances of the eyes." That night he was put up in the front bedroom off the dog run which divided the two sections of the house. (The children had been led sleepwalking into the back bedroom to stay with their parents.) His account is full of the lyric or obsessive detail that would characterize the best passages of *Let Us Now Praise Famous Men*: how by lamplight he read the inscriptions in the family Bible, the marriage and birth dates and the death of a six-month-old daughter; how he endured the persistent attacks of bedbugs and fleas. (Though Agee doesn't say so, he may have accepted it as a form of penance.) As he related, "Outside the vermin, my senses were taking in nothing but a deep-night, unmeditatable consciousness of a world which was newly touched and beautiful to me."

It is part of the legend that grew up around their book that Evans like Agee had stayed with the family. But the likelihood is probably that the fastidious Evans may have had a few meals with the Burroughses but stayed at more restful vermin-free quarters in a nearby hotel. The photographs he took over the next few weeks are all the evidence needed of a world as "newly touched" for him as for Agee, especially the photographs at the Burroughs farmstead. A series of formalized 35-mm shots seems to represent his preliminary try at the subject. They are far more carefully composed than the earlier 35-mm shots of the Tengle visit. Evans has taken some pains to compose the shots: a rear view of the farm-house and outbuildings with Allie Mae bringing in the milk, young Squeakie toddling behind her; photographs of young Lucille, rather too dressed up for the occasion, show her picking cotton in the family field. She is wearing a straw hat, sweater, and a print dress, and seems a bit posed, as if arranged rather than exemplifying the down-to-earth reality of the work. There is a more profound and troubling 35-mm photograph of Squeakie sleeping on the porch on a square of cloth, covered with a flour-sack except for his bare rump and legs. One foot is bandaged, perhaps from a cut or infection, the other has a noticeable scab. (One of Evans's photographs of Lily Fields shows her with a similarly bandaged foot.) Such details in Evans are rarely a matter of sentiment or propaganda for the plight of the disadvantaged; they are the riveting acknowledgment of everything that *is* and that pertains to the reality of a given moment or a chosen subject. An article for *Fortune* would require photographs meant to illustrate the hardships of a sharecropper's life, the details of the work in the field. The photos Evans took of Bud Fields in his torn trousers and old hat, a loose sweat band around the neck, standing in a field with the long trailing sack for carrying the bolls would be more to the point than the picture of Lucille in her print dress. A picture of Frank Tengle driving his wagon, loaded with cotton, to the gin mill would also be more appropriate.

In most ways, the Evans photographs of the Tengle and Fields families

conform to the images one would expect in a sobering article on the under-
class, unless, as may have proved to be the case, they could be considered
too dire an indictment of the failures of capitalism to appear in a presumably capitalist magazine. Evans's photographs of the Burroughs farm,
where, despite the poverty, a certain tidiness and order prevailed, have an
almost Vermeerlike quality of light, a sense of time stopped. Certainly they
are the opposite of those taken on the Tengles' porch, which Agee
described as "heavily littered with lard buckets, scraps of iron, bent wire,
torn rope, old odors, those no longer useful things which on a farm are
never thrown away." But one has the sense that Evans was more comfortable at the Burroughs place, and it shows in several of the interior
photographs, particularly the angled shot of the kitchen: the door ajar, the
floor swept, the table with its patterned oilcoth, and an oil lamp (probably
the glass kerosene lamp so fondly described in Agee's text of his first
overnight stay) and beyond it a kitchen cupboard (or "safe" as Agee duly
noted it was called in the South) with a crockery jar. The exchange of a
lamp (the kitchen lamp probably) served as part of a sequence of transi-
tions that Agee confessed would remain "beautiful in my remembrance and
which I can scarcely set down." Nonetheless he described how the family
had settled down in the room adjoining his and how

*... in a confusion of shufflings and of muted voices which overspreads the sleeping
of children like quiet wings; and rustlings of cloth, and sounding of bedsprings,
they restore themselves for sleeping: then a shuffling, a sliding of light, a soft
knock at the door; I come to it; Gudger [Burroughs] and I exchange our lamps,
speaking few words in nearly inaudible voices, while beyond his shoulder I feel
the deep dark breathing a soft and quiet prostration of bodies.*

Where Agee produced an aria of night sounds and intimate activities,
Evans saw a simple and earthy still life in the makeshift washstand just
outside the kitchen: a wash basin, a water bucket and an enamel cup, a
hanging towel made of flour sacking. He also provided views of the hearths
and the whitewashed fireplaces in the two bedrooms, including the objects
on the mantel shelves. In his text, Agee, with the practiced eye of an
appraiser, would make an even more itemized record of the objects,
including the "two small twin vases, very simply blown, of pebble-grained
iridescent glass. Exactly at center between them, a fluted saucer, with a

coarse lace edge of pressed milky glass which Louise's mother gave her to call her own and for which she cares more dearly than for anything else she possesses." He also notes, as Evans did, the homemade doily that Allie Mae cut from pattern-paper to hang on the mantel shelf in one of her efforts to dress up their living quarters. Strangely enough that intention is as clearly evident in the photograph as it is in the confirmation of Allie Mae's remark: "Oh, I do *hate* this house *so bad!* Seems like they ain't nothing in the whole world I can do to make it pretty!"

But what is apparent is that the dialogue between the photographs and Agee's text was far more collaborative and persistent than has been recognized, even down to the scattering of flies on the white sheeting on the bedsteads in the rear bedroom which Floyd and Allie Mae shared. Agee reported, "On each of these surfaces is a thin constellation of perhaps a dozen black flies. Once in a while several at once will move a sharp inch or two in straight lines, or one will suddenly spiral off and butt the window-screen." The flies would become essential elements, not happenstance, in Evans's photograph as well as in the text. This was made clear when the book was finally published and the engraver retouched the print in order to remove the spots before making the plate. Evans insisted the flies should be restored. Agee, when the family was at work in the fields, made a careful exploration of the house and the housekeeping, itemizing even the contents of bureau drawers and closets. (On the mantel of the rear bedroom: "A pink crescent celluloid comb: twenty-seven teeth, of which three are missing; sixteen imitation diamonds./ A nailfile./ A small bright mirror in a wire stand.") Whether Evans had photographed the fly-spotted bedsheet at Agee's suggestion, or whether he had photographed it on his own initiative remains one of those philosophical questions (Which came first, the chicken or the egg?), as pertinent to photography as to any other of the creative arts.

Alabama Cotton Tenant Farmer Wife, 1936

The most famous of the photographs of the Burroughs clan are the 8 x 10 portraits of Floyd and of Allie Mae, the first of which, taken on the step of the doorway to the rear bedroom, shows Floyd with curly hair, suggesting he had been caught unprepared, in contrast to the 35-mm portraits, in which he had plastered down his hair for the occasion. He is wearing a torn shirt, the photo cropped chest up, the head framed in the darkness of the doorway. A variant of this same shot shows Floyd sitting full length and barefooted with his daughter Lucille sitting in a chair a bit further down the

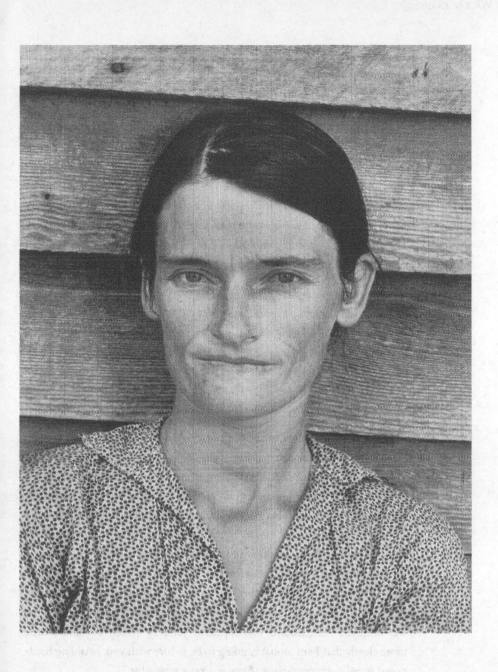

runway, both staring frankly and inquisitively at the camera. In one of the Allie Mae portraits (Evans made a sequence of nearly the same shots except for variations in her expression), there is only the slightest glimmer of a smile. It is a portrait pared down to the irreducible elements: the plain face, the insistent minuscule pattern of her dress, the bare grain of the wood clapboards. She is framed in near-noon glare, a plain madonna, hair pulled tight to the back. The sequence would become one of the most famous of Evans's photographs and, deservedly, an icon of documentary photography in the depression years. A hint of what was going on in the mind of the woman being photographed would come years later in an interview with Allie Mae Burroughs in the documentary film *Agee*. When asked about the two men who had entered their lives that summer, she remembered:

The big people you know, the big bugs around Moundville, they would tell us that they was spies from Russia, and that they was trying to get all they could out of the United States. I don't know what spies does, dear, but anyway we knowed that they wasn't going to hurt us, and they didn't. I don't know why they'd say such things about them. They just didn't know them was all . . . Afraid they might tell us some way to get by, tell us some way to make a better living, so we wouldn't have to dig it out with them, you see. It was the landlords mostly.

The most fascinating of the portraits, however, is the portrait of Lucille, framed from the neck up, wearing a wide collar, her head haloed in a straw hat. She is pictured against the vertical wood planking of one of the outbuildings in the compound. Her eyes serve as the most vivid focal point — luminous and youthful but decidedly questioning. If Evans and Agee had discussed this feature it would not be surprising; Agee made much of Lucille's young eyes in another of his soliloquies in *Famous Men*. It is almost a declaration of love, prompted by the "temperatureless, keen, serene and wise and pure gray eyes of yours, set so wide, between your square young temples . . ." In another moment of hyperbole, he confesses, "It is while I am watching you here, Louise, that suddenly yet very quietly I realize a little more clearly that I am probably going to be in love with you." Among hard-nosed social documentarians, Agee is a rank sensualist.

* * *

Lucille Burroughs,
1936.

Evans's group photograph of the Burroughs family, including Allie Mae's young married sister Emma who was visiting in midsummer, is not the most interesting of his Alabama photographs, but it has its significance. Emma was on the verge of moving to a farm in Mississippi with her husband and her visit was a sad occasion for the family. Everyone in the picture is properly dressed and groomed in their best Sunday clothes. The likelihood is that Floyd was instrumental in the taking of the photograph — and perhaps it shows. It is a bit slack and mundane for an Evans photograph. The family is posed against the side of the house in the bright sunlight. Floyd has his arms around the shoulders of his wife and his sister-in-law; the children, fresh and prim, are arranged on the wooden bench in front of them. The participants are frowning a bit in the glare, but Allie Mae, with a genuine smile of pleasure and pride in her family and sister, is wearing a best dress and stockings, even a pair of maryjane shoes with straps. It is the kind of photograph that Floyd would consider appropriate. Later critics were possibly right in thinking that such an ordinary, healthy-looking group would not serve the purposes of social propaganda and that was why Evans did not use it in his exhibition "American Photographs" or in *Let Us Now Praise Famous Men*. But in Evans's eye its very ordinariness would have been part of its documentary accuracy. The fact that he consented to take such a photograph more or less for the family's expectations has its importance. After all he had taken photographs of commercial portrait photographs before. That the family appear here with their hopes and ambitions, seen as they would prefer to be seen, is part of the message. The probability is that Evans sensed that the point was too subtle or too ironic to be appreciated by the mass audience.

Agee focused on a different aspect of the Burroughs family relations. Emma, who appears next to Floyd in the photograph, is one of the romanticized heroines in his book, along with Allie Mae; Tengle's forlorn and sad wife, Sadie; Margaret; Ruth Fields; and Lucille. It is plain that Agee finds Emma sexually attractive: "Her build is rather that of a young queen of a child's magic story who throughout has been coarsened by peasant and earth living and work." He notes her dime-store necklace, her cotton print dress, her cheap going-away paper suitcase. He understands that neither Emma nor Allie Mae is fond of their father's new younger wife. He believes that this is the reason that Emma, against her father's wishes, has married too young and to a man her father's age. Strangely and perhaps inevitably, during Emma's brief visit, he begins to fantasize about her having a sexual relationship not just with him, but (with suspicious generosity) with Evans and Floyd Burroughs as well. His support for this fantasy is that he believes Emma is attracted to all three. Emma, he believes, loves good times and towns and people her own age. In the little drama Agee concocts: "Each of us is attractive to Emma, both in sexual immediacy and as symbols or embodiments of a life she wants and knows she will never have; and each of us is fond of her and attracted toward her." He suspects that Floyd is "unconcealably attracted" to Emma but behaving as properly as the situation demands. Allie Mae, according to him, "gives no appearance of noticing the clumsy and shamefaced would-be-subtle demeanors of flirtation which George [Floyd] is stupid enough to believe she does not understand for what they are: for George [Floyd] would only be shocked should she give him open permission, and Emma could not be too well trusted either. So this sad comedy has been going on without comment from anyone." He concocts a fantasy for her: "if only Emma could spend her last few days alive having a gigantic good time in bed, with George [Floyd], a kind of man she is best used to, and with Walker and me, whom she is curious about and attracted to, and who are at the same moment tangible and friendly and not at all to be feared, and on the other hand have for her the mystery or glamour almost of mythological creatures." When the day came for Emma's departure there was a certain awkwardness at the breakfast table. Floyd, who had found some interim work at a local sawmill, got up to go. Agee relates:

Whether he would kiss Emma goodbye, as a sort of relative, was on everybody's mind. He came clumsily near it: she half got from her chair, and their bodies were suddenly and sharply drawn toward each other a few inches: but he was much too shy, and did not even touch her with the hand he reached out to shake hers. Annie Mae [Allie Mae] drawled, smiling, What's wrong with ye George [Floyd]; she ain't agoin' to bite ye; and everyone laughed, and Emma stood up and they embraced, laughing, and he kissed her on her suddenly turned cheek.

It is this subtext that gives a certain poignancy to Evans's family photograph, in which Floyd's arm rests lightly along Emma's shoulder. None of this, of course, was actually the burden of Evans's picture of the spruced-up family on a given day; nor was the fact that Agee had chosen the alias

329

Emma for Allie Mae's sister when that was the name of his own sister with whom Evans had had a sexual affair. Later, when Evans was asked about the Agee fantasy, he was quick to remark, "I blush and squirm every time I read that. God! In the first place, it wasn't in my mind at all. Agee never mentioned it. But my God, the enormity of such a suggestion! But that has to do with Agee and the fashion of the time." He was, in time, to encounter other equally strange aspects of Agee's vagrant sexuality.

*Burroughs
Kitchen,
Hale County,
Alabama,
1936*

The Cruel Radiance of What Is

15

"The trip was very hard," Agee wrote his mentor Father Flye from New York in early September, "and certainly one of the best things I've ever had happen to me." Back at work, however, he was less than certain of the results: "Writing what we found is a different matter. Impossible in any form and length *Fortune* can use; and I am now so stultified trying to do that, that I am afraid I've lost ability to make it right in my own way." His letter was by way of an apology for having failed to visit Flye and his wife as he had planned to do during his southern trip. He explained: "Everything there was unpredictable from day to day, I was half crazy with the heat and diet."

Evans was more fortunate; he had done the work of capturing the summer of 1936 on film, not that his part of the collaboration was finished. There were still the development of the films, the printing of the negatives, the incidental cropping and dodging, the final realization of what had been held captive, the images blossoming like ghosts in the developer trays. There were also, under the terms of his agreement with the FSA, the negatives and prints to be supplied to Stryker. Sometime during the next few months, Evans also put together a scrapbook of his sharecropper photographs. He had reason to feel satisfied. As he recognized later, what he had accomplished during the weeks shared with Agee and the three tenant families represented a cumulative achievement in his early work.

Flood Refugees, Forrest City, Arkansas, February, 1937

In Alabama, Agee had made notes on the spot and seems to have made a stab at beginning the *Fortune* article. In "A Country Letter," one of his soliloquies, he presents himself as having stayed awake, writing by lamplight in a child's copybook, while, in another room, the Burroughs family slept:

Just a half inch beyond the surface of this wall I face is another surface, one of the four walls which square and collaborate against the air [of] another room, and there lie sleeping, on two iron beds and on pallets on the floor, a man and his wife and her sister, and four children. . . . Their lamp is out, their light is done this long while . . .

Evans, confirming the picture, referred to the book as "night permeated." Night, he claimed, was Agee's time: "In Alabama he worked I don't know how late. Some parts of *Let Us Now Praise Famous Men* read as though they were written on the spot at night." (He had "A Country Letter" in mind.) Evans also concluded that later sections were largely written at night in New Jersey: "Literally the result shows this; some of the sections read best at night, far in the night." Just how much of the article or, for that matter, what portions of the book were written on the spot is open to question. The original manuscript version of the *Fortune* article reportedly has been lost, and the chronology of subsequent drafts and revisions of the book still needs definitive study. The published text is riddled with possible clues. The three segments of "On the Porch," which enclose the published text, for instance, carry a note indicating that they were written in 1937. Another note suggests that the segments were meant to form the beginning of a "much longer book" and confesses that "all other parts of this volume are intended as flashbacks, foretastes, illuminations and contradictions." Some descriptions in the book read as though Agee had Evans's detailed photographs in hand while writing the text. In one of the appendices to the book, Agee's replies to a 1939 questionnaire from *Partisan Review* dealing with writing and the writer's responsibilities in a possible world war are dated as late as the fall of 1940 to April 1941, only months before the publication of the book in September. The book still reads (as it was clearly intended to do) like a continuous work-in-progress.

Over the five-year period Agee spent writing toward the final text, he still had to resurrect much of the experience in prose, first against the deadline for the magazine, and then for the published text. In an undated note to Evans, he complained bitterly: "I am giving myself an awful fucking still after 6 weeks work to get a leverage on how to write this Alabama trip right. O well." Robert Fitzgerald's recollection was that Agee had turned in the article in September or early October, but that the magazine "did not have the courage to face in full the case he presented, since the case involved discomfort not only for the tenants but for *Fortune*." The article, in Evans's opinion, was "pretty thunderous" and it was by some estimates ten times longer than the editors had asked for. As Agee had guessed, it was evident that the article would not be used. Dwight Macdonald, by then a disaffected former Luce employee, maintained that the article fit neither the magazine's ambivalent "liberal" nor "conservative" mode and that it was "pessimistic, unconstructive, impractical, indignant, lyrical and always personal." Macdonald, in his pro-Marxist phase, already had had his run-in with the editors of *Fortune* when they tampered with his series of articles on the steel corporations, beginning with "Republic Steel," published in the December 1935 issue. The final segment of the series, covering U.S. Steel, carried a highly critical portrait of Myron Taylor, the company CEO, as well as equally critical speculations on monopoly capitalism. It was so heavily edited that Macdonald balked, writing vehemently to Ralph Ingersoll, then managing editor: "God damn it I'm getting sore. What earthly purpose is served by extracting all the points out of every sentence? If stories are to be edited like this why hire writers at all?" Finally, in protest — before Agee and Evans headed south on their assignment — he quit the magazine, fed up with the Luce operation. He confessed: "I was tempted, morally, to keep on selling out — I was by then getting $10,000 a year, an interesting salary in those primitive days — but it had become neurologically impossible: I kept falling asleep in the very act of prostitution."

That precedent hardly would have been lost on Agee when it came to the writing of his own troublesome article. *Time* editor T. S. Matthews recalled that the *Fortune* editors tried "chopping it in bits" and then finally gave up. But Evans, convinced of the complexity of Agee's motives, argued that "half unconsciously and half consciously Agee saw to it that it would *not* get into *Fortune*. He *made* it so that it would be unacceptable. Oh, I'm *sure* of it." Some months later, Russell Davenport, who took over as managing editor of *Fortune*, canceled the "Life and Circumstances" series altogether, killing any chances that the sharecropper article would be published at all. There followed several months in which Agee tried to wrest the article from the magazine's control without much initial success.

His dismay with text — any text, it seems — became a leitmotif in the random course of writing *Let Us Now Praise Famous Men*. In the early drafts, the language of some of the passages is more dramatic and intense than that of the later revisions. On one occasion he blurts out: "I wish I could write of a tenant's work: in such a way as to break your back with it and your heart if I could: but still more: in such a way that innocent of them though you are, you might go insane with shame and guilt that you are who you are. . . . Good God if I could only make even this *guilt* what it is." But even in the published text his dissatisfaction with words, with

335

language, remained. In an oft-quoted passage, with the grandstand humility that was one of Agee's strategies (endearing to some and irritating to others), he wrote: "If I could do it, I'd do no writing at all here. It would be photographs, the rest would be fragments of cloth, bits of cotton, lumps of earth, records of speech, pieces of wood and iron, phials of odors, plates of food and excrement." Few authors would have presented themselves to the reader insisting so on their inadequacies for the task. Agee had, in fact, turned his writing assignment into an intensive search for a new, more satisfactory medium.

* * *

For Evans, too, it was a fall and winter of failed hopes, deferred ambitions. He was traveling back and forth between New York and Washington. He and Ben Shahn, the latter still on loan from the Special Skills Division, were attempting to interest the powers that be, chiefly Rexford Tugwell, in various filmmaking projects that stretched out over a period of months and were cloudy in nature and uncertain of outcome. The success of Pare Lorentz's documentary film *The Plow That Broke the Plains*, promoting the agricultural policies of the New Deal, had stirred up possibilities of other Department of Agriculture films. There was also the possibility of an RA film on a suburban white-collar housing development in Berwyn Heights, Maryland, not far from Washington. Those prospects hung fire until the end of the year. While in Washington, too, Evans's interest was rekindled in the Civil War photographs of Mathew Brady. He had begun making a thorough study of them in the War Department's Signal Corp files, even to the point of making a list of a hundred or more of the war photographs from the six thousand or so prints in their collection as well as a hundred more of the civilian portraits. He was hoping to make prints and enlargements from the plates, some for himself, but primarily for the purpose of producing a small Brady exhibition. He had even gone as far as persuading the Resettlement Administration to let him make the prints on their time.

It was a roustabout existence. During his Washington sojourns, Evans roomed on 3213 M Street or occasionally stayed at the Blackstone Hotel. Finally in mid-winter he moved in with his sister and Tal Brewer in a house they had taken at 2921 Olive Avenue. In New York, he was in the process of moving out of the Bethune Street apartment and studio he had been intermittently sharing with Ben Shahn and Jay Leyda. Leyda had only recently returned from Russia. His work at the Moscow State Film School, his affiliation and friendship with Russian director Sergei Eisenstein, and his services for Alfred Barr in 1935 in securing works of the Russian constructivist artists Tatlin, Rodchenko, and Stepanova for an exhibition Barr was planning proved more than useful. He was appointed assistant curator of the Museum of Modern Art's newly established film department, bringing with him a fund of experience and knowledge about early filmmaking in Europe.

Among Evans's friends, it was a period of marital upsets, estrangements, separations. Shahn had left his wife, Tillie, and the two children and was living with Bernarda Bryson. Agee, too, according to Leyda, who had struck up an important friendship with him, was one of the transients camping out occasionally at the Bethune Street hostelry. Agee's four-year marriage to Via was in the process of breaking up and he had begun a passionate affair with Alma Mailman, a talented young musician whom he had first met through Via and the Saunders family. For the moment, Via Agee was tolerating her husband's romance, but unhappily. Leyda, too, was at an emotional stalemate, but for different reasons. In Russia he had met and married a dancer, Si-Lan Chen, who was nonetheless a fervid Marxist. Chen, who was performing in Norway, was expected to join her husband in the United States shortly.

It was Leyda's impression that toward the end of 1936, Evans was suffering through his own discontents: "Walker was at loose ends and didn't seem to know what to do. . . . Then [he] found this house on 92nd Street." Shuttling back and forth between Washington and New York, Evans found himself caught up in the household rearrangements that follow in the wake of the grander passions in the lives of one's friends. He seems to have felt some relief at finding the apartment at 491 East Ninety-second Street. It was on the second-floor back, overlooking the East River, and was in need of renovation, particularly since he wanted to use it as a working studio. Leyda, looking for new quarters in time for his wife's arrival, decided to take the second-floor front apartment.

A good part of Evans's correspondence with Leyda that fall and winter dealt with housekeeping matters at both the old and the new addresses. He was particularly worried that the new landlord might balk at his using the apartment as a photographic studio. Writing from Washington, he asked, "Do you think you could explain my peculiar 'amateur' photo situation to Electrician soon enough for possible big double sink in kitchen, but I want electric refrigerator too, and not stove? Be careful not to make me undesirable tenant, not to make it seem I'll open a commercial studio in that house." Typically, with his talent for enlisting friends, he hadn't arranged to have the electricity shut off in the old studio, had forgotten about the change-of-address cards, and in Washington, didn't have his checkbook handy, therefore couldn't send the five-dollar deposit on the new apartment. He asked Leyda if he would mind taking care of such matters. Later, he did at least send a check for twenty-five dollars for the rent deposit and the moving expenses, asking, "Would you like to supervise my moving for me in the meantime or would you rather leave it to me (Only I'm not sure I could get there)?" It was true, however, that at that particular time he was out in the field on an RA assignment. During one of his hurried New York

visits, he had, at least, made arrangements for the painting of the new apartment. "Everything seems O.K. darkroom and all," he said in an undated letter. "Also I caught what would have been a mistake — the walls were going to be stippled (a fancy art brush trick) so I changed to plain ordinary painting flat white some rooms, grey others. You'd better call him soon. I spoke about colors for you and bookshelves for you but forget what he said about shelves . . ." He was also solicitous about Leyda's comfort — whether at the Bethune Street address or the Ninety-second Street one is not clear: "If you're still sleeping in the cold front room and not using the back and not running the stove you are nuts." He seems to have taken a proprietary air in the matter of moving, sending Leyda a drawing of the Ninety-second street house: "He sent it to me," Leyda recalled, "to show me where all the families were living." No doubt Evans was grateful for his escape from the domestic upheavals of New York. That may be the import of his otherwise double-edged comments about his recent move to the Brewers' house in Washington: "I'm glad to be out of New York; here in this sweet provincial side street eating comfortable food in my sister's little Victorian house."

II

The more important matters were decidedly professional. On December 3, Evans wrote Leyda from Washington, outlining his prospects and difficulties: "The film for Resettlement is off; I'm sure Shahn told you since a telegram was sent to him there about it. Something else may be done with it, I don't know. I'm off on Civil War photographs and will do a little still shooting around here, weather permitting. Baltimore has something to do. A small quarrel with Shahn he may have related to you; hope not, as it's tiresome enough." The details of the quarrel have not surfaced, but it is clear that their Washington collaboration was a matter for nagging disagreements. At the end of the letter Evans referred to it again, attempting to rationalize his feelings: "I'm damned annoyed with Ben for various reasons. Of course it's not his fault we were stopped, that was just Washington — nobody's fault." Part of the problem, though Evans did not cite it, was that it was an election year and Rexford Tugwell, though a member of Roosevelt's original brain trust, was now considered too contro-

Evans with movie camera, near Greenbelt, Maryland, a community being constructed for resettlement of tenement dwellers October, 1936

versial and a distinct liability to the administration. Tugwell was in the process of being eased out of his position as both head of the Resettlement Administration and Under Secretary of the agricultural department. Although he offered his resignation to the double post early in the campaign, at Roosevelt's request he made the effective date December 31, 1936, well after the election. He was, in effect, in a lame-duck mode during the time Evans and Shahn were searching for filmmaking opportunities.

Considering Shahn's earlier misreading of the Cuban revolution, Evans may also have backed away from the political taint of Shahn's ideas for prospective films. Both he and Shahn were in touch with Leyda regarding their film projects, as evidenced in Evans's letters at the time. Evans seems to have occupied the post of middleman in subsequent discussions. (If so, the irony in that case was that Leyda's political views were every bit as leftward leaning as Shahn's.) In two undated letters to Leyda written from the Blackstone Hotel in Washington, it is clear that Evans was courting and favoring Leyda's opinions: "You'll be pleased to know," he wrote Leyda, "the whole plan has been scrapped for another which seems to me better." They had shown their initial results to a dozen or more officials, including Tugwell, from whom they had gotten "a properly negative reaction." But Evans sensed that Tugwell might be more receptive to a film that would leave out "all that crap about Washington and that special precious little housing project out in Maryland." As a result, he and Shahn quietly put together a prospectus for a film "about *people*, people and unemployment, people and slums, using employment office interviewer and questionnaire blanks as a device to jump off into various backgrounds, into unemployment, housing, child labor, farm tenant problems; any damn social situation you want." They intended to push their plan under various noses, "especially Tugwell's." But at the end of his letter Evans added a caustic postscript: "Actually Shahn is not the guy to admit it, you were so right about leaving out the first part of that scenario, the Washington stuff! . . . Many, many thanks again for helping so much." In a second letter, written possibly a week later just as he was leaving for a conference about the film, he offered another jibe: "By the way, a second indication of your ideas is to be found in our having put that cute half-ass cutting in first film sample. Leyda 2, Shahn 0."

It was in his December 3 letter that Evans gave the clearest account of his reasons for remaining in Washington: "Things now stand: I have 3 month job with gov't at pay enabling me to save a little, and at the moment I'm almost broke. I had thought I'd stick here because there's just about 3 months things to do that will interest me — and then you never can tell; someone may want a movie and this is a good place to uncover chances to do them." At the moment, the possibilities of making a film for the Department of Agriculture were still open: "The way they would have to work it would be to have someone (me) on their payroll who could shoot, direct himself, and compose the film. They could simply then pay for film and laboratory and write the expenses down, without the salary, as a very small item — Budgets — you've heard of them?"

Around the time that he moved into his sister's Victorian household, another possibility presented itself. Evans, this time, was cautious: "I think we are going to make a film, or try to. Don't know much about it yet and I would not like to have it known until the plan has been approved." One reason was that he suspected Pare Lorentz "would or might be sore." He was also particularly anxious to have Leyda's opinion: "I wonder if you will be interested in going over the beginnings of a scenario which we have, because I'll bring it up to New York in a week or so if you'd care to. I think you *will* see chances of something in it, else I wouldn't trouble you." (One possibility, since the dating of the Blackstone Hotel letters is uncertain, is that this was, in fact, the aforementioned Berwyn Heights project.) The opportunity, he said, was "not perfect of course, and won't be, even if finished with all our dreams inviolate, because it's to be a documentary about one of the resettlement projects for Washington white-collar workers near here; and as you may know, the Resettlement projects are very dim drops in the present bucket." Nonetheless he was eager to "get it by the bosses, so that I can get to work." He and Ben were to make a few sample shots immediately — probably within the week — then show the results to the necessary officials, including Tugwell. He had hopes, possibly based on the fact that that same day "Tugwell saw my sharecropper scrapbooks, seemed interested but he doesn't know much or care much about pictures or photographs or Art."

* * *

The ventures with Shahn were not the only film prospects Evans was entertaining. Jay Leyda and Agee had developed a fast friendship, with Leyda screening Russian films for the poet's benefit. The two were exploring the possibilities of future film projects. That was the tenor of Evans's bemused commentaries on the growing relationship between the two men. Agee, bogged down in uncertainties about the sharecropper article, was decidedly receptive to possible film projects. In his December 3 letter Evans wrote Leyda: "Thanks for your card about Agee's film thoughts. I was very glad you think as you do. Why do you ask me to find a subject to do with him? Do you mean he simply impressed you with impossible ideas, that now you'd like us to work on something as yet unborn? Yes, I'm interested." At the end of the letter, he repeated, "Lord, yes I would like to work with Agee and I certainly would like to make a film. I feel very let down over the cancellation of this last scenario." The nature of the proposed film Agee spelled out in a follow-up letter to Evans: "J. Leyda has seen or written you of possibility of short you and I might make for Nykino (what a name). I keep thinking a swell 20 minutes could be done out of tenant families, detail and country in the dead of winter." All the same, Agee's impressions of Leyda's abilities were not all that flattering. "He is a smart guy all right and a likeable one," he wrote Evans, "…I wd definitely not think a first rate director but very strong among second stringers and a hell of a lot more valuable than harmful to American pictures."

The Nykino referred to was a last-ditch effort of the Workers Film and Photo League, in which Leyda was an active member. Leyda referred to Nykino as "a descendant" of the league, which was run by Ralph Steiner, producer of *The World Today*, a short-lived left-wing alternative to *March of Time*, Luce's right-wing newsreel. The first sample that was run contained episodes on a rent strike in Long Island and a Ku Klux Klan rally. Evans's query about its activities was diffident: "Anyway I don't know a thing about 'The World Today,' never saw one. What do they want? I'll come up soon, can I see what they've done? I guess I know." The "I guess I know," is the telling comment. Evans's relationship with Leyda provides the most objective clues to Evans's attitudes toward politics and propaganda at the time. Aside from his work at MoMA, Leyda was also working as a film editor for Frontier Films, about which Leyda noted how Steiner and the young director Elia Kazan "were all swept away with excitement . . . because it was a new organization." But as far as Leyda could remember, Evans never availed himself of any connection with the operation: "We imagined the series would go on, and if Walker had come up with something he wanted to do, Frontier Films would probably have been able to do it." Strangely, too, Leyda was convinced that Agee's "*enormous* enthusiasm for films" had dampened Evans's interest in movie-making: "Jim would swamp the people in a room with his feelings about film. I've seen that happen with others who have a tendency to retreat. Walker admired Jim very much. Jim's being so very loud about film might have kept him away from it." Whether Leyda's account was accurate or not, it is true that either through lack of opportunity or inspiration, Evans never completely pursued his filmmaking ambitions. The idea for a film version of the tenant farmer book seems to have trailed off — on Evans's part — in a series of heartfelt apologies. In an undated letter written on Baltimore & Ohio Railroad stationery, Evans, following a brisk New York visit, apologized: "Bad day today couldn't phone, had hoped you-Agee-self triangle." He was sorry, he maintained, that "nothing was said about me and Agee and film and that was why I tried to meet all together. I do want to. Hail. Walker." But, for the record, that project never materialized.

III

On January 27, 1937, Roy Stryker suggested Evans take on a fresh assignment: photographing the recent devastating floods of the Mississippi River valley, around Tennessee and Arkansas. It was another governmental effort and another collaboration; this time he was joined by Edwin Locke, an RA photographer. That afternoon Evans had his first typhoid inoculation and that evening he had dinner with the Brewers, accompanied by Peter Sekaer, who was in Washington. Sekaer was expecting to make a trip to New Orleans and promised — seemingly at Evans's instigation — to ask a Danish compatriot there, Frans Blom, about Jane Ninas, who was a close friend of his. Oddly enough, Sekaer did see Jane during his winter visit to New Orleans but made no mention of Evans to her at all. Instead, he made a pass at Jane, which she promptly fended off. It was only many years later that she learned about the entry Evans had made that evening in the diary he kept during the early months of 1937. It was a time when she was suffering still with bouts of agoraphobia. It would have meant a good deal to her to know that, even then, Evans was still concerned about her.

On the twenty-eighth, still rooming at the M Street address, Evans learned of another possible collaboration through Ted Young (a government worker), who discussed a possible project with the WPA. No details, however, were indicated in his diary entry. Instead, Evans, always wary about sharing his professional thoughts, confessed to a certain uneasiness: "I told him perhaps too much about my ideas." That night and the next, still feeling "rotten" from his typhoid shots, he slept at his sister's house on Olive Avenue. It was not until mid-afternoon of January 30 that he finally got off on his trip.

*Flood Refugees,
Forrest City,
Arkansas,
February, 1937*

* * *

After the uncertainties of Washington, he was pleased to be on the road once more, driving until 10:30 P.M. when he reached Lexington, Virginia. "Relaxation," he noted in his diary, "good to be out again, good ride Shenandoah Valley; towns, houses, people." There was a heavy rain the following morning when he left at 9:00 A.M. for an all-day drive to Knoxville, followed by a second all-day drive before reaching Savannah, Tennessee, late in the evening. It probably says something about his state of mind on this trip that it was not until Tuesday, February 2, when he reached Memphis early in the afternoon, that he mentioned an unnamed traveling companion, presumably Edwin Locke, who was driving the car: "No signs of a flood as we came in, but we found part of the city is under." In his diary, Evans noted that he had had his second typhoid inoculation that afternoon and that he was waiting for Pare Lorentz or for "someone from his crew to call in from wherever they are." Lorentz, indeed, along with Willard Van Dyke, was in the process of shooting scenes of the flood damage for a documentary film, *The River*. The next notation in Evans's diary is curious: "Hopkins left this morning, will not be back." This suggests that another traveling companion might have been his old New Deal friend, Harry Hopkins, still the administrator of the WPA. Could Hopkins have been traveling with him to report to the president on the flood situation or did Evans meet him in Memphis? The possibility is that

the meeting might also have had some connection with the WPA project Ted Young had discussed with him only a few days earlier. It is at this point that Evans first mentions Edwin Locke. It was not a flattering notice: Locke, he claimed, "looks like a communist commissar in the Winter Palace." Evans would seldom have a high opinion of what he regarded as bureaucratic types.

February 3 was mostly a wasted day spent waiting for Lorentz to call, only to miss the call when it came because of the "stupidity" of the hotel clerks. It was not until 5:00 P.M. that they got underway, taking the train to Forrest City, Arkansas, where there were both refugee and livestock camps. The train was crowded with men in boots carrying boat motors and other paraphernalia. The highways were under water, but the train tracks were elevated above the flood level. Passing through the submerged landscape, he noted the water: "swift and deep and frightening." The trip to Forrest City took a wearying two and a half hours. On his route to the Arlington Hotel, Evans noted the military police in the street, the soldiers, the Red Cross personnel, the crowds of dispossessed refugees. The next morning, a sunny day, he and Locke visited the refugee camp for whites on a lot near the high school. Tents were being set up by a contingent of CCC men. Red Cross operatives pointedly asked him and Locke to be sure to include their insignia in the pictures. "Careful not to do this," Evans noted dryly. To Evans the refugees seemed thoroughly depressed, mostly worried about the future. He and Locke did a good deal of photographing, and were tired by the time they reached the much larger Negro camp on the other side of town. Evans found it more interesting; in fact, he would return several more times to photograph there. "Negroes really deflated," he wrote, "more so than I've ever seen them." In the dark interior of a cotton warehouse and using synchronized photo flashes, he made several shots of the refugees. In his diary he commented on the sick lying in an assortment of fancy iron beds. ("Their own?" he asked himself, perhaps reminded of the cast-iron beds in the tidier circumstances of the Burroughs homestead.) He caught the pitiful efforts of the dispossessed to make private spaces for themselves amid their scant, salvaged belongings: a woman turning her blank gaze upon the photographer as she sat in her disheveled best coat and hat at the foot of a bed with a makeshift canopy; another huddled under a patchwork quilt with a spittoon and a pair of battered shoes on the floor beside her. Evans confessed it had taken an effort to pry into the misery and bleak self-involvement of the refugees: "Felt completely ill-mannered but wanted at the same time to make just those pictures."

Locke, in a six-page letter to Stryker written that night on Hotel Chisca stationery, gave a dutiful report on their expedition. He noted that they had worked a full day from 6:00 in the morning until 5:30 P.M., then caught the 6:20 train back to Memphis. In a personal aside, Locke claimed: "So far all goes well. I had a job annoying Walker out of his lassitude, but today in Forrest City, Arkansas, he worked as I am sure he never has before."

For the next few days they made daily trips between Memphis and Forrest City photographing. On the fifth they traveled further into Arkansas, toward Marianna, presumably to meet up with Lorentz: "most of the way under water to the steps of the cars. Crept through." They arrived at their destination at 8:30 P.M. only to find that Lorentz was not there. Another case of missed connections. It was not until the next day that he had a phone conversation with Lorentz, who was back in Memphis. On the seventh, Evans and Locke took an early train back, reaching Memphis at noon and putting up at the William Lens hotel. Evans's diary entry was brief: "bathed, ate steak and loafed well." The following day was spent developing some of the Forrest City films ("Some good," he noted) and waiting for supplies.

* * *

After that, he was marooned at the William Lens. On the morning of the ninth, Evans woke with a bad case of influenza. "Will lose this week," he predicted, accurately enough. He remained in Memphis eight days, sick and weak, most of the time spent in bed. Locke, reporting to Stryker, wrote: "I am in a hell of a dilemma. Walker is down with the flu and has a good dose of it." For the time being, the project was stalled while Evans recuperated. By the fourteenth, Evans was able to take his last typhoid injection and the next day reported, "Up and out for a while, sun, river." By the sixteenth, when Locke's wife, Lorena, arrived, he claimed he felt better. At least by then he felt well enough to get on with the assignment. He left Memphis on the afternoon of the seventeenth.

That day, with a certain ebullience, he wrote Leyda: "I had the flu but the flood was damned interesting, highwater, refugees and all that." He also noted: "I am starting by motor back towards Washington but going slowly, working along the flooded river towns, taking about ten days." Flush with his government check he sent Leyda the twenty-five dollars to cover moving expenses for the new apartment, which he presumed "must be about ready now," including the five dollars he still owed on the deposit. "How are you, what doing?" he asked. "What is Agee doing, shall we talk about working on a film?"

On February 25 Evans returned to Washington. As the bare-bones itinerary of that part of the trip reveals, the assignment was something of a letdown. A note on March 20 reads: "Lunch with R. Stryker, extraordinary conversation." The "extraordinary conversation" with Roy Stryker, however, must have been related to the news that Evans's services with the Resettlement Administration were at an end. It could hardly have come as a shock: "Affairs very dubious in Washington," he had already informed Leyda. "I don't know what I'll be doing in March." The official announcement of March 23, 1937, simply stated: "Reasons for action: Services no longer needed." Whatever bitterness Evans may have held about his dismissal seems to have ripened over the years and was confined to the darker comments given in late interviews. The reality, as far as the contemporary documents reveal, was that for the next three or four years, Stryker was to be of some service to Evans, and Evans was to seek favors from him. As with photographs, time had a way of bleaching out old relationships. The random correspondence between the two remained cordial enough.

It had not been a successful assignment nor had it given Evans much satisfaction, partly because of his illness, partly perhaps because of a lack of interest in what he was doing. There was never the sense of accomplishment he had experienced in his earlier work for the Resettlement Administration and more certainly in the Alabama sharecropper photographs; nor, with the exception of a few of the images, did he promote the photographs he took in Arkansas and Tennessee. More important, as the 1973 Da Capo Press publication of Evans's FSA photographs admits, there was no definitive record of his work there. The distinctions between the photographs Evans took and those that Edwin Locke provided were muddled. A note for the Arkansas and Tennessee flood relief photographs reads: "The attribution to Walker Evans of all photographs in this section and the next is uncertain. FSA photographer Edwin Locke accompanied Evans to the Arkansas-Tennessee flood in 1937, and, despite considerable correspondence on the subject, confusion concerning the particular photographs taken by each has never been finally resolved." The records of the Prints and Photographs Division attributed all the photographs in that segment of the collection to Evans: "[B]ecause some are certainly by him and because there is no way to determine which if any are not his, all have been included in this catalogue." One might guess that the haphazard compositions of some of the 35-mm films (like the Ridgley photographs of the *Farmer's Home*) might be Locke's. Some of the more formally composed 4 x 5s are safely attributed to Evans, but there is no certainty. There are surer grounds for accepting the more dramatic shots that appeared in such early exhibitions as the FSA section of the 1938 "First International Photography Exposition," held at the Grand Central Palace, some of which were reproduced or mentioned in Edward Steichen's review of the FSA show within the show. Notably, "Flood Refugees, Forrest

Arkansas Flood Refugee, 1937

348

City, Arkansas, February 1937," which focuses on the parade of dark and shabby winter coats and the disembodied black hands holding tin plates and enamel-ware bowls of the faceless dispossessed waiting in a food line, or those of the sick women in their cast-iron beds, which Evans exhibited in his groundbreaking 1938 exhibition "American Photographs." Evans's quest for the topical and dramatic episode of the 1937 Mississippi flood was decidedly flawed. It lacked the signature of his work, what Agee would later perfectly describe as "the cruel radiance of what is."

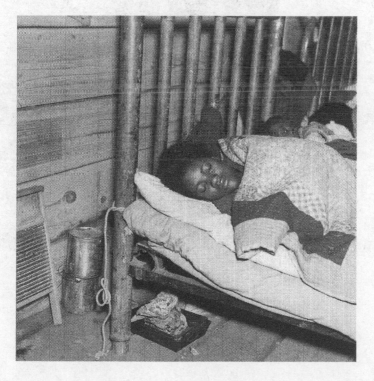

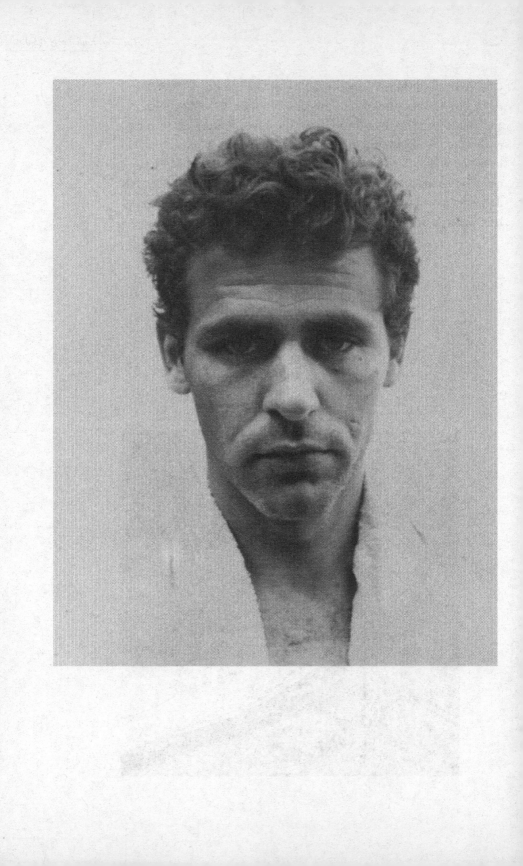

Evans believed in the importance of luck. The fact that Beaumont
Newhall, librarian at the Museum of Modern Art, was assembling a
historic exhibition, "Photography 1839–1937," proved to be an opportunity
on two counts, at least. Since the museum had no reputation in the field of
photography, both Barr and Newhall felt it would be a good idea to form
an international advisory committee to serve as sponsor. A calling card
with Newhall's title as Director, International Exhibition of Photography,
had even been devised. Evans's growing reputation fit into Newhall's plans
for the exhibition, which would include a full complement of contemporary photographers, including Paul Strand, Berenice Abbott, Ansel Adams,
Man Ray, and Edward Weston as well as works by photographers of the
past such as Nadar and Atget, calotypes by William Henry Fox Talbot, and
portraits by Julia Margaret Cameron and Americans Mathew Brady and
Alexander Gardner, and the western photographer Timothy O'Sullivan.
(Alfred Stieglitz, critical of the Modern from the beginning, had refused to
allow Newhall to use any of his work in this exhibition other than
published photogravures from *Camera Work*.)

On December 8, 1936, Newhall wrote to Evans in Washington asking
what photographs of his own he would like included in the Modern's show.
He also asked Evans's assistance in selecting works by Mathew Brady: "You
know much more about his work than I do and if it is not asking too much
of you, I should like to have you make a tentative selection of his work.
Also what do you know about Alex. Gardner." Evans's response was immediate. His reply, dated December 11, was brisk: He informed Newhall about
his recent studies of the Bradys in the Signal Corps collection and the
Library of Congress, both of which he had seen, as well as the negatives in
the L. C. Handy Studio ("the remains of the Brady commercial photo business, in the hands of relatives or something"). Pointing up his own plans
for making a collection of prints (the Signal Corps was selling not very
good prints for thirty or thirty-five cents apiece), he made it clear he would
prefer to make his own if he could get permission to use the negatives. On

James Agee,
Old Field
Point,
New York,
August, 1937

that score, he suggested that he and the museum could profitably work together. In fact, in a moment of magnanimity, he suggested that he might provide the Modern with a collection of Brady prints:

I could give the Museum a set of say a hundred prints for your permanent collection, and, I'd hope for a small Brady exhibition, sometime. Gift to the Museum from Resettlement Administration, selection and printing by me . . . Now a letter from the museum stating that this gift would be welcome would I think start opening the way to the negatives; I think Mrs. Roosevelt is the only person whose request will open the Signal Corps (War Dept.) and I think she'll do it.

Seemingly still unaware of Rexford Tugwell's pending resignation — one of the hazards of political wheeling and dealing — he suggested that he could get Tugwell to ask her but he needed to provide a good reason: "Tugwell is not interested in photography, doesn't know me or care about what I've been doing here; but he does care about education, will act for this idea from that side of it. It is forward of me to ask this, I'm sorry; still it's the best way to go about it, and it's worth doing." Evans indicated that he planned to be in New York in a week or so and "would love to have dinner" with the Newhalls, as they had asked. Then, in case Newhall was in a hurry, he made an itemized list of twenty-seven photographs from the Signal Corps files that he considered "especially good Bradys."

About his own work he was strangely reluctant; he made no mention at all about his own work, the prints Newhall had asked for the exhibition. Newhall hastily reprimanded him for overlooking the matter: "You said nothing in your letter about Evans prints from Evans negatives. Please do not overlook yourself. I very much want some of your things." On the other hand, Newhall was excited to hear about the possibility of a hundred Brady photographs for the museum collection: "If we could announce the gift at the time of the exhibition — that is sometime before April 18 — it would be swell publicity and would form the foundation for a permanent collection of old as well as modern things." About the Brady prints for the exhibition, he was sorry that he would have to limit them to ten; he explained that he already had a wealth of historical material. He suggested, however, that he would like an original Brady print "to show people what his things looked like." He made another suggestion: "If the plan goes through and we can have Evans prints of Brady negs, it will be very interesting to see the difference between an albumen print and a bromide or chloro-bromide print — that is unless you are thinking of making your own silver paper which is an idea it would be worthwhile keeping in mind." Newhall was clearly courting the photographer, but as it turned out Evans was less than grateful, even dilatory, about sending his own photographs. On January 18, 1937, Newhall was obliged to remind Evans: "Time is flying: the deadline of the catalogue approaches and I should appreciate very much receiving from you a half dozen prints for the exhibition. Will you please send some along (unmounted) as soon as convenient?" He also had to ask about the Brady prints: "How goes the Brady search? . . . Naturally I should like to know how you are progressing and what you have found. Will you please let me know as soon as you can?" As a teaser, perhaps, since it involved two of Evans's photographic heroes, Newhall mentioned that the Atget section of the show would match the Brady section: "that is there will be a case beneath the photos with his original albums, lent by Berenice Abbott."

On the twenty-seventh Evans wrote, apologizing for having held him up; he had been trying to make his prints on a special paper that would be a distinct improvement on the varieties he had previously used. "And just now government work has been piling in on me." That was true enough; the twenty-seventh was the day Roy Stryker had informed him of the assignment to photograph the flood areas in Arkansas and Tennessee. He also noted that Newhall had not specified a catalogue deadline; he promised, however, to send his photographs immediately or within the week. As to the Brady prints, he had found the Handy studio "pretty much of a shambles, both their files and their minds being buried in nineteenth-century cobwebs. Still you can have certain good original prints which I picked out (I bought one beauty for myself) by writing to Miss Evans there." If he had received Newhall's reply of January 28 in time, he may have been slightly miffed. Newhall, aside from mentioning that the deadline for the catalogue was February 6, noted that while he had asked Evans for six of his own photographs, "I am afraid that I shall have to cut it down to four. I do not want to have the walls too crowded and so, with a very few exceptions, I have limited the entries to four." Evans's diary note for January 30, the afternoon on which he left for Tennessee, indicates that that morning he had completed a last errand: "This morning requested

353

Miss Evans of Handy Studio to send 10 Brady prints, which I selected, to Museum for photo show." Quite possibly he had received Newhall's letter, since ten Brady prints was what Newhall had finally requested.

It was not the last of Evans's concerns about the "Photography 1839–1937" exhibition. As late as early March he was still sending possible photographs, or perhaps the only ones he managed to send, considering his illness while on assignment. Newhall, with a slight edge of remonstrance, wrote him on March 9:

Thanks for sending the three photographs for exhibition: "New York State Interior," "Alabama City Block," and "Minstrel Show Bill." These are fine pictures. I wish that we had received them in time to list in the catalogue, but I know how pressed you have been with your government work. After due consideration I decided that four pictures were not enough, and so I have catalogued six under your name, choosing available pictures which seemed to Alfred and myself representative of your work.

Actually Newhall listed seven photos, one of which, *Roadside Billboard, Cape Cod, 1931*, appears to be crossed out in the letter. The others were: *Moving Truck and Bureau Mirror, 1929*, *Photographers Window, Savannah, 1936*, *French Opera Barber Shop, Bethlehem PA, False Front*, and *New Circus Poster*, the last three of which were identified as the property of the Resettlement Administration. A further note indicated that since he had received the three photographs that morning, Newhall had decided to substitute the *Minstrel Showbill* for the *French Opera Barber Shop*. Newhall suggested that if Evans wanted substitutions made he should let him know before the week was out. He thanked him for the Brady material and hoped Evans might make it to the private opening at the museum on Tuesday evening, March 16. A note in Evans's hand on the reverse of the letter reads: "Thanks, however would rather not hang two billboard subjects so could you instead readmit 'Opera Barber Shop' and discard 'Cape Cod Billboard.'" The last-minute substitution appears to have been made, but not without some further contretemps. A letter from Frances Collins to Evans dated only "Wednesday" opens with the following zippy run-on paragraph:

Lissen: It will be all right about the prints. The others were about-to-be-hung and were included in the catalogue section on account of de Newhall said you were supposed to send a list of what you wanted in and then you didn't and the catalogue had to go to the printer and so Alfred brought over some that you had given Marga and E. Hitchings brought up some that she had around, and that's how it happened, and I'm sorry, but there was so much confusion and it was difficult as hell on account of B.N. and don't be sore because the new prints will go in the show, but the Bethlehem one of the river and houses on the opposite bank is so damn lovely, God, yes, exciting.

The undated "Thursday" letter Evans wrote to Jay Leyda — the one written on the Baltimore & Ohio Railroad stationery — quite probably had been written around the time that Newhall was organizing "Photography 1839-1937," which ran from March 17 to April 18 at the Modern. It was a well-received exhibition. *Time* magazine called the show's 814 exhibits "the most comprehensive exhibition of photography ever held in the U.S." *New York Times* critic Edward Alden Jewell was intrigued by the camera obscura built into the entranceway to the exhibi-

Frances Collins, 1938-39

tion which registered the visitors upside down on a framed sheet of ground glass, revealing the basic principle of photography "with full splendor." Lewis Mumford in *The New Yorker* praised Newhall for "ransacking the important collections for historic examples," and his catalogue as "one of the best short critical histories I know in any language." He was less impressed with the selection of contemporary photographers like Strand and Weston, Abbott and Evans, since "the most important modern photographer, Alfred Stieglitz, is not represented in this show by any of the work he has done during the last twenty-five years." Evans, for various reasons — perhaps the hoopla of the camera obscura or the installations by designer Herbert Matter — was disgruntled with the results: "The museum show of March," he wrote Leyda, "is depressing and embarrassing me more and more. I learn that Newhall has ambitions to become high paid photographer himself — hence commercial tie up. Merde."

An odd feature of this same letter is its passing indication that Agee and Lincoln Kirstein had been talking about a possible photographic exhibition. Evans told Leyda: "Jim says he discussed some photo show for next Sept. with Lincoln. He seems diffident about working on it but don't you think he would arrange or help arrange a good one? If you do please urge him to accept the responsibility. Plan I believe comes from Hurwitz Leo. I gather Jim has been offered director but am not sure of this. Anyway am all for it of course." It is at least possible that the exhibition Kirstein and Agee had discussed was an exhibition of Evans's photographs. His eagerness—"Anyway I am all for it of course"—tends to suggest this, just as Agee's diffidence suggests that Kirstein was the precipitating agent for promoting it. Perhaps it was mere coincidence, but a year later Kirstein was instrumental in promoting and providing the catalogue for an exhibition that would make Walker Evans a name to contend with in American photography.

* * *

The collaboration between Evans and Agee was, perhaps, never so sharply imaged, nor so mysteriously, as in the one or two portraits Evans made of Agee in the summer of 1937. The photographs, part of a series he made, presumably at a beach at Old Field Point on Long Island, tell us

Peggy Hobson

Wilder Hobson

James Agee

*All photos
taken at
Old Field
Point,
New York,
August, 1937*

little about the basic circumstances. But biographical sources indicate that Wilder and Peggy Hobson had rented a house there, that Hobson's marriage was on the rocks, that his father had died in the spring, that he had suffered through a damaging case of writer's block following an assignment in Japan with Archibald MacLeish and had quit his post at *Time* to take a job with its rival *Newsweek* — that he was eager for the companionship of old friends. There are, to be sure, bits of information to be gleaned from the sequence of photographs: that the shoot may have taken more than one day, since Peggy Hobson appears in two different bathing suits — or, perhaps, that she may have changed suits later in the same day and the photographs may have been taken at more than one location, since she is shown stretched out, like a fakir, on a field of very hard pebbles. (Both she and Wilder crop up haphazardly in several shots, suggesting that Evans was merely shooting at random.) There are also two or three portrait shots of Via, acknowledging that she was with Agee on the same August day. They are carefully posed photographs of her against an undistinguishable background.

In the most attractive of the Agee photographs, he is seen full face, a towel draped around his neck. He looks sullen, is unshaved, broad-browed, his hair tousled. He stares comfortably and knowingly at the photographer. The more remarkable prints, however, show him in much the same pose but with his eyes now narrowed and glittering; he is squinting. In the photograph, what appears to be the silhouette of the photographer has been captured in the lenses of Agee's eyes. The intensity of the latter photograph is undeniable; as if for once Evans had let down his guard in photographing one of his friends so directly. Evans was alert to Agee's sensuality, partly admiring and partly critical: "You know Agee was oversexed," he once remarked, late in life. "He was a very embarrassing man." But there is more fascination than embarrassment in this particular portrait. It could be the portrait of a young prizefighter with a day's growth of beard, slightly menacing; or the coffin portrait of a Coptic youth looking forward toward eternity. Whatever sensuality or sexuality it harbors is inherent, part of the subject in the way that the current of sensuality is inherent in any form of art that takes its impetus, however sublimated or disguised, from life.

The undistinguishable background in the portrait is the same that appears in the three or more photographs of Via. She is freckled, thoughtful, wearing a dark sportshirt. In one of them, Via, too, confronts the photographer, but more casually than her husband. Nothing seems amiss in most of these photographs. It is a summer day, or two, at a beach. There is the wide stretch of glaring sand and pebbles, only the mere promise of water in the distance. The emptiness and loneliness suggest that the beach is conducive to the nude bathing in which, some reports claim, the friends indulged on this particular occasion. In some of the photographs, Agee, as if by habit, appears garrulous, caught up in a nonstop gesturing conversation. But it is from other, later sources (letters, memoirs — the literary evidence) that one learns that appearances may not be what they seem in these photographs. Evans, for instance, maintained that Agee had made a mistake in taking up with Alma Mailman, whom he considered too young: "She'll be a high school girl twenty years from now, no matter what happens to her." (So, at least, an unpublished quasi-fictional version of Agee's courtship of Alma would have us believe. It is admissible testimony, as long as one recognizes that it is Agee's view of the circumstances, however false or accurate, tendentious or clouded. It is the product of his mind and motivations, not necessarily the absolute truth — nor even an exact transcription of Evans's thoughts, either.)

Tourist Motorcade in Havana, From Fortune *Six Days at Sea, September, 1937*

During his Long Island visit — or visits — Evans was taking Via out for drives in the surrounding towns, perhaps by way of consolation. And at some point, probably later, during the long summer of 1937 he and Via began an affair. Neither of them seemed to take this turn of events as absolutely serious. Via, reportedly, was tentative, aware she was not the only woman in Evans's life at the time: "With Walker you knew you were never the only one. He was discreet about it, but I knew there were others." True enough; Walker was also seeing Frances Collins, the head of the publications department at the Museum of Modern Art. The daughter of *New York Times* correspondent Simeon Strunsky, she was married to a young writer, Peter Collins. Then, too, the rumor still clung to him that he had a "girl" in New Orleans. There was a certain security in playing the field; Evans, however, would later chalk up such activities as the fashion of the time. It was, he claimed, "part of the first sexual revolution, and the violation, the innocent violation, reached enormous proportions. Everybody by rote went to bed with everybody else, and the result was an emotional desert and confusion." However, he issued a disclaimer: "I say 'everybody': I mean all the 'advanced' people — always. All the *sophisticated* and *emancipated* and *educated* people."

* * *

Although Agee was trying to curtail his activities at *Fortune* in 1937, that summer he became involved in the writing of three articles, one after another: for the March issue, "Posters by Cassandre," on the advertising posters of the French graphic designer A. M. Cassandre, and for June, "Smoke," a prophetic article on the effects of industrial pollution, one that clearly anticipated the concerns of environmentalists half a century later.

The third of Agee's articles, "Six Days at Sea," published in the September issue, was a minor masterpiece of travel writing, a sardonic, racy account of a Caribbean cruise on the Ward Line's *Oriente*. He and Via, brought along as traveling companion, and Evans, as photographer, had boarded the turboelectric liner on a bright early summer morning. From the beginning Agee's take on the cruise was definitely seriocomic. The *Oriente*, as he defined it, was "the sea-faring analogy to a second-string summer resort, a low-priced sedan, or the newest and best hotel in a provincial city." The

article contained the usual gloss of research department background: "Of the passenger traffic of all flags sailing from US ports in 1935 the cruising passengers accounted for ten per cent. In the same year, according to the Department of Commerce, 83,000 passengers left US ports on cruises." It was handled deftly enough, but the article, by turns, turned raucously funny and at times slyly sexual (or, in today's terminology, sexist). Agee noted the one hundred and thirty-two passengers, twenty of them traveling Cubans returning home, the rest mostly lower- to middle-bracket American tourists, some of them middle-aged married couples or pathetic spinsters. There was a large contingent of unattached young or middle-aged women and a smaller collection of desirable young males. Agee cast a wicked eye on a blond young man who resembled an airedale "sufficiently intelligent to count to ten, dance fox-trots, and graduate from a gentlemen's university." He and a duplicate male friend showed up "in naughty trunks, laid towels aside from their pretty shoulders, oiled themselves, and, after a brief warm up, began to play deck tennis furiously before the gradually assembling girls." Agee was a bit less caustic, more approving of the young women on the tour, mostly secretaries and clerks seemingly looking for husbands or a good time:

They strolled against the wind, they stood at the white rail with wind in their waved hair, they swung their new shoes from primly crossed knees, they lay back with shaded eyes, their crisp white skirts tucked beneath them in the flippant air . . . they lay supine, skull eyed in goggles; their cruel vermilion nails caught at the sunlight. They examined each other quietly but sharply, and from behind dark white-rimmed lenses affected to read drugstore fiction and watched those beautiful bouncing blond boys' bodies and indulged the long, long thoughts of youth. The airedales were fast and skillful, and explosive with such Anglo-Saxonisms as Sorry, Tough, Nice Work, Too Bad, Nice Going.

The seriocomic aspect of this particular assignment was that Agee, Evans, and Via decided to act as undercover observers — as spies, in other words — when they boarded ship one morning in early summer. This was, in fact, the same metaphor Agee chose to adopt when writing about his and Evans's adventures in Alabama. That they both thought there was some mileage to be gained from the concept is apparent; a few years later, Evans would essentially assume the same role when he began taking surreptitious photographs of unsuspecting passengers on the New York City subways. How successful they were on their Caribbean cruise is questionable; Evans, at least, could hardly have been invisible when he busily snapped pictures (nineteen of them were used as illustrations) of the forced gaiety of the passengers in their party hats, of others playing shuffleboard, of the girls on deck in their reclining chairs. Or once they had reached their destination — the day-and-a-half stopover at Havana. (Agee had struck the right preliminary chord when the *Oriente* shifted course eastward toward Cuba; he duly noted the "musical comedy blue of the Gulf Stream.") "Six Days at Sea" may have lacked the finer social distinctions of a Trollope novel, but it did have its own cutting edge as well as the bright verve of a 1930s Hollywood comedy. In Havana — they were to spend eighteen hours on their visit there — Evans snapped the *Oriente* tourists lounging at Sloppy Joe's Bar. Agee dubbed it "the Grant's Tomb of bars," noting that no self-respecting Cuban would be caught dead there. (Out of what fund of prior knowledge is unknown, unless Evans had alerted him to the fact.) Few of the tourists, Agee noted, ordered more than one drink, though Evans's photograph of the premises reveals them, glasses raised aloft, and convivial enough. He also showed them in a motorcade stopping traffic while standing in their touring cars to take in the sights, or herded like well-dressed sheep along avenues much tidier than those he had photographed a few years earlier. What his *Fortune* sequence lacked was the searching, starker enquiry of the photographs made for *The Crime of Cuba*: the grimmer statistics of the sleeping derelicts and drunks, the slums and *bohíos*. The streets in the better parts of town had been swept clean. Agee's account suggests that there had been no visits to the outlying slums and *bohíos* that Evans had so effectively photographed in 1933. Nor, in Evans's recollections, do there seem to be any mentions of the English secretary he had admired or the fate of the Fernández brothers. Having a few years earlier seen the country on the verge of revolution under the corrupt Machado regime, Evans had now had the opportunity of seeing what he had himself predicted, the equally corrupt benefits of the de facto Batista government.

The return trip to New York was expectably glum. Once the novelty of Havana had worn off, the passengers lost interest in the tea dances, the dressing for dinner. In Agee's words, "New acquaintances had run out of small talk and had no other and did not know how to get rid of each other." Things picked up with the farewell supper: Agee referred to it egregiously as "the last supper, with its tasseled menus, its signal flag, hats and noise-makers." It lasted too long and ended with some acrimonious exchanges between the disappointed young women, an argument between a married couple, the breaking of champagne glasses after a toast by a pair of snotty international smart set couples (one German couple and the other American) who had boarded the ship in Havana and kept themselves aloof from the other merrymakers. They ordered more champagne and more glasses and then proceeded to break them as well, even though a waiter had asked them as politely as possible to please refrain. Agee was slightly apologetic about his portrait of the tourists when the article finally appeared in the September issue of *Fortune*.

Words and images: A photographer, caught up in the moment of photographing, might turn retrospective in discussing his work. (Of course, it was still possible for Evans to alter the results of his negatives with later reprintings, croppings, or darkening of the contrasts, as a writer might edit or revise his earlier drafts.) When, later in life, Evans began to make known his thoughts (or words) about his photographic intentions, he took the retrospective approach. In a 1961 unpublished author's introductory note intended for the 1962 reissue of *American Photographs*, he referred to his efforts in the thirties (his own thirties as well):

The objective picture of America in the 1930ss made by Evans was neither journalistic nor political in technique and intention. It was reflective rather than tendentious and, in a certain way, disinterested. . . . Evans was, and is, interested in what any present time will look like as the past.

Even more important, Evans chose never to include the *Fortune* photographs of the Caribbean cruise in any of his exhibitions or exhibition catalogues. But they were, if not the best of his work, at least an honorable part of the objective picture of American life out of which he constructed a lengthy career.

17

No event had so decisive an effect on Walker Evans's career — certainly for better and in other ways, perhaps, for worse — than the 1938 publication of *Walker Evans: American Photographs* and the coincidental exhibition of one hundred of his photographs at The Museum of Modern Art. The origins of the book and the exhibition — the first one-man retrospective of a photographer at the museum — still raise questions of precedence. The book, more so than the exhibition, so firmly — and so completely — established Evans's reputation as a documentary photographer that he found it difficult to shake the limiting image.

Lincoln Kirstein, late in life, admitted to having financed the publication of the book. (If true, it would have been the most prominent of the supportive measures Kirstein had made on behalf of Evans's career.) But a contract dated May 6, 1938, and signed by Evans designates The Museum of Modern Art as publishers of the volume. It also gives the title of the book simply as *Photographs by Walker Evans* and notes that Evans was to "deliver to the publishers on or before the 31st day of May, 1938, a complete copy of the said work in its final form." The brisk deadline and the promised publication date ("on or before the 15th day of September 1938") suggest that work on the book had begun well before the contract date. The timetable, as far as one can determine from some of the surviving documents, is that the idea for the book at least had been in the works before March 29, when Tom Mabry, executive director at MOMA, was suggesting the possibility of an exhibition to accompany the book. Indeed, the museum seemed to be in the market for a major photographic exhibition for the opening of the fall season in its interim quarters at 14 West Forty-ninth Street. Its new modern building, designed by Edward Durrell Stone and Philip Johnson in the international style, was already under construction at the 11 West Fifty-third Street site.

The operations behind the mounting of Evans's restrospective suggest an almost Machiavellian scheme. Mabry's letter indicates that sometime in February Beaumont Newhall had been in Washington. With Roy Stryker's

Couple at Coney Island, New York, 1928

agreement, he had selected some eighty-six photographs from the FSA files, with plans for running an exhibition. Possibly Newhall wanted to match the success of his exhibition the year before. Mabry told Evans, "Since this selection has already been made, perhaps we should go ahead with it, although of course you know I would feel much safer to have your selection of the material." Presumably what was involved was an exhibition of the FSA photographers in general. What is surprising about the arrangement is that Stryker must have been preparing for a special exhibition of the FSA photographers, some eighty-one photographs, to be shown at the "First International Photography Exposition" at Grand Central Palace, slated to open on April 18. From Newhall, Mabry had also learned that Stryker was jealously guarding Evans's photographs of the Alabama tenant farmers, "wanting to release all of it at one time in some sort of impressive way." Mabry proposed another option: "What do you think of getting Stryker to let us have those photographs of your work and of giving a complete exhibition of them next fall." He mentioned that he had not yet discussed the matter with Director Alfred Barr, then busy with future exhibitions of his own, but he promised to do so in the near future. "It seems to me that if we publish a book of your photographs it might be wise to have an exhibition of your work simultaneously so that the book will have the same relation to our exhibition as our other catalogues have had. Both would help each other, I think." Mabry's letter does not altogether rule out the possibility that Kirstein had offered to finance the production of the book; it only indicates that the museum might serve as official publisher.

A month later, Mabry had evolved some definite suggestions for Lincoln Kirstein's covering essay for the book. Writing to Kirstein on April 29, reminding him of his promise to write the text, he confessed his own inadequacies: "You know much more about Walker's work than I do. However I should think that you might want to define as simply and clearly as possible the difference between Walker's work and the majority of photographers both 'documentary' and 'lyric.' Also I think that the article should not have an in memoriam flavor." One of his principal concerns was that Kirstein's piece should avoid "the canonization of the commonplace that documentary photography has turned into." His examples were photographer Margaret Bourke-White, the *Life* photographers, and a good many of the Federal Art Project photographers, whose works

were "just as bad to me as any kind of Herald Tribune beautiful baby contest photography." Nor was he altogether approving of the way Weston and Strand turned the commonplace into "something precious, exquisite, etched and fabulous," which was equally bad. Mabry was capable of maintaining other fine distinctions: "Incidentally, I think that some of Stieglitz's work is very good."

Evans himself (albeit late in life) was vague about the circumstances by which the book and the exhibition had come about. Little wonder: Learning about a possible exhibition of FSA photographers at the Modern that would certainly have ruled out the tantalizing proposal of an exhibition of his own work there when his book was published must have filled him with dismay. He may have been right when he insisted that both

Kirstein and Mabry were deeply involved in the success of the venture: "I believe that it was largely personal, that Lincoln Kirstein and Tom Mabry had a lot to do with that and sort of rammed it into the museum. . . . I had nothing to do with it. I don't even remember." He made it clear that Barr was not a determining factor: "Except that Alfred Barr was interested in some photography. I don't think he was particularly interested in me. He didn't even like me very much. He was a very very sensitive and intelligent man, although he was over-scholarly, he really had a mind for contemporary art and everything graphic — a true artist's mind for that."

Evans was in no doubt about how important the exhibition and, in particular, the publication of *American Photographs* was to his career: "It was like a calling card. It made it. The book particularly was like a passport for me. Sure. It established my style and everything. Oh Yes. And as time went on it became more and more important. It turned out to be a landmark, really." In later life he was more than generous in his praise of Kirstein's efforts when it came to the sequencing of photographs in the book: "I remember Lincoln helping me very much compose the thing. I would get stuck over a work, the layout of the book and he was so breezy and fast that he would untie all the knots in an afternoon and say come and do it this way and slap it in and it would be right." But it is important to note that the praise was part of an overall tribute to Kirstein's early recognition and support of his work. He gave a vivid account of Kirstein in the early phase of their friendship:

Kirstein was an aggressive, quite unrestrained young man. . . . He invaded you; you either had to throw him out or listen to him. As a matter of fact I thought at the time he was great and still do. Oddly enough, what happened was that this undergraduate was teaching me something about what I was doing — it was a typical Kirstein switcheroo, all permeated with tremendous spirit, flash, dash and a kind of seeming high jinks that covered a really penetrating intelligence about and articulation of all esthetic matters and their contemporary applications. It's hard to believe, but as I say the man was essentially explaining to me just what I was doing in my work. It was immensely helpful and hilariously audacious. Professor Kirstein.

That spring, events, at least as far as the publication of *American Photographs* was concerned, were developing with some speed. By May 4 —

two days before the contract was signed — Frances Collins, in charge of publications at the museum, wrote Evans: "Tom had a note from Lincoln. Lincoln says he will write a good piece about you. Lincoln is very excited about the book. He wants to call it A VISION OF AMERICA or A VIEW OF AMERICA. Lincoln sounds stirred and stormy: I ask God and St. Catherine that if Lincoln has to be handled it's you and Tom who will handle him." Her note indicates that the format of the book had been decided by then: "This is all there is to tell you about the book except that I have a dummy 7¾ by 8¾ which looks to be a good size and is — Joe [Blumenthal] says — very economical so far as paper is concerned: there's virtually no waste in the cutting. I'll let you know whatever else there is." This suggests that Evans had not specified the final format size which was an important factor in the scaling and cropping of individual prints. However, in a draft proposal for the original design, Evans had insisted on no reproductions, only lettering, on the dust jacket, and a possible reversal of the order of the two sections. By collecting all captions at the end of each section he allowed for maximum attention to the details of the photographs, which appeared opposite the numbered but otherwise blank white pages. Evans thereby insisted on the authority of the photographs themselves.

In her May 4 letter, Collins also brought up the question of the photographic plates: "New proofs came from Beck [the engraver] better than the first ones but still disheartening. . . . Joe suggests that if you were to make new prints: as glossy as possible: they could probably do better. I showed him the Ansel Adams book and he said, 'Oh, well, that's English engraving.' *What the hell.* Where does that leave us?" She was both knowledgeable and detailed in her suggestions. "The prints we send to the engraver, though, had better be mounted on any kind of mat so that thumbs don't land on them quite so regularly."

There was an element of concern on Evans's part about the *American Photographs* book. Writing to Stryker on June 15 — late in the proceedings — he noted, "The Mus. Mod. Art wants to publish me covering the range of ten years work. I am accepting although the book has to be arranged quickly. I have most of the Resettlement prints I want included here, no time to come to Washington about it. I told them to write to you about it, for permission, etc. It's a good idea, good as corrective. Hope you'll like it."

Strangely enough Evans said nothing about the exhibition. Nor was he altogether settled in his mind about the book a month later when he brought up the subject in a lengthy and tentative letter to Stryker which may not have been sent:

Dear Roy, One of the things I wanted to talk to you about, or at least to find out whether you understood clearly, is the matter of the extent of my freedom in the choice of pictures for this Museum book. I am quite sure this may be unnecessary, that is, I think you know well enough what I am about to say, but let us not take any chances: this is a book about and by me, and the number of Resettlement pictures I have decided to reproduce (with naturally, your permission and full credit acknowledgment) has been determined solely on the grounds of my opinion of their worth as pictures. They form a part of my work, all of which is to be represented. The Museum understands it this way, is bringing the thing out as an example of the work of an artist, is not interested in this respect in whom he has worked for or with.

Once again he insisted on his independence. Evans made no bones about his low opinion of Newhall. In a crossed-out segment, he added, "When I say Museum I do not mean the so-called curator of photography who as I told you has had and will have nothing to do with my book or exhibition and who as a matter of fact has not the right to use that title." The road to success, Evans seemed to imply, had to be traveled alone. Evidently, too, he had not forgotten that Newhall had been billed as the "Director" of the museum's "Photography 1839-1937" exhibition.

* * *

Originally, in the early stages of the planning for *American Photographs*, Evans wrote a long unsigned "note" to appear before the photographs of part two. In the end he decided to scrap it. What he chose not to say is instructive. He began with a borrowed quote from Charles Flato's essay on Mathew Brady from *Hound & Horn*: "Human beings . . . are far more important than elucidating factors in history: by themselves they have a greatness aside from the impressive structure of history." The human component, then, was intended to "illuminate the attitude" behind his selection of photographs. He went on: "There are moments and moments in history, and we do not need military battles to provide the images of conflicts, or to reveal the moments and changes, or again the conflicts which in passing become the body of the history of civilizations. But we do need more than the illustrations in the morning papers of our period."

From the beginning, a sense of time — of time passing — was a vital element of Evans's photography. The pictorial journalism of the moment, which included celebrity photography, was corrupt and commercial, he claimed. Worth noting is the fact that in neither his books nor his major exhibitions did Evans include photographs of friends or acquaintances (like Hart Crane or James Agee) or major celebrities, except for incidental appearances like the billboard illustrations of movie stars Anne Shirley and Carole Lombard (she of the black eye) in Atlanta, or the face of Kay Francis peering out from the magazine rack behind the black man-about-town in Havana. But even then, he was willing to concede that pictorial journalism and celebrity photographs might turn up records of value for future students of history. In *American Photographs*, however, he chose to represent something more valuable:

[T]hese anonymous people who come and go in the cities and who move on the land; it is on what they look like, now; what is in their faces and in the windows and the streets beside and around them; what they are wearing and what they are riding in, and how they are gesturing that we need to concentrate consciously with the camera.

It was a surprising, summary account of the photographs of people he finally chose for the opening segment of his book. (But what of the second segment, which consisted mostly of architectural photographs — frame houses, factories, gas stations? Clearly, for Evans, the works of man also represented man; it was one of Evans's subtler distinctions.) The original note might have given a warm, elegant testimony to the first decade of his photographic career, but Evans chose to delete it.

In the end, he opted for a brief author's introductory note, which began with acknowledgments to the Farm Security Administration; to *Harper's*, with whom he and Agee were negotiating for the publication of *Let Us Now Praise Famous Men*, crediting them for the several prints that appeared in *American Photographs*; and to *Hound & Horn*, where some of his earlier photographs had first been published. The principal importance of this introductory note was that Evans totally disavowed any esthetic or political influences that could be attributed to those sources:

The responsibility for the selection of the pictures used in this book has rested with the author, and the choice has been determined by his opinion: therefore they are presented without sponsorship or connection with the policies, aesthetic or political, of any of the institutions, publications or government agencies for which some of the work has been done.

It reads as a perhaps innocent reminder of the author's independence. But considering that it was to become in effect an esthetic credo for Evans's professional life and in some ways for his private life, it assumes major significance. It established at the beginning of his fame a reputation for reserve and cool distancing. Beyond that, Evans was content (probably well content) to leave the explanatory prose, esthetic claims, and critical writing to Kirstein.

* * *

Kirstein's essay proved to be an important feature of *American Photographs* and a contribution to the book's long-term public reception. There were good reasons for this: It was an impressive piece of writing, commented on in many of the reviews (both in agreement and condemnation). The essay began with a considered study of the history of photography and its fallibilities in the hands of current "art" photographers and candid camera addicts. Kirstein was intent on placing Evans in the context of the time, as an artist of "the unrelieved, bare-faced, revelatory fact." He went on: "It is 'straight' photography not only in technique but in the rigorous directness of its way of looking. All through the pictures in this book you will search in vain for an angle-shot." At some points, he pulled out all the stops, matching Evans's work with the Paris photos of Atget and the Civil War photographs of Brady. He recited the names of contemporaries who worked in different media but made comparisons between Evans's photographs and "the quartz and cameos of Marianne Moore, the lyrical case book of Dr. William Carlos Williams, the mural histories of Ben Shahn." He added: "The sculpture of the New Bedford ship-builders, the face-maps of itinerant portraitists . . . continue in his camera. We recognize in his photographs a way of seeing which has appeared persistently throughout the American past." Evans, Kirstein claimed, had no need to resort to tricks or dramatic angles because his subject matter was dramatic enough: "Even the inanimate things, bureau drawers, pots, tires, bricks, signs, seem waiting in their own patient dignity, posing for their picture."

Kirstein's characterizations seemed to be drawn as much from his appraisal of the man as from his recognition of the work: "The most characteristic single feature of Evans's work is its purity, or even its puritanism." He singled out the "purely protestant attitude" of Evans's photographs: "meagre, stripped, cold, and, on occasion, humorous." There were also times when Kirstein attributed to the photographer attitudes that might as easily have applied to himself: "It is also the naked, difficult, solitary attitude of a member revolting from his own class, who knows best what in it must be uncovered, cauterized and why." However, what Kirstein referred to as his own "pinkish flirtations," largely inspired by the physical attractions of Wirt Baker, a young organizer for the southern sharecroppers whom he had recently met, were to wane. Like Evans an admirer of Ben Shahn, Kirstein was still promoting the artist, but he was forced to admit that Shahn's "depthless indignation" over social causes "scared the wits out of me."

The most striking feature of Kirstein's critical approach was his insistence that the photographs were not to be viewed "as isolated pictures made by the camera turned indiscriminately here or there." Kirstein put forward the thesis that in intention and effect the photographs "exist as a collection of statements deriving from and presenting a consistent attitude. Looked at in sequence they are overwhelming in their exhaustiveness of detail, their poetry of contrast, and, for those who wish to see it, their moral implication." In effect, it was a variant of the program for the kind of photographic exhibition Agee had written up in his Guggenheim application. Perhaps one can attribute it to ideas that were circulating among those of Evans's friends who were eager to promote the book and the exhibition. Probably, too, it was significant that Agee, writing to Evans in June, should express an interest in the book and in Kirstein's essay: "I had heard from Via that you felt thoroughly well over Lincoln's introduction and needless to say, I wish also I might see it (the book I was thinking; the writing also) while it's being put together."

Among the various parties involved in the production of the book and the exhibition, there seemed to be a kind of dialectical argument in progress. In fact it is one of the failures of cultural histories that they often overlook the helpful or contradictory and sometimes misguided collaborative motivations of other artists, mentors, sponsors, editors, and critics who sustained, opposed, promoted the major reputations and the incredible achievements of modernism. Where Tom Mabry, for instance, decried other "documentary" and "lyric" photographers as compared to Evans, informing Kirstein that their work was little better than the baby pictures in a *Herald Tribune* photography contest, Evans could see some "accidental" documentary value even in pictorial journalism for "future students and examiners of the period." But he made the significant distinction: "only in time, when removed from their immediate contexts, will they serve the purpose under discussion." Kirstein, commenting on Evans's photographs "with all their clear, hideous and beautiful detail, their open insanity and pitiful grandeur," could ask, "What poet has said as much? What painter has shown as much?" He offered his own answer: "Only newspapers, the writers of popular music, the technicians of advertising and radio have in their blind energy accidentally, fortuitously, evoked for future historians such a powerful monument to our moment. And Evans's work has, in addition, intention, logic, continuity, climax, sense and perfection." Agee, in that network of interrelationships among New York friends, writing in *Let Us Now Praise Famous Men*, referred to himself as "a spy, traveling as a journalist" and Evans as "a counter-spy, traveling as a photographer." He also listed such mentors as William Blake, Ring Lardner, and Jesus Christ outlandishly as "unpaid agitators." Was it mere coincidence that Kirstein, in a neatly turned phrase, described Evans as "a conspirator against time and its hammers?"

The accuracy of those old reported discussions, the remembrance of former positions, of esthetic and political alignments, relevant at the time, are part of the not always reliable archeology of the cultural past. The circumstances surrounding the publication of *American Photographs* and the subsequent exhibition at The Museum of Modern Art (September 28–November 18) are not altogether recoverable except for the shards: ideas committed to paper in private notes, contemporary letters and reviews, memories later committed to tapes. Even then the circumstances are subject to the revisions of faulty memory and personal prejudice. Evans was willing to acknowledge the importance of Kirstein's appreciation of his work, including the essay he wrote for *American Photographs*. Late in life, in a taped interview, he admitted they meant "a great deal." He was expansive about the oddities of Kirstein's appreciation at the time: "In many ways he was able to tell me what I was doing, make me conscious of something I was doing unconsciously. That's why it seems original to you now. This was an unconscious vein I was working in and it took a fellow, an esthete like Kirstein, who was very bright, to pick out the rationale of that and articulate it for me." But he was still resolute — perhaps more so than ever — about the question of Kirstein's influence: "I don't think it influenced me; it just consolidated me."

He was lucky in his friends. In mid-September, Agee wrote him: "I wish you the luck of one good explosion of excitement over the show. I imagine it might solve everything." A day or two later, Agee had presumably seen the book. Evans must have expressed some sense of regret about it or dissatisfaction. Agee responded: "Simply by being published, bound, reproduced [the photographs] have a strange, thin part-death, which must or may be why you are partly disappointed." But he was full of praise: "It is one of the only 'great' and 'honest' or 'uncompromised' books of anywhere in this time, that I know of. It is also dangerous and I am very curious to see how far the dangerousness of so dangerous a thing can carry."

II

Significantly the major reviews focused on the book rather than the exhibition. William Carlos Williams, writing in the *New Republic*, took a personal approach: "I'm glad that Evans has promenaded his eyes about America rather than France in this case. We go about blind and deaf. We fight off convictions that we should welcome as water in the desert, could we possibly get ourselves into the right mind. The artist must save us. He's the only one who can." He was cautionary about Evans's sense of composition, which he found "of secondary importance in these clear statements." But he was resounding in his praise of Evans's accomplishment: "It is ourselves we see, ourselves lifted from a parochial setting. We see what we have not heretofore realized, ourselves made worthy in our anonymity." In the Sunday *New York Herald Tribune* books section, Carl Van Vechten, whom Evans had encountered in Muriel Draper's salon, started from the "unalterable" premise that great photographers were born, not educated. He went on to report: "If ever a photographer was born to use a lens it is Walker Evans. . . . He makes you see what he sees clearly. His eyes themselves are his lenses." Van Vechten claimed that "if everything in American civilization were destroyed except Walker Evans's photographs, they could tell us a good deal about American life. . . . As documentary evidence then, these pictures are valuable. But I place on them a much higher value than that, the value that lies in fine photography." In a highly ambivalent (or ambiguous) review in the *New York Times Book Review*, S. T. Williamson, noting Evans's success in the cult of the ugly, nonetheless wrote of his skill as a bafflingly expert technician: "His prints would put even Hollywood stills to shame for their clarity and no advertising agency would want better"—one of the odder tributes Evans would receive. Williamson went on to announce: "Some of his pictures haunt you long after the book is closed — two sullen boys with 'sez-you' expressions, a moronic youth and his girl in a parked roadster, and Mr. Evans's row of drab, depressing houses, as well as his squalid interiors." The critic however, came down on Kirstein's "boiled shirt introduction," taking offense at Kirstein's remark about the book: "The phsyiognomy of a nation is laid on your table." "Hardly," Williamson countered; it was the "bumps, warts, boils and blackheads" that showed, the blemishes of the physiognomy. As a book reviewer "singing for his supper" and not "some art commentator" he claimed he had pawed through a quarter of a million photographs in recent years. He had enough fingers and toes, he said, "on which to count photographers who have caught more of America than is presented in behalf of Mr. Evans." Kirstein did not fare well with some of the other critics either: Lewis Gannett in his "Books and Things" column in the *Herald Tribune* noted that Kirstein's "pretentiously arty essay seems out of place with these strong simple recordings of America."

Parked Car, Small Town, Main Street, 1932

It was one of the positive facets of the book that it brought the reviewers to single out and study individual photographs in detail. In that sense, Evans's insistence on sharply focused, uncaptioned prints was successful. David Wolff, in the left-wing *New Masses*, where one might have thought political correctness would have been the operative peg of the review, discussed the esthetic issues of Evans's case: "Our attention is compelled in these photographs by a combination of reticence, delicacy and a bitter surgical honesty; then what seems the most casual element becomes, as we study it, an irreducible point of the photograph." To illustrate the case Wolff chose the striking profile of the woman in the cloche hat in *Girl in Fulton Street*. "The face itself has a tragic and almost ferocious sensitivity, as if it were a kind of self-portrait of the artist; yet we see the other details: the three anonymous hats of the men just beyond, a steel arm of a crane, and especially the edge of the store window on which the girl is leaning, where the mixed and illusory reflections provide a kind of strip of confusion against which the girl's face looks back with such intensity." What he had singled out was one the still continuing fascinations of Evans's work, the counterpoint of image and reflection.

Wolff was not long in raising the political aspects of Evans work, seeing it as a revelation of "a certain hideous miscellaneousness of American life." His inventory was impressive, making it clear he had looked carefully — and had thought about — the subject matter:

... the used cars abandoned on a field; a confused and helpless back room, revealed through an open door; the tires, tubes and spare parts displayed on the front of a

garage; and the magic advertising words, the names, the signs, ubiquitous, ugly, meaningless, and powerful.

The special quality of Evans's photographs, Wolff maintained, was that they were also *facts* giving the work "the merciless edge of truth." Beyond their artistry, he noted, Evans's photographs have "the stature of documents and if we wish to understand ourselves we must look at them." It was a common note among some of the reviewers: Evans's sense of self- and national self-reflection. Peter Seitlin in *PM* denied that Evans was a "mere melancholy 'knocker.' His work is a logical expression of an honest man preoccupied with the cultural and aesthetic fate of his country and of an artist with the American Middle West in his bones." (Evans's connections with the Luce empire paid off; Seitlin's review was accompanied by three page-width illustrations, including *Joe's Auto Graveyard.*) Even the briefest mention of the book, a two-sentence notice by Eleanor Roosevelt in one of her "My Day" columns, obliquely sounded the same refrain: "Talking of photographs, a book has been published by The Museum of Modern Art called *American Photographs* by Walker Evans. It shows us contemporary America and I think all of us who care about our country will be deeply interested in this record." In some quarters the book was seen as having a national, if not necessarily patriotic, importance.

* * *

But not in all quarters: Evans's elevation as the first photographer to be given a one-man show at the Modern did not sit well with some of his professional rivals. Pare Lorentz, reviewing *American Photographs* in the December 17 issue of the *Saturday Review*, was determined to set the record straight. He considered the Modern's celebration — and especially Kirstein's essay — as misguided for singling out Evans from among the FSA photographers whose works were illustrated and accompanied by the Steichen essay in the 1939 *U.S. Camera Annual*, which Lorentz also reviewed. He was put off by Evans's or the museum's failure to acknowledge the importance of Roy Stryker's role in Evans's rise to fame. But Lorentz first took aim at Kirstein, who was "so far out of the realm of our understanding that we gather from his essay hardly more than that he thinks Mr. Evans is a fine photographer. With that we agree." He added, "But the facts are that until Professor Stryker employed him, along with Russell Lee, and Dorothy Lange, and Arthur Rothstein and Ben Shahn, and gave him an assignment, Mr. Evans had not found the wave length of his vision." Lorentz also argued that the photographs "should have been captioned." Of the eighty-seven photographs in the book, he noted, "almost half were taken at the instigation of Professor Stryker of the Farm Security Administration and were paid for by the U.S. Government." The numbers may be close to accurate, but the fact is that Evans made a point of working against the grain of the agency and its political intentions. On that subject, Evans was adamant until the end of his life. Stryker, he maintained, "Never directed me, I wouldn't let him." There is good reason to believe, too, that the directives about the subject matter for prints that Stryker sent out to other RA photographers owed some inspiration to the independent work Evans had been turning in. Stryker, who had seen the American Photographs show — and the book—"liked it a lot." He, too, took issue with Kirstein's essay. He wrote Evans: "I wish that Kirstein's article had been as good as the photographs."

The most determined of Evans's professional critics was the California photographer Ansel Adams. Writing to Georgia O'Keeffe, who had been so sympathetic to Evans's early efforts, Adams complained: "I think the book is atrocious. But not Evans's work in the true sense. . . . It's the putting of it all in a book of that kind — mixed social meanings, documentation, esthetics, sophistication (emotional slumming), etc. Just why the Museum would undertake to present *that* book is a mystery to me." O'Keeffe was not the only recipient of his rancor. Adams wrote photographer Edward Weston in the same vein: "I am so *goddam* mad over what people from the left tier think America is. Stinks, social and otherwise, are a poor excuse and imitation of the real beauty and power of the land and the real people inhabiting it. Evans has some beautiful things but they are lost in the struggle of social significance." It was not a new quarrel by any means. Four years earlier Adams had confided to Weston: "Your shells will be remembered long after [Walker] Evans' picture of two destitutes in a doorway." The lengthiest of his diatribes was sent to his patron, David McAlpin, who had also been the anonymous sponsor of Newhall's "Photography 1839-1937" exhibition. Adams, who considered himself a "bourgeois liberal," conceded that there were some "really swell photographs" in the book: ["But so few of the pictures are good photographs in any qualification that I do not believe the book should be called *American Photographs* and put out by an art organiza- tion.]... But see what happens — the 'esthetes' who are mostly pink because they lack the guts to be truly red, build up a good bit of smoke about a rather damp fire ... and indirectly and directly take their petulant jabs at the social order." As a parting shot, he took aim at Kirstein's text: "And I certainly do not like Kirstein's article in the book in question. So glib and so limited: Oh well."

III

The "American Photographs" exhibition was a different matter: more various, more problematic as a statement, less considered in format, more representative of the random nature of Evans's work over the prior decade. In making up the prints for both the book and the exhibition, Evans had the advantage of a capable young assistant. Sometime late in 1937 or in early 1938, Helen Levitt, an aspiring young photographer, had contacted him, wanting to show him her work. Brooklyn-born, around twenty-five when she introduced herself to Evans, she was at the beginning of a career in photography. She was aware of Evans's earlier work, having seen his Cuban photos in Carlton Beals's *The Crime of Cuba*. She believes she had also seen the three-man 1935 show at the Julien Levy Gallery in which Evans, Alvarez-Bravo, and Cartier-Bresson had appeared together. That she believes was her first view also of the photographs of Cartier-Bresson, whom she subsequently met at the studio of Willard Van Dyke. Early on, possibly in 1936, she had accompanied the French photographer on a shoot on the Brooklyn waterfront. It was largely Cartier-Bresson's example that encouraged her to adopt the 35-mm Leica instead of the used Voigtlander she had begun with.

Levitt had already worked in the studio of a commercial photographer in the Bronx who did photographs of weddings and bar mitzvahs, so she had some experience with darkroom work. She had also been granted dark- room privileges at the Workers' Film and Photo League. But it was not on her first meeting with Evans that the subject of her becoming a darkroom assistant came up. She does not recall precisely what photographs of her own she showed Evans, and confesses that she did not have all that many to show. But with the Leica, which she bought in 1936, she had already begun taking photographs of children in the streets and their childish graffiti on the sidewalks and the walls of buildings. What may have been her earliest Leica photograph was a candid shot of two gypsy girls in Central Park. What she does recall about that first meeting with Evans was that James Agee turned up at the Ninety-second Street studio. Agee's interest and enthusiasm for her work, as well as Evans's, sparked a friendship of some importance to all three of them.

When she did begin working for Evans, there was no pay involved, though he took her out to dinner on occasion when he had money and once made her a loan of fifty dollars. In time, she was given free use of his darkroom and enlarger for her own work, though she claims she did not use it all that often in the beginning. (A cause for later confusion, for some of her photographs of children's graffiti were later mistakenly attributed to Evans.) She vividly remembers Evans's habit of washing his prints in the bathtub and sticking them on the side of the tub to dry. She also remembers that it was Evans who later encouraged her to work for the WPA. Mostly her work on the prints for the *American Photographs* book and exhibition consisted of spotting; but she does not recall now which particular prints she may have made. Evans, she well remembers, was close-mouthed about himself, never mentioning his earlier activities — that he had, for instance, printed up some of the Mathew Brady photographs for Beaumont Newhall's historic exhibition. Nor did she ever see any Brady print on the walls of the Ninety-second Street apartment. (She does recall that there was one of Evans's baby pictures displayed.) Nor did she know that Peter Sekaer or John Cheever had served as his darkroom assistants. In time, Levitt would learn that there were well-defined compartments to Evans's social and private life.

* * *

For Evans, the retrospective exhibition at MoMA might well have been an anticlimax. But he took charge: Despite his reputation for shyness, he was adamant that he would do the installation himself. (One story has it that Beaumont Newhall had superimposed an initial installation that

Evans took down and redid himself.) The Evans show was the opening exhibition of the season at the museum's temporary quarters in the lower level concourse of Rockefeller Center. The other opening exhibitions were to be a show of Rouault prints and the first of the museum's industrial design exhibitions devoted to "Useful Objects under $5."

On August 24 Alfred Barr wrote Evans confirming the arrangements for the gallery. Barr had suggested Gallery 5 because of its better lighting conditions and because he felt there would be fewer difficulties with the installation. But Evans insisted on Gallery 1, with its alcoves near the entranceway. Barr agreed, but suggested that if the entrance gallery was too large, "the section which you come into first just at the right of the entrance

*Girl in
Fulton Street,
New York,
1929*

can be used for sculpture, which would have nothing to do with your photographs and would not I think compete with them in any way." Barr also offered the services of Dorothy Miller in planning the installation (she was at the moment out of town) "so that we can avoid last minute rushes and also competition with the other two exhibitions." It is not clear whether Miller in fact took part as offered. According to Newhall's recollection it was not until the last moment, the night before the private opening in fact, that Evans finally installed the show. Newhall had obligingly provided a large worktable and paper cutter supplies for what could only have been a fierce and terrific burst of energy and hard work, considering that there were one hundred photographs involved. (A checklist of

42nd St.,
1929

the photos exists, though curiously it proceeds in reverse order from number one hundred to one.) Evans chose a variety of formats: Some prints were framed with mats and mounted under glass. (A concession, perhaps, since Helen Levitt distinctly recalled that Evans, early on, told her he disliked showing photographs under glass.) Other prints were mounted and matted under glass without frames, and some, mounted on cardboard and cropped at the edges, were then glued directly to the walls. There are suggestions that Evans may indeed have had the help of a friend in putting up the show in one evening — a distinct probability considering the extent of the show and the time element involved. Lincoln Kirstein, in an interview, however, made it clear that he had taken no part in mounting the exhibition though he had helped organize the layout of the book. On the morning after, Newhall found the leavings of the heroic effort: a few empty Coca-Cola bottles and slivers of cropped prints left for the sweepers.

In the re-created version of the 1938 exhibition illustrated in *The Hungry Eye*, there are instances of pointed juxtapositions of one print and another scattered through the exhibition. The black woman in the dark coat at the Forty-second Street El steps (No. 10), for example, is definitely linked with No. 11, the Fulton Street flapper in the cloche hat and coat with the fur collar that so impressed the book reviewer for *PM* magazine. In the final segment of the installation, an overscale print of the *Tuscaloosa Wrecking Company*, itself a derelict structure advertising auto parts, provided a culminating image for the theme of the American automobile — *Joe's Auto Graveyard*, the angled cars on rain-wet *Main Street, Saratoga Springs; Parked Car, Small Town, Main Street; Garage in Southern City* — which threaded through the installation. But generally, the exhibition was more hurriedly composed, less intent on carrying out thematic variations.

Main Street, Saratoga Springs, New York, 1931

The most emphatic difference between the exhibition and the book was the sequence of thirteen photographs from the Alabama assignment which appeared midway in the exhibition. An out-of-sequence print also showed the hymn-singing Tengle family. Both this and the icon-portrait of Allie Mae Burroughs were variant prints of two photographs that had appeared in the book. That Evans had included so many of the Alabama photographs in the exhibition and not in the book perhaps indicated that he did not want to infringe on the material scheduled to be illustrated in *Let Us Now Praise Famous Men*.

On the night of the preview opening, September 27, according to Charles Fuller, Evans came to the door of the exhibition and then turned back, leaving the lighted space and gathered guests behind. On the edge of recognition, he had backed away. His retreat seems to be confirmed by the note Beaumont Newhall wrote Evans:

I'm sorry that I did not see you at the opening of your exhibition tonight, for I should have liked to congratulate you personally on the show. You are exhibiting a remarkable group of photographs and I am glad to have the chance to study them carefully.

Newhall had the further grace (all things considered) to compliment Evans on the installation: "It is so simple and straightforward — and daring. It is a severe test to present small prints on the expanse of a white wall; your prints live up to the exacting installation. It's a swell and impor-

tant show, and I'm proud of the museum for having given you the oppor-tunity." As an afterthought, he added that Stieglitz had written him some complimentary comments about the book "which I'll be glad to show you next time you're in the museum."

Due largely to Frances Collins's efforts as publicist for the book and show, Evans had gathered some remarkable advanced blurbs. Gilbert Seldes claimed, "There ought to be a thousand photographers of genius like Walker Evans to give us a picture of what America looks like — and what *it is*." Theodore Dreiser, too, thought the book represented the spirit of the country as well as its appearance: "I only wish that books like this about America were more frequent. They tell more about conditions here than volumes of prose." From France, Cartier-Bresson wrote Collins thanking her for the book, forwarding his good wishes to the photographer and noting that "l'intensité avec qu'il montre les gens et les endroits dans lequels ils vivent est bien émouvant." (The intensity with which he shows people and the places in which they live, is very moving.)

The coverage for the exhibition was mostly favorable. The reviewer for *Time* placed Evans among his more notable contemporaries: Stieglitz, Cartier-Bresson, and a relative newcomer, the Hungarian photographer Robert Capa. In the matter of influences, the reviewer noted the past master Mathew Brady and the movies of Eric von Stroheim and the Russian cinematographer, Dziga Vertov — names that suggest an insider's knowledge of Evans's tastes and interests not likely to have been gleaned from ordinary press releases. He hailed the photographer's exhibition and book as "the most significant event for the photographic art since Steichen went out of business." He seems to have seconded Kirstein's handy analogy that Evans's " view is clinical. Evans is a visual doctor, diagnostician rather than specialist." The *Time* reviewer praised Evans's selection of photographs as "many-sided, disinterested, clinical." In particular, he noted how the photographs:

caught the essential moment, memorized in detail some significant things: the early morning light on hundreds of back yards in an industrial city; four sour people on a Bronx bench on Sunday; a pompous Legionnaire with waxed mustaches, looking brave.

Edward Alden Jewell, in the Sunday, October 2, *New York Times*, noted

A Bench in the Bronx on Sunday, 1933

389

that although Evans's photographs might be deemed social documents, "the motivation seems, on the artist's part altogether esthetic. Sentimentality never obtrudes. The case is stated, brilliantly stated, in esthetic terms and there the matter ends." Evans, he said "never pictures for us a person or an object as a 'type.' Each lives a life of his or its own. . . . Carried to a certain point — far from inclusive, but richly, objectively, dispassionately drawn — this is a true portrait of America."

It remained for Tom Mabry, as executive director at the Modern and, perhaps, as Evans's helpful assistant in installing the exhibition, to give the most sober and most informed review of the book and the exhibition in the November 1 issue of *Harper's Bazaar*. An editor's note on the contributors' page plumped up the legend of the elusive artist: "We have no photograph of the photographer Walker Evans because he has a complex against publicity and has never posed for a picture of any kind." The puff was patently untrue — one of the bits of misinformation that help to create celebrity status.

From the outset, Mabry was prepared to claim that Evans "possesses perhaps the purest 'eye' of any photographer of our generation." People and architecture were his subjects, Mabry said. "The two play against each other, speak for each other; neither has any existence without the other." Mabry's observations often enough came from his relationship with the man. "Perhaps one clue to Evans's work," he stated, "is that his photographs are not symbols for something else; they are what they mean." The casual observer might not take them in at first, but on second sight "they electrify." "[I]f America has any character uniquely its own," he went on, "a quality of spirit, half squalid, half unbelievably beautiful, Walker Evans has found it within the context of his collection of photographs."

Like other critics Mabry concentrated on specific photographs, saw them as texts to be read, explicated:

Consider a few of them. The Coney Island girl: how calm her back is, and the seams of her stockings, so straight: and the main streets of Alabama towns, the conglomerate sun on Vicksburg's sidewalks, maybe people rest easy there. . . . And the little girl in a back yard: see her again, grown older on Fulton Street: the sharecropper's family singing hymns, the young lovers parked in an automobile . . .

What Mabry saw in Evans's work is its paradox, the power "which

*Coney Island
Boardwalk,
1929*

reveals a potential order and a morality at the very moment that it pictures the ordinary, the vulgar and the casually corrupt."

* * *

What Evans felt at the moment of his elevation as a major photographer of the American scene is not so readily defined. He chose not to speak for himself in *American Photographs*, deciding to let the work speak for him. He stole away from the opening night preview of his exhibition, reportedly circling the block one or two times before returning home. But the scattered documentation left from the weeks and months before the publication of his book — like debris left on a museum floor — offers some interesting clues. Among the handwritten notes and typed lists he made of the people who were to receive invitations to or announcements of the exhibition, there were the expectable names of worthies of the Roosevelt administration: Harold Ickes (whose official visage he had pasted into his scrapbook a few years before); Harry L. Hopkins; Secretary of Labor, "Madame" Frances Perkins; Rexford Tugwell; and Roy Stryker. Evans's connection with labor leader John L. Lewis remains obscure. Henry Allen Moe of the Guggenheim Foundation, understandably, might consider another application for a Guggenheim Fellowship. Caresse Crosby appears on the list, as does John Dos Passos. Sherwood Anderson's listing must have proved beneficial; seven of Evans's FSA photographs would be used in Anderson's 1940 volume, *Home Town*.

Evans remembered his earliest patrons and sponsors: Julien Levy, Gifford Cochran, Oliver Jennings, Adolph Dick, Charles Fuller. Some names recorded the down-and-out history of his Brooklyn and Bethune Street days: Hideo Noda, Ben Shahn and Moses Soyer, Beatrice Jacoby, Leonie and Harold Sterner, Paul and Dorothy Grotz, John Cheever. They were names that recorded his slow and painful ascent toward fame.

He also wrote out one or two trial lists of acknowledgments intended for the book: "The author wishes to thank the many persons for their various kinds of assistance, encouragement, cooperation, forbearance, perception, appreciation, criticism and education." (He had also listed "enmity" and "opposition," but thinking better of it, crossed them out.) The list included his sister and brother-in-law, his mother and father, Lincoln

Kirstein, Muriel Draper, Jay Leyda, James and Olivia Agee, Ernest Hemingway, and Joseph Verner Reed, among others. Newer acquaintances included Helen Levitt, Janice Loeb, Dorothy Miller, and the staff of The Museum of Modern Art. To his credit — or as testimony to the shrewdness of his observations of the world and its ways — he scribbled at the bottom of the page: "Omit names [of] prominent persons because no longer a subtle form of advertisement." Another draft of such acknowledgments was more expansive: "To Ralph Steiner for technical advice and instruction generously given to me"; "To Berenice Abbott for having been an honest and uncompromising artist from her beginning"; "To Hanns Skolle for early teaching"; "To Muriel Draper for stimulation." Various others, including Ernestine Evans, were remembered "for indefinable but more or less impersonal reasons — something like common standards, aims & values, directions." On the eve of recognition, he was perhaps unwittingly compiling a history of his life and career. Moments of generosity were mixed with the need to butter up those still in a position to further a career.

In the end, this cluster of connections — some amorous, some financial, a few denoting matters of loyalty — was finally scrapped. Among the names were the Jane Smith that had appeared on a spurious list of lenders to the exhibition and the Mrs. Paul Ninas that had been buried in the acknowledgments pages. What remained after all the siftings were the simple initials that Evans placed on the dedication page: " J.S.N."

Even that simple gesture had consequences. In a New Orleans bookstore, Christine Fairchild picked up a copy of *American Photographs* and, decoding the initials, showed it to Paul Ninas, who showed it to his wife, Jane, who had assumed that Walker Evans had all but forgotten her.

A Penitent Spy and an Apologetic Voyeur

18

"It was a project for love. . . . Nobody asked me to do that. Nobody paid me for doing it." So Evans remarked about one of the more secretive episodes of his career — his descent into the New York City subway to photograph unsuspecting passengers. There was an element of melodrama about it: The camera, a 35-mm Contax, the chrome painted a flat black, was strapped to his chest, hidden under his topcoat, the lens barely noticeable between two buttons. The long cord of the shutter release was strung down his right sleeve, where he could press it surreptitiously when he saw something worthwhile. He had begun on his project at least as early as February 15, 1938, the date established by the front-page headline of the *New York Daily News*, "Pal Tells How Gungirl Killed," which one of the passengers was reading.

But the idea for a subway series had come to him four years earlier as one item in a list of projects for a proposed photo unit for the WPA. Others included "New York society in the 1930s," "air views of the city," and "national groups." Coincidentally the list also included "children in the streets" and "chalk drawings," themes that Helen Levitt would later make her own and that may have stirred Evans's interest in her work to begin with. His list was written on the back of a blank check of the Bank of Manhattan Company tentatively dated 1934 or 1935.

Evans's subway series, then, had preceded the critical recognition of *American Photographs.* It continued at random over a four-year period, imposing interesting conditions for the exercise. Since he was making his shots on the sly, he picked the season, late fall or winter, when people were bundled up in heavy clothing, making Evans just another passenger while he kept his camera "under wraps." Seated, he focused on passengers directly across from him, generally limiting the results to bust-level portraits. Some shots were made at station stops when the train was not in motion and most of them at off hours when the cars were not crowded with standing passengers. On rare occasions he photographed from the front of the car, catching seated figures along the aisles or individuals

Subway Portrait, New York, 1938-1941

coming directly toward him. The trick was to avoid the jostling motion of the cars by using the camera's widest aperture to catch as much of the cars' artificial light as possible. It was an exercise in chance-portraiture, the choice of subjects determined by the accidental travelers who sat opposite him. In a series of draft texts and prefaces he wrote for later publication — later, that is, by some twenty or more years — he stressed the undercover nature of the effort and the anonymity of his subjects, nameless men and women, occasional children. (There were times, however, when it is clear that the man or woman across the aisle was staring quizzically at him or directly toward the lens.) Evans also hinted, several times, at the sexual implications of the activity, referring to himself variously as a "spy and voyeur in the swaying seat" or as a "penitent spy and apologetic voyeur." He noted the exposed situation of his fellow travelers: "The guard is down and the mask is off: even more than when in lone bedrooms (where there are mirrors). People's faces are in naked repose in the subway." But mirrors in Evans's work had other implications as well; from the beginning, they broached a philosophical question: the shadowy commerce between the real and the reflected image.

While engaged in the project, Evans managed to set aside the notion of publishing or exhibiting these photographs immediately. He may have been worried that he might be sued. Also, it was at the time illegal for photographers to take photographs on the subways without a police permit. Yet he felt, at least in later life, that there was an element of destiny in his choice: "It was a heaven sent exuberance — I see — that sent me down among the torn gum wrappers into the fetid, clattering, squealing cars underground. It was a driving innocence to want to record the people in the subway." He referred to the underground venture as "a sociological gold mine awaiting a major artist."

What is surprising, as with so many of Evans's career choices, is how much the subway series traces out a line Evans had begun earlier: the sequence of self-portraits he made while sitting in an automated photo machine and the anonymous portraits in the studio windows of commercial photographers he had rephotographed for himself. His earlier device of the right-angle viewfinder was the predecessor of the hidden camera used to conceal what he was doing in the subway. At the outset, Helen Levitt accompanied him on at least three or four occasions, serving as the kind of decoy

Jane Ninas had been during his earlier photographic stints around New Orleans. ("I was available and eager," she (Levitt) comments.) This was during the 1938 phase of the work, when Evans was using the Contax almost exclusively. Later he let her borrow the camera so she could take photographs in the subway on her own, which she did, also without a police permit. ("He was very generous that way," she recalls. Evans also loaned her his Speed Graphic, with which she took the photographs of children's graffiti.)

The subway sessions might last a few hours, Levitt recalled. There were intermissions when Evans felt the subjects were not particularly interesting or nothing seemed to be happening; they would get off at a stop, have a cigarette, and wait for the next train. After the shoot, he would go back to his apartment and develop the films. Possibly Evans was enjoying the undercover aspect of his self-imposed assignment, but Levitt's recollection was that he lacked energy or drive and needed to be pushed. He also seemed to rely on having a companion. She thinks that at the time Agee, too, was pushing him to keep on with the series.

Aboveground there was the broad context of a wider world; below, the focus was reduced to the confines of a subway car. The setting, in metaphorical terms, might have been a traveling coffin or hearse. There is good reason for thinking so. In 1937 Agee had published a poem called "Rapid Transit" in the February issue of the *Forum and Century*, and among Evans's papers there is a manuscript copy of the poem in Agee's hand with a mistaken homonym:

Squealing under city stone
The millions on the millions run,
Every one a life alone,
Every life a soul undone:
There all the poisons of the heart
Branch and abound like whirling brooks
And there through every useless art
Like spoiled meats on a butcher's hooks
Pore[sic] forth upon their frightful kind
The faces of each ruined child,
The wrecked demeanors of the mind
That now is tamed, and once was wild.

It is probably no coincidence either that Hart Crane had also used the subway earlier in "The Tunnel," a segment of *The Bridge* in which he raised up the ghostly figure of Edgar Allan Poe:

And why do I often meet your visage here,
Your eyes like agate lanterns — on and on
Below the toothpaste and the dandruff ads?

Evans, in discussing the subway series, would reach back to Daumier's *Third Class Carriage* as a precedent for what he was doing. He spoke of it as "a kind of snapshot of actual people sitting in a railway carriage in France in the mid-nineteenth century. Although he didn't use a camera, he [Daumier] sketched those people on the spot like a reporter and they probably saw him doing it. What of it?" But he was not so nonchalant himself; it was not until 1956 that he published a portfolio of eight of the photographs in the *Cambridge Review*, using the title of Agee's poem "Rapid Transit." And it was not until 1966 that he published eighty-nine of the subway prints accompanied by a posthumously published essay by Agee. In his text, in rearview retrospective terms, Agee stated that the pictures had been made "during the late thirties and early forties of the twentieth century" though the evidence indicates the essay had been written in October 1940. The title of the book was biblical: *Many Are Called*, based on Matt. 22: 14: "Many are called but few are chosen." As in *American Photographs*, the pictures were printed one to a page opposite blank but numbered pages. Agee's text noted the anonymous riders, each

an individual existence, as matchless as a thumbprint or a snowflake. Each wears garments which of themselves are exquisitely subtle uniforms and badges of their beings. Each carries in the posture of his body, in his hands, in his face, in the eyes, the signatures of a time and a place in the world upon a creature for whom the name immortal soul is one mild and vulgar metaphor.

Subway Portrait, New York, 1938–41

If there was an edge to Agee's religiosity, Evans took an even sharper, less sentimental view of it. Agee's friend Robert Fitzgerald maintained that "the religious sense of life is at the heart of all Agee's work." But he also noted that Evans, "who was not at all Christian, used to say that Agee had a greater taste for suffering than any man since Jesus Christ." Fitzgerald was of the opinion that Agee himself "would have appreciated Walker saying that."

* * *

However remote their subterranean aspects, Evans's subway photographs carried with them news of a war in Europe and politics at home. The newspaper on the lap of a matronly woman blazoned the headline "Kennedy Fights Aid Britain Bill," referring to Roosevelt's early 1941 effort to push the Lend Lease Act through Congress in order to help beleaguered Britain in its battle against Hitler, and to the ungrateful tactics of Joseph P. Kennedy, the former ambassador to the Court of St. James's, whom Roosevelt had appointed. In another photograph, a mother and daughter loll beneath a placard advertising the January concerts of the New York City Symphony Orchestra under the baton of the German refugee conductor, Otto Klemperer. Signs of the times. Other photographs hinted at less troubling events, but they had the incisiveness of a haiku poem: a dapper oriental-looking man wearing a dressy white scarf sits near a sign that reads: "Spitting on the floor of this car is a misdemeanor." The darkened windows of the subway car are splattered with rain. In Evans's photographs there is always more than meets the casual eye. For him, history is narrative, visual, and contrapuntal in its clues and details. As Evans recognized, the real world had a way of intruding below ground, even among the torn gum wrappers, the toothpaste and the dandruff ads.

Yet when the subway photographs were published years later, Evans passed over one of the surprising facets of his underground series: Some of the photos could also be read in sequence like connected stills in a movie. From frame to frame, there are animated conversations between passengers, fleeting changes of expression and mood, moments of frank curiosity (some of it directed at the secret photographer), the ensuing boredom of the ride. In these sequences petty human dramas unfold. Two women, one of them with a mannish hairdo, meet a male friend at the car entrance; they joke and carry on in lively fashion. The man departs; the women engage in confidences, laugh, stare at something at the other end of the car. The

*Subway
Portrait,
New York,
1938–41*

woman with the mannish cut — the most demonstrative of the pair — gets off at a subsequent stop; her companion sits glumly alone. (Still, the scenario might be read in a very different order — an alternative reading of the human text.) Underground, Evans could play the role of the private eye. His negative sleeves carry notations that suggest his fellow passengers were possible candidates for an unwritten novel: "Brooklyn youth," "Madonna of the social register," "Stenog and Wallace Beery type," "Sensitive young man," "Virgin teaser girls."

Even the epigraph Evans chose for *Many Are Called* had a certain mistaken bearing on his intentions. The text reads: "To a right-minded man, a crowded Cambridge horsecar is the nearest approach to heaven upon earth." First attributed to Henry James, Jr., it was corrected to read Henry James, Sr., on an erratum slip. That Evans chose it for his investigation of the underground subway, with its noise and grit and unwholesome air, says something about his sly perversity. But not altogether perverse, for Evans had a deep respect for Henry James, Jr., as well as for James Joyce, and felt a connection between a "great piece of writing and photography." Evans maintained: "There's no book but what's full of photography. James Joyce is. Henry James is. That's a pet subject of mine — how those men are unconscious photographers." James was also invoked in the draft texts of a maquette intended for possible publication in 1966: "The *subway*! 'Yes,' said Henry James: 'Yes,' roared Walt Whitman somewhere."

The idea and the imagery of *locomotion*, like the crowded Cambridge horsecar, run through Evans's work: His photographs of junked cars and parked cars and photographs taken from car windows would make a small metaphysical study. Later photographs would be taken from train windows. There would always be a continuing loyalty to chosen themes in Evans's work. Perhaps it was a literary inheritance. The most satisfying and probably the most poetic or profound of the images among the subway pictures is that of a blind accordianist proceeding step by step toward the cameraman. There are several prints and various croppings of the subject, indicating that Evans felt a special affinity for the subject. The musician, eyes closed, his mouth open as if singing, an enameled cup dangling from the accordian, makes his way along the aisle, past the barely interested riders in the car. In the maze of tunnels that made up the New York subway, confronting the blind musician, had Evans caught sight of himself as an Orpheus in the underground?

II

By the end of 1938 Evans was caught up in a strange weave of professional and personal matters. Finances were always a problem, but later in life, if not at the time, he was philosophic about his experiences: "I think that a depression is rather good for some kinds of artists; me included. It took away the temptation to be commercial and go into business. There wasn't any business." Among friends like Agee, he had gained a reputation for being uncompromising in his dedication. Writing to Father Flye, Agee praised Evans for the difficult life he was having as "a photographer and an 'artist' who will not sell out."

Agee was having his own problems. Throughout the summer of 1938 and into the fall, faced with imposed and subsequently deferred deadlines from his editor, Edward Aswell at *Harper's*, he had been struggling without success at the sharecropper book. He and Alma were living in a rented house in Frenchtown, New Jersey, where he had planned to settle down to work. His status reports to Evans, Father Flye, and Dwight Macdonald, however, provide a chronicle of restlessness and dissatisfaction. In July he wrote Evans that it was becoming physically impossible for him to get through even a sentence at a time. It was "very annoying and disturbing to me that I shouldn't manage to be fully and mentally eager to take hold of the work. Something is damned seriously wrong that I'm not." His pessimism deepened in August, when he wrote Father Flye: "My writing is in bad shape. The past five weeks have been completely sterile and I've just gotten a postponement of publication until the middle of winter and so, till November or December for more work, but even so I am in trouble near the bottom of borrowed money." He gave a detailed, if highbrow account of the problems he faced: "My trouble is, such a subject cannot be seriously looked at without intensifying itself toward a centre which is beyond what I, or anyone else is capable of writing of the whole problem and nature of existence. Trying to write it in terms of moral problems alone is more than I can possibly do." He was forced to trail off: "[W]ell, there's no use trying to talk about it. If I could make it what it ought to be made I would not be human." By September, he wrote Evans that he was reduced to the hope of "finding a way of doing the whole thing new from start to finish and am trying holding off in hope of some such crystallization." Unfortunately he

New York,
1938–41

felt "no excitement or vitality" about his work. Later, from Frenchtown, he wrote Dwight Macdonald that there were some signs of hope: "I am at last, after some strained and chaotic months, getting to work on the tenant book. This is a good place to live for a while." Personal matters also intervened. He informed Macdonald: "As you may have had wind of, Via and I are divorcing. I am here with Alma Mailman, whom you may but more likely do not know."

There were satisfying interludes, however, at the Frenchtown establishment. They bought inexpensive furniture at a country auction; among the cheap purchases, a wicker rocker and a large fourposter bed that proved to be too big to get into the upstairs bedrooms and so remained in the huge kitchen. As Alma remembered it, "Daytime was a little like playing house." In the warm weather they swam in a creek and played tennis. It would seem to be from this period that Agee wrote Evans in an undated note on a file card asking him to bring his Yellow Jacket racket and press: "I cannot

promise tennis for we have not yet investigated any of the 2 or 3 courts: but having two rackets and balls is at least, ha ha, half the battle." In the same note Agee informed Evans in a cryptic aside that two friends might be arriving on Saturday afternoon on the condition "that they do not spend the night & frustrate whatever triangular activities might otherwise obtain." Agee signed the note "JA and Consort."

He and Alma played cards and chess; occasionally they sketched one another. ("At night I'm starting to draw," he wrote Father Flye. "I now 'possess' and 'know' Alma's face . . . as well as I know my hand.") Agee took one of the upstairs rooms as his study, writing usually at night, and as Alma remembered it, without revisions. It was in the Frenchtown house, one night, that he came down late, pleased, to read her the passages of his autobiographical story "Knoxville: Summer 1915," which he had begun three years earlier. She was "as usual, moved by it and wholly uncritical." They listened to records and often played music together, Alma at the violin and Agee at the piano, plowing along with ardor and missed notes, through the first movement of Beethoven's violin concerto: "Jim's playing resembled his way of playing tennis. Hampered by lack of training, every once in a while he transcended his technical limitations with spurts of sheer physical and emotional bravura, with brilliant results." It was in Frenchtown, with a neatness and patience that surprised her, that Alma decided to make hand-bound copies of the string quartets of Haydn, Schubert, Brahms, and Mozart.

There were welcome visitors from New York that summer. Despite misgivings, Evans sent them a case of scotch when they settled in, then arrived as one of the first visitors to Frenchtown. He sat stoically through one of Alma's meals in which only the potatoes turned out edible. Helen Levitt and other New York friends like Robert Fitzgerald and Dwight Macdonald also came. Macdonald was then an editor at *Partisan Review*, and it was in the August-September 1938 issue of the magazine that the "Knoxville" story first appeared. Fitzgerald remembered that during the summer and through the fall Agee labored at his book, then titled *Three Tenant Families*, and read the various drafts to assembled guests. ("Jim wrote for the ear, wanted criticism from auditors.")

There are contradictory stories about the baby goat Agee bought for Alma. Its color was black and white, and it was tethered in the weedy backyard, though it conveniently cropped the grass in the front yard, giving the place the semblance of a tidy lawn. Newly weaned, it bleated continuously and was let into the kitchen to keep company with the family. On one occasion it was taken for an overnight visit to Evans's apartment at Ninety-second Street, where it was put up with a load of grass on the small roofed area outside the apartment window. Evans's displeasure was noticeable the moment he saw the goat being hauled upstairs with its load of grass; the visit lasted only one night. Alma was of the opinion that Agee had planned the surprise as a test of Evans's fastidiousness. But Alma had two versions of the goat story, the latter of which included two goats, the young one and the disreputable older male, which had been bought to keep the baby goat company and which also visited the Ninety-second Street apartment. In any event, the one or two goats were transients in the Agee household and met an unhappy end. The continuous bleating between the two became unbearable. After failing to find a suitable home for the animals, Agee and Alma reached a final solution. Putting the two goats in the car, they drove them to a local butcher who was pleased at the gift. It was to Alma's credit that in her account of the trip to the butchershop, she acknowledged that she and Agee were "silent and ashamed." Wilder Hobson, another of the visitors at Frenchtown, however, recalled that at least one of the goats had survived and that Agee brought it with him to the vacant house on St. James Place in Brooklyn that Hobson loaned the couple that winter. Neighborhood kids, he remembered, had scrawled a chalk message on the front steps: "The Man Who Lives Here Is a Loony."

* * *

For Agee's birthday on November 27, Evans sent unspecified gifts, including money for Alma. Agee was doubly pleased by the remembrance and by Evans's thoughtfulness toward Alma, particularly since he was aware that the two did not exactly hit it off together. In a separate note Alma thanked him, comically informing him that one-third of it "went to purchase a pretty wonderful pair of Frenchtown flannel pajamas, low in the crotch and extremely baggy and bow-legged in the knees." Agee was in a loving mood marred only by a recent visit with Wilder and Peggy Hobson because of "a sad feeling I got (and Alma) out of Wilder's reactions over his work relative to mine." Otherwise, Agee confessed, he was "in a nameday haze of outgoing tenderness and gratefulness towards you, them, Alma, Helen [Levitt], whoever feels love for me and whom I feel love for, including wanting to speak of it, which after fashion I now have."

His outpouring of love prompted one of his antic proposals for a sexual "orgy" among friends at Frenchtown. He had, he said, already broached the topic to the Hobsons: "I was a little (and a little too much) daunted by Wilder's and to a less extent Peggy's reaction, which was, however that they would come if it was staged." Agee's instructions turned official as if producing the agenda for an upcoming board meeting: "to convene whoever we would think good for it. (They to do likewise among their further acquaintance) for a party at Frenchtown, 2nd weekend of December, for essentially sexual purposes. Would you come? Would you bring friends? It would matter little whom or how many, since pairing is secondary." There is no indication that Evans accepted the invitation or that the Frenchtown orgy did in fact take place as scheduled.

The strangest aspect of Agee's proposal of a love-in was that, his divorce from Via having become final in November, he was planning to marry Alma, and did so on December 6 in a brisk ceremony in the dusty courthouse of Flemington, New Jersey, only days before the proposed orgy. It was not the only evidence of sexual largesse in Agee's correspondence at the time — even discounting the "triangular" possibilities hinted at in his earlier letter about prospective tennis matches in the country. For the next year or so sexual puns and innuendoes cropped up in his correspondence with Evans: "I have organized . . . an advanced sexual program," he announced in one such letter, "and we would appreciate if you will give us some advice on apertures." Another took a more apologetic approach: "Though I am still adolescent-capable of making myself and others trouble, I am getting over it," he suggested, while mentioning that further sexual encounters should be "purely chance pleasure if pure and independent chance so happens to shape them." By the end of 1938, he was still hoping Walker and Alma might be lured into a threesome in the interests of a sexual experiment that needed to be "learned, investigated, synchronized and tried." It was a heady season, one that justified Agee's cautionary remarks on moral issues in a December 21 letter to Father Flye: "The human race is incurably sick in more entangled ways than has even been suspected. . . ." In the same letter he announced to the cleric: "Alma and I were married early this month."

Barely a week later, in a moment of generosity, Agee was offering Evans not his wife, but an early draft of his book on the three sharecropper families. His long letter to Evans of December 27 was ripe with the Christmas spirit. He had been charmed by the sight of Alma decorating her first Christmas tree: "a pleasure people claim is to be had out of [only by] children." Agee was having second thoughts about the season: "Maybe there is really nothing at all wrong with Christmas except the English & their damned literary carol influences. Anyhow it took some wonderful holds on me this time. It always does to some extent but in mixed unpleasing ways and only by spasms. This was steady and unmixedly happy." Evans had sent a welcome package of books which Agee was pleased to receive. In turn, he reciprocated:

If you'd like it (and if you wouldn't by all means say so) I'd like to give you something which will be delayed, and will necessarily have a few strings attached: it

Subway
Portrait,
New York
1938-41

may also seem indecently egoistic (both 'personally' and 'classically,' I'd like to know your opinion)—that is when I'm done with it, whatever there is of the manuscript of the book. I feel so much the more diffident about it because I don't think much of it will be at all 'interesting' . . . But if you would like it, good.

The strings, as Agee explained, were simple enough. If at some time in the future he needed to go over the manuscript again he might need it back for a considerable period of time. There was a certain irony in the fact that Agee did indeed subsequently give Evans the early version of what became *Let Us Now Praise Famous Men,* and that in the course of several later domestic moves, Evans subsequently lost the manuscript.

The remainder of the Agees' stay in Frenchtown had an air of the hectic. Robert Fitzgerald recalled having seen one of Agee's journals in which Agee noted on December 1 that after the rent was paid, he would have only $12.52 in the world. But, fortunately, he also remembered, "*Fortune* came to the rescue with an assignment: the section on Brooklyn in an issue to be devoted to New York City." Wilder Hobson's offer of his vacant house, fully furnished, in Brooklyn's St. James Place, then, was highly opportune. The *Fortune* assignment was scheduled for the June 1939 issue of the magazine, but the Agees stayed on at Frenchtown till their lease expired early in 1939. The bleating goats having gone to their fate, they were replaced by a gentle hobo, Walter Clark, who showed up at the door one day, carrying his small store of belongings — a can of Campbell's pork and beans, a pair of potatoes, a whittled wooden spoon — tied up in a bundle attached to a thick stick. Agee took a fancy to him and when it proved impossible to get the vagrant into the local homeless shelter, which had closed for the season, Clark was allowed to stay in the house for the final weeks. As a treat he was taken to a movie. (The feature film with its glamorous movie stars left him awestruck, but Clark thoroughly enjoyed the Mickey Mouse cartoon.) After the movie they took him to a nearby restaurant where he eyed the extensive menu, then settled for his standard bill-of-fare, pork and beans. Alma claimed that she wanted to adopt him: "But, Jim, unlike me, saw the future responsibility this would inevitably bring, and which he did not want to face."

Their final departure from Frenchtown had a certain poignancy. Agee and Alma moved out on the day before the lease expired, leaving Clark to enjoy the last day by himself; but not before bestowing on him some final gifts: two quart bottles of whisky, a tin plate and tin eating utensils bought from a five-and-dime store, and six cans of pork and beans. Their final glimpse of their guest was of Clark sitting on the floor contemplating his treasures by candlelight, the electricity having already been shut off. They drove off with the van transporting their sparse furnishings to a farmhouse at nearby Stockton, New Jersey. They had rented it for the following summer and were allowed to store their furniture there over the winter. Alma sat beside the astonished driver of the van; she was taking with her in a "ketch-em-alive" trap five of the six mice (one had escaped) that had enjoyed the run of their kitchen at Frenchtown and that she had adopted. Her reasoning, probably accurate, was that new tenants would inevitably poison them. Instead, they were released to run free at Monks Farm in Stockton.

In Brooklyn Alma felt "misplaced." The four-story Hobson house was narrow, gloomy, and dark; the furniture, drab and heavy. She "felt lost and alone there most of the time," but they readily assembled a group of friends and married couples, mostly writers and editors, a few musicians, an occasional painter, all "pretty much of an age and of a kind." On Saturday nights, usually at someone's apartment, there were parties with drinks and dancing to records playing "hot jazz." According to Alma, Agee captured the Saturday night setting in an unpublished film treatment in which he described what might have been typical of many another party in the late thirties: an "easy, casual and very unserious kind of promiscuity among these people; the kind which rarely if ever goes beyond kissing and fondling in the kitchenette or the room where all the coats are piled on the bed."

* * *

When and where the much talked over assignation between Agee, Alma, and Evans took place, three in a bed, is a debatable matter. One might have expected that it took place in Frenchtown since it was an abiding concern in Agee's correspondence at the time, but according to Alma, it happened sometime in the summer of 1939, when she and Agee were living at Monk's Farm in Stockton, a run-down farmhouse that she found far more attractive than the Hobson place in Brooklyn. In her posthumously published memoir, *Always Straight Ahead,* she reports that it happened on one of Evans's visits. She felt uncomfortable about the whole business to begin with, but went along with it because Agee convinced her it was a genuine wish on his part "to bring together the two people he loved most." She was not sure what Walker thought or felt about her: "possibly jealousy, quite certainly bafflement about Jim's interest and love for me. Sexually, he probably thought me attractive, though I, on the other hand, had no such thoughts of Walker." It was Agee's hope, nonetheless, "that all would be resolved in that act of intimacy." As her account makes clear, it was not a fond memory:

The "experiment" however, did not last long. Less than five minutes after the three of us, naked on the bed, had begun tentatively to fumble with one another, Jim realized it was a mistake, that he did not want it. It was too late, though. He slipped off the bed and removed himself to a chair in the corner of the room, where for the next few minutes he sat crying — agonized sobbing it was, and I can only guess the reasons; probably a combination of love, jealousy, despair and self hatred, and possibly, knowing Jim, a generalized world grief. Walker and I soon disengaged ourselves and left to dress. I remember no talk or discussion about that incident — either then or later.

But Alma appears to have given a different story to Agee's biographer, Laurence Bergreen, indicating that the incident had taken place much later in 1939, when she and Agee had moved back to New York and were living in an apartment on Fifteenth Street near Greenwich Village. That story, too, presents certain contradictions since it was there that she learned she was pregnant, even perhaps late in her pregnancy — not the likeliest of times to be considering an amatory threesome. (Their son Joel was born on March 20, 1940, at the Lying-In Hospital in Manhattan.)

While Alma claimed that "no talk or discussion" about the incident took place after the stay at Stockton, it is clear that Agee had given the unhappy episode considerable thought, even some second thoughts. In a letter to Evans (possibly) dated late in 1939, Agee wrote: "I have caused each of you a certain amount of bother & am of course sorry and contemptuous of myself." He registered some moments of self-searching: "However much . . . you happen to like each other, good: I am enough of an infant homosexual or postdostoevskian to be glad. However much you don't, that's all right too: I am enough of a 'man' not to care to think particularly whether I care or not." In an undated note to Evans, possibly written earlier — or later — than the above, Agee reveals that he had other thoughts as well. The note indicates that Agee had made arrangements to stay overnight at (presumably) Evans's Ninety-second Street apartment while Alma was staying at her sister's place. Agee had arrived after Evans had gone to bed. The gist of the situation was that he and Alma were expecting to return to New Jersey, ostensibly to the farmhouse at Stockton: "I wish you could drive back with us, and stay longer," he told Evans, "we both look forward to the weekend." The more significant portion indicates that Agee had indeed suffered from some recent crisis or setback:

Thanks chiefly to a recrystallization of the libido I am pretty well on my ft. again: but my interest is in (learning?) to get there without any such benefit. A thing much on my mind just now is the extreme pleasure, and better still, of the night spent three on the bed. There was I think much more to communicate (etc?) on that than we ever happened to. I hope we may; and I rather than not, hope it will include Alma. I am wandering. Will you wake me when you wake? I am disappointed to have got back so late tonight. Love, Jim.

The note does not seem as distraught as the other evidence suggests. Its tenor depends somewhat on where it fits chronologically in Agee's correspondence with Evans. But the mordant truth is that Evans himself remained the most elusive of the participants in the affair. As far as present evidence suggests, he did not leave a paper trail of thoughts about the matter. It remains one of the more curious incidents in his lifetime. Either at the time of the supposed incident, or a bit later, he was caught up in an affair of sorts with Frances Collins, who was married at the time. And his prior affairs had been intimately — more than intimately — connected to Agee in ways that seem inexplicable. Having had an earlier affair with Agee's sister Emma, he then became involved with Agee's first wife, Via. In a moment of disintegration or despair, Agee tried to justify his own relationship with Via in a negative fashion: "Have you ever lived with a woman you felt no sexual love for, for five solid years?" So, at least, Agee asked in a reported conversation in the Bergreen biography, which offers no source or citation. Evans's response was: "I never intend to, either." Explaining his interim affair with Via, Evans suggested, "I can think of two reasons. She isn't in love with me; and I'm not in love with her." The explanation may have fit the eased sexual mores of the period. That too might explain Evans's participation in the sad episode with Alma and Agee in Stockton. Yet in this little vignette of extramarital or intramural love among friends there is a good deal that remains inexplicable, particularly since Evans's thoughts and memories of the incident are elusive at best. Alma, at least, tried to suggest an explanation: "I believe that suggestion of Jim's was an example of his personal need to live and feel intensely, to perpetuate as much as possible that intensity, and to compromise that need as little as possible." Evans was less direct. Once, in later life, he tried to establish a text for the entangled web of his relationship with Agee, but in not too convincing a fashion: "We had a great love for each other but, you know, between two normal males you don't express love so openly. It misleads a lot of people. But there is such a thing as a great love between two men which is a deepening in expression of friendship, and that's all." Like most explanations in the search for the self, it too was lacking.

Subway
Portrait,
New York
1938–41

An Apartment on the East Side

19

That Evans tended to be secretive about his affairs was no secret to his friends. How it came about that after his dedication of *American Photographs* to JSN he once again made contact with Jane Ninas is something of a mystery, other than the fact that it was through the agency of Billie Voorhees, who, under her maiden name, Billie Rainey, had been a friend and fellow student of Jane's at Sophie Newcomb. Rainey, a ceramicist, had only recently married sculptor Clark Voorhees. The two were living in Old Lyme, Connecticut, where Voorhees's father had been one of the impressionist painters associated with the Old Lyme school. Once the contact was made, Evans began sending private, sometimes ardent, notes to Jane in New Orleans under cover of Billie's letters. Jane's marriage was breaking up; she was unhappy with her situation as well as with Paul's drinking and his infidelities. Although moved by Walker's notes, she also worried that Paul might discover the ruse and regretfully destroyed the evidence. Her supposition was that Walker had written Billie, whom he had met on his earlier trips to New Orleans, to make inquiries about her and the letter must have been forwarded to Old Lyme. It was, in any event, evident that Walker was still interested in her and for that she was grateful.

The New York World's Fair, which opened in the spring of 1939, also figured in their eventual reunion. Holger Cahill and his wife, Dorothy Miller, had organized a giant exhibition of contemporary American art for the fair called "American Art Today." It was drawn largely from the various WPA art projects around the country. Among the works from the New Orleans contingent, Cahill had chosen one of Jane's paintings, a picture of a New Orleans cemetery. Jane's recollection was that it was Billie Voorhees, probably with Walker's encouragement, who invited her to come north for a visit. Ostensibly it was arranged so that she could also attend the fair and see her painting among the one thousand works displayed. Paul, in fact, made a bet that her first order of business would be to see her own painting. Her companion on the trip was to be Mona Kraut, a friend from boarding-school days, who was planning to visit her brother in New York.

Interior of 441 East 92nd Street, ink and brush drawing by Jane Ninas Evans Sargeant.

Jane did not drive at the time, so Mona elected to do the driving. In mid-June the two women set out from New Orleans in the none-too-reliable Chevy convertible Paul had inherited from his father. They were accompanied by an artist friend, Rudolf Staffel, who had been offered a teaching job at Temple University.

Evans, in a state of anticipation, had advised Jane to call him as soon as she reached Old Lyme. By June 22, not having heard from her, he wrote Billie. His opening words carried an edge of irritability: "Dear Billie, I guess I didn't make it clear enough to you how important it is to me to know about Jane's coming. Just now I'm on the rack over not hearing *anything*, very worried. Can you tell me what's happening? Anything, just a note." In his letter he indicated his "excitement and desire" to see Jane, footnoting it with asterisks as "practically unbearable." He was plainly impatient: "I have several things I have to consider which all depend on this possible visit, and they are important to me through various necessities. Hate bothering you — am already extremely grateful for all you've

done." "Please!" he added, "Soon; telegraph, write, telephone. Atwater 9-8175."

When Jane's call finally came (there was no telephone at the Voorheeses' and she phoned him from a pay phone in Hamburg Cove, near Old Lyme), he was relieved if not altogether satisfied. "Darling," he wrote her the following day, "you are terrible on the phone and so am I. Never mind. I want to see you Friday and am so low in money it has to be done all in one day and by train, and I will ask you about it when you call tomorrow morning." Apparently they were keeping their arrangements a secret from Billie's husband, Clark, who was inclined to be straight-laced in his younger days. "Do you think many letters coming typed . . . for you look strange? Will [Mona] mind much making it possible for us to see each other rain or shine Friday at the Saybrook station 10:45 daylight time in the morning." There were trains back from Saybrook at around six and eight in the evening, one of which he would have to catch. "That was a nervous day yesterday," he admitted, but he was "finally much relieved." Evans was, at the time, still working on the final details of the sharecropper book that he had already told Jane about, but he was hoping to go to the fair that night "to see a reputably good musical show." There were "many things to talk to you about." He sent his love.

After such anticipation, the first meeting was awkward and too brief. It was also hampered by the presence of Mona, who was serving as chauffeur, if not chaperone. Still, the tone of his letter to Billie made it clear that he was serious, and his note to Jane hinted at important matters to be discussed. With memories of their earlier break-up still in mind, Jane felt reluctant about committing herself. She also harbored some resentment for the way in which Evans had broken off their relationship three years earlier. But even after that first meeting — the three of them presumably had lunch somewhere, there were tentative attempts at conversation, then it was time to drop Walker off at the Saybrook station before his train arrived — Jane acknowledges that she had cried most of the night. Subsequent meetings followed: Evans drove up to Lyme with some frequency, took her to lunch, drove her around the countryside. She was clearly being courted and Evans did his best to persuade her to move to New York and stay with him — a move her friend Mona encouraged. On one of Walker's visits, they secretly went to a motel in Moosup and made

Jane drawing in kitchen studio, 92nd Street apartment

love for the first time since the break-up. Jane no longer remembers what story she concocted for Billie and Clark.

Not long after, she and Mona decided to pay a surprise visit to Evans's East Ninety-second Street apartment. Mona, having already stopped there on one of her visits to her brother, was familiar with the building. They pressed doorbells without getting a response. Knowing about the interior stairway, Mona made her way to the rooftop outside Evans's second-floor apartment. She climbed through a kitchen window and let Jane in through the front door. The two made themselves at home, played records on the phonograph. But the surprise was on them: In a short while Evans arrived accompanied by Frances Collins. It was another awkward moment in which everyone felt the need to act in a civilized fashion. Finally Frances took her leave, seemingly having come to the conclusion that Jane was the "someone else" Evans had already told her about. That night Jane stayed over in the apartment. In bed, in an unabashed tender moment, he wound a lock of her hair around his finger saying, "With this hair I thee wed." The next day, as she was packing to leave, he came to her and asked, "Will you stay?" She said yes. These were, possibly, the words Jane had been waiting to hear. One or two evenings later, as if it were a ceremonial event, Walker took her to a dinner party given by his friends the painter Calvert Coggeshall and his wife. Jane had no evening gown with her, but Mona came to the rescue, lending her a stylish one in a tartan plaid with sleeves that could be zippered on or off. When Walker saw her standing in the room, he broke down and cried.

* * *

As it happened Jane never went to the World's Fair with Walker nor with anyone else. Paul's taunt, she thinks, banished any desire she might have had to see her painting singled out in Flushing Meadows. Nor did she visit the exhibition "Art In Our Time," intended to celebrate the reopening of the Museum of Modern Art at its new quarters on West Fifty-third Street, even though it ran through September 30. As part of the exhibition of paintings, sculpture, prints, and drawings, there was also a photography show of "Seven Americans" mounted by Beaumont Newhall. It included seven of Evans's photographs, among them the battered cactus plant in the corner of the room in the house of the Portuguese family in Cape Cod, the forlorn Cuban woman with her sleeping children on a Havana doorstep, and the mysterious photograph of the truck with its cargo of a mirrored dressing table in lower Manhattan. The exhibition, unfortunately, was another of those occasions in which Newhall's good intentions rankled Evans's feelings. Newhall had come up with the idea of assigning a different wall color for each of the seven participants, the others being Berenice Abbott, Ansel Adams, Harold Edgerton, Man Ray, Ralph Steiner, and Brett Weston. Evans refused to exhibit his work against the dull red Newhall had chosen for his section. As Newhall well remembered: "He strenuously objected to showing his photographs against this color. Only through a third party was our needlessly acrimonious dispute ended. 'Mr. Evans,' I was told, 'will exhibit his photographs only on condition that he be allowed to hang them himself, but not in your presence.'" Newhall acceded and gave the night watchman instructions to allow Evans to hang the show himself: "Next morning we saw the result: Evans had dry-mounted each of his photographs on a large piece of white cardboard. When placed edge to edge the mounts completely covered the offending color." It mattered little to Evans, apparently, that Newhall had been generous in his mention of him in the catalogue text:

Walker Evans uses photography in a particularly sensitive way to comment upon our civilization. His choice of subject is eloquent, and his brilliant technique allows this subject-matter to be so readily grasped that the effect is often disquieting. In 1935 he helped outline the photographic policy of the Resettlement (now Farm Security) Administration.

It says something about Newhall's equanimity that in his later memoir, *Focus*, he acknowledged that Ansel Adams, also a purist, told him that the painted walls were not a happy choice.

In purely personal ways the exhibition was ill-fated. Intended to celebrate the Modern's tenth anniversary as well as salute the World's Fair, it resulted in the firing of Evans's two friends, Frances Collins and Thomas Mabry. Nelson Rockefeller, the newly named president of the museum, had planned a major event. The opening night, May 10, was a gala affair with engraved invitations and celebrity guests like Lillian Gish and

Salvador Dali. Several thousand guests attended. Frances Collins, however, considered it a snobbish affair and a slight to the staff since some of the less important staff members had not been invited. As a spoof, she issued her own in-house invitations, duly printed up by the obliging Joe Blumenthal of the Spiral Press, replete with a company motto, "Oil That Glitters Is Not Gold," and as the hostess who issued the invitation, "The Empress of Blandings," a pig made famous in a series of P. G. Wodehouse novels. As a further insult, there was a notation, "Better dresses 5th Floor." According to one story, Lincoln Kirstein had come across one of the bogus invitations and showed it to his friend Nelson. On opening night, he gave Collins an official "kiss of death" as he greeted her in her swank black evening gown. Not long after, she received official word that she had been fired, her job as manager of publications to be taken over by Monroe Wheeler, a friend of Kirstein's. Soon afterwards Tom Mabry, who had been the unfortunate bearer of the bad news, was also let go.

The palace revolution took place while Alfred Barr was in Europe, selecting works for the Modern's major retrospective of Picasso, and the museum staff was disturbed and demoralized by the sudden shake-up. As Newhall described it, "We did not know if Alfred was aware of this action or not. In our concern for our jobs we wired him." Fearing that the phones might be tapped, Newhall cabled Barr in Paris. He responded that the staff should sit tight until he returned. It was not until later that Barr explained, "It had to be done. I couldn't do it." Barr gave no further explanation. Newhall confessed, "Nor did I ask for one." For Francis Collins it was a double break. She wrote her friend and former Vassar classmate Margaret Scolari Barr that within twenty-four hours of quitting the museum, "I had the courage and ruthlessness to bring a sharp and inalterable end [to] two and a half years of intimacy with Walker, so that by Sunday night . . . I'd cut free from the wreckage and encumbrances that had been holding me down and stepped into a brave new world." She was, she said, ". . . glad to be free of Mr. Nelson Rockefeller *and* Mr. Walker Evans."

Jim and Alma Agee with Delmore Schwartz, Frenchtown, New Jersey, 1940

Jane guessed but did not ask Walker about his affair with Frances Collins. Strangely enough, Evans later volunteered the information about his three-in-the-bed episode with Agee and Alma. His uncharacteristic frankness (he also noted another earlier spur-of-the-moment threesome involving two women friends) suggests that he was in dead earnest about reestablishing his relationship with Jane and at some point felt a need to come clean about his intervening affairs.

But the confession about the unhappy "experiment" with Agee and Alma casts further doubt on Alma's recollection of its having taken place when she and Agee were living at Monk's Farm in Stockton. By then Jane had already arrived in Connecticut and Evans was courting her assiduously before the Agees left for Stockton, a move that took place sometime after June 27, when Agee wrote Father Flye from Brooklyn: "It is likely that by July Alma and I will be out of town about fifty miles for the summer. If so, I hope you will come and stay there all of the time you want to. . . . If we are here instead, stay with us." In the same letter, Agee confessed his dissatisfactions with the sharecropper book: "It has been a very bad three months here in New York. . . . The book is all done but a few pages, which I'm finishing a great deal too slowly. I feel almost nothing about it." Ironically Evans and Jane went out to spend an overnight at Monk's Farm when Father Flye was visiting there. Unlike Alma or some of Agee's other friends, Jane found Flye "a sweet, nice guy," a kind of father figure to Jim. The two, she thought, were a study in contrasts: Father Flye, a picture of health and morality; Agee, amoral if not immoral. She remembered the next morning at Stockton when she and Walker looked out of the bedroom window and caught sight of the priest in his trousers and undershirt doing exercises on the lawn.

II

That summer when Jane moved in with Evans, the apartment building at 441 East Ninety-second was one of several standing three or four stories high in more or less pleasant open space, except for the unsightly coal yard for the Ruppert Brewery. "It was all open up there," Jane remembered. "You'd get off the bus at 86th Street; you could see the river and sky." Their building was a hive of political and artistic activities: on their floor, the front apartment was still occupied by Jay Leyda and his dancer wife, Si-lan Chen. Si-lan was a committed Communist and in time the Leyda apartment became a haven for party meetings. Evans and Jane tended to avoid such get-togethers; Evans, wary of political commitments, was convinced the FBI had the Leydas under surveillance. It was not unjustified paranoia on Evans's part; a year later the FBI began a long-term file on Ben Shahn. It included reports by an informant about the bitter arguments Shahn and another politically minded photographer had in the photo lab of the Farm Security Agency, each calling the other a "soapbox Communist."

The third-floor apartment above the Evans's had been taken by FSA photographer Ed Locke and his wife, Lorena. A doctor and his French mistress were living in the third-floor front. (He reputedly had invented Tampax.) The entire fourth floor was occupied by Harry and Dorothy Harvey. Harry Harvey was the advertising executive who had invented the slogan "Lucky Strike: It's Toasted." Dorothy was one of the three attractive Dudley sisters formerly of Chicago. (Their father, a physician, had made a fortune in real estate.) In the twenties John Dos Passos had been charmed by the sisters when they were living a life of educated leisure in Sneeden's Landing on the Hudson. Dos Passos, in fact, had a mild crush on Caroline Dudley. All three women had lived or would live in Paris for a time. Caroline, married to an attaché of the American embassy in Paris, was the theatrical agent who introduced Josephine Baker to Europe. Having scouted the young black dancer and singer in New York, Dudley transported her to Paris, where Baker was starred in the Revue Nègre at the Théâtre des Champs-Elysées. Sisters Katharine and Dorothy, artists of some talent, worked on the sets for the October 2, 1925, opening, which launched Baker's career abroad. In Paris, Scott and Zelda Fitzgerald in their madcap years had attended Caroline's parties. In Paris, Katherine

Dudley was a friend and neighbor of Gertrude Stein. Dorothy Harvey became a writer and critic of some note. Her 1932 biography of Theodore Dreiser, *Forgotten Frontiers*, may have fallen by the wayside as far as the critics were concerned, but in 1934 Dos Passos tried to resurrect it as one of his choices for "Good Books That Almost Nobody Has Read" in an article Malcolm Cowley featured in *The New Republic*. By way of consolation, Dos Passos wrote Dorothy that the "critics are always glad to crap on anything that comes to them unintroduced and unbacked by some literary vested interest."

In the decade or so that Evans and Jane were associated with the Harveys, Dorothy was the hostess of a lively salon at 441 East Ninety-second, entertaining the likes of Alexander Calder and Carl Sandburg (both of whom also aroused the suspicions of the FBI). Evans, despite his aversion to photographing celebrities, made an exception when Dorothy called them to come up and meet the Chicago poet and biographer of Lincoln. Asked to sing some songs, Sandburg pleaded he had no guitar, so Jane went back to the apartment and brought up hers. Evans photographed the white-haired troubadour, angling around him as he sat in his starched white shirt and bow tie, in some sixty or more shots. For Jane the Harvey occupancy was a source of excitement by virtue of its "great connection with Paris." She suspected that Dorothy in her Paris days might have been the mistress of American painter Jules Pascin, since two of Pascin's nude drawings of her were prominently displayed in the apartment. And while in Paris in the early thirties, she and her husband, Harry, had become friendly with Henry Miller and Anaïs Nin. Dorothy also was well acquainted with Matisse and wrote an article about the second version of the Matisse mural *The Dance*, which was being shipped to the Barnes Museum in Merion, Pennsylvania. The museum housed the collection of Dr. Albert Barnes, the inventor of the antiseptic Argyrol. Due to faulty measurements provided by Barnes, the first version of the mural did not fit properly in the central gallery of the museum. Matisse, a steadfast artist, began the whole process over again. Interviewing Matisse about the commission, Dorothy was told: "It is a room for paintings: to treat my decoration like another picture would be out of place. My aim has been to translate paint into architecture, to make the fresco the equivalent of stone or cement." Dudley submitted her article to Lincoln Kirstein's *Hound & Horn*. Kirstein, eager to reproduce the photographs, found Dudley's article not quite up to his critical standards: "What I wanted was a much simpler, direct and impersonal account of Matisse's work as he told it to you, without any atmospheric embroidery. So I have taken the liberty of cutting your article and sending it back to you." He offered fifty dollars on publication. The edited version appeared in the January–March 1934 issue of the magazine. The French connections at the Harvey salon were to become even more evident with the outbreak of World War II and the subsequent surrender of France in June 1940, when the influx of French exiles and emigrés — the painters Marc Chagall and Max Ernst, the surrealist poet André Bréton, and the ubiquitous salonière Marcel Duchamp among them — helped transfer the Left Bank of Paris to the Upper East Side of New York and the Harvey salon.

Walker, at the time, was also caught up in the social swirl by another noted New York hostess, an old friend from his Bethune Street days, Margaret La Farge Osborn, who had a townhouse on East Sixty-first Street and a country house in Saunderstown, Rhode Island. Peggy Osborn was the sister of anthropologist Oliver La Farge and granddaughter of the artist John La Farge, the youthful friend of Henry James. Her husband, William, a top-ranking metallurgist on the research staff at Phelps Dodge, had been a classmate of Edmund Wilson's at Hill School and Princeton and was a long-term friend of the critic. In the late thirties, however, he was in the process of separating from his wife, and was not often on the scene. Peggy Osborn's salon was a bit more staid than the Harveys'; Jane had encountered some rather stuffy relatives there on occasion. But Peggy had advanced tastes in artists. It was at dinners there that Jane met such figures as the Chilean-born and Paris-trained surrealist painters Matta (Echauren) and Arshile Gorky, though not Gorky's friend, the promising sculptor Reuben Nakian. The new star of the Osborn salon was the Japanese-American sculptor Isamu Noguchi, who did a small yet impressive bust of her in Tennessee marble. Noguchi was temporarily ensconced in the studio of artist Harold Sterner, another figure in Peggy Osborn's entourage. An artist in the prestigious Marie Harriman Gallery now, Sterner's fortunes had risen since Evans knew him as the "awful husband" of Leonie Sterner, the "fascinating piece of cheese" of his Bethune Street days. Evans didn't like him any better, though Jane remembered they had subsequent lunches with Sterner, without his wife.

It was at Peggy Osborn's townhouse that the two met Djuna Barnes, author of the 1937 cult novel *Nightwood*. In November 1939, following the outbreak of war in Europe, Barnes returned to New York, her fare paid by the wealthy art collector Peggy Guggenheim. She arrived on the same boat as the French surrealist Yves Tanguy, another of the Guggenheim beneficiaries. Barnes, recovering from a breakdown spent in a nursing home in Paris, came home in a disturbed and depressed state. Sometime later she was one of the invited guests at a dinner party at Peggy's townhouse to which Evans and Jane were invited. If Evans had thoughts about the Parisian expatriate he did not commit them to paper. But Jane remembered the dinner at which some of Osborn's relatives were present, and Barnes, turning morose at the dinner table, moaned "Here we are eating like pigs when people are starving in Paris." The stylish and still attractive novelist was the first of the returning expatriates whom she and Evans had encountered during the early phase of what was then termed the "phony" war. It was also during this time, Jane remembers, that Hanns Skolle had made an unexpected visit to Ninety-second Street. Skolle was with one or two other people; they had talked about old times. But Jane had the distinct impression, now, that Walker looked down on Skolle, not considering him of the right social stratum.

* * *

In the early years on Ninety-second Street, Evans and Jane were happy together, passionate in their renewed love affair. In the mornings while Evans shaved, she sat in the bathroom chatting with him. They joked with each other, planning the day ahead. Evans's studio was no longer in the kitchen of the Ninety-second Street apartment, but in the darkroom he was sharing with Helen Levitt at her apartment at 201 East Ninety-third Street. The kitchen at the Ninety-second Street apartment now harbored, behind a hamper, an unexplained symbol: a no-longer functional piece from the engine of his mother's car. Jessie Crane Evans was currently living in an apartment in Washington, D.C., while working in a thrift shop. In time, as a cost-cutting effort, she moved to the suburb of Chevy Chase, Maryland, to stay with her daughter and son-in-law, Tal Brewer.

A pen-and-ink sketch Jane made of the living room at Ninety-second

Street shows the loosely organized clutter of two lives merging: an accumulation of furnishings, including a bureau with a radio installed in a top drawer, the dial protruding as a knob; a rosewood chair with an overstuffed cushion that had also belonged to Evans's mother; an English walking stick that served as a portable seat that he had found somewhere. Jane's studio was in a corner of the living room. In her sketch a line of stretched, primed but unpainted canvases hangs along the wall. Next to it is a cloth Halloween mask Evans had picked up on the street (more evidence of his search for street "finds"). Elsewhere, in a burst of domesticity, Jane had upholstered the cushion on top of a truncated wooden Ionic column, another of Walker's finds, that served as a stylish footstool. In photographs that Evans took of his various apartments and studios during the next several years, the footstool would make a modest appearance. Money was short in those first years when Jane set up housekeeping with him; Evans resorted to hocking one or more of his cameras in a local pawn shop. But there was help from friends better off than he; Peggy Osborn, for instance, gave Walker seventy-five dollars to buy clothes for Jane.

Agee, back from the summer in New Jersey, often turned up at night. A few times, strangely enough, he came with Via, from whom he was divorced. Jane recalls having made dinner for them. On other occasions he came with Alma, not yet visibly pregnant. On those occasions Agee read passages from the sharecropper book, which was at a crucial stage in their dealings with Harper & Brothers. She recalled one evening sitting on the sofa with Evans sitting on the floor next to her gently caressing her ankles while Agee read what he considered a terrific segment about a hotel toilet. Evans, however, decided it was not suitable. In any event the passage did not appear in the published version. At Harper's an in-house memorandum by one of the editors judged that the text contained too many objectionable passages and recommended that it be toned down. Edward Aswell thought that Agee's style was too disjunctive and unfocused but was still hopeful of publishing. Agee, hard up for money at the moment, was conciliatory but insisted that the in-house memorandum be published as part of the book by way of explaining any cuts in the text. Harper's could hardly go along with the suggestion. In the meantime, on September 8, Agee, low on funds, wrote Evans, asking for a loan: "More delays from Harper leaves me again without a cent, and because I can't stand asking the same people I've been asking again, I'm now asking you: could you loan me anything until (supposedly within a few days now) the money comes through from Harpers." Evans, too, was embroiled with the publishers — but over some of the engravings of the photographic plates, the most notable of which was the photograph of the Burroughs' bed. In the original the bedspread was visibly bespecked with flies, but one of the engravers had carefully removed the flies from the scene. Evans was insisting that they be restored.

At this stage of the proceedings, Agee was asking for Evans's editorial input, but Evans refused: "I said, 'Absolutely not. I won't touch it.' I saw things that needed to be done. But I thought it was too great and that its faults had better be left in it. Even though it *needed* it, it wasn't I who was going to touch it." But inevitably, the book was doomed at Harper & Brothers. At a meeting with Aswell — Agee had queried Wilder Hobson as to the proper dress code but then decided to go casual after all — he and Evans were told that the firm had decided to turn down the book. They were free to take it elsewhere, but Harper's expected to be reimbursed for the publishing advances already made and for the cost of the photoengravings if the book were published elsewhere. Agee wrote Father Flye that he felt "weak, sick, vindictive, powerless and guilty." In one of the more effective metaphors of his life, he complained that he had "missed irretrievably all the trains that I should have caught."

Evans, meanwhile, similarly stalled, reapplied for a Guggenheim Fellowship. He and Agee had applied for (and not gotten) one the year before. On October 28, he wrote Henry Allen Moe, the secretary general, about "re-presenting" his application. This time he made a brief no-nonsense statement as a substitute for his twice-rejected earlier application: "The applicant proposes to continue work in photography along lines he has been following for some years." He referred to the work already done in *American Photographs* published by the Museum of Modern Art, and explained: "Future work will concentrate somewhat more on cities and towns in this country, and will emphasize people. From this work, a book of reproductions will be made which is to be a catalog of people and environments of this time, general and anonymous, national rather than regional." On a separate page he included quotes from some of the reviews of *American Photographs*, explaining: "Certain written opinions concerning this work seem accurately to describe the applicant's purposes and intended function." It was clear that he was standing on his record of achievement and did not intend to present himself hat in hand.

* * *

It had come time for Jane to meet the Evans family. On the first visit, as Jane remembered it, they stayed with the Brewers and their son, Tad, in Chevy Chase, Maryland. (Jessie still had her apartment in Washington, then.) Fortunately, the family approved of her as a suitable candidate for Walker's wife. They were genuinely fearful that in his rebelliousness Walker might otherwise have chosen to marry a Jew or a black. In subsequent family visits, Jane was made well aware of the antagonism between mother and son. Jessie could be imperious, particularly so after she moved in with the Brewers, where she tended to be bossy, taking charge of the family's affairs. Her daughter, so Walker and Jane noticed, seemed to retreat to her bedroom more and more. Jessie's manner could be officious: "Walker," she might ask her son, "would you be kind enough to get me a handkerchief out of the top left-hand drawer in the bureau in my bedroom." Evans would take his revenge in comic ways, like the night in the living room when he insisted on reading aloud to the gathered family the more offensive passages of Molly Bloom's soliloquy in Joyce's *Ulysses*. His mother sat through the recital stony and silent.

Apartment at 441 East 92nd Street

Jane and Evans had already consulted a lawyer friend of Walker's about the most convenient way for her to divorce Paul. They had no money to travel to Reno and the lawyer advised them that it would be best to have Paul divorce Jane. For Paul's benefit, they had concocted the story that Jane was staying in Washington with Walker's sister. It now became Jane's duty to write Paul asking for the divorce, though Walker helped her compose the letter. Their cover story, however, worked against them. Paul decided that he would come to Washington and try to convince Jane to return to New Orleans with him — which he did, accompanied by Mona Kraut. "I suffered hellishly during all that," Jane remembered. She and Walker traveled down to Chevy Chase to await him. Walker advised her to pick a public place for the meeting. (Walker did not attend.) The final site was a mezzanine lounge in one of the bigger Washington hotels. Jane was nervous, even though Walker, beforehand, had given her a sedative. Nevertheless, she held firm in her decision. One of the inducements Paul offered in hope of Jane's return was that he was planning to take her on a trip to the Grand Canyon. She was not moved to change her mind. Still shaken after the ordeal, she returned to Chevy Chase, where she and Walker and the visiting Mona Kraus went for a swim. But the stress was not that easily relieved. In a moment of anger or frustration in young Tad's bedroom, she took off her wedding ring and threw it away. Jane Brewer carefully picked it up and returned it to her. For some time afterwards, Paul, still not convinced about her decision, continued to write her, seemingly as a friend sending news of New Orleans and word about her friends there. In time, however, he gave up. He sued her for divorce on the grounds of desertion.

Contemporary American Subjects

20

On March 27, 1940, Henry Allen Moe, secretary general of the Guggenheim Foundation, wrote Evans that he had been awarded a Guggenheim Fellowship. The stipend he received was a welcome two thousand dollars, though it was five hundred dollars less than the average award. It was for a period of one year, beginning that very spring. An article in the April 8 issue of the *New York Times* indicated that Evans was one of seventy-three "scholars" to win an award from among the 1,700 applicants competing that year. The official announcement listed him as "Photographer of New York City," whose project was: "To photograph contemporary American subjects." Among the judges in the fields of graphic and plastic arts were the regionalist American painters Charles Burchfield and Boardman Robinson and sculptor Mahonri Young. The *Times* article also noted: "Because of the war all the fellows appointed this year will work in the Western Hemisphere, except one whose studies take him to the Near East." It was significant that with Hitler, Mussolini, and Stalin on the march in Europe, Americans, both liberal and conservative, had begun to turn inward. It was more than a coincidence that in 1940 John Dos Passos, a stalwart liberal until the Spanish Civil War, had won a three-month extension of his earlier 1939 Guggenheim award for a project concerning an American theme, "the writing of a series of essays on the basis of the present American conceptions of freedom of thought." It resulted in his tribute to American democracy and its founding fathers *The Ground We Stand On*. Evans's application made it clear that he was not committed to any definite plan other than concentrating on American cities and towns and photographs of anonymous people. Privately, he was entertaining the idea that in the fall or winter he and Jane might make a trip to Georgia, one of the sites he had considered "a revelation" six years earlier. "Have to do something about that," he had noted then. In 1940, he was thinking particularly of Savannah.

There was other good news that spring. By the end of April, Evans and Agee had signed a new contract for *Let Us Now Praise Famous Men* with

Bridgeport Parade, 1941

Houghton Mifflin, the Boston publishing firm. Both were "hereinafter designated as the Authors," though payments were specified as 75 percent to Agee and 25 percent to Evans. The terms of the agreement were five hundred dollars on signing the contract and the standard royalties thereafter, depending on sales. (Officially, it seems, the fee was a payback for the advance already received from Harper's, which had undoubtedly been spent.) The offer had been arranged through the agency of Eunice Clark, former wife of Selden Rodman, the editor of *Common Sense*, who had published in his magazine a segment of the book, "On the Porch," accompanied by four photographs. As a literary scout, Clark had approached Paul Brooks, an editor at Houghton Mifflin. Brooks, a Harvard graduate, knew and had admired Agee's work on the Harvard *Advocate*. He and senior editor Lovell Thompson were noticeably enthusiastic about Agee's text — all the more so when Edward Aswell at Harper & Brothers, having been obliged to give the book up, wrote Thompson: "Let me tell you how greatly I envy you the privilege of publishing this book. It was a great blow to me personally that things turned out as they did. Agee is certainly one of the most remarkable writers I have ever known and the only one now living who, I feel sure, is an authentic genius." Houghton Mifflin also acquired the engravings from Harper's. Aswell spoke up for those: "I doubt if any engraver's plates were ever made under such careful and loving scrutiny." Nonetheless, Evans still insisted that the flies in the engraving of the Borroughses' bedstead be reconstituted and won his case. In the final preface Agee generously insisted on the parity of Evans's work: "The photographs are not illustrative. They, and the text, are coequal, mutually independent, and fully collaborative." One of the main editorial strictures, however — as Agee noted in his preface — was "that certain words be deleted which are illegal in Massachusetts." With some urging from Evans, apparently, Agee agreed to drop the more offensive terms—"fuck, shit, fart, piss, cunt, cock, ass"—from the long litany of Anglo-Saxon words "that a careful man will be watchful of, and by whose use and inflection he may take clear measurement of the nature, and the stature, and the causes, and the timbre, of the enemy." The others, including "god, love, loyalty, honor, beauty, duty, integrity, art," remained listed among the five hundred suspect words he posted toward the end of the book.

Blair Fuller,
Cornish, New
Hampshire

* * *

In mid-June, Evans had an assignment Jane could not recall. She thinks she might have been visiting with the Voorheeses in Old Lyme. He photographed the Fuller children, Blair and Jill, somewhere in a country setting. In the fields, the tall pasture grass has had an early mowing and was nearly dry. The children lounge in the grass, eager, attentive, staring quizzically at the photographer in the noonday glare. Jill Fuller cradles a hound puppy; Blair hugs a full grown boxer. After her divorce, Jane Fuller, Charlie's first wife, had married again. Her new husband was Cass Canfield of the Harper & Brothers publishing firm. His son, Cass Canfield, Jr., slightly older than the others, is photographed in the fields and again on the porch of the house where he sprawls casually in a chair. They are the attractive, well-dressed children of an idle afternoon in summer at what appears to be a rambling estate. The negative sleeves for the sequence, including other notations for some Burden children, the children of Douglas Burden, are dated June 21, 1940. It is Saturday, one day before

France officially surrendered to the Germans in the forest of Compiègne. A beaming Hitler presided over the ceremony in the same railroad car in which the Germans had been forced to sign the armistice in 1918.

In August, Evans received a check from the Guggenheim marked "increase of stipend" by way of Henry Allen Moe and he presently wrote to thank him. Whether he had requested it or whether it had been offered by Moe is not clear. Perhaps it was the five hundred dollars to make up the average payment of twenty-five hundred dollars received by other candidates of that year. It would not have been out of the ordinary for Moe to have done such a thing. He was well regarded in the field. Even a critic as difficult to satisfy as Edmund Wilson, who had served on an award jury with the officiating Moe, had high praise for the man: "I've always been struck by his sympathy and understanding for different kinds of people and his tact in dealing with them. . . . I am sure that if it weren't for his presence on these occasions the Guggenheim would be as badly handled as the Pulitzer Prize." Evans, apologizing for not having written Moe sooner — his letter was dated August 10 — explained: "I've had to interrupt affairs for a few days to take care of a small illness." What the small illness was is not mentioned, but Evans claimed he had "successfully disposed" of it.

A month later, on September 7, he wrote Moe again to alert him to a change of address. He had sublet his apartment, he noted, and could be reached now at 201 East Ninety-third Street. In anticipation of their trip to Savannah, he and Jane had sublet the Ninety-second Street apartment for several months to a married couple, friends of Alice Morris. At some point, in the gypsy fashion of the period, he and Jane stayed at the swank apartment of Calvert Coggeshall and his wealthy wife, Helen, whom, according to Jane, "everybody despised." Then Evans moved into the cramped Ninety-third Street workroom he shared with Helen Levitt. Strangely, Evans informed Moe that he was "preparing to leave New York to work in several Middle Western places." This may have been a ploy meant to satisfy one of Moe's concerns. As Edmund Wilson observed, Moe made the conditions for receiving awards as elastic as possible, never urging a recipient to travel to Europe if he didn't care to: "The only thing that he has tried to prevent is their staying in New York."

As it turned out, Evans's real plans, whatever they were, had to be canceled. He had a sudden attack of appendicitis and had to have an oper-

Helen Levitt,
c. 1938

ation — an "appendisodomy," as he roguishly informed Ernestine Evans in a letter. It was a serious illness, further complicated by the fact that he subsequently came down with pneumonia. Charlie Fuller, Jane remembered, generously paid to have Walker moved to a private room. On the night of the operation, Jane slept over at the apartment Alice Morris shared with literary critic Harvey Breit on East Seventy-fifth Street. Quarters there were cramped as well: At night she slept on a cot under the piano in their living room. Alice, then working at *Harper's Bazaar,* was to become a good and long-term friend of Jane's, though not without a certain amount of friendly needling along the way. Alice had a sharp tongue.

It was an awkward period; the Guggenheim funds had been practically used up and Evans, released from the hospital, stayed for a few days of recuperation at the LaFayette Hotel. In the twenties and thirties, the LaFayette had been one of the notable gathering places of Greenwich Village bohemia, partly for its continental café, though some complained that the drinks were overpriced and the waiters too surly. It was a site favored by the Ash Can School painters, notably John Sloan, who pictured it on a rainy night with patrons waiting for cabs. The baths at the hotel acquired a certain notoriety as a homosexual haunt, depicted in a sequence of randy watercolors by the otherwise fastidious American precisionist painter Charles Demuth. In the early forties it still had class; Jane and Evans dined there often. Following their brief stay at the hotel, they moved to Chevy Chase, Maryland, to stay with the Brewers for a period of a week or more.

For Evans, at thirty-seven, it might have seemed that the timing of his career moves had gone awry. Yet there were small gains to be registered. The publication of Sherwood Anderson's *Home Town* — Anderson's final book — included several illustrations from the FSA files, among them seven halftones by Evans. His FSA photographs had begun to serve him well in other ways. The WPA had initiated an ambitious program of producing state guidebooks, employing writers, artists, and photographers in the process. Evans's photographs appeared in guide books for Pennsylvania and Alabama that were published, respectively, in 1940 and 1941. Richard Wright, just then famous for his 1940 novel, *Native Son*, a searing account of growing up young and black in Chicago, published *Twelve Million Black Voices: A Folk History of the Negro in the United States*, with coauthor Edwin Rosskamp. The book was published with one of Evans's photographs on the dust jacket and another used as an illustration inside.

A more important opportunity was nevertheless an irritation for Evans. He received a hurried letter, dated October 10, 1940 from Jay Laughlin, the wealthy publisher of *New Directions*, asking for photographs to accompany Agee's text from the "Colon" chapter of *Let Us Now Praise Famous Men*. They were to be published in the annual *New Directions in Prose and Poetry, 1940*. Laughlin wrote him: "Jim writes that you would like to have some pictures in the book with it and that suits me fine, as I'm much interested in the general problem of the relationships between pictures and words." Laughlin, perhaps unfortunately but in passing, mentioned that the book would also include photographs by the writer and photographer Wright Morris, which Laughlin intended to bleed at the edges. He hoped Evans would answer right back as they were holding up on the pagination for the rest of the book. The letter rubbed Evans the wrong way and he took immediate offense. On the back of the letter he jotted down a few false starts in what appears to be white heat. The fullest response was blistering:

I am exceedingly tired of having rich sassy men who have never done anything of their own and never could do anything write the kind of toplofty self impor-

tant amateur pompous insensitive letter I have just received from you, with the appalling assumption behind and between the lines that I or any artist would be so grateful to break into your publication as to beg entrance on no terms at all, as you clearly assume I would do.

He must have thought better about sending it. Perhaps he discussed the matter with Agee. The twelve-page segment of Agee's text appeared in the published volume, accompanied by four of Evans's photographs.

In the meantime, publication of *Let Us Now Praise Famous Men* was proceeding, though not without further complications. Lovell Thompson wrote Evans thanking him for sending a new print for the photographic section of the book, which was to appear as an independent portfolio, as in *The Crime of Cuba*, except that the thirty-one photographs would be positioned at the front of the book. Thompson assured him: "Everything looks clear and simple and we will not deviate from your layout to any important extent without letting you know." But the hospital stay had caused delays, and Evans was still not sure whether the photographs would appear singly opposite a blank page — a more expensive proposition — or on facing pages in a spread. He was also concerned that the photographs should be credited to the Farm Security Administration. Writing to Thompson from Chevy Chase on November 17, he raised the issue again: "I have been waiting in the hope of hearing from you, first about the page placement: but now I am leaving Washington, and I believe Jim Agee must have come to Boston and then failed to send me your decision." By now, he was willing to concede: "In any case, I hope it is now not too late to use this new acknowledgment, immediately following the pictures, no matter how they are placed — singly or double-paged."

By the end of the year, both he and Agee were at a crossroads as far as the publication of their book was concerned. Originally scheduled for publication in January or February of 1941, it had been postponed until the following midsummer. Agee, writing to Robert Fitzgerald in December 1940, was depressed: "Everyone I see, myself included, is at a low grinding edge of quiet desperation. Nothing, in most cases, *out of the ordinary*, just the general average Thoreau was telling about, plus the dead ends of one of the most evil years in history, plus each individual's little specialty act." A father now, he was indulging in more than second thoughts about his marriage: "I must learn my ways in an exceedingly quiet marriage (which can be wonderful I've found but is basically not at all my style or apparent 'nature') or break from marriage and all close liaisons altogether and learn how to live alone & keep love at a bearable distance." The fact was that he had already become deeply involved with a new woman, Mia Fritsch, an Austrian emigrée who was working at *Fortune* as a researcher. There was in truth little that was quiet in his marriage over the coming months. There were scenes and recriminations. Alma, furious, made more than one attempt to run away. Once, Agee dragged her by the hair back to the apartment, then proceeded to punish himself by beating his head against a wall. And once, in the office at *Time*, where he was then working as a book reviewer, she made known her plans to leave him, taking Joel with her to Mexico, accompanied by Helen Levitt. Agee threatened to throw himself out the window. Refusing to be blackmailed, Alma stormed out to the elevator; then, fearful, returned to find the window open, but Agee hid behind the door, making her even more furious. Joel's first birthday in March marked a sad ending, as Alma recalled it in her memoir: "the three of us gazing solemnly at the one candle set in the middle of a cupcake and discussing the coming trip to Mexico with Helen."

II

It was Christmas by the time Evans and Jane returned to New York. Their apartment, however, was not available yet. Evans put up at the Wales Hotel for a time, while Jane once again stayed with Alice Morris at the Seventy-fifth Street apartment, where the two families celebrated Christmas together. When they did get back into their apartment, they found it a mess. In need of money once more, Evans contacted Henry Allen Moe about a renewal of his Guggenheim Fellowship and was told to reapply. His application on February 1 reported that he was now working on a book called *Faces of Men*, the subject of which would be "people in our time." Over the past year, he indicated, he had made a segment of the book, consisting of "semi-automatic" photographs taken in the New York subways "by a concealed camera method which I have devised particularly for this work." From some three hundred and fifty negatives made by this method he planned to submit seventy-five to the committee, some of which would be cropped as portrait photographs and others groups of individuals in the subway setting. The largest segment of the book would include photographs taken "in city streets and in various public places — under less special working conditions, technically." He intended to collect "a selection of literary texts, some just captions, some longer; and arrange a sequence of pictures and words. Some of this I want to write myself; some I want to be literally overheard spoken sentences or conversations." There is a text on the subway photographs furnished by Agee and dated October 1940 which may well have been written for the book Evans had in mind. In it Agee, after providing an account of Evans's method and intentions, mounted a psalm of praise for the anonymous passenger: "Each carries in the postures of his body, in his hands, in his face, in the eyes, the signatures of a time and a place in the world upon a creature for whom the name immortal soul is one mild and vulgar metaphor." But it was not until fifteen years later when Agee died and the *Cambridge Review* published eight of Evans's subway photographs in its Winter issue that the text was first used.

Evans, in his letter to Moe, also mentioned that he planned to spend another month taking photographs in the subway. Jane's recollection was that he had begun taking more subway photographs while he was staying at the Wales and that seems to be corroborated by the January dates of the newspaper headlines and some of the concert advertisements in the photographs. By the end of February, Helen Levitt, planning for her trip to Mexico, wanted to give up the Ninety-third Street apartment and studio. Evans found a new ground-floor workroom at 1683 York Avenue, where, on March 12, Moe wrote him to say that he had been reappointed to a fellowship of one thousand dollars for a period of six months beginning on April 1. Evans wrote Moe expressing his appreciation and suggesting that once he was settled into his new studio, he hoped Moe would pay him a visit: "I expect to have some things going that it may interest you to see."

It proved to be the beginning of a busy season. That spring he received two well-timed, if commercial, commissions. The first was a request to photograph the new Student Alumnae Building and the campus of Wheaton College in Norton, Massachusetts, for the book *Wheaton College Photographs*, published later that year. Founded in 1838, Wheaton was one of the oldest institutions in America for "the advanced education of females." The campus of Federal and Greek Revival structures had been expanded in the early twentieth century by architect Ralph Adams Cram in red-brick Georgian-Colonial style. It was dominated by Cram's 1917 Cole Memorial Chapel, with its three-tiered steeple, which Evans used as a focus for the series of photographs he took, twenty-four of which were used in the book. What had originally been a competition for a new art center had been the subject of an exhibition by the Museum of Modern Art in 1938 just prior to Evans's "American Photographs" exhibition. It had included drawings by such high-powered notables of the international style as Walter Gropius, Eero Saarinen, Richard Neutra, and Louis Kahn, but the winners were the more traditionalist young architects Richard Bennett and Caleb Hornbostel. When sufficient funds for the art center could not be raised, the winning team was given the assignment of designing the already funded Student Alumnae Building. Evans made an early trip to the site in late March, when stark leafless trees were still in evidence in the first set of photographs. He sent Jane a pair of comic, even racy telegrams on his arrival and again on the day of his departure. On March 25: "ARRIVED TEMPERATURE NORMAL REGION THICKLY SETTLED MISS YOU — UNSIGNED." Followed three days later by: "SEE YOU AROUND SEVEN TEMPERATURE BELOW NORMAL PLEASE START PULLMOTOR LOVE — W."

On a later excursion, in summer, perhaps, since the trees were in full leaf in the photographs, Jane traveled with him. They stayed at the Cambridge apartment of two women teachers from Wheaton who, according to Jane, "took to Walker like ducks to water." They were so charmed by his manners and poise they sold him their almost-new Ford for three hundred dollars. Jane paid half. The Wheaton assignment proved that Evans was thoroughly capable of producing respectable results on any commercial assigment if he chose. The photographs of the campus are fastidious in their detail; the interior shots of the new building are prim and proper but characteristically devoid of human beings. In the foreword to the book, the president of the college, J. Edgar Park, announced: "The college lends itself well to the talent of the photographer as three ages of architecture are here represented in buildings of real distinction, and the three styles meet here without disturbing the serenity of and the unity of the whole." Evans succeeded in proving the point, but, curiously, he balked at the president's word "talent" and asked that it be changed to "medium," which was was how it appeared in the final text. As it happened, an altogether different take on the interior views of the new building by an up-and-coming younger photographer, Ezra Stoller, appeared in *Architectural Forum* and *Interiors* magazines, showing the game room and other facilities in use, the figures — if somewhat stagily posed — providing a sense of space and scale. Evans's game room and parlor photographs, devoid of inhabitants, looked more like pristine stage sets. Jane's recollection of their Boston and Wheaton excursion, though it netted them an almost-new car and the opportunity to meet some pleasant people, had one mishap that illustrated Evans's concern for the proprieties. Invited for after-dinner drinks and conversation with President Park, Walker was in his element and made use of the opportunity. Jane, however, having spied a copy of the English magazine *Punch*, which she had never seen before, picked it up and idly paged through it. When they left, Walker gave her a round scolding for not paying attention.

Oddly, the difference between Evans's trim commercial work for the Wheaton College book and his talent for more challenging subjects would never be more sharply demonstrated than by his appearance — though minimal — in Berenice Abbott's *A Guide to Better Photography*, published the same year. At his best, Evans had the knack of including in his photographs the ephemera of the moment — advertisements, movie billboards, the trash in the streets, the current models of automobiles, the price of a meal in a restaurant, the style of a woman's hat, the headlines of the daily newspaper — everything that might fix a moment for posterity. At this stage of his career, he knew and subsumed all that with the same authority with which he clicked the shutter on his camera. The photographs Abbott selected to illustrate her points, along with works of her own, were photographs by major names of the contemporary scene: Cartier-Bresson, Strand, Weston, and Russell Lee. She also included works by such pioneers as Nadar, Southworth and Hawes, Mathew Brady, and Atget. In this lineup, Abbott's choice for her chapter on "Composition," a print of Evans's 1936 photograph *Bethlehem PA*, might well have confused or confounded an ordinary viewer. It was a clogged exposition of an industrial scene, one that perversely emphasized the layer by layer clutter of incident, from the gathered tombstones in the foreground cemetery, the seedy apartment houses beyond, next the row of smokestacks, and even further back a distant jumble of houses and factories. Yet, as Abbott pointed out in her text, the photograph was "a good example" of her Rule #6: "Not only lines, but also lights and shades need to be balanced. A large shadow should be relieved with a light area or another shadow of lesser intensity. Correct balance of light and shade unifies the photograph." In explicating the text of the photograph, Abbott acknowledged that the complexity of the forms and the interplay of various tones in the photograph "might well seem unrelated and chaotic, if the composition had not been brought to a focus by the placing of the large white cross. This solid, simple form creates balance and at the same time leads the eye back to the smaller cross and so to the smokestacks, which are the ultimate objective of the photographer's comment." But Evans's picture may have been even more complex than the matter of composition. He had indeed confronted the problem head on. Rather than prettifying the scene by shooting from a low angle and screening out the distant chaos by showing lots of serene sky, he compressed everything into a sequence of façades — the cemetery, the houses, the smokestacks, the clamoring distance beyond. Faced with such a scene, insisting upon the confusion, he turned the photograph into an evaluation of man's depredation of the environment and his crude efforts to establish a ramshackle sense of order in the midst of life and within view of impending death.

Movie Poster for Tobacco Road, Bridgeport, Connecticut, 1941

* * *

A more important commercial assignment fell his way late that spring. He was asked to photograph in Connecticut for an article titled "In Bridgeport's War Factories" to be published in the September 1941 issue of *Fortune*. It was not quite two years since the war had begun in Europe and local companies like Remington, Vought-Sikorsky Aircraft, and General Electric were now well into the war effort, producing armaments and supplies both for national defense and for the Allies, making shells, brass tubing, aluminum castings, and machine tools. The economic boom had generated an influx of workers and their families, creating a serious housing shortage. Young men from Pennsylvania coal mines had come north for the opportunity, sleeping in shifts, sometimes five to a room with three beds.

Restaurants were thriving along Main Street, and in the downtown districts shoppers crowded the streets. It was not a prepossessing subject but Evans, whose last assignment for *Fortune* had been four years earlier, must have considered it an important one. Over a period of two to three weeks in May and June, he set himself the task of photographing the city's bustling industrial sites and downtown stores, the swollen parking lots at the Vought-Sikorsky plant, the energetic shoppers on Main Street, workmen outside the factories on their lunch breaks, and a major parade, which Jane, who accompanied him on at least one of the shoots, believes was a Memorial Day parade. Contradictory evidence in the dating of the prints suggests it might otherwise have been the Fourth of July parade, billed in a press release as the "I Am An American Parade." The latter title seems to fit the all-out patriotic theme of perhaps the most notable of the photographs Evans took: four weighty Italian women in white uniforms being driven along the route in an open touring car with flags waving and a large sign on the door announcing "Love or Leave America." Whichever it turns out to be, it was an American festival — flags waving, crowds lining the streets, and the obligatory threesome of the battle for national independence: a bandaged warrior, a white-haired flag bearer, and the drummer boy all in Revolutionary War costumes.

In some instances Evans used his 35-mm Contax, an unnamed 4 x 5 camera and a 2¼ x 2¼ Rolleiflex. His random field notes indicate that on May 18, a Sunday morning, he photographed a Mansard house at West Avenue and Prospect Street. It was not unlike many another specimen of Victorian architecture he had taken, bright sunlight etching the porch railings and ornate columns. Over the next two days there were shots of a flagpole and flag in a playing field against a backdrop of row houses, a new housing development across the river, among others. What comes across in the Bridgeport photographs is the ordinariness of the city and the settings, and the fact that he was possibly making do with things he was comfortable with, had photographed in other cities and other times: the billboard for the City Savings Bank, a debonair couple picnicking alongside the motto "Savers Prosper," a movie poster for *Tobacco Road* with tenement houses in the background, people queuing up in front of another movie house showing *A Woman's Face*, starring Joan Crawford.

Spectators, Bridgeport, Parade, 1941

What seems otherwise inexplicable are the notations for the "dump of Fairfield Avenue." Jane remembered that when she was with him, she often stayed in the car sketching while Evans photographed, and that once, unaccountably, he had set up his tripod and camera in a dump among the tomato soup cans. Another time, while she was sketching by herself, a policeman had come up to the car and insisted on seeing what she was drawing, as if she were a spy. It was her first realization that even before America was at war, there was a suspicion abroad that spies might be keeping careful watch where defense industries were concerned. Among Evans's Bridgeport notes there is one that reads: "Submit negs & prints to Commander Alexander at Sikorski plant." Ads in the *Fortune* coverage announced products and tools that met defense specifications, and one for chain fencing suggested: "Like a ring of sentries an Anchor fence ensures protection for Government Contract Work." Signs of the times.

The photographs make a coherent sequence, long shots from above the marching groups; at street level, children neatly dressed sitting on the curb; a black shoeshine boy has climbed atop a primitively carved, boulder-sized war memorial; an excited little girl in a light summer dress stands, under glass, in a shop window looking out.

III

In mid-July 1941, the first copies of *Let Us Now Praise Famous Men* came off the press. After five years of deliberation, changes of publishers, accommodations in intention and design, it would have been hard not to admit that the actual publication of the book was anticlimactic. Up until virtually the final moment, Agee was registering last-minute changes in the text. Over the years it had acquired a kind of jerry-built structure. Yet it was to be a book very much about its time and about the character of the writer, his ambivalence and his sudden moments of inspiration. It was, and remains even now that it has become a classic text of the depression era, a continuous work-in-progress.

Reviewers of the book were far more likely to use Evans's photographs as the standard with which to criticize Agee's extravagant and unbridled text. Ralph Thompson in the *New York Times* claimed: "There never was a better argument for photography. . . . Mr. Evans says as much about tenant farmers . . . in his several dozen pictures as Mr. Agee says in his entire 150,000 words of text." Even a well-disposed critic like *Time*'s Jack Jessup, while claiming the book contained "some of the most exciting U.S. prose since Melville," complained that "Agee's chief failure is one Photographer Evans scrupulously avoids: he clumsily intrudes between his subject and his audience even when the subject is himself." Jessup classified the book as "a distinguished failure." The reviewer for *Partisan Review*, Paul Goodman, made much the same complaint — that Agee had intruded himself into the tenant farmers' lives with what he considered "insufferable arrogance." In the *Saturday Review*, Selden Rodman warned prospective readers about the opening pages: "If the reader does not like the kind of naked realism which is the truth as Walker Evans's camera-eye sees it he is through before he even reaches the text." Nonetheless he praised the combined "fury and humility" of Agee's writing. "Part of the greatness and unique quality of 'Let Us Now Praise Famous Men'," Rodman claimed, "is its structural failure, its overall failure as the 'work of art' it does not aim or presume to be and which from moment to moment it is." Even among friends, support was qualified. Dwight Macdonald saw it as "a young man's book — exuberant, angry, tender, willful to the point of perversity . . . with the most amazing variations in quality; most of it is extremely good, some of it as great prose as we have had since Hawthorne, and some of it turgid, mawkish, overwritten . . ." But principally, the book's lack of success — it sold little more than six hundred copies after its publication — was due to the mood of the country. With the war in Europe expanding — Hitler had invaded Russia in June 1941 — and the boom in defense contracts growing, the Great Depression was a thing of the past. The fate of tenant farmers was not the news of the moment.

The most sensitive review the book received appeared too late in any case to reverse the trend. Lionel Trilling's review in the Winter 1942 issue of the *Kenyon Review* was provocatively titled "Greatness with One Fault in It." At the outset, Trilling stated, "I feel sure that this is a great book." He then went on to call it "the most realistic and the most important moral effort of our American generation." He praised the "perfect *taste*" of Evans's photographs, "taking that word in its largest possible sense to mean tact, delicacy, justness of feeling, complete awareness and perfect respect." He particularly singled out Evans's portrait of Annie Mae Gudger (Allie Mae Burroughs):

The gaze of the woman returning our gaze checks our pity. . . . In this picture, Mrs. Gudger with all her misery and perhaps with her touch of pity for herself, simply refuses to be an object of your "social consciousness"; she refuses to be an object at all — everything in the picture proclaims her to be all subject. And this is true of all the Evans pictures of the Gudger, Woods and Ricketts families.

What he objected to as the "One Fault" was Agee's too-narrow focus on the presumably virtuous nature of the tenant farmers themselves. Agee, he concluded, was writing about them "as if there were no human unregenerateness in them, no flicker of malice or meanness, no darkness or wildness of feeling, only a sure and simple virtue, the growth, we must suppose of their hard, unlovely poverty." Yet at least once, in writing about the people of the rural South, meaning the people Agee most cared about there, he paints a much less flattering portrait: ". . . pretty nearly without exception you must reckon in traits, needs, diseases, and above all mere natural habits, differing from our own, of a casualness, apathy, self-interest, unconscious, offhand and deliberated cruelty, in relation toward extra human life and toward negroes, terrible enough to freeze your blood or break your heart or to propel you toward murder. . . ."

Resorters, Tourists, Emigrés

Their road to marriage was a circuitous one. Late in October, they traveled south, putting up at one of their favorite overnight stops in New Castle, Delaware. They were en route to another visit with the Brewers in Chevy Chase. Their decision to get married was a spur-of-the-moment thing. Walker, however, was decidedly against having his sister and brother-in-law serve as witnesses. Instead, Charlie Fuller, then working in Washington, was requisitioned for the job. The wedding took place on October 27, 1941, in the rectory of a Methodist church in nearby Rockville, Maryland. The minister, J. W. Rosenbeyer, having noticed on the marriage license that Jane was "A DIVORCED WOMAN" in capital letters and of no specified occupation, lectured her on the sanctity of marriage. The celebration back at the Brewers' house was modest to a fault. Evans had predicted his sister, Jane, would produce one bottle of champagne from the People's Drugstore. That turned out to be the case, though the family, including Evans's mother, was pleased that he had married a presentable woman. Evans and Jane, however, were eager to be on their way. Jane planned to inform her family in Fond du Lac in person and it would be a long trip in their recently acquired Ford. On the twenty-eighth, according to Evans's brief photo log, there was a stop at Frederic, Maryland, where Evans photographed a red barn. In a nostalgic mood, he made an overnight stay at Mercersburg, Pennsylvania, and drove Jane past the academy where years before he had been a student and where only six years earlier, in 1935, passing through, he had experienced the mild rush of reminiscences that made him realize he was still, if only partly, the seventeen-year-old boy in white flannel trousers. On the thirtieth Evans stopped again to photograph a "Carry Out Service" sign on a gas station west of Fort Wayne, Indiana — glimpses of America along the way. Jane was not altogether upset or surprised when Walker decided not to accompany her to Wisconsin to see her family. She had already come to the conclusion that it would probably have been an awkward situation, uncomfortable for both of them. Instead, Walker remained in Chicago, staying with Philip Rahv, the blustery and

*Resort
Photographer
at Work,
1941*

self-confident editor of the *Partisan Review*. (The magazine's coeditor, William Phillips, referred to Rahv as "a manic-impressive.") Rahv, recently married to Natalie Swann, was teaching for a term at the University of Chicago. Both Jane and Evans knew the couple through the parties of the magazine crowd in New York; occasionally the foursome went out to dinner together there.

In Chicago, Evans busied himself photographing tenement buildings at Forty-sixth Street and South Dearborn. More important, as his notes indicate, he caught sight of a blind couple near Maxwell Street walking toward him. The blind man in the dark suit has a tin cup dangling on a string from the neck of his guitar, while the woman holds out her cup in a gentle gesture. In the background, prominently displayed in a shop window, two mannequins are wearing bridal gowns and another is dressed as maid of honor. There appears to be no groom in the entourage.

* * *

Municipal Trailer Camp, Sarasota, Florida, 1941

Back in New York by the end of November, Walker finally consented to taking on a photographic assignment because of the persistence of his old nemesis Ernestine Evans. The journalist Karl A. Bickel had written a lively history of the less-well-known west coast of Florida titled *The Mangrove Coast* and needed illustrations. The book was scheduled for publication by Coward-McCann in 1942. Bickel, the retired president of the United Press Association, was a journalist of some note. He had been the media consultant for Charles Lindbergh during the grim days of the Lindbergh baby's kidnapping in 1932. Ernestine Evans assured the author that Walker was an ideal choice. Aside from Edward Weston, she wrote Bickel, Evans was "the most difficult artist in the country to deal with; but also he's so damned difficult and uncommercial that his product is the most interesting." Walker "says he can't and won't," she warned Bickel, "but I am allowing him another three days to reconsider." Bickel's book was a thoroughly readable affair, full of historical lore and local color, but as in earlier cases like the Cuban assignment, Evans may not have read the manuscript nor the galley proofs when he finally agreed to make the trip to Florida.

The long drive south had its problems; Evans suggested that every time they crossed another state line they perhaps should stop and celebrate.

Then on Thanksgiving Day, November 27, 1941, nearing Jacksonville, they developed engine trouble. Evans managed to get the car to a garage only to learn that he needed a part and the garage had none. A young mechanic offered to drive Walker to a junkyard in Jacksonville, where he could pick one up. Jane stayed behind sitting in the car, staving off hunger with a package of crackers. She sketched for a time as a relief from boredom. It was hardly the holiday they had planned. When the men returned and the part was properly installed, there was nothing to do but head on to Jacksonville, where they put up at a hotel. Both were too weary to celebrate. As a holiday gesture, however, Evans ordered a meal from the hotel kitchen and they dined alone in their room. They were on the road again the next day.

By November 30 they were in Sarasota, where Bickel and his wife were living in retirement. Evans at first busied himself with scouting a trailer park in Sarasota. The city, according to Bickel, boasted "the finest municipal trailer camp in the world." Evans's assessment of the trailer park turned out to be something closer to comic relief than sociological study. This was especially the case in his photograph of a man sitting on the porch of camp "Kum Ango" on Lot 14, with its flower boxes daintied up by borders of seashells. One could say that part of Evans's work, in effect, documented the curious nesting habits of homo sapiens.

Their month-long Florida jaunt ranged widely along the west coast. Sometimes the Bickels' live-in chauffeur, Ed, drove them to nearby areas. On most of the excursions, Jane accompanied Evans while he photographed. In Tampa and St. Petersburg Evans found familiar ground, taking photographs of auto graveyards and groups of elderly people sitting on benches along an esplanade. In St. Petersburg, too, he focused on another group of inhabitants, pelicans sitting solemnly on a pier. Judging by the overcoats worn by many of the elderly women, he and Jane had encountered a cold snap at this point in their excursion. But other photographs showed still energetic retirees in shirtsleeves playing at the shuffleboards or attending the races or waiting at corners for trolleys. Time seemed to hang heavily along the Gulf Coast.

One gets a few vivid clues as to what Evans was after in these photographs of what he labeled "Winter Resorters." They come from the instructions he sent the engraver for one of the plates. Two elderly women coated and hatted sit on a bench, sharing the same newspaper. One of them has a folded newspaper under her arm that Evans must have thought not sharp enough. In a note for the engraver Evans asked, "Can you make the words HOME EDITION legible without retouching?" At this stage of his career, Evans clearly intended that every telltale item in the reading of a photograph, every notation in his bill of particulars, should have its value. Despite his dislike of retouching, which became the motto of his photographic zeal, he nonetheless asked the engraver to black out the seven distracting triangles that formed a pattern along the bottom edge of the print; he considered them "unsightly." They do not appear in the illustrated plate. A third instance is more interesting still: "Try to get clearly the veins in the left leg of left woman, but without retouching." In the published photograph the veins appear enhanced a bit, though not noticeably enough to distract attention. In Evans's view, then, the whole field of an individual photograph might be read as a mine of information, both consciously sought or subliminally arrived at. Whatever else it might portend, this photograph of the two women (judging by physical appearances, they could be sisters) delivers a message about the debilities of age and the whisper of mortality. Evans, then, was not the absolute purist he sometimes pretended to be. From his program notes for this particular photograph, we learn — in fact have his word for it — the context of editing and decision also provides clues to meaning.

Evans had little sympathy for conventional landscape. He preferred to expose the oddities and freaks of nature, the rough edges of debilitated landscapes. In Florida, he found these in abundance. He photographed the messy impenetrable jungle of mangroves and vines at the water's edge; the twisted columns of banyan trees; clumps of cypresses in a swamp. If he hit upon a stand of skeletal leafless trees, he photographed one as if it were a bizarre Christmas tree, draped with tufts of Spanish moss and ornamented with the dark perched silhouettes of vultures. On a beach on the Gulf of Mexico, he photographed the wind-whipped blasted shapes of a series of palm trees. But what Jane remembered most was the photograph Walker took of a lone palm tree, listing to one side, bereft of all but a single frond. It was taken on December 7, the day the Japanese attacked Pearl Harbor. They did not hear the news until they returned from the beach. That night, not a night to celebrate, they had dinner at the local yacht club with Bickel and his wife.

* * *

Among the Florida photographs of people there is a sequence of a blind couple taken in City Hall Park in Tampa. They, too, are in overcoats warming themselves in the sun behind a makeshift counter on which a metal container for money stands. (It looks suspiciously like an old-fashioned spittoon.) The two appear to be deep in thought or maybe engaged in conversation. The pictures are significant; they form part of a trilogy of photographs of blind beggars Evans had taken within the past year or two: the blind accordionist in the New York subway, the recently photographed blind couple in Chicago, and now the blind pair in Tampa's City Hall Park. These happenstance finds surely offered him something more than mere ironic commentaries on sight and sightlessness in the eye of the beholding camera. Considering that early in his career Evans was struck by Paul Strand's 1916 photograph of the blind beggar woman, what unraveled sequence of associations does this 1941 reworking of the theme represent? As a man with literary inclinations, had he at the very least become a cataloguer of blindness in both the physical and metaphorical sense?

It is far easier to determine the meaning of another theme that Evans had been pursuing: the photographer at work. One has only to remember the signs painted on the photography studio in downtown New York, the man walking the streets with a signboard advertising a photo studio, or the penny-picture displays ripe with smiling faces in the windows of two photographers' studios in the South. On a pier in Florida Evans found the most comic and endearing example of the photographer-at-large. This one was a tall, thin, and gangly woman photographer wearing a turban who on a windy day — her dress is whipping up about her legs — bending like an awkward giraffe behind the tripod legs of her view camera, is taking a portrait shot. Evans photographed her several times, amidst her props, which were conveniently lined up along the edge of the pier: plastic palm trees, two hanging fake fish big enough to satisfy any fisherman's boast, imitation pelicans, a stuffed alligator, the prow of a speedboat, a cartoon bathing beauty on a striped towel with a cut-out space for the customer's head. The chance encounter with the photographer provided him with a lively satirical metaphor: the photographer as a purveyor of insidious or comic lies and dreams.

Store Display, Florida, 1941

In Tarpon Springs, they encountered a sizable colony of Greeks, many of them fishermen engaged in sponge-diving operations. Evans and Jane one day stopped for coffee or a coke in a Greek café there. To Jane's surprise she was the only woman in what turned out to be an all-male enclave. She could tell from the stares she received that her visit was considered out of order. Walker's photographic session in the area took in the wharves and boats tied up at the docks, the sponges arrayed along one of the wharfs. What caught Jane's eye, however, was a deep-sea diver's suit with bolted-down metal helmet slouched in a chair outside the Mermaid Curio Shoppe. She dearly wanted to make a painting from it: Walker, obligingly, took a set of photographs for her.

* * *

What may have been the most extended and possibly the most satisfying sequence of photographs for Evans were those associated with the Ringling Brothers Circus at Sarasota. He had made a sequence of photographs of the empty Ringling residence, Ca' d' Zan, looking like a Renaissance palace at the seaside. Patterned after the Doges Palace in Venice, the empty building, the former home of the deceased John and Mabel Ringling, was still in probate when he photographed it. He also photographed the sprawling coastal villa of Charles Ringling's widow. At the winter quarters of the circus, he took a whole series on the ornately carved and gilded circus wagons, some of them the worse for wear, like the

weathered United States wagon, carved with Indians and angels. Jane, too, had wanted a photograph of one of the wagons. Her later painting of it was hung in their apartment.

But the most exciting shoots, as Jane recalled, were the photographs of the animals. There is a portrait of two caged lions stately in their boredom and a throwback to the photographer's earlier interests — a torn circus poster of a lion's head. A pair of giraffes crane their heads above a wire fence; a baboon sulks in his cage. The most exciting moments came at the elephant kraal, when Evans set up his camera while the trainers put the lumbering animals through their paces, massive forelegs lifted as they sat on flimsy-looking seats or profiled in a mammoth chorus line. The gentleness with which they touched one another was astonishing.

Quite coincidentally, Evans's photographs of the elephant troupe could have been a preview of an elephant dance actually performed by the same animals at the opening of the circus the following April in Madison Square Garden. While Evans was in Florida, Lincoln Kirstein, in New York, was involved in the negotiations for an elephant ballet with choreography by George Balanchine and music by Igor Stravinsky. On December 24, a friend of Stravinsky's wrote the composer in Hollywood: "Two or three days ago in Town Hall, Lincoln Kirstein approached me and said, 'I saw Mr. North recently. He is the manager of the Ringling Brothers Circus and he wishes Balanchine to do a polka for the elephants and Stravinsky to write the music.'" (Balanchine had earlier collaborated with Stravinsky on the ballet "Jeu de Cartes," performed in 1937 by Kirstein's American Ballet Company.) One story had it that Stravinsky had asked how old the elephants, "those respectable quadrupeds," were. Told by Balanchine they were very young, he agreed to take on the commission. But Stravinsky was a wily businessman as well as a genius. As he wrote his New York friend, he had laid down certain conditions: "I also told [Balanchine] that if he was not in a great hurry, I could undertake to do this composition in March; that he should give me the time; that the Polka must not be long; and that he would have to see that I am paid very well."

The elephants, however, did not appear among the thirty-two illustrations from the Evans excursion when *The Mangrove Coast* was published in 1942. (Subsequent editions of the book dropped the illustrations altogether.) Nor did they appear in Alice Morris's article "The Circus at

Home," in the April 1942 issue of *Harper's Bazaar*, coincidental with the Madison Square Garden April 9 opening of the "Greatest Show on Earth" with the elephant ballet. Morris, however, did mention trainer Walter McClain putting "one of his pupils through difficult paces for the new elephant ballet — Balanchine choreography, Stravinsky music." Evans's photograph of the United States wagon served her for one of the "magnificent circus wagons of the past." She also used the photograph of the torn poster of the lion's head.

By Christmas eve, after a stop at Tallahassee, where he photographed plantation houses and groups of blacks on the city streets, Evans and Jane, heading north, were at Jacksonville, where they put up once more in a hotel. It would not be altogether untrue to think of their adventure in Florida between two holidays as an allegorical voyage on some Noah's ark with a cargo of aging tourists and wondrous beasts.

II

However much it was a winter of discontent, the first year of the war in America proved to be a significant event in American culture. The Stravinsky-Balanchine ballet for the elephants might seem one of the more comic illustrations of the merger of high art and American opportunity. (An unpublished account of the choreography suggests that fifty elephants [an exaggeration, surely] and fifty chorines all wearing tutus took part in the exercise.) At the April 9 premiere — for the benefit of the Army and Navy Relief Fund — the "Circus Polka" took four minutes to perform, in the course of which the lead elephant, Bessie, lifted Vera Zorina, Balanchine's wife-to-be, from its head to the center of the ring, there to dance the ballet with the attendant ballerinas. Ideally, a sequence of eighty-eight negatives of circus photographs taken at the 1942 opening of the new elephant ballet at Madison Square Garden, undated and unproofed as yet in the Evans archives at The Metropolitan Museum of Art, may prove to be Evans's follow-up to his Florida sequence. It is also well to remember how readily European artists and performers could adapt themselves to American possibilities. Although Balanchine and Stravinsky had earlier collaborated on such a classic and serious ballet as "Apollo," Balanchine had acquired Broadway status as a choreographer for his ballet numbers "Slaughter on

Tenth Avenue" and " La Princesse Zenobia Ballet" in the 1936 Rodgers and Hart musical *On Your Toes* (in which the dancer was his first wife, Tamara Geva). And Stravinsky, in Hollywood, had also tried his hand, without success, at writing scores for such films as *Jane Eyre* and *The Song of Bernadette*: "They want my name, not my music," Stravinsky complained.

Both artists were part of the emigration of artists, writers, architects, musicians, that having begun as a trickle in the early thirties around the time of Hitler's ascent to power, became a mainstream when the European war broke out. The sheer amount of individual talent that converged upon America in the succeeding years was imposing. Architects like Gropius and Mies van der Rohe, designers like Moholy Nagy and Herbert Bayer — refugees from the Bauhaus in its Weimar, Dessau, and Berlin phases — established themselves in Cambridge and Chicago and New York. In 1942, in New York, three exhibitions marked the undeniable presence of the European vanguard and its merger with vanguard American artists of the time. In March, the Pierre Matisse Gallery mounted an "Artists in Exile" exhibition, which included fourteen artists of whom most had arrived after the fall of France. An historic photograph taken at the gallery showed the radicals properly attired in business suits and ties: Matta, Ossip Zadkine, Yves Tanguy, Max Ernst, Marc Chagall, Fernand Léger, André Breton, Piet Mondrian, André Masson, Amédée Ozenfant, Jacques Lipchitz, Pavel Tchelitchew, Kurt Seligmann, Eugene Berman — a roll call of the different divisions of European modernism. Little wonder that Alfred Barr acknowledged that "New York during the war supplanted occupied Paris as the art center of the Western world." In October of that same year, at 451 Madison Avenue, Breton and Marcel Duchamp, the latter having returned that midsummer, mounted an exhibition, "First Papers of Surrealism," copping the title from the "first papers" required by immigrants to the United States. Breton hung the show, which added more names to the earlier Matisse list, including works by Duchamp, Hans Arp, Wilfredo Lam, Hans Bellmer, Alberto Giacometti. Frida Kahlo, Paul Klee, René Magritte, Juan Miró, and Henry Moore. A few young Americans, Robert Motherwell, William Baziotes, and the sculptor David Hare, joined the cast. Another novel feature was Duchamp's device of stringing the works of art together with twine until the entire installation looked like the interior of a continuous spider web. That same month, Peggy Guggenheim (who, soon after Pearl Harbor, had married Max Ernst, claiming, "I did not want to live in sin with an enemy alien") opened her Art of This Century Gallery. The installation for the surrealist gallery, designed by architect Frederick Kiesler, had the appearance of a dark tunnel with flashing lights, the paintings projecting from the walls on triangular supports and the sculptures, like Giacommeti's *Woman with Her Throat Cut*, mounted on overturned chair pedestals. In the abstract and cubist gallery, the paintings were hung on strings as if floating in space. As Guggenheim conceded: "If the pictures suffered from the fact that their setting was too spectacular and took away people's attention from them, it was at least a marvelous decor and created a terrific stir." The New York press had a heyday and the gallery was crowded daily.

Not all surrealists had chosen to take part in the surrealist encampment in New York. In Paris, Man Ray, at first convinced there would be no war, then lulled by the phony war of early 1940, managed to escape France in August by way of Biarritz, where he met his fellow American the composer Virgil Thomson. The two proceeded on to Lisbon, where they boarded the *Excambion*, a ship of the American Export Line. On the crowded voyage home, accompanied by Salvador Dali and his wife and the celebrated French film director René Clair and his wife, the little company slept on mattresses in the ship's library. Once established in New York, Thomson, with some reluctance, accepted the post of chief music critic for the *New York Herald Tribune*, a position he held with distinction and no little controversy as the country's most trenchant and knowledgeable critic. Man Ray, believing that "New York was twenty years behind Paris in its appreciation of contemporary art, and California was twenty years behind New York," nevertheless decided on California, even though he had, for the time being, given up photography in pursuit of art. René Clair, too, decided upon Hollywood, where he produced four films during his exile. The German film director Hans Richter, however, having arrived in the States in 1942, opted for New York, where he became the director of the Film Institute of City College, producing the film *Dreams That Money Can Buy*, with "dream" episodes by Léger, Man Ray, Duchamp, Ernst, and Alexander Calder. Man Ray's concession to his photographic past was a story titled "Ruth Roses and Revolvers," which had appeared in Charles Henri Ford's surrealist magazine *View*. Man Ray sent it as it had appeared in print to be "enacted" by the director. The filmed version was accompanied by a score by Darius Milhaud, another emigré composer then established at Mills College in Oakland, California.

* * *

"This is the only paper I see to write on. It takes pencil better than pen. I miss you and I am waiting for a phone call, you crook to get through to you, and I am sleepy and you are still not in." So Evans wrote Jane from Chevy Chase on one of his periodic visits to the Washington area during the first year or two of America's involvement in the war. In hopes of some kind of a war job, he sometimes stayed with the Brewers at Chevy Chase until his irritation with his sister, Jane, and his mother got the better of him, or at a hotel in Washington when he could get a room in the abnormally crowded capital. His letters give a sense of the buzz of the capital. In an April 1942 letter, written "Monday evening" from the Brewers' new house at 416 Cumberland Avenue, he claimed the house was "delightful and awful. Seems to be just as crowded and ill planned as all their other houses and I am sleeping on a cot in a small downstairs library." He added: "I can't see where you would have slept at all if you had come. What a world!" The next day he fared better, having moved to the Mayflower Hotel in Washington: "I am as you see in a grand hotel, atmosphere more suited to my tastes and needs. Here there are no children, only grown up crooks, spies and congressmen and cocottes."

In another Washington letter written five months later in early September, Evans was clearly dissatisfied with the Washington scene and his attempts to find useful work by way of his various connections there. (Jane was visiting the Voorheeses in Old Lyme, where as her part of the war effort she had planted a thriving victory garden, a source of fresh vegetables when she returned to New York.) Evans wrote her: "Must get out of here and return to civilized life. This is awful. Yesterday I saw people. Russell Hitchcock, Tom Mabry, Ben Shahn, Eddie Cahill: some by chance, some by design, and the head is full of messes of facts, hints, and information." There was a possibility he might get some poster work from the graphic arts department in one of the agencies or "become a petty officer in the Navy darkroom here. Etc., etc." He was invited to a party "to talk to more people about many things to do. Cahill who of course doesn't like me said nothing about that [Harry] Hopkins business. I'll try to see H. but don't want to wait around here very long. Want to rejoin the wife to put it mildly. This is no place for me."

Shahn, he reported, had invited him to have dinner at his house with "guess who Roy Stryker . . . Well I suppose I can learn something. It was sprung in such a way I couldn't very well get out of it — the next would be Peter Sekaer. Ach, I cannot write very well in this house at the moment. May as well stop and go down town and continue the rounds. I'm going to try to leave on some train on Saturday; but Steichen is coming back Monday. He's away now. I'm told I ought to see him. Ach. Hopkins seems more important to me, so we'll see. If he makes a date for next week that'll probably keep me drearily stomping around. Bah. Love, love." He sent hellos to Clark and Billie.

* * *

At an unexpected, even extraordinary, moment in New York's cultural history, Walker and Jane found themselves in the midst of things. Their connection with the French emigré artists was no further away than the Harvey apartment, two floors above, where they met the painter Ossip Zadkine and the sculptor Jacques Lipchitz. There, too, they were introduced to Georges Duthuit, critic and son-in-law of Henri Matisse, who was lecturing in the United States. (Married to Marguerite Matisse, who had remained behind in Paris, Duthuit was also the lover of Annie Harvey, though, discreetly, he lived elsewhere in Manhattan.) It was through Duthuit, Jane thinks, that they met André Breton, who early on paid a visit to Walker's York Avenue studio and seemed favorably impressed by his photographs, though Jane was not present and Walker characteristically said little about the visit. Jane also remembered that sometime before the end of the war she met Marc and Mme. Chagall at the Harveys' apartment. It happened one evening — she had been invited for after-dinner coffee on the terrace — and in the darkening twilight Dorothy Harvey inadvertently spilled scalding hot coffee in Chagall's lap. Dorothy rushed to wipe it up with a napkin, much to the alarm of Mme. Chagall, disturbed by the thought of an American hostess fussing about in privileged parts. On

461

another occasion, at some function at Peggy Guggenheim's, she and Evans were introduced to the white-haired, blue-eyed Max Ernst, but the meeting was little more than a polite handshake. None of these social occasions was earth-shaking, but they floated above a deeper trend. During the decade and more of the rise and fall of the Third Reich, according to one source, some 717 artists and 380 architects made the exodus to America. The presence of such luminaries in the United States, and the tradition of intellectual and esthetic authority they brought with them, had a profound effect on further developments of vanguard art and art criticism in America. Its most effective task, perhaps, was in breaking down the last traces of parochialism in the American cultural scene.

Though hardly a radical, Evans also had somehow drifted into the liberal and left-wing literary stream by way of his association with the writers of the *Partisan Review*. Throughout the decade of the forties the *Partisan Review* remained the most intellectual literary magazine of the period and perhaps the strongest anti-Stalinist voice in the American cultural establishment. In its heyday, it published the most distinguished list of writers, critics, and poets of the time: Saul Bellow, Paul Bowles, George Orwell, André Malraux, Stephen Spender, Hannah Arendt, Clement Greenberg, Elizabeth Bishop, Delmore Schwartz, Wallace Stevens, W. H. Auden. Through one connection or another, Evans and Jane became familiar with a number of its writers, among them Lionel and Diana Trilling, Mary McCarthy and her husband at the time, Edmund Wilson, who, if not a frequent contributor, thought highly of the magazine. Evans and Jane continued to have occasional dinners out with Rahv and his wife, Nathalie, now back from Chicago, though Jane found these occasions awkward. Rahv's furtive hand would slip under the table and down her leg while Nathalie and Walker sat opposite them.

Evans must have been pleased by the attention Lionel Trilling had paid him in his belated review of *Let Us Now Praise Famous Men* in the winter 1942 issue of the *Kenyon Review*. At some point in their long-term relationship with the Trillings, Evans, at Diana's urging, had made a series of portrait photographs of Lionel for a book jacket illustration. (It might have been for his 1943 study of E. M. Forster or as late as his more famous volume *The Liberal Imagination*.) That they were taken in one of Evans's studios is evidenced by the tripod for his camera that appears in many of the shots. That they were probably taken in the fall or winter months seems likely, given that in several of the photographs Trilling is bundled up in an overcoat. For some reason the photographs were never used. Jane thinks that Diana did not like them. There is, however, another sequence of photographs of both Diana and Lionel Trilling, with his shadowed profile behind the steering wheel in the darkened interior of an automobile as Diana leans in at the opened window as if discussing some last-minute business or errand. In the background is a parklike setting, seemingly in summer. As photographs, they catch an offhand moment of domesticity that is far more intriguing than the routine studio pictures of Trilling alone. Evans, perhaps, found them far more interesting as a couple.

Another friend during these years was Bernard Haggin, whom Evans introduced to Jane. Haggin was the brilliant, testy music critic who, having earlier written for *Hound & Horn*, was now the critic for the *New Republic*. His friendship was much appreciated since he regularly invited Evans and Jane to music and dance concerts in New York. If Evans was feeling worried or harassed, Haggin offered to get him to the ballet "for some distraction" or sent him and Jane tickets to the concert of the Budapest String Quartet at the YMHA. He invited them to his uptown apartment near Columbia University to hear his recordings of Rossini overtures; they, in turn, invited him to dinners at their Ninety-second Street apartment and introduced him to friends like Peggy and Wilder Hobson. Haggin's doggedness — and Evans's dilatoriness — in the relationship are revealed in the matter of the portrait photographs Evans made in 1942 for the dust jacket of Haggin's book, *Music on Records*, published in 1943. It was one of Evans's best formal portraits, showing the critic in an alert, intent, and seemingly equable mood. Haggin valued the portrait photograph. Unfortunately it had come back from the publisher scratched and spotted. Haggin's effort to get another print, for which he offered to pay, or even to retrieve the damaged original that he had brought to Evans for remounting, became a two-year ordeal that would become familiar to other friends of Evans's who made the mistake of returning a print if Evans asked for it. Haggin's repeated requests took the form of a reminder ("Your saying the other night that you were going to make a print of your Hart Crane photograph and that it was a simple matter to do it gives me the courage to remind you of the Haggin folder that you placed on your work-table last November. . . . They are among my most highly prized possessions; and I have been concerned about them."); an apology ("I'm not pressing you about my photographs; I'm merely preventing you from forgetting about them under pressure from other matters."); or a postscript with a gentle warning ("I shall continue to keep you from forgetting."). While it is not clear whether Evans finally delivered the originals from the "Haggin folder" or replaced them, the friendship continued on for some years. It was perhaps through Haggin that Evans made the acquaintance of the young photographer Rudy Burkhardt and the noted dance critic Edwin Denby, both of whom were protégés of Haggin. Jane recalls that Burkhardt only once turned up at their apartment on some matter of business, but suspects that no relationship developed there, largely because Evans was chary about relating to other photographers. But still, it was typical of the war years that writers and artists knew or knew of one another even if only on the basis of passing contacts. Sometimes those connections bore fruit and promoted the gospel of modernism in other ways. Virgil Thomson, for instance, ever alert to the value of literate criticism, hired Haggin to write a guest column on radio music and Denby to contribute columns on ballet for the *New York Herald Tribune*.

Despite the war — but more likely because of it — these were times when friends gathered together for talk. Jim Agee and his future wife, Mia, visited with them frequently. Jane, however, sensed that Mia did not particularly like Walker, that she disliked his fussiness and Eastern seaboard snobbishness. Another possibility, Jane felt, was that Mia was jealous of the relationship between Walker and her husband. But Jane and Agee got along as well as ever; like fellow conspirators, they shared their amusement at certain aspects of Evans's character: "Jim Agee and I used to laugh together saying 'Walker's becoming his mother.'" Mia and Agee crop up often in Evans's letters to Jane when she was up in Lyme tending to her victory garden. On June 18, 1942, for instance, he reported: "The evening you left I had dinner with Jim and Mia but Jim had to read all the time so I beat Mia at checkers so that is the scarlet bachelor life in the city. It was awful to come home to empty bed. I slept on your side and blotted everything out with intensive reading of War & Peace." It was clear that he was lonely: "You were lovely in your blue dress at the station and I understand OK about the flurry of getting on train and impossibility of such farewells." In a final note he added: "Do indeed miss you like hell and we will have a fine time when you get back. W." The following day he was in a more jovial mood:

Ach. I am sitting in our little kitchenette with the gently escaping gas moving the curls on the back of my neck and the rats making amiable gestures in the doorway to our little drawing room. It is Friday the fish day and there are no fish as usual. I have eaten your evening slippers (for the duration). Outside the window gay children are being run over in the streets, glad to give their lives to entertain me, for I have come to sit here in expectation of a phone call from the government. It doesn't come. Last night I stayed with Jim and Mia, not wanting to face another empty-bed-blues in our love nest. First though I took the precaution of dining with Peggy and Wilder off thick tenderloin and we drank to your health.

He reported on the incidents of his domestic life without her. He was trying to sell his movie camera; he was dutifully watering the plants on their roof garden; Ben Shahn had shown up unexpectedly and "quite seriously" had admired her picture of the circus wagon. There were "ghosts all over the place." Having driven Harvey Breit to a Forty-ninth Street rooming house to get his suitcases, he had now "come back to the love nest to contemplate." In an ironic moment he pondered their situation: "How bored you must be without me looking in the mirrors at my clothes and grousing about the house. Me, I smell your absence as I sprinkle your perfume on the plants." Intimacies were hinted at: "Please have all pleasures you can think of with my image. . . . I put myself in your hands before you left if you know what I mean." He concluded: "I will now get on with my career and we'll be rich when you come back."

22

In the spring of 1943, Evans, now thirty-nine, found work at Time Incorporated. The opportunity came by way of Wilder Hobson, then assistant editor of the "back-of-the-book," which included books, art, cinema, music, and theater. At the time Hobson was covering for editor Whittaker Chambers, Henry Luce's protégé, who was on sabbatical (with pay) for medical reasons. Chambers was recuperating from what his doctor first suspected was an angina attack but was later diagnosed as a serious case of overwork and nervous exhaustion. Chambers, who had defected from the Communist party after the 1939 Nazi-Soviet nonaggression pact, was in the process of cooperating with government investigators but was obsessed, fearful of being killed by some Soviet agent in retaliation — a not unwarranted fear considering the pickax murder of Leon Trotsky in Mexico in 1940 and the more recent suspicious death of another defector, Russian agent Walter Krivitsky, a friend of Chambers's who had begun testifying before the House Un-American Activities Committee. Ironically, the fierce anti-Communist crusade Chambers was launching in his albeit anonymous book reviews and articles for *Time* would have made him a likely target for political attack. Chambers would strike up a friendship of sorts with Evans when he returned to the magazine in June, a few months after Evans had joined the staff.

At *Time* Evans, hired to cover cinema, must certainly have found the work congenial, considering his early and continuing interest in film, newsreels, and documentaries. It was an ideal situation, all things considered; his literary interests served him well in the new post. Jim Agee, though technically still writing movie reviews at *Time*, had also recently been hired to review films by the rival *Nation*, which had offices on Vesey Street in lower Manhattan. There, with greater freedom, unhampered by the anonymous, adjectival *Time* style, he gained a certain cult status. But he also faced competition from its staff of high-powered cultural critics: Diana Trilling, its fiction critic; Clement Greenberg, who covered art; Mary McCarthy, who wrote about theater; and Bernard Haggin, the magazine's regular music critic. Diana Trilling never wrote at the magazine's office — the books were sent to her apartment — which spared her the usual office politics. Nevertheless, at parties and casual meetings she was able to make her own sharp assessments of her fellow critics. Haggin she considered "an angry man; it took considerable patience to be friends with him." Like Evans and Jane, she and her husband Lionel were invited to Haggin's evenings of recorded music, very carefully planned concerts held in Haggin's apartment near Fort Tryon Park. The Trillings' long friendship with Haggin suffered a "premonitory threat" when Diana wrote a piece for the *Nation* on Caruso. It was made clear to her that while she might discuss music in Haggin's presence, it was a matter of trespass if she wrote about it in public print. The friendship with Haggin ended soon after the Trillings' son was born. Haggin, she claimed, "was not prepared to accept the competition for our attention," though the ostensible reason was that, since Haggin did not drink, she had been remiss for "providing liquor for our guests who drank but never having chocolates for him."

About Agee, Diana had been forewarned: ". . . although we sometimes spent an evening with him, we learned that it was dangerous to invite Agee to our apartment for a visit because he never went home." Under the influence of alcohol or in his exuberance about a subject, he stayed and stayed. "He seduced language, he made love to language and showered it with gifts, often unwisely. Drink never impeded his talk; liquor was its ally." She and Lionel preferred Evans: "He had a harder intelligence than Agee." She particularly liked him because he was the best dancer in their intellectual community. Fellow critic Clement Greenberg, writing about *Let Us Now Praise Famous Men*, was full of praise for Evans, but also had reservations about Agee. Greenberg thought him too talkative, too eager to discuss his activities. He considered him an "unrealized great writer." The admiration was double-edged: "He [Agee] had the ability to be sincere without being honest."

When both Evans and Agee worked at the *Time* offices on the fiftieth floor of the tower at 9 Rockefeller Center, it was a hive of activity among writers and editors, predominantly male, and the mostly female researchers. A recent newcomer to the staff, James Stern, an Englishman hired to cover the art scene, had a brisk remembrance of Agee:

Jim sitting in that bolt upright posture, head nevertheless bent in intense concentration, pencil — always pencil — careering back and forth across the page in that tiny, totally legible hand. And then one morning of seeing Walker crouched in equal concentration beside his friend in such a position that even a stranger's eye would recognize it at once as that of the pupil. Agee teaching Evans? What? A language known as Timese.

The work week stretched from Thursday to Monday evening, when the magazine went to press. It was a lively scene: along the long corridors the office doors were invitingly open for quick conversations among the staff who oftentimes lunched, four to six together, at pubs and restaurants, notably the nearby Maison de Winter and the Ristorante del Pezzo around the corner. Stern thought it a privilege to have been hired (at the suggestion of another staff member, his friend, the English novelist Nigel Dennis) not just for the money but also for the company of such writers as Dennis, Agee, and Evans; theater critic Louis Kronenberger; and music critic Winthrop Sargeant. Stern and his wife, Tania, became good friends of Walker and Jane, though he slyly described Walker as a "diffident dandy." He claimed that Walker's "initial interest in me derived from one particular Savile Row suit, which he so coveted that I promised to leave it to him in my will."

That the work at *Time* coincided with a cutback in his photographic output in these years was not altogether coincidental or happenstance.

Bernard Haggin, 1941

Gasoline rationing — the standard allowance was four gallons a week, for instance — curtailed his freedom of movement. Much of Evans's earlier photography had depended on his mobility, the long trips meandering through the countryside, the need to transport bulky equipment like his view camera and tripod. (As certain of his letters to Jane indicate, he was beginning to look for convenient spots in Old Lyme or Saybrook to put up his car, at least for the winter.) Now he found it just as convenient — perhaps even more convenient — to be at work writing. There were occasions, to be sure, early in the war years, when he took photographs for friends and acquaintances, like the summer photographs of the Fuller and Burden children and Cass Canfield, Jr., in Bedford and studio portraits of friends in their military uniforms, like a naval lieutenant, and other unidentified acquaintances. But generally during the two years Evans worked at *Time*, he cut back on his photographic work.

Despite his occasional grousing, he seems to have taken a deep and steady interest in his work at the magazine. Not long after his arrival, for instance, he sent Wilder Hobson the following memorandum: "I would readily accept Hobson's invitation to cuss Cinema if I had been doing it long enough to have many objections — as it is, not much." Yet he managed to produce a three-page note with suggestions that were general: "I'd like to see Cinema rather more loose and daring when it may be so with taste and in compliment to intelligence of readers. I believe surprise and excitement of manner need not cheapen tone." Other suggestions were particular.

Hollywood men now working in Government and Army: how they took up their jobs when making the change; what they wanted to do as well as what they are doing. Or: Axis is using films in South America for propaganda. Time letter from there suggests possibilities I would like to go into if facts are available, without much tie to news: what films: are they good; do they get around; how and by whom are they being fought or competed with. Suggest Cinema might be allowed to expand some in such a story on subject of propaganda films.

His early reviews were serious and perhaps cautious. He and Agee seemed to be engaged in friendly competition when they reviewed the same films, Evans in *Time* and Agee in the *Nation*. They agreed on the excellence of *Desert Victory*, a British documentary covering Montgomery's

1942 campaign against Rommel in North Africa. Evans thought it "the finest film of actual combat that has come out of this war." He praised the Hollywood-trained Scots director David MacDonald for the night battle on a desert stretch before El Alamein: first the sappers and then the bayonet-bearing infantrymen moving forward while artillery flashes split the night sky and then bombardment reaching a staggering crescendo. "Meant to be unbearable, it is that," Evans conceded. "By placement, timing and delivery, this is also the most intelligent passage in the picture." Unlike Agee, Evans commented on the technical aspects of the film: "the 200,000 exposed feet reduced into an order, flow, and sequence as correct as those of well written music." The narration, both in style and delivery, he considered "a model for non-fiction films." Agee's review covered many of the same points, though he seems to have sat through the 60-minute film twice. Agee, too, fastened on the barrage sequence, recalling: "The natural sound rises, in one scene, to a solid attempt to annihilate the audience which a friend of mine has properly compared with Beethoven. The second time I heard it, it was muted into a defeat of this intention." Agee advised the viewer: "I urge that by every means possible you require that it be given full blast. It is the first serious attempt to make an audience participate in the war. No audience should be spared it." The likelihood is that both men had seen the screening together. Jane suspects that that was probably the case. She remembers certainly that Walker and Agee discussed films frequently. She, however, never attended a screening with Walker; the theaters usually scheduled them in the mornings.

More instructive, perhaps, are the reviews that both wrote for *Mission to Moscow*, the Warner Brothers film, adapted from former Ambassador to Moscow Joseph E. Davies's memoir of the same title. In the film Davies was played by Walter Houston, his wife by "sweet-faced" Ann Harding. Evans was not impressed by the impersonations of such international figures as von Ribbentrop, Stalin, Litvinov, Bukarin, and the usual walk-ons merely listed as "flower girl," "1st young man," "2nd young woman," and "fat German." He was sardonic about the tributes awarded Davies at his farewell dinner ("You have done what no other Ambassador has done.") and such episodes as the "grand surprise interview with Stalin" and the ambassador's return to America "to stump the country in behalf of the truth about Russia." Cut into the Hollywood reenactments, Evans noted, were clips of "Soviet industrial life, army maneuvers, Red Square demonstrations, and factual films of World War II as it broke over Europe. The picture ends in a sudden tone of Biblical fervor conveyed to the screen by swelling music and illustrated by pasteboard silhouette dream-city." He made it clear he was not buying the propaganda. He also noted what was left out: "Missing is the important Soviet-U.S. debt question; omitted is all mention of Communism. But for many moviegoers the picture may collapse on a simpler account: that of being a bore for the money."

Though Agee started off his May 22 review in the *Nation* commending the effort as possibly "the first time that moving pictures have even flexed their muscles in a human crisis," his criticisms took precedence as well: "We can only suspect through rumor and internal inference, that the Stalinists here stole or were handed such a march that the film is almost describable as the first Soviet production to come from a major American studio." The makers of the film had produced, he claimed, "a great glad two-million-dollar bowl of canned borscht." But he had not altogether given up on his notion of the Soviet Union "as the one nation during the past decade which not only understood fascism but desired to destroy it, and which not only desired peace but had some ideas how it might be preserved." That pretty much discounted any problematic references to the German-Soviet nonaggression pact, the carving up of Poland, and later the invasion of Finland. Agee, however, did own up to the fact that the Stalinist purge trials posed certain difficulties for him: "About the trials I am not qualified to speak. . . . I am unable to trust the politicians of either camp or any other to supply me, the world in general, or even their closest associates with the truth." The latter statement may account for the fact that Diana Trilling, writing in her late memoir *The Beginning of the Journey*, comparing the two reviews of *Mission to Moscow*, claimed that "it was Evans who recognized its bias. Agee took refuge in his accustomed pure-mindedness from having to deal with the political message of the film."

Evans could be sly, as in his review of *Slightly Dangerous*, "a mildly loony comedy starring full-sailed Lana Turner and sandpapered Robert Young." In another reference to the full-breasted actress he described the dialogue as "laundered snow white for all possible audiences." He then noted: "But her management of a standard old-fashioned camisole more than avenges this modest attempt at censorship." The notable bit in the film was a steal by actor Alan Mowbray, "listed quite sufficiently as an 'English Gentleman,' dislocating the rest of the film by a monumental, effortless detachment towards Robert Young, his own surroundings, and the comedy at hand." On the other hand Evans fully appreciated *The Ox Bow Incident*, an unusual Western starring Henry Fonda, Dana Andrews, and Anthony Quinn, the climax of which was a brutal lynching. He praised "Walter Van Tillburg's excellent sagebrush yarn" except for its "occasional thoughtless detail," specifically the very obvious fake tree in the lynching scene. In the low-key rivalry he and Evans seemed to be engaged in, Agee at first stated he had missed the screening of the movie: "I regret having missed *The Ox Bow Incident* and for the moment can only pass on the word of trustworthy people that it is worth seeing. . . ." Three weeks later, when he did review it, he began his discussion with a teaser: "After a good deal of effort to get it on to paper and into feasible space, I'm afraid it is wiser to give up, saying only as follows. *Ox Bow* is one of the best and most interesting pictures I have seen for a long time and it disappointed me." His reasons: the "occasional flagrant mistakes, like the phonily gnarled lynching tree." He also disliked the film's "literariness and theatricality." He ended up, however, by admitting: "I find the same arteriosclerotic fault-of-attitude harming still better things — nearly all the good writing of this century, the films of Pudovkin and Pabst, and some of the music of Brahms."

One of the more unusual aspects of Agee's movie reviews was that he felt no qualms about giving his friend and rival reviewer a puff in the pages of the *Nation*. Reviewing an army orientation film, Frank Capra's *Prelude to War*, he found it verbose, with too many narrative overvoices, most of which sounded like the "flunked divinity students who are the normal cantors for our nonfiction films." He went on to complain that "too many of the shots devoted to demonstrating that John Q. Public's country is a horse of a different color, were indeed of another color, glossy and insipid; but I blame this less on the country than on the fact that few of us, conspicuously excepting Walker Evans, have yet learned how to make a camera show what a country it is."

Evans's days as a *Time* movie critic gave him a toehold in the sprawling Luce empire; from it he was able to take on occasional book reviews: an August 9 review of the reprint of Andreas Vesalius's sixteenth-century *De Humani Corporis Fabrica* (*The Fabric of the Human Body*), whose Jan van

Calcar illustrations of skeletons must have been as familiar and appreciated as the anatomical prints he had included in the early scrapbooks he and Hanns Skolle had assembled. The editors of the volume, he noted, failed to indicate that the reprinted woodcuts were "stylistic forerunners of surrealism; the fantastic effects produced by some of the exposed anatomies have their counterparts in the work of several modern painters, notably Giorgio de Chirico, Salvador Dali." It was a bit of oneupmanship he may have enjoyed. He also had occasion to review the combat photographs by Eliot Elisofon in an exhibition at the Museum of Modern Art. One of the more unusual of these excursions, taken on when James Stern moved on from reviewing art exhibitions to book reviewing, was a review of an exhibition of Georgia O'Keeffe's recent paintings at Stieglitz's gallery, An American Place. The show featured her New Mexican landscapes, including a series of bone paintings, which Evans declared "quasi mystical," singling out *Pelvis III* as a "swatch of blue sky seen through the gape of sun-baked bones." O'Keeffe, discussing the painting in her catalogue text, confessed that she was most interested "in the holes in the bones — what I saw through them — particularly the blue . . . that blue that will always be there as it is now after all man's destruction is finished." If Evans, a decade and a half after his first meeting with the artist, was still charmed by her and her work, he seems to have been miffed still by Stieglitz's early indifference on seeing his photographs. His review carried the taint of his first encounter with O'Keeffe's husband: "Dealer Stieglitz," he wrote, "also handles all O'Keeffe sales. . . . These are usually accompanied by a resounding clang of the cash register." It was surely as a little twist of the knife that he added: "The money must be accompanied by certain spiritual, emotional, and intellectual qualifications satisfactory to Dealer Stieglitz."

* * *

Evans's letters to Jane when she was away at Lyme suggest the routine of his life at *Time*. In an early letter, he adopted the magazine's review headings: "Cinema (Evans) *Walker Misses Jane* (92nd Street Productions)." His "Report" followed: "I went Friday to Wilder and Peggy to dinner. Bernard was there, but so was V. Agee. We ate chicken and drank whisky. Saturday I watered the plants, O.K. not bad chore. Dragged around this office with a slight hangover, ate dinner alone at the Tree G's but Jim Stern sat with me

Peggy Osborn,
New York,
1944

for a while." He had fallen asleep while reading *Mission to Moscow*, the next day he made a stab at writing about Tyrone Power, probably a review of *Crash Dive*, the film the actor made prior to his enlistment in the Marine Corps.

His letters were apt to be laced through with sexual innuendos: "Miss you like hell, have indescribable thought[s?] about private intimacies. Come home for demonstration." "No news, nothing happening except daily erections." "Nothing to report. I am merely writing for the sake of cluttering up the mail. I am sitting naked in the bedroom feeling rather good." Jane's absences were cause for other plaintive reports: "I miss you. Our beautiful home misses you. The hose on the living room floor misses you. We love you." "Write me and think about the same things I think one of which is we ought to be together this minute preferably in bed with all that love."

Evans kept her up to date on the current gossip: "Alma would let Jim have Joel the son up here if he will stop living with Mia. Crazy business." "So Wilder says come home with me and I went home with him and then we went to a cocktail party for the purpose of having martinis which tasted good and then Wilder said stay to dinner which I did but it wasn't very good and Wilder and Peggy got into a fight and Peggy said she'd marry me if I'd ask her." He listed casual invitations to the theater or dinner: "Am going to a theater opening with Margaret Marshall tonight. Am lonely while in the apartment." (Margaret Marshall was the editor of the "back-of-the-book" at the *Nation*.) "Bernard took me to the ballet, a good program you would have liked. Will tell about later. Don't forget to ask about putting car up there *if convenient*." "Will see Peggy [Osborn] Monday for dinner. It seems Noguchi and somehow Gorky have made her unhappy as if I cared do you?" He sent news of his work: "I am spending the afternoon working on a story about Winston Churchill as a painter, that is what art means around here. I may go to the McDonalds and I may not." *Time*'s efficient researchers may have dug up an interesting item in their Churchill researches. Evans had bought himself a pair of silk underpants: "You may not like them but they are silk and luxurious and Churchill wore pants like them. Cost no more than the usual." The McDonalds he mentioned were John McDonald, a staff writer at *Fortune* whom Evans had met earlier through the Trillings, and his wife, Dorothy Eisner, who was a painter. Like many of Evans's friends at Time Inc., McDonald was a political activist; he had been Trotsky's assistant in Mexico. The pair lived in New Jersey, where Evans was often invited. "Played tennis today twice at McDonald's. . . . felt this is my last Sunday, so I took myself out there for the night. There were some funny people there rather pretentious pompous sort but they left."

Despite the war, or because of it, the staff members at Time Inc. were a very social group, though Jane noticed that rather too much of the talk was about office matters. Occasionally she and Walker had lunch with

another Luce protégé, T. S. Matthews, the managing editor of *Time*. Matthews, tall, handsome, and patrician, educated at Princeton and Oxford, was married to a Proctor & Gamble heiress. Before coming to *Time*, he had worked at *The New Republic* with Edmund Wilson. Matthews's mission was to upgrade the style of writing in the magazine. A good *Time* story, in his view, was "clear without being flat, readable without being libellous, intelligent without being snobbish, critical without being cruel." He was an admirer of Agee's prose and when Agee's cover story on Ingrid Bergman, whose role as Maria in the movie version of Hemingway's *For Whom the Bell Tolls* was creating a stir, Matthews sent a memo to "All Writers & Researchers" announcing that while he would not claim it was a "model Time story" it definitely had a "quality we would all like to see more of in Time: humaneness."

It was at the Agees' that Jane and Evans did their socializing with Whittaker Chambers, though Chambers regularly avoided the more liberal members of the staff and was adept at purging members from the book review staff, including Weldon Kees and Saul Bellow, the latter lasting only one day on the job. He nonetheless had struck up a friendship with Agee which proved effective in damping down Agee's earlier sympathies for the Soviet Union. It was through Evans, however, that Jane learned about Chambers's oftentimes reclusive, sometimes paranoid, behavior. Walker told her that when he and Agee lunched with the former Communist agent, Chambers always made a point of sitting with his back to the wall in any restaurant they went to.

Among the other members of the New York intellectual community, Evans and Jane had once visited Edmund Wilson and Mary McCarthy when they were living near Gramercy Park at some point shortly after the birth of their son, Reuel. But it was not until Walker's first vacation at *Time*, perhaps in 1943 or 1944, that they had an unexpected meeting with the couple on Cape Cod. Whatever the year, she and Walker were staying at a pleasant inn at Wellfleet. Because of the gas shortage they had to rent bicycles on the Cape. One day, however, picking up a pack of cigarettes at a store, they met Mary McCarthy, who was glad to see someone from New York. In Wellfleet Mary would drive them to the local beach. They were also invited to dinner. Jane found Wilson a bit overpowering, however. When he asked what she was reading and she mentioned she was reading

John McDonald & Dorothy Eisner McDonald, c. 1945

through a set of Dickens, Wilson was very interested and they had a lively conversation. She was relieved to be able to talk about it, particularly since Walker, who "despised" Dickens, shuddered when the subject came up and made a point of talking to Mary.

Later that evening, back at the inn, she and Walker had had a big fight over the fact that she didn't seem to care whether she had a wedding ring. At their spur-of-the-moment marriage in 1941, Walker had picked up a wedding ring at the five-and-ten, but Jane had never pressed the issue of getting one after that, put off she thinks by the fact that the Napoleonic code as practiced in Louisiana made it seem that a wife was one more of her husband's possessions. Walker however had noticed that Mary McCarthy had a proper wedding ring and that was what had started the argument. It was a big fight, she remembered, and for a day or two a source of concerted unhappiness. After that it seemed to be a forgotten issue.

* * *

It had been some time since Evans had heard from Lincoln Kirstein but out of the blue he wrote Evans a comic and grumpy letter. Since their last contact, Kirstein, like Evans, had married in whirlwind fashion in 1941 (to Fidelma Cadmus, the sister of painter Paul Cadmus), and had traveled extensively in South America, sometimes in the company of Nelson Rockefeller, collecting Latin American paintings and sculpture for the collection of the Museum of Modern Art, resulting in its 1943 exhibition, for which Kirstein wrote the catalogue text. During that same period he toured South America with the American Ballet Caravan (combining his American Ballet Company with the Ballet Caravan); founded a new magazine, *Dance Index*; and published a novel, *For My Brother*, based on his experiences in Mexico. He also joined the Army and while stationed at Ford Belvoir, Virginia, arranged an exhibition and wrote the catalogue for "American Battle Painting: 1776-1918," shown at the National Gallery of Art in Washington, D.C.

Prior to being sent overseas, Kirstein wrote Evans at the offices at *Time*. The date, April 1, 1944, was of some significance. The intention was decidedly comic, but there was a legitimate grievance at the heart of it. The magazine had recently published a piece about the activities of the Mexican muralist David Alfaro Siqueiros, an artist with fervid Communist leanings, who was organizing a program of South American artists in the fight against fascism called "Art for Victory." Kirstein had met the artist in Chile and had also written an article about him which had appeared in the December 1943 issue of the *Magazine of Art*. In it, Kirstein had rather minimized the part that Siqueiros had played in an abortive attack on the home of Leon Trotsky in Coyocán, Mexico, following which — after the murder of Trotsky — Siqueiros was questioned and jailed, then released on grounds of insufficient evidence. The article in *Time* covered many of these details. It mentioned that Siqueiros was planning to visit the United States in hopes of enlisting American artists in his cause. The anonymous article had been written by a stringer in Mexico City. It was on the basis of that *Time* article that Kirstein wrote his old friend, "Walker Evans, Art or Something Editor," whom he addressed as "Dear Sir":

Knowing that you only work there, do the work and then some phoney rewrite man like TR Matthews [sic] or Wilder re-writes your re-written stuff and makes it sound like time sounds, I do not rise to protest but simply to state as you no doubt do not care to be reminded that the words you put in my mouth about Siqueiros being "the most important pictoric work since the cubist Revolution of 1911" is invented out of the whole cloth. Pictoric is a word like shit that I never use, and it hurts awful to be thought to use Timese.

Tell your lousy boss, whoever he is, or show him this, that there must be some law against lying about soldiers in uniform who are giving their all that Luce may wave. I protest. I PROTEST. Also the article is the usual miracle of inaccuracy. . . .

When Siqueiros is in NY, I personally will give you both a champagne dinner in Rockefeller Centre Plaza.

Also you are quite a little S.O.B on your own for not making a poor old soldier the two fotos he wanted in the service of his country while you lie and snipe in the easy etc. Don't bother now, I have some alright ones I got from Underwood and Underwood.

Consider this the end of a beautiful friendship.

* * *

It is not from the photographs Evans took of Jane — Jane in the New Orleans street in the early years when they first met, Jane in the Ninety-second Street apartment, Jane recovering from a cold, wearing the bedjacket her mother made for her — that we sense the man in love as much as the photographer documenting a moment in his domestic life, or, in one case, according to Jane herself, Evans simply was testing out a new brand of film. There is, it seems, an element of restraint, a chill; he is cautious about divulging his feelings in the process. It is difficult, for instance, to think of him as taking a series of intimate photographs such as those Stieglitz took of Georgia O'Keeffe in the early years of their relationship in 1918 and then at random through to the early 1930s. Stieglitz explores every aspect O'Keeffe's personality and her body. She is posed, clothed or partially nude and completely nude, in front of her large watercolor abstractions or in a thin embroidered kimono, her hair loosened and falling down to her shoulders. He is fascinated — and has probably posed her thus — with her hands unbuttoning the button of a jacket, or holding a corn cob, or caressing the chrome hub and spokes of a dark Ford V8 — arty, undoubtedly, but a conjunction that bears the imprint of the sexual and symbolic reduced to negotiable terms, as if the camera eye were a hand traveling down, appraising the rounded forms, the curves, the crevices. One has to look hard to find that concentration of the erotic in Evans in the photographs he took of his wives or the incidental women he might have loved or admired. Some years later (in his late fifties) he attempted a series of nude shots of a young thing he knew, sprawled like a skinny maja on a bed. She appears uncomfortable; the photographer catches her awkwardness. The photographs do not appear to be hurried at all — there is no way of telling from the photographs themselves — but there is a sense of an imminent threat of a policeman's knock on a motel door.

It is from his letters to Jane while he is away or she is away that one gets the hint of their intimacy, a touch of humor, or even the ribaldry of Evans in love. Even then the moments of intimacy are shuffled into the context of gossip and office news, the state of the apartment or the weather. In June 1944 he spends several days visiting with Jimmy and Tania Stern and then with Wilder Hobson and his wife, Verna, at a cottage on Fire

Island. He reports:

Dear Wifemate. There is a boat leaving in a half hour to get this letter on. Fire Island much more cut off than one imagined. No phones at all, no elec, and no heterosexual people (except us). How are you, wish I could call you up. I miss you. We do nothing, just what I like. [A] wonderful white beach . . . the sun, the thundering ocean. I am twice as brown already in one day.

The war inevitably intrudes, but only for the moment: "Today there was a practice air invasion of Sayville across the bay, parachutes plus all, extremely exciting to watch. Glider's too, plus smoke screens." He has had word of the death of a young pianist, a remarkably good one named Robert Pitney, a very good friend of Alice Morris's. It was at her apartment that he and Jane had heard him play. Bernard Haggin thought him remarkable as well: "I found it very sad to think about, I liked him. Alice plus Bernard will be horrified." His days are spent strolling along the beach: "I relax, do not even read. You hear the surf banging all the time. I'm in my element." He is still a gatherer: "I have a magnificent collection of shells, stones, driftwood, bottles from beaches. I made a sketch but not yet a painting." The letters continue: "We do nothing. I made a drawing. I have desires directed straight to you. Life is slow, airy, sunlit . . . "

In October, when Jane goes to Wisconsin to visit her parents in Fond du Lac, there is a moment of panic that he tries to turn comic:

All is forgiven. I just got scared. We will avoid that sort of thing after this by telegraphing automatically words of arrival on trips. But jeez this time I didn't know whether you'd been put off the train for to berth a wounded soldier or made off with like the newspapers say beautiful girls (that's you) are by lust-mad soldiers. (2 cases last week ended in murder) anyway the post office never pays good attention to postcards and I didn't get yours until Monday, almost a week after you left. At that, one was lost, never came at all. Let us communicate by air mail, at least, in future. Put card in env. If you must send cards.

The last remark, as Jane begins to learn, is a reminder of duties shirked. Evans expects her to write him when she travels, or to be at home when he calls.

"Kisses." Another letter begins, " I'm at the orifice. No news . . . I sleep fairly well, considering."

...And Fortune: The Road Taken

23

No single explanation accounts for Walker Evans's lengthy career at *Fortune* magazine. In September 1945, following his two-year stint at *Time*, he was offered a position at *Fortune*, which on the surface, at least, furthered his photographic career and served his literary interests as well. Ralph Delahaye Paine, another of Henry Luce's favored Yale graduates and, at Time Inc., managing editor of *Fortune*, was the apparent motivating force behind the offer. His choice was seconded by associate editor Katherine Hamill, a friend of Evans's on the staff. Hamill had been the principal researcher for one of the most famous and controversial articles to appear in *Fortune*, "Arms and the Men," an exposé of European arms manufacturers which had appeared in the March 1934 issue. She was also the author of an article on the Williamsburg and Harlem River housing projects in the August 1939 issue of *Harper's Bazaar*. It was illustrated with seven photographs by Evans and carried a portrait of him as well as a brief biographical sketch.

According to one source Luce was also pleased with the Evans appointment. After having founded the magazine in 1930, Luce expressed his dissatisfaction with business types as writers, even for a magazine promoting the values of big business: "Of necessity," he claimed, "we made the discovery that it is easier to turn poets into business journalists than to turn bookkeepers into writers." Consequently he staffed the magazine with poets like Archibald MacLeish and James Agee, and versatile, politically minded writers like Dwight Macdonald — a bolder approach for a high style capitalist magazine than he has been given credit for. Evans was the first staff photographer hired by the magazine, though Luce had earlier favored such free-lance photographers as Margaret Bourke-White and Erich Salomon for a number of special assignments. The magazine also carried articles that featured American artists such as Charles Burchfield and Jacob Lawrence.

From the beginning Evans was given a more or less free hand in proposing subjects, wrote his own copy for the portfolios he produced, and

"Chicago: A Camera Exploration," Fortune, *February, 1947. (This image unpublished.)*

485

eventually assigned other photographers, some of them friends, for a variety of staff articles. He was relieved of a good deal of the darkroom work, not often the best practice for an artist who wants to keep in touch with the medium, tedious though it might be, while continuing to learn from the process itself. His films were sent out to commercial laboratories to be developed and printed. For about the first decade or so Evans usually did his own layouts and was rather profligate about ordering photostats—"thirty of everything," as Roland Campbell, a member of the *Fortune* art department, recalled. (After 1954, Campbell worked regularly with Evans on the layouts.) And as Leslie K. Baier, who interviewed Evans's colleagues at the magazine in preparing her dissertation on Evans's years at *Fortune*, learned, Evans didn't trust the printers to follow his instructions. He had a bad habit, when specifying image size and cropping for the layouts, of "trimming his negatives to the desired image with scissors or glass and a blade." As a result, the edges didn't meet at strict right angles and created more problems for the printers than the one Evans sought to avoid.

From virtually the beginning of his career as staff photographer at *Fortune*, Evans was of two minds about his position there. He recognized both the opportunities and the security the job provided him. With a certain ebullience he once acknowledged, "At *Fortune*, they realize I'm a writer too." (He was not shy about what he considered the talents he brought to his job: "Why, if I know what I want," he boasted, "I can photograph it even from the back of a moving car. If it's there, it's there.") But in time he found reasons to complain, for instance, of "a certain satanic naivete in the very top editorial directions of Time Incorporated, perceptible only from below." He made a point of mentioning that "intelligent, gifted employees were expected to work hard and long hours under crushing pressure at many tasks no man with a mind could put his heart into." Despite the quibbling, he remained on the job for twenty-one years. It is of some significance that the two longest and best paid opportunities in his career were the three years he was employed by the federal government, working for the Farm Security Administration, and the twenty-three years he spent at Time Inc. Evans conceded that the Time Inc. post had its benefits: "I think it sort of kept me alive, kept my hand in. Really there was a duality there that was a little sad and a little embarrassing at its worst; and that is that I don't think they quite knew how to use me. There was some good will on their part, some on mine; some ill will too." In the end, he felt the magazine hadn't made the best use of his talents: ". . . they didn't really make what I would call really creative or intelligent use of me. I think they realize it more and more now. It's the fault of that kind of system of group journalism and the group mind." It is worth noting that in the remaining ten years of his marriage to Jane, while on the staff of *Fortune*, not once did Evans bring home a copy of the magazine.

Yet it would be a mistake to think of him as playing a walk-through role in a convenient long-term job. There is evidence of the time and effort he put into his contributions as a professional photographer as well as what he had to offer as a writer. In his early short stories and translations and in the texts he supplied for articles, reviews, and catalogues as well as the portfolios he contributed to *Fortune*, it was his habit to make preliminary notes and numerous revisions before final drafts were completed, even though, as in his work at Time Inc., he knew there would always be further editorial revisions. Over the years he was conscientious as well about the memoranda he submitted for *Time* and *Fortune* both. A case in point was the December 3, 1945 memorandum he sent suggesting photographic illustrations for a possible portfolio on the atomic bomb. Evans obviously counted on the efficient Time Inc. research staff to dig up material on various subjects. The atomic bomb had already been a cover story in the August 20, 1945 issue of *Time* and illustrated in *Life* as well. For *Time*, T. S. Matthews had assigned Agee to write one of the articles in the issue, an overview of the bombing of Hiroshima and Nagasaki, which Agee characterized as "an event so much more enormous that, relative to it, the war itself shrank to minor significance." It created something of a stir both publicly and among the Time Inc. staff. Agee, who had mixed feelings about the war to begin with, was appalled by the consequences of Hiroshima: "When the bomb split open the universe and revealed the prospect of the infinitely extraordinary," he wrote, "it also revealed the oldest, simplest, commonest, most neglected and most important of facts: that each man is eternally and above all else responsible for his own soul. . . ." Matthews regarded the piece as vindication of his faith in Agee and of the *Time* style as well: "When people tell me . . . that *Time* was always written in some form of pidgin English, I remember Agee — and this piece in particular."

Evans's memorandum, ostensibly for *Fortune*, covered the pictorial possibilities — images drawn from scientific documents, records, and texts. The coverage of the event for *Fortune* might have seemed something of an anticlimax at Time Inc., but Evans launched into the subject hopefully: "Preliminary research reveals plenty of material for an arresting portfolio on the bomb," he wrote. "It also reveals that photographs I shall make should be supplemented with existing pictures dealing with nuclear physics as well as the bomb project themselves. Example — possibly the lead picture — the astounding, beautiful, (if familiar) Army still photograph of the 40,000 ft. cloud which arose at Nagasaki." Evans was nothing if not alert to the rivalry among the various sister publications at Time Inc. One of his problems was to come up with visual material not used before. He carefully pointed out: "The finest Nagasaki cloud photo I find to be one not used in LIFE domestic issues." He also suggested other "exciting" and "mysterious" possibilities: "1) laboratory microphotographs of atom scintillation, 2) flashes made on fluorescent screens when struck by flying atomic particles, 3) streaks across photo plates marking paths of atoms." In his memorandum, there was undeniably an element of salesmanship, the talents of the pitchman customary to the job. But even so, he had serious points to make: "The portfolio will make scientific and historical sense without including any 'dull but important' pictures. Emphasis throughout will be on quality and interest of each picture." Evans's preliminary list of the portfolio illustrations indicates his alert attention to specific possibilities:

The Nagasaki cloud column.

The corona of the sun (an incandescence maintained by an atomic energy process).

An atom smasher.

Uranium

Einstein's famous "mass energy equation, $E = mc^2$," written in chalk on a black ground.

Oak Ridge, Tenn.: selected scenes and objects at the plant.

Los Alamos, N.M.

the laboratory—"probably the best-equipped physics lab in the world" (Smyth)

Also the remains of the steel tower from which first bomb was detonated, also precise close-up detail of the seared ground in the crater.

Also the old ranch house, scene of first assembly of first bomb.

In the planning stage, at least, he was expected to travel, supplementing the documentary material with photographs of his own. He mentions a pending trip to "cover Oak Ridge, Tenn. and Los Alamos, N.M." But there is no record that he made such a trip. It is clear that in putting together his memorandum he had at least looked over two or three relevant scientific texts, and that he was intrigued by certain visual possibilities: "a careful study of water (hydrogen), cheapest substance on earth, which may become a source of atomic energy or, end with one of the strange, abstract combinations of streaks left on photographic plates by paths of atoms." The last item, one that he had suggested earlier, he noted, came from the Smyth Report, *Atomic Energy for Military Purposes*, where it was described as the "closest approach that can be made to 'seeing' an atom." If nothing else, work at *Fortune* was an education about the world of business and the new technology that the war had necessitated. At the end of World War II, then, having elected to put his talents to work as a photographer in the service of American journalism, Evans made a choice that had consequences he may or may not have thought through. Particularly since he stayed so long on the job, it had particular critical consequences, promoting the view that his most important work was behind him with the "American Photographs" exhibition and the publication of *Let Us Now Praise Famous Men*. At *Fortune* he attended staff meetings where he made suggestions for upcoming theme issues. For some articles he supplied only the photographs; for others that he proposed he wrote both the text and supplied the illustrations.

The two earliest articles Evans illustrated in his new post at *Fortune* would be a misleading index of what his career at the magazine would be. The first was "The Small Shop," which appeared in the November 1945 issue. As the lead indicated, "It is the philosophy and the pleasure of Mr. and Mrs. Phelps, craftsmen of leather, of New York City. The profits, moreover, are comfortable." The article covered four pages with one color illustration and four black and whites. A second article, "The Boom in Ballet," in the December issue, acknowledged the surge of interest in ballet in America, due in part to the promotional skills of his friend Lincoln

*Labor
Anonymous,
Detroit, 1946*

Kirstein. But, once again, if ballet was viewed as a marketable commodity it was not the full-fledged business opportunity one might expect in a business magazine of the period. Evans photographed the warm up for Jerome Robbins's ballet *Fancy Free* and the Metropolitan Opera's rehearsal of *Giselle* including photographs of Alicia Markova. Both series of photographs were not terribly striking. However, his record of the graffiti backstage underscores his love for the vernacular. Evans apparently supplemented these with a sequence of rather dour portraits of Lincoln Kirstein, just returned from his military service overseas, now sitting in his office at the School of American Ballet.

The major portfolios Evans produced in 1946 during his first stint at *Fortune* were more substantial, notably "Homes of Americans — Portfolio," a ten-page spread with a text by Wilder Hobson, now on the editorial board of *Fortune*, which appeared in April 1946. Evans selected the photographs. It was, in effect, something he could feel comfortable with, a reprise of his Farm Security Administration days. He chose FSA photographs by Russell Lee, Jack Delano, Jack Vachon, Arthur Rothstein, and Marion Post

Wolcott, thirty-three photographs in all, including seven of his own black-and-whites. Among them he included a photograph of the Burroughs farmhouse. The significance of the piece was that it was in a vein — how Americans live, from the meanest working-class homesteads to the swank interiors of the homes of artist and writer friends — that Evans would mine throughout his career. Two months later, in the baseball season (he and Jane were fans of the New York Giants and attended the games with some regularity), Evans provided in the July issue seven black-and-white illustrations for "The Yankees. The player's the thing, as thousands cheer, but it takes brains to make even a winning club pay a profit."

In the summer of 1946, according to the Time Inc.'s in-house publication "FYI," Evans headed west in his car "on a felicitous mission to follow, on behalf of *Fortune*, where his sharp eye led him." Away from home and office on this jaunt, he gathered material for two of the signature articles he produced for *Fortune*, "Labor Anonymous," scheduled for the November 1946 issue on labor in the United States, and "Chicago: A Camera Exploration," in the February 1947 issue devoted to Chicago and

Pittsburgh. It was quite probably one of the virtues of Evans's approach to his *Fortune* assignments that he covered them without preconceived ideas, content to explore the territory — as he emphasized in the Chicago title. From Pittsburgh on July 28, he sent a first batch of films asking that they be developed and contact prints made to be sent on to the Chicago office of *Fortune* marked "Hold for Arrival." In Detroit by August 3, he sent off a second batch, presumably the "Labor Anonymous" photographs.

The Detroit feature in its way was an extension of Evans's subway series, but he captured the figures in action — an exercise in mobility that he did not often use in his usually more static shots. Workers are shown striding along a street from a fixed vantage point, only a few of whom stare back at the offending photographer. The backdrop appears to be a wooden wall of the type built around a construction site. Unlike the subway series there are no telltale distractions and only a few clues, such as clothing, that reveal style or time of the year. Otherwise he presents Everyman off to work. The mobility captured in these photographs perhaps offers an interesting clue. The figure in action was the province of Henri Cartier-Bresson, who arrived in New York at the beginning of a cross-country tour. In 1946 and 1947, Cartier-Bresson would photograph the American scene and such noted American celebrities as William Faulkner in Oxford, Mississippi; Truman Capote in New Orleans; Saul Steinberg in Vermont; a young black woman in a flowered hat on Easter Sunday in Harlem; an elderly woman in Cape Cod on the Fourth of July wearing the American flag draped from her neck because her flag pole had broken; the beaches of California; a rainy day street scene in Chicago — venues that had been or soon would become territories that Evans made his own as well. Given Cartier-Bresson's friendship with Helen Levitt, who accompanied him on some of his New York jaunts, it seems unlikely that Evans was totally unaware of his rival's presence in the country as he scouted the American scene. Or that, conversely, Cartier-Bresson might not have been alerted to the possibilities before him after seeing, say, Evans's photograph of a black woman shopper on a Chicago street wearing a fancy hat in his *Fortune* portfolio.

Evans may well have written the brief text for "Labor Anonymous," no more than a page-and-a-half in length in the edited version. This seems to have been wired to him for approval at the North Michigan Avenue offices of Time Inc. on September 12, 1946, just as the November issue was going

Women Shoppers, Randolph Street, Chicago, 1946

to press:

The American worker, as he passes here, [usually] unaware of Walker Evans' camera, is a decidedly various fellow. His blood flows from many sources. His features tend now toward the peasant and now toward the patrician. His hat is sometimes a hat and sometime he has moulded it into a sort of defiant signature. It is this diversity, perhaps, which makes him, in the mass, the most resourceful and versatile body of labor in the world. If the war proved anything, it demonstrated that American labor can learn new operations with extraordinary rapidity and speedily carry them to the highest pitch of productive efficiency.

Though it may often lack the craftsmanly traditions of the older worlds, American labor's wide spectrum of temperaments rises to meet almost any challenge: in labor as in investment portfolios, diversification pays off. There is another thing to be noted about these street portraits. Here are none of those worn, lustreless, desolated faces we have seen so frequently in recent photographs of the exhausted masses of Europe. Most of the men on these pages would seem to have a solid degree of self-possession. By the grace of providence and the efforts of millions including themselves, they are citizens of a victorious and powerful nation, and they appear to have preserved a sense of themselves as individuals. When editorialists lump them as "labor," these laborers can no doubt laugh that off.

The two-page article carried eleven black-and-white photographs. (At the time, he was using his Rolleiflex, the 2¼ x 2¼ prints ideal for the concise format of a two-page spread, the scowling man with the floppy hat and bakery box noted in the text, appropriately merging word and picture.)

Evans's Chicago exploration was one of the most considerable and colorful of his efforts at *Fortune* to date. His easy familiarity with the city was obviously an asset, and the photographs he took tended toward the unusual, what he called the sights "that meet a leisured and untethered

eye." He leaned heavily on the city's history — especially the Chicago World's Columbian Exposition of 1893, for a lengthy quote from Henry Adams, and on the site of its Century of Progress Exposition of 1933 — for his photographs of what was now in part a dump "strewn with assorted relics of the big show," where he photographed its huge marble sculptures left standing in the weeds, noting that as you approach at dusk "rats smartly abandon their little businesses." His coverage was apparently meant to be a series of little perversities; a photograph of a makeshift peanut stand made from a baby carriage appeared on page 119, captioned *Sunday in an Alley*. And, if one is to believe what he claimed in a much later interview, his shots of heavy-duty women shoppers were meant to be "rather anti-feminist pictures. Unappetizing women going by with materialism in their minds and their arms full of packages."

*   *   *

Despite his affiliation with the Luce empire, Evans was receiving favorable attention in important quarters, notably in Clement Greenberg's columns in the *Nation*. Reviewing the 1944 exhibition "Art in Progress" at the Museum of Modern Art, Greenberg, the country's most demanding art critic, took issue with one aspect of the photographic portion of the show: "I found nothing to quarrel with in the photography section except that Ansel Adams is given an undeserved amount of space, while only nine of Walker Evans's prints are shown. Evans is certainly our greatest living photographer after Stieglitz." Two years later, covering an exhibition of Edward Weston's photographs at the Modern, Greenberg suggested that "Weston's failure is a failure to select." He went on to assert:

Sunday in an Alley, Chicago, 1946

If one wants to see modern photography at its best let him look at the work of Walker Evans, whose photographs have not one-half the physical finish of Weston's. Evans is an artist above all because of his original grasp of the anecdote. He knows modern painting as well as Weston does, but he also knows modern literature. And in more than one way photography is closer today to literature than it is to the other graphic arts. (It would be illuminating, perhaps to draw a parallel between photography and prose in their respective historical and aesthetic relations to painting and poetry.) The final moral is: let photography be

495

"literary."

It was still a time when reputations in American art could be established by such incremental notices.

II

In mid-August 1947, the *Fortune* article "One Newspaper Town," about Paducah, Kentucky, was on the stands when Evans took off on a cross-country trip to California. His photographs for the Paducah article constituted another of his Main Street investigations: shots of the commercial quarter of the city, views of downtown, random women shoppers, storefronts, and some streets as eerily silent as Sunday mornings. There was also a sequence of views of a paddleboat and waiting figures on the bank of the Ohio River.

His 1947 trip west seems to have been initiated by John Becker, his former New York gallery dealer, now living in California. Becker had recommended him to give lessons in photography to Florence Homolka, wife of character actor Oscar Homolka. From Chicago on August 17 he wrote Jane about a serious mishap: "My girl, I seem to have forgotten everything: the September rent, my jewel box with cufflinks, money for you, those films," all of which suggested he was ill-prepared for his takeoff. Chicago was so hot that "this morning I changed into bathing trunks in the station men's room and under overcoat took a taxi to the Oak St. beach, had a wonderful swim." Since he hadn't money enough in his bank account to pay the $34.50 rent check for September, he asked Jane to make out a check for it when it came due: "I have to pay for my room as soon as I arrive and may not collect from my pupil immediately."

On Sunday evening from aboard "The Chief" on the Santa Fé line he wrote her again: "My girl, (section 2); the 'Chief' is indeed a triumph of something — mechanical anyway. But the *noise!* the *people!*" At the moment, he noted, the train was "tooling across Missouri." It was a beautiful clear hot day and he was waiting for a seat in the diner. Back from dinner, he alerted her to the fringe benefits of the journalist profession, courtesy of the Santa Fé railroad: "I ordered a magnificent steak and when I called for the check was told it was compliments of the assistant to the vice president of the railroad." Jane was not to do anything about the left-behind films until he tried in Los Angeles. He thought, too, that he could probably pick up a pair of cufflinks there that would be "wearable." There were no interesting women aboard the whole blasted stainless-steel train and because it was Sunday he couldn't even buy a drink. Luckily he had his flask handy. "A man?"—the question mark was relevant—"tried to pick me up. My God," he wrote her, "there are Hollywoodist moviest people aboard."

The next day he was speeding through Colorado to Gallup, New Mexico: "Well Gee Zuss: what a landscape . . . Really the god damnedest thing you ever saw." He had thought of retiring in La Junta, Colorado, but now had changed his mind: "I propose to come out to New Mexico in car — not only for the scenery but what they say is true: it makes you feel good. The air. The light is of course unbelievably beautiful." He was not a fan of the scenic or the picturesque: "The Indians are pretty extraordinary too," he wrote. "They sleep, as in a *New Yorker* cartoon. Head between knees under big hats." It was the fantastic red rock formations against turquoise skies with pure white floating clouds that got to him: "Holy Cats." (For all Evans's huff about the spuriousness of Stieglitz's famous cloud studies, it is clear that he had made a few cloud photographs of his own when passing through New Mexico.) The only place he hadn't liked was Albuquerque "which it's got a main street too big & modern and just like Fond du Lac, Paducah, Terre Haute and all the rest." He had spent most of the day "at the open door between coaches, you know, my favorite railroading stand. This time I tried snapping pictures at the sights." He had also done four sketches representing the four states of Illinois, Missouri, Colorado, and Arizona. Unfortunately the train was "infested" with tourists: "Does anybody know why tourists are so repulsive?" Wrapping up the newsy letter, he wrote: "Tune in again: what will happen to Walker in Hollywood? Will he get the money? Will he beat the rap?"

He was just as lively when he reached the coast. From Olympic Boulevard in Beverly Hills, he wrote Jane: "Well I swan and great Scott. California is inexbelievable to the extreme. Shall I belate my adventures?" No one had met him at the station and he had taxied to the suite of rooms Florence Homolka had reserved for him. "The landlady announced that 'my friend' had called from the station saying she'd missed me." Florence, however, was on her way: "Out came fat, distraught Florence. On top of missing me she'd been copped for speeding and hadn't had any breakfast so she wasn't in exactly precisely good shape." Evans therefore hadn't the heart to mention that on the train he had picked up a newspaper and read that Oscar Homolka was suing his ex-wife "for the asserted loss of much of his personal property, including a liquor supply." He was demanding $22,442 in damages. "Well I always say other crimes other climes," Evans wrote. "So I gave her a pull at my platinum flask and away we went for her breakfast." He had, he said, more or less expected what followed: "beside a swimming pool dotted with sportcoated movie moguls, all telephoning from their tables, a three inch filet mignon, french fried potatoes and some sort of species of cream puffs & pots of coffee," after which he managed to get away and spend the day, alone, exploring. It was "great fun, as it always is for me. Looking about in new places, alone, was my most passionate diversion for years, and I've missed it lately. Beverly Hills is of course feerightful."

That night at the Homolka "manse" for dinner there was a certain amount of confusion. Having gotten the news, Florence Homolka was on the phone in a long conversation with her New York lawyer: "So I looked at a poor but large Dali on the wall and talked to her two handsome, impishly out of hand boys." The air of "ghastly luxury" did not escape his assessing eye: "Gardens, patios, telephones, mirrors, art & books all over the place. Slices of cold roast beef an inch thick, absolutely tasteless." The servant, he noticed, trembled while serving. Finally: "There was just a little talk about the camera I brought, then I left."

He decided, after all, that he needed the items he forgot to bring with him. He sent a thirteen-point list of what was wanted with details about where they were to be found in the apartment: the cufflinks in the black jewel box, ". . . be sure oval silver links are in it and not in some shirt lying around"; a gray flannel shirt on the shelf over the radio; a little coverless address book "if you can find it which I doubt because I think it isn't there"; and rolls of Super XX, Ansco Color, and 35-mm Ansco Supreme films "to be found also on radio shelves, or if not there in the small black leather camera case stored on shelf under pants collection. I do not want any 35-mm *color*." The list went on for three pages, ending: "Oh well, add on a couple of paint rags if there are any around." (Quite probably Evans did not remember that his mother used to give such detailed instructions when she asked him to get her a handkerchief from the top drawer of the bureau in her bedroom.) Further instructions suggested how she might get the zippered canvas bag to the post office: "Remember please I want it Air Parcel Post, even though costly."

In his letters to Jane there is evidence that she missed him, was feeling lonely or left out, even that there might have been a taint of impersonality in his letters. That seems to account for the tenor of his later responses: "you gotta not feel so bad, please miss. But sure stay where you are until you feel like country life again, you'll like that too when you get there. I'll be back in no time, and, presumably, the car will be running like crazy then — if I can find the dough to pay for it." In another letter he told her: "But listen you got no business feeling about 'impersonality' so stop it — it's bad for me too. After all, what about my writing every day — me who never wrote a letter in his life. . . . Stop it, you're OK and remember there's things I need too that aren't troubles, misunderstandings, difficulties, complications, and I been doing things to have them." The canvas bag arrived "and a great event it was and I thank you from middle of heart you did it for me. You're a geniass. Love, personal, you dope, W."

* * *

Money was an ongoing problem, he hoped that either Florence Homolka or Johnny Becker, whom he visited at his seaside cabin, where he was living "in sin" with a pretty girl, would put him in the way of some "portrait hacking or something besides this teaching." He had, however, developed a certain respect for Florence Homolka. "She's a good egg and quite bright," he wrote Jane, "But she has some reason to hide it."

There were some enjoyable days alone at the beach at Santa Monica: "It is of course spectacular. High clay bluff, enormous surf, lotsa young beautiful blond tanned boys & girls all tall, clean & vacant as the roast beef." All of which, he recognized, "has been said before — though perhaps not so well — by other master prosateurs." In the capital of lush youth and sexuality, his bedside reading, appropriately or not, was Hesketh Pearson's biography of Oscar Wilde, which he had found "quite good." He also had bought himself a pocket-size set of Winsor & Newton watercolors: "Want to set down those memory quick sight sketches, in color, of train window views . . . I think my sketches are worth it."

His photographs of the beach at Santa Monica constitute another of his exercises, combining his ardor for swimming and sun bathing with a rationalized sociological study. (A selection of the photographs would be published as such, some five years later, in Fleur Cowles's flashy magazine venture *Flair Annual 1953*.) The Santa Monica series was a happy field day: He photographed a pair of bathing beauties from the back, slender and tanned, trim buttocks sculptured by the overhead sun, standing before a concession advertising in painted capital letters CANDY APPLES. He photographed them aft and fore; a lucky accident too good to pass up. Another series captures a pair of women and other bathers passing under a latticework canopy, marvels of geometric light and shadow in which the human element is entrapped. (One could make a minor study of Evans's fascination with geometric patterns, beginning with his women in zebra-stripe dresses.) Nor did he overlook the male sex: there are studies of lithe young males lined up at an outdoor shower or balancing their girlfriends aloft in displays of athletic prowess. On the beach at Santa Monica, youth was on display for the forty-four-year-old photographer who was perhaps beginning to feel his age. "I just lay [sic] in the sun, surrounded on all sides by the inevitable seaside bathing girls," he wrote Jane. "The whole thing carries me back to my Riviera period — which I don't like."

Santa Monica, California, 1947

In that light, and considering that he had just bought himself a Winsor & Newton paint box, the series of photographs he did of a young boy, no more than seven or eight, an amateur artist on the beach with a workbench and easel made from a packing box, has some private and comic implications. In some photographs, a woman — perhaps the boy's mother — sits beside him as he dabs at a Kandinsky-like abstract watercolor or gouache on a broad piece of paper. The boy also turns around to pose proudly and inquisitively for the photographer, his work on display behind him. But wait: in the corner of another photograph, just the woman's hand appears holding what seems to be a paintbrush and there is a merest glimpse of a childish caricature of a human figure. Is she perhaps the artist of the caricature? This little series, depending upon the chronological sequence of the photographs, may or may not have been finally reduced to one of Evans's paradigms: a photograph in which there is no human figure — the artist is absent, the biographical clues reduced to scanty terms. We see the box and

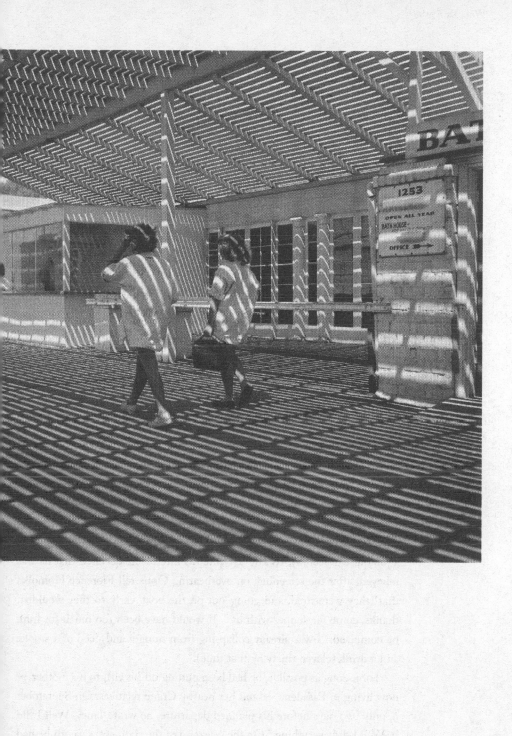

easel, the abstract painting, the water cans, the paintbrushes at the ready, a tiny stool in the foreground, and on the sand the even more childish watercolor of the figure with a circle head and dots for the eyes and mouth. Beside it is the boy's toy truck. Beyond it an empty beach stretches away to the curling lips of incoming waves. The mystery of art and the inconsequential artist.

Another relevant highlight of the California trip was a screening at the Hal Roach Studios of the film *Open City*, which Evans had seen and thought "quite good." There were other rewards, too: amid the assembled people he noted Jean Renoir, filmmaker son of Auguste Renoir; the dancer Sono Osato; and playwright Clifford Odets. Evans was also aware of a somewhat hushed atmosphere and a long mysterious wait: "For good reason, for at almost nine in trotted a little bouncing white-headed man accompanied by a flashing lovely in sky blue evening wraps — Chaplin and Oona":

It was an entrance. The man was, in this small circle, completely aware of his royalty, and at home because he knew everyone in the screening room except me. So he put on a little act, a jolly bouncing, assured but in no way distinguished showman scene, not easy to describe. Enough to say it was based on that royalty and that the whole room, used as it was to seeing him, would hang on every word, glue eyes to every gesture. I must say, one likes to see such power.

Evans sized up the actor in self-referential terms: "He is shorter than I am." He specified the "delicate" features, the "eyes and lips showing this the most." He noted the white flannel jacket Chaplin wore, "frankly a showman's uniform"—a mild criticism of one dandy by another. He described Chaplin's wife as well: "The Oona: very young, and holding quite a job quite gracefully, I'd say." Despite his interest he declared that he was relieved, after the screening, on overhearing Oona tell Florence Homolka that "they were tired, and going 'out on the boat' early so they wouldn't, thanks, come for supper with us." It would have been too much for him, he confessed; "I was already collapsing from hunger and need of a smoke and a drink (eleven thirty by that time)."

For as long as possible, he had been putting off his visit to his mother — now living in Pasadena — and her nearby Crane relatives. On September 9, only two days before his planned departure, he wrote Jane: "Well I did it. Well I did everything." On the weekend of the sixth and seventh he had traveled to Pasadena. Aldous Huxley, he noted, had called it " 'the city of the living dead' and boy oh boy is he right, the livingest deadest being the two Crane families and their vermiform appendix Mrs. W.E. Jr." The other thing he had done was to have a "big old angry tooth pulled" after having suffered with it through the whole weekend: "The less said about that," he wrote Jane, "the better, but you might be amused by the family visit — which was of course much worse an experience than the tooth pulling, I can tell you, Kiddo."

He wasn't quite prepared, he said, "for the degradation I found — age, relative poverty, mental deterioration, and deep-dyed narrow provinciality in the younger ones."

His letter was a paean of irritation: "The whole god damned lot of the old fucks drove over here to get me Saturday morning. I got an immediate impression of false teeth, dandruff, adenoids, varicose veins and halitosis of the eardrums. They gabbed at me in their nasal voices, they bickered among themselves about the way home (they all detest each other). They all got possessive about me." By the time he got to Pasadena, he had a terrific headache and no appetite for the fussy lunch they put before him. At the same time his toothache kicked in. "So I put on some sort of act about that which saved me." The family spent much of the day trying to find a dentist who would extract the tooth, but without any luck. The meal that night in a liquorless restaurant gave him indigestion. It was followed by a visit to one of his Crane cousins, eight adults sitting around in a circle with all the windows closed for two hours. "I simply drew a blank, couldn't possibly remember what the hell anyone talked about during that season in hell." Fortunately the next day there was a Sunday drive to Santa Barbara, where he managed, at the beach, to take a swim by himself. The disintegration of the Robert Cranes ("who were once pretty hot stuff. He had a $40,000 salary, the top clubs and all that") gave him pause for thought: "But its really interesting how fast the top bourgeois crust can melt and how empty in this period and finished it is anyway." What the family didn't see "was how fatal it has been that all the women have ruled the men right out of their masculinity, independence, courage, will and at last, brains even."

What he hadn't given Jane, he realized, were the "net effects" of his visit with his mother:

But they are good on me, clearing up inner complications which I needed to get at, and revealing some interesting, and really relieving things I didn't even know about — pertaining to who and what I am, what my background is good for and what is bad for, etc. Tell you when I see you. Anyway that's all to the good.

Due to his infected tooth, he warned Jane, he hadn't felt much like swimming and as a result he had lost "one of the deepest most beootiful tans you ever saw. . . . It was supposed to excite you beyond endurance, but now you'll have to find something else about me." After a final working session with Florence Homolka, he was planning to take the train on Thursday afternoon, the eleventh, arriving in New York on Sunday on The Century.

It had been — after all — an experience.

Walker Evans,
Santa Monica,
California, 1947

"If It's There, It's There."

24

At the end of 1947 Evans was given a second important retrospective, this time at the Art Institute of Chicago. Less than a decade earlier Evans's major exhibition, the 1938 "American Photographs" show at The Museum of Modern Art, had established him as a presence in American photography. The Chicago exhibition, which ran from November 14, 1947, to January 4, 1948, may have done a good deal to affiliate him, in the critical mind, with Time Inc. It reportedly included some seventy-five photographs, several of which had been taken during his brief 1946 stint at the Chicago offices of the Luce empire. The impetus for the show seems to have been his "Chicago" portfolio in the February issue of *Fortune*. The exhibition was promoted by Carl O. Schniewind, Curator of Prints and Drawings at the Art Institute of Chicago, who wrote him after seeing the portfolio, suggesting that a show of his photographs might produce an effect "somewhat like holding a mirror up to the people of Chicago. I feel they need it." Evans, considering it a good idea also, responded, "Let's shake Chicago back down to the swamps from which it grew."

Back in New York after his California trip, Evans, selecting the prints for the show, wrote Schniewind a detailed letter concerning the mounting of the exhibition. He had distinct preferences, was even finicky. For the mats he chose "cold, pure white with a matte surface." If possible, he wanted glass with no blue or green or yellowish tint: "Do not think me outrageously fussy — I only wish to state some of my experiences with materials and aiming for perfection." About dry-mounting, he thought it "just the thing, provided the tissue never shows at the picture borders. That takes care as you know. That infinitesimal edging of shiny tissue that sometimes peeks over print edges is like a flat note in a violin solo, to me, or shall we say, a slur upon a lady's name?"

Originally, Schniewind had asked for "about sixty-five photographs." While no definitive checklist for the Chicago retrospective seems to exist, a preliminary listing dated November 25 does list some sixty-five prints, twenty-three of which were recent photographs from Evans's 1946 stint in

Family Plot,
Mayfield,
Kentucky, 1947

the Chicago office of *Time*, and one — of the blind couple on Halsted Street — dates from his 1941 visit. Evans later also sent eighteen more photographs, perhaps borrowed from the collection of The Museum of Modern Art. In a letter to Schniewind, dated October 22, Evans indicates that he was considering this: "The great Steichen who is now in charge of them, yesterday consented to lend what I may want."

At another point Schniewind sent Evans a telegram listing titles for some thirty photographs. These were for a possible feature in *Life*. But it appears to have been later dropped, perhaps because *Time* decided to cover the exhibition in its December 15 issue. The Schniewind list ranged over Evans's earlier photographs, from *Two Men*, dated 1929; several of the

Halsted Street, Chicago, 1946

Havana photographs of 1933; the 1941 parade watchers in Bridgeport; up to works as recent as his 1945 photograph of a fisherman's bedroom in Biloxi, Mississippi. One of the Chicago photographs, titled *What No Garters?* referred to a slogan on a billboard at a State Street burlesque house on a rainy day. The poster featured "Red Hot" Ginger Britton in "Souls in Pawn." Too raunchy probably for the *Fortune* portfolio, it was nevertheless included in the exhibition, testimony to what Tom Mabry (who may have had had some unspecified involvement in the Chicago show) once termed Evans's eye for the "casually corrupt."

But other photographs from that particular sequence, not included in the show, caught sight of a yawning soldier apparently leaving the theater while a civilian stares at the billboards before making up his mind whether to enter. Commenting on his Chicago photographs Evans admitted: "In Chicago I wandered around, not even looking for things to photograph, not consciously, but then something would strike me, and that would be it. As simple as that." But not so simple. Evans knew as well as any photographer that the individual photograph without its sequence shimmers with ambiguity. The soldier may only have been loitering at the entrance; the civilian may not have gone in either. We are given the hesitancy of commitment. Individual photographs may present a realm of appearances and suppositions, not necessarily the verifiable fact. The honky-tonk theater on that rainy day might have revealed only the premise of frustrated desire. A movie sequence would have actually shown the civilian buying his ticket, the soldier exiting out of the theater door.

One item, listed as *Family Plot Mayfield Kentucky*, finally offers the key to a mysterious sequence of graveyard photographs Evans made, presumably circa 1945, of the "Woodbridge" family monuments in Mayfield, Kentucky. With what *The New Yorker* writer Murdock Pemberton called "the verity of type" — meaning that once a piece of misinformation is published, it develops an insidious life of its own, appearing and reappearing elsewhere in print ad infinitum — so the identifications of the "Woodbridge" monuments that have appeared in captions and catalogues over many years now should be laid to rest. As confirmed by the November 25 checklist for the Chicago retrospective, the family name is Wooldridge; the monuments are located in Mayfield, Kentucky; and the date when Evans took his photographs is 1947. The most plausible explanation now is that Evans took his photographs of the Wooldridge family plot earlier in the spring of 1947 while he was staying with the Paxtons in Paducah. Mayfield, about a half hour's drive south, is the county seat of Graves County. Schniewind was correct in linking the Mayfield photograph with the Castellucci gravestone, also included in the Chicago show, which Evans had photographed in Bethlehem, Pennsylvania, in 1935. How much Evans was aware of the local history of the monument and the mistaken legends surrounding it even then is a moot point. It is possible that the Paxtons might have alerted him to its nearby location and told him something about its history. In one of the photographs a woman and a young girl can be seen moving among the statues. Might it have been Evelyn Paxton and one of her daughters? Or merely some other visitors at the site?

What No Garters? Chicago, 1946

The sequence picturing monuments for eleven members of the Wooldridge clan, presided over by Henry G. Wooldridge, is one of the most striking of Evans's life-long graveside ruminations. Dubbed locally as the "Strange Procession That Never Moves," it is a near life-size family transfixed in sandstone by a primitivist local sculptor. It was commissioned by Henry G. Wooldridge some years before his death in 1899, rather like a local pharaoh overseeing the building of his tomb. The family plot in fact contained two effigies of him: one of marble carved in Italy and shipped to America, which showed him at a lectern, his hand on a closed book presumed to be the Bible (despite the fact that he was not considered an essentially religious man); the other, in sandstone, which showed him in the hunting mode, astride his favorite horse, Fop, in pursuit of his stationary hound "Bob." The dog is in pursuit of a stationary fox. (Elsewhere on the plot his hound "Towhead" pursues a deer.) Ironically, Wooldridge is the only family member actually buried in the Maplewood Cemetery plot. (He insisted that he be buried in an aboveground tomb and not below the earth.) His widowed mother, three sisters, and four brothers, along with two of his favorite great-nieces, are also represented by individual statues, though all were buried elsewhere. The simple stylization of the women's dresses, which Evans noted in taking photographs from the back of the ensemble, gave the sculptures a surprisingly sleek, modernist look. At the time he made his photographs the plot was cordoned off with wire fencing, which meant he had to use a certain ingenuity in focusing on the statues themselves, while avoiding the unnecessary business of the

surrounding plots. The photographs, taken with his Rolleiflex, suggest the eerie stolidity and calm of the stone population, all facing solemnly toward eternity, a strange and poignant instance of American idiosyncrasy.

* * *

The article on the Evans retrospective that appeared in the December 15, 1947, issue of *Time* had been initiated by Serrell Hillman of the Chicago staff, who wrote Evans on November 12, 1947, "I hope to hell they do it." But as Hillman acknowledged a week later, Evans was to be "seen"—that is interviewed — by members of the New York staff (notably Manon Gaulin and Alexander Eliot), and there wasn't too much for him to do on the story. He had, however, "spent hours today going over your stuff: and God, it really is terrific." Hugh Edwards, Associate Curator of Prints and Drawings, he reported, "has a case of real hero worship for you."

The *Time* story, titled "Puritan Explorer," described Evans as a "wry shy little man with an air of worried thoughtfulness." It credited him with being "one of the top half dozen photographers alive." With some accuracy it tallied up certain virtues of his photographs, their "antiseptic brilliance of black, white and gray. Chill as glass, they had no more charm than a newsreel, but the quiet clarity of each print gave their commonplace subject matter the impact and beauty of things seen for the first time." The piece noted his distaste for the medium itself as compared to the joys of painting, mentioning that he had begun to paint at age four: "And as a matter of fact I still paint once in a while. There's a sensuous gratification in handling the tools. Cameras on the other hand are cold machinery, developing chemicals smell bad, and the darkroom is torture." There the editors tidied up the prose a bit, omitting one of Evans's waggish asides. His comment in the original interview was: "Chemicals smell bad and machinery is cold. Darkness is torture, and probably immoral to boot." The story also indicated that Evans had "explored the face of the U.S. for Government projects, for *Fortune* and to illustrate books (*Let Us Now Praise Famous Men*), photographing its muck and loveliness, miseries and grandeur, all with the same puritanical detachment." It acknowledged his continuing dedication to the photographic medium with an Evans quote: "After 20-odd years of work I still have great difficulty maintaining enough calm to operate well, at moments when some sort of perfection is in sight."

Three men with mules and wagon, "Faulkner's Mississippi," Vogue, *October 1, 1948*

Just as interesting as the sparse quotes from Evans that were actually used in the article were the quotes not used — and relegated to the *Time* morgue three months later in February 1948. The interviews flesh out the briskly edited public persona of the article. They provide a summation of the man in mid-career. Not that there wasn't a self-serving element in the statements Evans made (as would be the case in any media interview). "How can I tell you about myself," Evans stated in a typed copy of the first interview, dated November 21. "It would be too embarrassing for instance to (say) that I don't belong to any church but that I have my religion inside me." Nor, he admitted, could he tell the interviewer how he went about his work: "I speak from very unhappy experience. I used to analyze it, to try to figure out just exactly what I was doing all the time and that inhibited me, terribly, until I found out I didn't need to go through all that at all." There were other embarrassments: "My work is like making love, if you'll forgive me. It has to spring from the moment, from what I feel at the moment. That's all."

His off-the-record remarks contained a few assessments of fellow photographers that understandably did not appear in the published piece: "Technique interests me of course . . . more than it does Henri (Cartier-Bresson), for example, though I admire his work very much. But less than it does Weston and Ansel Adams and Strand, none of whom I admire. (Off the record.)" His boldest onslaught on the contemporary photographic scene was blunt. The only photographers he felt had something original to say were Cartier-Bresson, Helen Levitt, and himself. Evans conceded that his background was more literary than anything, much influenced by the French symbolist poets: "You'll have to make what you can of that, I'm afraid," he added.

Three days later, in another response, he was more expansive about his past career. His first adult photograph, he said, was the "first one that did not look like someone else's photograph." Unfortunately he did not remember when this was. Asked about his favorite writers, he came up with a hodgepodge of modernists and traditionalists: the early prose of Tolstoy and Christopher Isherwood, James Joyce's *Portrait of the Artist As a*

Young Man, Rémy de Gourmont's essays, Ring Lardner and Jules LaForgue, nineteenth-century English writer Sydney Smith, the prose imagery of James Agee.

Confronted with an interview intended to sum up his thoughts and his opinions, he presumably gave an honest accounting — as honest as could be under the circumstances. The interview version of his published remark about his years of work as a photographer had more force than the edited *Time* story. The difference is subtle but he was speaking in the act as it were: "After 20-odd years of work I still somehow have great difficulty maintaining enough calm to operate at moments when some sort of perfection is in sight but not yet caught." In the creative arts if ambition still outdistances achievement it may well be a good sign.

* * *

That many of Evans's major photographs had been taken in the South, that he seemed to have a sensitivity to the region, proved to be an asset for an important assignment from *Vogue* magazine. In 1948, William Faulkner, after a sojourn as a screenwriter in Hollywood, published his first novel in several years, *Intruder in the Dust*, a controversial work in which a man of mixed blood, Lucas Beauchamp, wrongfully accused of murder, is defended by a southern white lawyer and acquitted. Evans, who had photographed frequently in Louisiana and Alabama, Georgia and Mississippi, even in Faulkner's hometown of Oxford, Mississippi in 1936, was a reasonable choice for photographing "Faulkner's Mississippi," the article that appeared as a six-page spread in the October 1, 1948 issue of *Vogue*. Feature editor Allene Talmey was assigned to produce, on the basis of the galley proofs, a six-page story, the text derived largely from Faulkner's novels and stories (*Intruder*, *Light in August*, *Sanctuary*, "The Bear"). Evans was to provide the appropriate photographs. (Jane, who had accompanied Walker to dinner at Talmey's apartment, recalled: "I don't know how she plucked Walker out of nowhere but she did to go on this trip. I wasn't invited.") Talmey, presumably already familiar with some of the descriptive passages from the Faulkner texts, accompanied Evans, along with another staff member, in the late spring. It was a fairly extensive tour, judging from the seventy-one photographs, mostly made with his Rolleiflex, that Evans assembled for a dummy mock-up he titled "Faulkner's Country" and dated June 1948. Many of the various sites in Mississippi he was already familiar with — Edwards and Vicksburg, for instance. But he also took a few shots from an automobile window, as he had years before in New Orleans. The subjects were also familiar — ruined plantation houses, muleteams in the plowed fields, tenant farm houses with dog-trots, crossroads stores, four-square Negro churches, cemeteries and stone monuments — all certifying that these were part of Evans's territory as well as Faulkner's.

Both the Faulkner texts selected by the editors and the Evans imagery carried the drowse of late spring or early summer heat and somnolence lying over the land. The greatest irony about the photographs is that there were none from Faulkner's hometown nor, it seems, did the editors traveling with him insist on it, though Faulkner's imaginary Jefferson City, actually Oxford, would have been en route from a locale like Ripley, in which he was working. Whether this was due to Evans's long-term distaste for the very idea of tracking down celebrities is not clear. The former executor of Evans's estate, photographer John Hill, recalled that Evans once told him that although he admired Walker Percy, another notable southern writer, he would never in a million years knock at the writer's door intending to take pictures. Instead, perhaps, at the cemetery in Ripley, Evans managed to make an evasive Faulkner connection by taking photographs of the monument to Faulkner's great-grandfather Colonel William C. Falkner (without the "u") who had been shot dead on the main street of the town as a result of a feud with a business partner.

All the more unusual, then, that at some later point Faulkner became familiar with one or more of Evans's photographs of the Wooldridge family monuments and found them a source of inspiration for passages in a short story or sketch, "Sepulture South: Gaslight," published in the December 1954 issue of *Harper's Bazaar* while Alice Morris was still fiction editor there. The story is the brooding recollection of a teenage boy remembering his grandfather's funeral and the family plot with effigies of his grandfather, grandmother, and other family relatives seemingly patterned after the Wooldridge plot, though in marble and not the local sandstone:

effigies of the actual people themselves as they had been in life, in marble now, durable, impervious, heroic in size, towering above their dust in the implacable tradition of our strong, uncompromising, grimly ebullient Baptist-Methodist Protestantism, carved in Italian stone by expensive craftsmen and shipped the long costly way by sea back to become one more among the invincible sentinels guarding the temple of our Southern mores . . .

The Evans photograph that accompanied the opening page of the Faulkner story was a full-page bleed though a reverse print of the negative. Appropriately, however, merging word and image, it provided a close match for the fictional effigies of the family in Faulkner's story. In a remarkable passage, the boy, obviously grown older, returns three or four times a year, uncertain of why he comes back to see them:

. . . looming among the lush green of summer and the regal blaze of fall and the rain and ruin of winter before spring would bloom again, stained now, a little darkened by time and weather and endurance but still serene, impervious, remote, gazing at nothing, not like sentinels, not defending the living from the dead by means of their vast ton-measured weight and mass, but rather the dead from the living, shielding instead the vacant and dissolving bones, the harmless and defenseless dust, from the anguish and grief and inhumanity of mankind.

II

At *Fortune*, Evans was coming up in the ranks. In July, after nearly three years on the job and with what appears to have been a general overhaul of the magazine now under consideration, he wrote a long semi-solemn memorandum to Managing Editor Ralph Delahaye Paine: "I ask indulgence, official nonsense is beyond me. Instead I'm writing a discursive letter which shall not be entirely playful if I can make a few points." He began with a general criticism of the use of photography in *Fortune*: "The magazine does too much, thus diluting the photographer's concentration and penetration. Then after having ordered too much, it prints too many pictures, thus diluting the visual impact of the piece itself." After considering the writing and editorial performance of the magazine, he concluded that "this part of it is way ahead of the art." He was not above using the photographs of the "One Newspaper Town" story as an example of such failures. His particular gripe was the cluster of photographs of Ed Paxton,

Jr., and Sr., along with the shots of the *Sun Democrat* plant and its radio affiliate. After having laid out the rest of the story's pictures rather atmospherically: "Well, we stuck these tag picture-notes almost postage-stamp size all together in a little knot that became, visually, quite illegible." There should be as much concern for the pictures as for the prose, he maintained. Citing *Time* as another example, he claimed: "The Time literary *mind* is ahead of the Time visual mind." It was necessary then for "the literary mind to alter its thinking about the visual. I've seen signs that something like this could be done without any broken lobes at all."

Proposing a similar program for *Fortune*, he realized, was coming "too close to the perilous question of taste not to fall into mention of it." He rose to the occasion: "You know the danger — as lief question a man's endowment with a sense of humor or his possession of a full set of real teeth and enviable procreative powers." At Time Inc., where men generally predominated in matters of policy, the metaphors of authority naturally tended toward the "procreative." But it was on the issue of taste that Evans presented his professional credo of the moment:

Taste, let us admit, is a rather arrogant thing. If you have it, you have to use it arrogantly. But your arrogance may be so quiet and assured as to be unnoticeable: then, strange to say, people like it and fall in with you. Almost everybody likes a show of knowing taste — people learn something from it. Is there a greater pleasure?

His criticisms bore fruit. On September 27, 1948 Paine sent a memo to the *Fortune* staff: "This is to confirm the appointment of Walker Evans to an assignment he has been working on unofficially for the past few months — namely Special Photographic Editor. The real assignment is to develop a distinctive photography for the new *Fortune*." For certain selected stories Evans was to take "full responsibility for photographic illustrations," assigning and directing the photographer, choosing the pictures, and supervising layout for the final approval of the art director and the managing editor. On other stories chosen by the art director, Evans would work in an advisory capacity, directing the photographers and selecting the photographs for first layouts. Another of his tasks was the supervision of a compilation of sources, "great pictures" that would be particularly appropriate to *Fortune*, pictures to be used for lead stories and in the short article

517

section of the magazine.

The criticisms he had put forward were based on his broadening experience at the magazine. At *Fortune* during these years he had had some notable successes and had taken on new ventures. As early as November 1945, he produced a first color photograph for the article "The Small Shop." Then in September 1950, in "Along the Right of Way," he produced his first major color portfolio, even though it included only four color and three black-and-white illustrations: eastern and midwestern scenes seen through train windows, subjects already congenial to Evans, and what he referred to in his three-paragraph text as "the rich pastime of window-gazing." These were precursors for a good deal of the color work Evans would develop more extensively throughout the 1950s. It was noticeable — and would be true of many of his color photographs — that he preferred subjects weathered by time and accident rather than the bright, glossy chromatics favored by amateurs of the growing fad for commercial color films. For the remainder of his life, Evans distanced himself from the easy autumn-leaves-and-blue-sky school of color photography.

Throughout this period of his career in journalism, he still produced black-and-white photographs. Among the major portfolios he assembled for *Fortune* was the May 1948 "Main Street Looking North from Courthouse Square," on a subject of abiding interest for him — picture postcards. It carried eighteen examples from the growing hoard of cards he had begun collecting in the late 1920s. The illustrations dated from the turn of the century, 1890 to 1910. It was in essence an archival look at the American postcard but also an essay on the American main street, which in the emerging postwar age of superhighways, motel chains, and malls, was already becoming a thing of the past.

Poland Springs House, Poland Springs, Maine, 1949

Another was "Summer North of Boston," in the August 1949 issue, for which he again provided both the photographs and the text. It was an homage to the legendary resort hotels situated within a triangle that Evans described from Swampscott, Massachusetts; Bretton Woods, New Hampshire; and Bar Harbor, Maine. Two of the sites could claim international importance: Wentworth-by-the-Sea near Portsmouth, New Hampshire, where delegates drew up the treaty concluding the Russo-Japanese War of 1904-1905; and the Mount Washington Hotel, where, more recently, the Bretton Woods International Economic Conference was held in 1944. The major photograph of the portfolio was the two-page spread devoted to the sprawling Poland Springs House in Maine, "designed with the prodigality of a Wagner opera and the verve of a Sousa march." Evans's account of it, with its three hundred rooms, outlying stables and gazebos, golf links and tennis courts, was expansive. Its mix of architectural forms "manages to bring you Carcassonne and Italian Baroque, Caesar Augustus, Pericles, and Chester A. Arthur all at once." His exuberance rippled through the text. Jane recalled that he had enjoyed it so much that they lingered on for an extra day at the hotel's expense. But other excursions to hotels in Massachusetts also gave him great pleasure: trips to the Ocean View in Swampscott and the Oceanside in Magnolia. "They gave him great luxury everywhere, which was right up Walker's alley." Summer hotels were an expansive subject. "Catch one of these gay land arks in the late day sunlight, under a fleeced sky," Evans advised. "This is the nation's uttermost dream of secular grandeur; this clapboard castle, turreted, porticoed, balustraded, oriflammed."

III

In the late winter or early spring of 1949-50, Evans and Jane were obliged to move from 441 East Ninety-second Street. The apartment house was sold to make way for a new building for the American Society for the

Prevention of Cruelty to Animals. It was not an easy move. Though Walker had found new quarters downtown in the West Village, Jane was miserable there; she could hear conversations through the thin walls and the loud music in the next-door apartment. Within a month or two, Evans somehow managed to break the lease and they moved to his top-floor studio at 1666 York Avenue, a cold-water flat with a kerosene stove in the kitchen. In the winter, as in other railroad flats, they were living in cramped quarters. The bathtub was installed in the kitchen with a wide-board cover that served as a counter of sorts. Jane's studio was now in the kitchen as well. In the summers, though Evans had no great appreciation for country living, they could retreat to the cottage that Jane and Clark Voorhees had put together from a transported garage re-installed on the Voorheeses' property in Old Lyme.

The moves, dictated by changing times, marked the end of a ten-year period when, living together and then married, they had been part of the renewal of modernist art in America and the wartime influx of European artists. They had frequented the salons of Dorothy Harvey only floors above them and the Upper East Side apartment of Peggy Osborn, where artists and intellectuals were a steady mix. In that heady time, they partied with the writers and critics of the *Partisan Review*, the *Nation*, and the *New Republic*. Evans's career and reputation, reinforced by his association with Time Inc., expanded as well, even began reaching an international audience. In 1948, for instance, Dwight Macdonald wrote a lengthy reappraisal of the out-of-print *Let Us Now Praise Famous Men* that appeared in the spring issue of his new magazine *Politics*. In 1941, Macdonald had originally seen it as "a young man's book — exuberant, angry, tender, willful to the point of perversity." Now he considered it "one of the most interesting and important American books of the last fifteen years." The times and political options — including Macdonald's own views — had changed considerably: "The great thing about Agee's text and Evans's photographs," he now claimed, "is that they dare to state the truth about these trapped people, without the usual Progressive-superficialities about 'solving problems.' (All they need is a TVA.) They have given us a *Works and Days* of our times." The occasion for this reappraisal may have been the fact — also a feather in his own cap — that he was now able to report: "Oddly enough — or perhaps not at all oddly — the book is being revived in Paris. When

Simone de Beauvoir was over here, I lent her my copy. She read it, was impressed, and has had some of it translated for *Les Temps Modernes.* A French edition might do better than the American."

"Politics" was the operative word of the moment in the immediate postwar period. Nothing revealed the shifting alliances of culture and politics, the strange bedfellows of the cold war period, better than the Whittaker Chambers-Alger Hiss appearances before the House Un-American Activities Committee, in which Chambers, the former Communist agent turned archconservative, exposed the political past of the highly honored former State Department official. (In the pages of *Time*, Hiss was always referred to as the "adviser to Franklin Roosevelt at Yalta," furthering the image of a New Deal linkage with the conspiracy.) Evans's political views were as ambivalent as ever. He had no commitment either to the New Deal bureaucracy or to left-wing leaning friends like Ben Shahn. Jane remembered that it was not until they had moved into the apartment at 1666 York Avenue, and only with her encouragement, that Walker deigned to vote. Even then, the first important election of the period in which Evans took part had him so nerved up that he had to write down everything about the process, taking it with him to the voting booth.

It was not altogether strange then that with the beginnings of the Chambers-Hiss case in 1948, and for complicated personal reasons, Evans and Jane had sided with Chambers, believing that Hiss was guilty. (Stranger even, perhaps, was the fact that Agee too believed in Chambers's accusations.) Nor was this a simple alignment on Evans's part. He took the matter seriously enough to bone up on the case during its lengthy process. A letter from Bernard Haggin dated November 25, 1949 reminded Evans to try to get him "that complete set of reports on last summer's Hiss trial." Three years later, Haggin was still writing Evans: "I also did want to hear what answer you had got — if you got any — to those questions you had put indirectly to W. Chambers." The case with its undercurrents of guilt and political betrayal, hints of possible homosexual complications between Chambers and Hiss, continued on in Evans's mind for a long time. It also was the source of a decisive break in Jane's wary friendship with Bernard Haggin. In another casualty of the political climate during the height of the Chambers affair, Jane altogether innocently passed on some remark or recent rumor about the death of the Russian defector Walter Krivitsky, a friend and confidant of Chambers, who had died mysteriously in a Washington hotel before testifying before the House Un-American Activities Committee. Officially ruled a suicide, Chambers was convinced Krivitsky had been killed by Russian agents. Haggin, hearing Jane's remark, had exploded, "You stupid woman, what do you know about it?" Deeply hurt, she no longer invited him to dinner, and preferred not to see him.

Late in Evans's life, in an interview with T. S. Matthews, the subject of Chambers and his residence at *Time* inevitably came up. So too did the relationship between Chambers and Agee who once shared an office together—"a very odd pair indeed," as Matthews acknowledged. ". . . They were both night owls. They both preferred to work at night and they usually worked all night when they did work. I never understood really what their friendship was founded on. Something very personal to themselves."

"Yeah," Evans countered. "In the matter of balance of relationships it was something like a couple of constellations. Agee and Chambers and the pull between them." At the time of the interview, Evans tended to write off his relationship to Chambers as principally a result of his own friendship with Agee. But he conceded that Chambers "used to do an awful lot for me. . . . Occasionally when I made a [howler] and produced an extremely wrong piece of copy, he'd rewrite the whole thing in about ten minutes and it would come out pure Chambers and it would be right." Still, he claimed, "Chambers and I didn't have much of a relation. I was fascinated by him, and again, I was influenced by Jim's attitude toward him."

Perhaps the eeriest account of Whittaker Chambers's effect on Evans occurs in an undated transcript of a dream Evans once had in which Chambers played a significant role. In the preface to the dream, Evans was in the company of a figure of his past, Joseph Verner Reed, the possibly envied millionaire who, after the war, was appointed to an ambassadorial post in London. In the dream, Evans was expecting to attend a board meeting of a social welfare group with his friend Reed, but learned that the group only wanted him to appear later at 5:00 P.M.

Whittaker Chambers slyly appears and sidles up to me. He and I have been playing cat and mouse with one another during all our acquaintance. I fear him but he dominates me. He has some secret conspiratorial information somehow concerning the board which he will make me reveal. His information is of great national and historical significance. Chambers is an outcast now, after the Hiss-Chambers case and trials. He is using me to try to make a comeback in established circles. He arranges to be seen with me in various presentable groups. I am ambivalent toward him responding to his great charm, emphatic intelligence and psychological power, but recoiling from him because of his deviousness, his illicit, underhand manipulation of me for his own ends. He talks brilliantly, wittily, knowingly, dropping sinister hints of inside important knowledge.

Like all dreams, characters merge, incidents are transposed, the past is fused to the immediate present, the circumstances of a day before are displaced to the past; sexual complications occur or are hinted at or glossed over by metaphors. But there is no denying that the character of Whittaker Chambers had, for Evans, assumed sinister implications.

Whittaker Chambers

Couples

25

On October, 20, 1950, Edward Steichen, director of the Department of Photography at The Museum of Modern Art, organized a symposium on the subject "What Is Modern Photography?" Among the ten invited panelists, including Evans, were the painters and photographers Ben Shahn and Charles Sheeler as well as photographers Irving Penn and Aaron Siskind. The session, well attended, provided a summing up of the status of photography from its early history to the present. Evans, in his brief talk, spoke of his own beginnings during the modernist phase of the twenties, which featured "atonality and cacophony in music, abstractions and various distortions in painting, incommunicable subjective imagery in poetry and automatic writing in prose." But he understood as well that at the very moment the shutter clicked, temporality became one of the subjects of any photograph. He confirmed the classic premise that "a good picture shows a relation to its period." The discussion was broadcast overseas on the Voice of America and aired locally on WNYC, the public radio station. Steichen, writing Evans on October 30, thanked him for his "generous and valuable" contribution to the affair, noting that the "house was sold out even beyond its capacity and the evening showed a profit." Therefore the department was sharing the wealth with the participants. Steichen enclosed a check for twenty-five dollars.

Jane and Walker at 1666 York Avenue, 1953

Evans's career at *Fortune* thus far indicated that much had changed in the role of the documentary photographer from his earlier years when, fresh from his trip to Paris, he had begun photographing the streets of New York and on occasion tried out the look of abstraction considered stylish among vanguard photographers. His career in effect was an example of the gradual assimilation of the documentary approach by the media and of how the Luce empire was playing its part in the shifting cultural values of the time. The pictorial approach would have even greater impact in the televised future.

That it was a time for taking stock professionally was not unusual; Evans was a man in his late forties and just past the midpoint of his career.

Professionally he was in better financial circumstances than he had been for some time. And he was aware of the vulnerabilities of other colleagues. Ralph Steiner, for instance, who had returned from a five-year stint in Hollywood during which he had given up his regular practice of still photography, was in straitened circumstances. Evans, feeling he owed Steiner a debt of gratitude, was instrumental in hiring him to photograph the full-page color photographs of corporate executives that were a regular feature of *Fortune*'s coverage in the early 1950s. Steiner found the assignments rewarding. In his memoir, *Point of View*, written in the brisk short takes of a stand-up comic, he acknowledged that Evans "sort of saved my life." Happy to have the opportunity of photographing top executives around the country, he noted: "I never found in several years a big executive who wasn't anxious to do what I asked in order to get his face on the first page of *Fortune*." The corporate image was a serious matter in the postwar world. Steiner acknowledged that Evans sometimes accompanied him on these photographic assignments. "But he never came with me when I photographed the heads of industries. Nor did he ever, over the years, comment pro or con about the quality or interest of my photographs."

It was true enough; Evans had mixed feelings about such assignments. He told his old friend Paul Grotz that he did not regard them as an important part of his work, that he "was amused by the reactions of self-conscious businessmen who tried to display an air of authority although they felt vulnerable when confronted by his camera." He was typically ambivalent about the task. In California in 1947 he had complained to Jane about the business of "portrait hacking." But actually from November 1951 through May 1954 Evans regularly supplied *Fortune* with monthly portraits of chief executives of the most important American corporations: Craig of AT&T, McCaffrey of International Harvester, Towe of American Cyanimid, Hood of U.S. Steel, Supplee of Atlantic Refining — some twenty-four photographs, most of them in color. He was on the road a good deal of the time in fact. There were members of the staff who envied him his freedom. Max Gschwind, an assistant director of the *Fortune* Art Department, remembered, "Walker'd go out to photograph for two months' time, and he'd never show up at the office.... And one day he would trundle in and would try to sell the story he had gone out to do. Very often he would succeed." By most accounts his office was something of a way station. Gschwind remembered it as an interior room that looked like a storage closet, outfitted with a canvas chair and a hot plate. Steiner's report of Evans at work differs slightly but is also that of a somewhat cavalier operator:

As I remember it, there was nothing in the room to make it Walker's; a standard chair, desk, lamp and no name on the door. I once asked Walker how he operated since he seemed so little connected with the magazine. He told me that twice a year he would take the managing editor out to lunch and would suggest picture story ideas. They were almost always accepted. And the ideas were usually those which would include a trip that Walker wanted to take.

His summary account of Evans on the road was more caustic: "As research, I'm sure he ate in the very best restaurants." Whether Evans intentionally created the image of himself as the autocrat on the staff, the man who chose the rare assignments and was paid to travel the country and occasionally abroad, is not altogether clear. Nevertheless, he must have had some intrinsic value to management. He stayed on at *Fortune* for twenty-one years.

There was other evidence that Evans was taking stock. In October 1952, he reviewed Cartier-Bresson's major photographic study *The Decisive Moment* for the *New York Times Book Review*. The book illustrated the wide range of the photographer's travels in China, India, the United States, and Mexico as well as in England, France, and Spain; the exotic locales; the vivid action shots of subjects everywhere — a skill that Cartier-Bresson had mastered, all in keeping with the implications of the title. It would hardly be altogether wrong to assume that Evans harbored a certain envy for Cartier-Bresson's achievements. His review was concise — and pointed. He noted the "discovery" of the photographer in the 1930s by what he termed "this or that local esthete of influence." He sharpened up the precise qualifying adverb: "He was relatively unharmed by the experience." There was no doubt that Evans's years at Time Inc. had given an edge to his literary style. But, he added, "The esthetes were right. Cartier-Bresson was and is a true man of the eye. More, he was one of the few innovators in photography." This was balanced by a necessary admonition or two: "Camera portraiture of celebrities," he noted, "is the riskiest of fields: people are so ready to look at the famous that the artist is tempted into mere photographic name-dropping. Cartier-Bresson can stumble over this too; his picture of Saul Steinberg though mildly witty seems nothing much." He made it plain that he did not favor portraits of the famous but that he was also well aware of the great virtue of Cartier-Bresson's portraits of the painter and theatrical designer "Bebe" Berard "awash in his hotel bedding . . . a lesson in how to give odor full and high to a photograph," and that of Jean-Paul Sartre "in conversation, out somewhere in the soft Paris air," which he dubbed "perhaps the best of the portraits." After the qualified praise, there was a reminder that a seasoned photographer was writing the review: "I happen to think that if you must photograph person-alities, this neo-newspaper style is the way to do it."

It says something that this five-paragraph review went through several careful typescript revisions and presumably as many rougher handwritten drafts — if Evans followed his usual procedure as a writer. He was as exacting about the adjectives he chose as about stalking the right camera angle as a photographer. He found the heliogravure plates "breathtaking," and praised Cartier-Bresson's "peculiar" ability in a fourteen-page preface to write an essay that was "quite devoid of rubbish and ego."

That he regarded the review as a form of self-definition seems clear from a note he appended to the copy of the published review he sent *Fortune* Managing Editor Ralph Delahaye Paine: "Del, Overlook immod-esty of my attaching this: I really want you to see what I say here. W.E."

* * *

In mid-Christmas season 1950, Evans had word from Jim Agee in California that he had suffered a heart attack serious enough to put him in the hospital for several weeks and interrupt work on the screenplay for C. S. Forester's novel *The African Queen*, on which he had been collabo-rating with John Huston. The movie, directed by Huston and starring Humphrey Bogart and Katharine Hepburn, would be released in 1952. Before learning of the heart attack, Evans had written Agee asking if he knew "a good color man"—probably for a *Fortune* assignment. He needed someone who would "do a job for $300 and expenses." Agee, writing from his hospital bed in Santa Barbara — the letter was dated only "Sunday Night" — said that he had asked a photographer but the answer had been no, at least not for the money. Still eager to be of help he said he would ask

Huston if he knew of someone else. Only then did Agee proceed to the more alarming news:

As you doubtless have heard, I'm in a hospital with the effects of a heart attack — one of the most majestic things to be afflicted by, that I can think of. The least one can do is drop dead, and apparently that is fairly often done. However, I got off light.

Four weeks in hospital & strictly in bed, then a few more weeks' slow convalescence, & I'll presumably be all right (or virtually so) if I'm careful. Quite an order and quite a show at 41, but so far, outside of occasional depressed moments, I don't much mind. I guess I'm still feeling too lucky at being alive and at not being turned into a permanent invalid.

The cause of the attack might be attributable to the fact that for some time Agee had been drinking and smoking heavily, even more so in Hollywood. Also he was playing strenuous, even demonic, tennis matches with Huston. And he had been indulging in an another of his intermittent affairs while away from home, this time an obsessive affair with a screenwriter named Pat Scallon, a woman much younger than he. In the manner in which stories and rumors converge, magnetized by some personal episode, Evans later learned, by way of Jay Leyda, that Huston had sneaked a bottle of whisky up to Agee's hospital room so they could continue working on the screenplay. Evans considered this "appalling" though admitting the possibility that the story might be hearsay. Huston, however, later maintained that he and Agee had "just finished" the script when the heart attack occurred. Even though Agee, in the hospital, had begged him for a cigarette, for instance, he claimed he had answered, "No Jim, I can't do that. You know you're not supposed to have cigarettes now." There is evidence in Laurence Bergreen's biography of Agee that Agee acknowledged that he and Huston had completed only a portion of the script: "The first hundred [pages] were mine and brought it through almost exactly half the story. The last 60 pages, except a few scenes and interpolations, were Huston's." Soon after Agee's heart attack, Huston hired a young screenwriter, Peter Viertel, to collaborate on completing the script.

In his hospital letter Agee informed Evans that Mia would be arriving in Los Angeles that night. Stalled in a hospital bed, it was time for serious reflection: "Christ how I wish I could pray and mean, 'From all adulterous liaisons and deceptions of the trustful, and divisions of the heart, good Lord deliver us.' I couldn't. But how lousy it is. It is bad enough when as seems to be usual, only one woman is loved." He didn't like hurting anyone, he acknowledged, least of all his wife, because of her *"genuine* nobility." He had, however, mixed feelings about Pat and himself. "There's nothing about the *genuine* that bores me or that I less than love and revere. But I do also like messier mixtures, being one myself."

Agee made one of his unusual requests. Pat would be in New York in the near future: "I may ask you to see her a little if you will — or again I may not. It isn't very often that of two close friends, one likes the other's mistress particularly — let alone wife or what not — so why try, or be concerned. And yet, come to think of it I really do like Jane and you really do like Mia." In the haze of loving kindness that furthered Agee's emotional attachments, there were some misconceptions in those pronouncements. Neither Jane nor Walker felt quite comfortable with Mia, much as they loved Jim. Evans, according to Jane, sensed that Mia disliked him, perhaps was jealous of his prior relationship with her husband. She didn't seem to warm up to people from Agee's past. And though Mia made a point of inviting Jane to their apartment, there was an undercurrent of hostility; Mia seemed to bristle in her company. Jane remembered an occasion when Agee had asked them to dinner one evening. When they arrived it was clear Agee and Mia had had an argument. Agee had apparently not told her he had invited them to dinner and she made no move to prepare a meal. To ease the situation, Evans and Jane suggested taking their hosts out to a nearby restaurant, but Agee insisted on cooking the meal himself — he had already bought the steaks — and Jane had offered to help in the kitchen since Mia had remained resolutely in her chair. It was an awkward evening.

Mia Agee

Agee's heart attack was not the end of his Hollywood saga unfortunately. Despite the fact that he had told her about his on-going affair with Pat Scallon, Mia remained with him through the recovery period before returning to New York. Agee stayed behind, still hoping to continue his film work. He had made connections with some of the literary lights of Hollywood — Dorothy Parker, Christopher Isherwood, and Aldous Huxley — at the salon of former screenwriter Salka Viertel, the mother of

Peter Viertel. At the same time his affair with Pat was becoming more difficult; there were dramatic confrontations. He was back to drinking heavily again, and smoking, and was even more negligent about his personal appearance. In October, he had a second heart attack, this time a milder one. Once again Mia returned to Los Angeles with their two daughters, Teresa and Andrea Maria, giving his life some semblance of order.

II

From their letters, it is difficult to tell that Evans and Jane were a couple drifting apart. Their correspondence, written during the intervals when Evans was away traveling, was lively. Jane no longer accompanied him on such trips — or only rarely. In the letters, the terms of endearment remained steadfast. But Jane felt the separations keenly. She remembers that there were weeks at a time when Walker was off on assignments while she remained at home. She saw friends, mostly women friends — Eleanor Fitzgerald, Robert's now discarded wife, and Alice Morris. But she might have been a woman living alone with her black cat Boss. There were days when she took a book to read in Carl Schurz Park, just to get out of the apartment and be among people.

In the spring of 1951 Evans was off photographing once again in Chicago for the portfolio "Chicago River: The Creek That Made a City Grow," which appeared in the August issue with eight color photographs and five black-and-whites. "Dear Husband," she wrote him early in May, "Not very much excitement since you left — we're still here though."

She and Boss had been indulging in a common New York City practice, spraying for roaches under the kitchen sink, "a weary chore — and we only got two cockroaches."

Boss had been "so gay last night, maybe to celebrate your departure that I couldn't read at all and had to play ball in your room and explore the front room all evening." The latter remark appears to have been an inside joke, for according to Jane the cat "adored" Evans, jumped on his shoulder at night when Walker came home and was ritually paraded around the rooms. True, Boss definitely "liked" her and purred around her; but then she was the provider of meals. It was cold, Jane wrote Evans; "Come home. Love, love. Your wife."

When she wrote again, she remarked, "Gosh you've only been gone a week and it feels like much more — very empty around here. We improved the shining hours by putting Drano down the bathtub pipe today — twice — We don't think it's very much better." On a Monday, she wrote him again that Boss was mad with her: "I tried to paint him today and I got his rear and hind legs and tail all fine and then he got up and left — so I tried to explain to him and put him back and told him to stay but that outraged him and his hair started to fall so I gave up and took out what I'd done — and we were both sad."

In the early 1950s she was finally receiving a bit of welcome recognition with her painting. The Kraushaar Gallery had taken some recent work — an interior view of the Ninety-second Street apartment, some still lifes, signed with her maiden name Jane Smith — and she had been included in group exhibitions there. "I have a couple of paintings at a 57th Street gallery — *at last*," she wrote Jim and Mia Agee at Christmastime, 1951. (The Agees had remained in California following his second heart attack.) Both she and Walker had loved the perfume they sent her, she told them: "It couldn't have come at a better time." All the more so because of a domestic mishap: the oil man had dropped a gallon of fuel in the kitchen "and I spent two hours with papers, kleenex and paper napkins and then mopping it three times — everything stank and tasted of oil and your perfume was a great consolation.". . . "We miss you," she ended.

In August 1953, while Walker remained in New York, Jane had hurried out to Fond du Lac because her father was seriously ill. "Well today I am a man — I've had it," she wrote him soon after her arrival on a Saturday noon. She had gotten to the hospital, "but my father was in a coma and didn't know me. We sat and listened to his ghastly breathing for a while and then I made mother come home — she hadn't slept for two nights — she went to sleep right after supper and I went to bed about nine." Early the next morning there was a call from the hospital saying her father was very low, "so we threw on some clothes, got a taxi and tore out there — He died just before we reached his room — To my own dying day I'll be haunted by his face. There it was — real death — not the play kind at funerals." Writing on the day before the funeral, she recounted the inevitable details of a death in the family, the ritual arrangements, the necessary phone calls, the neighborly condolences: "people started coming and the whole day went in an awful numbness, talking to people. The funeral's tomorrow and today I'm trying to keep mother a little quiet — she's been wonderful but today she's beginning to come apart at the seams." On the Thursday after the funeral, she wrote him that, all things considered, she expected to remain for three weeks; she was trying to convince her mother to stay on in the house rather than move to an apartment. The will had to be probated; she was packing up things in cartons. "When I get back to New York," she told him, "I want to go to the Stork Club every night and live on the Staten Island ferry or join a convent. The last six months are beginning to tell on my supply of self discipline." Fond du Lac was as deadly dull as ever, she said, the weather had been dismal. Perhaps the erosion of their marriage had begun to show through in her letters while they were apart. "It's rained like hell in the middle west for five days," she wrote him, adding "if that helps you on golf courses."

* * *

Perhaps there is no single date or event to which the breakup of a marriage or the failure of a relationship can be assigned, no deciding argument after which nothing can be repaired. The rest, after all, may be a continental drift of the emotions. But it had come nonetheless, the gradual erosion of their life together. What Jane remembered was the loneliness, which was growing insupportable — the times when he called from the office to say he would not be home for supper. At times she felt like an "unpaid domestic." There were the cutting remarks. The happier days of their marriage were being buried under the slag of arguments intended to wound and wounding, grievances now becoming permanent, an indifference building like a wall, stone by stone. She began going to an analyst who proved to be less than helpful. Walker, who had no faith in the procedure, didn't believe in it, could only be persuaded to attend one joint session. His major complaint seemed to be: "She's taking my friends away from me." In the long aftermath following the break-up, she would feel guilty for not having tried harder and felt the heavier burden of realizing she still loved him.

She had friends whom she saw with some regularity. Mona Kraut, now married to a sculptor, Harold Ambellan, had come back into her life. She and her husband lived in the same apartment building where Alice Morris lived. At one point in her peregrinations and marriages, Mona had posed in the nude for Jane, whose sketches had later been turned over to the prints and drawings collection at the Kraushaar Gallery. Jane's relationship with Mona had its ups and downs. When Walker was off on his trip to Chicago, Jane wrote him: "Mona called up at last today and was so surprised that I hadn't gone to Chicago — ugh! I gave her the very small treatment and said nothing but mmmm and uh-huh — she wants me to have dinner with her — which I won't." But when Jane's father had died, Mona had sent a sympathy note to her mother in Fond du Lac: "Mona did something so good — she wrote a note to mother right away and sent her a check for $25." Jane and Harold frequently attended life-study classes together. Through John and Dorothy McDonald, she had become acquainted with the painter William Kienbusch and his painter girlfriend Dorothy Andrews, who had a wide circle of artist friends and gave notable parties. Walker had little interest in the Kienbusch-Andrews circle, which included a number of abstractionist artists. Jane's impression was that Walker considered it too bohemian. Among the other artists Jane became familiar with in the early fifties, several of whom showed at the Kraushaar Gallery, were the painters John Heliker and Robert Lahotan, with whom

Evans was also friendly.

The most important of her friendships at the time proved to be with Winthrop Sargeant, Walker's friend from Time Inc. He and Walker lunched together often enough to be referred to in the office as "The Gold Dust Twins." They were also members of the circle, including Hobson and Solow, who lunched with Whittaker Chambers during the period that led to the Chambers-Alger Hiss trials. Sargeant, who considered Chambers "undoubtedly a rather fanatical fellow" both in his Communist and anti-Communist phases, nonetheless found him a "widely read, highly intelligent man and a good writer." In his memoir, "In Spite of Myself," Sargeant claimed: "I have always had to protect Chambers's reputation from the assaults of my liberal friends. Whatever he did, I am positive that it was in a spirit of righteousness. Driven by genuine fears for his country."

Sargeant had begun his career as a musician, playing second violin for the New York Symphony and then the New York Philharmonic under both Toscanini and Furtwangler. From there he had branched out into writing music criticism for various New York newspapers. Later he served as music critic for *Time*. But there he became increasingly dissatisfied with the anonymous reviewing policies of the magazine and moved on to *Life* as a senior editor. He was entrusted with such major stories as a profile of the Indian leader Jawaharlal Nehru, the result of an extended assignment in India, as well as feature pieces on Hollywood and the movie celebrities. Sargeant had been through two unhappy and unsatisfactory marriages — the last with Georgia Graham, Martha Graham's sister. He suffered through two breakdowns and two bouts with psychiatrists, the second time verging on periods of suicidal thoughts. After Sargeant's divorce from Georgia, Walker and Jane tried to set him up with suitable dates, but with not much success. Jokingly, but with an undercurrent of seriousness, he warned Evans, "If you don't treat that wife of yours right, I'll take her away from you." It was Sargeant now, rather than Bernard Haggin, who, with Walker's blessing, invited Jane to concerts and performances of the ballet.

What Walker truly felt about the growing relationship between his wife and Winthrop Sargeant is something of a mystery. Perhaps he considered it another case of Jane's taking his friends away. It was a period Jane once characterized as Walker's having been "wildly unfaithful." But she never felt that Evans encouraged the relationship with Winthrop as a means of bowing out of their marriage. Years later, after Evans's death, a series of negatives taken during this period turned up in the archives, revealing that Evans had on several occasions surreptitiously photographed her without her being aware of it. The deception was not after all an unusual practice for him: In New Orleans, he had aimed the camera at her while sneaking photographs of others with his right-angle viewfinder; in the New York subways he had hidden his camera while taking photographs of innocent subway riders. Nor was it unusual that he hadn't shown her the negatives or prints, since he maintained a separate studio at 1681 York Avenue. Some of the most affecting photographs were from a series taken while she was painting a picture in her kitchen studio at the York Avenue apartment. She stands engrossed in her work, arm outstretched toward the easel, brush in hand; or sometimes pauses, looking reflectively at the work. (They appear to be Rolleiflex shots; she thinks Evans must have taken them through the window-size opening cut through the wall between the bedroom and the kitchen.) In a moment of domesticity, Evans also took a sequence of photographs of Boss sitting placidly at the kitchen window, the remains of a meal and a vase of roses visible on the nearby table. In another sequence, Evans caught Jane in the front yard of her "cottage" at Old Lyme on a summer morning. She is wearing one of Walker's shirttails as pajamas, her hair is down to her shoulders, and Boss, tail up in a question mark, wanders in, exploring the territory, wanting to be petted. For Jane now, poignantly, the photographs have become souvenirs of happier times, proof that even in the difficult phases of their marriage, there was still an undercurrent of love and respect which must have prompted Walker to take them.

Jane at easel, 1953

It was during this time, too, that he made a series of party photographs taken in the York Avenue living room with its bookcases and cumbersome oil stove. Agee is there and Alice Morris and an unidentified man (one of the fugitive personae who register like ghosts in intimate photographs). Agee is looking over a book and he and Jane are laughing. The book is her childhood copy of *The Wizard of Oz,* in which she had inscribed her name — Jane Alice Smith — with a bevy of hyphenated letters. A homey scene from New York City life circa 1953. It is a vein of photography — parties and apartments — that Evans seems to have adopted in midcareer while working at Time Inc.: domestic scenes and photographs of artists and writers of his acquaintance, celebrities-to-be or well on their way — a still

unexplored record of the cultural life of the time and an unrecognized aspect of his work that might well have begun years before when he first photographed the remains of a party at Muriel Draper's apartment. Jane was certainly aware that he was taking these shots, but she does not remember who might have taken some of the shots in which Walker does appear. In another sequence she and Walker are sitting relaxed in the living room, Walker in an armchair, Jane sitting on the floor beside him. Walker breaks out in an irrepressible laugh; she sits grinning beside him, secure and at ease — more proof that love had still been lingering in the quiet corners of their relationship. Jane does not recall who might have taken the sequence. She thinks it might have been Herman Landshoff, an older commercial photographer who, with his wife Ursula, befriended Walker and made a point of inviting Jane to dinner often when Walker was away. Or perhaps it might have been Robert Frank, the young Swiss photographer whom Evans had recently met and was encouraging. Frank and his wife, Mary, a young sculptor, daughter of English music critic Edwin Lockspeiser, had attended some of the parties at 1666 York Avenue. Walker and Jane had begun to see something of the young couple and their children, Pablo and Andrea, at their loft apartment downtown.

III

In midsummer of 1954 Evans made a trip to London and Paris, partly for business and partly for pleasure. It was his first trip abroad since 1926 and, while they hadn't precisely decided against Jane's accompanying him, she had a real dread of becoming seasick on a long ocean voyage, particularly in public, a holdover from her agoraphobia. So it was left at that. Evans was booked on the French liner *Liberté*. Jane did, however, go with him to the pier and to say their good-byes in the cabin. When it was time to leave, Walker had grabbed her. "Come with me!" he said. "Come with me!" It was an improbability at that last moment, but Jane felt it was a genuine appeal, that Walker too was feeling some anxiety at their separation. She hoped that it was so.

Soon after Evans's departure she took a trip to Maine to spend a week or so with Dorothy Andrews, who had invited her to join two other guests, young male sculptors of her entourage. Early one morning, they set off in Dorothy's car for Bath, where Bill Kienbusch (who had a studio there as well), was living on the opposite side of the street.

From England, Walker's letters seemed hectic: "Wow. What a rush," he wrote her. He was avoiding contact with the *Time/Life* people: "I keep out of the London office. Went to one party there that's all — but there I found Nigel [Dennis], who is a joy really." Dennis and a writer friend, Constantine Fitzgibbon, had been persuading him to "get an English publisher interested in my making a book on London & England. So, dates and appointments. Meantime trying to get something done on color pictures of sport. My God no rest." London was crowded, the hotels full, and in Paris, too, he had heard. He planned to move on to Paris as soon as he photographed the artist John Piper for some project Anthony West, then working for *Harper's Bazaar*, was engaged in. Though nothing immediate resulted from these English prospects, and no book was forthcoming, he did, over the next few years and on subsequent trips, gather in a portfolio of photographs on English subjects. Evans had gotten Jane's letter from Maine and was glad that it had ended happily. "5:30 A.M. You?" he commented presumably on the start of her trek. "That's good news about Sarge," he added. " — is he really going to do it? I'll lose my influential contact at *Life*, but I don't care." Jane had apparently written him that Sargeant had been offered a position as music critic at the *New Yorker* and was seriously considering taking it. "Today for the first time," he told her, "I slumped into wishing to be back on terra firma. I've known I'd be homesick some but put it down with all this busy-ness. . . . Go, all the time go, then fall into bed." He was looking forward to Paris, might be leaving in a few days. "Well, I miss you and the Boss something terrible now," he wrote her.

Jane's letter to him, after her return to New York, was something of a letdown:

"It's beastly hot and everyone but Alice is gone for the Glorious Fourth, so it will be dull around here." She and Alice were planning to go to the movies on the holiday. Mostly her letter was a litany of chores and household reports: she had an appointment with the dentist to have her teeth cleaned; she received a frenzied telegraph from Walker's mother wanting to know where he was and how he was, "so I wired back that you were in England on a business trip"; she had paid for his London call and let the rest of the telephone bill go; the state income tax was due and Mona was lending her money to pay it; the check that was supposed to come from *Harper's Bazaar* hadn't arrived and Alice was going to make a fuss at the magazine because of the delay; the key for the mailbox at the 1681 studio got stuck in the lock, though she was able to pull out his gas and electric bill. She had gotten one of Walker's letters from Paris: "sorry it's a disappointment." The one bright spot in this catalogue of woes was that one of Dorothy Andrews's sculptor friends had taken her to a baseball game, the Brooklyn Dodgers against the New York Giants, and the Giants had won and were now in first place by four games: "Probably won't last, but it's wonderful for now." The Boss was in splendid form, she told him, "—but bored. He misses you and the firecrackers are beginning to bother him. By Monday he'll be a wreck." She sent her love.

In Paris Walker had met up with Dorothy and Annie Harvey, now living there. They were staying in Katherine Dudley's apartment, "but nonetheless it looks just like the place on Ninety-second street. They ask about you and send salutes. It was rather a subdued evening. Of course D[orothy] when A[nnie] was out of room said 'You ought to look up Georges — of course we don't see him — but you ought to.'" After some trouble he had found a good clean cheap hotel, "in my rightful neighborhood, that is." It was the Hotel Pas de Calais on the rue des Saints Pères on the Left Bank. He was suffering from an upset stomach and it was so cold that a fire was necessary. He was wearing a Burberry, a sweater and a woolen scarf. "My God, on July 7!" "But I like Paris — better now than at first. It's not as delightful as it was, but it's still fascinating and beautiful. I don't do much but walk around; and I carry my pocket camera." He thought Jane might like to paint in Paris—"but it would make you think a lot of New Orleans. Better of course; but you'd feel you'd seen it." He had been to a printing establishment "where the big color posters of exhibitions are printed and got some of them. You are getting a lovely Renoir." The trip had obviously brought back memories of when he had been there, a younger man. "Ach one could go on about what Paris looks and feels like — and what it looked and felt like in 1926. I'd say a lot of obvious things, so I'll skip it and tell you later if you can bear it." Time was running out, "and I'll be on the boat before I know it."

In London, he had booked passage back, tourist class, on the *Liberté*, sailing on July 13 and arriving in New York on Monday, July 19. The return, he wrote Jane, "will be hell — over the propellers. Poor old man — born 1st class." But aboard ship, Evans, who had a way with him, struck up a relationship with the ship's purser who, catching sight of him coming up on deck from tourist class, asked what he was doing down there. When Evans told him, the purser remarked, "Well, we should do something about that. We need someone like you to dance with the old ladies up here." Evans was accordingly bumped up to better quarters. He would always manage to live with style.

A Season of Endings

26

On May 16, 1955, James Agee died in a New York taxicab en route to his doctor's office. He had been suffering from a series of debilitating angina attacks, was on nitroglycerin tablets, had troubling dreams and premonitions of death. Still there wasn't a great deal of evidence that he was being cautious enough or cutting back on his destructive life-style. That morning in the cab, he had a heart attack so sudden and painful he passed out. The frightened cab driver drove him across town to Roosevelt Hospital, but it was too late. Agee had suffered a coronary occlusion and was pronounced dead on arrival, a casualty among strangers. Mia, summoned to the hospital, was at first not allowed to see the body, but insisted on identifying her husband. (Staff members, it seemed, were afraid she might become hysterical.) Father Flye, then in Kansas, was called. He agreed to conduct the funeral service and arrived the following morning by plane. Jane learned of Agee's death while attending the opening of a sculpture show at a Fifty-seventh Street gallery later that afternoon. (The artist was the sculptor friend of Dorothy Andrews with whom she had attended the Giants game.) She immediately phoned Walker — who was having drinks with wealthy friends Courtney and Trini Barnes uptown (another instance of their going their separate ways socially). They had planned to dine out together that evening but, stunned and grieving, they decided to go home together and open a can of soup. Frances Collins, now married to Denver Lindley, had phoned Walker. As far as Jane knew she might have been a ghost from the past, they saw so little of her. Frances commented: "It takes a great event to see one another nowadays."

The funeral was held on the nineteenth at St. Luke's Chapel in Greenwich Village. On this spring day, there was a congregation of a hundred or more: Mia and the two girls, the rest friends and colleagues. Walker and Jane attended, as well as Wilder Hobson, Eleanor Fitzgerald, and Helen Levitt. What surprised Jane was the sight of Christine Fairchild, Paul's former mistress, now married and living in New York, sitting in the pew in front of her and Walker. What connection Christine

Portrait of Evans by Jane Ninas Evans Sargeant, January, 1954

543

had with Agee — though they had met once or twice in New Orleans through her — Jane wasn't sure. But it was a reminder, it seemed, one more bit of evidence of earlier times and earlier relationships converging on a present that was much changed. What Jane remembered of Father Flye's sermon was his passing remark that Agee had "gone on ahead of us." The phrase stuck in her mind, because Agee, at forty-five, having lived hard, careless of health and body, was the first of their group to die. What seemed to be the only personal observation Father Flye allowed himself in the service was a reminder: "It's not the custom of this church to eulogize its dead. I can only say that those who knew James Agee will never forget him." After the funeral Evans went on to Hillsdale for the burial — one of the smaller number of friends, including Helen Levitt, who traveled the many miles to the farm Agee had bought, where he was laid to rest.

The *New York Times* obituary referred to Agee as "a poet, critic and sensitive writer in many media." It singled out his more recent work as a film critic and screenwriter. In citing his *Let Us Now Praise Famous Men*, the obituary noted, "Many critics gave the book high praise but Ralph Thompson, writing in the *New York Times*, attacked it as 'arrogant, mannered, precious, gross.'" That criticism was balanced by the kinder, more intriguing words of a reviewer of Agee's 1951 novel *The Morning Watch*, who found the book "in tone, imagery and movement . . . something of a dark poem."

It was a sign of Agee's general improvidence that, as his biographer Laurence Bergreen would claim, Agee left no will or life insurance and only $450 in a savings account. His friends and acquaintances, among them Evans, Jimmy Stern, Lillian Hellman, David McDowell, and Frank Taylor, organized the James Agee Trust Fund to provide for the three children, including Joel, who learned of his father's death in East Berlin, where he was living with his mother and Bodo Uhse. Young Joel, then fifteen, having heard the news by phone, had been planning to return to the States to visit his father. Alma was struck by his bitter comment, "Well, I guess there's no reason for me to go the United States now."

* * *

It was not a happy time for Jane. She remembers the years 1954 and 1955 as encompassing "the worst parts of the marriage." It didn't help, either, that her one constant companion, Boss, died in the winter of 1954. The absence was all the more noticeable at the kitchen window where Boss sat in front of the view, the parade of backyards stretching toward the massive bulk of Doctor's Hospital, the clothes on the clotheslines hanging like pennants.

Close friends were aware that things were not going well with the marriage. Jim Agee had been particularly sympathetic, a consoling friend who was now gone. He had once asked her out to lunch and Walker knew about it. She and Jim met at a restaurant near the Time-Life building that the staff frequented. While the two of them were at lunch, Walker had come in, presumably for lunch. Seeing them together, he simply turned around and walked out again without even a nod. To other friends like Wilder Hobson, Jane confessed that she was thinking of leaving Evans but didn't know where to go or what to do. Hobson offered to look into the possibility of a job at Princeton, where he and Verna were living, perhaps in the university library there. But it was hard to know what Walker felt or thought; it wasn't discussed. She felt upset, angry, and ignored. But after Agee's death she stayed on not wanting to make the move. What bewilders her even now is the way that their correspondence in those last bitter years screened the dissatisfaction and the unhappiness. The letters Evans wrote her while on his 1954 trip to London and Paris and the one or two she sent him at the time — forgotten letters that came to her attention again in 1997 — were affectionate and unconcerned, full of civility. They gave barely a hint of what was happening between them. They are, seemingly, innocence itself. Only in one letter from Jane is there any evidence to the contrary. It is written to Evans in November 1954, when, after his return from Paris and apparently in response to his mother's worried telegram, he dutifully took the train to California to visit her. Jane wrote him in the old, easy, semi-comic way: "Darl, Ain't got nothing to say." She had taken his trousers to Atlas, the tailor: "He said you wanted button holes — I said no, new zippers — he said button holes — and so we decided to wait till you come back. Sorry." Toward the end the tone darkens somewhat. On Sunday night she had a dismal supper with Alice who was "depressed and full of complaints and I wasn't fun — same stuff — sad — sad." The night of the letter, she was planning to go to dinner at Mona's and then to sketch class with Harold: "They're cold," she wrote. "I hope it's not too awful with you — Lonely here. Love. Love. J." Evidence that letters written at the time — like photographs — may conceal as much as they reveal. Histories based on such documents can be false or misleading.

But the process of letting go had not quite run its course. She and Winthrop had begun their affair sometime before Walker's trip to Europe. Despite her guilt about the deception — and she did feel guilty — she was well aware that Walker had been unfaithful too. It was not until three months after Agee's death that she finally made up her mind to leave Walker. In August, over a weekend that Evans had decided to spend at the cottage in Old Lyme — whether alone or with company, she didn't know — Jane made up her mind to leave. She hired a mover to pack up the books and clothing she had decided to take with her. Around noon on Monday morning, Walker called from Grand Central Station on his way to work. It was then that she told him she was leaving, that she had made a reservation at the Barbizon Hotel. He was nonplussed, said he was planning to spend the next weekend with her in Old Lyme. Jane gave her reasons: "I don't think you even like me any more. Winthrop wants to marry me." "You're bettering yourself," Walker countered. She answered, "I hadn't thought of it in those terms." She advised him not to come home right away, since the mover was still packing her things. That night Evans called her at the Barbizon, telling her, "I don't want you to move in with Winthrop." But it was clearly over; she doesn't remember the rest of the conversation, what she said, what he said. Within a day or two she moved to Winthrop's apartment.

Legalities consumed the next few months; the papers for a legal separation were drafted, dated for November 1955: "Whereas, differences having arisen between them, the husband and wife are now and for some time have been living separate and apart from each other . . . " It was noted that "the parties have heretofore made a division of their tangible personal property and it is agreed that each shall hereafter own and enjoy, free from all claim of the other, all their tangible personal property in accordance with that division." In the event of an application for divorce: "the parties agree that neither of them will make an application to the court for alimony, maintenance, support, counsel fees, settlement of property rights or financial obligations." (The agreement, however, was not officially signed until December 5.) At some point a divorce in Arkansas was under consideration, at least on Walker's part. He scribbled down pages of notes: questions to ask the lawyer; questions to ask Jane. They were cool and considered queries: "Would a lawyer representing a future wife object to my Arkansas divorce?" was first on the list. He wondered whether an Arkansas divorce would be solid, permanently, in all places, forever; also if there were an advantage in having his wife become the plaintiff. From Jane he wanted to know what grounds she intended to give as cause and whether he would get papers in evidence of the divorce. Also, did she have the marriage license? But he never questioned her on those points. A series of other notes suggests that the Arkansas divorce was dropped when he learned that he would have to be represented in Arkansas and that Jane would have to comply with the residency requirements there. But by that time, there was no communication between the two.

Evans sent a stiff and formal letter to Winthrop, offering to pay for the legal fees, an offer that was rejected. His letter had included a bitter postscript addressed to Jane: "From now on I will consider you dead."

The lawyers recommended the divorce be obtained in Juárez, Mexico, and the necessary papers were forwarded to lawyers in El Paso, Texas. Winthrop would be getting time off from the *New Yorker* in December, so he and Jane decided to take the train for Texas then. There was no need for Walker to attend. So, on December 21, Jane and Winthrop, accompanied by two El Paso lawyers, crossed the bridge to Juárez, where she signed the final divorce papers. On the same day, the two were married by a local judge with a pair of old Indian women serving as witnesses. The marriage ceremony was brief, conducted in Spanish. By Christmas day, she and Winthrop were on the train to New York.

Evans's little 1955 Leathersmith of London engagement book, consisting of entries dating only from November 28 to December 31, indicates that he did a fair amount of socializing during that holiday season: dinners and evening appointments with Trini and Courtney Barnes, or Milly Knox , or the Landshoffs; a lunch with Bernard Haggin at Barbetta's; an evening at the Metropolitan Opera; a party at the Breits'. He dined twice with Eliza Parkinson, the niece of a founder of The Museum of Modern Art, who had a house on Fisher's Island off the Connecticut coast to which he was often invited. These were the names — and many others as the circle widened — that appeared in his engagement books in subsequent years. There was, of course, no mention of Jane or Winthrop among the growing entries in the appointment books he now regularly kept. Friends told Jane that he refused to mention her name and was not happy when other people did. It was from Billie Voorhees that she learned that Evans, who was frequently invited to dinner at their house in Old Lyme, once asked her where she got the recipe for a particularly delicious meal she had served. Billie had had to tell him, "It's a recipe from the nameless one."

II

Late in life, at a panel discussion at Yale, Evans admitted that he did not remember when he first met the young Swiss photographer Robert Frank. But he was generous in stating the importance of the meeting: "I was looking for somebody to take what I started back in the South." Curiously, he mentioned, "I thought of spending 5 or 7 years in New Orleans and I was exhausted and this guy picked me up a little bit by showing me he could say the truth . . ." Frank himself suggested it might have been around 1953 or 1954 and noted that Evans had helped him to get the Guggenheim Fellowship he was awarded in 1955. That year and the next, when the award was renewed, he traveled through America gathering the photographs that made up his controversial, now classic, 1959 book, *The Americans.*

Robert Frank and Mary Lockspeiser Frank

Frank had arrived in America in March 1947 at age twenty-three with a portfolio of forty photographs which he showed to Alexey Brodovitch, the art director of *Harper's Bazaar.* Brodovitch, decidedly impressed, hired him as one of the magazine's stable of fashion photographers, which then included Richard Avedon and Louise Dahl-Wolfe. From the States, in 1948, he made a six-month liberating trip to Peru, where, with his Leica and Rolleiflex, he photographed Indians in the Andes, traveling with them without benefit of a translator. He found it "the beginning of a whole new way of photographing" as a kind of silent witness. He referred to it as the best trip he ever made: "I didn't talk to anybody for maybe a month." In 1950, Edward Steichen had included him in a survey exhibition at The Museum of Modern Art, and in 1952, under Steichen's auspices, he was traveling in Europe with the director as a consultant for two upcoming shows, a survey of European photography and the famed "Family of Man" exhibition of 1955. (Frank had some photographs in the exhibition.) Evans, though asked, declined to appear in the show, opposed to the broad romanticized view of mankind it promoted; he preferred the individual and particular, not the sweeping generalities espoused by Steichen. It was, nonetheless, the most successful and talked-about photographic exhibition of its time, with record-breaking attendance figures at the Modern; in further editions it traveled to Japan, France, Russia, and India, gathering crowds everywhere.

When the two men did meet, around 1953, Frank was already familiar with the fifty-year-old photographer's work by way of *American Photographs*. Frank was then married to Mary Lockspeiser. The pair had two children, Andrea and Pablo. Evans was clearly impressed with the younger photographer's work and, serving as a consultant in photography for the Guggenheim Foundation at the time, encouraged Frank to apply for a grant. His January 20, 1955, recommendation letter was persuasive: "This man is probably the most gifted of the younger photographers today," he wrote Henry Allen Moe. "Anyway I think he is. I know his work quite well." He reiterated: "Robert Frank is a born photographer, if there is such a thing." As evidence, he mentioned two examples: a series of photographs on the life of a coal miner Frank had made in Wales, a few years earlier,

"and currently, a journalistic commission he executed for me at *Fortune*, of the Pennsylvania Railroad's Congressional Limited train. Both these projects — one freely inspired, one commercial — are creative, thorough, and intelligent." The *Fortune* assignment seems to have been completed sometime earlier though it did not appear in print until the November 1955 issue of the magazine, where the ten black-and-white photographs by Frank were accompanies by a text by Evans himself.

Working with Evans was a study in contrasts. Frank remembered helping him on one of the classic portfolios that appeared in the July 1955 *Fortune*, "Beauties of the Common Tool," a collection of tin snips, a brick-layer's pointing trowel, a baby terrier crate opener, among others, each photographed pristinely against a white shadowless backdrop. At first Evans sent Frank out to buy the likely subjects, then accompanied him, the two of them walking up and down Second Avenue. They would stand and look in the windows of hardware shops, discussing various pieces. "Then if he saw something that interested him we might go inside." Evans would turn aside the salesperson while he looked some more. (If he didn't like the salesman, they would leave.) When he finally decided on a tool, he would buy several in different sizes. The photographs were made in his York Avenue studio. "I was surprised to see what a Rube Goldberg set-up he made," Frank remembered. "Seamless paper held up by clothes pins, tools supported on a dowel. . . . An 8 x 10 camera on a shaky tripod over the set up. Whenever a subway would pass then everything shook and we would have to wait for the vibrations to stop."

On the road for other assignments, the process was equally circumspect and well-considered. Frank would drive:

Tin Snips by J. Wiss & Sons Co. $1.85, "Beauties of the Common Tool," Fortune, July, 1955

At some point Walker would say 'Stop right here.' Then he would get out and go walk some distance up the road — quite a few hundred yards. He would take no equipment. Maybe stand and look for quite a while. When he came back to the car he would say tomorrow at such and such a time, the light will be right and we will come back. . . . I would never be asked to get out of the car.

On the return trip, they found the best hotel in the area and checked in.

It was a far different, less risky operation than the one Frank experienced while crisscrossing the country in the fall of 1955 taking the

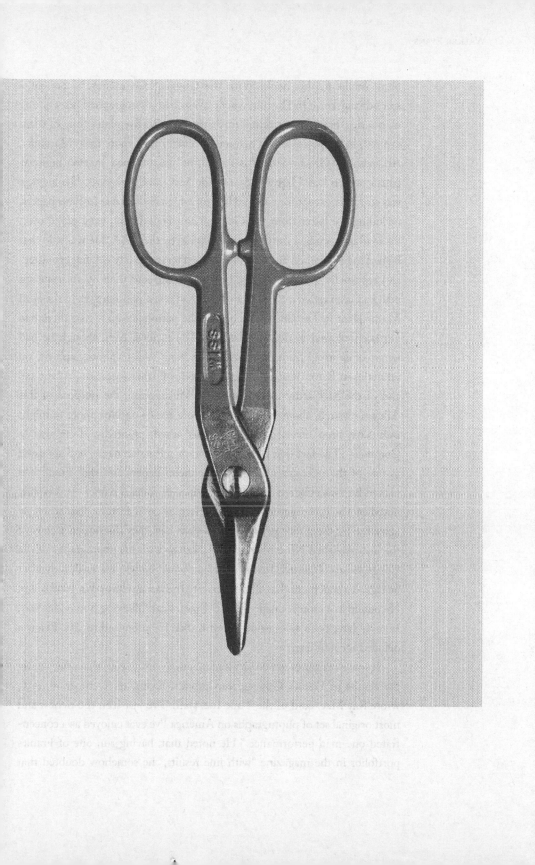

photographs for his book. With the Guggenheim money he bought a secondhand Ford. In Detroit, where Evans had photographed his working men series, Frank was arrested for having two license plates (one of them expired) in his possession. Then on November 7, en route from Marianna, Arkansas, to Greenwood, Mississippi, he was stopped by two highway patrol cars on U.S. Highway 65, outside McGehee, Arkansas. His luggage was searched, except for a locked bag for which the key was lost; his papers, including the letter from the Guggenheim Foundation, were pored over; his road map studied for the routes marked by the AAA. He was told that he had to be detained and was then locked up in the city jail, fingerprinted, and repeatedly questioned, first by a lieutenant and then by an inspector who had been called in. The fact that he had taken photographs in the Ford Motor plant in Detroit, which one of the patrolmen on a visit there had not been allowed to do, was considered suspicious. Even though he had letters of approval from Standard Oil in New York to photograph the oil refineries in Baton Rouge, it was a cause for further suspicion. At the tail end of the McCarthy investigations in Washington, the purpose of this Arkansas search, about which Frank wrote Evans on November 9, might well have been revealed when he was asked, pointedly, if he was "a Commie." (The fact that Alexy Brodovitch, a Russian name, had appeared as one of the references in his Guggenheim papers and that Frank had named his two children Pablo and Andrea — foreign names — was duly noted by the investigators.) It was a piece of good fortune that when he agreed to let the police pry open his locked bag, they discovered a copy of the just published November issue of *Fortune* with his photographs of the Congressional Limited. It was midnight when he was released, only after he signed a statement that all his property had been returned in good order. He put up in a motel outside town, the patrol car following him on his way. It could have been an episode out of Kafka. He promised to give Evans a detailed account later.

It was a matter of generosity and genuine enthusiasm, that after seeing the results of Frank's Guggenheim project, Evans, on October 16, 1956, wrote Ray Mackland of the Time Inc. staff: "I've just seen the richest and most original set of photographs on America I've ever enjoyed as a concentrated one-man performance." He noted that, having run one of Frank's portfolios in the magazine "with fine results," he somehow doubted that

Fortune, as a business magazine, could do justice to the new work in the right way: "I think these pictures are really daring and grown-up work. As you may know, Frank is not a salesman (neither am I); but I think he will come to see you anyway." He hoped "my writing to you is not far out of order, but my enthusiasm leads me to signal this set as an outstanding picture event." Was there a slight edge of ambivalence in Evans's memo, a suggestion that despite the high praise, he had been confronted by a very talented young rival, now traveling the roads he had once traveled? Where Evans in Beaufort, South Carolina, had focused on the cluster of signs on a porch where Lafayette had once slept, Frank, twenty years later in Beaufort, had captured a black woman seated in the fields at dusk, and the interior of a bereft café with a huge jukebox and a black baby crawling on the floor. Evans had put him on to certain sites and even advised him on marking out the route from Chattanooga, Tennessee, across Alabama and into Mississippi. ("About that, great questioning," Frank informed him referring to his bout with the patrolmen.) The chilled dispassionate eye Evans had brought to eighty-seven subjects in *American Photographs* was not the brooding private, personal feeling one senses in the eighty-three photographs of Frank's *The Americans*. Considering how vulnerable he might then have felt following his divorce from Jane and his ambivalence about his career at Time Inc., it would have been hard for Evans not to have felt some measure of self-questioning.

One gets a sense of that when, in lieu of the "Family of Man" exhibition, Steichen, in January 1956, included Evans as one of the participants in the series "Diogenes with a Camera" which he was presenting at The Museum of Modern Art. Evans was teamed with Alvarez-Bravo, with whom he had shown twenty years earlier at the Julien Levy Gallery, and the German photographer August Sander. On the wall label, written by Evans for his nine photographs, after stating that "Valid photography" was too serious a matter to speak about seriously, he went on to contend "what it is *not* can be stated with the utmost finality." He ticked off the message:

It is not the image of Secretary Dulles descending from a plane. It is not cute cats, nor touchdowns, nor nudes; motherhood; arrangements of manufacturer's products. Under no circumstances is it anything ever anywhere near a beach. In short it is not a lie — a cliché — somebody else's idea. It is prime vision combined with quality of feeling, no less.

Under this dictum or banner, one would have to overlook or dismiss a good many of his own photographs, though in some respects it addressed his reservations about the whole "Family of Man" exhibition, his distaste for celebrity photographs. In one wall label, Evans had, more or less, his credo, and, in his deceptive way, had forgiven himself the same sins he was complaining against.

Walker's friendship with Frank and his family continued for some years; there are photographs of the couple, and at some point Evans, indulging in his photographs of parties, began to make quick shots in the manner of Frank. But at this point Evans must have begun to realize that he was now confronting the young, that his private or personal life was in something of a shambles, that he had shifted his career into a commercial drive — which paid well enough for once — but which meant that he was performing services he probably felt were demeaning. If he had thought about himself and his career at that moment, he might have understood the contradictions of his personality most keenly. But at that moment he was encouraging a young photographer, assigning him to certain opportunities, and was once again in the field himself, usually with Frank. Evans liked working with Frank because he didn't talk very much. There must have been an air of the Chaplinesque about these ventures, but there must also have been a kind of self-criticism that he himself would never take such risks and dangers as Frank did, that Frank was far more venturesome if not to use the word *brave*. When *The Americans* came out it was, among other things, a commentary upon his own view of America twenty years before, an update of most of the scenes that Evans had chosen. Making a protégé of Frank was a very generous gesture, but it was also indicative of some measure of Evans's pride in the fact that his own photography had been so influential in the mix that Frank had arrived at. Had Evans retreated into thinking that way? Was he becoming more concerned about his historical place? Concentrating as he did on his engagement book and the lengthy entries in his journals and diaries, it would seem that he could have begun to consider himself in this light as a result of the interactions with Frank.

Publisher's Note

James Mellow died on November 23, 1997 before finishing the final drafts of the last chapters. The following summary lists the most important events in Walker Evans's life and career from 1957 through his death in 1975. For the full chronology of his life, see pages 623–630.

Isabelle Evans,
163 East 94th Street,
Christmas, 1960

1957-1975: A Summary

27

James Mellow died on November 23, 1997 before finishing the final drafts of the last chapters. The following chronology lists the most important events in Walker Evans's life and career from 1957 through his death in 1975. For the full chronology of his life, see pages 623–630.

1957

Reviews a portfolio of photographs by Robert Frank to be published in *U.S. Camera Annual* (1958). Earlier, he wrote the introduction for a portfolio of Frank's pictures in *Fortune* ("The Congressional," November 1955).

The young photographer Lee Friedlander seeks out Evans; a friendship develops. Evans admires Friedlander and helps promote his work; Friedlander advises Evans on such matters as lenses for 35-mm cameras. Later the two will take working trips together, and Friedlander helps Evans to paying work.

Two color portfolios of Evans's photographs appear in *Fortune*; *Sports Illustrated* illustrates two articles with his photographs. One of the *Fortune* portfolios, "Before They Disappear" (March 1957), features close photographs of railroad insignias in sunlight, photographs that suggest an interest in color and design. Kodachrome transparencies made for one of the *Sports Illustrated* pieces, "Henley Forever" (about the Henley Regatta), so concentrate on spectators' costumes that color relationships seem as much a concern as the nominal subject of the assignment.

1958

Publishes three portfolios of his own photographs in *Fortune*, writes the text for an article in *Sports Illustrated*, and contributes three portfolios of his photographs to *Architectural Forum*. One

557

of these, "Gallery: Color Accidents" (January 1958) presents color photographs not as journalistic illustrations, but as pictures to be looked at for their own interest. This portfolio is Evans's first public acknowledgment that color photography is an artistic medium he might want to use (though color pictures have been finding their way into his files for years).

1959

In Evans's diary, the single word "Socializing" heads a list of dinner parties and dates with friends, some prominent socially or artistically. Through his friend, the photographer Herman Landschoff, Evans meets Isabelle Boeschenstein von Steiger, a young Swiss woman working in fashion design. She is in New York City with her husband, Alex von Steiger, an aspiring photographer. The acquaintance soon becomes a serious courtship.

Awarded a second Guggenheim Fellowship, for an application to produce a book of pictures of America (not to be cliches of beauty), with extended captions and text. Henry Allen Moe's letter to Evans announcing his award mentions only "creative photography." Writes a letter in support of the Guggenheim application of Robert Frank.

Begins a series of photographs of Third Avenue, New York City, from bus windows. Also, begins to photograph Third Avenue shop fronts from street level.

Travels with his friend, photographer and designer Ben Schultz, to Grand Rapids, Michigan. Makes photographs of an antique car rally for *Sports Illustrated*.

Orders a Nikon F 35-mm, single-lens reflex camera, charged to *Fortune*'s account.

1960

Writes a letter applying to the Ford Foundation Fellowship Program for Studies in the Creative Arts. Proposes a "book of documentary, non-artistic photographs, with text, essay, and extended captions, recording American society as it looks today." Goes on to explain, "My book will remain unscholarly, yet it will not be pictorial journalism. Simply, it aims at actuality in depth, and at contemporary truth and reality."[1] The application is not successful.

A second edition of *Let Us Now Praise Famous Men* is issued by Houghton Mifflin. The number of photographs is increased from thirty-one to sixty-two, and the book contains a carefully-written essay by Evans describing James Agee in 1936.

Photographs warehouses in Brooklyn and Manhattan in June.

Travels to Detroit by train to photograph Buick, Lincoln, Ford, and Dodge plants in August.

Photographs in Maine, on the Cranberry Isles, in late August.

Marries Isabelle von Steiger in October at the home of architect Mott Schmidt in Katonah, New York.

Fortune publishes one essay with black-and-white pictures by Evans, "Summer at Harbor Point," and one in color, "On the Waterfront."

Warranty cards show that in late 1959 and early 1960 Evans buys two normal-lens (80-mm) and one telephoto (135-mm) twin-lens Rolleiflex cameras from Royaltone, a professional camera store in New York City.

1961

In January he photographs for *Fortune* portfolio of distressed areas to be called "People and Places in Trouble." In making some of these pictures he experiments with 35-mm camera using a 21-mm lens, very wide angle at the time.

Visits Lee Friedlander in New City, New York in March.

Photographs in auto junkyards in Connecticut in May and June.

In July, a Jaguar sedan is registered in Evans's name. Letters to

Isabelle suggest that at least some of his recent fellowship money may have been directed toward this purchase.

Architectural Forum publishes a portfolio of Evans's pictures of southern churches under the title "Primitive churches."

1962

The Museum of Modern Art publishes a second edition of *Walker Evans: American Photographs*, printing the pictures with the same copper letterpress plates used for the first edition. The second edition, redesigned by Bert Clarke, has a picture on the dustjacket instead of the bold type of the original. The new edition begins with an introductory note by Monroe Wheeler, most of which—including the observation that Evans's work is "reflective rather than tendentious"—was written by Evans himself.

"Walker Evans: The Unposed Portrait," a portfolio of Evans's subway pictures, appears in *Harper's Bazaar*, largely due to the interest of art director Marvin Israel.

Fortune publishes "The Auto Junkyard," with eight color photographs; *Architectural Forum* publishes "The American Warehouse," with black-and-white pictures and essay by Evans.

Publishes two magazine portfolios drawing on postcards, which he began collecting in the late 1920s or early 1930s. "Come on Down," in *Architectural Forum*, reproduces seven postcards from his collection—one so large it extends across the gutter of the magazine spread—accompanied by Evans's text. "When 'Downtown' Was a Beautiful Mess," in *Fortune*, consists of eight reproductions of postcards plus Evans's text, which is as much imaginative evocation of turn-of-the-century "downtown" as it is the description of postcards.

For *Vogue* he photographs Gordon Wasson, a senior vice president at J. P. Morgan, in his office at 23 Wall Street; also officers of the Carnegie Corporation and of the Ford, Rockefeller, and Guggenheim Foundations.

Receives a Carnegie Corporation Award.

Introduced to the young photographer Diane Arbus by Marvin Israel. He is impressed by her work and later writes in support of her application for a Guggenheim Fellowship.

Photographs in Cape May, New Jersey in June; in July he works in Maine, in Damariscotta and New Castle, and on the Cranberry Isles.

Buys a black Leica M-2 35-mm camera from Royaltone, in New York City. Soon after he buys another; he uses them with a normal (50-mm) and moderate wide-angle (35-mm) lenses.

Photographs the interior of Pennsylvania Station in New York City, in September.

Travels to California in October. On the return trip, aboard the Santa Fe Super Chief, he photographs Colorado and Arizona landscapes from the train windows.

1963

Harper's Bazaar publishes "Those Little Screens. A photographic essay by Lee Friedlander with a comment by Walker Evans."

Mademoiselle publishes five Evans photographs in "Collectors' Items," an article on collecting.

Makes more than 400 2¼ x 2¼ and 35-mm black-and-white negatives for a proposed but unpublished series for *Fortune* to be called "Men's Fashion on New York City Streets."

Also makes photographs that go unpublished of the Chicago railyards, Container Corporation, and Bethlehem Steel.

Makes family portraits and other pictures for the Fred Dupee family.

1964

Goes to Yale University, to give a lecture with the title "Lyric

Documentary" on March 11. The painter Jack Tworkov, who had heard Evans give a similar talk at the Century Association, suggested Evans as a possible lecturer in a series put on by the School of Art and Architecture and organized by architecture professor Charles Brewer. Speaking to a full house in Lecture Room 100 of the Yale Art Gallery (a formal auditorium, the largest lecture room in the building), Evans shows slides and discusses examples of vernacular images that please his eye—images like postcards, which, in attempting to document some humble fact, bring into play an instinctive, untrained style that accounts for their strong appeal. His last slide is one of his own photographs, "Westchester, New York, Farmhouse, 1931."

Shortly after Evans's lecture a campaign begins, led by Professor of Graphic Design Alvin Eisenman, to convince Evans to teach at Yale. Eisenman recalls asking Evans many times before

Evans with students at Yale Summer School of Music and Art, Norfolk Connectiut, 1964.

receiving the answer he was after. Evans agrees to try teaching for a year.

In May, Evans begins a four-year commission documenting Brown Brothers Harriman & Co., a private banking concern. Invited to undertake this project by John Kouwenhoven, Evans (for his convenience) leaves some camera equipment at the Brown Brothers offices. He later recalled that he visited from time to time, on his own schedule, to have lunch and photograph.

Visiting Artist at the Yale Summer School of Music and Art in Norfolk, Connecticut. He and Isabelle stay in the grand "White House," formerly the Battel-Stoeckel mansion; he talks informally to students.

Photographs in Maine, Vermont, and Connecticut in August, making many pictures of stone architecture, grave markers, and ruins.

His sister, Jane, dies on September 12, and Evans flies to Florida.

Begins to teach at Yale as Professor in the Department of Graphic Design on September 21. His colleagues in photography include Thomas A. Brown, John T. Hill (on fellowship leave), Herbert Matter, and Joe Watson. He meets Norman Ives, a graphic designer, whose collages and collection of type forms and old printing he admires.

An exhibition of Evans's photographs organized by Hugh Edwards is shown at the Art Institute of Chicago.

1965

Meets Leslie Katz, a writer who is establishing Eakins Press to publish high quality books on the arts. Katz is also an enthusiastic, perceptive student and champion of American art. He has developed a considerable interest in Evans's work without realizing the photographer is still alive, and is delighted to meet him. Katz hopes a book of Evans's photographs can follow the first offering from Eakins Press, a facsimile of the 1855 edition of Walt Whitman's *Leaves of Grass*.

Evans and Isabelle begin a house in Lyme, on the site of the small shack that had belonged to Evans's first wife, Jane Ninas. He tells friends he has worked on the design of the angular, modern structure himself, along with Yale architecture student Robert Busser, who appears in Evans's diary as early as 1962. Jane's original shack was burned down to clear the small property for the new house, but Evans eventually has another rustic one-room shack built behind the main house.

Isabelle and Evans's friends begin to worry about his drinking. After one dinner with the couple in New York, John McDonald returns to Evans's apartment and insists that he face his problem. Isabelle arranges for a November stay at Regent's Hospital in New York City, where Evans goes to dry out. Later he remembered being "knocked out" with drugs; when he came to, he was fed a delicious meal and then knocked out again. He recalled leaving after two weeks of this regimen, cured, he said, but with an Anabuse prescription for good measure.[2]

Fortune publishes Evans's last portfolio, "American Masonry," with seven photographs, all color.

1966

Visits the new house in Lyme, possibly to check on progress, in January.

Attends a dinner at the Museum of Modern Art in New York City, also in January. Lincoln Kirstein and Ben Shahn are present.

In April he receives an advance from Time-Life Books for work on a Library of America book, *The Gateway States*. At the suggestion of the book's designer Ben Schultz, editor Oliver Allen asks Evans to spend much of May photographing architecture in the mid-Hudson Valley. His diary records at least nine days of photography, during which he works in Poughkeepsie,

Evans house in Lyme, Connecticut, 1967

who shows mostly paintings in his oeuvre, also handles works by
the photographers Brassaï and Henri Cartier-Bresson.

In late December he heads to London to meet Jacobs. They stay

Rhinebeck, Hudson, Kingston, Hyde Park, and Albany.

"Walker Evans' Subway Photographs," an exhibition of his
subway photographs from the late thirties and early forties, is held
at MoMA in New York City. Houghton Mifflin publishes *Many
Are Called*, a book of the subway photographs with an introductory essay written in 1940 by James Agee. Eighty-eight portraits
of individuals or groups plus one view down the aisle of a subway
car appear without captions. None of the texts drafted by Evans
over the years to appear with these pictures is used. In a 1960
letter Evans refers to his improvised technique for working in the
subway as "a useful method of sampling a metropolitan population."[3] Another point of reference for this astonishing collection
of portraits may be Evans's 1936 photo of a penny-picture display
in a photographer's studio window: an early maquette of the cover
of a proposed book of subway pictures (*The Passengers*) suggests
this link. The book is dedicated to Agee.

Eakins Press publishes *Message from the Interior*, a book with
photographs of the interiors of ten American rooms, plus a view
of the inside of a burned building and a detail of a battered circus

565

wagon. An oversize book, fourteen inches square, it contains rich
full-page reproductions printed by the Photogravure and Color
Company in sheet-fed gravure (a time-consuming process which,
as commercial practice, was on the verge of extinction in this
country). The book has no text except for titles (collected on one
page in the back of the book), a four-paragraph afterword by John
Szarkowski, Director of the Department of Photography at
MoMA, and an epigraph from *Matisse: L' exactitude n'est pas la
verité*. The book is dedicated to Isabelle.

Let Us Now Praise Famous Men appears in paperback.

Has a one-man show at Robert Schoelkopf Gallery on Madison
Avenue in New York City. Schoelkopf, a knowledgeable dealer
who shows mostly painting and sculpture, also handles work by
the photographers Brassai and Henri Cartier-Bresson.

In late December he flies to London to meet Isabelle. They stay
with James and Tania Stern, an old friend from Time Inc.,
through the year's end, and then travel on to Switzerland to visit
Isabelle's family.

*Evans party
at new house,
Lyme,
Connecticut,
1967*

1967

The Exchange National Bank of Chicago purchases 13 prints from Evans.

Lectures at the University of Southern California at Santa Cruz.

Has dinner with John Szarkowski in October. A retrospective at MoMA and funding are discussed.

In November, Isabelle gives a large party—combination house-warming and birthday party for Evans—in Lyme. He is in evening dress, and musicians play in the studio.

1968

Diary notes a barn with fading paint along the Boston Post Road near his house in Lyme. As the surface paint fades, an old TEXACO sign painted earlier shows with increasing clarity. He photographs this curious instance of reverse fading, using a wide-angle Rolleiflex and color film, at 5:30 P.M. on April 19.

Williams College makes Evans an honorary Doctor of Letters.

Elected Fellow of the American Academy of Arts and Letters.

A young photographer named Virginia Hubbard comes to New Haven to show her work to Evans.

In July, Evans has surgery at Yale-New Haven Hospital to remove gallstones.

Arnold Crane, a Chicago lawyer and private collector, buys a large number of prints and other material directly from Evans. Much of this purchase eventually passes to the collection of The J. Paul Getty Museum.

Partners in Banking: An Historical Portrait of a Great Private Bank, Brown Brothers Harriman & Co., 1818–1968 is published by Doubleday. The text is by John Kouwenhoven; Evans contributes more than fifty photographs.

*Evans with
students, 1966*

1969

Quality: Its Image in the Arts, edited by Louis Kronenberger, is
published by Atheneum. Evans contributes the chapter on
photography, a description of the state of the medium. He includes
21 photographs, each accompanied by a brief essay. Younger artists
mentioned include Arbus, Frank, Friedlander, and Virginia Hubbard.
A color picture showing an assortment of hand-lettered signs is identified as "photographer unknown"; it is almost certainly by Evans. The
accompanying dismissive commentary on the vulgarity of color is
likely ironic, and may be meant to apply to the other color photograph included, a lush study of a male and motorcycle by Marie
Cosindas.

Thomas Dabney Mabry, longtime friend and executive director of
MoMA during Evans's "American Photographs" exhibition, dies
suddenly in September. Evans travels to Kentucky for the funeral.

1970

"Walker Evans: Paintings and Photographs", an exhibition at

the Century Association, is organized by A. Hyatt Mayor.

Continues to plan for his retrospective at MoMA. Curator John Szarkowski decides to use new prints from Evans's negatives rather than "vintage" examples. The museum's department of photographic services makes proof prints of several hundred negatives; Jim Dow, a young photographer, works with Evans to make the exhibition prints.

Norman Ives, a School of Art colleague, works with Evans to choose fourteen photographs for a limited-edition portfolio. After many tests prints, 100 prints of each selected negative are contact-printed by a team led by Thomas Brown.

1971

A large retrospective of Evans's photographs, curated by John Szarkowski, opens at MoMA in January. Many of the pictures shown date from the 1930s, but some—including one of the two poster images—were made as recently as 1970. The exhibition of more than 200 prints is mounted in the first-floor galleries and is accompanied by a handsomely printed hardcover catalogue. The introductory essay by Szarkowski is at once a perceptive comment on Evans's work and a tribute to a close friend. The show travels to seven other venues; photographers too young to have known *American Photographs* discover, and are affected by, Evans's vision.

Has his second exhibition at Robert Schoelkopf Gallery.

Leslie Katz conducts a lengthy taped interview of Evans, who helps edit it for publication in *Art in America*. Deftly prompted by Katz, Evans provides the most complete, expansive discussion he has ever given of his artistic work and thought.

Meets with Alvin Eisenman in early spring to discuss a possible successor as senior faculty member in photography after Evans retires. They agree to invite Diane Arbus to come as Visiting Artist; she declines to visit.

Robert Frank visits Yale in May. He sits in on Evans's class; the discussion is taped and later edited and published in *Still/3* (1973).

Travels to Nova Scotia to visit Robert Frank, and to photograph.

Begins his last academic year as a regular Yale faculty member, leading a seminar open to graduate students and advanced undergraduates on Mondays, and a seminar in Trumbull College on Tuesdays.

Meets Alan Trachtenberg, who is in his first year at Yale as Professor of American Studies. Trachtenberg is beginning to write with increasing frequency on photography, and he introduces Evans to other academics interested in his photographs.

In December, the Yale Art Gallery presents "Walker Evans: Forty Years," also a retrospective exhibition. Evans, who influences the choice of pictures, includes much recent work, including a generous selection of prints from his recent trips to Nova Scotia. Chooses many photographs of roadside signs, and part of the gallery contains actual roadside signs, mounted in white wooden frames. Nearby, Evans offers two paragraphs of explanatory (or provocative) text, which assert the artist's claim on the objects that attract him— a claim equally valid whether he merely takes a picture or actually lifts the thing itself.

"Walker Evans: Fourteen Photographs," a limited-edition portfolio, is published by Ives-Sillman, New Haven publishers of portfolios of silk-screen prints by Josef Albers, among others. The introductory statement is by Robert Penn Warren. Of the proposed 100 sets, 88 are dry-mounted onto debossed museum boards, numbered, signed, and assembled into boxed sets.

Evans's photographic work at this time is done mostly with his set of 2¼ x 2¼ Rolleiflex twin-lens reflexes (he carries a case containing two cameras with normal 80-mm lenses, two with telephoto 135-mm lenses, and one, eventually two, with 55-mm wide-angle lenses). In the field, he works mainly in black-and-white. Begins to bring home objects, especially roadside and other kinds of signs, to photograph in his yard; in this work he sometimes uses color as well as black-and-white. Some of the actual camera work is done by assistants or friends, but Evans directs the process. Also collects discarded paper ephemera, pull-tabs from beverage cans, driftwood, and other rubbish for use in assemblages inspired by Cornell, Ives, and others.

Paul Cummings interviews Evans for the Archives of American Art.

1972

Travels to the Virginia Eastern Shore to photograph in late March. Works in 2¼ x 2¼ black-and-white and 35-mm color, using Leicas. Continues to acquire signs, and carries a toolbag in the back of his Chevrolet Vega station wagon.

Vogue commissions a portrait of Leon Edel by Evans for a proposed story. Goes to Edel's apartment with an assistant; using a pair of Rolleiflexes (he works with one while the assistant reloads the other) he exposes seven rolls of twelve-exposure film while keeping up an uninterrupted conversation with Edel about Henry James. Submits eight or ten prints, which he judges to be "competent work,"[4] to the magazine; the pictures are accepted but the story never runs.

Isabelle now spends most of her time in the New York apartment on East Seventy-third Street. She is manager of the designer salon at Bonwit Teller. Her weekend visits to Lyme are less frequent.

Accepts the invitation of Matthew Wysocki, a collector of folk art, dance photographer, and Director of Visual Studies at The Hopkins Center at Dartmouth College, to be Artist-in-Residence for the fall term of 1972. After a brief trip to London and leading a traveling workshop to Martha's Vineyard for Yale students, Evans reports for duty in mid-October. Has a studio in the Hopkins Center, where he works with his growing collection of found objects. Chauffered by Wysocki, he also explores the countryside around Hanover, making black-and-white photographs of churches and domestic interiors.

An exhibition of Evans's photographs is presented at the Jaffe-Friede Gallery in The Hopkins Center at Dartmouth, accompanied by a small illustrated catalogue.

Shortly after his sixty-ninth birthday Evans is checked into Mary Hitchcock Hospital in Hanover, New Hampshire, with a perforated ulcer. Surgery in late November removes the remainder of his stomach, and a substitute is fashioned from his upper small intestine. Recovery is slow. One of the night-shift doctors who visits him is the son of a man who worked to bring Kodak Tri-X film to market; Evans relishes the coincidence.

1973

Sent home to be looked after by a group of friends and students who take care of his housekeeping, meals, prescription medications, medical bills, and other needs. A local friend, a doctor in Old Saybrook who is nearly blind, has agreed to keep his eye on Evans.

Receives a grant from the Rothko Foundation, and the Schoelkopf Gallery cancels a show of work from the estate of Gaston Lachaise to offer Evans a date in spring for an exhibition.

A copy of a new Eakins Press book, *The Sculpture of Elie Nadelman* by Lincoln Kirstein, arrives by mail in Old Lyme. Signed by Kirstein and inscribed to Evans, it is their first direct communication in some years.

After a lengthy convalescence involving psychiatric treatment, Evans recovers his health and sufficient strength to live on his own, resume work, and travel. His first trip is to visit Christopher and Evie Clarkson in St. Martins, French Antilles.

Writes an introductory essay for Lee Friedlander's portfolio, "15 Photographs by Lee Friedlander." When asked by a young friend about his choice of the word *quotidian*, Evans replies with a smile that he always likes to use one word that sends them to the dictionary.

April exhibition of photographs at Schoelkopf Gallery presents black-and-white pictures from his entire career. Some enlargements of his 8 x 10 negatives are shown in Schoelkopf's front room, and a selection of recent work, including some pictures from New Hampshire and Virginia, is included.

Divorce from Isabelle is recorded in New Haven on April 25.

Travels to Decatur, Georgia, to have dental work done by Dr. Benjamin Hill, who accepts photographs in lieu of fees and is also his host. Buys a Polaroid SX-70 color camera, which is being test-marketed in the Atlanta area. Photographs with his Rolleiflexes.

Travels to England for several weeks, staying in the London flat of Robert Lowell, who is married to Evans's old friend Lady Caroline Blackwood. Visits them in the country, photographing the family in color with his SX-70, as well as in black-and-white, with a Leica. Also photographs with Rolleiflexes, at Brighton and at other locations.

Leads another fall traveling workshop for Yale students, this time to the Eastern Shore of Virginia. Photographs here with his Rolleiflexes for the last time. Begins to use the color Polaroid exclusively, photographing some architectural views, but mostly signs, bits of discarded rubbish, and the faces of friends and the students he encounters at lectures. Polaroid Corporation notices his interest, and begins to supply him with free film and duplication services.

1974

Travels to Oberlin College, the University of Texas, and other schools to lecture. On these trips he photographs with his color Polaroid.

"Walker Evans: Photographs from the 'Let Us Now Praise Famous Men' Project" is presented in the Michener Gallery of the Humanities Center at the University of Texas in Austin. During Evans's visit to the exhibition, Garry Winogrand, who is

573

teaching there, invites him home to dinner. Asks Winogrand for a signed copy of his book *The Animals*.

Returns to St. Martins, where he photographs with his SX-70.

The National Institute of Arts and Letters presents Evans its Award for Distinguished Service to the Arts, with a citation by Lionel Trilling.

Double Elephant publishes "Walker Evans: Selected Photographs," a portfolio of fifteen photographs with Lionel Trilling's citation as introduction. The portfolio, edited and produced by Lee Friedlander, is a boxed set of overmatted enlargements printed by a team led by Richard Benson.

Evans beachcombing, Old Black Point, 1974

Davis Pratt, Curator of Photographs at Harvard University's Fogg Museum, introduces Bobbi Carrey to Evans. A young photographer with a knowledge of archival materials and procedures, Carrey visits Lyme, to work at organizing the negatives and prints. Her visits last most of the summer.

In September, Evans takes a New Haven apartment with Jerry Thompson, a part-time assistant and friend. He begins to hint to a few close friends that he may have a large sale in the works.

Leads another traveling workshop of Yale students to Martha's Vineyard. Shortly after his return, he sells all his prints and an option for the purchase of his negatives to dealer George Rinhart and his partner, Thomas Bergen.

Spends more time in New Haven, photographing regularly and energetically with his color Polaroid. Makes more than 2,000 pictures of friends, students, strangers, old signs, and letter forms. He plans (among other projects) an alphabet book, a collection to include a witty color photograph of each letter of the alphabet. On his daily outings he searches hand-lettered parking lot signs and scrawled graffiti for good examples. These color details and portraits are not exhibited as a group during his lifetime, but this body of work receives his focused, sustained attention; it is a serious effort, and represents a significant late development in his work.

Has begun to drink again; by his seventy-first birthday he is obviously in trouble. Friends worry; James Mellow visits the New Haven apartment to interview Evans for the *New York Times*, and his published description of Evans sipping a tumbler of Remy Martin leaves little room for doubt. By the time the interview appears on December 1, Evans has, on the advice of his psychiatrist, checked into Yale-New Haven Hospital's psychiatric unit for a full physical and mental evaluation. There he suffers a fall, breaking his collarbone and requiring his transfer to a medical ward, where he contracts pneumonia. After a month, he transfers to Gaylord Hospital in Wallingford for rehabilitation.

1975

Discharged February 7, 1975, and returns to the New Haven apartment.

Virginia Hubbard, who now has a fifteen-month-old son, comes to New Haven and lives in the apartment. Listless and uncommunicative, Evans shows little interest in resuming an active life.

Announces his intention to keep a long-standing engagement to speak at Radcliffe College in April. With considerable effort and against all odds, Evans, in the company of a student companion, travels to Boston by train on April 8.

Dapper in a gray plaid suit and sporting a luxuriously full white beard, Evans answers questions about his life and work with coherent, even forceful replies, offering reflective asides on a variety of subjects, such as the havoc wrought on the central nervous system by alcohol. He and the talk are well received.

Shaky but triumphant, he takes the train back to New Haven alone on April 9. Later that night he suffers a massive stroke. Unconscious but surrounded by a small circle of friends, he dies during the early morning hours of April 10.

His will, written the night before his 1972 surgery in Hanover, names three equal heirs: Frances Lindley (formerly Frances Collins), Eliza Mabry (Tom's daughter, and Evans's goddaughter), and Virginia Hubbard. John Hill, who will manage Evans's artistic legacy until museums vie for that responsibility twenty years later, is designated executor.

This summary of Evans's life from 1957 to 1975 was drawn on notes left by James Mellow, but also on chronologies published in Walker Evans: *Subways and Streets*, by Sara Greenough (National Gallery of Art, 1991); *Walker Evans: The Getty Museum Collection* by Judith Keller (The J. Paul Getty Trust, 1995), and *Walker Evans: The Hungry Eye* by Gilles Mora and John T. Hill (Abrams, 1993). A substantial part of the account of events after 1971 has been taken from *The Last Years of Walker Evans* by Jerry L. Thompson (Thames and Hudson, 1997), or from notes assembled when that book was in preparation.

1 WE to Ford Foundation, April 29, 1960. WE Archive, WEA/MMA.
2 Conversation with JLT, ca. 1973.
3 WE to Ford Foundation, April 29, 1960. WE Archive, WEA/MMA.
4 Conversation with JLT, 1972.

*   *   *

"The American photographer Walker Evans, who died on April 10 at the age of seventy-one, was one of the greatest artists of his generation. He was also, in my opinion, one of the most widely misunderstood — misunderstood in the way that photography itself was so often misunderstood in his lifetime. Like many great artists, he was a difficult man, often indeed a devious man, and never more devious than at those moments — and they were not infrequent — when he allowed his work to pass into the world and be praised as something he knew it was not. He was an artist who traveled, as it were, incognito, sometimes amused, sometimes cynical, sometimes merely resigned to what the world had made of his accomplishments. He was very far from being immune to vanity or the appetite we all share for praise, recognition, and preferment — he certainly savored to the full his well-earned position as a classic — but he was disinclined by temperament and intelligence to mistake the world's word for the precise measure of his artistic worth. To no other figure of our time does Rilke's dictum about the paradox of celebrity — that fame is but the sum of misunderstandings that accumulate around a well-known name — apply with greater force."

> *from Hilton Kramer's "Walker Evans:*
> *A Devious Giant of Photography,"*
> New York Times, *April 20, 1975,*
> Sect. 2, pp. 1, 33.

Notes

The following abbreviations are used in the Notes

AA	Ansel Adams		* * *
BN	Beaumont Newhall		
BS	Ben Shahn	*ALWC*	*A Life Without Consequences*
CB	Carleton Beals	*FF*	*Letters of James Agee*
DM	Dwight Macdonald		*to Father Flye*
EH	Ernest Hemingway	*FM*	*Let Us Now Praise Famous*
EP	Ezra Pound		*Men*
ES	Elizabeth Skolle	*MAC*	*Many Are Called*
FC	Frances Collins	*WEAW*	*Walker Evans at Work*
FF	Father Flye	*WEF*	*Walker Evans at* Fortune
HC	Hart Crane		
HS	Hanns Skolle		* * *
JA	James Agee	AAA	Archives of American Art,
JDP	John Dos Passos		Smithsonian Institution
JES	Jane Evans Sargeant (Jane	FSA	Farm Security
	Ninas Evans)		Administration
JH	John Hill	MoMA	Museum of Modern Art,
JL	Jay Leyda		New York
JRM	James R. Mellow	NYPLPA	New York Public Library for
JS	John Szarkowski		the Performing Arts
JT	Jerry Thompson	Ransom	Harry Ransom Humanities
LB	Lesley K. Baier		Research Center,
LK	Leslie Katz		University of Texas at Austin
MR	Man Ray	Tamiment	Tamiment Institute Library,
PS	Peter Sekaer		New York University
RS	Roy Stryker	WEA/MMA	Walker Evans Archive, The
WE	Walker Evans		Metropolitan Museum of Art

I: School Years

31 "were very sympathetic and good women. They were wonderful"; WE/LK taped interview, for "Interview with Walker Evans," *Art in America* (March–April 1971), pp. 82–89, WEA/MMA.

31 "until I discovered the choice of being bad"; Ibid.

31 "That was a big thing"; Ibid.

31	"I did have a box camera and I developed film"; Ibid.
31–32	"But I was both graphic and visual in school"; Ibid.
32	"I'm a natural painter"; Ibid.
32	"I also went through a period of insecurity"; Ibid.
32	"I had to get over that"; Ibid.
33	"Observant boy remembers classic portico"; WE diary, June 3, 1935, WEA/MMA.
33	"completely over looked the gingerbread wing"; Ibid.
33	"visited Mercerburg Academy – deserted, touched by a mild rush"; WE diary, June 3, 1935, WEA/MMA.
34	"I started reading at Andover with a real love of reading"; Ibid.
34	"although I left in good standing"; Ibid.

2: The Incandescent Center

37	"I went there" Beaumont Newhall, ed., *Photography: Essays and Images*, 1980, p. 314.
37	"One lived in a sort of"; Ibid., p. 315.
38	"My best regards"; Hanns Skolle to WE, April, 1926; WEA/MMA.
38	Argument with his mother; JES/JRM interview, Jan. 6, 1994; also JT/JRM interview, Jan. 5, 1994.
38	"Any man of my age"; Newhall, p. 315.
38	"Figure what was going on"; Ibid.
38	"Your intention to write"; HS to WE April 27, 1926; WEA/MMA.
38	"Chère Avis"; June 1926; WEA/MMA.
39	"Mais helas"; June 1926; WEA/MMA.
39	"Alors que dire"; Ibid.
40	"Disgust in the boat train"; WEA/MMA.
41	"Problem of JCE"; Evans's list; WEA/MMA.
42	"Their impact was immediate"; Berenice Abott, *The World of Atget* (1964), intro, viii ff.
43	"Upon my word"; HS to WE, October 18, 1926, WEA/MMA.
43	"Acknowledged that they showed 'something'"; LK tapes: 1–3, for *Art in America*, WEA/MMA.
43	"certain people"; interview, WEA/MMA.
44	Hemingway in Paris; "All these personages"; JRM, *Hemingway: A Life Without Consequences* (1992), p. 306; Janet Flanner, *Paris Was Yesterday, 1925–1939* (1972), p. 12.
47	"I wanted you to swim"; ZSF to FSF, in JRM, *Invented Lives* (1984), p. 272.
48	"bull fighting"; *ALWC,* p. 333.
48	"All people went to Europe"; LK interview transcript; p. 21, WEA/MMA.
49	"I don't write to you"; undated note on back of Skolle letter dated July 29, 1926, WEA/MMA.
50	"You see I'd done a lot"; LK interview transcript, p. 5, WEA/MMA.
50	"How are the literary"; HS to WE; July 29, 1926, WEA/MMA.
50	"I fear you made"; HS to WE, Oct. 18, 1926, WEA/MMA.
51	"I knew she would get thick ankles"; Evans, "A Love Story," WEA/MMA.

52   "After that the sea"; Ibid.

52   "Voici mon journal"; WE, homework assignment dated August 7, 1926, WEA/MMA.

53   "tourmente, serre par la sante perverse"; Ibid.

53   "femmes affamees"; WE, undated assignment, ca. August 1926, WEA/MMA.

54   "I was really anti-American"; LK interview transcript, p. 16, WEA/MMA.

54   "Culture and art"; Ibid., p. 20.

54   "ridiculous woman"; WE, homework assignment dated November 12, 1926, WEA/MMA.

55   "Life was not a series of parties"; Francis Steegmuller, *Cocteau: A Biography* (1970), p. 372.

56   "Damn good"; HS to WE, Feb. 1927, WEA/MMA.

56   "Become sedate, old bean"; Ibid.

57   "Gide's prose style"; LK tapescript, WEA/MMA, p. 5.

57   "It seems to me"; WE translation, p. 3, WEA/MMA.

57   "And before sinking into sleep"; Bussy's Modern Library translation, p. 19.

3: Standing Aside

63   "of huge dimensions"; HS to WE, February 1927, WEA/MMA.

63   "Walker Evans, a figment of my mind"; "A Story in Which Something Happens"; 1927, WEA/MMA.

64   "Hanns Skolle listened in the evening"; Ibid.

64   "found me in the New York Society Library"; Ibid., p. 2.

64   "Ellie married Hanns"; Ibid., pp. 2–3.

64   "Hanns had lost the conviction"; Ibid.

65   "The appalling red thing"; Ibid., p. 5.

65   "I was surprised"; Ibid.

65   "Hanns grew fonder of the piano"; Ibid.

65   "escape from the saucepan"; ES to WE, July 14, 1927, WEA/MMA.

65   The horticultural project begun at Stamford; Postmarked envelopes addressed to WE, c/o HL Cornish, 335 Fairfield Ave, Stamford, from July 17 to Sept. 20, 1927, WEA/MMA.

66   "forget-me nuts"; HS to WE, May 1929; "damned peanut bulbs"; Feb. 15, 1930, WEA/MMA.

66–67   "Yes, take my advice"; HS to WE, undated 1927–1928, WEA/MMA.

67   "By Jove"; HS to WE, Sat. July 23, 1927, WEA/MMA.

67   "under the stinking influence"; HS to WE, Aug. 21, 1927, WEA/MMA.

67   *Ulysses* collage; HS to WE, Aug. 21, 1927, WEA/MMA.

67   "irascible giraffe"; HS mss; "Cinema, Deviation Number I", WEA/MMA.

67   "I think you would do well"; HS to WE, undated, Cos Cob stationery. Since the Skolles were planning to move to Colorado in Sept. 1928, the letter would have to have been ca. 1927, WEA/MMA.

68   "For Hanns, I am 'sa femme'"; ES to WE, Aug. 1928, WEA/MMA.

69   "long islandish labours"; HS to WE, June 1928, WEA/MMA.

70   "Respectueux souveneirs"; ES to WE, early July 1928, WEA/MMA.

70   "I shall come in town with automobile"; WE to HS, July 11, 1928, WEA/MMA.

70   "The joys of country-life"; HS to WE, undated July 1928, WEA/MMA.

71   "In general, things are not quite"; HS to WE, Aug. 1927, WEA/MMA.

72   "Bonne chance et à bientôt"; ES to WE, Aug. 1928, WEA/MMA.

72   "It was hinted in some quarters"; HS to WE, Aug. 1928, WEA/MMA.

72   "They are not even in the attic"; WE to HS, Aug. 14, 1928, WEA/MMA.

72   "There are also two girls"; Ibid.

74   "I was standing aside"; Newhall, pp. 313–314.

75   "I always remember"; Ibid., p. 313.

75   "The direct expression of today"; see Sue Davidson Lowe, *Stieglitz: A Memoir Biography* (1983), p. 201.

75   "The photogravures in this number"; Alfred Stieglitz quoted in *Camera Work*, June 1917, p. 17.

75–76 "I remember going out of there"; LK interview transcript for *Art in America*, WEA/MMA.

76   "Isn't it fine"; Edmund Wilson, *The Twenties*, (1975), p. 375.

76   "Oh yes, I was a passionate photographer"; Evans corrected typescript, 4.

76   "a semi-conscious reaction"; LK, WE corrected transcript, 16; Other transcript, p. 15. *Art in America*, pp. 84–85, WEA/MMA.

77   "Walker and I used to take"; HS/LB interview; May 23, 1979, Corrales, NM.

77   "were of two kinds"; Ibid.

77   "always extremely keen on everything"; Ibid.

77   "On one of our walks"; HS/LB interview, May 23, 1979.

78   "Just imagine looking out of your window"; John Unterecker, *Voyager—Hart Crane* (1969), pp. 356–357.

79   "God no. Perish the thought!"; WE/LK interview, WEA/MMA.

79   "Kindly give bearer 1 pint of gin"; HC note, undated. WEA/MMA.

79   "who saved 'The Bridge' "; HS/LB interview, May 23, 1979.

79   "Stick your patent name"; Waldo Frank, ed., HC's *Complete Poems* (1946), p. 15.

80   "Till elevators drop us"; HC, *The Bridge* (1930), p. 3.

80   "It's me for the navy"; Brom Weber, ed., *Crane Letters* (1952), p. 330; "the 20th of the 28th at the A.M. 7-thirtieth."

80   "There's Scott's Emulsion"; Unterecker, p. 563.

81   "Like greased lightning"; Ibid., p. 569.

81   "I fake it"; Ibid.

81   "Walker had a lot of friends then"; HS/LB interview, May 23, 1979, WEA/MMA.

81   "To Walker Evans"; HS to WE note, translations and clipping, late Dec. 1928, WEA/MMA.

81   "A child! Oh yes, a child!" Ibid; HS translation, WEA/MMA.

81   "and his head fell in"; undated clipping, Ibid.

81   "Tough going after Lady Chatterley"; HS to WE, Jan. 23–26, 1929, WEA/MMA.

81   "Thursday spent figuring best way"; WE to HS, Jan. 25 "nom de dieu" 1929, WEA/MMA.

81–82   "I could see it through his violent"; Ibid.

83   "very casually"; Ibid.

83   "highly pleased"; HS to WE, postmarked Jan. 29, 1929, WEA/MMA.

83   "from five to midnight"; WE to HS, Jan. 30, 1929, WEA/MMA.

83   "Thanks for…No thanks for"; Ibid.

83–84   "Situation very satisfactory here"; WE to HS, Feb. 6, 1929, WEA/MMA.

84   "Perhaps you'd better send me"; Ibid.

4: Words, Etc.

87   "undoubtedly one of the most insistently 'artistic' "; Louis Kronenberger, ed., *Quality: Its Image in the Arts* (1967), p. 206.

87   "There is reason to believe"; See drafts and notes titled "The Seeing-eye Man," WEA/MMA.

88   "not a business"; Lowe, p. 278.

88   "a very nice conversation"; JT interview with author, tape #14; Jan. 31, 1973, courtesy of Jerry Thompson.

88   "Saw Stieglitz again"; WE to HS, March 17, 1929, WEA/MMA.

89   "ribbon of talk"; Edmund Wilson, *American Earthquake* (1958), p. 100.

89   "When I knew Walker"; HS/LB interview, WEA/MMA.

90   "Did you ever see Stieglitz's photos"; WE to HS; June 28, 1929, WEA/MMA.

91   "You know, really, when you come"; WE/LK interview transcript, p. 25, WEA/MMA.

92   "My job"; WE to HS; Feb., 1929, WEA/MMA.

92   "Have decided to continue"; "Brooms," ca. February 1929, WEA/MMA.

92   "Couldn't buy anything"; Ibid.

93   *"Brooms* is remarkably good"; HS to WE, Feb. 11, 1929, WEA/MMA.

93   "Most encouraging"; WE to HS, Feb., 1929, WEA/MMA.

93   "got a decent letter"; WE to HS, March 25, 1929, WEA/MMA.

94   "Thanks for that superbest of all treats"; HS to WE, Feb. 20, 1929, WEA/MMA.

94   "I suppose you and I would both"; WE to HS, toward the end of Feb. 1929 for certain, WEA/MMA.

94   *Sons and Lovers* "made a very deep impression"; WE to HS, March 3, 1929, WEA/MMA.

94   " 'Plumed Serpent' ugly"; HS to WE, March 9, 1929, WEA/MMA.

94   "It's a hum-dinger!"; HS to WE, March 1, 1929, WEA/MMA.

94   "Excellent observations on D.H. Lawrence"; WE to HS, March 3, 1929, WEA/MMA.

94   "Did a very successful watercolor"; HS to WE.

95   "It is a large picture, I hope"; WE to HS, March 25, 1929, WEA/MMA.

95   "I was very pleased"; HS to WE, April ?, 1929, WEA/MMA.

95   "The Denver Museum"; HS to WE, May 1929, WEA/MMA.

95	"Permanent loan means"; WE to HS, May 24, 1929, WEA/MMA.
95	"Paul Grotz is coming here to live"; WE to HS, March 3, 1929, WEA/MMA.
95	"The whole thing sounds"; Ibid.
96	"a subversive…insidious book"; WE to HS, March 25, 1929, WEA/MMA.
96	"More impressed than at first"; WE to HS, April 16, 1929, WEA/MMA.
96	"You will have received"; WE to HS, March 17, 1929, WEA/MMA.
97	"Rented a house here"; WE to HS, May 24, 1929, WEA/MMA.
97	"We came back to my place"; WE to HS, July 14, 1929, WEA/MMA.
97	"I'll never manage"; WE to HS, May 3, 1929, WEA/MMA.
97	"Summer has been a success so far"; WE to HS, July 24, 1929, WEA/MMA.
98	"I met one Angel Flores"; WE to HS, July 14, 1929, WEA/MMA.
98	"Flores is a man of taste"; Ibid.
98	"like a slut from the streets"; *"Moravagine," Alhambra*; Aug. 1929, p. 34.
98	"Carnal visions pursued me"; Ibid., p. 35.
98	"Walker Evans is uneducated"; *Alhambra*, Aug. 1929.
100	"A prolonged *Walpurgishnacht*"; Angel Flores to Maxim Lieber, Aug. 24, 1929, WEA/MMA.
100	"Dear old BROOMS"; WE to HS, March 11, 1930, WEA/MMA.
100	Meeting of HC and García Lorca; Ian Gibson, *Federico García Lorca: A Life* (1985–87), p. 271.
101	"Anyway my mind has been completely put to rest"; WE to HS, Ibid.
101	"Hart Crane is in very bad shape"; WE to HS, Nov. 1929, WEA/MMA.
102	"Thank heaven"; Ibid.
102	"remarkable coincidence"; HC to Joseph Stella, Jan. 24, 1929, *Crane Letters*, p. 334.
104	"By the way, will you see"; HC to Caresse Crosby, Dec. 26, 1929, *Crane Letters*, p. 347
104	The Gauguin, Seurat, Cézanne and Van Gogh was the premiere exhibition at the new Museum of Modern Art; Nov. 1929 on the twelfth floor of the Hecksher Building on s/w corner of Fifth Ave. and 57th St. See Jan. 1930 letter to HS about the show, WEA/MMA.

5: The Center of Things

107	"the liquid soap squirters"; WE to HS, "the end of November" 1929, WEA/MMA.
107	"I am not working downtown anymore"; WE to HS, Feb. 24, 1930, WEA/MMA.
107	"interesting and amusing person"; WE to HS, Feb. 24, 1930, WEA/MMA.
108	"has married the lady"; WE to HS, Jan. 11, 1930.
108	"was better than ever"; WE to HS, Jan. 11, 1930, WEA/MMA.
108	"a great stampede of the art world"; WE to HS, Jan. 11, 1930, WEA/MMA.
108	"I used to try"; "Puritan Explorer," *Time*, Dec. 15, 1947, p. 73; Chicago exhibition "Leaving Things As They Are," 1987.
108	"I am learning something about photography"; WE to HS, "Feb twenty five

nineteen thirty," WEA/MMA.

109   "no reflection of light"; WE to HS, March 11, 1930, WEA/MMA.

109   "I need some good criticism"; WE to HS, May 7, 1930, WEA/MMA.

109   "Tableau No. 2 is disgusting"; HS to WE, Feb. 15, 1930, WEA/MMA.

110   "Besides amusing me beyond words"; WE to HS, Jan. 11, 1930, WEA/MMA.

110   "I got fed up with Crane"; WE to HS, May 7, 1930. WE's May letter is in response to eight letters from HS dating from March 20 to April 2, WEA/MMA.

111   "since I have borrowed"; Ibid.

111   "Couldn't say what happened"; WE to HS, June 19, 1930, WEA/MMA.

111   "pretty good, of course, but he has nowhere near your depth"; WE to HS, June 19, 1930, WEA/MMA.

111   "You would like Berenice Abbott"; WE to HS, Feb. 25, 1930, WEA/MMA.

112   "Berenice Abbott let a French publisher"; WE to HS, June 19, 1930, WEA/MMA.

112   "Further news is not worth recording"; Ibid.

112   "*un remarquable champ d'experience*"; *La Revue Moderne,* Paris, Nov. 14, 1930, pp. 24–25.

113   "I was, with Ben"; WE/JT tape, side 1 and 2.

113   "fire in apartment"; James T. Soby, *Ben Shahn: His Graphic Art* (1957), p. 20.

113   "a tough Jew"; WE/JT interview transcript, side 2, courtesy of Jerry Thompson.

114   "peculiar landscape"; WE to HS, June 19, 1930.

115   "But we manage"; WE to HS "Thursday night" [The mentions of the "Boston Exhibition" indicate that the date is late November and before Thanksgiving Day], WEA/MMA.

116   "The only thing one goes out for"; Ibid.

118   "I think I incorporated"; LK interview for *WEAW,* p. 70.

119   "happier"; Kirstein, *Mosaic,* p. 66.

120   " 'Tis the white stag, Fame"; *The Hound and Horn,* vol. I. (September 1927).

120   "a pair of rich fahrts and not getting paid"; Ibid., p. 13.

120   "Evans photos. good"; Ezra Pound to Lincoln Kirstein, Oct. 22, 1930; Ibid., p. 53.

121   "Photography exists in the contemporary consciousness"; Introductory Note from the exhibition catalogue for "Photography 1930"; Harvard Society for Contemporary Art, Nov. 7–29, 1930.

121   "Is it art or is it caricature"; WE to HS, "Thursday Night," Nov. 1930, WEA/MMA.

6: The Indigenous Past

124   "I enjoy your parties"; Letter to Edmund Wilson, March 17, 1930, WEA/MMA.

124   "large, blonde, faintly Churchillian baby"; Nicholas Jenkins, ed., *By With To & From: A Lincoln Kirstein Reader* (1991), p. 34.

124   "I often used his description"; Ibid., p. 31.

125   "had the curious New York Manner"; Kirstein diary, NYPLPA.

125   "It slightly embarasses me"; Kirstein diary, November 12, 1931, NYPLPA.

125   "and horrifying him by acting camp"; Ibid., August 1, 1931.

125   "transparently flirtatious . . ." Ibid., n.d., pp. 39–40.

126   "Walker and I took the bus"; Ibid., p. 130.

126   "went over to 14th Street"; Ibid., pp. 119–120.

127   "Walker first took me as a convict"; Ibid., p. 131.

128   "It's not a novel . . ." Ibid., p. 131.

129   "Dinner with Walker Evans"; Ibid., p. 124.

130   "lurid metaphor in the bright lights"; Ibid., p. 124.

131   "stale white calla lillies"; Gilles Mora and John T. Hill,
        Walker Evans: The Hungry Eye (1993), p. 65.

131   "Suggested he come up"; Kirstein diary, p. 177, NYPLPA.

132   "I so much wanted"; Ibid., p. 191.

132   "Spoke to Joe of trying"; Ibid. p. 212.

132   "incipient rape"; Ibid., p. 211.

132   "extraordinary tale"; Ibid. p. 217.

133   "doubtful novel"; WE to HS, May 19, 1932, WEA/MMA.

133   "he can't even see"; Kirstein diary, p. 217, NYPLPA.

133   "One of Walker Evans's convictions"; Ibid., p. 229.

133   "Patient, penitence, muffled apologies"; BWTF, p. 44.

134   "He achieved, she said"; Kirstein diary, pp. 335–336, NYPLPA.

134   "liked each other at once"; Ibid., p. 231.

135   "Lechery presupposed"; Ibid., p. 258.

136   "Colorless, pleasant before and exerting"; Ibid., pp. 259–261.

136–37 "Jack Wheelwright and Walker Evans"; Ibid., pp. 263–264.

137   "The Victorian houses that Jack Wheelwright"; Ibid., p. 265.

138   "not too interested in people"; Kirstein/JRM interview, June 20, 1991.

138   "Walker Evans I find"; Kirstein diary, p. 265, NYPLPA.

138   "for fear she would read"; Ibid., pp. 265–267.

138   "Tonight Walker was feeling"; Ibid., p. 267.

140   "Ralph Steiner the photographer"; WE to HS, July 4, 1931, WEA/MMA.

140   "To see Walker Evans"; Kirstein diary, p. 294, NYPLPA.

141   "Dreadful goings on"; WE to HS, May 11, 1931, WEA/MMA.

141   "two coats of brilliant black"; Ibid.

141   "This pleased me"; Ibid., pp. 315–316.

141   "I don't much want to see"; Ibid., p. 324.

141   "architecturally speaking"; Ibid., p. 328.

142   "Increasingly bored with Evans"; Ibid., p. 329.

142   "great precision"; Ibid., p. 329.

142   "silent, exercising to the full"; Ibid., p. 330.

142–143 "The work itself"; Kirstein to Lewis Mumford, June 30, 1931, NYPLPA.

143   "She is nice in a way"; Frederick Brown, *An Impersonation of Angels: A Biography
        of Jean Cocteau* (1968), p. 243.

143   "I said I had not yet explored"; Kirstein diary, p. 357, NYPLPA.

143   "Augmented the series"; WE to HS, July 4, 1931, WEA/MMA.

143	"indeed a good book"; Ibid.
145	"jig-saw gothic"; Ibid., October 2, 1931.
145	"Walker Evans has done some magnificent"; letter dated October 7, 1931, *The Hound & Horn Letters*, Mitzi Berger Hamovitch, ed. (1982).
145	"Thousands of men sell apples"; Kirstein diary, November 12, 1931, NYPLPA.
146	*"Dec. 30, [1931]: To New York"*; Ibid., p. 81.

7: Voyages

149	"gentlemen, flanneled fools"; WE to HS, Jan. 1, 1932, WEA/MMA.
150	"Four tiled bathrooms"; Ibid.
150–151	"My eye ceases to select"; Ibid.
151	"called piggly-wiggly"; Ibid.
151	"I must say, your convincing descriptions"; HS to WE, March 30, 1932, WEA/MMA.
151	"The Pacific Ocean is like"; WE to HS, Jan. 1, 1932, WEA/MMA.
151	"a dreadful conglomeration"; WE to HS, continuation of Jan. 1, 1932 letter, WEA/MMA.
152	"It is to be doubted"; Charles Roberts Anderson, *Melville in the South Seas* (1966), p. 51.
152	"Pitoyable"; WE to HS, Jan. 1, 1932 ff, WEA/MMA.
153	"But we were gay"; Ibid.
154	"The sadness of the Marquesans"; Ibid.
155	"The thing is, I went in fear"; WE to HS, May 19, 1932, WEA/MMA.
155	Evans warned about venereal disease; told to Norman Ives (per JH to JRM, Feb. 1995).
155	He had shunned the native women; JES/JRM interview, June 15, 1991.
155	Male dancers; Reel 3, 4, WEA/MMA.
156	"Telephoto closeup"; Reel notations, WEA/MMA.
156	"Movies are more difficult"; WE to HS, May 19, 1932, WEA/MMA.
157	"For Christ's sake come in"; WE, "The Italics Are Mine," p. 1, WEA/MMA.
157	"Come and meet my friends"; Ibid.
157	*"An underdog past"*; WE, "The Italics Are Mine", p. 3, WEA/MMA.
158	"My plans are less protuberant"; Ibid., p. 4.
159	"All I've got to do"; WE, "The Italics Are Mine", p. 2, WEA/MMA.
160	"Letter to Hanns Skolle"; April 4, 5, 6, 7th, 1932, WEA/MMA.
161	"Yes, Havana has something about it"; HS to WE, July 2, 1932, WEA/MMA.
161	"There was nothing much"; WE to HS, April 4, 5, 6, 7th, 1932, WEA/MMA.
161	"I'm not going to make it"; Unterecker, pp. 683–84.
162	"Hart Crane did away with himself"; WE to HS, May 19, 1932, WEA/MMA.
163	Levy had introduced Atget's work to America; Julien Levy, *Memoirs of an Art Gallery* (1959), p. 93.
164	Levy mentions Evans only once; Ibid., p. 69.
164	Levy claimed . . . that it was he; Levy, pp. 78, 116.

164   "a sort of New York Atget"; *New York Times,* Feb. 4, 1932.

164–165   "jigsaw details"; *Brooklyn Daily Eagle,* Feb. 7, 1932.

165   "What else, I should like to know"; Ibid.

165   "proof that the camera"; *The Art News Sunday,* Feb. 7, 1932.

165   "is to reveal in the most ordinary subject"; *Brooklyn Times,* Jan. 31, 1932.

167   "an incredible study of chaos"; *New York Times,* May 8, 1932.

167   "spunge off a few crumbs"; WE to HS, May 19, 1932, WEA/MMA.

168   "You remember the 'Men Working' idea?"; Ibid.

168   "We are both doing rather extraordinary things"; HS to WE, March 30, 1932, WEA/MMA.

169   "I do think you and I"; Ibid.

169   "Sacco and Venzetti in coffins"; Ibid.

8: Cuba Libre

173   Ernestine Evans/Stalin; Walter Duranty, *I Write As I Please,* (1935), pp. 198–199.

174   Gonzáles Rubiera; Carleton Beals, *The Crime of Cuba* (1933), p. 299, Russell Porter, *New York Times,* Feb. 4, 1933.

174   "No tire más" ("Don't shoot anymore"); R. H. Phillips, *Cuban Sideshow.* Havana: Cuban Press (1935), p. 15, and R. Hart Phillips, *Cuba, Island of Paradox,* pp. 7–9; Hugh Thomas, *Cuba, or, The Pursuit of Freedom* (1959), p. 607.

175   As early as March, through EE; see J. Jefferson Jones to CB, n.d., 1933, WEA/MMA.

175   "more truly than ever what an important thing"; Walter Goodwin to CB, April 26, 1933, WEA/MMA.

175   "I am sure the boy"; Walter Goodwin to CB, May 4, 1933, WEA/MMA.

176   "The political situation was critical"; WE, 1933 diary, n.d., WEA/MMA.

176   "When you are still bewildered"; Ibid.

177   The Alhambra Theater; Gibson, p. 292; Molina Rejo, Beals, p. 36.

178   "heavy, shouldered guns"; WE, 1933 diary, n.d., WEA/MMA.

178   " 'They' would suspect something and follow me"; Ibid.

178   "He said good! We will go to lunch"; Ibid.

179   "and I was thinking about his good latin face"; Ibid.

179   "Is this man knocking around between money, sex, boredom"; Ibid.

179   "I had a wonderful time with Hemingway"; *WEAW,* p. 82; Boston interview, August 4, 1971.

180   "Photographically speaking the face of a celebrity is a cliché"; "Much to Hemingway's delight I might add"; Mellow, "Walker Evans Captures the Unvarnished Truth," *New York Times,* Dec. 1, 1974, pp. 36–38.

180   "I had a very instinctive bond between him and me"; LK interview transcript, p. 46, WEA/MMA.

180   "We were both working against Machado"; EH to Harvey Breit; July 4, July 20, 1952, Princeton University Library.

182   "They were nice-looking fellows"; Hemingway, *To Have and Have Not,* 3ff.

182   "They were good-looking fellows"; Ibid., p. 6.

183   "Missed Machiavelli the Ferrara"; WE to CB, June 25, 1933, WEA/MMA; WE, *Havana, 1933* (1989), p. 5.

183   "All is fiction"; HB, pp. 277–278.

185   "Those people have no self-pity"; *WEAW*, p. 82.

187   "Your eye is a collector"; U. of Michigan tape, October 29, 1971, University of Michigan and WEA/MMA.

187   "None of the pictures with people is posed"; Dustjacket blurb, *The Crime of Cuba*.

189   "I had better write you"; 1933 diary, July 21–Aug. 2, WEA/MMA.

190   "The number of prints"; WE to CB, June 25, 1933, p. 2, WEA/MMA.

192   "Especial mention should be made"; *New York Times Book Review*, Aug. 20, 1933.

9: Seeing Red

195   "Hungry, so walked to see Noda"; WE diary, July 13, 1933, WEA/MMA.

195   "very bad"; Ibid.

195   "Leonie attracts me"; Ibid.

196   "I feel careless about it"; Ibid.

196   "So much Jew, me so much Nordic"; WE diary, July 14, 1933, WEA/MMA.

197   "[Ruth] promptly went into a madcap mood"; Ibid.

197   "I think she lost interest"; Ibid.

197   "Tonight at least crystallized an attitude in me"; Ibid., July 16, 1933, WEA/MMA.

197   "Since nothing is important to her"; Ibid., July 17, 1933, WEA/MMA.

198   "Mysterious Leonie"; Ibid., July 21–Aug. 2, 1933, WEA/MMA.

199   "I didn't like it"; Ibid., Aug. 4–5, 1933, WEA/MMA.

199   "small amount of money"; Ibid.

199   "Leonie Sterner has ditched me"; Ibid.

199   "We got nowhere"; Ibid., Aug. 9–11, 1933, WEA/MMA.

199   "Leonie Sterner, Peggy Osborne reappears"; WE diary, Aug. 19–22, 1933, WEA/MMA.

199   "In the restaurant we talked"; WE diary, July 14, 1933, WEA/MMA.

199   "Ben's private dilemma"; WE diary, Aug. 8, 1933, WEA/MMA.

200   "Roosevelt may do something"; WE diary, July 20, 1933, WEA/MMA.

200   "Berlin bad, Ernestine bad, me somehow good"; Ibid., WEA/MMA.

200   "Let myself be led around"; WE diary, July 18, 1933, WEA/MMA.

200   "I dislike other men's wives in that condition"; WE diary, July 21–Aug. 2, 1933, WEA/MMA.

200   "The government launches the National Recovery idea"; Ibid.

200   "America is changing"; WE to HS, April 20, 1933, WEA/MMA.

201   "It's important because at the moment there is *nothing* doing"; Ibid.

201   "I could support myself copying paintings"; Ibid.

201   "but not yet really a film"; Ibid.

201   "Murphy is dumb as they come"; Ibid.

201   "No money for eating"; WE diary, July 17, 1933, WEA/MMA.

202   "Spending pennies"; Ibid., July 21, 1933.

202   "How I eat three times a day is a mystery"; Ibid., July 21–Aug. 2, 1933.

202   "Your telephone is disconnected"; Ibid.

202   "Mrs. Evans writes that she wants to send me some money"; Ibid., Aug. 4–5, 1933.

202   "I don't remember two days running"; WE diary, Aug. 4–5, 1933, WEA/MMA.

202   "a few petty borrowings and scrapings"; Ibid., July 21–Aug. 2, 1933.

202   "Incredibly set up by Frida's appreciation"; Ibid.

202   "He insists we have a telephone here"; Ibid., Aug. 4–5, 1933.

202   "Shahn is working with Rivera on a mural"; WE to HS, April 20, 1933, WEA/MMA.

203   "the organized Soviet masses, with their youth"; Diego Rivera, *Portrait of America*, pp. 28, 24, 32.

203   "reactionary" and "counterrevolutionary." Hayden Herrera, *Frida, A Biography of Frida Kahlo* (1983), p. 166; see Diego Rivera, *My Life: An Autobiography* (1960), p. 210.

204   "was caught in no man's land"; Bertram Wolfe, *Fabulous Life of Diego Rivera*, footnote 329, the 1963 version; see page 366 in the 1939 version.

206   "gave me a nice puff"; WE diary, Aug. 6–7, 1933, WEA/MMA.

206   "Thank the lord"; Ibid., Aug. 17, 1933.

206   "Curiously unemotional about him"; Ibid., Aug. 6–7, 1933.

207   "victimized"; LB interview, May 23, 1980, WEA/MMA.

207   "about background, revolution, communism"; WE diary, July 15, 1933, WEA/MMA.

207   "poison…or at least he accuses me of trying"; Ibid., July 21, 1933, WEA/MMA.

207–208 "I didn't like him"; Ibid., July 16, 1933.

208   "Full moon, Westchester, misty valleys"; Ibid., Aug. 4–5, 1933, WEA/MMA.

208   "I was just able to go through with it"; Ibid., July 19, 1933, WEA/MMA.

208   "One of the good guys"; Kirstein/JRM phone conversation; March 23, 1933.

209   "charm, his untamed outrage"; Kirstein, *Mosaic: Memoirs* (1994), p. 182.

209   "It sounds very much like"; WE diary, Aug. 6–7, 1933, WEA/MMA.

209   "Got two dollars out of the bank"; Ibid., July 21–Aug. 2, 1933.

209   Ailments, "My stomach is bad"; (Aug. 4–5), drinking milk (Aug. 6–7), WE diary, WEA/MMA.

209   "I have had a new pain"; Ibid.

209   "I am told"; Ibid., Aug. 19-22, 1933.

209   "Asks me to send photos"; Ibid., July 21–Aug. 2, 1933.

209   "I've rarely spent so much time"; Ibid., Aug. 6–7, 1933.

210   "Cuban news more and more exciting"; Ibid., Aug. 6–7, 1933.

210   "No sales"; Ibid., Aug. 8, 1933.

210   "if American society is still functioning"; Ibid., Aug. 12, 1933.

210   "The terrible things which happened"; Phillips, *Cuba, Island of Paradox*, p. 40.

211   "Report on American rich"; WE diary, Aug. 13, 1933, WEA/MMA.

211     $68, "undreamed of riches"; Ibid., Aug. 18, 1933.

211   "If they use some, I'll be rich"; Ibid., Aug. 14, 1933.

211   "Shahn of course thinks"; Ibid., Aug. 14, 1933.

10: The Politics of the Vernacular

213   "I'm interested in what's called vernacular"; LK, "Interview with Walker Evans," *Art in America*, March–April, 1971, p. 88.

213   "If I hadn't known him"; Kirstein/JRM interview, April 12, 1995.

213   "Talked about a show"; Kirstein diary, Nov. 9, 1933, NYPLPA.

213   Newsreel theater: LK interview transcript, p. 12, WEA/MMA.

213   "Documentary?"; LK/WE interview; *Art in America*, p. 87; see also *Art in America* transcript, p. 60, 62, etc., WEA/MMA.

214   "philistines"; LK/WE interview, *Art in America*, p. 87.

214   "Photography is in essence"; Kirstein, *MoMA Bulletin*, December 1933.

214   "Evans's style is based on moral virtues"; Ibid.

216   He had no recollection: Kirstein/JRM interview, April 1995.

216   "The focus was sharpened until so precise"; Ibid.

216   "Any further relation of such a character"; Lloyd Goodrich, *Edward Hopper* (1949), p. 162.

216   "In its most limited sense"; Ibid.

216   "This is a case of parallel"; WE/Jonathan Goell interview, Museum of Fine Arts, Boston: [n.d.].

216–217   "disappointing. His work is careful"; WE to JL, Nov. 22, 1933, Tamiment. Unfortunately, Evans seems to have made no mention of another exhibition of a photographer whose works would have been more in his line, Henri Cartier-Bresson, who exhibited at the Julien Levy Gallery in the fall of 1933. Perhaps he did not see the show, though that *seems* unlikely.

219   "Julien Levy has shown me your note"; EE to JL, April 24, [1934], Tamiment.

220   "On receipt of your cable"; Ibid.

220   "I'm sure it all means"; WE to JL; Nov. 22, 1933, Tamiment.

221   "I motored down"; WE to EE, unfinished letter, February 1934, Tamiment.

221   "What do I want to do"; Ibid.

223   Automobiles and the automobile landscape; Ibid.

223   "You ought to see West Palm Beach and die"; Ibid.

224   "I am in a lousy resort hotel living room"; WE to JL, Feb. 21–March 27, 1934, Tamiment.

224   "was never active politically"; JL/LB interview, May 23, 1980, Tamiment.

225   "after I had declined the honor"; WE to JL, Nov. 22, 1933, Tamiment.

225   "Such whirligig changes"; Dwight Macdonald, *Memoirs of a Revolutionist: Essays in Political Criticism* (1957), p. 9; see also, James B. Gilbert, *Writers and Partisans: A History of Literary Radicalism in America* (1968), p. 172, ff.

225   "not to worry"; Michael Wreszin, *A Rebel in Defense of Tradition: The Life and Politics of Dwight Macdonald* (1994), pp. 30–31.

225   "disgusted by humanity"; DM to Nancy Rodman, July 16, 1934, Ibid.

225   "bathed in a clean capitalist pool"; Ibid.

II: Jane

229   "Cochran's American Vitruvius"; WE diary, April 18, 1935, WEA/MMA.

230   "depressing, unappetising"; WE, 2-page diary note, Feb. 5, 1935, WEA/MMA.

232   "extraordinary charm"; JES/JRM interview, June 15, 1997.

232   "He was very witty"; JES/JRM interview, June 15, 1991.

234   "The most sophisticated example"; *WEAW*, p. 113.

238   "Suddenly Walker pushed me up against a fence"; JES/JRM interview,
       June 15, 1991.

238   "more wildly and openly"; Ibid.

239   "bestirring themselves industriously"; Julia Mood Peterkin, "A Plantation
       Christmas," *Country Gentleman Magazine*, December, 1929.

239   "as they pick"; Ibid., p. 8.

239   "weathered by long years of rain"; Ibid., p. 11.

239   "[F]ive dozen or so finished"; WE diary, April 7, 1935, WEA/MMA.

239   forty prints: WE diary, April 9, 1935, WEA/MMA.

240   "a moral photography"; *New York Sun*, April 1935. Actually, Lloyd/Levy had
       referred to it as "amoral photography," quite a different thing.

240   actually a pseudonym for gallery-owner Julien Levy; Levy, *Memoirs*, pp. 48–49.

241   "Barr so nice and so confused"; WE diary, April 13, 1935, WEA/MMA.

241   "Tom knows what he is doing"; Ibid.

241–242 "The Museum has been fortunate"; *Museum of Modern Art Bulletin*,
       March–April 1935.

242   "C. wriggled lamely"; WE diary, April 18, 1935, WEA/MMA.

242   "Apparently all the first-rate publishers"; Ibid., April 2, 1935.

242   "Feeling of life disappearing"; Ibid., April 17, 1935.

242   "a photo taking arrangement"; Ibid., April 14, 1935.

243   "From here to Memorial Day"; Ibid., April 19, 1935.

I2: Love in the Thirties

245   "Postcards to Morrie, Cheever, Ben"; WE diary loose leaves: Feb. 4–5, 1935,
       WEA/MMA.

245   Cheever's argument with Kirstein: Scott Donaldson, *John Cheever: A Biography*
       (1988), p. 48.
       "When I was twenty-one"; Cheever to Allan Gurganus, March 28, 1974,
       Ben Cheever, ed., *The Letters of John Cheever* (1988), p. 304.

245   mostly women friends; see Frances Lindley's opinion, Donaldson, p. 68.

246   "because he couldn't believe"; Susan Cheever, *Home Before Dark* (1984), p. 23.

246   Beatrice Jacoby; phone interview with Beatrice Jacoby Perenchief, Sept. 21, 1992.

247   Tad Brewer was born in NY, March 16, 1932; T. Brewer to JRM Feb. 25, 1994.

248   "I do not doubt but the majesty"; Walt Whitman in JS, *Walker Evans*, MoMA, 1971.

240   "The only authentic photograph"; WE postcard, WEA/MMA.

249   "In the 1900's sending and saving"; ms postcard article, WEA/MMA.

249 "Main Street Looking North"; *Fortune,* May 1948, pp. 102–106.

249–250 "Your Ma and I stopped"; WE postcard, WEA/MMA.

250 "Hm"; WE to JT, ca. late 1973, courtesy of Jerry Thompson.

250 "Evening at Agee's unpardonably dull"; WE diary, April 5, 1935, WEA/MMA.

250 "poetic gift"; Laurence Bergreen, *James Agee: A Life* (1984), p. 139.

251 "hymn of praise"; Ibid., p. 143.

251 "Cleaning and pressing would"; James Agee, *Let Us Now Praise Famous Men: Three Tenant Families* (1941), pp. xli–xlii.

251 "He seemed to model"; Ibid., p. xlii.

252 "an open palm"; Paul Ashdown, ed., *James Agee: Selected Journalism* (1985), pp. 42–43.

252 "It is no chance"; *BWTF,* p. 229.

252 "For *Fortune*"; Agee to Father Flye, June 6, 1935; *The Letters of James Agee to Father Flye* (1971), p. 75.

252 "Add gentlemen of the persuasion"; Ashdown, p. 99.

253 "Saratoga runs less to the hot"; Ibid., p. 111.

253 "Keeps his real name or number"; Ibid., p. 103

253 "And every next morning the streets"; Ibid., p. 113.

254 "Evening Emma Agee came"; WE diary, April 6–8, 1935, WEA/MMA.

254 "Emma came again tonight"; Ibid., April 10–12, 1935.

254 "I can't remember having the nerve"; Interview, JES/JRM, Salisbury, CT, May 12, 1993.

255 "Roosevelt has almost no taste"; Daniel Aaron and Robert Bendiner, eds., *The Strenuous Decades: A Social and Intellectual Record of the 1930's* (1970), p. 121. His Secretary of Labor, Frances Perkins, remarked, "The pictures he selected from the art project for his office, while not the worst in the collection, were certainly not good."

256 "Mean never [to] make"; *WEAW,* p. 112.

257 "and do some work (as expert!)"; WE diary, June 8, 1935, WEA/MMA.

257 "Not only was she trying"; Taped interview, JES/JRM, May 12, 1993.

257 "work both sides of the street"; Colin Westerbeck, *Bystander: A History of Street Photography* (1994), p. 259.

258 "It always took a *long* time"; Taped interview, JES/JRM, May 12, 1993.

258 "Went to Morgantown, loaded holders in photographers darkroom there"; WE diary, July 2, 1935, WEA/MMA.

259 "wonderful rows of frame houses"; Ibid., June 29, 1935.

259 "very typically" became amorous; Phone interview, JES, Aug. 23, 1995.

260 Much affection for Jane"; WE diary, July 3, 1935, WEA/MMA.

260 "leisure, solace (what?)"; Ibid., July 4, 1935.

260 "very bad, my fault, stupid of me"; Ibid.

260 "hot, depleted, unsexed"; WE diary, July 6, 1935, WEA/MMA.

261 "slight depression, not thinking of J."; Ibid., July 7, 1935.

261 "some interiors"; Ibid.

262 "Rather discouraging, not getting much"; WE diary, July 9, 1935, WEA/MMA.

262   "cold and terrifying"; Ibid., July 10, 1935.

262   "worked badly and listlessly"; Ibid., July 11, 1935.

263   "As a joke on myself"; Ibid., July 12, 1935.

263   "mad unnecesssary"; Ibid., July 13, 1935.

263   "touched by a mild rush of reminiscence"; Ibid.

263   "Discovered that some things"; Ibid.

I3: A Subsidized Freedom

265   "Typical Washington day"; WE diary, July 15, 1935, WEA/MMA.

265   "I went down there"; Cummings interview transcript, p. 20, AAA.

265   [One third of the works were Hine's] Westerbeck, p. 248.

265   "was mine and Stryker's"; William Stott, *Documentary Expressions and Thirties America* (1973), p. 212.

265   "Truth is the objective"; Ibid., p. 14.

265–266   "A good documentary"; Ibid., p. 29.

266   "not the America"; Ibid., p. 50.

266   "It was crazy, you know"; Cummings interview transcript, p. 20, AAA.

266   "give a damn"; Stott, p. 281.

266   "Well, a subsidized freedom"; Op. cit., p.20.

266   "E.E. wired admonishingly"; WE diary, July 23, 1935, WEA/MMA.

266   "Look good"; Ibid., July 27, 1935.

266   "dispirited and worried"; Ibid., July 26, 1935.

267   "that the only really satisfactory prints"; WE to John Carter, Aug. 17, 1935, *WEAW*, p. 112.

267   "exceedingly interested"; Ibid.

267   "Thank God letter from J."; WE diary, July 22, 1935, WEA/MMA.

268   "Considerable excitement"; Ibid., Sept.10, 1935.

268   "Bad letter from J."; Ibid., July 25, 1935.

268   "beer, poor conversation"; Ibid., Aug. 17, 1935.

269   Hiring Peter Sekaer: Elizabeth Sekaer Rothschild/JRM phone interview, Sept. 19, 1995.

269   "Mr. Walker Evans has agreed"; *WEAW*, p. 113.

269   "Job looks excellent"; WE diary, Oct. 9, 1935, WEA/MMA.

269   A diary note; Ibid., Aug. 30, 1935.

270   "art and culture" in America; Ibid., Oct. 11, 1935.

270   "great reservoir"; Stott, p. 118.

270   Berenice Abbott's West 53rd Street studio; Julia Van Haaften/JRM phone interview, Oct. 3, 1995; WE diary, Sept. 18–19, 1935, WEA/MMA.

270   "He could wrap Mr. Stryker"; Cummings interview transcript, p. 18, AAA.

270   Tillie Shahn, Lou Block; Clarence Pearson Hornung, *Treasury of American Design*, 1976.

270   Shahn's fixed lens Leica; Westerbeck, p. 259.

270   "That always irritated me"; Cummings interview transcript, p. 18, AAA.

270–271   "Shahn's Scott's Run photographs"; Westerbeck, pp. 233, 234.

271   "Walker Evans's pictures"; Ibid., p. 285.

271   Stryker's agency supplied photographs to *Fortune* etc.; Ibid., p. 254.

272   "Still photography, of a general sociological nature"; *WEAW,* p. 113.

273   "We were working at a pretty white heat"; Stott, p. 282.

275   "inexplicable"; WE diary, Nov. 3, 1935, WEA/MMA.

275   "take no prisoners attitude"; Phone conversation with JES, Summer 1995.

275   "epic vistas"; JT to JRM, Aug. 25, 1995.

277   "a simple complaint"; *WEAW,* p. 12.

280   "It's transcendent. You feel it"; LK interview, *Art in America,* p. 82.

281   "with some 32 rolls"; Gehman, *The Morning Call,* Feb. 22, 1990; mss. p. 4.

281   "I developed my own eye"; Cummings interview transcript, p. 20, AAA.

281   "I look at those other photographs"; Bill Ferris, *Images of the South: Visits with Eudora Welty and Walker Evans* (1978), p. 33.

281–282   "a mining town on a hill"; WE diary, misdated Nov. 18, 1935. Crossed out and redated "See Nov. 29," WEA/MMA.

282   "The hotel chambermaids"; WE diary, Nov. 29, 1935, WEA/MMA.

282   "complex, pictorially rich"; *WEAW,* p. 113.

282   "Hills in this city"; Ibid.

282   "had been waylaid"; Roy Stryker to WE, Dec. 10, 1935; Stryker Papers, University of Louisville. Appears to have been addressed to Nashville.

282   "[Y]ou must push as hard as possible"; Gehman, Feb. 22, 1990.

283   "Come Back Boss Man"; WE diary, Dec. 18–19, 1935, WEA/MMA.

284   "out of obvious evil"; JES/JRM interview, n.d. 1995.

284   "It was just tension"; JES/JRM interview, May 12, 1933.

285   "You can always count"; PS to WE, Dec. 26, 1935, WEA/MMA.

285   "Still not so much as a postal from you"; PS to WE, Jan. 2, 1936, WEA/MMA.

286   "Of course, we concede your right"; RS to WE, Feb. 1936, *WEAW,* p. 118.

286   "I am informed that you"; Ibid.

286   "This will give you a chance"; Ibid., p. 119.

289   "Behind the window screen"; Annemette Sørensen, *Peter Sekaer: New Deal Photography* (1990), p. 61.

289   "when word came"; Ibid.

290   "Do you think that coat's warm enough"; JS/JRM interview; May 12, 1993; confirmed, phone interview Nov. 7, 1995.

292   *The Voice of Bugle Ann; Hungry Eye,* p. 308. Sekaer in his *New Deal Photography* caption (Catalogue 57) mistakes the tag line as the title of the film: "'Love Is Young' is playing at the movies. Vicksburg."

292   "I am fascinated by man's work"; Radcliffe College talk transcript, WEA/MMA. Dustjacket for WE, *First and Last* (1978).

293   "Of course I remember Vicksburg"; Ferris, p. 33.

294   Paul Ninas threatens Evans; JES/JRM, phone interview, Nov. 7, 1995.

301   "Negroes are used to build roads"; Sørensen, p. 51.

302   "so many/I had not thought"; T.S. Eliot, *Complete Poems, 1909–1935* (1932), p. 71.

302   The *Penny Picture Display* negatives; see JT, "Walker Evans: Some Notes on His Way of Working," *WEAW,* p. 14.

I4: A Curious Piece of Work

308   "One day Jim appeared"; Robert Fitzgerald, *The Third Kind of Knowledge* (1993), p. 62.

308   "The best break I ever had"; Cassidy, Spears, Robert Coles, *Agee, His Life Remembered* (1985), p. 56; dated June 18, 1936.

308   "eagerly grabbed by Agee but not by me"; LK, *Art in America*, p. 32.

308   "The problem is one of staying out"; Stott, p. 320.

308   "I was interested, selfishly"; Ibid., p. 319.

308   "didn't really know what role"; Katz, p. 32.

308   "subterfuge"; Cummings interview transcript, October 13, 1971, p. 28, AAA.

309   Leave of absence from *Fortune*; Stott, p. 349.

309   "During July and August 1936"; FM, p. xlv.

309   "Sure, of course, take all the snaps"; Ibid., p. 25.

310   "An you, you ben doin much coltn lately"; Ibid., p. 28.

310   "it tore itself like a dance"; Ibid., p. 29.

310   "something with some life to it."; Ibid., p. 30.

310   "in a perversion of self-torture"; Ibid., pp. 29–30.

311   "next to unassisted and weaponless consciousness"; Ibid., p. 11.

311   "Awnk, awnk"; Ibid., p. 35.

311   "as if he were a dog masturbating"; Ibid., p. 37.

312   "Without appearing to look "; Ibid., p. 39.

312   "Their faces were secret, soft,"; Ibid., p. 42.

312   Harmon was forced to admit; Dale Maharidge, *And Their Children After Them: The Legacy of "Let Us Now Praise Famous Men," James Agee, WE, and the Rise and Fall of Cotton in the South* (1989), p. 20.

312   "I should have been back"; Ibid., p. 372.

313   "how much slower white people are; Ibid., p. 362.

313   "[We] told them exactly what we were doing."; Spears, p. 58.

315   "the terrible structure of the tripod"; Ibid., p. 364.

315   "Walker made a picture of this"; Ibid., p. 364.

315   "the children standing like columns"; Ibid., p. 365.

315   "whose eyes go to bed"; Ibid., p. 372.

316   "Your father will not let you"; Ibid., p. 368.

316   "The background is a tall bush"; Ibid., p. 369.

316   kept the Tengles from their dinner; Ibid., p. 362.

317   "Why, that dirty son-of-a-bitch"; Ibid., p. 79.

317   "But all this while,"; FM, p. 365.

318   "whose goodness and understanding"; FM, p. 373.

318   "walk through lobbies whose provincial slickness"; Ibid.

318   "first walked in the late brilliant June"; Ibid., p. 374.

318   "I knew I very badly wanted"; Ibid., pp. 375–376.

318   "All the porches were empty"; Ibid., p. 379.

319   "the slow blue dangerous and secret small town eyes"; Ibid., p. 373.

319   "talking low in sexual voices"; Ibid., p. 281.

319   "Of all the christbitten places"; Ibid., p. 377.

319   "You understand, taint I don't trust yuns"; Ibid., p. 371.

319   "His yellow eyes and very slow way"; Ibid., p. 385.

320   "devil hisself was after her"; Ibid., p. 399.

320   "as if a definite avoidance"; Ibid., p. 403.

320–321   "Our voices and our bodies take shape"; Ibid., p. 403.

321   "can fill you with love"; Ibid., p. 406.

321   "I had a least half-contrived this."; Ibid., p. 411.

321   "superior"; Ibid., p. 414.

321   "not of our creating"; Ibid., p. 417.

322   "Outside the vermin"; Ibid., p. 427.

323   "heavily littered with lard buckets"; Ibid., p. 76.

323   "safe"; Ibid., p. 179.

323   "beautiful in my remembrance"; Ibid., p. 419.

323   "in a confusion of shufflings"; Ibid., p. 419.

324   "two small twin vases"; Ibid., p. 163.

324   "Oh, I do *hate* this house *so bad*"; Ibid., p. 210.

324   "On each of these surfaces"; Ibid., pp. 170–171.

324   "A pink crescent celluloid comb"; Ibid., p. 172.

326   "The big people, you know, the big bugs"; Spears, p. 62.

326   "temperatureless, keen, serene and wise and pure gray eyes"; Ibid., p. 368.

326   "It is while I am watching you"; Ibid., p. 369.

328   "Her build is rather that of a young queen"; Ibid., p. 59.

329   "Each of us is attractive to Emma"; Ibid., p. 61.

329   "gives no appearance of noticing"; Ibid.

329   "if only Emma could spend"; Ibid., p. 62.

329   "Whether he would kiss Emma goodbye"; Ibid., p. 63.

330   "I blush and squirm every time"; Stott, p. 318; see also p. 265.

15: The Cruel Radiance of What Is

333   "The trip was very hard"; JA to Father Flye; Sept. 8, 1936. *The Letters of James Agee to Father Flye* (1971), p. 94.

333   "Just a half inch beyond the surface"; *FM*, p. 57.

333–334   "night-permeated"; Ibid., p. xliii.

334   "a much longer book"; "all other parts of this volume"; Ibid., pp. 244–245.

334   "I am giving myself an awful fucking"; Bergreen, p. 180.

334   "did not have the courage"; Fitzgerald, p. 86.

334   "pretty thunderous"; Stott, p. 262.

334   "liberal" nor its "conservative" mode; Macdonald, p. 262, Spring 1948.

335   "God damn it I'm getting sore"; Wrezin, p. 52.

335   "the Steel sell-out"; See DM to Dinsmore Wheeler. June 10, 1936; Wreszin, p. 53.

335   "chopping it in bits"; Stott, p. 262.

335   "half consciously"; see also Stott, p. 262.

336   "I wish I could write of a tenant's work"; Ibid., p. 293.

336   "If I could do it"; *FM,* p. 13.

337   "Walker was at loose ends"; JL/LB interview, May 23, 1980, courtesy LB.

338   "Do you think you could explain"; WE to JL, Dec. 22, 1936, Tamiment.

338   "Would you like to supervise"; WE to JL, Feb. 17, 1937, Tamiment.

339   "Everything seems O.K. darkroom and all"; WE to JL, n.d., Tamiment.

339   "If you're still sleeping"; WE to JL, Dec. 3, 1937, Tamiment.

339   "He sent it to me"; JL/LB interview, May 23, 1980, courtesy of Leslie Baird.

339   "I'm glad to be out of New York"; WE to JL, after Feb. 17, 1937, Tamiment.

339   "The film for Resettlement is off"; WE to JL, Dec. 3, 1936, Tamiment.

339   "I'm damned annoyed with Ben for various reasons"; Ibid.

340   Tugwell resignation; see Kenneth S. Davis, *FDR: Into the Storm, 1937–1940* (1993), pp. 7–8.

340   "You'll be pleased to know"; WE to JL, Sunday, ca. late 1936, Tamiment.

340   "especially Tugwell's"; "Sunday" Blackstone Hotel, 1936, Tamiment.

340   "Actually Shahn"; Ibid.

340   "By the way, a second indication"; WE to JL, c. late 1936, Tamiment. Both the previous letter above an this one may have been written around the same time as Evans's Dec. 3, 1936 letter to Leyda, since in the "Sunday" letter and the Dec. 3rd, Evans mentions that he has a three month period of work ahead of him.

341   "Things now stand"; WE to JL, Dec. 3, 1936, Tamiment.

341   "I think we are going to make a film"; WE to JL, n.d. but from the 2921 Olive Street address, Tamiment.

341   "I wonder if you will be interested"; Ibid.

342   "Thanks for your card about Agee's film thoughts"; WE to JL, Dec. 3, 1936, Tamiment.

342   "J. Leyda has seen or written you"; JA to WE, n.d., Ransom, Belinda Rathbone, *Walker Evans: A Biography* (1995), p. 145.

342   "He is a smart guy all right"; JA to WE, probably late 1936, Ransom; Bergreen, p. 181.

342   "a descendant" of the League; JL/LB interview transcript, p. 5, courtesy of Leslie Baird.

342   "Anyway I don't know"; WE to JL, Dec. 3, 1936; Tamiment.

343   "were all swept away"; JL/LB interview transcript, p. 5, courtesy of Leslie Baird.

343   "enormous enthusiasm for films"; Ibid., p. 2.

343   "Bad day today couldn't phone"; WE to JL, "Thurs." Baltimore & Ohio stationery, Tamiment.

343   Sekaer's meeting with Jane in New Orleans; JES/JRM interview.

343   "I told him perhaps too much about my ideas"; WE diary, Jan. 28, 1937, WEA/MMA.

343   "No signs of a flood as we came in"; WE diary, Feb. 2, 1937, WEA/MMA.

345   "looks like a communist commissar in the Winter Palace"; Ibid.

345   "swift and deep and frightening"; Ibid., Feb. 3, 1937, WEA/MMA.

346   "Careful not to do this"; Ibid., Feb. 4, 1937, WEA/MMA.

346   "Their own?"; Ibid.

346   "So far all goes well"; Edwin Locke to RAS, Feb. 4, 1937; Rathbone, p. 146.

347   "bathed, ate steak, and loafed well"; WE diary, Feb. 7, 1937, WEA/MMA.

347   "Some good"; Ibid., Feb. 8, 1937.

347   "Will lose this week"; Ibid., Feb. 9, 1937.

347   "I am in a hell of a dilemma"; Edwin Locke to RAS; Feb. 11, 1937; Stryker
       Papers, University of Louisville.

347   "Up and out for a while, sun, river"; WE diary, Feb. 14, 1937, WEA/MMA.

347   "I had the flu but the flood was damned interesting"; WE to JL, Feb. 17, 1937,
       Tamiment. His diary for the remainder of the trip; WE diary, Feb.17, 1937,
       WEA/MMA.

348   "affairs very dubious in Washington"; WE to JL, Feb. 17, 1937, Tamiment.

348   "Reasons for action"; March 24, 1937, National Personnel Records Center, St.
       Louis; Rathbone, p. 147.

348   "The attribution to Walker Evans"; Maddox, Walker Evans Photographs for
       the Farm Security Administration, 1935–1938 (1973), note on page for items
       #412, 413.

350   "the cruel radiance of what is"; *FM*, p. 11.

I6: Untitled

351   "You know much more about his work"; BN to WE, Dec. 8, 1936, MoMA.

351   "the remains of the Brady"; WE to BN, Dec. 11, 1936, MoMA.

352   "I could give the Museum a set of"; Ibid.

352   "Tugwell is not interested in photography"; Ibid.

352   "you said nothing in your letter"; BN to WE, Dec. 12, 1936, MoMA.

352   "If we could announce the gift"; Ibid.

352   "to show people what his things looked like"; Ibid.

353   "Time is flying"; BN to WE, Jan. 18, 1937, MoMA.

353   "How goes the Brady search"; Ibid.

353   "that is there will be a case beneath"; Ibid.

353   "And just now government"; WE to J. Newhall, Jan. 27, 1937, MoMA.

353   "pretty much a shambles"; Ibid.

353   "I am afraid that I shall have to cut"; BN to WE, Jan. 28, 1937.

353–354 "This morning requested Miss Evans..."; WE diary, Jan. 30, 1937, WEA/MMA.

354   "Thanks for sending the three..."; BN to WE, March 9, 1937, MoMA.

355   "Lissen: It will be all right..."; Frances Collins to WE, Wed., n.d., MoMA.

355   "The most comprehensive exhibition..."; *Time* magazine, October 3, 1938.

356   "Ransacking the important collections"; BN, *Focus: Memoirs of a Life in
       Photography* (1953), p. 53.

358   "You know Agee was oversexed"; WE/Stott tape transcript, around p. 154,
       University of Texas at Austin.

359   "She'll be a high school girl twenty years"; Bergreen, p. 187.

360   "With Walker you knew you were never"; Rathbone, p. 151.

360   "part of the first sexual revolution"; Stott, pp. 318–319.

360   "the sea-faring analogy"; Ibid., p. 142.

361   "of the passenger traffic of all flags"; Ibid., p. 142.

361-362   "sufficiently intelligent to count to ten"; Ibid., p. 139.

362   "in naughty trunks, laid towels aside"; Ibid., pp.143–144.

362   "the musical comedy blue of the Gulf Stream"; Ibid., p. 148.

363   "the Grant's Tomb of bars"; Ibid., p. 153.

363   "New acquaintances"; Ashdown, p. 153.

17: A Way of Seeing

367   "deliver to the publishers"; Contract dated May 6, 1938; WEA/MMA.

368   "Since this selection has already been made"; Thomas Mabry to WE, March 29, 1938, WEA/MMA.

368   "You know much more about Walker's work"; Mabry to Kirstein: April 29, 1938; Office of the Registrar MoMA; Keller, *Walker Evans*, p. 129.

370   "I believe that it was largely personal"; LK/WE interview transcript, p. 33, WEA/MMA.

370   "It was like a calling card"; Cummings interview transcript, p. 33, AAA.

370   "I remember Lincoln helping me"; Katz edited transcript, pp. 33–34, WEA/MMA.

370   "Kirstein was an aggressive quite unrestrained young man..."; *Art in America*, p. 83; also Douglas R. Nickel, "American Photographs Revisited," *American Art*, Spring 1992, p. 90.

371   "Tom had a note from Lincoln"; FC to WE: May 4, 1938, WEA/MMA; Blumenthal of Spiral Press, *WEAW*, 150.

371   "New proofs came from Beck"; Ibid.

371   "The Mus. Mod. Art wants to publish"; WE to RES, June 15, 1938; Stryker Papers, University of Louisville.

372   "Dear Roy, One of the things"; WE to RES; July 16, 1938; 441 E. 93nd St.; WEA/MMA.

372   "Human beings...are far more important"; *WEAW*, p. 151.

373   "[T]hese anonymous people who come and go"; Ibid.

374   "The responsibility for the selection of the pictures"; Ibid.

374   "the unrelieved, bare-faced, revelatory fact"; Kirstein essay in WE, *American Photographs* (1988), p. 196.

374   "It is 'straight' photography"; Ibid., p. 197.

374   "The quartz and cameos of Marianne Moore"; Ibid., pp. 197–198.

375   "Even the inanimate things, bureau drawers"; p. Ibid., 197.

375   "The most characteristic single feature"; Ibid., 197.

375   "pinkish flirtations"; Kirstein, *Mosaic*, p. 181.

375   "scared the wits out of me"; Ibid., p. 183.

375 "as isolated pictures made by the camera"; Ibid., p. 193.

375 "I had heard from Via"; JA to WE, June 20, 1938 Ransom; Rathbone, p. 159.

376 "accidental...future students and examiners of the period"; *WEAW*, p. 151.

376 "only in time"; Ibid.

376 "with all their clear, hideous and beautiful detail"; WE, *American Photographs*, p. 193.

376 "a spy, traveling as a journalist"; *FM*, p. liv.

376 "a conspirator against time and its hammers"; Op. cit., p. 196.

377 "a great deal"; LK/WE, pp. 13–14, WEA/MMA.

377 "In many ways he was able to tell me"; Ibid.

377 "I wish you the luck"; JA to WE, Sept. 13 or 14, 1938, Ransom.

377 "Simply by being published"; JA to WE, Sept., 15, 1938, Ransom.

377 "I'm glad that Evans has promenaded his eyes"; *The New Republic*, Oct. 12, 1938.

378 "unalterable...If ever a photographer"; Carl Van Vechten, *New York Herald Tribune Books*, Oct. (16), 1938, p. 4.

378 "His prints would put even Hollywood stills to shame"; S.T. Williamson, *New York Times Book Review*, Nov. 27, 1938, p. 6.

378 "Some of the prints haunt you"; Ibid.

378 "The physiognamy of a nation";BN, *American Photographs*, p. 198.

378 "Hardly...bumps, warts, boils and blackheads"; S.T. Williamson, *New York Times Book Review*, Nov. 27, 1938, p. 6.

378 "pretentiously arty essay"; Lewis Gannett, *New York Herald Tribune*, Nov. 25, 1938.

378–379 "Our attention is compelled in these photographs"; David Wolff, *The New Masses*, Oct. 4, 1938.

379 "the used cars abandoned on a field"; Ibid.

380 "Talking of photographs"; Eleanor Roosevelt, "My Day," *New York Telegram*, Sept. 30, 1938.

380–381 "so far out of the realm of our understanding"; Pare Lorentz, *The Saturday Review*, Dec. 19, 1938, p. 6.

381 "Never directed me"; WE/Stott tapes.

381 "liked it a lot"; Roy Stryker to WE, Nov. 9, 1938. Stryker Papers, AAA.

381 "I think the book is atrocious"; Nancy Newhall, *Ansel Adams: The Eloquent Light* (1963).

381 "I am so *goddam* mad over what people from the left tier"; Ansel Adams to Edward Weston: Nov. 1938; BN, *Focus: Memoirs of a Life in Photography* (1993), p. 163.

381 "Your shells will be remembered"; Mary Street Alinder et al., *Ansel Adams: Letters and Images* (1988), p. 74.

381 "bourgeois liberal...But so few pictures"; Adams to David McAlpin, Nov. 4, 1938, in Ansel Adams, *Letters*, p. 109.

384 "the section which you come into first"; Alfred Barr to WE, Aug. 24, 1938, WEA/MMA.

388 On the night of the preview opening: Rathbone, p. 163; but she gives it as a Saturday; MoMA press release says public opening Wednesday, Sept. 28.

388 "I'm sorry that I did not see you"; BN to WE, Sept. 27, 1938, MoMA and

WEA/MMA.

389   "There ought to be"; Clipping n.d., MoMA.

389   "I only wish"; Theodore Dreiser to MoMA, Oct. 8, 1939; MoMA.

389   "l'intensité avec qu'il montre"; Henri Cartier-Bresson to Frances Collins, Oct. 30, 1938, MoMA.

389   "the most significant event"; *Time*, Oct. 3, 1938.

389   "view is clinical"; *American Photographs*, p. 194.

389   "caught the essential moment"; *Time*, Oct. 3, 1938.

390   "the motivation seems, on the artist's part"; Jewell, *New York Times*, Oct. 2, 1938.

390   "We have no photograph of the photographer"; Mabry, *Harper's Bazaar*, Nov. 1, 1938.

390   "possesses perhaps the 'purest' eye"; Ibid., p. 84.

390   "Consider a few of them. The Coney Island girl"; Ibid.

392   He stole away from the opening night preview; Rathbone, p. 163.

392   Among the handwritten notes and typed lists: These and the following notations are from WE's papers related to the American Photographs exhibition and book in the archives of the Metropolitan Museum of Art.

392   "The author wishes to thank"; WE note, n.d., WEA/MMA.

393   "Omit names [of] prominent persons"; Ibid.

393   Another draft of such acknowledgments; WE note, n.d., WEA/MMA.

393   Among the names was the Jane Smith: WE note, n.d., WEA/MMA. The list of "Lenders" included Noda, Beatrice Jacoby, Ernestine Evans, the Agees, Gifford Cochran, Dorothy Miller, Frances Collins, none of whom were officially named as lenders to the exhibition. "J.S.N."; JES/JRM interview.

18: A Penitent Spy and an Apologetic Voyeur

395   "It was a project for love"; Paul Cummings, *Artists in Their Own Words: Interviews with Paul Cummings* (1979), pp. 38–39.

395   "Pal Tells How Gungirl Killed"; Greenough, p. 43.

395   "New York society in the 1930's"; *WEAW*, p. 107.

395   "under wraps"; Ibid., p. 127.

396   The trick was to avoid; see note on Jerry Thompson in Judith Keller, *The Walker Evans Collection*, The J. Paul Getty Museum, p. 188.

396   "spy and voyeur in the swaying seat," "penitent spy," "the guard is down"; Greenough, p. 127.

396   "It was a heavensent exuberance"; Ibid.

396   "a sociological gold mine"; Ibid.

397   "I was available and eager"; Helen Levitt, phone interview with JRM, Oct. 23, 1996.

397   "He was very generous that way"; Ibid.

397   "Squealing under city stone"; Agee, ms. copy "Rapid Transit," WEA/MMA.

398   "And why do I often meet your visage here"; *Complete Poems of Hart Crane*, p. 56.

398   "a kind of snapshot"; Katz, *Art in America*, p. 86.

399   "an individual existence"; *MAC*, introduction. In 1966, the Museum of Modern

Art, Oct. 5–Dec. 11, which included forty-one of his subway photographs.

399   "the religious sense of life is at the heart"; Spears, p. 167.

399   "Kennedy Fights Aid Britain Bill"; *MAC*, pp. 16, 77.

400   "Spitting on the floor of this car"; Ibid., p. 125.

400   Yet when the subway photographs were published: The closest that he may have come to showing a sequence of two frames of a man and woman on the Lexington Avenue Local, which he showed in the MoMA exhibition in 1966, but as Sara Greenough notes may or may not have been the work of the Modern's installation. [Greenough, p. 38.]

401   "To a right-minded man"; *MAC*, epigraph page.

401   "great piece of writing and photography"; Cummings interview transcript, p. 41, AAA.

401   "The *subway!* 'Yes,' said Henry James"; Greenough, p. 127.

402   "I think that a depression"; Op. cit., p. 45.

402   "a photographer an an artist"; JA to Father Flye, Jan. 13, 1939; Frenchtown, *FF*, p. 113.

402   "very annoying and disturbing to me"; JA to WE; July 1, 1938; Ransom.

402   "My writing is in bad shape"; JA to FF; Aug. 12, 1938, *FF*, 104.

402   "finding a way of doing the whole thing new"; JA to WE; Sept. 15, 1938, Ransom.

403   "I am at last"; Spears and Cassidy, Robert Coles, *Agee: His Life Remembered*, p. 105.

403   "Daytime was a little like playing house"; Alma Neuman, *Always Straight Ahead: A Memoir* (1993), p. 32.

404   "At night I'm starting to draw"; JA to FF, *FF*, p. 115.

404   "as usual, moved by it and wholly uncritical"; Neuman, p. 35.

404   "Jim's playing resembled his way of playing tennis"; Ibid., p. 33.

404   "Jim wrote for the ear, wanted criticism from auditors"; Fitzgerald, p. 88.

405   On one occasion"; Spears, p. 110.

405   "silent and ashamed"; Neuman, p. 37.

405   "The Man Who Lives Here Is a Loony"; Fitzgerald, p. 89.

405   "went to purchase a pretty wonderful pair"; Alma Mailman to WE, ca. November 27, [1938], WEA/MMA.

405   "a sad feeling I got (and Alma); JA to WE, Ibid.

407   "I have organized…an advanced sexual program"; JA to WE, late 1939?; Bergreen, p. 234.

407   "Though I am still adolescent-capable"; JA to WE, September 1939; Ibid.

407   "learned, investigated, synchronized and tried"; JA to WE, December 1938; Bergreen, p.226.

407   "the human race is incurably sick"; JA to WE, December 21, 1938, *FF*.

407   "a pleasure people claim is to be had [only by] children"; JA to WE, December 27, 1938, WEA/MMA.

407   "If you'd like it"; Ibid.

408   "*Fortune* came to the rescue"; Fitzgerald, p. 88.

408   "But Jim, unlike me"; Neuman, p. 41.

409   "misplaced…felt lost and alone"; Ibid., p. 43.

410   "to bring together the two people he loved most"; Neuman, p. 44.

410   "The 'experiment,' however, did not last long"; Ibid., p. 44.

410   "I have caused each of you"; Bergreen, p. 239; JA to WE, late 1939, Ransom.

411   "I wish you could drive back with us"; JA to WE, n.d., ca. Summer 1939, WEA/MMA.

411   "Have you ever lived with a woman"; Bergreen, p. 203; presumably fall of 1937.

412   "I believe that suggestion of Jim's"; Neuman, p. 57.

412   "We had a great love for each other"; Ferris, p. 33.

19: An Apartment on the East Side

415   Paul, in fact, made a bet; JES/JRM taped interview, May 12, 1993, WEA/MMA, courtesy of JES.

416   "Dear Billie, I guess I didn't make it clear enough"; JA to Billie Voorhees, June 22, 1939, WES/MMA, courtesy Jane Sargeant.

417   "Darling, you are terrible on the phone"; JA to JES. "Wednesday morning," ca. late June 1939.]

418   "With this hair I thee wed"; JES/JRM taped interview, May 12, 1993.

419   "He strenuously objected"; Newhall, *Focus,* p. 56.

420   "Oil That Glitters"; Russell Lynes, *Good Old Modern: An Intimate Portrait of the Museum of Modern Art* (1973), p. 207.

420   "We did not know"; Newhall, *Focus,* p. 59.

420   "I had the courage and ruthlessness"; Jane Collins to Marga Barr, July 28, 1939. MoMA Archives, Margaret Scolari Barr Papers.

421   "It is likely that by July"; JA to FF, June 27, 1939, *FF.*

421   "a sweet, nice guy"; JES/JRM taped interview, May 12, 1993.

422   "It was all open up there"; Ibid.

422   "soapbox Communist"; Herbert Mitgang, *Dangerous Dossiers* (1996), p. 213.

422   "Lucky Strike: It's Toasted"; Ironically, the slogan had appeared in Evans's 1930 photograph "Broadway Composition."

423   "critics are always glad to crap on anything"; JDP to Dorothy Dudley, Mar. 10, 1933, University of Rochester Library.

423   "It is a room for paintings"; Alfred H. Barr, *Matisse, His Art and His Public* (1951), p. 241.

423   "What I wanted was a much simpler"; LK to Dorothy Dudley Harvey, October 2, 1933. Kirstein Papers, YCAL.

424   *Hound & Horn;* Jan.–March 1934; 298–303.

424   Her husband, William, a top-ranking metalurgist; conversation with David Osborn, their son, by author, December 15, 1996; see also Edmund Wilson, *The Thirties.*

424   "awful husband," "fascinating piece of cheese"; WE diary, WEA/MMA.

425   They joked with each other; conversation with JES by the author.

426   "More delays from Harper"; JA to WE, September 8, 1939, Ransom.

427   "I said 'Absolutely not' "; Stott, p. 264.

427   "weak, sick, vindictive"; JA to FF, *FF,* p. 121; Bergreen, p. 235.

427   "The applicant proposes." WE. Application for Guggenheim Fellowship,

October 28, 1939, courtesy of the Guggenheim Foundation.

428   "Walker, would you be kind enough"; JES conversation with author.

428   "I suffered hellishly during all that"; Ibid.

20: Contemporary American Subjects

431   Guggenheim Fellowship: Henry Allen Moe to WE, March 27, 1940, courtesy of the Guggenheim Foundation.

431   "scholars"; *New York Times*, April 8, 1940.

431   "the writing of a series"; Virginia Spencer Carr, *Dos Passos: A Life* (1984), pp. 394, 399.

431   "a revelation...Have to do something"; WE, *WEAW*, p. 98.

432   "Let me tell you"; Edward Aswell to Paul Brooks, July 8, 1940, uncatalogued, Houghton Library.

432   "I doubt if any engraver's plates"; Aswell to Paul Brooks, July 8, 1940.

432   "The photographs are not illustrative"; *FM*, p. xlvii.

432   "that certain words be deleted"; Ibid., p. xlvi.

432   "fuck, shit, fart"; Stott, p. 264.

432   "god, love, loyalty, honor"; *FM*, pp. 456–458.

434   "increase of stipend"; WE to Henry Allen Moe, August 10, 1940, courtesy of the Guggenheim Foundation.

434   "I've always been struck"; Edmund Wilson, *Letters on Literature and Politics, 1895–1972* edited by Elena Wilson (1977), pp. 305–306.

434   "I've had to interrupt affairs"; WE to Henry Allen Moe, August 10, 1940, courtesy of the Guggenheim Foundation.

434   "everybody despised"; Phone interview with JES; Jan. 4, 1997.

434   "preparing to leave New York to work"; WE to Henry Allen Moe, September 7, 1940, courtesy of the Guggenheim Foundation.

434   "The only thing he has tried to prevent"; Wilson, *Letters*, p. 306.

435   an "appendisodomy"; WE to EE, n.d.; Ernestine Evans Papers, Rare Book and Manuscript Library, Columbia University.

436   "Jim writes that you would like"; Jay Laughlin to WE, October 10, 1940; WEA/MMA.

436–437   "I am exceedingly tired"; n.d. note by WE on verso of Laughlin letter.

437   "Everything looks clear and simple"; Lovell Thompson to WE, October 4, 1940. WEA/MMA.

437   "I have been waiting"; WE to Lovell Thompson, November 17, 1940, WEA/MMA.

437   "Everyone I see, myself included"; JA to Robert Fitzgerald, December 1940, in Spears, p. 119.

438   "I must learn my ways in an exceedingly quiet marriage"; Ibid., see also Fitzgerald, p. 94.

438   Agee quarrels with Alma...hiding behind the doors; Bergreen, p. 248.

438   "the three of us gazing solemnly"; Neuman, p. 58.

438   "people in our time"; WE to Henry Allen Moe, February 1, 1941, courtesy of the

Guggenheim Foundation.

439   "Each carries in the postures of his body"; Greenough, p. 128.

439   "I expect to have some things"; WE to Henry Allen Moe, March 17, 1941, courtesy of the Guggenheim Foundation.

440   "ARRIVED TEMPERATURE NORMAL"; WE to JES, March 25, 1941.

440   "SEE YOU AROUND SEVEN"; WE to JES, March 28, 1941, WEA/MMA.

440   "took to Walker like ducks to water"; JES/JRM taped interview, June 15, 1991.

440   "The college lends itself"; Keller, p. 243.

441   Walker gave her a round scolding; JES taped interview, June 15, 1991.

442   "Not only lines"; Berenice Abbott, *A Guide to Better Photography* (1941), p. 95.

442   "might well seem unrelated and chaotic"; Ibid., p. 100.

442   "In Bridgeport's War Factories"; *Fortune*, September 1941, pp. 87–92, 156, 158–62.

444   "I Am An American Parade"; "General Order No. 1"; July 2, 1941, WEA/MMA.

444   "dump of Fairfield Avenue"; WE field note, May 18, 1941, WEA/MMA.

444   "Submit negs & prints"; Ibid., n.d.

445   "Like a ring of sentries"; *Fortune*, op. cit., p. 158.

446   "There never was"; *New York Times*, August 19, 1941, p. 19, 1 ill.R, 186.
       Fitzgerald, 97. [Robert Fitzgerald on leave from *Time* having originally been
       assigned the book to review and had turned his review in only to learn from Jessup
       who had assigned it to him that it was considered too reverent and, with that,
       Fitzgerald agreed. His review eventually appeared in *Furioso* two years later.]

446   "insufferable arrogance"; Stott, p. 304. See *Partisan Review*, Jan.–Feb., 1942, pp.
       86–87.

446   "If the reader does not like"; Rodman, "The Poetry of Poverty," *Saturday Review*,
       August 23, 1941, p. 6, 1 ill.

446   "a young man's book"; Macdonald, *Memoirs of a Revolutionist*.

447   "The most realistic and most important"; Lionel Trilling quote, Houghton
       Mifflin press release.

447   "The gaze of the woman"; Stott, p. 277.

447   "as if there were no human unregenerateness"; Ibid., p. 305.

447   "pretty nearly without exception"; *FM*, pp. 216–217.

2I: Resorters, Tourists, Emigrés

449   "A DIVORCED WOMAN"; Marriage License, Oct. 27. 1941, WEA/MMA.

449   champagne from the People's Drugstore; JES to JRM phone conversation,
       March 25, 1997.

450   "a manic-impressive"; William Barrett, *The Truants: Adventures Among the
       Intellectuals* (1982), p. 38.

450   Bickel and Lindbergh; Keller, p. 257.

450   "the most difficult artist"; EE to Karl Bickel; n.d. Rare Book and Manuscript
       Library, Columbia University.

452   "the finest municipal trailer camp in the world"; Karl A. Bickel, *The Mangrove
       Coast: The Story of the West Coast of Florida* (1942), p. 297.

452   "Can you make the words HOME EDITION"; Keller, p. 259.

453   Pearl Harbor Day; Phone conversation, JES to JRM.

453   "Blind Couple in Tampa City Hall's Square"; Keller, p. 959.

456   "Two or three days ago"; Samuel Dushkin to Igor Stravinsky, December 24, 1941, in Stravinsky, *Selected Correspondence,* translated and edited by Robert Craft (1982–)Volume II, p. 311.

456   "those respectable quadrupeds"; Igor Stravinsky to Samuel Dushkin, December 29, 1941, Ibid.

456   "I also told [Balanchine]"; Igor Stravinsky to Samuel Dushkin, December 29, 1941, Ibid.

458   *On Your Toes,* Robert Garis, *Following Balanchine* (1995), p. 187.

458   "They want my name, not my music"; *Time,* July 26, 1997. Kobler, p. 195.

458   An historic photograph; William Rubin, *Dada, Surrealism, and Their Heritage* (1968), p. 158.

458   "New York during the war"; Peggy Guggenheim, *Confessions of an Art Addict* (1960), p. 13.

458   "First Papers of Surrealism"; Rubin, Op. cit., p. 160

458   "I did not want to live in sin"; Guggenheim, *Confessions,* p. 91.

459   "If the pictures suffered"; Guggenheim, *Out of This Century* (1979), p. 274.

459   "New York was twenty years behind Paris"; Neil Baldwin, *Man Ray, American Artist* (1988), p. 245. Man Ray, *Self Portrait* (1963), p. 335.

460   "This is the only paper I see to write on"; WE to JES, "Monday evening" 1942, WEA/MMA.

460   "I am as you as you see"; Ibid.

460   "Must get out of here"; WE to JES. "Thursday morning" [1942], WEA/MMA.

462   717 artists and 380 architects; Alice Goldfarb Marquis, *Alfred H. Barr Jr.: Missionary for the Modern* (1989), p. 187.

463   Rahv's furtive hand; JNE taped interview with JRM, June 15, 1991, side A.

464   "for some distraction"; B.H. Haggin to WE, April 17, 1996, WEA/MMA.

464   "I'm not pressing you"; B.H. Haggin to WE, March 25, 1947, WEA/MMA.

465   "Jim Agee and I"; second May 1993 tape.

465   "The evening you left I had dinner"; WE to JNE, June 18, 1942, WEA/MMA.

465   "Ach. I am sitting in our little kitchenette"; WE to JNE, June 19, 1942, WEA/MMA.

466   "quite seriously"; Ibid.

466   "ghosts all over the place"; Ibid., June 16, 1942, WEA/MMA.

22: Of Time . . .

470   "an angry man"; Diana Trilling, *Reviewing the Forties* (1978), p. 292.

470   "providing liquor for our guests"; Ibid.

470   "although we sometimes spent an evening"; Ibid., p. 293.

470   "He had a harder intelligence than Agee"; Ibid.

470   "unrealized great writer"; Bergreen, p. 271.

471   "Jim sitting in that bolt upright posture"; Stern, "Walker Evans, a Memoir," *London Magazine*, August–September, 1977.

471   "diffident dandy"; Ibid.

472   four gallons a week: Fussell introduction to Trilling, p. vii.

472   As certain of his letters to Jane indicate; see WE to JES, Sept. 1943, WEA/MMA.

472   "I would readily accept Hobson's invitation"; WE to Wilder Hobson; Memo date?

472   "Hollywood men now working"; Ibid.

473   "the finest film of actual combat"; text, March 26, 1943; issue, April 12, 1943, p. 95.

473   "Meant to be unbearable, it is that"; Ibid.

473   "The natural sound rises"; JA, *Agee on Film*, Vol. I (1958), p. 34.

473   "I urge that by every means possible"; Ibid.

474   "We can only suspect through rumor and internal reference"; Agee, *On Film*, p. 37.

474   "About the trials I am not qualified to speak"; Ibid., p. 39.

474   "it was Evans who recognized its bias"; D. Trilling, *Reviewing the Forties*, p. 293.

474   "a mildly loony comedy starring full-sailed Lana Turner"; text, April 1, 1943, MMA.

475   "Walter Van Tillburg's excellent sagebrush yarn"; *Time*, May 3, 1943, p. 94.

475   "I regret having missed"; Agee, *On Film*, p. 42.

475   "After a good deal of effort"; Ibid., p. 44.

475   "flunked divinity students"; Ibid., p. 41.

476   "stylistic forerunners of surrealism"; *Time*, Aug. 9, 1943.

476   Eliot Elisofon….; BR, p. 193.

476   "quasi mystical"; Ibid., *Time*, Feb. 5, 1946, p. 86.

476   "in the holes in the bones"; *Georgia O'Keeffe*, Viking Press, plate 76, but a 1944 date for the painting.

476   "Dealer Stieglitz"; BR, p. 196; *Time*, Feb. 5, 1945; p. 86. *Georgia O'Keeffe*, Ibid.

476   "Cinema (Evans) *Walker Misses Jane* (92nd Street Productions)"; WE to JNE, April 18, 1943, WEA/MMA.

477   "Miss you like hell, have indescribable thought[s?]"; Ibid.

477   "Nothing to report. I am merely writing"; WE to JES, Sunday night, bedtime, 1943, WEA/MMA.

477   "I miss you. Our beautiful home misses you"; WE to JES, May 11, 1943, WEA/MMA.

477   "Write me and think about the same things"; WE to JES, June 12, 1943, WEA/MMA.

477   "Alma would let Jim have Joel"; WE to JES, May 3, 1943, WEA/MMA.

477   "So Wilder says come home with me"; WE to JES, June 12, 1943, WEA/MMA.

477   "Am going to a theater opening"; WE to JES, May 3, 1943, WEA/MMA.

477   "Bernard took me to the ballet"; WE to JES, May 11, 1943, WEA/MMA.

478   "Will see Peggy [Osborne]," WE to JES.

478   "I am spending the afternoon"; WE to JES, June 12, 1943, WEA/MMA.

478   "You may not like them"; WE to JES, Sunday night bedtime, 1943, WEA/MMA.

478   "Played tennis today twice at McDonalds'" WE to JES, Ibid.

479   "clear without being flat"; T.S. Matthews, memorandum, July 31, 1943, WEA/MMA.

479   adept at purging members; see Sam Tanenhaus, *Whittaker Chambers: A Biography* (1997), p. 560, n. 44.

480   The fight over the wedding ring; Phone conversation with JES, April 20, 1997.

481   "Walker Evans, Art of Something Editor"; Kirstein to WE, April 1, 1944, NYPLPA.

23: . . . And Fortune: The Road Taken

485   Ralph Delahaye Paine as managing editor of *Fortune* as of 1941; Elson, p. 452; also Policy Committee member of *Time*; Elson, p. 360; Baier, p. 11.

485   according to one source Luce was also pleased: Baier, *Evans at* Fortune, p. 11.

485   "that it is easier to turn poets into business journalists"; Elson, p. 137.

486   "thirty of everything"; Baier, p. 13.

486   "trimming his negatives"; Baier, p. 15.

486   "At *Fortune*, they realize I'm a writer too"; *Time* interview with WE, Nov. 21, 1947.

486   "Why, if I know what I want"; Ibid.

486   "a certain satanic naivete in the very top editorial directions"; Szarkowski, p. 18.

486–487   "I think it sort of kept me alive"; Cummings interview, p. 32.

487   not once while he was on the staff of *Fortune*; JES/JRM, interview, July 8, 1997.

487   atomic bomb story in *Time*; August 20, 1945, p. 19.

487   "an event so much more enormous that"; Bergreen, p. 295.

487   "When the bomb split open"; Ibid., p. 295.

487   "When people tell me…"; Bergreen, p. 296, and David Madden, ed., *Remembering James Agee* (1974), p. 116.

488   "Preliminary research reveals plenty of material"; WE memorandum to Deborah Calkins and Will Bartin December 3, 1945; Evans Archive, MMA.

488   The Nagasaki cloud column; Ibid.

489   "It is the philosophy and the pleasure of Mr. and Mrs. Phelps, craftsmen"; *Fortune*, November 1945, pp. 158–161.

491   "The Yankees. The player's the thing"; *Fortune*, July 1946, pp. 130–39ff.

492   "on a felicitous mission"; BR, FYI, Jan. 13, 1947.

492   "Hold for Arrival"; WE to Mrs. Sweet, July 28, 1946, WEA/MMA.

493   "The American worker, as he passes here"; wire to WE, Sept. 12, 1947, WEA/MMA.

495   "that meet a leisured and untethered eye"; Ibid., p. 112.

495   "strewn with assorted relics of the big show"; Ibid., p. 121.

495   Sunday in an Alley; Ibid.

495   "rather anti-feminist pictures"; WE, Limerick interview, 1973, WEA/MMA.

495   "I found nothing"; Greenberg, *The Nation*, June 10, 1944.

495   "Weston's failure"; Greenberg, *The Nation*, March 9, 1946.

496   "One Newspaper Town"; *Fortune*, August 1946, pp. 102–107.

496   "My girl, I seem to have forgotten everything"; WE to JES, August 17(?) [1947], WEA/MMA.

496	"My girl (section 2)"; WE to JES, "Sunday Evening;" [August 17? 1947], WEA/MMA.
497	"But the *noise!* the *people!*"; Ibid.
497	"Well Gee Zuss: what a landscape"; WE to JES, "Wednesday evening, August 20, 1947, MMA.
497	"Does anybody know why tourists are so repulsive?"; Ibid.
497	"Well I swan and great Scott"; WE to JES, "Thursday" August 21, [1947], WEA/MMA.
498	"So I looked at a poor but large Dali on the wall"; Ibid.
498	"...be sure oval silver links are in it"; Ibid.
499	"you gotta not feel so bad, please miss"; Ibid.
499	"But listen you got no business feeling"; WE to JES, "Wednesday Afternoon"; [August, n.d., 1947], WEA/MMA.
499	"in sin"; WE to JES, August 22, [1947], WEA/MMA.
499	"portrait hacking or something"; WE to JES, August 21, [1947] WEA/MMA.
499	"She's a good egg and quite bright"; WE to JES, "Monday," misdated September 9, [1947]; s/b perhaps September 8 or Tuesday, September 9, WEA/MMA.
499	"It is of course spectacular"; WE to JES, August 21, [1947], WEA/MMA.
499	"quite good"; Ibid.
499–500	"Want to set down those memory quick sight sketches"; Ibid.
472	"I just lay (sic) in the sun"; WE to JES, August 22, 1947.
502	"For good reason, for at almost nine"; Ibid.
502	"It was an entrance"; Ibid.
502-503	"Well I did it. Well I did everything,"; WE to JES, "Monday," misdated September 9, [1947]; s/b perhaps September 8 or Tuesday, September 9, MMA.
503	"for the degradation I found–"; Ibid.
504	"But they are good on me"; Ibid.

24: "If It's There, It's There."

507	"somewhat like holding a mirror"; Schniewind to WE Feb. 11, 1947, Art Institute of Chicago.
507	"Let's shake Chicago back down"; WE to Schniewind, Sept. 2, 1947, Art Institute of Chicago.
507	"cold, pure white with a matte surface"; WE to Schniewind. October 17, 1947, Art Institute of Chicago.
509	"casually corrupt."; Mabry, "Walker Evans' Photographs of America", *Harper's Bazaar*, November 1, 1938.
509	"In Chicago I wandered around"; WE/*Time* interview; Nov. 21, 1947; typed copy.
509	The Woodbridge family monuments: In some instances this sequence of photographs has been dated 1945 or ca. 1945; the location given as Manfield, Kentucky, or Biloxi, Mississippi and the family name given as Woolbridge.
511	"I hope to hell they do it"; Serrell Hillman to WE, November 12, 1947, Time Inc.

511   "spent hours today going over your stuff"; Ibid., November 19, 1947, Time Inc.

511   "wry shy little man with an air of worried thoughtfulness"; *Time*, December 15, 1947, p. 73.

512   "Chemicals smell bad and machinery is cold"; WE interview, November 24,1947, Time Inc.

512   "explored the face of the U.S."; *Time*, December 15, 1947, p. 7.

512   "After 20-odd years of work"; Ibid.

512   "How can I tell you about myself"; WE interview, November 21, 1947, Time Inc.

512   "first one that did not look like someone else's photograph"; November 27, 1947 int. Manon Gaulin-Alex Eliot interview; Time Inc.

514   "After 20-odd years of work I still"; WE typed interview November 24, 1947, Time Inc.

514   Faulkner and Evans: Evans's library included a number of Faulkner's writings.

514   "I don't know how she plucked Walker out of nowhere"; JES/JRM taped interview, June 1, 1991.

515   "effigies of the actual people themselves"; Faulkner, "Sepulture South: Gaslight," *Harper's Bazaar*, December 1954, p. 140.

516   "looming among the lush green of summer"; Ibid., p. 141.

516   "I ask indulgence, official nonsense is beyond me"; WE to Ralph Delahaye Paine, July 23, 1948; *WEAW*, p. 180.

517   "Well, we stuck these tag picture-notes"; Ibid.

517   "The Time literary *mind* is ahead of the Time visual mind"; Ibid., p. 181.

517   "This is to confirm the appointment of Walker Evans"; *WEAW*, p. 182. This memorandum is dated September 27, 1948.

517   "full responsibility for photographic illustrations"; Ibid.

518   "the rich pastime of window-gazing"; *Fortune*, September, 1950.

519   "designed with the prodigality of a Wagner opera"; *Fortune*, August 1949, p. 76.

519   "They gave him great luxury everywhere"; JES/JRM taped interview June 15, 1991 [100.ff.].

519   "Catch one of these gay land arks"; *Fortune*, August 1949, p. 75.

520   "a young man's book"; Chapter XXII, p. 18. [20ff Houghton Mifflin publicity release].

520   "one of the most interesting and important American books"; Macdonald, *Memoirs of a Revolutionist*, p. 263.

521   "adviser to Franklin Roosevelt at Yalta"; W. A. Swanberg, *Luce and His Empire* (1972), p. 287.

521   "that complete set of reports on last summer's Hiss trial"; Haggin to WE, November 25, 1949.

521   "I also did want to hear"; Haggin to WE, July 12, 1952.

522   "a very odd pair indeed"; WE/Matthews interview [undated, but late].

522   "Yeah...In the matter of balance of relationships"; Ibid.

522   "Whittaker Chambers slyly appears and sidles up to me"; Undated transcript of a dream, WEA/MMA.

25: Couples

525   "atonality and cacophony in music"; Rathbone, p. 218.

525   "generous and valuable" contribution; Edward Steichen to WE, October 30, 1950, MoMA.

526   "sort of saved my life"; Ralph Steiner, *Point of View* (1978), p. 28.

526   "But he never"; Ibid.

526   "was amused by the reactions"; Baier, p. 59.

496   "portrait hacking"; WE to JES, August 21, 1947, WEA/MMA.

497   "Walker'd go out to photograph"; Baier, p. 12.

527   "As I remember it"; Steiner, p. 28.

527   "As research, I'm sure he ate"; Ibid.

527   "discovery"…"this and that local esthete"; *New York Times Sunday Book Review*, October 1952, p. 7.

528   "awash in his hotel bedding"; Ibid.

528   "Del, Overlook immodesty of my attaching this"; undated note on clipping, WEA/MMA.

528   "a good color man"; JA to WE, [possibly January 21, 1951], Ransom.

529   "appalling"; WE to TS Matthews tape.

529   "just finished," "No Jim, I can't do that"; Spears and Cassidy, p. 153.

529   "The first hundred [pages] were mine"; Bergreen, p. 355.

530   "Christ how I wish I could pray and mean"; JA to WE, [possibly January 25, 1951], Ransom.

530   "I may ask you to see her a little if you will"; Ibid.

532   "Dear Husband,"… "Not very much excitement"; JES to WE, [May 4,1951] WEA/MMA.

532   "Gosh you've only been gone a week"; JES to WE, n.d. [1951], WEA/MMA.

532   "I tried to paint him"; JES to WE, n.d. "Mon–" [1951], WEA/MMA.

532   "I have a couple of paintings"; JES to Mia and Jim Agee, n.d.;Christmas [1952?]

533   "When I get back to New York"; JES to WE, Thurs. August 6, 1954, WEA/MMA.

534   "unpaid domestic."; JES to JRM phone conversation, October 24, 1997.

534   "Mona called up at last today"; JES to WE, [May 1951], WEA/MMA.

534   "Mona did something so good"; JES to WE, Thursday, August 6, 1953, (postmarked Fond du Lac, Wisc., August 6), WEA/MMA.

535   "undoubtedly a rather fanatical fellow"; Winthrop Sargeant, *In Spite of Myself* (1970), p. 235.

535   "If you don't treat that wife of yours right"; JES/JRM phone interview, October 7, 1997.

538   "Come with me!"; Ibid.

538   "Wow. What a rush"; WE to JES, Tues. 22 or 23, [1954], WEA/MMA

539   "That's good news about Sarge"; Ibid.

539   "It's beastly hot and everyone but Alice is gone"; JES to WE, July 3, 1954, WEA/MMA

539   "[P]robably won't last, but it's"; Ibid.

540   "but nonetheless it looks just like"; WE to JES, July 7,1954, WEA/MMA.

540   "will be hell–over the propellers" ; WE to JES, Tues. 22 or 23 [June 1954], WEA/MMA.

540   "Well, we should do something about that"; JES to JRM phone interview, Oct.

26: A Season of Endings

543   on nitroglycerin tablets; Cf, Bergreen, pp. 401–407.

543   "It takes a great event"; JES/JRM, phone interview, Nov. 11, 1997.

544   "gone on ahead of us"; Ibid.

544   "It's not the custom of this church"; Bergreen, p. 407.

544   "a poet, critic and sensitive writer in many media"; *New York Times*, May 18, 1955.

544   "in tone, imagery and movement...something of a dark poem"; Ibid.

544   "Well, I guess there's no reason"; Neuman, p. 147.

545   "the worst parts of the marriage"; JES/JRM, phone interview, Nov. 11, 1997.

545   "Darl, Ain't got nothing to say"; JRS to WE, postmarked November 30, 1954, WEA/MMA

545   "depressed and full of complaints"; Ibid.

546   "I don't think you even like me any more." JES/JRM, phone interview, Nov. 11, 1997.

546   "Whereas, differences having arisen between them"; undated notes ca. Nov. 1955, WEA/MMA.

547   "From now on I will consider you dead"; Nov. 11, 14, 1997 phone interview.

548   "I was looking for somebody"; panel discussion, Yale University, May 5, 1971.

548   "the beginning of a whole new way of photographing"; Westerbeck, p. 352.

547   "I didn't talk to anybody for maybe a month"; Ibid.

549   "This man is probably the most gifted"; WE to Henry Allen Moe, January 20, 1955, courtesy of the Guggenheim Foundation.

550   "then if he saw something"; Robert Frank to John Hill interview; undated.

550   "I was surprised to see what a Rube Goldberg set-up"; Ibid.

550   "At some point Walker would say"; Ibid.

552   if he was "a Commie"; Robert Frank to WE, November 9, 1955, WEA/MMA.

552   "I've just seen the richest and most original"; WE to Ray Mackland, October 16, 1956, WEA/MMA.

553   "About that, great questioning"; Robert Frank to WE, November 9, 1955, WEA/MMA.

List of Illustrations

All photographic prints are silver gelatin images unless otherwise noted.
All reproduction rights for images made by Walker Evans are controlled by the
Metropolitan Museum of Art, including those taken from private collections unless
otherwise noted. All reproductions are from WEA/MMA unless otherwise noted.
Captions written posthumously for identification are enclosed in square brackets [ ].

49   Walker Evans
Hanns Skolle, New York, 1929.
Private collection

54   Walker Evans
[Shadow self-portrait, Juan-les-Pins, France, January 1927]
Private collection

58–59   Photographer unknown.
Evans with friends, South of France, 1927

62   Photographer unknown, possibly self-portrait.
Walker Evans, Columbia Heights, Brooklyn, 1928.
Private collection.

66   Photographer unknown, probably Hanns Skolle.
Evans in East 14th Street studio, New York, 1927.

69   Photographer unknown.
Evans at New York, Hospital, June 1928.
Private collection

71   Photographer unknown, possibly Walker Evans.
Evans's sister Jane with her husband Talbot Brewer, circa 1929.

73   Hanns Skolle. American, born Germany, 1903–1980.
Portrait of Elizabeth Skolle.
Medium and size unknown (copy photograph by Walker Evans).

74   Walker Evans
Lindbergh Day Parade, New York, 13 June 1927.

86   Paul Grotz. American, born Germany, 1903–1990.
Walker Evans, Darien, Connecticut, 1928–29.

89   Walker Evans.
Port of New York
Wall Street Windows
[Family on Street Corner, As Seen from Above]

90   Walker Evans.
Paul Grotz, 1929.
Private collection

99   Walker Evans.
Building and Crane, 1929. New York.

103   Walker Evans.
Hart Crane, New York, 1929.

106   Walker Evans.
Brooklyn Bridge, 1928–29.

108   Walker Evans.
[Photomat Portrait of Evans, New York City, 1929–30.]

110   Walker Evans.
Berenice Abbott, New York, 1929–30.

191   Photographer unknown.
[Tintype of Evans with young woman, possibly Dorothy Butcher, Havana 1933.]
Image of this tintype is reverse reading.

194   Walker Evans.
[Detail of Diego Rivera Mural for the New Workers School, as cropped by Evans.]

198   Walker Evans.
Ben Shahn, 1933.

201   Photographer unknown.
Ernestine Evans, 1930s.

205   Walker Evans.
[Panel from Diego Rivera's Mural for the New Workers School, 1933.]

206   Photographer unknown, possibly Walker Evans.
Jay Leyda, circa 1933.
Courtesy of Tamiment Institute Library, New York University.

212   Walker Evans.
Maine Pump, 1933.

215   Walker Evans.
Wooden Gothic Near Nyack, New York, 1931.

217   Walker Evans.
Gothic Gate Cottage, Near Poughkeepsie, New York, 1931.

218   Paul Grotz. American, born Germany, 1903–90.
[Evans Photographing Chrysler Building Construction, 1929.]

222   Walker Evans.
Billboard Painter, Florida, circa 1934.

230   Walker Evans.
[Jane Smith Ninas, Bourbon Street, New Orleans, 1935.]

231   Walker Evans.
Savannah Negro Quarter, 1935.

233   Walker Evans.
[Levee Scene, Vicinity New Orleans, 1935.]

234   Walker Evans.
The Breakfast Room, Belle Grove Plantation, 1935. White Castle, Louisiana.

236   Walker Evans.
Sidewalk and Shopfront, New Orleans, 1935.

243   Walker Evans.
[Jane Ninas, Belle Grove Plantation, White Castle, Louisiana, 1935.]

244   Walker Evans.
Hudson Street Boarding House Detail, New York, 1931.
[John Cheever's Room.]

296   Walker Evans.
        Houses and Billboards in Atlanta, 1936.

299   Walker Evans.
        Penny Picture Display, Savannah, 1936.

301   Janice Loeb. American, dates unavailable.
        Walker Evans, 1936.

304   Walker Evans.
        Signs, South Carolina, 1936.
        Collection: Library of Congress

306   Walker Evans.
        Tenant Farmer with Daughter, Hale County, Alabama, 1936.
        [Floyd Burroughs with Daughter Lucille]
        Private collection

314   Walker Evans.
        [Floyd Burroughs on the Tengle family porch, 1936.]
        Collection: Library of Congress

315   Walker Evans.
        Alabama Cotton Tenant Farmer's Wife, 1936.
        Collection: Library of Congress

317   Walker Evans.
        [Lucille Burroughs, Hale County, Alabama,1936.]
        Collection: Library of Congress

331   Walker Evans.
        Burroughs Kitchen, Hale County, Alabama, 1936.
        Collection: Library of Congress

332   Walker Evans.
        Flood Refugees, Forrest City, Arkansas, February 1937.
        Collection: Library of Congress

338   Ben Shahn.
        [Evans with movie camera, near Greenbelt, Maryland, a community being
        constructed for resettlement of tenement dwellers, October 1936.]
        Courtesy of the Fogg Museum, Harvard Univeristy Art Museums, Gift of
        Bernarda Bryson Shahn. Image © President and Fellows of Harvard College,
        Harvard University.

345   Walker Evans.
        Flood Refugees, Forrest City, Arkansas, February 1937.
        Collection: Library of Congress

349   Walker Evans.
        Arkansas Flood Refugee, 1937.
        Collection: Library of Congress

350   Walker Evans.
        James Agee, Old Field Point, New York, August 1937.

414   Jane Nina Evans Sargeant.
Interior of 441 East 92nd Street, New York.
Ink and brush drawing, 30.2 x 22.8 cm. (12 x 9 in.)
Courtesy of the Historic New Orleans Collection.

416   Walker Evans.
[Jane Drawing in Kitchen Studio, 92nd Street Apartment.]

421   Helen Levitt. American, 1913– .
Jim and Alma Agee with Delmore Schwartz, Stockton New Jersey, 1939.
© Helen Levitt. Courtesy of the artist.

429   Walker Evans.
[Apartment at 441 East 92nd Street.]

430   Walker Evans.
Bridgeport Parade.
Fortune, "Bridgeport's War Factories," September 1941.

433   Walker Evans.
Blair Fuller, Cornish, New Hampshire.

435   Emma Agee. American, 1913–82.
Helen Levitt, W. Greenwich Village, New York, circa 1938.
Courtesy of Helen Levitt.

443   Walker Evans.
[Movie poster for Tobacco Road, Bridgeport, Connecticut, 1941.]

445   Walker Evans.
[Spectators, Bridgeport Parade]
Fortune, "Bridgeport's War Factories," September 1941.
Collection: Dr. Benjamin A. Hill

448   Walker Evans.
Resort Photographer at Work, 1941.
From *The Mangrove Coast,* Carl A. Bickel.

455   Walker Evans.
Store Display, Florida, 1941. [Diver's suit in chair.]
Variant cropping appears in *The Mangrove Coast.*

462   Walker Evans.
Lionel Trilling, circa 1941.

467   Walker Evans.
Gulf of Mexico, 1941.
From *The Mangrove Coast.*

468   Walker Evans.
[James Agee and Eleanor Clark, circa 1943.]

477   Walker Evans.
Peggy Osborn, circa 1944.

    478   Walker Evans.
John McDonald. and Dorothy Eisner McDonald, circa 1945.

542 Jane Ninas Evans Sargeant. American, 1913– .
Walker Evans. January, 1954.
Brush and ink drawing, 35.4 x 25.2 cm. (14 x 10 in.)

549 Walker Evans.
Robert Frank and Mary Lockspeiser Frank, New York, 1953.

551 Walker Evans.
Tin Snips by J. Wiss & Sons Co. $1.85
From "Beauties of the Common Tool," *Fortune,* July 1955.

556 Walker Evans.
Isabelle Evans, 163 East 94th Street, Christmas 1960.

562 John Hill. American, 1934– .
Evans talking to students at the Yale Summer School of Music and Art,
Norfolk, Connecticut, 1964.
© courtesy of the artist

565 John Hill.
New house, Lyme, Connecticut, 1967.
© courtesy of the artist

566 John Hill.
Evans party, Lyme, Connecticut, 1967.
© courtesy of the artist

568 Peter Koster. American, 1946–
Evans talking with students, Yale Art & Architecture Building, 1966.

574 Marcia Due. American, 1947– .
Evans beach combing. Old Black Point, Easter 1974.
© courtesy of the artist

652 Don Fehr. American, 1957–.
Augie Capaccio and James Mellow, Rockport, Massachusetts, 1993.
© courtesy of the artist

A Brief Chronology

1903   Born 3 November, St. Louis, Missouri. Family moves to Kenilworth, affluent Chicago suburb, and later to Toledo, Ohio.

1922   Graduates from Phillips Academy, Andover, Massachusetts. Briefly attends Williams College, Williamstown, Massachusetts.

1923   Moves to New York City, working at various clerical jobs. Meets
1926   German-born artist Hanns Skolle, with whom he corresponds for some years.

1926   Travels to Paris to pursue writing career and French studies at
1927   the Sorbonne. Tours France and Italy taking a few photographs.

1927   Returns to New York City, sharing a studio with Hanns Skolle. Continues writing and begins to consider photography seriously. Works at clerical jobs in investment house.

        Meets Ralph Steiner, who instructs Evans in photographic techniques. They share interest in vernacular subjects including advertising displays and billboards. Evans shows influence of European constructivism, possibly from Paul Grotz, Evans's artist friend from Germany.

1929   Meets Lincoln Kirstein, who becomes a most important promoter, mentor and philosophical guide—and provides access to power. Evans now living in Brooklyn with Grotz. He begins a series of the Brooklyn Bridge pictures and environs with a small camera.

        Meets poet Hart Crane, who is living in Brooklyn.

1930   Hart Crane's poem *The Bridge*, published by the Black Sun Press in Paris, illustrated with three photogravures by Evans.

Begins using large format cameras, 5 x 7 and 6½ x 8½.

Meets Berenice Abbott, who introduces him to the work of Eugène Atget; these images become a major influence.

Work published in *Architectural Review, Creative Arts* and *Hound & Horn*, the literary magazine founded by Lincoln Kirstein.

1931   Begins recording Victorian architecture at the suggestion of Lincoln Kirstein and assisted by John Brooks Wheelwright. The series continues for several years.

Exhibits with Margaret Bourke-White and Ralph Steiner at the John Becker Gallery in New York.

1932   Sails to Tahiti, acting as photographer for a group of wealthy tourists. Uses a small handheld camera, a large format 6½ x 8½ and, for the first time, a movie camera.

Exhibits with George Platt Lynes at the Julien Levy Gallery in New York.

1933   Spends two or more weeks in Havana documenting the general social scene to illustrate Carlton Beals's *The Crime of Cuba*. 31 images selected and sequenced by Evans for this volume.

Museum of Modern Art exhibits "Walker Evans: Photographs of 19th Century Houses," first one-man photographic exhibition mounted by a major museum in the United States.

1934   Begins small assignments from *Fortune* magazine including the "Communist Party Summer Camp."

Travels to Florida on assignment to document resort community and finds interest in roadside scenes.

1935   Makes approximately 500 photographs for "African Negro Art" at the Museum of Modern Art. Commissioned to produce 17 sets of 477 images.

Contracted by Gifford Cochran to illustrate a book about
Southern antebellum architecture. Sets up base for this in New
Orleans. Meets artist Jane Ninas and begins courtship.

Begins work for the government agency, the Resettlement
Administration (later becomes the Farm Security Administration).
Hired to record social conditions of the Depression.

He travels widely in the South and central states using primarily
an 8 x 10 camera, supplemented by 35-mm and 4 x 5 cameras.

1936   Continues work in the South for the FSA. Granted a three-week
        leave from the government agency to work with James Agee
        documenting the conditions of rural southern families for a
        Fortune magazine essay. Intentional rawness of the writing causes
        rejection by the magazine. Using this material, Agee and Evans
        begin a book, later to be called *Let Us Now Praise Famous Men.*

1937   Continues limited work for FSA, including a document of
        Mississippi River flood refugees in Arkansas.

        Relationship becomes strained between Evans and
        administration of FSA.

        Evans's work included in MoMA exhibition,
        "Photography: 1837–1937."

1938   Exhibition at the Museum of Modern Art, "Walker Evans:
        American Photographs," with a publication of the same name,
        both with the assistance of Lincoln Kirstein, Frances Collins and
        Thomas Mabry. Acclaimed a major artist.

        Using a concealed 35-mm camera, Evans begins making portraits
        on New York subways.

        FSA terminates relationship with Evans.

        Application for Guggenheim Fellowship denied.

1939   Asked by Beaumont Newhall to contribute prints to the MoMA exhibition "Art in Our Time."

1940   Receives Guggenheim Fellowship.

1941   Extension of Guggenheim Fellowship allows him to complete series of New York City subway portraits.

Publication of *Let Us Now Praise Famous Men* by Houghton Mifflin, co-authored by James Agee and Evans.

Marries Jane Smith Ninas.

Travels to Florida to photograph for Carl A. Bickel's book *The Mangrove Coast*.

First major essay for Fortune, *Bridgeport's War Factories*.

1942   Publication of *The Mangrove Coast* by Carl A. Bickel, with 32 photographs by Evans.

Smaller cameras used more frequently, mainly 2¼ x 2¼ and 35-mm.

1943
——   Reviews books, art and cinema for *Time* magazine.
1945

1945   Becomes a full-time staff photographer for *Fortune* magazine.

1947   The Art Institute of Chicago mounts retrospective exhibition of Walker Evans's work.

1948   Becomes *Fortune*'s Special Photographic Editor. Asked to create a distinctive and unifying photographic style for the magazine. Controls his own projects, including pictures, layout and text.

1950   Begins generating his own assignments.

1953   The Bollingen Foundation publishes *African Folk Tales and Sculpture*, 113 Evans photographs taken in 1935.

1954   Invited to membership in the Century Association.

1955   Death of James Agee.
Divorce of Jane Smith Ninas and Evans.

1956   Museum of Modern Art exhibit "Diogenes with a Camera III," includes Evans's work.

Travels to British Isles for *Sports Illustrated*. Photographs golf at St. Andrews and the Henley Royal Regatta in Cambridge.

1958   *Architectural Forum* publishes "Color Accidents," 6 photographs and text by Evans, first publication of his attention to color as more than a descriptive element.

1959   Receives second Guggenheim Fellowship.

1960   Second edition of *Let Us Now Praise Famous Men* published by Houghton Mifflin. Increases number of photographs from 31 to 62.

Marries Isabelle Boeschenstein von Steiger, Katonah, New York.

1962   Second edition of *American Photographs* published by MoMA, accompanied by an exhibition of images selected from the book.

1963   Selects and sequences photographs to illustrate *My Years at General Motors*, the Alfred Sloan biography by John McDonald.

1964   Invited by Yale University School of Art and Architecture as part of a lecture series. Illustrates the lecture, "The Lyric Documentary," with vernacular photographic images from his postcard collection.

Begins teaching photography at the Yale School of Art and Architecture as Professor of Graphic Design.

1965   Retires from *Fortune*.

Meets Leslie Katz, publisher and director of Eakins Press.

1966   "Walker Evans Subway Photographs" exhibited at the Museum of Modern Art. Coincidentally, Houghton Mifflin publishes *Many Are Called,* a collection of New York subway portraits.

Message from the Interior, 12 images in sheet-fed gravure with an afterword by John Szarkowski, published by the Eakins Press.

Exhibition of 40 prints at the Robert Schoelkopf Gallery.

Moves to new house in Lyme, Connecticut.

1968   Becomes Fellow, American Academy of Arts and Letters.

Receives an honorary degree from Williams College.

1969   *Quality, Its Image in the Arts,* edited by Louis Kronenberger, published by Atheneum, includes an essay by Evans on photography. Ends by proclaiming vulgarity of color photography.

Photographs in Nova Scotia while visiting Robert Frank.

1970   Edits and prepares work for upcoming MoMA retrospective.

1971   Major retrospective of 200 images exhibited at the Museum of Modern Art. Catalog introduction by John Szarkowski. Acclamation brings a wide rediscovery of Evans.

"Walker Evans: Forty Years," an exhibition at the Yale University Art Gallery, includes signs and advertisements collected by Evans.

Ives-Sillman publishes portfolio of 14 signed prints by Evans.

Leslie Katz records a lengthy interview with Evans, edited by Evans and published in *Art in America*, September 1971. Contains a clear and concise summary of Evans's aesthetic.

Interview recorded for Archives of American Art.

1972   Retires from Yale. Continues traveling workshops.

Travels to London.

Artist in Residence, Dartmouth College. Exhibits work at
Hopkins Center, Dartmouth College.

Collections of signs and printed ephemera increases. Also, begins
audio recording as experimentation in verbal or aural snapshots.

Undergoes surgery for perforated ulcer at Mary Hitchcock
Hospital in Hanover, New Hampshire.

1973   Returns to his home in Lyme to recover.

Exhibition at Schoelkopf Gallery.

Evans and Isabelle Boeschenstein von Steiger are divorced.

Travels to Georgia, buys his first Polaroid SX-70 color camera.
Continues collecting signs.

Travels to London, visits friends and photographs with color
Polaroid and 2¼ x 2¼ and 35-mm cameras.

Returns to Hale County, Alabama with photographer
Bill Christenberry. Works in Polaroid color.

1974   Continues traveling workshops with Yale students.

Yale alumni magazine publishes Evans interview in which he
full embraces color photography.

Lectures at Oberlin College, University of Texas at Austin and
Rhode Island School of Design, Providence.

Receives Distinguished Service Award from the American
Academy Institute. Lionel Trilling delivers introduction.

Publication of the Double Elephant Portfolio, 15 prints edited
and directed by Lee Friedlander.

Continues intense production with Polaroid color, producing well over 2000 images.

Health degenerates.

1975   Shares an apartment in New Haven. Sells entire print collection to a dealer with an option for later purchase of negatives.

8 April. With a student companion and against reason and odds, Evans travels by train to Boston where he gives an evening lecture at Radcliffe College. Evans and talk enthusiastically received.

9 April. Elated, he returns to New Haven by train.

10 April. Dies of a stroke in the early morning hours at the Yale New Haven Hospital.

1975
1994   The Estate of Walker Evans publishes the following:
Walker Evans, First and Last, Harper & Row, New York, 1978
Walker Evans at Work, Harper & Row, New York, 1982
Walker Evans, Havana, 1933, Pantheon, 1989
Walker Evans, The Hungry Eye, Harry N. Abrams, 1993

Published with the cooperation of the Estate:
Walker Evans, Amerika, Schirmer/Mosel, 1990, Rizzoli, 1991
Walker Evans, The Brooklyn Bridge, a portfolio of nine hand-pulled gravure prints, Eakins Press, 1994

Various exhibitions and smaller publications also produced by the Estate are listed in *Walker Evans: The Getty Museum Collection*, 1995.

1994   The Metropolitan Museum of Art acquires Walker Evans Archive.

Selected Bibliography

Abbott, Berenice. *A Guide to Better Photography*. New York: Crown Publishers, 1941.

Agee, James and Walker Evans. *Let Us Now Praise Famous Men: Three Tenant Families*. Boston: Houghton Mifflin, 1941.

Ashdown, Paul, ed. *James Agee: Selected Journalism*. Knoxville: University of Tennessee Press, 1985.

Baier, Lesliy K. *Walker Evans at Fortune, 1945–1965*. Wellesley, MA: Wellesley College Museum, 1977.

Beals, Carleton. *The Crime of Cuba*. Philadelphia and London: J.B. Lippincott, 1933.

Bergreen, Laurence. *James Agee—A Life*. New York: E.P. Dutton, 1984.

Bickel, Karl. *The Mangrove Coast: The Story of the West Coast of Florida*. New York: Coward-McCann, 1942.

Brown, Frederick. *An Impersonation of Angels: A Biography of Jean Cocteau*. New York: The Viking Press, 1968.

Crane, Hart. *The Bridge*. Paris: Black Sun Press, 1930.

——. *The Collected Poems of Hart Crane*. Edited by Waldo Frank. New York: Liveright, 1946.

——. *The Complete Poems and Selected Letters and Prose of Hart Crane*. Edited by Brom Weber. New York: Liveright, 1966.

Evans, Walker. *American Photographs*. Essay by Lincoln Kirstein. New York: The Museum of Modern Art, 1938.

——. *Many Are Called*. Introduction by James Agee. Boston: Houghton Mifflin, 1966.

——. *Walker Evans*. Introduction by John Szarkowski. New York: Museum of Modern Art, 1971.

——. *First and Last*. New York: Harper & Row, 1978.

——. *Walker Evans: Signs*. Introduction by Andrei Codrescu. Malibu, CA: J. Paul Getty Museum Publications, 1998.

——, and William Christenberry. *Of Time and Place*. Fort Worth, Texas: Amon Carter Museum, 1990.

Ferris, Bill. *Images of the South: Visits with Eudora Welty and Walker Evans*. Memphis, TN: Center for Southern Folklore, 1977.

Fitzgerald, Robert. *The Third Kind of Knowledge: Memoirs & Selected Writings*. Edited by Penelope Laurans Fitzgerald. New York: New Directions, 1993.

Gibson, Ian. *Federico García Lorca*. New York: Pantheon Books, 1933.

Greenough, Sarah. *Subways and Streets*. Washington, D.C.: National Gallery of Art, 1991.

Guggenheim, Peggy. *Out of This Century: Confessions of an Art Addict*. Foreword by Gore Vidal. Introduction by Alfred H. Barr, Jr. New York: Universe Books, 1979.

Hagen, Charles. *America: The Black Years (FSA) Photo Poche No. 4*. Paris: Centre National de la Photographie, 1983.

Herera, Hayden. *Frida: A Biography of Frida Kahlo.* New York: Harper & Row, 1983.

Katz, Leslie. " Interview with Walker Evans," *Art in America* (March–April, 1971): 82-89.

Keller, Judith. *Walker Evans: The Getty Museum Collection.* Malibu, Ca.: J. Paul Getty Museum, 1995.

Kirstein, Lincoln. *By With To & From: A Lincoln Kirstein Reader.* Edited by Nicholas Jenkins. New York: Farrar, Straus & Giroux, 1991.

——. *Mosaic: Memoirs.* New York: Farrar, Straus & Giroux, 1994.

Kronenberger, Louis, ed., *Qualtiy: Its Image in the Arts.* New York: Atheneum, 1969. Essay on photography by Evans.

Lowe, Sue Davidson. *Stieglitz: A Memoir/Biography.* New York: Farrar, Straus & Giroux, 1983.

Macdonald, Dwight. *Memoirs of a Revolutionist.* New York: Meridian Books, 1958.

Maddox, Jerold C. *Message from the Interior.* Afterword by John Szarkowski. New York: Eakins Press, 1966.

——. *Walker Evans: Photographs for the Farm Security Administration: 1935-1938.* New York: Da Capo Press, 1973.

Mora, Gilles. *Walker Evans: Havana 1933.* New York: Pantheon, 1989.

——, and John T. Hill. *Walker Evans: The Hungry Eye.* New York: Harry Abrams, 1993.

Neuman, Alma. *Always Straight Ahead: A Memior.* Baton Rouge and London: Louisiana State University Press, 1993.

Papageorge, Tod. *Walker Evans and Robert Frank: An Essay on Influence.* New Haven: Yale University Art Gallery, 1981.

Park, Marlene, and Gerald E. Markowitz. *New Deal for Art: The Government Art Projects of the 1930s with Examples from New York City and State.* Hamilton, NY: Gallery Association of New York State, Inc., 1977.

——. *Photography: Essays and Images.* Edited by Beaumont Newhall. New York: Museum of Modern Art, 1980.

Rathbone, Belinda. *Walker Evans: A Biography.* New York: Houghton Mifflin, 1995.

Rivera, Diego. *Portrait of America.* Explanatory text by Bertram D. Wolfe. New York: Covici Friede, 1934.

Rosenheim, Jeff. *Walker Evans and Jane Ninas in New Orleans, 1935-1936.* New Orleans: The Historic New Orleans Collection, 1991.

Rosenheim, Jeff and Vicente Todoli. *Walker Evans, 1928-1974.* Madrid: Ministerio De Cultura, Direccion General De Belles Artes y Archives, 1983.

Sargeant, Winthrop. *In Spite of Myself: A Personal Memoir.* Garden City, NY: Doubleday and Co., 1970.

Sørenson, Annemette. *Peter Sekaer: New Deal Photography.* Copenhagen: The Royal Library, 1990.

Sontag, Susan. *On Photography.* New York: Farrar, Straus & Giroux, 1973.

Stott, William. *Documentary Expressions and Thirties America.* New York and London: Oxford University Press, 1973.

Thompson, Jerry. *The Last Years of Walker Evans.* New York: Thames & Hudson, 1997.

——, and John Hill. *Walker Evans at Work.* New York: Harper & Row, 1982.

Tractenberg, Alan. *Brooklyn Bridge: Fact and Symbol.* Chicago and London: University of Chicago Press, 1979.

Unterecker, John. *Voyager—A Life of Hart Crane.* New York: Farrar, Straus & Giroux, 1969.

Ward, J.A. *American Silences: The Realism of James Agee, Walker Evans, and Edward Hopper.* Baton Rouge and London: Louisiana State University Press, 1985.

Westerbeck, Colin, and Joel Meyerowitz. *Bystander: A History of Street Photography.* Boston: Bullfinch Press, 1994.

Wolfe, Bertram D. *The Fabulous Life of Diego Rivera.* New York: Stein and Day, 1963.

Index

Augie Capaccio
and James Mellow,
Rockport, Massachusetts,
1993

Photograph by Don Fehr

James R. Mellow (1926-1997) is one of America's most esteemed biographers. He is universally regarded as a supreme stylist and a master of biographical portraiture. About his craft he has said that writing "about the past is like attempting to restore an old house: you can never bring it back to what it once was, but you can hope to make it livable again." That metaphor aptly describes Mr. Mellow's entire oeuvre, which includes a string of distinguished biographies, including *Nathanial Hawthorne in His Times*, winner of the 1983 National Book Award for biography, and a trilogy of biographies on writers of the Lost Generation, which includes the masterpiece *Charmed Circle: Gertrude Stein & Company*, a finalist for the National Book Award, *Invented Lives: F. Scott Fitzgerald*, and *Hemingway: A Life Without Consequences*. In addition, he has also published books on Picasso and Jim Dine. In his forty-year career as a writer, art critic, and biographer, he has written for the *New York Times, Architectural Digest, Art International, Gourmet, Arts Magazine*, among other publications. Mr. Mellow's biographical style is well honed and very distinct. It is perhaps best encapsulated in his obituary, written by Mel Gussow of *The New York Times*: "For Mr. Mellow, accuracy and atmosphere were paramount. He once wrote that the biographer 'wants the life, against all the reasonable odds, to have the verisimilitude of a period photograph: the exact hour of a certain afternoon, the forgotten details in place, the casual smile or anxious look fixed forever in its particular time.' He added, 'In other words, everything.'"

Notes on the Type

Around 1720, after some years as an engraver of guns, William Caslon opened a type foundry in London. Caslon's types were immediately recognized for their natural elegance, simplicity and legibility. His work established England as a primary source of type and printing, which broke its dependence on Europe.

As an example of Caslon's wide appeal, Benjamin Franklin caused the first authenticated copies of the Declaration of Independence to be printed using Caslon types. This typeface was the choice of the late 18th century literati and today *The New Yorker* magazine continues to print in Caslon.

Excepting a brief fall from favor in the early 19th century, Caslon's design continues to have a remarkable life. Dozens of foundries and designers have issued variants bearing Caslon's name but rarely his sophistication.

Many of Walker Evans's photographs show his delight in the nuances and subtexts of letters and words. In his first book, American Photographs, Caslon all caps announce the style and impact of the unadorned and muscular images inside. Evans may have selected this type but it is more likely to be the hand of Joseph Blumenthal, master typographer and printer of the volume. In either case the chemistry between text and pictures is brilliant in their shared color and structure.

With this history in mind and realizing the timeless quality of the pairing, Caslon was again the choice for this book. The text is set in 10 point Adobe Caslon with old style figures. The Roman display sizes used for chapter titles and jacket are Matthew Carter's new drawing, Big Caslon. Jacket italics are Caslon 540.

Design by John T. and Dorothy O. Hill.
Typesetting by FoxPrint, Winsted, Connecticut.
Digital photo scanning by GIST, New Haven, Connecticut.

CPSIA information can be obtained
at www.ICGtesting.com
Printed in the USA
LVHW031541121119
637135LV00006B/733/P